MASTERING EXCEL 2000 PREMIUM EDITION

BY MINDY C. MARTIN, STEVEN M. H̶A̶̶̶̶̶̶̶̶̶, AND BETH KLINGHER

1328 pages
ISBN: 0-7821-2317-1
$39.99

Written for the real Excel aficionado, this definitive, solutions-oriented reference takes you to the next skill level. This Premium Edition delivers all the fundamental concepts plus full coverage of advanced topics such as VBA programming, Web publishing, and Office integration. Create timesaving, productivity-enhancing macros based on VBA and write your own VBA code. Import and analyze information from the Internet/intranet. Featuring advanced tips and methods, this book gives you everything you need to master the Excel environment. The accompanying CD-ROM is packed with useful software and all the sample workbooks discussed in the text.

MASTERING MICROSOFT OUTLOOK 2000

BY GINI COURTER AND ANNETTE MARQUIS

816 pages
ISBN: 0-7821-2472-0
$34.99

Written for business people who really want to go beyond the basics, this definitive guide to Outlook quickly moves into intermediate and advanced features. Challenging topics include security, e-mail decoding, using Outlook with the Web, integrating Outlook with other Office applications, compatibility with e-mail services, setting up Outlook for a LAN and as an Exchange Server client, and much more. With a comprehensive troubleshooting section, this is the Outlook book users will turn to for answers to the tough questions. It covers Outlook for stand-alone LANs and Exchange Server environments, plus Outlook Express.

Microsoft® Office
2000 Complete

SYBEX® SAN FRANCISCO ▸ PARIS ▸ DÜSSELDORF ▸ SOEST ▸ LONDON

Associate Publisher: Amy Romanoff

Contracts and Licensing Manager: Kristine O'Callaghan

Developmental Editor: Sherry Bonelli

Compilation Editors: Davina Baum, Dann McDorman

Compilation Technical Editors: Keith Giddeon, Pamela Hahn

Editors: Brianne Agatep, Laura Arendal, Andy Carroll, Pat Coleman, Jim Compton, Ed Copony, Anamary Ehlen, Dann McDorman, Vivian Perry, Emily Wolman, Kim Wimpsett

Technical Editors: Maryann Brown, Margaret Brundy, B.K. DeLong, Susan Glinert, Russ Jacobs, Julia Kelly, Will Kelly, Tom Maxwell, Rima Regas, Tyler Regas

Book Designer: Maureen Forys, Happenstance Type-O-Rama

Graphic Illustrator: Tony Jonick

Electronic Publishing Specialist: Robin Kibby

Production Coordinator: Shannon Murphy

Indexer: Matthew Spence

Cover Designer: Design Site

Cover Illustration: Design Site

Library of Congress Card Number: 99-60016
ISBN: 0-7821-2411-9

Manufactured in Canada
10 9 8 7 6 5 4 3 2 1

TRADEMARKS

SYBEX has attempted throughout this book to distinguish proprietary trademarks from descriptive terms by following the capitalization style used by the manufacturer.

Netscape Communications, the Netscape Communications logo, Netscape, and Netscape Navigator are trademarks of Netscape Communications Corporation.

Netscape Communications Corporation has not authorized, sponsored, endorsed, or approved this publication and is not responsible for its content. Netscape and the Netscape Communications Corporate Logos are trademarks and trade names of Netscape Communications Corporation. All other product names and/or logos are trademarks of their respective owners.

The author and publisher have made their best efforts to prepare this book, and the content is based upon final release software whenever possible. Portions of the manuscript may be based upon pre-release versions supplied by software manufacturer(s). The author and the publisher make no representation or warranties of any kind with regard to the completeness or accuracy of the contents herein and accept no liability of any kind including but not limited to performance, merchantability, fitness for any particular purpose, or any losses or damages of any kind caused or alleged to be caused directly or indirectly from this book.

Photographs and illustrations used in this book have been downloaded from publicly accessible file archives and are used in this book for news reportage purposes only to demonstrate the variety of graphics resources available via electronic access. Text and images available over the Internet may be subject to copyright and other rights owned by third parties. Online availability of text and images does not imply that they may be reused without the permission of rights holders, although the Copyright Act does permit certain unauthorized reuse as fair use under 17 U.S.C. Section 107.

ACKNOWLEDGMENTS

This book incorporates the work of many people, inside and outside Sybex.

Amy Romanoff and Sherry Bonelli defined the book's overall structure and contents. Davina Baum and Dann McDorman compiled and adapted all the material for publication in this book.

A large team of editors, developmental editors, project editors, and technical editors helped to put together the various books from which *Microsoft Office 2000 Complete* was compiled: Maureen Adams, Cheryl Applewood, Sherry Bonelli, and Melanie Spiller handled developmental tasks; Brianne Agatep, Laura Arendal, Raquel Baker, Andy Carroll, Elizabeth Clevenger, Pat Coleman, Jim Compton, Ed Copony, Anamary Ehlen, Malka Geffen, Dann McDorman, Diane Lowery, Ben Miller, Vivian Perry, Kim Wimpsett, and Emily Wolman all contributed to editing or project editing; and Maryann Brown, Margaret Brundy, B.K. DeLong, Susan Glinert, Russ Jacobs, Julia Kelly, Will Kelly, Tom Maxwell, Rima Regas, and Tyler Regas provided technical edits. Keith Giddeon and Pamela Hahn deserve particular thanks for their help in shaping the book's outline and updating material.

The *Microsoft Office 2000 Complete* production team of desktop publisher Robin Kibby and production coordinator Shannon Murphy worked with speed and accuracy to turn the manuscript files and illustrations into the handsome book you're now reading. Ellen Bliss and Dan Schiff also helped in various ways to keep the project moving.

Finally, our most important thanks go to the contributors who agreed to have their work excerpted in *Microsoft Office 2000 Complete*: Pat Coleman; Gini Courter and Annette Marquis; Christian Crumlish; Peter Dyson; Guy Hart-Davis; Ron Mansfield and J.W. Olsen; Mindy Martin, Steven Hansen, and Beth Klingher; Katherine Murray; Celeste Robinson; and Gene Weisskopf. Without their efforts, this book would not exist.

CONTENTS AT A GLANCE

TABLE OF CONTENTS

Chapter 9 □ Writing Formulas   **281**

Part IV ▶ Database Creation with Access 2000   423

Chapter 13 □ Access Basics   425

Part V ▸ Managing Your Time with Outlook 2000 523

Chapter 16 □ Managing Contacts with Outlook 525

Part VII ▸ Exploring the Internet 711

Chapter 21 ▫ Getting on the Internet 713

Chapter 22 ▫ An Introduction to Internet Explorer 723

Part VIII ▸ Introduction to Web Publishing 793

Part IX ▶ Discover Windows 98   857

Chapter 26 ▫ Windows 98 Command and Feature Reference   859

Part X ▶ Appendix   936

Appendix ▫ Installing Microsoft Office 2000   939

INTRODUCTION

*M*icrosoft Office 2000 Complete is a one-of-a-kind computer book—valuable both for the breadth of its content and for its low price. This thousand-page compilation of information from a dozen Sybex books provides comprehensive coverage of the new Office 2000 suite of products. This book, unique in the computer book world, was created with several goals in mind:

- Offering a thorough guide that covers the important user-level features of the Office suite at an affordable price

- Helping you become familiar with the essentials of Office 2000 so you can choose an advanced Office book with confidence

- Acquainting you with some of Sybex's best authors—their writing styles and teaching skills, and the level of expertise they bring to their books—so you can easily find a match for your interests as you delve deeper into Office use

Microsoft Office 2000 Complete is designed to provide all the essential information you'll need to get the most from Office, while at the same time inviting you to explore the even greater depths and wider coverage of material in the original books.

If you've read other computer "how-to" books, you've seen that there are many possible approaches to the task of showing how to use software and hardware effectively. The books from which *Microsoft Office 2000 Complete* was compiled represent a range of the approaches to teaching that Sybex and its authors have developed—from the quick, concise *No Experience Required* style to the exhaustively thorough *Mastering* style. As you read through various chapters of *Microsoft Office 2000 Complete*, you'll see which approach works best for you. You'll also see what these books have in common: a commitment to clarity, accuracy, and practicality.

You'll find in these pages ample evidence of the high quality of Sybex's authors. Unlike publishers who produce "books by committee," Sybex encourages authors to write in individual voices that reflect their own experience with the software at hand and with the evolution of today's personal computers. Nearly every book represented here is the work of a single writer or a pair of close collaborators, and you are getting the benefit of each author's direct experience.

In adapting the various source materials for inclusion in *Microsoft Office 2000 Complete*, the compilers preserved these individual voices and perspectives. Chapters were edited only to minimize duplication and to add sections so that you're sure to get coverage of cutting-edge developments.

WHO CAN BENEFIT FROM THIS BOOK?

Microsoft Office 2000 Complete is designed to meet the needs of a wide range of computer users. Therefore, while you *could* read this book from beginning to end, all of you may not *need* to read every chapter. The Table of Contents and the Index will guide you to the subjects you're looking for.

Beginners   Even if you have only a little familiarity with computers and their basic terminology, this book will get you using the Office applications you need.

Intermediate users   Chances are, you already know how to perform routine operations with Office. You also know that there is always more to learn about working effectively, and you want to get up to speed on new features in Office 2000. Throughout this book you'll find instructions for just about anything you want to do. Nearly every chapter has nuggets of knowledge from which you can benefit.

Advanced users   If you've worked extensively with Office, you'll appreciate this book as a reference, and as a guide to further work with the Office suite.

HOW THIS BOOK IS ORGANIZED

Microsoft Office 2000 Complete has 26 chapters and one appendix.

Part I: Word 2000 Essentials   In the first five chapters, you'll learn the basic concepts of Word 2000, such as how to create documents, how to format them nicely, how to add zippy graphics, and finally, how to print your magnus opus.

Part II: Working with Numbers with Excel 2000   Part II
will give you the tools to go the distance with Excel. You'll get a
comprehensive tour of all of Excel's features, and you'll find
yourself crunching the numbers in no time.

Part III: Creating Presentations with PowerPoint 2000
Part III delves into the fantastic world of graphic presentations.
PowerPoint gives you many ways to develop dynamic and
engaging slide shows, and these three chapters will give you the
push you need to get started.

Part IV: Database Creation with Access 2000   The three
chapters in Part IV will have you navigating Access databases in
no time. You'll get a tour of the basics of Access, as well as suggestions as to how to plan a database from scratch and how to
find your own style for creating tables.

Part V: Managing Your Time with Outlook 2000   Part V
covers the three key tools that Outlook gives you: managing
contacts, sending e-mail, and scheduling your time.

Part VI: Using Publisher 2000   This part outlines the capabilities that this robust tool can give you. With Publisher, you
can create fabulous publications that will catch the eye of the
reader.

Part VII: Exploring the Internet   The Internet is an integral
part of today's computing world, and Office 2000 does not
ignore it. Part VII explores Internet basics to get you started, as
well as how Internet Explorer 5 can deepen your experience.

Part VIII: Introduction to Web Publishing   Now that you
have the basics down, you can start getting your hands dirty
with real Web experience. HTML and FrontPage can get you up
on the Web in seconds flat.

Part IX: Discover Windows 98   If you've bought your PC
recently, you most likely are seeing the world through the eyes
of Windows 98. This little part will serve as your instant reference to the commands and features of your operating system.

Part X: Appendix   You want to work with Office 2000?
Well, the first thing you'll have to do is install it. Use this
appendix as your guide to getting yourself up and running
with this extensive suite of programs.

A Few Typographical Conventions

When an operation requires a series of choices from menus or dialog boxes, the ➤ symbol is used to guide you through the instructions, like this: "Select Programs ➤ Accessories ➤ System Tools ➤ System Information." The items the ➤ symbol separates may be menu names, toolbar icons, check boxes, or other elements of the Windows interface—any place you can make a selection.

This typeface is used to identify Internet URLs and HTML code, and **boldface type** is used whenever you need to type something into a text box.

You'll find these types of special notes throughout the book:

TIP

You'll see a lot of these—quicker and smarter ways to accomplish a task, which the authors have based on their experience using Office.

NOTE

You'll see these Notes, too. They usually represent alternate ways to accomplish a task or some additional information that needs to be highlighted.

WARNING

In a very few places you'll see a Warning like this one. When you see a Warning, pay attention to it!

YOU'LL ALSO SEE "SIDEBAR" BOXES LIKE THIS

These boxed sections provide added explanation of special topics that are noted briefly in the surrounding discussion, but that you may want to explore separately. Each sidebar has a heading that announces the topic so you can quickly decide whether it's something you need to know about.

FOR MORE INFORMATION...

See the Sybex Web site, `www.sybex.com`, to learn more about all of the books that went into *Microsoft Office 2000 Complete*. On the site's Catalog page, you'll find links to any book you're interested in.

We hope you enjoy this book and find it useful. Happy computing!

PART i
WORD 2000 ESSENTIALS

Chapter 1

WORD 2000 BASICS

In this chapter, you'll get started with Word. You'll start by setting up the screen so you're working comfortably and can see what you need to see. I'll discuss how to use the menus and the toolbars, and how to choose which toolbars to display on screen and how to change their shape and location. You'll start a basic document so you have something to look at. Then I'll discuss the various views that Word provides for looking at your documents and when you may want to use each of these views. After that, we'll look at how you get Help when using Word. Finally, you'll exit Word.

Adapted from *Word 2000 No Experience Required*
by Guy Hart-Davis

0-7821-2400-3   448 pages $19.99

STARTING WORD

You can start Word in any of several ways:

- ▶ If you have the Office Shortcut Bar displayed, click the Word button on it.

- ▶ Choose Start ➤ Programs ➤ Microsoft Word.

- ▶ If you have a shortcut to Word on the Windows Desktop, click or double-click it (depending on whether you're using the Web-style Desktop or the "Windows Classic" style).

- ▶ If you have a shortcut to Word on the Quick Launch toolbar, click it.

TIP

To create a shortcut to Word on the Desktop or the Quick Launch toolbar, choose Start ➤ Programs to display the Programs submenu. Then hold down the Ctrl key, click the Microsoft Word menu item, and drag it to the Desktop or to a position on the Quick Launch toolbar, as appropriate. Because you can keep the Quick Launch toolbar available all the time you're working in Windows, this is the easiest way to launch Word regularly.

SETTING UP YOUR SCREEN

Before we get into working with documents, let's quickly look at how Word appears on the screen (see Figure 1.1).

I'll discuss most of these features in the rest of this chapter. The following list discusses the features that will be familiar if you've used other Windows applications and points to the discussion of the topics treated in more depth later in this chapter.

- ▶ The title bar shows the name of the document in the window, followed by *Microsoft Word*.

- ▶ The menu bar provides access to the commands on the menus.

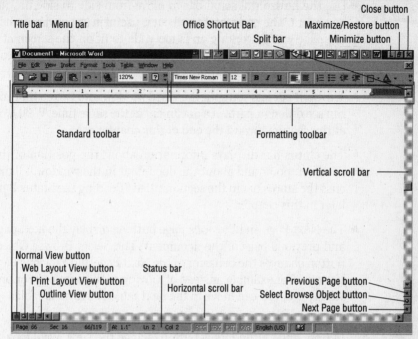

FIGURE 1.1: The elements of the Word window. The Office Shortcut Bar appears only if you have Microsoft Office installed and running on your computer.

- ▶ The toolbars provide access to assorted commands. We'll look at how to work with them a little later in this chapter.

- ▶ You use the Maximize/Restore, Minimize, and Close buttons to resize or close the Word window. We'll look at working with windows next.

- ▶ Use the vertical scroll bar to move backward and forward in your document. You can click the up-arrow button and down-arrow button to scroll one line at a time. Alternatively, drag the scroll box (technically known as the *thumb*) to move quickly through the document. As you drag the scroll box, Word displays a ScreenTip showing the page number and the heading that you're scrolling by, as illustrated here.

Page: 38
Saving Private Data

▶ Use the horizontal scroll bar to move from side to side in your document. The horizontal scroll bar is useful in layout views when the page you're working on is too wide to fit on the screen at a readable magnification. As with the vertical scroll bar, you can either click the scroll buttons or drag the scroll box.

▶ The Split bar lets you split the Word window into two so that you can see different parts of a document at the same time. We'll look at this feature toward the end of this chapter.

▶ The status bar displays information about the position of the insertion point and about the document in the window. I'll discuss the status bar in the section titled "Reading the Status Bar" later in this chapter.

▶ The Next Page and Previous Page buttons display the next page and previous page of the document. The Select Browse Object button changes the behavior of the Next Page and Previous Page buttons. For example, instead of moving to the next page or previous page, you can move to the next table or previous table.

▶ The Normal View button, Web Layout button, Print Layout View button, and Outline View button change the view. We'll look at the three main views later in this chapter.

Using the Menus

To display a menu, click it with the mouse or press the Alt key followed by the underlined letter on the menu (for example, press Alt and then F to display the File menu). To close a menu without choosing a command, click the menu's name again, or click in the document window, or press Alt again, or press Esc.

To choose an item from a menu, click it with the mouse, or press the key for the underlined letter, or use ↓ and ↑ to move the highlight to it and press Enter.

If a menu item is shown in gray embossed letters rather than black letters, it is currently unavailable. For example, the Footnotes item on the View menu will be unavailable until you create a footnote in the document.

Word's menus are *two-stage* and *adaptive:* They appear in two stages, and they change as you use them. At first, when you display a menu, Word shows only the most-used commands on the menu to keep the menu as brief as possible. If you don't choose one of the items within a second or so, Word displays the rest of the menu. This is disconcerting at first, but you may get used to it pretty quickly. If you don't get used to it or if you don't like the effect, you can make Word display the menus normally, as you'll see in a moment.

The last item on the short version of the menu has two arrows pointing downward, indicating that further menu items are available. You can either click this item to display the rest of the menu or wait for Word to display it, as described in the previous paragraph.

The most-used items on the menu are shown in the regular medium gray of most Windows menus. The less-used items appear in a lighter gray. But the first time you use one of the lighter-gray items, Word promotes it to the regular gray and includes it in the short version of the menu from then on. Word also promotes the menu items you use most frequently toward the top of the menu, changing the order of the menu items somewhat. If you're used to regular menu behavior, this can make it harder for you to find the items you need on the menus.

BACK FROM THE FUTURE I: GETTING FULL MENUS AND NON-ADAPTIVE MENUS

If you don't like the new two-stage, adaptive menus, you can make them behave like "normal" menus in previous versions of Word (and in most other Windows applications):

1. Choose Tools ➤ Customize to display the Customize dialog box.

2. Click the Options tab to display it (if it isn't already displayed).

3. In the Personalized Menus And Toolbars area, clear the Menus Show Recently Used Commands First check box. This will gray out the Show Full Menus After A Short Delay check box, and will make Word show the full menu at once.

4. Click the Close button to close the Customize dialog box.

Using Toolbars

Word comes with a variety of toolbars containing buttons that give you quick access to actions—everything from italicizing your text to running a mail merge. To see what a button represents, you can display a ScreenTip by moving the mouse pointer over a button and holding it there for a moment.

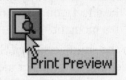

By default, Word displays the Standard and Formatting toolbars, arranging them to share the screen with their most commonly used buttons visible (depending on the screen resolution and window size you are using). But you can easily choose to display other toolbars (such as the Tables And Borders toolbar or the Drawing toolbar) if you need them. Alternatively, you can hide the Standard and Formatting toolbars to give yourself more screen real estate.

Like many Windows applications, Word can display its toolbars and the menu bar as either *docked* panels attached to one side of the screen or as free-floating (or *undocked*) panels that you can drag anywhere on your screen. At the right-hand end of the visible part of any docked toolbar (or the lower end of a vertically docked toolbar), Word displays the More Buttons button: a minimal button with a single downward-pointing arrow. When part of a toolbar is hidden by another toolbar, Word displays >> on the More Buttons button. Click the More Buttons button to display a panel containing the remaining buttons.

Like the menus, Word's toolbars are adaptive. When you use a button that was previously on a hidden part of a toolbar, Word will promote it to the displayed part of the toolbar. If two toolbars are sharing a row across the screen, part of the toolbar that the button was not on may be removed to make space for the button you used.

BACK FROM THE FUTURE II: DISPLAYING THE FULL STANDARD TOOLBAR AND FORMATTING TOOLBAR

If you're used to using most of the buttons on the Standard toolbar and the Formatting toolbar in previous versions of Word, you may find it awkward to have them competing for space on the same line. Here's how to tell Word to display them separately:

1. Choose Tools ➤ Customize to display the Customize dialog box.

2. Click the Options tab to display it (if it isn't already displayed).

3. Clear the Standard And Formatting Toolbars Share One Row check box.

4. Click the Close button to close the Customize dialog box.

One more thing you can do in the Customize dialog box is reset your toolbars and menus to their default settings. To do so, click the Reset My Usage Data button.

Displaying and Hiding Toolbars

To display and hide toolbars:

▶ With the mouse, right-click anywhere in the menu bar or in a displayed toolbar to display a list of toolbars. Checkmarks will appear next to those currently displayed. Click next to a displayed toolbar to hide it or next to a hidden toolbar to display it.

▶ With the keyboard (or the mouse), choose View ➤ Toolbars to display the list of toolbars. Again, checkmarks will appear next to those toolbars currently displayed. Use ↓ and ↑ (or move the mouse pointer) to move the highlight to the displayed toolbar you want to hide or the hidden toolbar you want to display, then press Enter (or click the highlighted item).

TIP

Unless you have a huge monitor or high screen resolution (or both), hide tool-bars when you don't need immediate access to them so that you have more of the screen available for working in.

Moving and Reshaping Toolbars

Word can display its toolbars and the menu bar either attached to one side of the screen or as free-floating. Docked toolbars can overlap each other, which means that you can arrange them to save space on screen. Figure 1.2 shows toolbars arranged somewhat improbably on screen, demonstrating the possibilities.

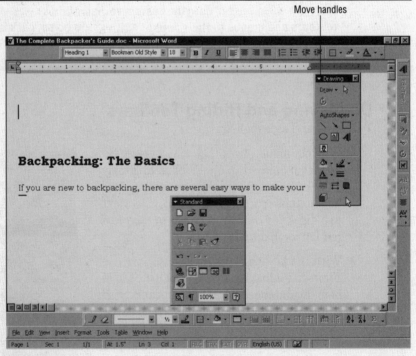

FIGURE 1.2:   You can display your toolbars at any extremity of the Word screen, or you can place them plumb in the middle.

To move a toolbar or the menu bar from its current position, click the move handle at its left end (or its top end, if it's positioned vertically) or in any space in the toolbar or menu bar not occupied by a button or menu item and drag it where you want it—either to one of the edges, in which case it will snap into position, or to the middle of the screen.

To uncover more of a docked toolbar that is obscured by another docked toolbar, drag the move handle of the toolbar that is doing the obscuring.

TIP

You can dock a floating toolbar (or the floating menu bar) by double-clicking its title bar.

To reshape a floating toolbar or floating menu bar, move the mouse pointer over one of its borders until the pointer turns into a double-ended arrow, then click and drag to resize the toolbar. Because of the shape of their buttons or menu names, toolbars and the menu bar resize in jumps rather than smoothly like windows do.

Reading the Status Bar

The status bar (see Figure 1.3) provides the following information from left to right:

- ▶ The number of the page the insertion point is currently on.

- ▶ The number of the section the insertion point is currently in.

- ▶ The current page number and the number of pages in the whole document.

- ▶ The vertical position of the insertion point from the top of the page (for example, **At 4.2"**).

- ▶ The *column number*—the number of characters between the current position of the insertion point and the left margin (for example, **Col 36**).

- ▶ Whether macro-recording mode is on (the REC indicator will be darkened if it is).

▶ Whether change-tracking is on (the TRK indicator will be darkened if it is). Change-tracking is also known as *revision marking*.

▶ Whether extend-selection mode is on (the EXT indicator will be darkened if it is). We'll look at extend-selection mode later in this chapter.

▶ Whether Overtype mode is on (the OVR indicator will be darkened if it is). We'll look at Overtype mode later in this chapter as well.

▶ The language the current selection (or the text at the position of the insertion point) is formatted as—for example, **English (US)**.

▶ The state of spell-checking and grammar-checking in the document. While Word is checking the spelling and grammar as you work, you'll see a pen moving across the page on the icon. When Word has finished checking, you'll see a red cross on the right-hand page of the icon if there's a spelling or grammar problem, and a red checkmark if Word considers all to be well.

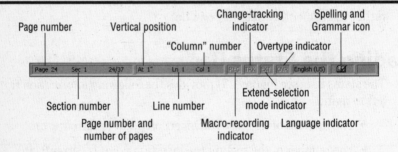

FIGURE 1.3:   The status bar provides information about the position of the insertion point, the document, and what Word is currently doing.

Displaying and Hiding the Status Bar and Scroll Bars

To adjust the amount of free space you have on screen, you can hide and redisplay the status bar and scroll bars as necessary. I find the status bar and vertical scroll bar more or less indispensable, but usually get rid of the horizontal scroll bar:

1. Choose Tools ➢ Options to display the Options dialog box.

2. Click the View tab to bring it to the front of the dialog box if it's not already displayed.

3. In the Show group box, clear the Status Bar, Horizontal Scroll Bar, and Vertical Scroll Bar check boxes to hide the status bar and scroll bars. Select these check boxes to display the status bar and scroll bars.

4. Click the OK button to close the Options dialog box.

Displaying and Hiding the Rulers

To help you position your text optimally on the page, Word offers a horizontal ruler in Normal view and Web Layout view and both horizontal and vertical rulers in Print Layout view and Print Preview. The horizontal ruler displays margin stops and tab stops for the current paragraph or selected paragraphs.

You can either display the ruler on screen all the time or keep it hidden but available. To toggle the display of the ruler on and off, choose View ➢ Ruler. To pop up the horizontal ruler momentarily, move the mouse pointer to the thin, light-gray bar at the top of the current document window:

The ruler will appear automatically so that you can view text positioning or work with tabs:

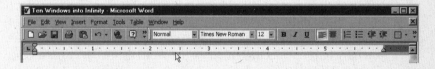

The ruler will disappear when you move the mouse pointer away from it.

To pop up the vertical ruler in Print Layout view or Print Preview, move the mouse pointer to the thin, light-gray bar at the left edge of the current document window. The vertical ruler will appear automatically, and will disappear when you move the pointer away again.

NOTE

These pop-up rulers are controlled by the Provide Feedback With Animation check box on the General tab of the Options dialog box. To prevent the rulers from popping up, select Tools ➢ Options to display the Options dialog box, click the General tab, clear the Provide Feedback With Animation check box, and choose the OK button.

Understanding and Arranging Windows

In this section, we'll look at how Word uses windows and how you work with them.

How Word Handles Windows

To work effectively in Word, you need to understand how Word handles windows when you have more than one document open. Word 2000 (and other Office 2000 applications, such as Excel and PowerPoint) uses a different arrangement of windows than previous versions. Previous versions kept all document windows within one main window, the application window. Only the main application window appeared on the Taskbar, identifying itself as *Microsoft Word* and the name of the document that was currently active in it—for example, *Microsoft Word—September Report Memo*.

Now, each document appears in a separate document window, and each document window appears as a separate icon on the Taskbar, identified by the name of the document: For example, one document window might be identified as *September Report Memo*, another as *Letter to Mom*, and a third *Ode to the Bosnians*. This makes it easier to switch from one open document to another by using the Taskbar. However, not having an application window as such can make it confusing as to when you're closing a document and when you're closing Word itself. When you have only one document open, the Word menu bar grows a Close Window button at its right-hand end, as shown in Figure 1.4. By clicking this Close Window button, you can close the document rather than Word. (As soon as you open another document, the Close Window button disappears.) Clicking the Close button on the title bar of the window closes Word.

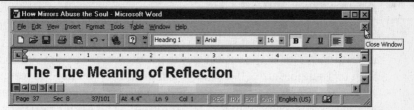

FIGURE 1.4: When only one document is open, Word displays a Close Window button at the right-hand end of the menu bar. Clicking this Close Window button closes the document; clicking the Close button on the window's title bar closes the application.

Switching from One Document Window to Another

If you have the Taskbar displayed, the easiest way to switch from one document window to another is to click the Taskbar icon for the window you want to activate. Alternatively, you can press Alt+Tab to *coolswitch* (switch quickly) through all the Word windows and other running applications. You can also use the Window menu in Word to move between document windows. The Window menu lists the first nine document windows you have open; you can activate any of these document windows by choosing its item from the menu. If you have more than nine documents open (which, under normal circumstances, you'll seldom need to), the Window menu will include a More Windows item that displays the Activate dialog box shown in Figure 1.5. Either double-click the listing for the window you want or select the listing and choose the OK button.

FIGURE 1.5: When you have more than nine documents open, Word provides the Activate dialog box as a way of moving from one document to another.

Arranging Windows

As usual in any Windows application, you can resize the Word document windows to any size that suits you by dragging the borders or corners of any window. This is the easiest way to get the windows you want to work with to a suitable size. (If a window is maximized, you need to restore it to a non-maximized state before you can resize it.) You can also arrange windows by choosing Window ➢ Arrange All. The Arrange All command *tiles* the windows on the Desktop, giving each as equal a share of space as possible. Unfortunately, Arrange All tiles two or three windows by dividing the screen horizontally rather than vertically, which typically makes them too small to do much work in.

You can also arrange Word document windows, together with any other windows of your choice, by using the Cascade Windows, Tile Windows Horizontally, and Tile Windows Vertically items on the context menu on the Windows Taskbar. (To display the context menu, right-click in an open space in the Taskbar.) These commands work on any windows that are not minimized. For example, to arrange two Word windows side by side, right-click in any open space in the Taskbar and choose Tile Windows Vertically from the context menu.

For most purposes, you'll usually do best to maximize the Word window so you have as much space as possible to work in. Unless you have a huge monitor (or need to see other applications while you work in Word), I suggest maximizing the Word window by clicking the Maximize button on the title bar. Once you've maximized the Word window, Word will replace the Maximize button with the Restore button; click the Restore button to restore the window to the size it was before it was last maximized.

You may also want to use Zoom to enlarge or shrink the display. If so, go on to the next section.

VIEWING THE DOCUMENT

Word offers five main ways of viewing your documents, each of which has its strengths and weaknesses: Normal view, Web Layout view, Print Layout view, Print Preview, and Outline view. In the following sections, I'll describe each view briefly. In conjunction with the five views, there are two features that you can use: split-screen view and the Document Map. I'll discuss these as well.

Normal View

Normal view provides the easiest view of the text and other elements on screen and is probably the view you'll spend most of your time using when creating and editing documents. In Normal view, Word approximates the fonts and other formatting that you'll see when you print your document, but adapts the document so that you can see as much of it as possible on your screen. In Normal view, you don't see the margins of the paper, the headers and footers, or the footnotes and comments. Word can also wrap the text horizontally to the size of the window so that no text disappears off the side of the screen.

 To switch the document to Normal view, choose View ➤ Normal or click the Normal View button at the left end of the horizontal scroll bar.

Web Layout View

Web Layout view is designed for creating and reading online documents. Web Layout view (see Figure 1.6) splits the screen vertically, displaying the Document Map (a collapsible outline of the document) in the left pane and the document itself in the right pane at an easily readable size.

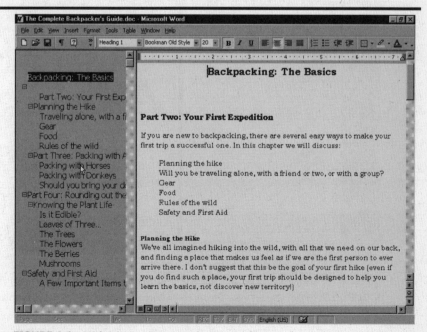

FIGURE 1.6:   Web Layout view provides special features for working with online documents.

To switch to Web Layout view, choose View ➤ Web Layout or click the Web Layout View button on the horizontal scroll bar.

Print Layout View

Print Layout view is useful for getting an idea of how your documents will look when you print them. In Print Layout view, Word shows you the margins of the sheet or sheets of paper you're working on, any headers or footers, and any footnotes or comments. Word doesn't wrap text to the size of the window, as doing so would change the page from its print format.

To switch to Print Layout view, choose View ➤ Print Layout or click the Print Layout View button on the horizontal scroll bar. You'll see an approximation of the layout of your document, complete with margins (see Figure 1.7). If necessary, zoom to a more appropriate zoom percentage (see the section titled "Zooming the View" a couple of blocks south of here).

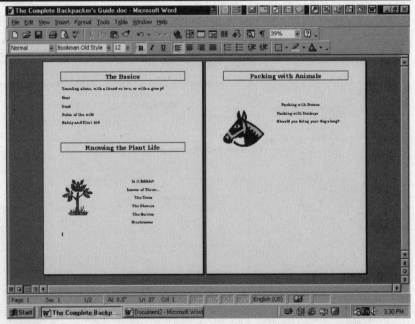

FIGURE 1.7: Print Layout view shows you where each element in your document will appear when printed.

Print Preview

Word's Print Preview provides a way for you to scan your documents on screen for formatting mistakes before you commit them to paper. Print Preview shows you, as closely as Word can, the effect you'll get when you print your document on the currently selected printer. We'll look at Print Preview in detail in Chapter 4.

Outline View

Word's Outline view lets you collapse your documents to a specified number of heading levels—for example, you can choose to view only the first-level heads in your documents or the first three levels of heads. Outline view is very useful for structuring long documents.

Split-Screen View

Word also offers split-screen view, in which the screen is divided into two panes. You can use a different view in each pane, display a different part of the document in each pane, and zoom each pane to a different zoom percentage. Split-screen view is especially useful when you need to see two separate parts of a document (for example, the beginning and the end) on screen at the same time.

To split the screen, choose Window ➤ Split (see Figure 1.8). The mouse pointer will change to a double-headed arrow pointing up and down and dragging a thick gray line. Move the line up or down the screen to where you want to split it, then click to place the line.

To reunite the split screen, choose Window ➤ Remove Split.

TIP

To split the window in half quickly, double-click the split bar—the tiny horizontal bar at the top of the vertical scroll bar. Double-click the bar dividing the screen to remove the split.

Document Map

The Document Map, shown in Figure 1.6 earlier in this chapter, is a prime component of Web Layout view. You can also use the Document Map with Normal view, Print Layout view, and Outline view (though it is largely redundant for Outline view). You cannot use the Document Map with Print Preview.

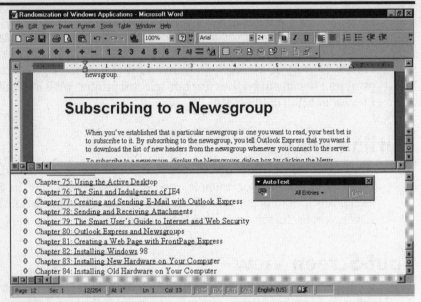

FIGURE 1.8: Choose Window ➤ Split to split the screen into two panes. You can then work in a different view or at a different zoom percentage in each pane.

The Document Map consists of an outline pane that shows the outline of the document. The outline consists of the various levels of headings in the document (you define headings by using the Heading 1 through Heading 9 styles). You can collapse and expand the outline to show different levels of headings by clicking the plus sign or minus sign in the little box to the left of any heading that has subheadings. You can right-click in the Document Map to display a context menu of commands, including commands to collapse or expand the Document Map to show a specified number of levels of heading. For example, to display three levels of headings in the Document Map, right-click in it and choose Show Heading 3 from the context menu. You can click a heading in the Document Map to display that part of the document in the main pane of the Word window.

Zooming the View

In any of Word's views, you can use the Zoom feature to increase or decrease the size of the display. Word lets you set any zoom percentage between 10 percent and 500 percent of full size.

You can use either the Zoom box on the Standard toolbar or the Zoom dialog box to set the zoom percentage.

Zooming with the Zoom Box on the Standard Toolbar

To zoom the view with the Zoom box on the Standard toolbar:

1. Display the Standard toolbar if it isn't visible.

2. Click the button to the right of the Zoom box to display a drop-down list of zoom percentages.

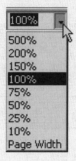

3. Choose a zoom percentage from the drop-down list or type in a different percentage (between 10 percent and 500 percent).

Zooming with the Zoom Dialog Box

To zoom the view with the Zoom dialog box:

1. Choose View ➢ Zoom to display the Zoom dialog box (see Figure 1.9).

2. In the Zoom To box, choose the zoom percentage you want:

    ▸ To zoom to 200 percent, 100 percent, 75 percent, Page Width, Text Width, or Whole Page (which is available only in Print Layout view and Print Preview), click the appropriate option button in the Zoom To box.

    ▸ To display more than one page at a time (only in Print Layout view and Print Preview), click the monitor next to the Many Pages option button and drag through the grid it displays to indicate the configuration of pages you want to view: 2×2 pages, 2×3 pages, and so on. You'll have more display options for a document that contains many pages than a document that contains only a few.

▶ To display the page or pages at a precise zoom percentage of your choosing, adjust the setting in the Percent box at the bottom-left corner of the Zoom dialog box.

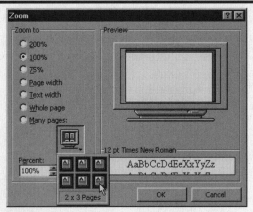

FIGURE 1.9: In the Zoom dialog box, choose the zoom percentage you want in the Zoom To box.

3. Click the OK button to apply the zoom percentage to the document.

GETTING HELP

 Word comes with a sophisticated Help system designed to answer questions you have about working with Word. You can get help by using the Office Assistant or by accessing the Microsoft Word Help application directly.

The Office Assistant is the default interface for the Microsoft Office Help application. The Office Assistant consists of animated characters and graphics such as Rocky, the dog seen in Figure 1.10. Click the Office Assistant to display the prompt balloon shown in the left part of Figure 1.10. (If the Office Assistant is hiding, you can summon it by pressing the F1 key, clicking the Microsoft Word Help button on the Standard toolbar, or choosing Help ➤ Show The Office Assistant.)

Type into the text box at the bottom of the Office Assistant balloon, then press Enter or click the Search button to display the list of topics that the Office Assistant associates with that topic.

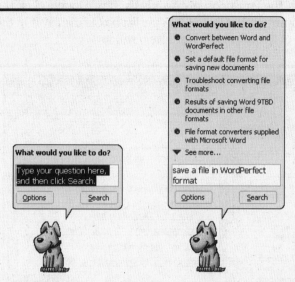

FIGURE 1.10:   Use the Office Assistant to access Word's Help system.

If one of the Office Assistant's suggestions is suitable, click it to display the Microsoft Word Help window with instructions or advice for the procedure or topic you chose. If there's a See More button toward the bottom of the Office Assistant's balloon, you can click that to display further related topics.

To find further topics from the Microsoft Word Help window, click the Show button to display the left panel of the Microsoft Word Help window (see Figure 1.11).

▶ The Contents tab of this panel contains a list of the topics in the Word Help file. To expand any topic, click the + sign to the left of it. To collapse an expanded topic, click the – sign to the left of it.

▶ The Answer Wizard tab provides a way to search for Help topics without using the Office Assistant. Enter your question, or relevant words, in the What Would You Like To Do? text box, then click the Search button. Double-click the topic in the Select Topic To Display list box to display the topic in the main part of the Microsoft Word Help window.

▶ The Index tab provides an alphabetical list of the keywords in the Help file. Either type one or more keywords in the Type Keywords text box and press Enter, or click the Search button, or select a keyword in the Or Choose Keywords list box. Double-click the topic you want in the Choose A Topic list box to display it in the main part of the Microsoft Word Help window.

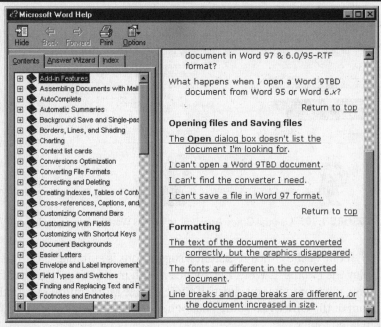

FIGURE 1.11:   Use the left panel of the Microsoft Word Help application window to access further information.

To move backward and forward between the Help topics you've been working with, use the Back and Forward buttons on the toolbar of the Microsoft Word Help window. The Forward button will become available only when you've used the Back button.

To close the Microsoft Word Help application, click its Close button.

DOWNSIZING YOUR OFFICE: GETTING RID OF THE OFFICE ASSISTANT

If you prefer not to use the Office Assistant, you can turn it off by right-clicking it and choosing Options from the context menu to display the Office Assistant dialog box. On the Options tab, clear the Use The Office Assistant check box, then click the OK button to close the Office Assistant dialog box. You can then click the Microsoft Word Help button or choose Help ➤ Microsoft Word Help to display the Microsoft Word Help window without the intervention of the Office Assistant.

To start using the Office Assistant again, choose Help ➤ Show The Office Assistant.

EXITING WORD

When you finish working in Word, choose File ➤ Exit to exit and get back to the Windows Desktop. If you have unsaved documents, Word or the Office Assistant will prompt you to save them. For the moment, choose No, because in this chapter you've been working only with a scratch document. In the next chapter, we'll look at how to save a document.

WHAT'S NEXT

Now that you have the basics down, you're ready to delve into the real thing. In the next chapter, we'll work more in depth with Word documents. This involves creating and saving a new document, using the Undo and Redo features, entering text, dates, or special characters, selecting text, and saving and closing the document.

Chapter 2

CREATING SIMPLE WORD DOCUMENTS

I n this chapter, we'll look at how to work with Word documents. You'll create a new Word document and save it to disk. After that, I'll discuss how to close a document you've been working on and how to reopen that document or open another document. Along the way, I'll discuss the most common things you'll want to do in documents you create: Enter text in them, undo mistakes you've made, and insert information such as dates or special characters.

Adapted from *Word 2000 No Experience Required*
by Guy Hart-Davis
0-7821-2400-3   448 pages $19.99

CREATING A NEW DOCUMENT

As you saw in Chapter 1, when you run Word, it opens a new blank document and names it Document1.

 To create a new document based on the default template (Blank Document), click the New Blank Document button on the Standard toolbar or press Ctrl+N. Word will open a new document named Document*x*–Document2, Document3, and so on.

At other times, you'll probably want to create a new document based on a template that already contains some text or that provides a different look and feel than the default template. A *template* is the skeleton upon which a document is based. To create a new document based on a different template:

1. Choose File ➢ New. Word will display the New dialog box (see Figure 2.1).

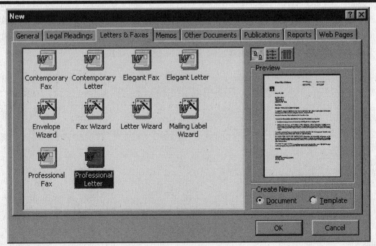

FIGURE 2.1:   To create a new document based on a template other than Blank Document, choose File ➢ New and select the template in the New dialog box.

2. In the Create New group box at the lower-right corner of the New dialog box, make sure that the Document option button is selected rather than the Template option button. (You use the Template option button for creating a new template.)

3. In the New dialog box, choose the tab that contains the type of document you want to create: General, Legal Pleadings, Letters & Faxes, Memos, Other Documents, Publications, Reports, or Web Pages.

> ▶ If you didn't install all the templates that Word offers, you may not see all of these tabs in the New dialog box. Then again, if you or someone else has created more templates in another folder, you may see more tabs than those listed here.

> ▶ To see a preview of a template in the tab you chose, click a template. The preview will appear in the box on the right side of the New dialog box.

NOTE

A *template* is a special type of document that you use to produce documents that share the same look or contents. Templates can contain styles, AutoText entries, toolbars, and macros. By basing a document on a different template, you can change its styles instantly, change its look completely, and virtually typeset it differently, in seconds. (Word calls this "attaching" a template to a document.) Take a look at the Preview box as you click some of the templates offered to get an idea of the different templates available.

> ▶ You can choose between three views of the templates available by clicking any of the three buttons above the Preview box. The leftmost button gives the Large Icons view; the second gives the List view; and the third gives the Details view.

TIP

Details view offers the most information of the three views, and you can sort the templates by name, size, type, or date last modified by clicking the buttons at the top of the columns.

4. To start a document based on the template you chose, double-click the icon or listing for the template, or click it once and then click the OK button.

WORKING WITH TEXT

As in most word-processing applications, Word's basic unit is the paragraph. These aren't paragraphs as people generally understand them: A paragraph in Word consists of a paragraph mark (made by pressing the Enter key) and any text (or graphic) between it and the previous paragraph mark (or the beginning of the document). In other words, a paragraph consists of anything (text, a graphic, space, or even nothing at all) that appears between two paragraph marks, up to and including the second paragraph mark. Strange as it seems, a paragraph mark with nothing between it and the previous paragraph mark is considered a full paragraph. You can treat each paragraph as a unit for formatting with styles or for moving and copying.

Each blank document you create contains one paragraph, which is located at the start of the document. You can add as many paragraphs to a document as you need.

TIP

If you don't see paragraph marks on your screen, click the ¶ button on the Standard toolbar. This is the Show/Hide ¶ button and it toggles the display of spaces, tabs, paragraph marks, and the like. Some people find it easier to work with these marks displayed; others find them distracting. You can also display and hide these marks by pressing Ctrl+Shift+8.

Entering Text

To enter text into your document, position the insertion point where you want the text to appear and type it in. Word will automatically wrap text as it reaches the end of a line, so you don't need to press the Enter key when you get there. Press the Enter key when you need to start a new paragraph.

NOTE

If you're working in Normal view (discussed in Chapter 1), Word will adjust the display of the text to suit the screen and window size you are working with, rather than display the text as it will appear when you print it out. For precise layout, you'll need to work in Print Layout view (View ➤ Print Layout) rather than Normal view.

If you want to move to a new line without starting a new paragraph—for example, so there is no extra space between lines—press Shift+Enter to start a new line within the same paragraph.

As you reach the end of a page, Word will automatically break text onto the next page. If you want, you can start a new page at any point by inserting a page break. To do so, press Ctrl+Enter.

In Print Layout view, Web Layout view, and Print Preview, Word 2000 provides a new feature called Click and Type that enables you to double-click where you want to enter text on the page. Word automatically enters any blank paragraphs and tabs required to position the insertion point where you double-clicked, and changes the alignment of the paragraph if necessary. (If there are already superfluous blank paragraphs or tabs beyond where you double-clicked, Word removes them automatically.) For example, to create a centered heading one-third of the way down the fresh page in a new blank document, double-click one-third of the way down the page and in the middle of the line. Word will place the insertion point there, add blank paragraphs from the top of the page to the line of the heading, and apply center alignment. You can then create a right-aligned paragraph at the bottom of the page by double-clicking at the right margin toward the bottom of the page.

The mouse pointer displays the type of alignment that Click and Type will implement if you double-click in that area: centering around the horizontal middle of the page, right alignment near to the right margin, and left alignment everywhere else.

Insert and Overtype Modes

Word offers two *modes* (methods of behavior) for adding text to your documents: Insert mode and Overtype mode. In *Insert mode* (the default mode), characters you type are inserted into the text at the insertion point, pushing along any characters to the right of the insertion point. If you want to type over existing text in Insert mode, select the text using either the mouse or the keyboard (see the next section for instructions on selecting text) and type in the text you want to insert in its place. In Insert mode, the OVR indicator on the status bar is dimmed.

In *Overtype mode*, any character you type replaces the character (if any) to the immediate right of the insertion point. When Word is in Overtype mode, the OVR indicator on the status bar is active (darkened), as shown here.

To toggle between Insert mode and Overtype mode, double-click the OVR indicator on the status bar or press the Insert key. Alternatively, choose Tools ➤ Options to display the Options dialog box, click the Edit tab to display it, select the Overtype Mode check box, and click the OK button.

Moving the Insertion Point

In Word, you can move the insertion point using the mouse, the keyboard, or a combination of the two. In most situations, you can use whichever means you prefer, though you will probably find the mouse easier for some operations and the keyboard easier for others.

Using the Mouse

To position the insertion point using the mouse, simply move the insertion point to where you want it, and click.

Use the vertical scroll bar to move up and down through your document (or, if you have an IntelliMouse or other scrolling mouse, use the mouse's roller). When you scroll with the scroll bar (the thumb) in a multipage document, Word will display a small box next to the scroll bar showing which page and heading you're scrolling past. Use the horizontal scroll bar to move from side to side as necessary.

TIP

If you often need to scroll horizontally in Normal view to see the full width of your documents, turn on Word's Wrap To Window option, which makes the text fit into the current window size, regardless of width. To turn on Wrap To Window, choose Tools ➤ Options, click the View tab, and select the Wrap To Window check box. Click the OK button to close the Options dialog box.

Click the Next Page and Previous Page buttons at the foot of the vertical scroll bar to move to the next page and previous page. Make sure that these buttons are black, which indicates that Word is browsing by pages. If they're blue, Word is browsing by a different item, such as sections or comments; clicking the buttons while they are blue will take you to the next (or previous) section or comment in the document. To reset Word to browse by pages, click the Object Browser button between the Next and

Previous buttons and choose the Browse By Page button in the Object Browser list, as shown here.

NOTE

The Object Browser is a feature introduced in Word 97 that allows you to choose which type of item you want to navigate to in the document. You can move to the previous or next field, endnote, footnote, comment, section, page, Go To item, Find item, edit, heading, graphic, or table. This provides a way of moving quickly from one instance of an item to the next or previous instance. For example, if you need to check each table in a document, choose Table from the Object Browser list and then use the Previous and Next buttons to navigate from table to table.

Using Keyboard Shortcuts

Word offers a number of keystroke combinations to move the insertion point swiftly through the document without removing your hands from the keyboard. Besides ← to move left one character, → to move right one character, ↑ to move up one line, and ↓ to move down one line, you can use the following:

Keystroke	Action
Ctrl+→	One word to the right
Ctrl+←	One word to the left
Ctrl+↑	To the beginning of the current paragraph or (if the insertion point is at the beginning of a paragraph) to the beginning of the previous paragraph
Ctrl+↓	To the beginning of the next paragraph

Keystroke	Action
End	To the end of the current line
Ctrl+End	To the end of the document
Home	To the start of the current line
Ctrl+Home	To the start of the document
PageUp	Up one screen's worth of text
PageDown	Down one screen's worth of text
Ctrl+PageUp	To the first character on the current screen
Ctrl+PageDown	To the last character on the current screen

TIP

You can quickly move to the last three places you edited in a document by pressing Shift+F5 (Go Back) once, twice, or three times. This is especially useful when you open a document and need to return to the point at which you were last working.

Selecting Text

Word offers a number of different ways to select text: You can use the keyboard, the mouse, or the two in combination. You'll find that some ways of selecting text work better than others with certain equipment; experiment to find which are the fastest and most comfortable methods for you.

Selected text appears highlighted in reverse video—for example, if your normal text is black on a white background, selected text will be white on a black background.

Selecting Text with the Mouse

The simplest way to select text with the mouse is to position the insertion point at the beginning or end of the block you want to select, then click and drag to the end or beginning of the block.

TIP

Word offers an automatic word-selection feature to help you select whole words more quickly with the mouse. When this feature is switched on, as soon as you drag the mouse pointer from one word to the next, Word will select the whole of the first word and the whole of the second; when the mouse pointer reaches the third, it selects that too, and so on. To temporarily override automatic word selection, hold down the Alt key before you click and drag. To turn off automatic word selection, choose Tools ➢ Options to display the Options dialog box. Click the Edit tab to bring it to the front of the dialog box, and clear the When Selecting, Automatically Select Entire Word check box. Then click the OK button. To turn automatic word selection on, select the When Selecting, Automatically Select Entire Word check box.

You can also select text with multiple clicks:

- ▶ Double-click in a word to select it.
- ▶ Triple-click in a paragraph to select it.
- ▶ Ctrl+click in a sentence to select it.

In the *selection bar* on the left side of the screen (where the insertion point turns from an I-beam to an arrow pointing up and to the right), you can click to select text as follows:

- ▶ Click once to select the line the arrow is pointing at.
- ▶ Double-click to select the paragraph the arrow is pointing at.
- ▶ Triple-click (or Ctrl+click once) to select the entire document.

Selecting Text with the Keyboard

To select text with the keyboard, hold down the Shift key and move the insertion point by using the keyboard shortcuts listed in the section titled "Using Keyboard Shortcuts" earlier in this chapter.

SELECTING TEXT WITH THE EXTEND SELECTION FEATURE

You can also select text by using Word's Extend Selection feature, though for most uses it's slow and clumsy. Press the F8 key once to enter Extend Selection mode; you'll see EXT appear undimmed on the status bar. Press F8 a second time to select the current word, a

CONTINUED ➡

third time to select the current sentence, a fourth time to select the current paragraph, and a fifth time to select the whole document. Then press the Esc key to turn off Extend Selection mode.

Extend Selection also works with other keys on the keyboard: To select a sentence, press F8 at the beginning of the sentence and then press the punctuation mark that appears at the end of the sentence. To select some text, position the insertion point at the beginning of that text, press F8, and then press the letter up to which you want to select. If there is another instance of the letter before the one you want to select, press the letter again.

To select a paragraph, place the insertion point at the start of the paragraph, press F8, and then press the Enter key.

Selecting Text with the Mouse and Keyboard

Word also offers ways to select text using the mouse and keyboard together. These techniques are well worth trying out, as you can quickly select awkward blocks of text—for example, if you want to select a few sentences from a paragraph or to select columns of characters.

To select a block of text using the mouse and the keyboard, position the insertion point at the start (or end) of a block and click. Then move the insertion point to the end (or start) of the block—scroll if necessary with the mouse roller or the scroll bar, but don't use the keyboard—hold down the Shift key, then click again.

To select columns of characters, hold down the Alt key and click and drag from one end of the block to the other (see Figure 2.2). This technique can be very useful for getting rid of extra spaces or tabs used to align text.

NOTE
Selecting text in a table works a little differently from selecting regular text. Play around a little to get comforable with tables.

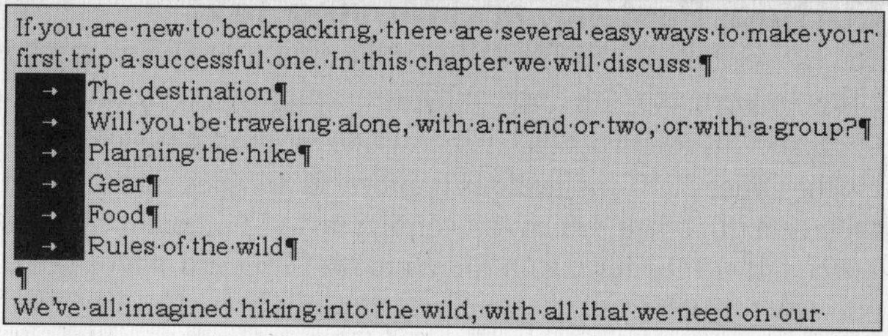

> If·you·are·new·to·backpacking,·there·are·several·easy·ways·to·make·your·
> first·trip·a·successful·one.·In·this·chapter·we·will·discuss:¶
>   → The·destination¶
>   → Will·you·be·traveling·alone,·with·a·friend·or·two,·or·with·a·group?¶
>   → Planning·the·hike¶
>   → Gear¶
>   → Food¶
>   → Rules·of·the·wild¶
> ¶
> We've·all·imagined·hiking·into·the·wild,·with·all·that·we·need·on·our·

FIGURE 2.2:   To select columns of characters without selecting whole lines, hold down the Alt key and drag through the block.

Deleting Text

Word lets you delete text swiftly and easily:

- ▶ To delete a block of text, simply select it and press the Delete key.

- ▶ To delete the character to the left of the insertion point, press the Backspace key.

- ▶ To delete the character to the right of the insertion point, press the Delete key.

- ▶ To delete the word to the right of the insertion point, press Ctrl+Delete. This actually deletes from the insertion point to the beginning of the next word (or the end of the line, if the current word is the last one in the line); so if the insertion point is in a word when you press Ctrl+Delete, you won't delete the whole word.

- ▶ To delete the word to the left of the insertion point, press Ctrl+Backspace. Again, if the insertion point isn't at the end of the word, only the part of the word to the left of the insertion point will be deleted.

TIP

You can also delete selected text by choosing Edit ➢ Clear or by right-clicking in the selection and choosing Cut from the context menu that appears. (Some context menus—which are different for different elements of Word documents—don't have a Cut command.)

Cutting, Pasting, and Moving Text

You can easily copy and move text (and graphics) around your document either by using the Cut, Copy, and Paste commands or by using Word's drag-and-drop feature, which lets you copy or move text using your mouse.

The Office 2000 applications improve on previous versions by having their own Clipboard, which can contain up to 12 different copied or cut items, rather than relying on the Windows Clipboard, which can contain only one text item and one graphical item at a time. This new Office Clipboard is implemented as a toolbar, and its contents are available to each of the Office applications. As shown in Figure 2.3, the Office Clipboard uses icons to indicate the type of information each of the 12 storage containers holds: a Word document icon for text from a Word document, an Excel spreadsheet icon to indicate cells from a spreadsheet, an Excel chart icon to indicate a chart, a PowerPoint slide icon to indicate a slide from a presentation, and so on.

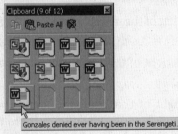

FIGURE 2.3:   The new Office Clipboard can contain up to 12 items of different types. To see a simplified version of the contents of an item on the Clipboard, move the mouse pointer over it so that a ScreenTip appears.

As you cut or copy items, they are added to the Office Clipboard until it contains 12 items. When you cut or copy a thirteenth item, Word or the Office Assistant will warn you that copying this item will drop the first item from the Clipboard. Choose OK or Cancel.

You can paste any individual item from the Clipboard to the current position of the insertion point by clicking it. Alternatively, you can paste all the items from the Clipboard by clicking the Paste All button on the Clipboard's toolbar. The Paste All command is useful for gathering a number of items in sequence—for example, you might want to cull a dozen headings or paragraphs from a report to create a summary.

When the Clipboard is full, or nearing full, you can remove all the items from the Clipboard by clicking the Clear Clipboard button on the Clipboard's toolbar.

The most recent text item or graphical item on the Office Clipboard is also placed on the Windows Clipboard, so that you can transfer information to and from non-Office programs much as before. Likewise, the current text or graphical item on the Windows Clipboard is also placed on the Office Clipboard.

 Cut   The Cut command removes the selected text (or graphics) from the Word document and places it on the Office Clipboard and Windows Clipboard. From there, you can paste it into another part of the document, into another document, or into another application. To cut the current selection, click the Cut button, right-click and choose Cut from the context menu, choose Edit ➢ Cut, or press Ctrl+X.

 Copy   The Copy command copies the selected text (or graphics) to the Office Clipboard and the Windows Clipboard. From there, you can paste it into another part of the document, into another document, or into another application. To copy the current selection, click the Copy button, right-click and choose Copy from the context menu, choose Edit ➢ Copy, or press Ctrl+C.

 Paste   The Paste command pastes a copy of the Windows Clipboard's contents into your Word document at the insertion point. To paste the contents of the Windows Clipboard, right-click and choose Paste from the context menu, click the Paste button, choose Edit ➢ Paste, or press Ctrl+V.

USING UNDO AND REDO

Word provides an Undo feature that can undo one or more of the last actions that you've taken, and a Redo feature that can redo anything that you've just chosen to undo.

To undo the last action you've taken, click the Undo button on the Standard toolbar, press Ctrl+Z, or choose Edit ➢ Undo.

To undo more than one action, click the arrow to the right of the Undo button and choose the number of actions to undo from the drop-down list, as shown here.

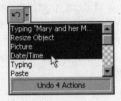

To redo a single action, click the Redo button on the Standard toolbar, press Ctrl+Y, or choose Edit ➤ Redo. (Often, the Redo button is on the part of the Standard toolbar that is covered by the Formatting toolbar.) To redo more than one action, click the arrow to the right of the Redo button and choose the number of actions to redo from the drop-down list.

When there is no action that can be undone, the Undo button will be dimmed and unavailable. When there is no undone action that can be redone, the Redo button will be dimmed and unavailable.

WARNING

There are a few actions that Word *can't* undo, including File ➤ Save, File ➤ Close, and a number of others. If you find yourself needing to undo an action that Word says it cannot undo, you may need to resort to closing the document without saving changes to it. You will lose all changes made since the last time you saved it — but if you've done something truly horrible to the document, this sacrifice may be worthwhile. (This is another argument for saving your documents frequently, preferably after just enough reflection to be sure you haven't ruined them.)

INSERTING A DATE

To insert a date in a document:

1. Position the insertion point where you want the date to appear. (If necessary, use the Click and Type feature to position the insertion point.)

2. Choose Insert ➤ Date And Time to display the Date And Time dialog box (see Figure 2.4).

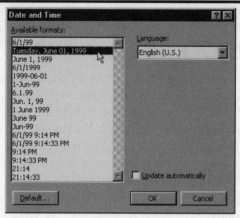

FIGURE 2.4: Use the Date And Time dialog box to quickly insert a date in a document.

3. In the Available Formats list box, choose the date format that you want to use.

  ▶ The Language drop-down list box will show the language you're currently working in. You can choose another language—for example, *English (Australian)* instead of *English (US)*—to see the date formats available for that language.

  ▶ If you want to make the date format in the Available Formats list box the default date format, click the Default button, and then choose the Yes button in the confirmation dialog box that appears. Word will then select that date format automatically every time you display the Date And Time dialog box.

4. If you want the date to be updated every time the document is opened, select the Update Automatically check box. This is useful for documents such as reports, which you often want to bear the date (and perhaps the time) on which they were printed, not the date on which they were created. For documents such as business letters and memos, on the other hand, you usually will want to make sure this check box is cleared, so that the date you insert remains the same no matter when you open or print the document.

5. Click the OK button to insert the date in your document.

INSERTING SYMBOLS AND SPECIAL CHARACTERS

Word offers enough symbols and special characters for you to typeset almost any document. Symbols can be any character from multiplication or division signs to the fancy ➤ arrow Sybex uses to indicate menu commands. Special characters are a subset of symbols that include em dashes (—) and en dashes (–), trademark symbols (™), and the like—symbols that Microsoft thinks you might want to insert more frequently and with less effort than the symbols relegated to the Symbols tab.

To insert a symbol or special character at the insertion point or in place of the current selection:

1. Choose Insert ➤ Symbol to display the Symbol dialog box (see Figure 2.5).

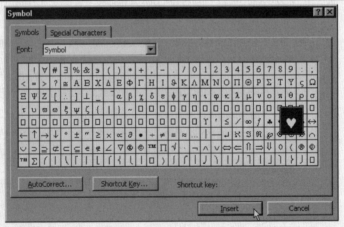

FIGURE 2.5: In the Symbol dialog box, choose the symbol or special character to insert and then click the Insert button.

2. To insert a symbol, click the Symbols tab to bring it to the front of the dialog box (if it isn't already there) and then choose the symbol to insert from the box.

   ▶ Use the Font drop-down list to pick the font you want to see in the dialog box. For some fonts, a Subset drop-down list will appear to the right of the Font drop-down list; you can also choose a different subset of the font from this drop-down list.

▶ To enlarge a character so you can see it more clearly, click it once. An enlarged version of it will pop out at you. You can then move the zoom box around the Symbols dialog box by using ↓, ↑, ←, and →, or by clicking it and dragging with the mouse.

NOTE

Word will display a shortcut key for the symbol (if there is one) to the right of the Shortcut Key button. If you're often inserting a particular symbol, you can use the shortcut key instead—or you can create a shortcut key of your own. You can also create an AutoCorrect entry, which can be a handy way of inserting symbols in text.

3. To insert a special character, click the Special Characters tab to bring it to the front (unless it's already there). Choose the character to insert from the list box (see Figure 2.6).

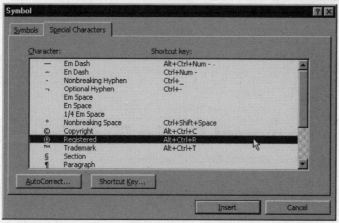

FIGURE 2.6:   Choose a special character from the Special Characters tab of the Symbol dialog box and then click the Insert button.

4. To insert the symbol or special character, click the Insert button. Word will insert the character, and the Cancel button will change to a Close button.

▶ You can also insert a symbol or special character by double-clicking it.

5. To insert more symbols or special characters, repeat steps 2 through 4.

6. Click the Close button to close the Symbol dialog box.

If you find yourself inserting a particular symbol or special character frequently, you can create a shortcut key combination for placing it more quickly. As you can see in the Symbol dialog box, many of the symbols and special characters already have shortcut keys assigned, but you can replace these with more convenient keyboard shortcuts of your own if you prefer.

SAVING A WORD DOCUMENT

The first time you save a Word document, you assign it a name and choose the folder in which to save it. Thereafter, when you save the document, Word uses that name and folder and does not prompt you for changes to them—unless you decide to save the file under a different name or in a different folder, in which case you need to use the File ≻ Save As command rather than File ≻ Save. I'll discuss this in a moment.

TIP
You can also save different versions of the same document in the same file.

Saving a Document for the First Time

To save a Word document for the first time:

1. Click the Save button or choose File ≻ Save. Word will display the Save As dialog box (see Figure 2.7).

NOTE
In dialog boxes that show filenames, you'll see file extensions (e.g., .DOC at the end of a Word filename) only if you chose to see them in Windows Explorer. To display extensions in Explorer, choose View ≻ Options and clear the Hide MS-DOS File Extensions For File Types That Are Registered check box on the View tab of the Options dialog box or the Folder Options dialog box (these vary among Windows 95, Windows 98, and NT Workstation 4). Then click the OK button.

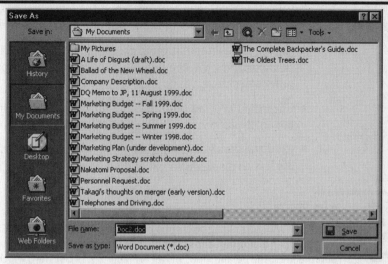

FIGURE 2.7: In the Save As dialog box, choose the folder in which to save your file, then enter a name for the file.

2. In the Save In box at the top of the Save As dialog box, choose the folder in which to save the document.

▶ Click the drop-down list button to the right of the Save In drop-down list to display the drop-down list of computers, folders, and locations accessible from your computer.

▶ Click the Up One Level button (or press the Backspace key with the focus on the folder list) to move up one level of folders, or double-click a folder to open it and display its contents.

▶ Click the Back button (the button with the blue arrow pointing to the left) to move to the folder you were in previously. This button works like the Back button in Internet Explorer (or any other Web browser). When you display the ScreenTip for this button, it will show the name of the folder to which clicking the button will take you.

▶ Click the History button in the left panel of the dialog box to display the list of documents and folders you've worked with recently. (This list of documents is stored as links in the \Office\Recent\ folder.)

- ▶ Click the My Documents button in the left panel of the dialog box to display the \My Documents\ folder.

- ▶ Click the Desktop button in the left panel of the dialog box to display the computers and folders on your computer's desktop.

- ▶ Click the Favorites button in the left panel of the dialog box to display your list of Favorite folders and documents.

- ▶ Click the Web Folders button in the left panel of the dialog box to display your list of Web folders.

TIP

Like many Windows dialog boxes that provide access to files, Word's Save dialog box, Open dialog box, and others provide various ways in which to view and sort the files. The default view, shown in Figure 2.7, is List view, which shows an unadorned list of filenames. For more information, click the View drop-down list button and choose Details to show Details view, which shows the Name, Size, Type (for example, Microsoft Word Document), and Modified (i.e., last-modified) date for each file. You can also choose View ➤ Properties to show a panel of properties on the right-hand side of the dialog box or View ➤ Preview to display a preview panel on the right-hand side of the dialog box. To sort the files, choose View ➤ Arrange Icons and then By Name, By Type, By Size, or By Date, as appropriate, from the submenu. In Details view, you can click the column headings to sort the files by that column: Click once for ascending sort order, and click again to reverse the order.

3. In the File Name text box, enter a name for your file.

- ▶ With Windows 95, Windows 98, and Windows NT's capacity for long filenames, you can enter a thorough and descriptive name—up to 255 characters, including the path to the file (i.e., the name of the folder or folders in which to save the file).

- ▶ You can't use the following characters in filenames (if you do try to use one of these, Word will advise you of the problem):

Colon	:
Backslash	\
Forward slash	/
Greater-than sign	>

Less-than sign	<
Asterisk	*
Question mark	?
Double quotation mark	"
Pipe symbol	|

4. Click the Save button to save the file.

TIP

To save all open documents at once, hold down one of the Shift keys on your keyboard, then, with your mouse, choose File ➢ Save All. Word will save each document that contains unsaved changes, prompting you for filenames for any document that has never been saved. If you have made changes to any of the templates on which the documents are based, Word will prompt you to save the template as well.

5. If Word displays a Properties dialog box for the document (see Figure 2.8), you can enter identifying information on the Summary tab.

▶ In the Title box, Word displays the first paragraph of the document (or a section of it, if it's long). You'll often want to change this.

▶ In the Author and Company boxes, Word displays the username from the User Information tab of the Options dialog box.

▶ Use the Subject box to describe the subject of the document and enter any keywords that will help you remember the document in the Keywords box.

▶ Fill in other boxes as desired, then click OK to close the Properties dialog box and save the file.

NOTE

Whether the Properties dialog box appears depends on the Prompt For Document Properties setting on the Save tab of the Options dialog box. To have Word automatically prompt you for summary information, choose Tools ➢ Options, click the Save tab, select the Prompt For Document Properties check box, and click OK.

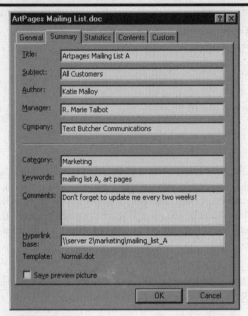

FIGURE 2.8: You can enter identifying information in the Properties dialog box.

Saving a Document Again

 To save a document that you've saved before, click the Save button, choose File ➤ Save, or press Ctrl+S (the shortcut for Save). Word will save the document without consulting you about the location or filename.

Saving a Document under Another Name

One of the easiest ways to make a copy of a Word document is to open it and save it under a different name. This technique can be particularly useful if you've made changes to the document but don't want to replace the original document—for example, if you think you might need to revert to the original document and you've forgotten to make a backup before making your changes. The Save As command can also be useful for copying a document to a different folder or drive—for example, if you want to copy a document to a floppy drive or to a network drive.

To save a document under a different name or to a different folder:

1. Choose File ➤ Save As to display the Save As dialog box.

Part I

2. Enter a different name for the document in the File Name box or choose a different folder in the Save In area.

3. Click the Save button to save the document.

If the folder you chose already contains a document of the same name, Word will ask whether you want to overwrite it. Choose Yes or No. If you choose No, Word will return you to the Save As dialog box so that you can choose a different name or different folder.

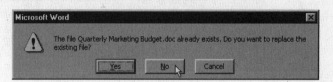

SAVING A WORD DOCUMENT IN A DIFFERENT FORMAT

Word lets you save documents in formats (file types) other than Word— for example, the file formats of other word processors. To save a file in a different format, you need to have Word's converter file for that format installed on your computer. If you don't, Word will prompt you to install the converter. Choose the Yes button, and the Windows installer will install the converter in question and notify you when it has finished doing so.

To save an existing file in a different format:

1. Choose File ➤ Save As. Word will display the Save As dialog box.

2. Scroll down the Save As Type drop-down list and choose the file type you want to save the current document as.

3. If you want, enter a different filename for the file.

4. Click the Save button or press Enter.

NOTE

If you haven't saved the file before, you can choose File ➤ Save instead of File ➤ Save As to open the Save As dialog box. You'll also need to specify a name for the document.

Closing a Document

To close the current document, choose File ➤ Close, press Ctrl+F4, or click the Close button on the document window. If the document contains unsaved changes, Word will prompt you to save them and will close the document when you're finished.

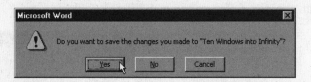

If the document has been saved before and if there are no new changes, Word will simply close the document. If you've created a new document but never changed it or saved it, Word will close it without prompting you to save it.

TIP

To close all open documents at once, hold down one of the Shift keys on your keyboard, then, with your mouse, choose File ➤ Close All. (Interestingly enough, the Close All choice appears on the File menu even when you have only one file open in Word.)

Opening a Word Document

To open a Word document:

1. Click the Open button on the Standard toolbar, choose File ➤ Open, or press Ctrl+O. Word will display the Open dialog box (see Figure 2.9). The Open dialog box provides several methods of navigating to the folder and file you want to open.

2. If you're already in the right folder, proceed to step 3. If not, use the techniques described for the Save As dialog box in the section titled "Saving Documents for the First Time" to navigate to the folder holding the document you want to open. You'll notice that the Open dialog box has a Look In drop-down list rather than a Save In drop-down list, but otherwise everything works the same.

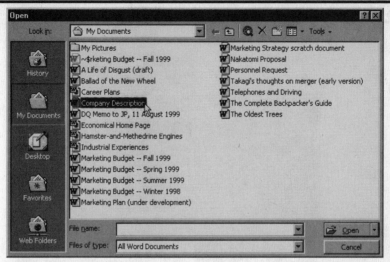

FIGURE 2.9: In the Open dialog box, use the Look In box to navigate to the folder that contains the document you want to open, then highlight the document and click the Open button.

3. Choose the document to open, then click the Open button.

TIP

To open several documents at once, click the first one in the Open dialog box to select it. Then, to select contiguous documents, hold down Shift and click the last document in the sequence to select it and all the ones between it and the first document. Then click the Open button. To select noncontiguous documents, hold down Ctrl and click each document you want to open and then click the Open button. (You can also combine the two methods of selection: First use Shift+click to select a sequence of documents, then use Ctrl+click to select others. To deselect documents within the range you have selected, use Ctrl+click.)

Opening Word Documents Using Windows Techniques

Windows 95, Windows 98, and Windows NT 4 offer several ways to open a Word document quickly. If you've used the document recently, pop up the Start menu, choose Documents, and choose the document from the list of the fifteen most recently used files (as shown here). If Word is already open, Windows will just open the document for you; if Word isn't open, Windows will open Word and the document at the same time.

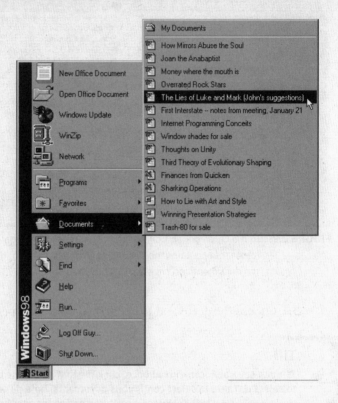

In Windows 98, the Documents menu also provides a shortcut to the \My Documents\ folder, the default location for storing your documents in Windows 98. In Windows NT 4 with Internet Explorer 4 or Internet Explorer 5 installed, the Documents menu provides a shortcut to the \Personal\ folder, the default location for storing your documents in NT. Click the My Documents shortcut or the Personal shortcut to display that folder in an Explorer window, from which you can launch a document by double-clicking.

If you need to open a Word document frequently but can't be sure that it will always be among your fifteen-most-wanted files on the Start menu's Documents menu, you can create an icon for it on the Desktop. To do so, either right-click the Desktop, choose New ➤ Shortcut, and then Browse for the document in the Create Shortcut dialog box; or, more simply, open an Explorer window, find the Word document you want to keep handy, and right-drag it to the Desktop. Windows will invite you to create a shortcut to the document; go right ahead.

TIP

To quickly open one of the documents you worked on most recently from inside Word, pull down the File menu and choose one of the most recently used documents listed at the bottom of the menu. (By default, Word lists four files, but you can change this by using Tools ➢ Options, selecting the General tab, and changing the number in the Entries box for the Recently Used File List. Alternatively, you can turn off the display of recently used documents by clearing the Recently Used File List check box.

To keep a document in an even more handy place than the Desktop, you can create a shortcut for it on a Quick Launch toolbar if you're using the Active Desktop. To do so, open an Explorer window, find the document, right-drag it to the Quick Launch toolbar in question, and choose Create Shortcut Here from the resulting context menu. You'll then be able to launch the document (and Word, if it isn't already running) by clicking the icon on the Quick Launch toolbar.

Finding Word Documents

The Open dialog box also lets you quickly search your computer for documents that contain a certain word or phrase that matches a certain description. This can be useful when you need to find a document whose name or location you've forgotten but whose contents you can remember.

To search for a document:

1. Choose File ➢ Open or click the Open button on the Standard toolbar to display the Open dialog box.

2. If you know which folder the document is in, navigate to that folder in the Open dialog box.

3. Make sure the Files Of Type drop-down list at the bottom of the Open dialog box is showing the type or types of files you want to search for. If you're searching for Word documents, templates, or Web pages, you'll probably want the All Word Documents choice.

4. Click the Tools button (located toward the upper-right corner of the Open dialog box) and choose Find from the

drop-down menu, or press Ctrl+F, to display the Find dialog box (see Figure 2.10). The Find Files That Match These Criteria list box will display what Word is currently set to search for. For example, if you chose All Word Documents in the previous step, the Find Files That Match These Criteria list box will display *Files of type is All Word Documents*.

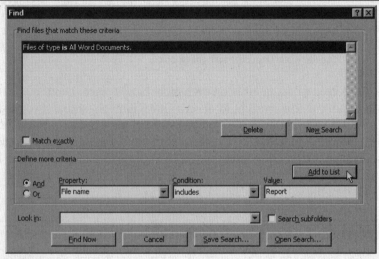

FIGURE 2.10: Use the Find dialog box to locate a document by name, by part of its name, by a word or phrase it contains, or by its properties.

5. In the Define More Criteria group box, choose a criterion on which to search:

    ▶ To refine a search, make sure the And option button is selected. (Use the Or option button to search for files that meet either of two criteria.)

    ▶ In the Property drop-down list, choose the property of the file for which you want to specify information. The default is File Name, which you use to search for a file by its name. You can also choose other properties such as Author, Company, Comments, Keywords, Last Modified, Subject, Title, and other document properties. These correspond to the information that Word displays on the five tabs of the Properties dialog box. As an example, say you want to search for Word documents whose names include the word *Report*. You would choose File Name in the Property drop-down list.

▶ In the Condition drop-down list, choose a suitable condition for the property you chose. The options in the Condition drop-down list vary depending on the property: For text properties such as File Name or Author, the list contains options such as Includes, Begins With, and Ends With, while for temporal properties such as Last Modified, you'll see choices such as Yesterday, Today, Last Month, and so on. In our example search, you would choose Includes in the Condition drop-down list.

▶ In the Value text box, enter the information with which to compare the property. The Value text box will be dimmed and unavailable for temporal conditions and some other conditions. In our example search, you would enter **Report** in the Value text box.

▶ Click the Add To List button to add the criterion to the list of criteria. The Find Files That Match These Criteria list box will change to reflect the criterion you specified. In our example, it will now read *File name includes Report. Files of type is All Word Documents.*

TIP

One of the most useful properties to use in a search is the Text Or Property property, which enables you to search for a document by one or more of the words in it. With the Text Or Property property, you can specify Includes Words, Includes Phrase, or Includes Near Each Other in the Condition drop-down list. For example, if you need to locate all documents with the words *Khyber Pass* in them, you would choose Text Or Property in the Property drop-down list and Includes Phrase in the Condition drop-down list, then enter **Khyber Pass** in the Value text box.

6. If necessary, add further criteria by repeating step 5.

7. In the Look In drop-down list, make sure that an appropriate folder or drive is selected. (The Look In drop-down list will show the folder you chose in step 2.) To change the drive, click the drop-down list button and choose the drive from the resulting list.

8. Select the Search Subfolders check box if you want the search to include subfolders of the folder or drive you chose. Unless you're sure of the folder that contains the document, it's usually a good idea to select this check box.

9. If you think you'll want to save this set of search criteria, click the Save Search button to display the Save Search dialog box. Enter a name for the search criteria in the Name For This Search text box and click the OK button.

10. Click the Find Now button to search for files that match the criteria you specified. Word will display the files it finds in the Open dialog box. Choose the file you want and click the Open button to open it.

To use a saved search, display the Find dialog box as described above, then click the Open Search button to display the Open Search dialog box. Select the search you want to use and click the Open button to open it. You can then add search criteria if necessary, or click the Find Now button to run the search.

OPENING A NON-WORD DOCUMENT

Word can open files saved in a number of other formats, from plain-text ASCII files to spreadsheets (for example, Lotus 1-2-3) to calendar and address books. To open a file saved in a format other than Word, you need to have the appropriate converter file installed on your computer so that Word can read the file. Generally speaking, the easiest way to tell if you have the right converter installed for a particular file format is to try to open the file; if Word cannot open it, it will prompt you to install the converter. Choose the Yes button. The Windows Installer will install the converter and will notify you when it has finished doing so.

To open a document saved in a format other than Word:

1. Select File ➢ Open to display the Open dialog box.

2. Choose the folder containing the document you want to open.

3. Click the drop-down list button on the Files Of Type list box at the bottom left-hand corner of the Open dialog box. From

the list, select the type of file that you want to open. If Word doesn't list the file that you want to open, choose All Files (*.*) from the drop-down list to display all the files in the folder.

4. Choose the file in the main window of the Open dialog box, then click the Open button or press Enter to open the file.

What's Next

OK, so you've mastered basic Word tasks, you can cut, copy, and paste like a pro, and you're opening and closing documents all over the place. What's the next thing you'll want to do? Format your documents, of course! The next chapter will instruct you on such topics as formatting characters and words, formatting paragraphs, using tabs, using language formatting, setting up the page, and applying borders and shading.

Chapter 3
FORMATTING DOCUMENTS

Word supplies you with enough formatting options to create anything from simple, typewriter-style documents up to a complex newsletter or book. The basic types of formatting options start with character formatting (how the individual letters look) and move through paragraph formatting (how paragraphs appear on the page) to style formatting (a combination of character and paragraph formatting, among other formatting) and, finally, page setup. In this chapter, we'll look at character formatting, paragraph formatting, and page setup.

Adapted from *Word 2000 No Experience Required* by Guy Hart-Davis

0-7821-2400-3   448 pages $19.99

CHARACTER FORMATTING

Character formatting is formatting that you can apply to one or more characters. A character is a letter, a number, a symbol, a space, or an object (such as a graphic). Character formatting consists of:

- ▶ Character attributes (properties), such as bold, italic, underline, and strikethrough

- ▶ Fonts (also known as typefaces) such as Courier New, Times New Roman, and Arial

- ▶ Point size—the size of the font

- ▶ Character spacing such as superscripts and subscripts (vertical spacing), and kerning (horizontal spacing)

You can apply character formatting in several ways: by using the Font dialog box, keyboard shortcuts, or the Formatting toolbar. Each of these methods has advantages and disadvantages depending on what you're doing when you decide to start applying formatting and how much of it you need to apply. We'll look at each of them in turn.

Character Formatting Using the Font Dialog Box

The Font dialog box offers you the most control over font formatting, providing all the character-formatting options together in one handy location.

To set character formatting using the Font dialog box:

1. Select the text whose formatting you want to change.

   - ▶ If you want to change the formatting of just one word, place the insertion point inside it.

2. Right-click in the text and choose Font from the context menu, or choose Format ➢ Font, to display the Font dialog box (see Figure 3.1). If the Font tab isn't displayed, click it to bring it to the front of the dialog box.

3. Choose the formatting options you want from the Font tab:

   - ▶ In the Font list box, choose the font for the text.

   - ▶ In the Font Style list box, choose the font style: Regular, Italic, Bold, or Bold Italic.

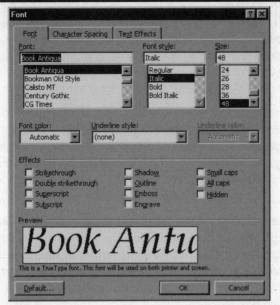

FIGURE 3.1: The Font dialog box gives you quick access to all the character formatting options Word offers.

TIP
Watch the Preview box at the bottom of the dialog box to see approximately how your text will look.

▶ In the Size box, choose the font size you want. To choose a font size that Word doesn't list, type it into the top Size box—for example, enter **13** to produce 13-point text. (Word offers 12-point and 14-point options in the list box, but no 13-point.)

▶ In the Underline box, choose the underlining style you want. The styles are mostly self-explanatory, with the possible exception of these two: (none) removes any existing underline, while Words Only adds a single underline underneath words, with no underline underneath spaces. If you apply underlining, you can select the color for the underline by using the Underline Color drop-down list. Automatic applies the default color (typically that of the current font). For colors beyond those shown on the drop-down panel, click the More Colors button on the panel, select the color you want on either the Standard tab or the Custom tab of the Colors dialog box, and click the OK button to apply the color.

▶ For any special effects, select the check boxes in the Effects area for Strikethrough, Double Strikethrough, Superscript, Subscript, Shadow, Outline, Emboss, Engrave, Small Caps, All Caps, or Hidden. (Hidden text is invisible under normal viewing conditions and does not print unless you choose to include it.)

▶ Finally, choose a color for your text from the Font Color drop-down list. This will affect the text on screen—and on printouts if you have a color printer. Again, you can choose colors other than those on the drop-down palette by clicking the More Colors button to display the Colors dialog box.

4. For special effects, adjust the settings on the Character Spacing tab of the Font dialog box.

▶ The Scale drop-down list controls the horizontal scaling of the text. By default, this is set to 100%—full size. You can change this value to anything from 1% to 600% to squeeze or stretch the text horizontally.

▶ The Spacing option controls the horizontal placement of letters relative to each other—closer to each other or farther apart—by adjusting the space between the letters. From the Spacing drop-down list, you can choose Expanded or Condensed, then use the up and down spinner arrows in the By box to adjust the degree of expansion or condensation. (Alternatively, simply click the spinner arrows and let Word worry about making the Spacing drop-list match your choice.) Again, watch the Preview box for a simulation of the effect your current choices will have.

▶ The Position option controls the vertical placement of letters relative to the baseline they're theoretically resting on. From the Position list, you can choose Normal,

Raised, or Lowered, then use the spinner arrows in the By box to raise or lower the letters—or simply click the spinner arrows and let Word determine whether the text is Normal, Raised, or Lowered.

▶ To turn on automatic kerning for fonts above a certain size, select the Kerning For Fonts check box and adjust the point size in the Points And Above box if necessary.

NOTE

Kerning is adjusting the space between letters so that no letter appears too far from its neighbor. For example, if you type **WAVE** in a large font size without kerning, Word will leave enough space between the *W* and the *A*, and the *A* and the *V*, for you to slalom a small truck through. With kerning, you'll only be able to get a motorcycle through the gap.

5. To really enliven a document, try one of the six options on the Text Effects tab of the Font dialog box: Blinking Background, Las Vegas Lights, Marching Black Ants, Marching Red Ants, Shimmer, and Sparkle Text. Use these options in moderation for best effect on Web pages, and be aware that they can look bad in printed documents. To remove an animation, select (none) in the Animations list box.

6. When you've finished making your choices in the Font dialog box, click the OK button to close the dialog box and apply your changes to the selected text or current word.

Setting a New Default Font

To set a new default font for all documents based on the current template, make all your choices on the Font and Character Spacing tabs (you probably won't want to set any Text Effects options as defaults) of the Font dialog box, then click the Default button (on any tab). Word will display a message box to confirm that you want to change the default font. Click the Yes button to make the change.

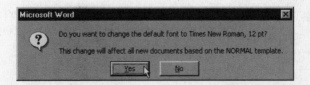

Character Formatting Using the Formatting Toolbar

The Formatting toolbar offers a quick way to apply some of the most-used character formatting options: font, font size, bold, italic, underline, highlighting, and font color (see Figure 3.2).

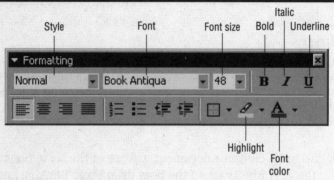

FIGURE 3.2: The Formatting toolbar provides a quick way to apply formatting to your documents.

To change fonts with the Formatting toolbar, select the text you want to affect, then click the drop-down list button on the Font box and select the new font from the list that appears.

▶ The fonts you've used most recently will be listed at the top of the list, with an alphabetical listing of all the fonts underneath.

▶ To move quickly down the list of fonts, type the first letter of the font's name.

To change font size, select the text to change, then click the drop-down list button on the Font Size box and select the font size from the list that appears. To choose a font size that Word doesn't list, type it into the Font Size box and press Enter.

TIP

To change the font or font size of just one word, you don't need to select it—just placing the insertion point within the word does the trick.

To apply bold, italic, or underline, select the text you want to emphasize, then click the Bold, Italic, or Underline button on the Formatting toolbar. When you've applied one of these attributes, the relevant button will appear to be pushed in.

To remove bold, italic, or underline, select the emphasized text, then click the Bold, Italic, or Underline button again to remove the formatting.

 To apply highlighting to one instance of text, select the text, then click the Highlight button.

To apply highlighting to several instances of text easily, click the Highlight button before selecting any text. Your mouse pointer will take on a little highlighter pen when moved into the document window. Click and drag this over text to highlight it.

To turn the highlighting off, click the Highlight button again or press the Esc key.

To change the color of the highlighting, click the drop-down list arrow next to the Highlight button and choose another color from the list. (The default color for highlighting is the classic fluorescent yellow—Enhanced French Headlamp, as it's known in the trade—beloved of anyone who's ever had a highlighter pen break in their shirt pocket.)

To remove highlighting, click and drag the highlighter pen over the highlighted text.

To change the font color of the current selection or current word, click the Font Color drop-down palette button and choose the color you want from the palette. You can then apply that color quickly to selected text by clicking the Font Color button.

Character Formatting Using Keyboard Shortcuts

Word offers a number of keyboard shortcuts for formatting text with the keyboard. For all of them, select the text you want to affect first, unless you want to affect only the word in which the insertion point is currently resting.

Shortcut	Effect
Ctrl+Shift+.	Increase font size (in steps)
Ctrl+Shift+,	Decrease font size (in steps)

Shortcut	Effect
Ctrl+]	Increase font size by 1 point
Ctrl+[	Decrease font size by 1 point
Shift+F3	Change case (cycle)
Ctrl+Shift+A	All capitals
Ctrl+Shift+K	Small capitals
Ctrl+B	Bold
Ctrl+U	Underline
Ctrl+Shift+W	Underline (single words)
Ctrl+Shift+D	Double-underline
Ctrl+Shift+H	Hidden text
Ctrl+I	Italic
Ctrl+=	Subscript
Ctrl+Shift+= (i.e., Ctrl++)	Superscript
Ctrl+Shift+Z	Remove formatting
Ctrl+Shift+Q	Change to Symbol font

PARAGRAPH FORMATTING

With paragraph formatting, you can set a number of parameters that influence how your paragraphs look:

► Alignment

► Indentation

► Line spacing

► Text flow

► Tabs

The following sections of this chapter discuss each of these paragraph formatting options in turn.

Setting Alignment

Word provides the standard four kinds of paragraph alignment: left-aligned (the default and normal alignment), centered, right-aligned (aligned with the right margin), and justified (aligned with both the left margin and the right margin). Alignment is also called *justification*.

There are several ways to set paragraph alignment: You can align new text (more exactly, a new paragraph) quickly in Print Layout view, you can use the alignment buttons on the Formatting toolbar, you can use the keyboard shortcuts, or you can use the options in the Paragraph dialog box. Using the buttons on the Formatting toolbar is the easiest way of aligning existing text.

Aligning New Text Using Click and Type

If you need to quickly align a new paragraph you're adding to a page, your best bet is to use the Click and Type feature, which we examined in Chapter 2. Double-click to place the insertion point where you want it in blank space on the page, and Word handles the intervening paragraphs, any necessary tabs, and the alignment automatically.

Setting Alignment Using the Formatting Toolbar

To set alignment using the Formatting toolbar:

1. Place the insertion point in the paragraph that you want to align. To align more than one paragraph, select all the paragraphs you want to align.

2. Click the Align Left, Center, Align Right, or Justify button on the Formatting toolbar (see Figure 3.3).

FIGURE 3.3: To quickly align the current paragraph or selected text, click the appropriate button on the Formatting toolbar.

Setting Alignment Using Keyboard Shortcuts

When you're typing, the quickest way to set the alignment of paragraphs is by using these keyboard shortcuts:

Shortcut	Effect
Ctrl+L	Align left
Ctrl+E	Center
Ctrl+R	Align right
Ctrl+J	Justify

Setting Alignment Using the Paragraph Dialog Box

The third way to set alignment—and usually the slowest—is to use the Paragraph dialog box. Why discuss this? Because you're very likely to be making other formatting changes in the Paragraph dialog box, so sometimes you may find it useful to set alignment there too.

To set alignment using the Paragraph dialog box:

1. Place the insertion point in the paragraph you want to align. To align several paragraphs, select all the paragraphs you want to align.

2. Right-click and choose Paragraph from the context menu, or choose Format ➤ Paragraph, to display the Paragraph dialog box (see Figure 3.4).

3. Choose the alignment you want from the Alignment drop-down list.

4. Click the OK button to close the Paragraph dialog box.

Setting Indents

As with setting alignment, you can set indents in more than one way. Again, the quickest way is with the ruler, but you can also use the Paragraph dialog box and keyboard shortcuts.

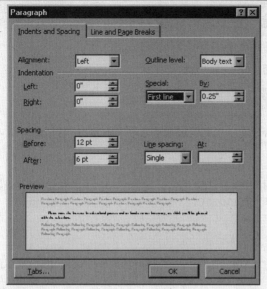

FIGURE 3.4:   In the Paragraph dialog box, you can set many paragraph-
formatting options, including alignment.

Before we get into setting indents, you need to know a little about how
Word handles them. Briefly, the size of the page you're working with is
set via the Page Setup dialog box, which we'll examine in the section titled
"Page Setup" later in this chapter. For most documents, Word starts you
off with an 8½" × 11" page–standard letter-sized paper. You can then set
top, bottom, left, and right margins for the page. Again, Word starts you
off with default margins, but you can set your own margins whenever you
want (we'll examine this in "Page Setup" too). Any indents you set are relative to the margins, not to the edges of the page. You can set both positive
indents (in from the margin) and negative indents (out from the margin).

Setting Indents with the Ruler

To set indents using the ruler, click and drag the indent markers on it
(see Figure 3.5).

  ▶ The first-line indent marker (the downward-pointing arrow) spec-
    ifies the indentation of the first line of the paragraph (this could
    be a hanging indent).

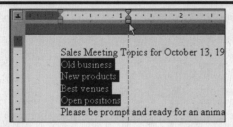

FIGURE 3.5:   Click and drag the indent markers on the ruler to change the indentation of the current paragraph or selected paragraphs.

▶ The left indent marker (the upward-pointing arrow) specifies the position of the left indent.

NOTE

To move the left indent marker and first-line indent marker together, drag the left indent marker by the square box at its base rather than by the upward-pointing mark. Dragging by the upward-pointing mark will move the left indent marker but leave the first-line indent marker where it was.

▶ The right indent marker specifies the position of the right indent.

Setting Indents with the Paragraph Dialog Box

Depending on whether you have a graphical or literal mindset, you may find setting indents in the Paragraph dialog box easier than setting them with the ruler.

To set paragraph indents with the Paragraph dialog box:

1. Place the insertion point in the paragraph for which you want to set indents. To set indents for several paragraphs, select all the paragraphs you want to set indents for.

2. Right-click and choose Paragraph from the context menu, or choose Format ➤ Paragraph, to display the Paragraph dialog box.

3. Make sure the Indents And Spacing tab is selected (if it's not visible, click it to bring it in front of the Line And Page Breaks tab).

4. In the Left box, enter the distance to indent the paragraph from the left margin.

5. In the Right box, enter the distance to indent the paragraph from the right margin.

6. In the Special box, choose from (none), First Line, and Hanging:

    ▶ (none) formats the paragraph as a regular paragraph, with indents controlled solely by the Left and Right settings.

    ▶ First Line adds an indent to the first line of the paragraph. This indent is in addition to the Left setting. For example, if you choose a Left setting of 0.5″ and a First Line setting of 0.5″, the first line of the paragraph will be indented one inch. By using a first-line indent, you can avoid having to type a tab at the beginning of a paragraph.

    ▶ Hanging makes the first line of the paragraph hang out to the left of the rest of the paragraph. (This is sometimes referred to as an *outdent*.) Hanging indents are great for bulleted or numbered paragraphs—the bullet or number hangs out to the left of the paragraph, and the wrapped lines of the paragraph align neatly with the first line.

    Figure 3.6 illustrates the different types of indentation Word provides for paragraphs.

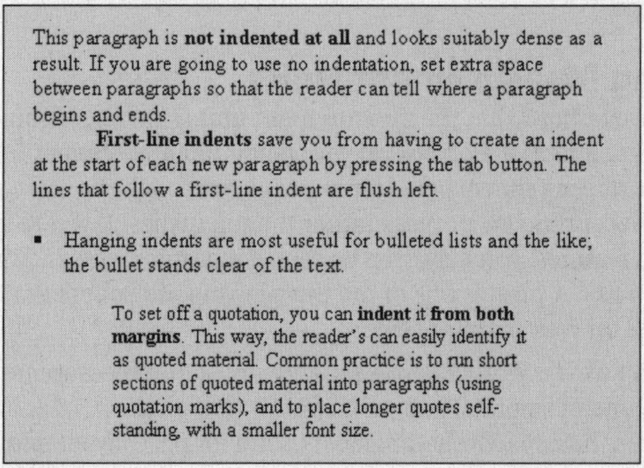

This paragraph is **not indented at all** and looks suitably dense as a result. If you are going to use no indentation, set extra space between paragraphs so that the reader can tell where a paragraph begins and ends.

First-line indents save you from having to create an indent at the start of each new paragraph by pressing the tab button. The lines that follow a first-line indent are flush left.

▪ Hanging indents are most useful for bulleted lists and the like; the bullet stands clear of the text.

To set off a quotation, you can **indent** it **from both margins**. This way, the reader's can easily identify it as quoted material. Common practice is to run short sections of quoted material into paragraphs (using quotation marks), and to place longer quotes self-standing, with a smaller font size.

FIGURE 3.6: Word provides these different types of indentation for formatting paragraphs.

7. If you chose a Special setting of First Line or Hanging, enter a measurement in the By box.

8. Click the OK button to close the Paragraph dialog box.

TIP

When setting indents, you can use negative values for Left and Right indents to make the text protrude beyond the margin. Negative indents can be useful for special effects, but if you find yourself using them all the time, you probably need to adjust your margins. One other thing—for obvious reasons, you can't set a negative hanging indent, no matter how hard you try.

Setting Indents by Using Keyboard Shortcuts

Here are the keyboard shortcuts for setting indents:

Shortcut	Effect
Ctrl+M	Indent from the left
Ctrl+Shift+M	Remove indent from the left
Ctrl+T	Create (or increase) a hanging indent
Ctrl+Shift+T	Reduce (or remove) a hanging indent
Ctrl+Q	Remove paragraph formatting

Choosing Measurement Units

You may have noticed that the measurement units (inches, centimeters, etc.) in the Paragraph dialog box on your computer are different from those in the screens shown here—for example, you might be seeing measurements in centimeters or picas rather than in inches. If you're using Word's Web features, you may even be seeing measurements in pixels (abbreviated *px*). A pixel is one of the tiny glowing phosphors that create what you see on your monitor screen.

If so, don't worry. Word lets you work in any of four measurements: inches, centimeters, points, and picas. Points and picas—$\frac{1}{72}$ of an inch and $\frac{1}{6}$ of an inch, respectively—are most useful for page layout and typesetting, but if you're not doing those, you might want to switch between inches and centimeters.

To change your measurement units:

1. Choose Tools ➤ Options to display the Options dialog box.

2. Click the General tab to bring it to the front.

3. Choose Inches, Centimeters, Millimeters, Points, or Picas as your measurement unit from the Measurement Units drop-down list.

4. Click the OK button to close the Options dialog box.

Setting Line Spacing

In most documents, Word starts you off with single-spaced lines, with only enough spacing between the lines to prevent the descenders on characters in one line from touching the ascenders on characters in the next line. You can change the line spacing of all or part of a document by using either the Paragraph dialog box or keyboard shortcuts:

1. Place the insertion point in the paragraph you want to adjust, or select several paragraphs whose line spacing you want to change.

   ▶ To select the whole document quickly, choose Edit ➤ Select All, or hold down the Ctrl key and click once in the selection bar at the left edge of the Word window. Alternatively, press Ctrl+5 (that's the 5 on the numeric keypad, not the 5 above the letters R and T).

2. Right-click in the selection and choose Paragraph from the context menu, or choose Format ➤ Paragraph, to display the Paragraph dialog box (shown in Figure 3.4).

3. If the Indents And Spacing tab isn't at the front of the Paragraph dialog box, click it to bring it to the front.

4. Use the Line Spacing drop-down list to choose the line spacing you want:

Line Spacing	Effect
Single	Single spacing, based on the point size of the font.
1.5 lines	Line-and-a-half spacing, based on the point size of the font.

Part i

Line Spacing	Effect
Double	Double spacing based on the point size of the font.
At least	Sets a minimum spacing for the lines, measured in points. This can be useful for including fonts of different sizes in a paragraph or for including in-line graphics.
Exactly	Sets the exact spacing for the lines, measured in points.
Multiple	Multiple line spacing, set by the number in the At box to the right of the Line Spacing drop-down list. For example, to use triple line spacing, enter **3** in the At box; to use quadruple line spacing, enter **4**.

5. If you chose At Least, Exactly, or Multiple in the Line Spacing drop-down list, adjust the setting in the At box if necessary.

6. Click the OK button to apply the line spacing setting to the chosen text.

TIP

To set line spacing with the keyboard, press Ctrl+1 to single-space the selected paragraphs, Ctrl+5 to set 1.5-line spacing, and Ctrl+2 to double-space paragraphs.

Setting Spacing before and after Paragraphs

As well as setting the line spacing within any paragraph, you can adjust the amount of space before and after any paragraph to position it more effectively on the page. So instead of using two blank lines (i.e., two extra paragraphs with no text) before a heading and one blank line afterward, you can adjust the paragraph spacing to give the heading plenty of space without using any blank lines.

Part I

TIP

The easiest way to set consistent spacing before and after paragraphs of a particular type is to use Word's *styles*.

To set the spacing before and after a paragraph:

1. Place the insertion point in the paragraph whose spacing you want to adjust, or select several paragraphs to adjust their spacing all at once.

2. Right-click and choose Paragraph from the context menu, or choose Format ➤ Paragraph, to display the Paragraph dialog box (shown in Figure 3.4).

3. Make sure the Indents And Spacing tab is foremost. If it isn't, click it to bring it to the front.

4. In the Spacing box, choose a Before setting to specify the number of points of space before the selected paragraph. Watch the Preview box for the approximate effect this change will have.

5. Choose an After setting to specify the number of points of space after the current paragraph. Again, watch the Preview box.

NOTE

The Before setting for a paragraph adds to the After setting for the paragraph before it; it does not change it. For example, if the previous paragraph has an After setting of 12 points, and you specify a Before setting of 12 points for the current paragraph, you'll end up with 24 points of space between the two paragraphs (in addition to the line spacing you've set).

6. Click the OK button to close the Paragraph dialog box and apply the changes.

TIP

To quickly add or remove one line worth of space before a paragraph, select the paragraph or place the cursor within it and press Ctrl+0 (Ctrl+zero).

Using the Text Flow Options

Word offers six options for controlling how your text flows from page to page in the document. To select these options, click in the paragraph you want to apply them to or select a number of paragraphs. Then choose Format ➤ Paragraph to display the Paragraph dialog box, click the Line And Page Breaks tab to bring it to the front of the dialog box (unless it's already at the front), and select the options you want to use:

Widow/Orphan Control	A *widow* (in typesetting parlance) is when the last line of a paragraph appears by itself at the top of a page; an *orphan* is when the first line of a paragraph appears by itself at the foot of a page. Leave the Widow/Orphan Control box selected to have Word rearrange your documents to avoid widows and orphans.
Keep Lines Together	Tells Word to prevent the paragraph from breaking over a page. If the whole paragraph will not fit on the current page, Word moves it to the next page. If you write long paragraphs, choosing the Keep Lines Together option can produce painfully short pages.
Keep With Next	Tells Word to prevent a page break from occurring between the selected paragraph and the next paragraph. This option can be useful for making sure that a heading appears on the same page as the paragraph of text following it or that an illustration appears together with its caption—but be careful not to set Keep With Next for body text paragraphs or other paragraphs that will need to flow normally from page to page.

Page Break Before	Tells Word to force a page break before the current paragraph. This is useful for making sure that, for example, each section of a report starts on a new page.
Suppress Line Numbers	Tells Word to turn off line numbers for the current paragraph. This applies only if you are using line numbering in your document.
Don't Hyphenate	Tells Word to skip the current paragraph when applying automatic hyphenation.

When you've chosen the options you want, click the OK button to apply them to the paragraph or paragraphs.

Setting Tabs

To align the text in your documents, Word provides five kinds of tabs:

- ▶ Left-aligned
- ▶ Centered
- ▶ Right-aligned
- ▶ Decimal-aligned
- ▶ Bar (a vertical line at the tab's position)

Setting Tabs Using the Ruler

The quickest way to set tabs for the current paragraph, or for a few paragraphs, is to use the ruler. If the ruler isn't visible, choose View ➤ Ruler to display it, or simply pop it up by sliding the mouse pointer onto the gray bar at the top of the screen once you've selected the paragraphs you want to work on.

Adding a Tab   To add a tab:

1. Display the ruler if necessary.

2. Place the insertion point in a single paragraph or select the paragraphs to which you want to add the tab.

Part i

3. Choose the type of tab you want by clicking the tab selector button at the left end of the ruler to cycle through left tab, center tab, right tab, and decimal tab.

4. Click the ruler in the location where you want to add the tab. The tab mark will appear in the ruler:

TIP

When adding a tab, you can click with either the left or the right mouse button. For moving or removing a tab, only the left button works.

Moving a Tab   To move a tab, display the ruler if necessary, then click the tab marker and drag it to where you want it.

Removing a Tab   To remove a tab, display the ruler if it's not visible, then click the marker for the tab you want to remove and drag it into the document. The tab marker will disappear from the ruler.

Setting Tabs Using the Tabs Dialog Box

When you need to check exactly where the tabs are in a paragraph, or if you set too many tabs in the ruler and get confused, turn to the Tabs dialog box to clear everything up. First, place the insertion point in a single paragraph or select the paragraphs whose tabs you want to change, then choose Format ➤ Tabs to display the Tabs dialog box (see Figure 3.7) and follow the procedures described in the next sections.

TIP

To quickly display the Tabs dialog box, double-click an existing tab in the bottom half of the ruler. (If you double-click in any open space in the bottom half of the ruler, the first click will place a new tab for you; if you double-click in the top half of the ruler, Word will display the Page Setup dialog box.) You can also get to the Tabs dialog box quickly by clicking the Tabs button on either panel of the Paragraph dialog box.

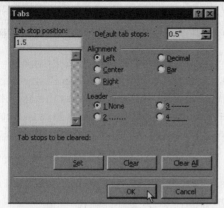

FIGURE 3.7: The Tabs dialog box gives you fine control over the placement and types of tabs in your document.

Setting Default Tabs To set different spacing for default tabs, adjust the setting in the Default Tab Stops box at the top of the Tabs dialog box. For example, a setting of 1″ will produce tabs at 1″, 2″, 3″, and so on.

Setting Tabs To set tabs:

1. Enter a position in the Tab Stop Position box.

   ▶ If you're using the default unit of measurement set in the copy of Word you're using, you don't need to specify the units.

   ▶ If you want to use another unit of measurement, specify it: for example, 2.3″, 11cm, 22pi, 128pt, 66px.

2. Specify the tab alignment in the Alignment box: Left, Center, Right, Decimal, or Bar. (Bar inserts a vertical bar (|) at the tab stop.)

3. In the Leader area, specify a tab leader if you want one: periods, hyphens, or underlines leading up to the tabbed text. (Periods are often used as tab leaders for tables of contents, between the heading and the page number.) Choose the None option button to remove leaders from a tab.

4. Click the Set button.

Part i

5. Repeat steps 1 through 4 to specify more tabs if necessary.

6. Click the OK button to close the Tabs dialog box and apply the tabs you set.

Clearing Tabs   To clear a tab, select it in the Tab Stop Position list and click the Clear button. Word will list the tab you chose in the Tab Stops To Be Cleared area of the Tabs dialog box. Choose other tabs to clear if necessary, then click the OK button.   To clear all tabs, simply click the Clear All button, then click the OK button.

Moving Tabs   To move tabs using the Tabs dialog box, you need to clear them from their current position and then set them elsewhere—you can't move them as such. (To move tabs easily, use the ruler method described earlier in this chapter.)

LANGUAGE FORMATTING

You can format text as being written in a language other than English. Not only can you spell-check text written in other languages, but you can use the Find feature to search for text formatted in those languages for quick reference.   To format selected text as another language:

1. Choose Tools ➤ Language ➤ Set Language to display the Language dialog box (see Figure 3.8).

FIGURE 3.8: In the Language dialog box, choose the language in which to format the selected text, then click OK.

2. In the Mark Selected Text As list box, choose the language in which to format the text.

   ▶ Selecting the Do Not Check Spelling Or Grammar check box tells Word not to use the spell checker and other proofing tools on the selected text. This can be useful for one-off technical terms that you don't want to add to your custom dictionaries. But if you find the spell checker suddenly failing to catch blatant spelling errors, check to see if the Do Not Check Spelling Or Grammar check box is selected for the text in question.

WARNING

If Word does not have the dictionary files installed for a language that you have formatted text as, it will display a warning message box when you run a spell-check on the text. After checking other text formatted as languages that it recognizes, Word will then tell you that the spell-check is complete. This can be deceptive, because it will not have checked the text for whose language it does not have the dictionary.

3. Click the OK button to apply the language formatting to the selected text.

TIP

You can also apply language formatting from the Spelling context menu: Right-click a word with the wavy red underline and choose Language from the context menu. Then either select a language from the list of languages you've been using, or choose Set Language to display the Language dialog box.

PAGE SETUP

If you're ever going to print a document, you need to tell Word how it should appear on the page. You can change the margins, paper size, layout of the paper, and even which printer tray the paper comes from (as we will see in Chapter 4).

NOTE

The best time to set paper size is at the beginning of a project. While you can change it at any time during a project without trouble, having the right size (and orientation) of paper from the start will help you lay out your material.

To alter the page setup, double-click in the top half of the horizontal ruler (or anywhere in the vertical ruler), or choose File ➤ Page Setup, to display the Page Setup dialog box, then follow the instructions for setting margins, paper size, and paper orientation in the next sections. If you want to change the page setup for only one section of a document, place the insertion point in the section you want to change before displaying the Page Setup dialog box. Alternatively, you can choose This Point Forward from the Apply To drop-down list on any tab of the Page Setup dialog box to change the page setup for the rest of the document.

TIP

To quickly display the Page Setup dialog box, double-click in the top half of the ruler. (Double-clicking in the bottom half of the ruler displays the Tabs dialog box, so be precise.)

Setting Margins

To set the margins for your document, click the Margins tab in the Page Setup dialog box (see Figure 3.9). In the boxes for Top, Bottom, Left, and Right margins, use the spinner arrows to enter the measurement you want for each margin; alternatively, type in a measurement.

If you're typesetting documents (rather than simply using the word processor to put them together), you may want to select the Mirror Margins check box. This makes the two inner-margin measurements the same as each other, and the two outer-margin measurements the same as each other. It also changes the Left and Right settings in the column under Margins in the Page Setup dialog box to Inside and Outside, respectively. (If you're having trouble visualizing the effect that mirror margins produce, try opening a few books on your bookshelf and looking to see if the margins will mirror each other when the book is closed. This book doesn't use mirror margins, but many others do.)

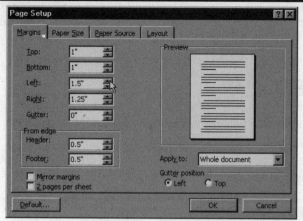

FIGURE 3.9:   The Margins tab of the Page Setup dialog box

To print two pages per sheet of paper, select the 2 Pages Per Sheet check box. This is especially useful with the Landscape paper orientation (discussed in the section titled "Setting Paper Orientation") for creating folded booklets on standard letter-sized paper. When you select 2 Pages Per Sheet, the Mirror Margins check box becomes dimmed and unavailable.

The *gutter measurement* is the space that your document will have on the inside of each facing page. For example, if you're working with mirror-margin facing pages, you could choose to have a gutter measurement of 1" and inside and outside margins of 1.25". That way, your documents would appear with a 1.25" left margin on left-hand pages, a 1.25" right margin on right-hand pages, and a 2.25" margin on the inside of each page (the gutter plus the margin setting). The two Gutter Position option buttons (Left and Top) control where Word positions the gutter margin on your pages. The default position of the gutter margin is left, but you can change the gutter margin to the top by selecting the Top option button. When Top is selected, the Mirror Margins and 2 Pages Per Sheet check boxes are dimmed and unavailable.

TIP

Use gutters for documents you're planning to bind. That way, you can be sure that you won't end up with text bound unreadably into the spine of the book.

Use the Preview box in the Page Setup dialog box to get an idea of how your document will look when you print it. (There's more on printing in Chapter 4.)

Setting Paper Size

Word lets you print on paper of various sizes, offering a Custom option to allow you to set a paper size of your own, in addition to various standard paper and envelope sizes.

To change the size of the paper you're printing on, click the Paper Size tab of the Page Setup dialog box (see Figure 3.10).

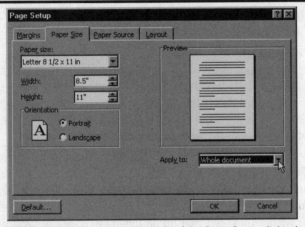

FIGURE 3.10:   The Paper Size tab of the Page Setup dialog box

In the Paper Size drop-down list box, choose the size of paper you'll be working with (for example, Letter 8½ × 11 in). If you can't find the width and height of paper you want, use the Width and Height boxes to set the width and height of the paper you're using; Word will automatically set the Paper Size box to Custom Size.

Setting Paper Orientation

To change the orientation of the page you're working on, click the Paper Size tab of the Page Setup dialog and choose Portrait or Landscape in the Orientation group box. (Portrait is taller than it is wide; Landscape is wider than it is tall.)

BORDERS AND SHADING

If a part of your document—whether it be text, a graphic, or an entire page—needs a little more emphasis, you can select it and add borders and shading by using either the Tables And Borders toolbar or the Borders And Shading dialog box. In general, the Tables And Borders toolbar is easier to use, as you can immediately see the effects it's producing.

Adding Borders and Shading Using the Tables And Borders Toolbar

To display the Tables And Borders toolbar, right-click the menu bar or any displayed toolbar and choose Tables And Borders from the context menu. Figure 3.11 shows the Tables And Borders toolbar with the buttons related to borders and shading identified.

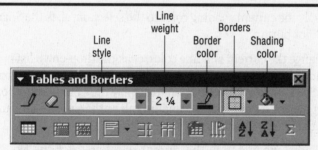

FIGURE 3.11: Use the border-related buttons on the Tables And Borders toolbar to apply borders.

First, choose the style of border you want to apply:

▶ Click the Line Style button and choose a suitable style of line from the drop-down list: single, dotted, dashed, dotted-and-dashed, multiple lines, and so on.

▶ Click the Line Weight button and choose a suitable weight from the drop-down list.

▶ Click the Border Color button and choose a color from the palette of available colors. The Automatic choice applies the default color of border for the font color of the text or object selected. To see more colors, click the More Line Colors button to display the Colors dialog box, select a color on either the Standard tab or the Custom tab, and click the OK button to apply it.

Next, apply the border:

▶ To apply the current style of border to the current selection, just click the Border button.

▶ To apply a different style of border, click the drop-down list button and choose a type of border from the border palette. If you're not clear which style of border one of the buttons on the palette represents, hover the mouse pointer over it to display the Screen-Tip for the button.

▶ To remove the border from the current selection, click the No Border button on the border palette.

Then apply shading if you want to:

▶ To apply the current shading color to the selection, click the Shading Color button.

▶ To change the current shading color, click the drop-down list button and choose a color from the palette. To see more fill colors, click the More Fill Colors button to display the Colors dialog box, select a color on either the Standard tab or the Custom tab, and click the OK button to apply it.

▶ To remove shading from the current selection, click the No Fill button on the Shading Color palette.

Adding Borders and Shading Using the Borders And Shading Dialog Box

For more control over the borders and shading you apply, use the Borders And Shading dialog box:

1. Select the text or objects to which you want to apply borders or shading and choose Format ➤ Borders And Shading to display the Borders And Shading dialog box (see Figure 3.12).

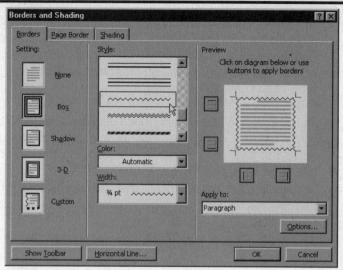

FIGURE 3.12: Apply borders and shading to items from the Borders And Shading dialog box.

2. On the Borders tab, choose the type of border you want to add from the options displayed:

   ▶ In the Settings area, choose one of the settings: None, Box, Shadow, Grid (for tables and cells), 3-D (not available for tables and cells), or Custom. Watch the effect in the Preview box.

   ▶ Next, choose the type of line you want from the Style list, choose a color from the Color drop-down list, and choose a weight from the Width drop-down list. To change one of the lines, click the appropriate icon in the Preview area to apply it or remove it.

   ▶ For text, you can choose Text or Paragraph in the Apply To drop-down list below the Preview area. If you apply the border to a paragraph, you can specify the distance of the border from the text by clicking the Options button and specifying Top, Bottom, Left, and Right settings in the Border And Shading Options dialog box. Then click the OK button.

3. On the Page Border tab, choose the type of border you want to add to the page. The controls on this tab work in the same way as those described in step 2. The important difference is that the Apply To drop-down list allows you to choose between the Whole Document, This Section, This Section– First Page Only, and This Section–All Except First Page. Again, clicking the Options button displays the Border And Shading Options dialog box, which allows you to place the border precisely on the page. The Art drop-down list provides decorative page borders suitable for cards, notices, and the like. Depending on your installation of Office, you may need to install the Art files separately; if so, choose Yes when Word prompts you to do so, and the Windows Installer will handle the process.

4. On the Shading tab, choose the type of shading to add:

   ▶ Choose the color for the shading from the Fill palette.

   ▶ Choose a style and color for the pattern in the Style And Color drop-down list boxes in the Patterns area.

   ▶ Finally, use the Apply To list to specify whether to apply the shading to the paragraph or just to selected text.

WARNING

Go easy with shading on printed documents, especially if you're using a mono-chrome printer. Any shading over 20 percent will completely mask text on most black-and-white printouts (even if it looks wonderfully artistic on screen). For Web documents, you can be a little more liberal with shading, but be careful not to make the pages difficult to read.

5. Click OK to close the Borders And Shading dialog box and apply your changes to the selection.

Removing Borders and Shading

To remove borders and shading, select the item, then choose Format ➢ Borders And Shading to display the Borders And Shading dialog box. Then:

▶ To remove a border, choose None in the Settings area on the Borders tab.

▶ To remove a page border, choose None in the Settings area on the Page Border tab.

▶ To remove shading, choose No Fill in the Fill palette and Clear in the Style drop-down list on the Shading tab.

Click OK to close the Borders And Shading dialog box.

Inserting Decorative Horizontal Lines

To insert a decorative horizontal line in a document:

1. Choose Format ➤ Borders And Shading to display the Borders And Shading dialog box.

2. Click the Horizontal Lines button on any one of the three tabs. Word will close the Borders And Shading dialog box and display the Horizontal Line dialog box.

3. On the Pictures tab, select the style of line you want.

4. Click the OK button to insert the line and close the Horizontal Line dialog box.

WHAT'S NEXT

You've mastered the tips and tricks necessary to get your documents to look good on the computer screen, and so in the next chapter we'll cover how to print them out perfectly so that you can show all your friends. Chapter 4 will deal with all aspects of printing your document, including previewing the document, printing multiple copies or a range of pages, collating, and printing labels and envelopes.

Chapter 4

PREVIEWING AND PRINTING DOCUMENTS

Printing can be quite simple or relatively involved, depending what you want to do. In this chapter, we will discuss printing common pages, envelopes, labels, and other kinds of documents in a variety of printing environments. We will discuss how to preview your documents before you print them, how to cancel a print job in midstream when you change your mind or don't like the results that you are seeing on your first few pages of the job, and more.

We also discuss various kinds of printing tasks you can accomplish with Microsoft Word, beginning with simple projects and then moving to more complex circumstances. First, though, in the brief next section, let's ensure that your computer system is ready to print.

Adapted from *Mastering Word 2000 Premium Edition* by Ron Mansfield and J.W. Olsen

ISBN 0-7821-2314-7   1120 pages $39.99

FIRST THINGS FIRST

Before you begin printing, you must be sure that your printer or printers are properly cabled to your computer and that you have set up Windows for printing. See the documentation that came with your printer and, if necessary, also check out your Windows documentation for the details that apply to your hardware.

TIP

It is always good to save before you print. Occasionally, printing problems can lock up a computer, and you might lose unsaved changes if you must restart your system. Do what the pros do: Get into the habit of pressing Ctrl+S or clicking the Save button on Word's Standard toolbar before you print. Personally, I've developed a reflex habit of pressing Ctrl+S whenever I do almost anything other than entering text—before printing, before switching between Word documents, before switching from Word to another application, and even before performing more complex chores in Word itself.

After your printer is set up, before you tell Word to print a document, be sure that your printer is turned on, loaded with supplies, and, if applicable, warmed up. Most printers have a ready light that indicates that the printer is ready to do its thing. The remainder of this chapter assumes that your printer is set up and ready to print.

WHY'D IT DO THAT?

One of life's little mysteries for new (and many not-so-new) Word users is why Word asks you whether to save changes to a document after printing, even though you may not have made any changes to the document. What Word is really asking is whether you want to save the date of last printing, which it hides in a statistical area in your file.

To check out this and other statistics for a current document, use File ➤ Properties and then click the Statistics tab from the dialog box that appears.

CONTINUED ➞

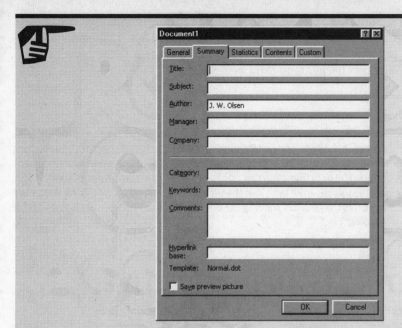

To check the properties of a Word document that is not currently open, select File ➤ Open, navigate to the desired file, right-click that file, and then select Properties from the context menu. In this case, Word automatically brings the Statistics tab information to the forefront, so you don't have to click it.

INTRODUCING BASIC PRINTING

If you want to print only a single copy of a basic document to your default printer, open the document in Word with File ➤ Open and then do one of the following:

- ▶ Select File ➤ Print
- ▶ Press Ctrl+P
- ▶ Click the Print button on Word's Standard toolbar

The status area on the bottom of Word's window will chart the progress as your document prints. Page numbers and a little animated printer icon tell you how many pages have been sent to the printer or to the Windows background printing feature.

TIP

Assuming you have Word and Windows set up for background printing (discussed in the "Background Printing" section later in this chapter), you can continue working in Word or in another Windows application while your document prints. The only thing you can't do is work on the current Word document during the usually brief time that the little printer icon on the Windows status bar indicates that Word is sending the document to the Windows background print spooler.

PRINTING IS AN INTERACTIVE SPORT

Although printing can be as simple as described in the preceding section, it is a good idea to get into the habit of using Word's Page Setup dialog box, and possibly the Print dialog box, whenever you begin a new document—particularly if you work with a variety of printers, paper sizes, and document designs. (These dialog boxes are discussed and illustrated in the sections that follow.) Otherwise, if you wait until you have finished working on a document before choosing a printer, your page and line endings may change considerably from those you initially saw on your screen. This can result in anything from a minor annoyance to big-time disaster.

For example, if you write a long document, create a table of contents, and then change printers or choose different printing features, the line and page breaks may change. You will need to redo the table of contents so that it agrees with the newly formatted pages. The following printer decisions affect pagination and should be selected or determined when you begin a project. (Other changes affect the appearance of printed pages, but have little impact on pagination and other printing-related issues.)

► Page Setup options (such as paper source)

► Printer model

► Paper size

- ▶ Reduction or enlargement (scaling)
- ▶ Page orientation
- ▶ Margins
- ▶ Gutters
- ▶ Larger or smaller print area
- ▶ Printing or not printing hidden Word text
- ▶ Printing or not printing footnotes and endnotes
- ▶ Font substitution options
- ▶ The phase of the moon

Print Dialog Box Options

You use the Print dialog box to tell Word a variety of details about your current printing task, such as which printer to use, which pages to print, and how many copies to print. We discuss these options in the following sections. But first, you must access the Print dialog box. To do so, select File ➤ Print or use the Ctrl+P shortcut. Word displays the dialog box shown in Figure 4.1.

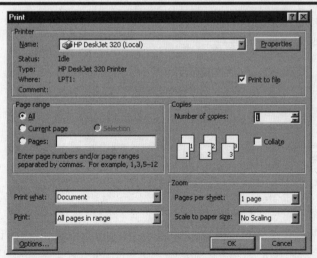

FIGURE 4.1: The Print dialog box appears when you choose to print a document.

Choosing an Installed Printer

If you have only one printer and it works properly on your system, you can skip to the next section, "Choosing What to Print." Otherwise, to choose a previously installed printer for your current document, follow these steps after opening the Print dialog box as indicated in the preceding section.

1. Notice the drop-down pick list of printers in the Printer section of the Print dialog box. Click the downward-pointing arrow next to the pick list to see the installed printers on your system and choose the one you want to use.

2. If the printer you have chosen has options (letter quality versus draft quality, lighter or darker, and so on), you can usually reach these by clicking the dialog box's Properties button. Figure 4.2 shows the user-settable properties for an HP DeskJet 320 printer.

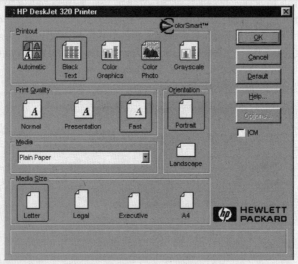

FIGURE 4.2: For many printers, you can set properties similar to those indicated here.

3. When you are finished adjusting the printer's settings, click the dialog box's OK button. You may have to click OK more than once to get back to the Print dialog box. When you click the OK button in the Print dialog box, the dialog box closes and your document prints. Reward yourself with a cup of coffee.

Choosing What to Print

Normally, you will want to print all or part of your document by itself.
However, sometimes you may want to print other things, such as the document's annotations or other information. Use the Print What drop-
down pick list in the Print dialog box to select any of the following
options:

- ▶ Document
- ▶ Document properties
- ▶ Comments
- ▶ Styles
- ▶ AutoText entries (typing shortcuts)
- ▶ Key assignments (keyboard shortcuts)

Choosing How Many Copies to Print

To specify more than one copy of whatever you intend to print, either
type a number in the Copies text box in the Print dialog box or click the
upward- or downward-pointing arrows next to that text box to display the
number of copies you want.

Choosing Whether to Collate

If you request multiple copies (five copies of a 10-page document, for
instance) and do not choose the Collate option on the Print dialog box,
Word will print all five copies of page 1, then all five copies of page 2, and
so on. You will need to hand-collate them to make orderly sets. If you choose
the Collate option, Word will print all pages of the first copy of the document in order, then all pages of the second copy, and so forth.

Collating may or may not increase overall printing time depending on
your printer and a number of other factors; you will have to experiment.
However, even if you lose a little print time, the nuisance of avoiding
hand collating may be worth the loss.

Choosing a Page Range

To print an entire document, be sure that the All radio button in the Page
Range region of the Print dialog box is marked. To print only the page in
your document currently containing the insertion point, click the Current

Page button. To print selected text, select the text before opening the Print dialog box. Then, click the Selection button in the Page Range area. This choice will be inaccessible unless you have selected something in your document.

To print a range of pages (pages 6–10 in a 50-page document, for instance), type the first and last page number in the Pages text box separated with hyphens (*6–10* in this example). Or, to print specific, individual pages, list them separated by commas (*3,5,8,* for instance). Ranges and single pages can be combined in a single print job. So entering *6–10,13,19,42–44* will work, too.

Choosing to Print All, Odd, or Even Pages

Many of my Word pages are odd. But, we're not really talking about weirdness here.

Normally, Word prints all pages in order. But if you want to print two-sided sheets of paper or if you have other reasons to separate odd and even pages, use the drop-down Print pick list at the bottom of the Print dialog box to specify Odd Pages or Even Pages. For example, you might first print all odd-numbered pages and then put the sheets of paper back in the printer facing the opposite direction to print the even-numbered pages on the other side. This technique quickly saves both paper and storage space for mega projects.

Choosing to Print to a File

You can send a "printed" version of a document to a file on a disk instead of to a printer. This technique is sometimes used when you want to take a document to a service bureau for typesetting or other special services. A print file contains all the information needed to allow printing even if the other computer does not have exactly the same fonts used to create the file (or even a copy of Word itself).

It is wise to do a test run before trying this technique on large or urgent documents, because print-to-disk files contain many land mines. Consider providing your service bureau with copies of the original Word document files and a printed copy of them as well as the print-to-disk files. The printed copy visually provides the desired results, while the Word document files can be used if necessary to tweak the files before the document is typeset or processed in other ways.

TIP

When planning to send print-to-disk files to a service bureau, check with the vendor before you even begin your document to determine their needs and to avoid problems before they occur. Service bureaus can have widely differing needs, and even in the best of circumstances, problems can and regularly do arise.

To print a document to a disk file, check the Print to File checkbox in the Printer region of the Print dialog box. The dialog box shown in Figure 4.3 appears, in which you specify the name of the file in which to save the print-to-disk copy of your document.

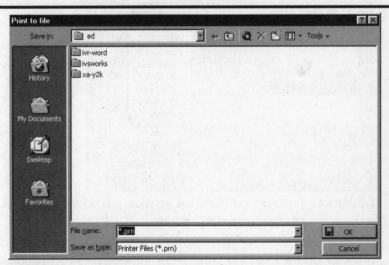

FIGURE 4.3: Enter a filename in this dialog box to save a print-to-disk copy of your document.

TIP

The disk size of print-to-disk files can mushroom, particularly if they contain graphics. Consider printing small ranges of pages to multiple files if you need to transport print files on floppy disks. You will need to experiment, because the disk space required per page can vary widely, even among several pages of the same document.

Two-Tray Printers

If your printer has two paper sources (such as two trays, or a tray and a "pass-through" feature), Word can switch sources as needed. To prepare your document for two-tray and similar features, follow these steps:

1. Select File ➢ Page Setup. A dialog box appears.

2. Select the Paper Source tab in the dialog box. The dialog box now looks like Figure 4.4.

FIGURE 4.4:   The Page Setup dialog box lets you access multiple paper sources for printers that offer that feature.

3. Set the First Page, Other Pages, and perhaps Apply To options as appropriate for your needs.

4. Click the OK button in the dialog box. The dialog box closes and your preferences are stored.

Other Printing Options

Word offers still more printer options—enough to satisfy even the most compulsive techie addicts among us. These options can be reached by choosing the Print tab in Word's Options dialog box shown in Figure 4.5. These options are discussed individually in the following sections.

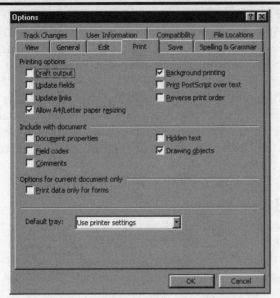

FIGURE 4.5:   The Print tab in the Options dialog box lets you set a variety of printing-related preferences.

You display the Options dialog box either by choosing Tools ➢ Options and then clicking the Print tab or by clicking the Options button in the Print dialog box. These settings remain in place after you choose them for future documents until you change them. This is sort of a set 'em and forget 'em thing.

Draft Output

The Draft Output option can speed printing. Its effect varies from printer to printer. Everything may be printed in a single font, as efficiently as possible and at the expense of appearance. In any case, think of this option as a down-and-dirty tool.

Update Fields and Update Links

With the Update Fields and Update Links options, you determine when and if Word's fields and links are updated before printing.

Allow A4/Letter Paper Resizing

Check the Allow A4/Letter Paper Resizing option if you want Word to automatically adjust the printout of your document to fit a different size of paper. For example, you would use this option if you work in the United States, where we generally use 8.5″ × 11″ paper, and are exchanging documents with someone in another country, where A4 often is the standard paper size. Only the printed copy is affected when you enable this option; the formatted document itself is not. If you want to change the margins on your monitor, too, you must explicitly do so. (Chapter 3 covers formatting further.)

Background Printing

A check in the Background Printing checkbox causes Word to use the Windows Background printing feature, which lets you work on other things while your document prints in the background. On computers with modest resources (especially minimal memory), this can make the computer uncomfortably sluggish or sometimes even lead to other, more serious symptoms. If you experience problems, you may want to try turning off background printing. Typically, background printing does not slow the speed of the printing itself, because background printing attempts to feed the printer with enough of a document to keep the printer chugging away at its top speed.

Print PostScript over Text

This option is only needed when you are printing a converted Word for Macintosh document. The option causes Word to print PostScript code over text rather than under it, which can be useful if a graphic has been included in encapsulated PostScript form. The option applies when the document contains a Print field.

TIP

Don't worry about this option unless you are printing to a PostScript device and even then only after you encounter a problem.

Reverse Print Order

Use Reverse Print Order to print documents from last page to first page. This is a handy feature for printers that output pages face up, which means that without this feature you must manually reverse the order of pages to get the first page of a document on top. I'm sure you can think of more inviting ways to get your daily exercise.

Include with Document

The Include with Document choices in the Print tab of the Options dialog box are self-explanatory. Click the checkbox next to the associated item (summary information, annotations, and so on) to place a checkmark in the box so that the associated item will print along with the document's contents. Clicking a checkmark again removes the checkmark and prevents the associated item from printing. Here are the choices involved:

- ▶ Document properties
- ▶ Field codes
- ▶ Comments
- ▶ Hidden text
- ▶ Drawing objects

Options for Current Document Only

The options that appear in the Options for Current Document Only region of the dialog box vary with the contents of your document. A common option here lets you print data within a Word form without printing the related form, too. If other options appear in this region related to a particular option, try right-clicking the item and selecting the What's This? context menu option.

Default Tray

Use this choice to force a paper source other than the standard tray of your printer for special needs (such as a cover letter that you want to print on your business letterhead). Obviously, the selected printer must have more than one paper source for this to be useful. You might need to press a button or two on your printer to feed paper from the auxiliary tray. Consult your printer's documentation.

USING PRINT PREVIEW

You aren't required to use Word's Print Preview feature before you print a document. For short documents or for documents that are quite unadorned (perhaps containing nothing more than paragraphs of Normal style text), Print Preview may be more of a time waster than a time saver. But sometimes, especially for more a complex project, previewing your document before printing it may save you time, paper, and aggravation.

To enter Print Preview mode, Choose File ➤ Print Preview (or use one of the keyboard shortcuts, Ctrl+Alt+I and Ctrl+F2). Print Preview gives you an excellent idea of how your document will look when it is printed. You will be able to see margins and, if your document contains headers, footers, line numbers, and other embellishments, you will see them, too, as illustrated in Figure 4.6.

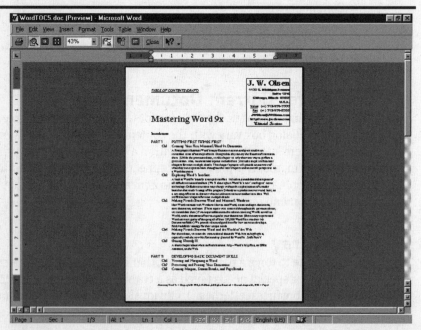

FIGURE 4.6: Use Print Preview to get an overview of how a document will print, including its header and footer.

Notice the toolbar buttons along the top of the Print Preview window. With them, you can control many of Print Preview's functions. As always, if you forget a button's function, pointing to it without clicking will display button help. The following is a brief outline of the functionality of these buttons (from left to right).

Part i

Print   The Print button on the Print Preview toolbar prints a single copy of the document without opening the Print dialog box. (If you need to set options on the Print dialog box, discussed earlier in this chapter, choose File ➤ Print or press Ctrl+P just as you would do while in any other Word view.)

Magnifier   The Magnifier button lets you zoom in to better read small portions of the page and zoom out to get a bird's-eye view of one or more pages.

One Page   The One Page button previews a single page even if you are working with a multiple-page document.

Multiple Pages   The Multiple Pages button lets you specify the number of miniaturized pages you want to see simultaneously. Pressing this button drops down a toolbar from which you can select how many pages you want to appear at the same time. In Figure 4.7, all three pages of a three-page document are viewed simultaneously.

Zoom Control   The Zoom Control (the text box that displays a percentage value) tells you the current enlargement or reduction factor and lets you select a variety of zoom levels from a drop-down pick list. You can also click in the text box and enter a value of your own. (Often, the preset zoom levels don't quite meet your needs. Experiment. You may be surprised how handy entering a value of your choice may be.)

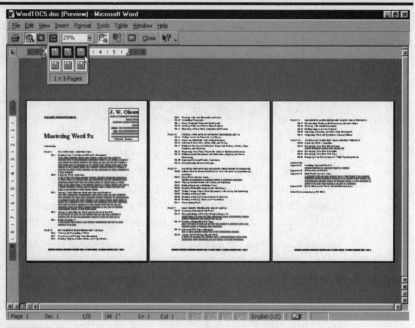

FIGURE 4.7: The Multiple Pages feature lets you specify how many of a document's pages you want to preview simultaneously.

View Rulers   You click the View Rulers button to toggle the Print Preview rulers that you can see in Figure 4.7. These rulers indicate the margins for your current document. You can adjust these margins. (Try this option, too. Often, eliminating the rulers provides just enough extra screen real estate to let you enlarge a document enough to make it much easier to preview in detail.)

Shrink to Fit   When you press the cool Shrink to Fit button (to the right of the View Rulers button), Word attempts to tighten and tweak a document that ends with a mostly white page. For example, Figure 4.8 shows how Word proposes to tighten the three pages shown in Figure 4.7 into two, fuller pages. Occasionally, Word can't successfully shrink a document. If it can't, it will tell you so.

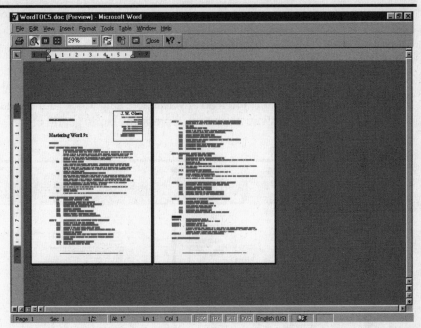

Part i

FIGURE 4.8: Word's Shrink to Fit button often removes those ugly, short last pages of documents. Compare this figure to the way the same document would have been printed as shown in Figure 4.7.

NOTE

To undo the results of Shrink to Fit, choose Edit ➢ Undo Shrink to Fit or press Ctrl+Z.

Full Screen The Full Screen button removes most of the Print Preview clutter (menu bar, title bar, status bar, and so on) so that you can see a bigger version of your document. Again, seeing a larger version of a document may be just enough to significantly aid you in previewing the details of a document. Pressing the Full Screen button a second time returns the hidden controls. Figure 4.9 illustrates Print Preview in Full Screen view.

Close Button   The Print Preview toolbar's Close button takes you back to the previous view you were using before entering Print Preview. Pressing your Esc key has the same effect.

Help Button   The Help button morphs your mouse cursor into a question mark. Point to the item of interest (the vertical ruler, for instance) to read any available help. Click your mouse anywhere in Word's window or press any key to get rid of the pop-up help.

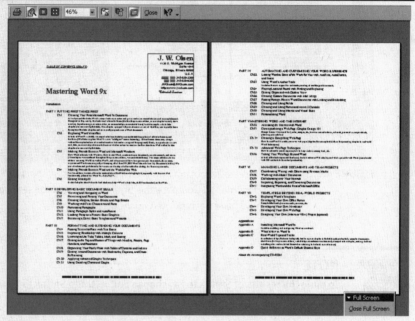

FIGURE 4.9:   Print Preview's Full Screen button lets you see your document in more detail by removing much of Word's screen clutter.

TIP

Pressing Esc is a quick way to exit Print Preview and return to the view you were using before entering Print Preview. You can also select a view from the View menu or click the Close button on Print Preview's toolbar to exit.

Here is a down-and-dirty way to adjust print-time margins while you are working in Print Preview:

1. Display the rulers if they are not already visible by clicking the View Ruler button on the Print Preview toolbar.

2. Point to the place near the top or bottom of the vertical ruler on the left edge of your screen where the white portion of the ruler meets the gray portion. (This point designates one of your margins.) The cursor lets you know that you have successfully found the margin by morphing into an arrow with two arrowheads pointing in opposite directions.

3. Hold down your primary mouse button (normally the left button). A dashed line denoting the margin appears across your screen, as illustrated in Figure 4.10.

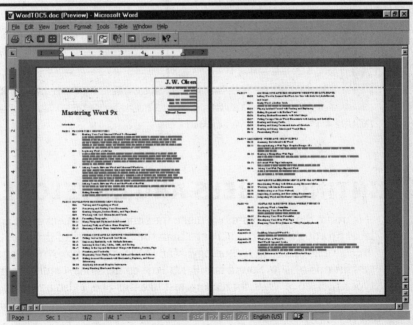

FIGURE 4.10: Drag a margin handle to adjust the margins.

4. While continuing to hold down the mouse button, drag the white portion of the ruler (and the dashed line, which tags along for the ride) up or down to where you want the new margin to be.

5. Release the mouse button. Word adjusts the margin, moving the text up or down, as illustrated in Figure 4.11.

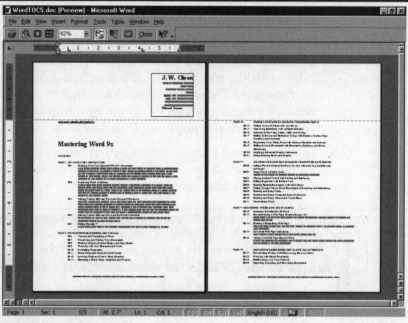

FIGURE 4.11: The margin is adjusted.

PRINTING LABELS AND ENVELOPES

It is ironic that our computers make the simple tasks of envelope and label printing more of a challenge than the typewriters of the past. So much for advances in technology! Many offices keep typewriters around just for this reason. Sound familiar? (True confessions: I still have my typewriter, circa 1979, for reasons just like this one. I also have a special label printer and label software attached to one of my computers for similar reasons.)

But computerized envelope and label printing really is not so bad after you get the hang of it, and you can set up documents that remember the recipe for you. If you don't have a typewriter kicking around, give the instructions described here a try before marching out to buy a typewriter. You may actually prefer using your computer for envelopes and labels.

Word has envelope, label, and list-management features that you may find quite useful. But before we get into the specifics, here are some general tips:

▶ Use preprinted window envelopes whenever possible to avoid envelope printing altogether. Set up letterheads, invoices, and other documents with the inside address properly positioned for standard window envelopes.

▶ Ask your letterhead designer to take your computer printer into consideration. Running a list of preprinted information along the left side of letterhead may not allow you to properly position inside addresses, and some paper stock and ink won't work properly in some computer printers.

▶ Choose envelopes designed for your printer. These supplies are easy to find these days, and many office-supply stores and mail-order paper sellers stock them. Laser-friendly envelopes have flaps and glue that minimize jamming. Ink-jet-savvy envelopes are made of paper stock that won't fuzz up your characters or cause them to smear.

▶ Purchase an envelope tray or feeder for your printer if you print many of them.

Printing Envelopes

Word can print addresses on envelopes by looking for the addresses in your documents (the inside address of a letter, for instance), or you can manually type an address in Word's Envelopes and Labels dialog box. For example, Word correctly inserted the Delivery Address textbox's contents in Figure 4.12 based on the letter in Word's document window. The Return Address details were completed manually.

To open the Envelopes and Labels dialog box depicted in Figure 4.12, choose Tools ➤ Envelopes and Labels. In this dialog box you can do the following:

▶ Print envelopes containing single-use addresses that you type into the dialog box itself

▶ Copy an address from your document for envelope printing

▶ Type envelope addresses and have Word store them in your letters or other Word documents

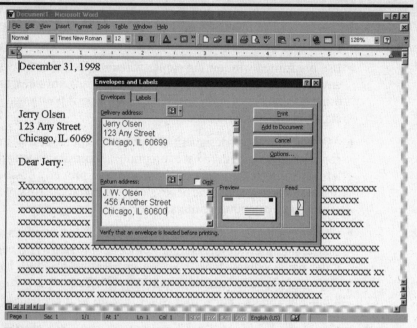

FIGURE 4.12: Word can pull addresses from your document, or you can enter them by hand.

Setting Up a Return Address

If your envelopes have preprinted return addresses, you can skip this task. But if you want to use unprinted envelopes and have Word print your return address in the upper-left corner of an envelope, follow these steps:

1. Choose the printer you plan to use from the File ➤ Print dialog box if you have more than one printer.

2. Open the Envelopes and Labels dialog box by choosing Tools ➤ Envelopes and Labels.

3. Click the dialog box's Envelopes tab if it is not foremost. Word displays the dialog box that was shown in Figure 4.12.

4. If Word finds an address in the current Word document, you will see it in the Delivery Address portion of the dialog box. Otherwise, you can enter one by hand.

5. Type your return address in the text box labeled Return Address. (Part of the address already may be entered, based on your Word User Info details.)

6. When you are happy with the spelling and appearance of your return address, try test printing on a standard #10 (4.125″ × 8.5″) envelope. Word assumes that you can center-feed envelopes in your printer. If that's not possible, click the envelope in the Feed section of the dialog box to display the Envelope Options dialog box, shown in Figure 4.13.

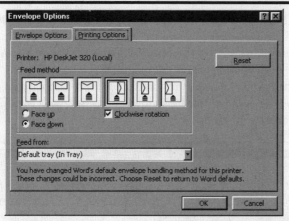

FIGURE 4.13: You can change envelope printing options in this dialog box.

7. Select the desired options for your printer; then click the OK button. The Envelope Options dialog box closes.

8. Place an envelope in your printer.

9. Click the Print button in the Envelopes and Labels dialog box. Your envelope prints.

TIP

In typical situations, Word usually guesses the delivery address correctly. If, however, you have several addresses in your document, Word might get confused. One way around this is to select (highlight) the correct delivery address with your mouse before you invoke Tools ➢ Envelopes.

Suppressing a Return Address

If you always plan to use envelopes that contain preprinted return addresses, you can make sure that nothing prints in that portion of your envelope by ensuring that the Return Address text box in the Envelopes and Labels dialog box is blank. On the other hand, if you expect to use preprinted envelopes part of the time and unprinted envelopes at other times, you can enter a return address and, when necessary, suppress its printing by placing a checkmark in the Omit checkbox of the dialog box, which is sort of like having the best of both worlds.

Storing an Envelope Page with Your Documents

Clicking the Add to Document button in the Envelopes and Labels dialog box inserts an envelope page at the beginning of your document. Word takes care of all of the details. Doing so means that if you print the document in the future, you can also automatically print its associated envelope. Take a look at how all of this looks in Print Preview with two "pages" showing, as illustrated in Figure 4.14.

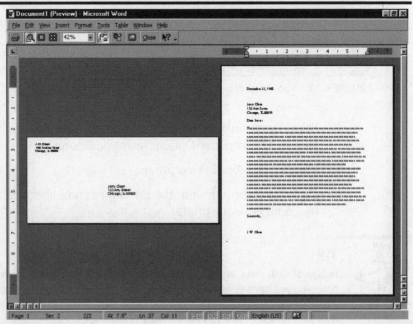

FIGURE 4.14: Word will store an envelope's text as part of your document file if you ask politely.

Changing Addresses

After you have inserted an envelope page in a document, you can change the envelope and inside address (the recipient's address at the top of your letter) at any time. Here's how:

1. Open the document.

2. Make the address change in the inside address. *Or* choose Tools ➤ Envelopes and Labels and make your changes there.

WARNING

If you change the Delivery Address in the Envelopes and Labels dialog box and then click the Change Document button, Word updates the envelope but *not* the inside address in the main portion of your document.

3. Click the Change Document button on the dialog box. (This is the same button that was labeled Add to Document in Figure 4.12. Only its name has been changed to protect the innocent.) The envelope is changed.

Envelope Sizes, Fonts, and Other Options

Word lets you specify envelope sizes (both standard and custom), fonts for delivery and return addresses, and more. The options are selected from two tabs in the Envelope Options dialog box, which you access through the following steps.

1. Select Tools ➤ Envelopes and Labels. The Envelopes and Labels dialog box opens.

2. Click the Options button on the dialog box. The Envelopes dialog box appears.

3. Click the Envelope Options tab on the dialog box. The dialog box is shown in Figure 4.15.

4. Proceed with setting any of the options described next.

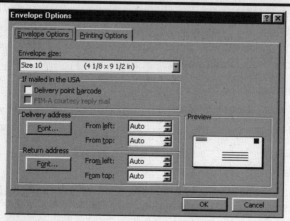

FIGURE 4.15: You can set several envelope printing options from this dialog box.

You can choose from any of the standard envelope sizes listed in the drop-down pick list or specify a custom size by typing dimensions or selecting Custom Size in the drop-down Envelope Size pick list in the Envelope Size dialog box. If you select Custom Size from the pick list, a pop-up dialog box lets you enter your envelope's dimensions.

If you are sending mail within the United States, you can ask Word to print bar codes on your envelopes. Bar codes can speed automated mail sorting, reduce delivery time, and reduce mail-handling errors. Word supports both POSTNET bar codes (for regular mail) and FIM-A (for business-reply mail). Both types of codes are illustrated in Figure 4.16.

FIGURE 4.16: This envelope contains a FIM-A (business-reply) bar code near its top and a POSTNET (automated postal routing) bar code just above the delivery address.

The remaining options depicted in Figure 4.15 let you change the font and the positioning for either the delivery address or the return address. These options are self-explanatory. Experiment with them if you aren't satisfied with Word's default values. The Preview region of the dialog box visually approximates the results of your changes.

Printing Labels

Label printing is similar to envelope printing, except that you have even more options. For instance, you can print single labels or sheets of labels. Word knows the dimensions for many industry-standard label stocks.

Simple label printing is a lot like envelope printing. Here are the general steps:

1. Select the address in your document if it has one. (This step is optional.)

2. Choose Tools ➤ Envelopes and Labels. The Envelopes and Labels dialog box appears.

3. Click the Labels tab if it is not already foremost. You will see the options illustrated in Figure 4.17.

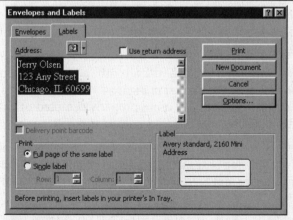

FIGURE 4.17: You perform the basic steps to print a label from this dialog box.

4. If you selected an address in step 1 or if Word finds one on its own, you will see it in the dialog box; if not, type an address in the Address text box.

5. Choose the desired options in the main Labels tab. To print a single label on a multilabel sheet, click Single Label and specify the row and column position of the label on your labels sheet. Choose to print or not print a bar code and return address.

6. To select different label sizes, click the Options button. The dialog box illustrated in Figure 4.18 appears.

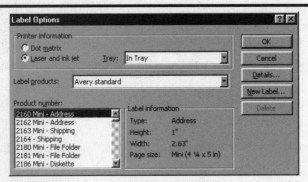

FIGURE 4.18:   The Label Options dialog box lets you fine-tune your labeling requirements.

7. Select the requirements for your labels. ·For even more detailed options (wow!), click the Details button. The new dialog box, shown in Figure 4.19, appears.

8. You will only need to muck with all of the additional options in the dialog box presented in Figure 4.19 if *all* the labels of the current type are not quite properly centered on your sheets of labels.

9. When you have made your choices, if any, click the OK buttons of all dialog boxes until you return to the Labels tab of the Envelopes and Labels dialog box that was illustrated in Figure 4.17.

10. Insert a label or sheet of labels of the proper style into your printer.

11. Click the Print button on the dialog box. Your labels print.

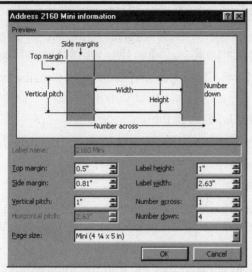

FIGURE 4.19: Guess what? More detailed label options—decisions, decisions...

THE PROPER CARE AND FEEDING OF LABELS

It is a good idea to do a trial run of labels by practicing on plain paper. Hold the test pages up to a light source behind a sheet of label stock to see how they line up. If all looks well, you can print on the considerably more expensive label stock.

Normally, you can put partially used sheets of labels through your printer once or twice more, but you run a risk of jamming and possibly damaging your printer. It is often wiser to print full sheets and file the unused labels for the next time you mail something to the same recipient—or to discard partially printed sheets or use them for other purposes. Label paper stock isn't cheap, but your printer is much more of an investment. Label stock can be mighty mean to printers.

Including Graphics on Envelopes

You can print graphics on envelopes. It is a great way to add logos, special messages, business reply art, yadda, yadda. Here are the general steps:

1. Choose Tools ➣ Envelopes and Labels. The dialog box appears.

2. Select the Envelope tab in the dialog box.

3. Click the Add to Document button (which may be labeled as Change Document—it doesn't matter).

4. Switch to View ➣ Print Layout view.

5. Paste or create a graphic, and then drag it where you want it. (You can use the Insert ➣ Picture command described in the Chapter 5.)

6. Make any other changes that you want (rearrange or reformat lines of text in the inside address, for instance).

7. Save your changes with your document or as a template (as discussed in a moment).

Figure 4.20 illustrates a Print Preview view of the results after a graphic was inserted into the envelope shown in Figure 4.16.

FIGURE 4.20:   You can add a graphic to your envelopes.

At this point, the envelope is one-of-a-kind and in a separate section at the top of your current document. You can either save the document and print the envelope along with the rest of the document or save the document as a template for repeated use.

But there's one other possibility. If you want your glorious artwork to appear on *all* your envelopes, you can select the art and create a special AutoText entry called EnvelopeExtra 1 or EnvelopeExtra 2.

Labels and Large Mailing Lists

When mailing to many addresses, consider using Word's Mail Merge feature. To preview these labels, follow these general steps:

1. In a document, type the name, address, and so forth that you want on the label.

2. Format the information, adding graphics if you want, as discussed in the preceding section.

3. Select the label, including the graphic.

4. Select Tools ➤ Envelopes and Labels. The dialog box opens.

5. Select the right label size and make any other appropriate changes as discussed in the "Printing Labels" section earlier in this chapter.

6. Click New Document on the Labels tab. Your labels will appear in the document, which you can preview.

FORMATTING LABELS

There is no easy way to insert art or change the font, size, or other elements of character appearance in the Labels tab (even though you can do these things with envelopes). This means that name tags, video-spine labels, and similar specialty labels can look rather nondescript.

There is a workaround to this problem (clicking the Add to Document button and then editing the individual labels in the document). This approach isn't too practical for larger projects, however.

Formatting all labels in a given document is a breeze. Select them all, make them look terrific, and then print them. They won't look different from one another, but the labels for a given mailing—name badges for a conference, for example—can have a great look that is unique to that event.

Checking—and Changing—the Status of Printing Documents

With background printing at work (see the "Background Printing" section earlier in this chapter), you can check and change the status of multiple print jobs. Your options are to pause or cancel active printing tasks.

To check the status of currently printing jobs, to pause them, or to cancel them, follow these steps:

1. Double-click the printer's icon in the Windows Taskbar. A printer window appears.

2. Right-click any jobs you want to pause or cancel. A context menu appears.

3. Click the desired option from the pop-up context menu to pause or cancel the jobs.

4. Use the printer menus for other options, if desired.

5. To return to Word, hold down the Alt key and press Tab as many times as necessary for Word to be selected.

TIP

A quick way to cancel *all* pending print jobs (whether invoked from Word or otherwise) is to choose Printer ➢ Close from your printer's window or to click the standard Windows Close button in the upper-right corner of that window. Either way, Windows asks you to confirm that you want to cancel all pending print jobs before it closes the Printer window.

What's Next

Now that you're a pro in Word's printing features, we can go on to fancier stuff, like graphics. You'll be able to pretty up your documents with all sorts of art, and soon you'll be using the Picture toolbar, resizing and cropping graphics, and adding balloon callouts left and right.

Chapter 5

Looking Pretty As a Picture: Basic Graphics

I f you adhere to the adage that a picture is worth a thousand words, you will be delighted to know that Microsoft Word lets you import graphics created with other software as well as draw, place, resize, reposition, and embellish graphics. You can use your own drawings, charts from spreadsheet packages, photos that you run through a computer scanner, and just about any other computer-compatible art form or object. Word even comes with some clip art that you can use to begin your graphics library. This chapter contains all you need to know to start creating and using art in Word.

Adapted from *Mastering Word 2000 Premium Edition* by Ron Mansfield and J.W. Olsen

ISBN 0-7821-2314-7   1120 pages $39.99

First Things First

Word's graphics tools break down into two categories: those for *bitmap graphics* and those for *vector images*. Roughly speaking, bitmap graphics can be thought of as "painted" images or pictures, while vector graphics can be thought of as line drawings—things like you might sketch with a pen or pencil, such as a series of lines, ovals, rectangles, and freehand scribbles.

Because of the technical differences between bitmap and vector images, you generally use different tools in Word to work with each of them. If you are working with a bitmap graphic, most of what you will want to know is found in the sections beginning at the "Using Insert Picture" section in this chapter. If you are working with a vector graphic, most of what you will want to know begins in the "Using Word's Drawing Tools" section later in this chapter. However, because of some overlap in graphic tools and techniques in Word, you may want to familiarize yourself with both major discussions.

If the tools described in one of these major discussions don't seem to work with your current graphic, check out the other major discussion. Graphics newbies sometimes confuse the two categories of graphics. Vector graphics created by a pro can look remarkably like a "real" picture (bitmap) image. On the flip side, a bitmap conceivably could contain an image as simple as a black line on a white background—and thus be mistaken for a vector image.

GETTING OFF ON THE RIGHT GRAPHICAL FOOT

The effects of many or most graphic-related commands can be quite unexpected, even for experienced users. Therefore, you should use File ➤ Save or its keyboard shortcut, Ctrl+S, frequently when working with graphics. In fact, working with graphics is a great reason to save a copy of your document under a unique filename with File ➤ Save As at each stage of graphic manipulation, from inserting the graphic into your document through each stage of editing the graphic. That way, you can revert to the last "good" copy of the document—not merely the copy before your last save command. If you have *really* worked yourself into a graphical corner, merely going back one step may do you little or no good.

IMPORTING GRAPHICS

Like text, computer art is stored in disk files. Unfortunately, different graphics products store their creations in dozens of different file formats. Part of the reason for this is historic. Different vendors sought to lock users into their proprietary formats, hoping that you and others who access your graphics would be a captive audience for their products. Also, patent issues were a factor. Rather than pay royalties to a competitor, vendors would design their own format. And of course, the legendary programmer ego entered the picture. ("My format is better than your format, na-na-na-na-na.")

But plenty of entirely justifiable reasons led to some of the graphics format flavors. For example, in some cases (such as on the Internet), the size of files is critical, because smaller files transfer to viewers faster. In other cases (such as photos destined for slick advertising brochures), maximum quality may be all that matters. Still other formats were developed to permit editable layers of images in a single graphic. (Perhaps you want to superimpose a hat on a model for an ad. Later, your client wants you to substitute a different model—but keep the hat.) Yet other formats were devised to permit animated graphics, such as spinning logos. The list of needs goes on and on.

Fortunately, Word contains a number of built-in graphic translators, so that it can enter the Tower of Babel of graphic file formats and allow you to insert their images into Word documents. Therefore, usually you do not need to worry yourself about the format. However, if you do encounter a graphic file whose format Word does not understand, you can use any of many fine third-party file conversion utilities. (Many such utilities also let you modify the appearance of graphics far, far beyond the features offered by a word processor—the right tool for the right job, as another adage goes....)

SOURCES OF ARTWORK

You have many ways to obtain the artwork to include in your Word documents. Here are some of them:

- ▶ Create your own artwork. We discuss some of Word's intrinsic drawing tools in later sections of this chapter; but if you are serious about creating your own graphics, you will soon decide that you need a third-party program specifically designed for this purpose. (You almost certainly have the rather anemic Paint program that ships with Windows. Usually, it is found on your Start Menu at Start ➤ Accessories ➤ Paint.) If you have licensed Microsoft Office rather than just Word, check out the promising PhotoDraw 2000. It may meet many of your graphics needs.

▶ Word arrives with a variety of clip art. To see what is provided, select Insert ➤ Picture ➤ Clip Art and browse the dialog box that appears. (If you did not install Word's full clip art collection when you installed Word, you may want to use Word's installer again at this time.)

▶ You can purchase gorgeous third-party artwork collections—many free or at a steal of a price, others quite expensive—on the Internet, from retail computer stores, from ads in major computer magazines, and elsewhere.

▶ If you have a scanner attached to your computer, you can create computer graphic files from printed images or, in some cases, from photographic slides. The price of basic scanners has dropped to a relative pittance in the last year or two.

NOTE

Be sure that you understand and honor copyright restrictions when you use graphics. With today's technology, it is all too easy to rob others—and many people don't even realize that they are doing so. Some people assume, for example, that they are free to use artwork that they copy from Web pages, from files that are part of software programs on their computer, and so forth. In almost all cases, though, such artwork is copyrighted even if it is not accompanied by a traditional copyright symbol.

USING INSERT PICTURE

The easiest way to become comfortable working with graphics in Word—and to get hooked on doing so—is to import an existing image or two into a document. You can do so either by choosing an image from Word's clip art library or by browsing all graphic files on your disk for the desired image. Figure 5.1 illustrates the results of both of the basic picture insertion techniques described in this section.

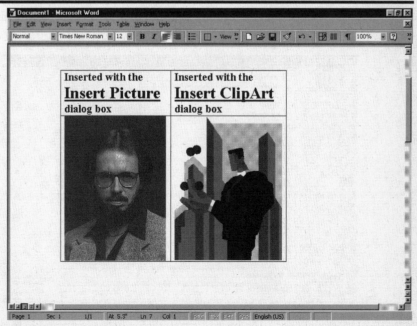

FIGURE 5.1: The end effect of both primary Insert Picture commands is comparable.

TIP

If you are just beginning to work with pictures, working on a throw-away document is good advice, in part because you won't worry if you muddle the results and in part because you will feel much freer to creatively experiment and learn Word's capabilities.

The originals of the two images in Figure 5.1 differed in size. As you will see in the "Resizing Graphics" section later in this chapter, resizing images to suit given purposes—in this case so that they are of comparable size—is even easier and faster than inserting them. Finally, this figure demonstrates that you can insert a graphic virtually anywhere you want in a Word document—in this case, in cells of a table so that they align with no effort on my part.

Next, we'll discuss each of these slightly different procedures (Insert ➤ Picture ➤ From File and Insert ➤ Picture ➤ Clip Art). In both cases, however, you begin by placing the insertion point where you want your graphic to appear. (Until you become familiar with inserting objects into Word documents, it is safest to place your insertion point on a blank line.)

To browse your disk and insert any graphic file that you find, the next step is to select Insert ➤ Picture ➤ From File. The Insert Picture dialog box appears.

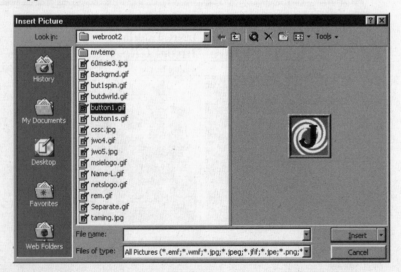

As you will note, the Insert Picture dialog box is comparable to the familiar Open dialog box that you use to open a Word document. Simply browse your hard disk as usual until you find a desired graphic file. Then, press the Insert button. Your graphic appears at the insertion point in your document.

NOTE

If you are looking for a practice graphic to insert, browse to your Windows folder with the Insert Picture dialog box. Several files of filetype .bmp reside in that folder.

THE ALTERNATE ROAD TO TIPPERARY

If the Picture toolbar is visible, you can also reach the Insert Picture dialog box by clicking—guess what?—the Insert Picture toolbar button (the first button on the left). To display the Picture toolbar, select View ➢ Toolbars ➢ Picture.

To insert a graphic from Word's clip art library, after placing the insertion point where you want the graphic to appear, select Insert ➢ Picture ➢ Clip Art. The Insert ClipArt dialog box appears.

In the Insert ClipArt dialog box, after ensuring that the Pictures tab is selected, click a category. After the images in that category appear, click the desired image. Finally, from the pop-up menu that appears, click the top button. (The ToolTip that appears if you hover your cursor over that button reads: Insert Clip.) The selected image appears at the insertion point in your document.

INSERTING GRAPHICS FROM THIRD-PARTY PROGRAMS INTO WORD WITH THE WINDOWS CLIPBOARD

If you have created, edited, or simply opened a graphic file in a third-party program (such as the Paint program that ships with Windows), here is the procedure to more directly insert the graphic into a Word document via the Windows Clipboard:

1. Start or switch to the third-party program.

2. If you have more than one graphic opened in that program, select the graphic of interest. (In most programs, you do so by clicking the graphic).

3. Copy the graphic to the Windows Clipboard. (In most programs, you do so by selecting Edit ≻ Copy or using its keyboard shortcut, Ctrl+C.)

4. Start or switch to Word.

5. With the desired document into which you want to insert the graphic open, place the insertion point where you want the graphic to appear.

6. Select Edit ≻ Paste or its keyboard shortcut, Ctrl+V. The graphic is inserted.

After you have inserted a graphic by any of the methods described in this section, you almost always will find that you want to reposition, resize, or embellish the image. These procedures are discussed in the following sections.

USING THE PICTURE TOOLBAR

As indicated in the "The Alternate Road to Tipperary" sidebar in the preceding section, you can use Word's Picture toolbar to insert a picture into your document. However, you will find several additional handy tools on the same toolbar.

The most effective way to observe the effects of the toolbar's features is simply to experiment with them on a sample graphic in a discardable document. In general, you first must select one or more graphics by clicking them. (To select multiple graphics, hold down your Shift key as you click each image.) In many cases, clicking the same button multiple times increases the effect of the button.

Here is a quick introduction to the effects of the Picture toolbar's buttons, from left to right as they appear in the graphic of the toolbar as illustrated in the "The Alternate Road to Tipperary" sidebar in the preceding section. To make the toolbar visible, select View ➤ Toolbars ➤ Picture.

Insert Picture   This button lets you insert a picture, as described in the preceding section.

Image Control   This button drops down a small menu with these choices:

Automatic   Lets Word control the overall look of your image. Unless one of the alternate choices is applicable, use this choice. (If you have not used one of the alternatives, you don't need to click this one.)

Grayscale   The colors in your image are converted to varying shades of gray in the range from pure white to solid black. This option is handy for better visualizing how your image may look if later printed to a black-and-white printer. It also can create a strikingly different, appealing feel for a picture.

Black & White   The colors in your image are converted to black and white—no shades of gray. Sometimes, you may need to use this option to better print a color image on a black-and-white printer. Other times, this option may produce an artsy special effect.

Watermark   Your image is greatly "lightened." The results are suitable for placing a picture "behind" text and other elements of a document—much like a conventional stationery watermark.

More Contrast   Word attempts to increase the contrast between the colors of your image each time you click this button.

Less Contrast   Word attempts to reduce the contrast among the colors of your image each time you click this button.

More Brightness   Word attempts to increase the brightness or brilliance of the colors of your image each time you click this button.

Less Brightness   Word attempts to decrease the brightness or brilliance of the colors of your image each time you click this button.

Crop   You use this button to trim some of the edges of your image, much like taking a pair of scissors to a printed photograph. For more information, see the "Cropping Graphics or Surrounding Them with Extra Space" section later in this chapter.

Line Style   For bordered graphics, this button lets you set the style (generally the width) of the border.

Text Wrapping   This button lets you determine how text in your document wraps around your image.

Format Picture   This button pops up the Format Picture dialog box. From that dialog box, you have an alternate way to control many of the other features on the Picture toolbar—and more. You will run into uses for the Format Picture dialog box in various sections later in this chapter.

Set Transparent Color   For images in some graphic formats, you can set one color as *transparent*. That is, whatever appears behind it in your document will show through like through a window. This is particularly useful for Web pages and other places where you might have a background color or background image. For example, my Web site displays my name in a banner graphic rather than as ordinary text, because I want to control exactly how it appears regardless of what fonts visitors might have on their computers. I've added a subdued speckled appearance to the font and color that I use for my name. However, because a graphic is rectangular and because I want my name to appear on the background rather than on a slab of color that, in turn, is on the background, I set the white color of that slab as transparent so that the background image shows through.

Also, doing so means that the inside of each letter of my name (such as inside the *O* of *Olsen*)—which, like the rest of the slab, was white in the original graphic—lets my background image show through. The net result is that only the actual letters of my name appear in color, floating directly on the background image.

Reset Picture   If you have experimented with the toolbar buttons' effects on an image until the image is hopelessly far from what you want (that is, a simple Edit ➢ Undo can't bail you out), click this button to restore your original image.

WARNING

Often, the effects of Picture toolbar features on a given image are hard to judge until you try them. So remember the admonition of saving your document with File ➢ Save (Ctrl+S) before experimenting. Also, if you don't like an effect *immediately* after trying it, remember, too, the magic of Edit ➢ Undo (Ctrl+Z). See also the discussion of the Reset Picture button in this section.

RESIZING GRAPHICS

When you select a graphic in a Word document by clicking it, the image is surrounded by a box containing eight handles—one in each corner and one centered on each side of an outline box that appears. When you position the mouse cursor on a handle, the cursor morphs into a two-headed arrow.

You can increase or decrease the size of the entire graphic proportionally by clicking a *corner* handle and then, while holding down your mouse button, dragging that handle to a new position. When you release the mouse button, the graphic is resized accordingly.

NOTE

Sizing a graphic proportionally means that as the size of the graphic changes, its width and height retain the same proportions relative to each other. That is, if the height becomes three times larger, the width becomes three times larger as well. Otherwise, the image will be distorted.

You also can click a handle in the center of one of the four sides of a graphic and then, while holding down your mouse button, drag it. When you do so, the graphic's vertical size changes if you drag the handle on the top or bottom of the image. If you drag the handle on the right or left, the graphic's horizontal size changes. However, because you are resizing only one dimension of the two-dimensioned image, dragging a side handle distorts the image. Whether this is desirable or not depends on your objective. It also depends on the nature of the graphic. A distorted photograph is quite a different matter than some kinds of logos, for example.

Figure 5.2 illustrates an original logo as the top-left image and an original photo as the bottom-left image. The center image on each line is an enlargement of its original image, created by dragging a corner handle. Notice that, other than size, both of the center images look identical to the originals. By contrast, the images on the right were created by dragging the handles on the top edges of the images. Notice how the images are distorted. The photo on the right looks quite hideous. (Are you creating an advertisement for an amusement park house of mirrors?) The logo on the right looks strikingly different from the original, but it is not inherently inappropriate. The distorted version of the original graphic could be used as a logo.

FIGURE 5.2: The center images were created by dragging a corner handle. The right images were distorted by dragging top-side handles.

Some graphics are even more obvious candidates for distorted enlargements or reductions. The graphic on the left of Figure 5.3 is a standard Word clip art image. The graphic on the right was intentionally distorted by moving the handle on the right side of the image. Which image is desirable depends entirely on your intended use.

FIGURE 5.3:   The image on the right distorts the original clip art on the left for an intended purpose.

CROPPING GRAPHICS OR SURROUNDING THEM WITH EXTRA SPACE

Cropping a graphic is like taking a pair of scissors to a photographic print: Doing so resizes the print, but in the process it removes part of the image along one or more of its rectangular edges. In Word, you have two ways to crop graphics, the Crop button on the Picture toolbar and the Format Picture dialog box. The Crop button is better for visually altering a graphic—often the best approach for quickly inserting graphics into everyday documents. The Format Picture dialog box is better if you want to crop or expand the space surrounding a graphic by specifying an exact amount of space to crop or add—often better when you have multiple graphics to insert and you want them to occupy the identical space on a page. The dialog box approach also is better when your document design requirements require exact sizing, such as in a catalog destined for commercial printing.

In contrast to cropping, adding white space is somewhat like affixing the photographic print to a larger sheet of paper or matting. Doing so, in effect, resizes the total area occupied by the print without increasing the size of the actual image. Just as you might use this technique to fit, for example, a 5″ × 7″ print into an 8″ × 10″ picture frame, in Word you usually add white space around the image so that it looks better—perhaps to add some "breathing room" between an image and surrounding text and other objects. You use either of the same two tools and techniques to surround a graphic with extra space as you do to crop a graphic.

Figure 5.4 shows the results of both cropping and adding white space to the original graphic in the upper-left corner. Extra white space has been added to the exact copy of the original in the upper-right corner, which is indicated by the border box—which otherwise would tightly fit the graphic. (The box and its handles won't print. They appear only because the image was selected before capturing the screen shot to highlight the increased size of the region occupied by the graphic.) The two bottom graphics in Figure 5.4 illustrate cropped copies of the original graphic.

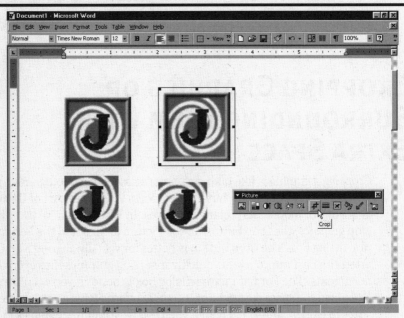

FIGURE 5.4: White space has been added around one copy of the original image, while two other copies have been cropped.

The next two sections explain how to use the two tools that can either crop or add surrounding space to a graphic. Thereafter, in the "Recovering from Cropping or Adding Space" section we discuss how to extricate yourself from disastrous results when cropping (or adding extra space to) a graphic. It isn't a matter of if, but when, you will run into this problem. Fortunately, the remedy usually is quick and painless. Regardless, especially before cropping a graphic, you should save your document with File ➢ Save (Ctrl+S), just to be safe.

Cropping or Adding Space with the Crop Button

To crop a portion of a graphic or to add space around it with the Crop Button method, follow these general steps:

1. If the Picture toolbar (see Figure 5.4) is not visible, display it by selecting View ➤ Toolbars ➤ Picture. The Picture toolbar appears.

2. Select the desired graphic by clicking it. A border with eight handles appears.

3. Click the Crop button on the Picture toolbar (highlighted in Figure 5.4). Your cursor morphs into a do-dad that looks like the Crop button.

4. Click a handle on the selected graphic and, while holding down the mouse button, drag the handle to where you want that side or corner of the graphic to move. If you drag the handle toward the center of the graphic, the graphic will be cropped accordingly. If you move the handle away from the center of the graphic, space will be added around the graphic.

TIP

Dragging a handle on the middle of any of the four sides of a graphic crops or expands the space for that side. Dragging any of the four corner handles crops or expands the space on both corresponding sides. For example, dragging the upper-left handle crops or expands the space on both the top and left sides of the graphic.

5. When the handle of the graphic is where desired, release the mouse button. The graphic is cropped or surrounded by extra space.

TIP

If you are dissatisfied with the results of cropping or expanding the space of a graphic, see the "Recovering from Cropping or Adding Space" section later in this chapter.

Cropping or Adding Space with the Format Picture Dialog Box

To crop a portion of a graphic or to add space around it with the Format Picture dialog box method, follow these general steps:

1. Select the graphic to crop or to surround with extra space by clicking it. A border with eight handles appears.

TIP

If you want to crop or add space around a graphic more precisely, display Word's rulers before beginning the procedure in this section by selecting View ➤ Ruler. The horizontal and vertical rulers appear.

2. Select Format ➤ Picture. (Alternately, you can click the Format Picture button on the toolbar displayed in Figure 5.4.) The Picture tab page of the Format Picture dialog box displayed in Figure 5.5 appears.

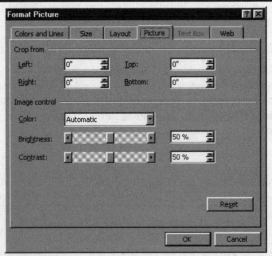

FIGURE 5.5: You can specify precise cropping or extra space values with the Format Picture dialog box.

3. Enter the precise amount of space that you want to crop or to surround as extra space in any combination of the four text boxes in the Crop From region of the dialog box.

TIP

A positive value in a Crop From text box crops the corresponding side, while a negative value adds space to that side. You can enter positive values for some sides and negative values for other sides. For typical image size and document margins, you likely will be working in small fractions of an inch. For example, the bottom-left graphic in Figure 5.4 was cropped by only .07", while the bottom-right graphic was cropped by precisely .1".

4. Click the OK button. Your selected graphic is cropped or expanded. (If you have set positive values for some sides but negative values for other sides, some sides are cropped while space is added on the other sides.)

TIP

If you are dissatisfied with the results of cropping or expanding the space of a graphic, see the next section.

Recovering from Cropping or Adding Space

Often, you may not be quite satisfied with the exact cropping of, or extra space added to, a graphic. This is especially critical in the case of cropping, because you have lost some of your graphic's content. Extra white space is not such a critical matter, because all that you really need to do is remove the "nothingness" represented by additional space.

Word provides three solutions to either of these situations. Each of these solutions is explained in this section.

TIP

A proverbial ounce of prevention is worth a kilogram of cure when working with potentially destructive commands. See the "First Things First" section earlier in this chapter about how to avoid a real mess when working with a graphic in an important document.

If you simply want to restore a graphic's original contents (perhaps to try again to crop or add space) and you make this decision before doing anything else with the document containing your graphic, your old faithful Edit ➤ Undo command (Ctrl+Z) is the easiest solution.

If you want to restore a graphic's original content, but Word's Undo command is no longer available to restore your graphic because you have otherwise worked in the document containing the graphic, follow these steps:

1. Select the offending graphic by clicking it. A border with eight handles appears.

2. Select Format ➤ Picture. (Alternately, you can click the Format Picture button on the toolbar displayed in Figure 5.4.) The Picture tab page of the Format Picture dialog box displayed in Figure 5.5 appears.

3. Click the Reset button.

4. Click the OK button. Your graphic is restored.

If you previously added extra space around a graphic rather than cropped it, you can use the third solution to remove some or all of that space—or even to add additional space. Simply follow the procedure to add space described in the "Cropping or Adding Space with the Crop Button" section earlier in this chapter and then drag the appropriate border handle or handles to alter the size of the extra space that you previously added.

While the third solution isn't guaranteed to restore your graphic to the absolutely exact original dimensions, you may find the approach sufficient. But if you find yourself getting into a deeper and deeper mess when attempting to remove extra space by this dragging method—and sometime you will—your fall-back remedy is to revert to the Format Picture alternative described in this section.

USING WORD'S DRAWING TOOLS

While Word is no match for a dedicated, full-fledged application when drawing your own objects, Word does provide ample tools to create basic graphics. Besides a freehand drawing tool, Word supplies basic shapes, such as rectangles and ovals, that you can insert into your document and then manipulate their size and shape. Word also provides a modest supply of additional drawings, which you can supplement as discussed in the "Sources of Artwork" section early in this chapter.

You also can create *text boxes*, which hold text that you can manipulate like drawn graphics, such as by placing them at an angle off the invisible horizontal plane of ordinary text or by giving them special properties, such as a pseudoshadow.

To use Word's drawing tools, you begin by displaying the Drawing toolbar if it is not already visible. To make it visible, click the Draw button on the Standard toolbar or select View ➤ Toolbars ➤ Drawing. (If your Word document contains a drawing that you want to modify, double-click the graphic.) The Drawing toolbar depicted in Figure 5.6 appears. You can then use the various toolbar buttons to create or edit your drawing as discussed in the following sections.

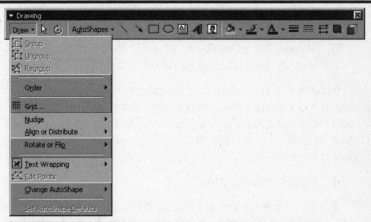

FIGURE 5.6: Use the Drawing toolbar to create or edit drawings.

Drawing Lovely Lines and Shapely Shapes

To draw lines and shapes in Word, you use the Drawing toolbar (described and illustrated in the preceding section). First, you click a drawing button (line, oval, or rectangle) and then you use your mouse as the drawing tool.

Follow this procedure to create a straight line:

1. Click the Line button.

2. Click but do not release the mouse button where you want one end of the line.

3. Drag the line to where you want it to end.

4. Release the mouse button. Your line is drawn.

Follow this procedure to create any shape of rectangle, including a precise square:

1. Click the rectangle button.

2. If you want to create a precise square, press a Shift button and hold it down while you continue with the following steps.

3. Click but do not release the mouse button where you want one corner of the rectangle.

4. Drag the rectangle to where you want its opposite corner. (For example, if you clicked the upper-left corner in step 3, drag the rectangle to the lower-right corner.)

5. Release the mouse button (and Shift key, if you pressed it in step 2). Your rectangle is drawn.

You can create an oval with its long dimension either vertical or horizontal, but not in any other orientation. (You can, however, rotate an oval to another orientation after you create it. See the "Rotating and Flipping Objects" section later in this chapter.) You can also create a precise circle. Follow this procedure to create any type of oval:

1. Click the oval button.

2. If you want to create a precise circle, press a Shift button and hold it down while you continue with the following steps.

3. Click but do not release the mouse button where you want the topmost, bottom-most, left-most, or right-most point of your oval.

4. Drag the oval to where you want its opposite point. (For example, if you clicked the left-most point of the oval, drag the oval to its right-most point.)

5. (If you are holding down the Shift key to create a circle, skip this step.) Your oval will look weird—with little height, if you drew it horizontally in steps 3 and 4, or with little width. So, while continuing to hold down the mouse button, drag your cursor to give your oval height or width. If you dragged your oval horizontally in step 4, drag it vertically now; otherwise, drag it vertically.

6. Release the mouse button (and Shift key, if you pressed it in step 2). Your oval is drawn.

Drawing More Complex Shapes

You can use the drop-down AutoShapes menu on the Drawing toolbar to create more sophisticated shapes than those represented by buttons on the main toolbar. The choices are too numerous to list or describe all of them here, but you can quickly acquaint yourself with them visually by clicking the AutoShapes button on the Drawing toolbar. From the drop-down menu that appears (see Figure 5.7), click the various menu items to view the available shapes palettes.

Part i

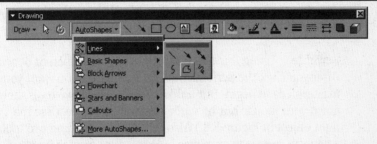

FIGURE 5.7:   The AutoShapes menu leads to many different shapes to augment those represented by buttons on the main Drawing toolbar.

Be sure not to overlook the three buttons on the bottom row of the Lines palette (shown in Figure 5.7). These three buttons, from left to right, are called Curve, Freeform, and Scribble. If you can't find an appropriate object elsewhere to meet your current need, you can draw the object with these three tools. You also use two of these three tools slightly differently than in the procedures described in the preceding section. Following is a description of each of these tools; the possible results of using them are shown in Figure 5.8.

Curve   Click where you want to begin your curved line (such as the top point on the left of the left object in Figure 5.8). Drag your line to where you want it to sharply bend (such as the lowest point on the left of the object). The line will appear straight. Click again, the line curves. Repeat this process as often as necessary to create the next portions of your curvy line (such as the top-right point of this object). Each time you click, Word turns your newest straight line into a curved line. After all of the curvaceous sections of your line are in place, press your Escape key to turn off curve drawing.

Freeform   The Freeform tool works exactly like the curve tool, except that each segment of your object remains a straight line from each point where you clicked to the next point where you clicked. (See the middle object in Figure 5.8.) Press the Escape key to turn off Freeform drawing. Think of it as connecting the dots on a grade-school picture. Back to the future.

TIP

For both Curve and Freeform tools, if you complete the last segment of your object by clicking precisely where you clicked to begin the object, your object is completed without pressing your Escape key.

Scribble   Using this tool is like drawing with a pen or pencil. After you click the Scribble button, click where you want your masterpiece to begin. But unlike the preceding two tools, hold down your mouse button while you, well, scribble. (See the right object in Figure 5.8.) Also unlike the preceding two tools, when you release your mouse button, your object is finished.

FIGURE 5.8:   These three hand-drawn objects were created (from left to right) with AutoShapes's Curve, Freeform, and Scribble tools.

Because you are drawing freehand lines as you create objects with these three tools, often you don't get quite the results that you wanted. (Alas, we aren't all accomplished artists, and unlike professional drawing programs, Word does not supply a drawing eraser tool.) Note the imperfect triangle on the left in Figure 5.9.

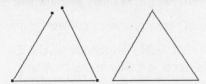

FIGURE 5.9:   Edit Points lets you morph the imperfect triangle on the left into the object on the right.

Because you can't simply stop in the middle of using these freehand tools to undo a slightly misplaced point, you must first complete your freehand drawing and then use this special drawing editing procedure:

1. Click the Select Objects button toward the left of the Drawing toolbar. (It looks like an arrow.) Your cursor morphs into that arrow.

2. Select the object that you want to edit by carefully positioning the cursor over any line of the object. When your cursor is correctly positioned, an arrow with two arrowheads pointing in opposite directions appears on the tip of your cursor.

3. Click your mouse. Tiny black handles appear. (If you created the object with the Curve or Freeform tools, these handles appear each place that you clicked while drawing it. With the Scribbler tool, Word inserts handles where it chooses—often many of them in the case of particularly curvaceous scribbles.)

4. Click one of these handles and continue to hold down your mouse button while you move the handle where you want it. The associated line or lines follow along for the ride.

5. When the handle is in the desired spot, release the mouse button. Your drawing is edited.

For example, in the duplicate object on the right in Figure 5.9, you can click the handle on the top-right and drag it onto the top-left handle. Voilà—a real triangle!

Creating *Really* Complex Shapes

If you want to insert some fancy clip art instead of the more modest shapes discussed in the preceding two sections, follow these general steps:

1. Place the insertion point where you want to insert an object.

2. If the Drawing toolbar isn't visible, display it. (See the "Using Word's Drawing Tools" section earlier in this chapter.)

3. Click the AutoShapes button. A drop-down menu appears.

4. Click the More AutoShapes menu choice. The More Auto-Shapes dialog box appears.

5. If necessary, expand the dialog box (as done in Figure 5.10) to make it easier to browse the objects and to access the toolbar buttons in the dialog box. (The simplest way to do this is to click the Maximize button—the middle button of the three buttons in the upper-right corner of the dialog box.)

6. Click the desired object to select it. A pop-up button menu appears. (See Figure 5.10.)

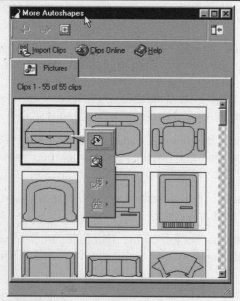

FIGURE 5.10: You can insert clip art as drawings via this dialog box.

7. Click the Insert Clip button (the top button). The object appears at the insertion point in your document.

8. If you want to insert additional objects from the dialog box, repeat steps 4 and 5 as many times as desired. (Word places each object next to the preceding object that you selected in your document. You can reposition them, if desired, later. (See the "Moving or Copying Objects" section later in this chapter.)

9. Click the Close button (the right button of the three buttons in the upper-right corner of the dialog box). The dialog box closes.

Selecting Objects

To work with a drawing after you create it (such as to resize, move, or duplicate it), you first must select it. Oddly, how you select it depends on the nature of the object. There are three different ways to select an object. (If the apparently correct approach doesn't work, try one of the others.)

▶ For lines—or any freehand objects in which the beginning point and ending point (the first and last places you clicked to draw your object) do *not* touch—click very carefully on any part of the line. (You will know that your cursor is directly over the line when an arrow with two arrowheads pointing in opposite directions appears at the tip of your cursor.)

▶ For geometric objects (rectangles, ovals, or similar shapes—or freehand objects where your beginning and ending points *do* touch)—click anywhere inside the object. (The same arrow with two arrowheads pointing in opposite directions indicates that you're in a geometric object.)

▶ For clip art (see preceding section), you follow the procedure for geometric objects. However, this only works if the Select Objects button on the Drawing toolbar (which looks like an arrow) is not selected (that is, it is not depressed).

SELECTING MULTIPLE OBJECTS SIMULTANEOUSLY

Selecting multiple objects simultaneously (to delete several at once, for example) is as inconsistent as selecting individual objects. You can select lines or geometric shapes (as defined in this section). To do so, select one of these objects and then hold down a Shift key while you continue to select additional objects. (Clicking outside any of the selected objects deselects all of them.)

You can't select multiple clip art objects to work on them simultaneously. The only exception is that you can use Edit ➤ Select All to select everything in a document (clip art, drawings, text—the whole enchilada), to copy it to the Windows Clipboard, for example.

Resizing Objects

To resize drawing objects of any ilk, follow this general procedure:

1. Select an object. (See the preceding section.) Eight handles appear around the graphic—one on each corner and one along each of its four sides.

2. Grab one of the handles and, without releasing your mouse button, drag it to its new location. (See the general discussion about working with handles in the "Resizing Graphics" section earlier in this chapter. In this respect, pictures and drawings function similarly.)

Moving or Copying Objects

You will find many reasons to move or copy objects. Besides moving them around to obtain a desired effect, you may need several instances of the same object. It is easier and your results will be more consistent if you create, size, and otherwise prepare one instance of the object and then make copies of it than if you individually prepare separate objects.

To move or copy objects, follow these general steps:

1. Select the object or objects to move. (See the "Selecting Objects" section earlier in this chapter.)

2. Position your mouse cursor over one of the selected objects, avoiding the object's handles. (If the object is *not* clip art, you

can tell that your cursor is correctly positioned when an arrow with two arrowheads pointing in opposite directions appears at the cursor's tip.)

3. Right-click at that position and continue to hold the button down as you drag the object or objects to the desired location.

4. Release the mouse button. A context menu pops up.

5. Select whether to move or make a copy of the object or objects at the new location.

TIP

Except for clip art, if you want to move rather than copy objects, you can click rather than right-click in step 3 of the procedure in this section. The context menu in steps 4 and 5 will not appear, and you can't choose to copy the objects.

ALIGNING MOVED OBJECTS

If you have used flowcharting or other diagramming software, you know how utterly frustrating it was to align objects until the programming gods and goddesses gave us snap-to grids. Objects placed near the horizontal and vertical lines of such grids magically gravitate to the precise positions of those lines, as if drawn by magnets. Fortunately, now Microsoft has given us a similar feature in Word's drawing toolkit, albeit in Word's case, the grid lines are invisible.

What good are snap-to grid lines? Imagine that you have drawn a series of objects and want them aligned horizontally and vertically. Tweaking their position by manually moving them tiny fractions of an inch is as much of a royal pain in the azimuth as aligning a dozen pictures on your living room wall.

To automate the alignment of drawings, begin by selecting the Draw button on the Drawing toolbar and then click Grid from the dropdown menu that appears. Then, from the Drawing Grid dialog box that appears, click to place a check mark next to Snap Object to Grid and then click the OK button. (You can optionally set the spacing of your invisible drawing grid before clicking OK.)

CONTINUED ➡

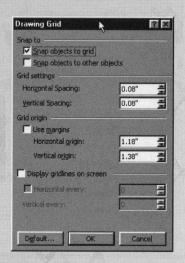

Note that using the Drawing Grid dialog box does not align *exist-ing* drawing objects. This isn't necessarily bad, because sometimes you may not want Word to enforce alignment. So you can turn this feature on and off as specific sets of objects require it.

Layering Multiple Drawing Objects

Layering is an essential drawing concept when you move beyond a simple line, rectangle, or oval. Consider the two hen-scratched houses that I constructed, one behind each other, in Figure 5.11.

For Figure 5.11, I originally created a house with simple rectangles and a triangle for the roof. Because I "built" the basic framework of a house first and then added windows and a door, I didn't have to be concerned about layers. When you place one object over another object, Word automatically places subsequent objects on top of existing objects.

I then decided to create a second house behind the first one. In this simplistic example, I could have created the second house in its entirety and simply let the second house be the one in front. However, in a more complex drawing, that could mean substantial extra work. Instead, all that the house in the background needs is its basic framework (a rectangle and a triangle)

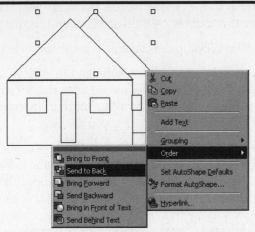

FIGURE 5.11:   Layering permits you to make objects appear in front of and behind each other.

plus one window. So I built only those elements, then exploited the layering feature to move the second house's window all the way to the back, and then did the same with the rectangle of the house (which effectively placed it behind its window, so the window would be visible).

Next I selected the triangular roof of the second house (shown as selected in Figure 5.11 by its visible handles). Finally, from the menu that appears in the figure, I moved the triangle to the very back, too. The net result: The second house I built is now behind the original house.

NOTE

I could have selected multiple objects (in this case both the triangle and the rectangle of the second house) and moved them all the way to the back simultaneously. In the real world, though, selecting multiple objects requires a little more thoughtful planning to avoid potentially unexpected results as layers are freely tossed around.

The general procedure to move a drawing layer forward or backward is as follows:

1. Select the object or objects to move forward or backward. (See the "Selecting Objects" section earlier in this chapter.)

2. Either right-click one of the selected objects or click the Draw button on the Drawing toolbar. (I explain ways to display the

Drawing toolbar in the "Using Word's Drawing Tools" section earlier in this chapter.) A drop-down menu appears.

3. Click Order from the drop-down menu. A submenu appears.

4. Click the appropriate item on the submenu to achieve the effect that you want. (See the discussion after these steps.) Your selected object or objects move forward or backward, depending on the submenu item that you choose.

The options on the submenu in the procedure in this section are generally self-explanatory. However, the difference between Bring to Front and Bring Forward (or between Send to Back and Send Backward) may warrant clarification. Bring to Front (or Send to Back) means to move the selected objects all the way to the front (or back), while the other two options only move the selected objects one layer forward (or backward) each time you select them.

WARNING

It is easy to "lose" an object (especially when moving multiple objects to new layers simultaneously). The experience feels a little like losing a pen in the sea of papers on an overflowing desk. I did so with a window of a house while playing with Figure 5.11. The solution is to move some objects (usually the larger ones) all the way to the back to expose the lost object to view, and then to more carefully determine which layers you must move forward or backward to maneuver all objects to their desired layers without losing access to any object.

Grouping and Ungrouping Drawing Objects

Sometimes, you will want Word to treat multiple drawing objects as a single object. This makes it easier to move and resize complex elements. I could have done this with each of the two houses in my example in the preceding section. That would have made simpler work of the project by allowing me to build each house separately and then place one in front. (To carry the example to its ideal extreme, I could have created one house, grouped its elements, copied the grouped object, and then positioned one of the copies in front of the other.)

The procedure to *group* multiple objects (that is, to allow all of the objects to be moved or otherwise manipulated at the same time) is as follows:

1. Select the objects that you want to group. (See the "Selecting Multiple Objects Simultaneously" sidebar in the "Selecting Objects" section earlier in this chapter.)

2. Either right-click one of the selected objects or click the Draw button on the Drawing toolbar. (For ways to display the Drawing toolbar, see the "Using Word's Drawing Tools" section earlier in this chapter.) A drop-down menu appears.

3. Click Grouping from the drop-down menu. A submenu appears. (See Figure 5.12.)

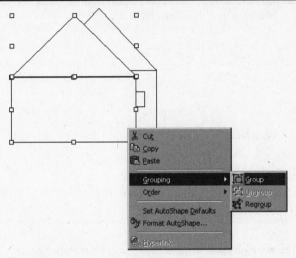

FIGURE 5.12:   Group or ungroup multiple drawing objects from this menu.

4. Click Group from the submenu. The selected objects behave as a group when you apply future commands to them.

EXTRA CREDIT FOR WORKING WITH GROUPED DRAWING OBJECTS

If you select multiple objects, they will move together as if grouped. However, if you click only one object, you can move it independently.

To ungroup grouped objects, follow the procedure in this section, but click Ungroup rather than Group in step 4. Thereafter, the selected objects behave only as their original, individual objects when you apply future commands to them.

Rotating and Flipping Objects

You likely will want to change the orientation of objects by rotating them to the right or left, by flipping them horizontally or vertically, or by freeform rotation. Figure 5.13 shows the results of all of the available ways to flip or rotate an object. In this case, that object is a simple line drawing created with Word's Curve tool.

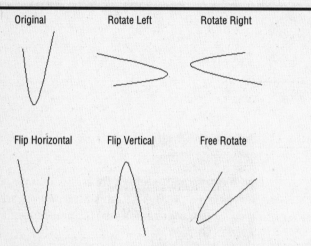

FIGURE 5.13: You can alter the orientation of an object in many ways.

As you will note from Figure 5.13, rotating an object causes it to rotate 90 degrees each time you use the Rotate Left or Rotate Right tool. To use either of these tools twice on the same object cumulatively rotates the object 180 degrees—that is, turns it upside down. To use either of these tools three times cumulatively rotates the object 270 degrees—that is, doing so has the same effect as having used the other rotate tool once. The Free Rotate tool lets you manually rotate an object to any angle.

Here is the general procedure to rotate or flip an object:

1. Select the object or objects that you want to reorient. (See the "Selecting Objects" section earlier in this chapter.)

TIP

If you want to use the Free Rotate tool, you can substitute clicking the button by that name (which contains a circular icon) on the Drawing toolbar for steps 2–4 in the procedure in this section.

2. Click the Draw button on the Drawing toolbar. (For ways to display the Drawing toolbar, see the "Using Word's Drawing Tools" section earlier in this chapter.) A drop-down menu appears.

3. Click the Rotate or Flip item from the drop-down menu. A submenu appears. (See Figure 5.14.)

FIGURE 5.14:   You flip or rotate drawing objects with this menu.

4. Click the desired rotate or flip effect from the submenu. Unless you select Free Rotate, your object or objects are rotated or flipped, and you are done with this procedure.

5. If you selected Free Rotate, colored handles appear around the selected object or objects. (Depending on your Windows display color scheme, these handles probably will be green.) Grab one of these handles and hold down your mouse button while you drag the object or objects to rotate them. (You will know that you have successfully positioned your cursor directly over a handle when it is surrounded with a circular cursor and your regular arrow cursor disappears.) If you selected multiple objects in step 1, all objects rotate in unison, providing the odd sensation of propeller blades spinning.

6. Release your mouse button. If you aren't satisfied with your results, you may grab a handle and rotate your selected object or objects repeatedly until you are satisfied.

7. When you are satisfied, exit Free Rotate mode in any of these ways:

   ▶ Click outside any of the selected objects. (This is the easiest way.)

▶ While your cursor is positioned over one of the colored handles, right-click and then select Exit Rotate Mode from the context menu that appears.

▶ Click the Free Rotate button on the Drawing toolbar.

Adding Balloon Callouts

Callouts allow you to attach any of several "balloon"-style text boxes to a drawing or picture. As illustrated by Figure 5.15, callouts can resemble the speech or thought balloons of cartoon fame.

FIGURE 5.15:   Callouts add fancy text boxes to drawings or pictures.

Here are the general steps to add a callout:

1. Select a drawing or a picture to which you want to add a callout.

2. Click the AutoShapes button on the Drawing toolbar. (For ways to display the Drawing toolbar, see the "Using Word's Drawing Tools" section earlier in this chapter.) A drop-down menu appears.

3. Choose Callouts from the menu. A palette of callouts appears.

4. Click the desired callout.

5. Click in your document where you want the callout. (Don't worry precisely where you click. You probably will need to move it slightly next in this procedure anyway.) Your callout appears, with a text box containing the insertion point at which you can insert text. (The text box will disappear and be replaced by your chosen callout later in the procedure.)

6. If necessary, resize or reposition the text box.

7. Enter your text. (Most normal Word text tools are available to you.)

8. If necessary, again resize or reposition the text box to best fit your text.

9. Click outside the callout. The text box disappears and is replaced by the callout that you selected in step 4.

10. If you want to reposition the portion of the callout that does not contain text (in Figure 5.15, this portion is the three small "clouds" between the man and the cloud containing the text), click that portion of the callout. One or more colored, diamond-shaped handles appear. (Depending on your Windows display color scheme, that color probably is yellow.)

11. Click a colored handle and, while holding down your mouse button, drag the handle to where you want it.

12. Release the mouse button. The portion of the callout with handles is repositioned.

13. If necessary, repeat any of the various steps in this procedure to reposition portions of the callout, resize the text-box portion of the callout, or modify your callout's text. (You may want to drag different handles of your callout or its text box. Dragging different handles causes different effects.)

14. Click outside all portions of your callout. Your callout is done.

TIP

After completing a callout, you may at any time click either the text portion to edit the text box, which will reappear, or outside the text portion, to again edit the portion that you clicked. *Hint:* If you want to edit both portions, click the portion that does *not* contain text to have immediate access to edit either portion.

Using Other Drawing Toolbar Features

Most of the buttons on the Drawing toolbar have been discussed throughout several sections in this chapter. In this final section, let's look at each of the remaining buttons found on the right side of the toolbar illustrated in Figure 5.16.

FIGURE 5.16: The Drawing toolbar contains several style features.

The general procedure to use any of these features is to select the drawing to which you want to apply a feature and then to click the desired button. In the case of the three color-related features, the associated button displays the color that will be applied if you click it. If you prefer a different color, click the downward-pointing arrow associated with the desired button and select from a color palette that appears. (These palettes also offer ways to select no color.) In the other cases, clicking the associated button leads to a drop-down palette of options. An effect is applied only when you click a choice on the palette. In a couple of cases, a drop-down palette contains buttons that lead to other opportunities to modify your drawing in some delightfully striking ways. A few side excursions to explore can be well rewarded.

TIP

Your best bet in working with the special effects described in this section is to experiment in a throw-away document. But if you're feeling brave or in a rush, be sure to save your document with File ➤ Save (Ctrl+S) before applying effects. And as always, remember that if you *immediately* use Edit ➤ Undo (Ctrl+Z), you can remove the most recently applied effect.

The following buttons are on the Drawing toolbar, from left to right beginning with the Fill Color button:

Fill Color   This button fills your drawing with the selected color.

Line Color   This button modifies the color of the lines in your drawing.

Font Color   This button changes the color of the text in your drawing. Note that you either must choose your font's color before entering your text, or select the text and then choose the color to apply to it.

Line Style   This button lets you alter the type of lines that comprise your drawing (generally to make them thicker or thinner).

Dash Style   This button lets you replace the solid lines of your drawing with any of a variety of lines—dashed, dotted, or a combination of dotted and dashed that looks like Morse code.

Arrow Style   This button lets you replace the normal arrowheads in your drawing with less common styles. Some of these styles don't look like arrowheads at all, but like dots and diamonds. These alternatives are most commonly associated with certain lines useful in flowcharts.

Shadow   This button lets you place pseudo-shadows behind your drawings.

3-D   This final Drawing toolbar button offers a variety of interesting 3-D effects for your drawings.

WHAT'S NEXT

Congratulations! You've completed your tour of Microsoft Word 2000. Now it's time to move on to the next stop in the Office 2000 tour: Excel. You'll be a pro at navigating your way around the application, manipulating data, and writing formulas in no time!

PART ii
WORKING WITH NUMBERS
WITH EXCEL 2000

Chapter 6

FINDING YOUR WAY AROUND IN EXCEL

This chapter introduces you to the essentials of Excel. If you're new to spreadsheets, this material will give you a quick boost up the learning curve. If you're already familiar with another spreadsheet program, the information in this skill will help you make the transition to Excel.

Adapted from *Excel 2000: No Experience Required* by Gene Weisskopf

ISBN 0-7821-2374-0   432 pages $19.99

STARTING AND CLOSING EXCEL

You can start Excel in several ways:

- ▶ Choose Start ➤ Programs ➤ Microsoft Excel, which opens Excel and a blank document.

- ▶ Select Excel from the Office shortcut bar, which opens Excel and a blank document.

- ▶ Double-click an Excel document icon, which opens Excel and that document.

- ▶ Choose Start ➤ Open Office Document to open the Open Office Document dialog box, and then select an existing workbook.

- ▶ Choose Start ➤ New Office Document to open the New Office Document dialog box, click the General tab, and then select Blank Workbook.

Once Excel is running, you'll find it as easy to use as any well designed Windows program. For example, choosing File ➤ Save saves your current document, choosing Edit ➤ Copy and then Edit ➤ Paste copies data, and the Help menu contains online documentation and the answers to your questions. When you're ready to close Excel, you can:

- ▶ Choose File ➤ Exit.

- ▶ Click the Close button at the right side of Excel's title bar.

- ▶ Double-click the Control menu box, or choose Close from the Control menu.

If you have not saved an open document in which you've made changes, Excel prompts you to do so before it closes.

LOOKING AT EXCEL'S WORKBOOKS, WORKSHEETS, AND CELLS

An Excel document is called a *workbook*, which is the basic file in Excel, and each workbook can contain multiple pages, which are called *worksheets*. The active worksheet is displayed in the document window. Figure 6.1 shows the Excel application window with a worksheet open in the document window.

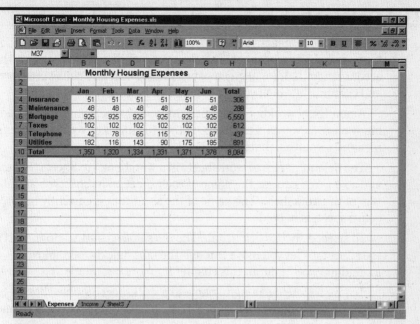

FIGURE 6.1: A worksheet open in Excel

You no doubt recognize many of the standard Windows controls and components. The title bar is at the top, with its Minimize, Maximize, and Close buttons on the right side. Beneath it is the menu bar with the commands File, Edit, View, and so on. Beneath the menu bar are two *toolbars*, which include a variety of buttons for performing common Excel tasks (you'll learn more about toolbars later in this chapter).

In the main body of Excel's application window is the Monthly Housing Expenses worksheet. You use the horizontal and vertical scroll bars to navigate through the rows and columns of each worksheet in the workbook.

NOTE

You can hide or display many components. Use either the commands on the View menu or the settings in the View tab of the Options dialog box (choose Tools ➢ Options).

Using Worksheets within a Workbook

The basic work area in an Excel workbook is a *worksheet*, which is sometimes called a spreadsheet. The electronic worksheet is based on the accountant's traditional green paper spreadsheet and consists of rows and columns in which you enter data and formulas.

A new Excel workbook contains three worksheets, and you can add as many more as you care to create—within the limits of your computer's memory resources, that is.

The default names of worksheets in a workbook are Sheet1, Sheet2, and so on. You can see the name of each sheet on its *sheet tab* at the bottom of the worksheet. The name of the sheet that is currently in use, the *active* sheet, is in bold.

To select a sheet, click its tab. The *tab scrolling* buttons to the left of the sheet tabs let you move through the tabs quickly (see "Moving around in Excel" later in this chapter for more information).

To give a more meaningful name to a worksheet, double-click its tab and type a new name. In Figure 6.1, the names of the first and second sheets are Expenses and Income.

Understanding Cells in a Worksheet

Each worksheet in Excel is made up of rows and columns. The rows are identified by numbers, labeled down the left side of the worksheet in the heading area. In Figure 6.1, you can see only 26 rows of the 65,536 rows in each worksheet (yes, that really is a lot!).

The columns are identified by letters, labeled across the top of the sheet in the heading area. Each worksheet has a total of 256 columns; you can see columns A through M in Figure 6.1. Column Z is followed by columns AA, AB, AC, and column AZ is followed by BA, BB, BC, and so on, out through column IV.

At the junction of each row and column is a *cell*, and it is in the cells that you enter data, including text, numbers, and formulas. You refer to a cell by its *address* in formulas, commands, and so on. To refer to a cell:

On the current sheet   Specify its column and row. For example, cell H4 is at the junction of column H and row 4.

On another sheet in the same workbook   Include the sheet name before the cell address with an exclamation point as a separator. For example, the address Sheet3!A15 refers to cell A15 on Sheet3.

In another workbook   Precede the cell address and sheet name with the workbook's filename, enclosed in square brackets. For example, the address [Sample.xls] Sheet2!B12 refers to cell B12 on Sheet2 in the workbook named Sample.xls.

Finally, hiding behind all the cells, worksheets, and workbooks is Excel's powerful calculating engine that can update thousands of your formulas in less time than it takes you to reach for a calculator. Without your even lifting a finger, Excel will keep track of all changes you make to the worksheet and update your formulas accordingly. All you have to do is sit back and be creative while Excel handles the number crunching.

EXPLORING THE EXCEL WINDOW

In Excel you can interact with the program by using menu commands and shortcuts, the Formula bar, and the status bar.

Accessing Commands in Excel

In Excel you can generally issue commands in two ways—through the menu bar and from shortcut menus.

Browsing through the menus is an easy way for you to take a quick tour of Excel's commands. Some menu commands also have shortcut keystrokes, such as Ctrl+S for File ➢ Save and Ctrl+C for Edit ➢ Copy. The shortcuts for all commands that have them are listed next to the command on the menu. But you may find that shortcuts really don't save all that much time or effort compared with the usual ways of accessing menus in Windows.

Excel also supports shortcut menus. Right-click a cell, a chart, a toolbar, or just about anything else to display a shortcut menu of commands you can select. You can also click a cell and press Shift+F10 to display a shortcut menu.

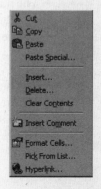

TIP

Shortcut menus list only commands that are relevant to the object you click (perhaps not every possible command, but the most commonly used ones). For example, the shortcut menu for a cell displays Cut and Copy, but not Save, Exit, or New Window.

Using the Formula Bar to See What's Inside

Beneath the toolbar and just above the worksheet is the Formula bar. It serves two important functions in Excel.

First, you can enter and revise data within the Formula bar for the current cell in the active worksheet. Second, the Formula bar displays whatever is *inside* the current cell. Here, you can see the formula =SUM(B5:G5) in the Formula bar. That formula is inside the selected cell, H5, and the selected cell displays only the *result* of that formula, 288. (Formulas are discussed in the section "Entering Data and Formulas into a Cell" later in this chapter and in more detail in Chapter 9.)

On the worksheet, and on paper when you print it, you really can't tell that there's a formula behind the value. To peek behind the scenes, keep your eye on the Formula bar as you're working in Excel.

At the left side of the Formula bar is the *Name Box*, which displays several types of names and addresses (you don't have to absorb all this right now; feel free to come back later on!):

▶ The address of the currently selected cell.

▶ The number of rows and columns you are selecting when you are selecting a range of cells, such as by dragging over them with the mouse.

▶ The name of the selected drawing or chart object.

▶ The named ranges in the workbook, which are accessed by clicking the Name Box's list arrow. When you can click a named range, Excel selects that range of cells (see Chapter 8 for a discussion of names).

Watching the Status Bar to Keep Informed

Excel's *status bar* is at the very bottom of the application window. It displays various messages that keep you in touch with Excel.

Ready   CAPS NUM

NOTE

On your computer, you might see the Windows 95/98 taskbar displayed at the bottom of the screen. On the computer used to write this book and capture the screens for its figures, the taskbar has been hidden to avoid complicating the illustrations. You can hide your Windows taskbar by choosing Start ➢ Settings ➢ Taskbar, and choosing Auto Hide. The taskbar will appear only when you point to the bottom of your screen.

The indicator on the left side of the status bar shows the current state of the program. Ready indicates that you can perform any action. Other indicators include Edit, when you're editing a cell; Enter, when you're entering new data into a cell; and Point, when you're pointing to a cell while writing a formula.

The right side of the status bar displays the current state of several toggle keys, including CAPS when Caps Lock is on and NUM when Num Lock is on.

Using AutoCalculate to Get a Quick Answer

Excel has a great feature called AutoCalculate that displays the total of the numbers in the currently selected cells. Figure 6.2 shows an example in which five cells, B4:B8, have been selected. The AutoCalculate indicator displays Sum=1168 on the status bar. This is the quickest way to see a total without writing a formula.

But wait, there's more! You can change the calculation that AutoCalculate performs by right-clicking on the AutoCalculate indicator and selecting an arithmetical operation from its shortcut menu. Otherwise, choose None to turn it off. You can see the AutoCalculate shortcut menu in Figure 6.2.

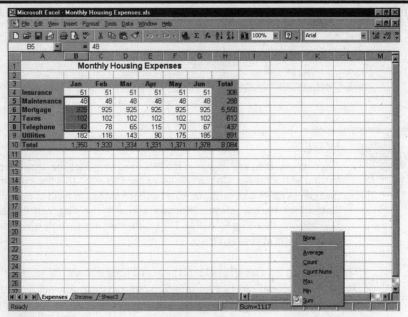

FIGURE 6.2: The AutoCalculate feature displays the sum of the selected cells.

WORKING WITH CELLS

When you select a cell, that cell is then the *active* cell and is enclosed in a thick border. Its row and column will appear sculpted in the row and column headings to help you identify its position in the worksheet. Its contents, if it has any, are shown in the Formula bar. You can enter data only in the active cell.

You can select a cell in several ways, but here are the three you'll use most often (others are discussed in Chapter 8):

▶ Click the cell with the mouse.

▶ Move to the cell with the keyboard arrow keys.

▶ Choose Edit ➢ Go To (or press F5 or Ctrl+G) to open the Go To dialog box, enter the address you want to go to in the Reference field, and click OK. This is especially handy when you want to go to a distant location, such as M1205.

To select multiple cells (a range), drag over the cells with your mouse. You can also use the Shift+arrow key method if you like to keep your hands on the keyboard. A range's address is defined by its upper-left and lower-right cells, such as A1:D9. To deselect a range, simply select another cell.

Entering Data and Formulas into a Cell

Earlier I mentioned that there are a total of 65,536 cells in a worksheet. I'll use that number shortly to show you how to enter a formula in a cell. But first you need to know the following about data entry:

▶ You can enter a bit more than 32,000 text characters in a cell; a formula can be a maximum of 1024 characters.

▶ To cancel your data entry before you press Enter, press Esc, which will leave the cell unchanged.

▶ To cancel an action after you've already made it, choose Edit ➢ Undo or click the Undo button on the toolbar. Using the Undo drop-down list, you can undo any of the most recent 16 changes you've made in Excel. Choose Edit ➢ Redo or click the Redo button to undo the effects of the Undo command.

▶ You can erase the contents of a cell by selecting the cell and pressing Delete or by choosing Edit ➢ Clear ➢ Contents.

▸ When entering numbers or formulas, you don't have to worry about how they look on the display, because you can format a cell to make a number appear just about any way you want to see it.

Now, let's calculate how many cells are in a worksheet. We'll use this example again later.

1. Click the Sheet1 tab to make it active. Select cell A1, which is always a good place to start.

2. Type **65536** and press Enter to move to the cell below. (See the section "Moving around in Excel" later in this chapter to learn why the selection moves when you press Enter.)

3. In cell A2, type **256** and press Enter.

4. In cell A3, type the formula **=A1*A2** and press Enter (be sure to include the equals sign—it's important).

Cell A1 contains the number of rows in a worksheet, and cell A2 contains the number of columns in a worksheet. You begin a formula in Excel with the equals sign; the asterisk denotes multiplication. This formula, then, multiplies the number of rows by the number of columns, and presto—it displays the result as 16777216 in cell A3. That's 16 million-plus cells, probably a few million more than you'll ever need! (You will find much more information about writing formulas in Chapter 9.)

A3		=	=A1*A2	
	A	B	C	D
1	65536			
2	256			
3	16777216			
4				

Editing a Cell

Let's revise the formula in cell A3 of our example to calculate the total number of cells in a new workbook:

1. Double-click cell A3 to edit its contents within the worksheet.

2. Press End to place the insertion point at the end of the formula, and then type ***3**.

3. Press Enter to put the revised formula back into the cell.

Now the formula results in 50331648—that's 50 million cells in each new workbook. Wow.

TIP

The ability to process formulas that contain numbers or to reference other cells and display the results instantly is the heart of Excel's power.

To get another taste of Excel's power, try this. Enter a different number in cell A1 or A2 and watch the result of the formula in A3. It might have changed too quickly for you to notice, but its result is different now, right?

Excel recalculates a formula when the data it references change, and it will do this for *every* formula in every worksheet in the workbook, as well as in any other open workbooks! When you have created a workbook with thousands of cells containing data and formulas, you will really appreciate Excel's power.

Enhancing a Cell

Here's a quick look at one way you can change the *display* of a cell without affecting its contents, using the worksheet from the previous example:

1. Select cells A1:A3—click cell A1 and drag to cell A3.

2. Right-click anywhere within the selected cells, and then select Format Cells from the shortcut menu to open the Format Cells dialog box, as shown in Figure 6.3.

3. Click the Number tab. As you make choices here, watch the Sample field to see how numbers will be displayed.

4. In the Category list of numeric formats, select Number.

5. Click the Use 1000 Separator check box, and set Decimal Places to 0, as shown in Figure 6.3.

6. Click OK.

FIGURE 6.3: You can change the way Excel displays numbers by applying a numeric format, which does not affect the value of the numbers themselves.

Notice that the numbers greater than one thousand in cells A1 and A3 are displayed with a comma to separate the thousands. However, if you select either of those cells and then look on the Formula bar, you'll see that the number within the cell does not contain a comma. Only the display of the number has changed.

NOTE

While playing with the numbers, you may find that a cell displays not the number but only pound signs: #######. The problem is that the column is not wide enough to display the number (or the numeric result of the formula) in the numeric format you have chosen. To fix this, you can change the format, widen the column, or use a smaller font.

MOVING AROUND IN EXCEL

As you've seen, Excel worksheets are big—really, really big. The part you see on the screen is only a very small piece of a worksheet. To go to another part of any of the worksheets, all you need to do is select a cell in that area. In most cases, you can use your mouse, your keyboard, or a command.

Moving Cell by Cell

To move from one cell to another:

- ▶ Press one of the arrow keys.

- ▶ Click the arrow at either end of a scroll bar to scroll the window in the direction of the arrow. You can then select a cell.

- ▶ Make a selection, press Scroll Lock on your keyboard, and use the arrow keys to scroll the worksheet window without affecting the selection. When you're finished, be sure to press Scroll Lock again to turn it off.

- ▶ If your mouse has a scrolling wheel, such as Microsoft's Intelli-Mouse, you can use the wheel in the usual ways to scroll up or down through the window.

- ▶ Press Enter. You can disable this feature—or change the direction in which the selection moves—by choosing Tools ➢ Options to open the Options dialog box and then clicking the Move Selection after Enter check box and selecting a direction.

- ▶ First, select the range of cells in which you want to edit data. Pressing Enter moves the selection down a cell, but only within that range. From the bottom of one column, the selection will move to the top of the next. Press Shift+Enter to move up a cell, or press Tab or Shift+Tab to move a column to the right or left.

Moving Screen by Screen

To move a screen at a time:

- ▶ Press Page Down or Page Up.

- ▶ Click within a scroll bar outside the scroll box.

- ▶ Drag a scroll box to move to that relative position in the occupied worksheet. If row 100 is the last occupied row, dragging the scroll box halfway down the vertical scroll bar displays the portion of the worksheet around row 50.

NOTE

When you drag a scroll box, a ScrollTip tells you exactly which row or column will be displayed when you stop scrolling.

Moving between Worksheets

In addition to clicking the Sheet tab to open a worksheet, you can press Ctrl+Page Up or Ctrl+Page Down to move between sheets. If you've added more sheets to a workbook, you'll find that there isn't enough room to display more than about a half-dozen sheet tabs at one time. But you can use the four tab-scrolling buttons to the left of the sheet tabs to display more tabs.

The two outside buttons display the sheet tabs starting from the first sheet or the last sheet in the workbook. The two inner buttons display one more sheet tab in the chosen direction.

You can also show more or fewer sheet tabs by dragging the tab split box either left or right. Double-click it to display the default number of sheet tabs.

If there are many worksheets in use in the workbook and scrolling through the tabs would be a bit of a pain, right-click a tab-scrolling button to display a list of all the worksheets in the workbook. Click one, and you're there.

Moving in Large Jumps

You'll probably most often use the Go To dialog box (see Figure 6.4) to move in large jumps. (Choose Edit ➤ Go To to open the Go To dialog box.) Simply type the address you want to go to into the Reference field, and click OK. Otherwise, you can select one of the named ranges in the workbook (cells that you have named for convenience, as discussed in Chapter 8), as well as the last four addresses from which you chose the Go To command (a quick way to return to places you've been).

Another way to go to and select an address or named range is with the Name Box on the left side of the Formula bar. Select the box, type a range name or cell address, and press Enter. You can also open its drop-down list of range names (if there are any ranges in the workbook) and select one.

FIGURE 6.4:   In the Go To dialog box, you can select or type the name or address you want to go to.

Here are several other neat ways for getting to places fast:

▶ Press Home to move to the beginning of the current row.

▶ Press Ctrl+Home to move to cell A1 in the current worksheet.

▶ Press Ctrl+End or End and then Home to move to the cell in the last occupied row and column of the worksheet. (This method will show you the farthest extent of the occupied worksheet.)

▶ Press Ctrl+arrow key or End, and then click an arrow key to move as far as possible in the given direction, based on whether cells in that row or column are occupied. Play with this one both while the active cell is occupied and while it's unoccupied to see how it works. You can also double-click one of the four edges of the active cell's selection border to get a similar result.

▶ Press End and then press Enter to move to the last occupied cell in the current row.

Moving between Workbooks

You can work with multiple workbooks at the same time in Excel, just as you can work with multiple documents in Microsoft Word. Switching between workbooks is really just a matter of switching between windows:

▶ If the other workbook is visible on the screen, click within it.

▶ Select a workbook from the Window menu.

▶ Press Ctrl+F6 to switch to the next window.

Using the Toolbars

A new feature in Excel 2000 is the Personal toolbar, which is installed by default. In one row, the Personal toolbar combines buttons from the Standard toolbar and the Formatting toolbar. Of course, there isn't enough room to display all the buttons from both these toolbars, so Excel displays those you use the most. Thus, the Personal toolbar is constantly changing, depending on how you work.

If you need a button that isn't displayed, simply click the More Buttons button to display the rest of the buttons normally found on the Standard or Formatting toolbars. Figure 6.5 shows the results of clicking the More Buttons button at the end of the Standard toolbar portion of the Personal toolbar. Notice that the Personal toolbar includes two More Buttons buttons—one in the middle and one at the far right. Figure 6.6 shows the list of buttons that is displayed when you click Add or Remove Buttons. To add or remove a button, simply click it. If you want to reset the toolbar to its original (default) state, click Reset Toolbar.

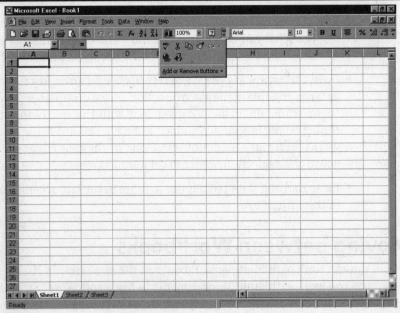

FIGURE 6.5: The Personal toolbar

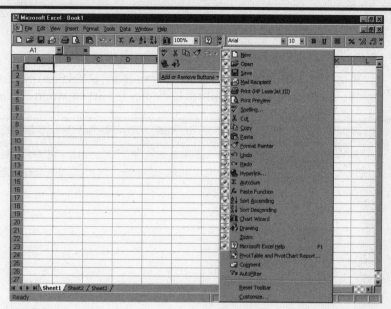

FIGURE 6.6: The results of clicking the Add or Remove Buttons button

I used the Personal toolbar while writing this book, and all the figures and graphics show the Personal toolbar. Of course, my Personal toolbar displays those buttons that I have most recently used, so it will look different from yours. You can, however, choose to display the Standard and Formatting toolbars in two rows, as they appeared in previous versions of Excel. To do so, follow these steps:

1. Right-click anywhere on the Personal toolbar to open the Customize dialog box, and then click the Options tab.

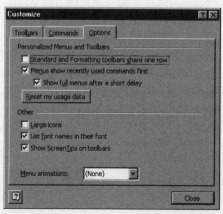

2. Clear the Standard and Formatting Toolbars Share One Row check box.

3. Click Close.

Besides the Standard and Formatting toolbars, Excel has 12 other toolbars. Choose View ➤ Toolbars to display the list shown in Figure 6.7.

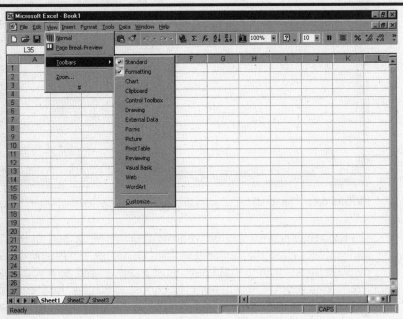

FIGURE 6.7: Click the name of a toolbar to display it or hide it.

By default, toolbars appear beneath the menu bar, but you can place them anywhere on the screen and adjust their shape. Simply point to the toolbar's handle on the left side of the toolbar and drag it where you want it. If you drag the toolbar to an edge of the screen, the toolbar will "dock" against that edge. Otherwise, you can change the shape of the toolbar and its position within the window to suit your work habits.

When a button has a drop-down palette of choices, like the Borders and Fill Color buttons on the Formatting toolbar, you can tear off the palette and keep it available on the screen. Just drag its border away from the toolbar. The palette has its own Close button.

USING THE MENUS

As you work, Excel 2000 also personalizes your menus to reflect the commands you most recently used. By default, Excel displays short menus. To see all the commands on a menu, hold down the mouse button after you open a menu, or click the More Buttons button at the bottom of a menu. Figure 6.8 shows the short File menu, and Figure 6.9 shows the long File menu.

New...	Ctrl+N
Open...	Ctrl+O
Close	
Save	Ctrl+S
Save As...	
Save as Web Page...	
Web Page Preview	
Page Setup...	
Print Area	▶
Print Preview	
Print...	Ctrl+P
Send To	▶
1 D:\Ex...\Monthly Housing Expenses.xls	
2 D:\Excel book\Gene's files\f0101.xls	
3 D:\NER Author Re...\Loan Calculator.xls	
4 D:\NER Author Review\S...\meisters.xls	
Exit	

FIGURE 6.8: The short File menu

Part ii

To reset your menus to their default state, follow these steps:

1. Choose Tools ➤ Customize to open the Customize dialog box.

2. Click the Options tab.

3. Click Reset My Usage Data.

4. When Excel asks if you're sure you want to do this, click Yes.

5. Click Close.

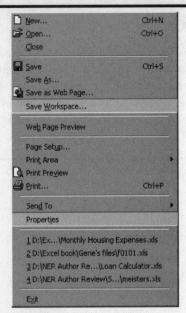

FIGURE 6.9: The long File menu

Getting Help

Its abundance of online help is one of the reasons people like to use Excel, especially new users. In Excel 2000, you can get help in three main ways:

Office Assistant   A quirky, animated character that answers your questions.

Help topics   Countless pages of information about Excel, which you can access through a table of contents or an index or by asking questions of the Answer Wizard.

World Wide Web   If you have access to the Internet, you can tap into Microsoft's online help at various Web sites.

You'll also find help in a variety of other places and styles:

▶ Point at the name of a button on the toolbar to display a descriptive ScreenTip.

▶ To see a ScreenTip about an item on the Excel screen or a command on its menus, choose Help ➢ What's This (Shift+F1) and then click the item or command.

▶ To get help on an option in a dialog box, click the question mark in the upper-right corner and then click the option. A ScreenTip describes that option. Most dialog boxes also have a Help button that explains how to work with their settings.

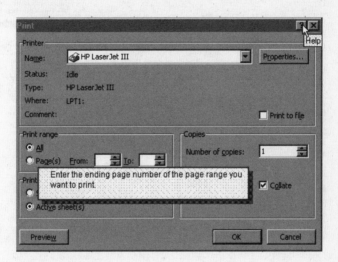

Accessing the Office Assistant

Excel and the other programs in Microsoft Office extend their online help capabilities with the Office Assistant. This perky, user-friendly, always-at-the-ready, "Yes Sir!" kind of help system goes a big step further in the world of online help. Some will say that it goes way too far, but you can decide for yourself.

TIP

While you're trying out the Assistant, you might do your co-workers a favor by turning down your computer's speakers! Alternatively, you can clear the Make Sounds check box on the Options tab of the Assistant's Options dialog box. This change affects the Assistant in all other Microsoft Office applications on your computer.

You access the Assistant for the first time by choosing Help ➤ Show Office Assistant. After you access the Assistant from the Help menu, you can click the Office Assistant button on the toolbar for future help.

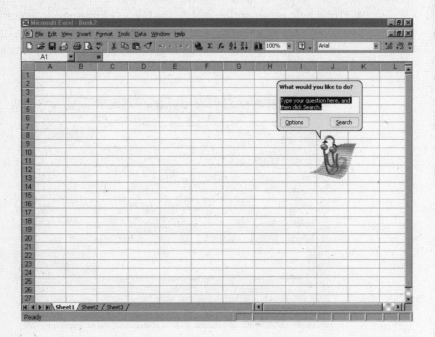

Once you've gotten over the animation of the Assistant, you'll find several ways to get help:

Ask a Question   Type your question (be concise) and click the Search button. The Assistant will present you with several suggested help topics that may answer your question. Clicking one will bring up the relevant help screen. For example, try "How do I widen a column?" or "How do I use the Assistant?"

Tips   While you're working in Excel, you may see a light bulb appear in the Assistant from time to time. Click the bulb to display a helpful tip about what you're doing. If the Assistant isn't open, you'll see the light bulb in the Office Assistant button on the Standard toolbar. Click the button to open the Assistant, and then click the light bulb to get the tip.

Wizards   When a Wizard is helping you perform a task in Excel (Wizards are discussed a little later), you can have the Assistant stand on the side and kibbitz with explanations and helpful tips.

Relevant help   When the Assistant is open, you can click it to have it offer help about the current task. When you're performing a task for the first time, the Assistant displays a light bulb. Clicking the light bulb or the Assistant displays relevant help topics.

The Office Assistant is an interesting and lively way to get help while you're working in Excel. If your Assistant gets annoying, you can adjust or disable many of its features. Simply click the Assistant, click the Options button to open the Office Assistant dialog box, and choose the Options tab.

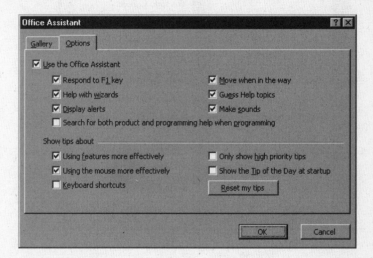

You can then fine-tune the Assistant to suit your needs (but don't you dare peek at the Gallery tab, or you'll twiddle away as much time as I did...just kidding). You can also right-click the Assistant and then click Hide on the shortcut menu to hide the Assistant.

Using Help Topics

You can access the main body of help, shown in Figure 6.10, by pressing F1, which sidesteps the Assistant.

TIP

If the F1 key displays and hides the Office Assistant, click the Office Assistant, click the Options button to open the Office Assistant dialog box, clear the Respond to F1 Key check box, and then click OK.

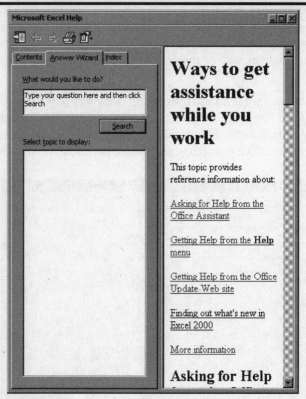

FIGURE 6.10:   You can display the Help window by pressing F1.

The Help window opens in the size and shape in which it was last used. Here are a couple of ways to adjust the views of the Help window to get the most out of the Help feature.

▶ Click the Maximize button so that the Help window covers the entire screen.

▶ Choose Window ➢ Arrange, select Tiled, and then click OK to display the Help and workbook windows side by side.

If multiple Excel windows are open, choosing Arrange tiles all of them. The Help window has three tabs:

Contents   Displays a table of contents of all the available help topics in Excel.

Answer Wizard   Lets you find a topic by typing a question.

Index   Displays a list of topics related to a word that you enter. Double-click one of them to display help on that topic.

 Click the Hide button to hide the tabs and view the entire Help window.

Finding Help on the World Wide Web

If you're connected to the Internet's World Wide Web (would you admit it if you weren't?), Excel can find helpful information for you on Microsoft's Web sites. Choose Help ➤ Office on the Web to open your Web browser and access the Microsoft Office site.

Calling on Wizards to Lend a Hand

Excel is a huge program with lots and lots of features. The Wizards help you with some of the more common tasks that can seem rather complex the first time you use them (or each time if you rarely perform the tasks).

A Wizard is simply an automated question-and-answer session that walks you through the steps to complete a task; you'll also find Wizards in the other programs in Microsoft Office. A Wizard explains what is required at each step, prompts you for your response, and then moves on to the next step.

Some Wizards appear automatically—for example, when you choose Insert ➤ Chart. In this case, the Wizard guides you through the steps that are required to create a chart based on your worksheet.

To find other Wizards and *add-ins* (optional accessory programs), choose Tools ➤ Add-Ins. Once the add-ins are selected and installed, you can find them under the appropriate menus. For example, the Template Wizard is on the Data menu after it is installed.

This chapter has introduced you to many of the Excel features that you will use on a daily basis. I hope that you've also begun to tinker with any features or odds and ends that pique your interest. The best way to learn about Excel is to read and experiment.

WHAT'S NEXT

Chapter 7 will take you one step further on your tour of Excel. Now that you know the basics, you can get started with entering and editing data, which is what Excel is all about.

Part ii

Chapter 7

ENTERING AND EDITING DATA

No matter how elaborate your Excel worksheet may be, the most important component is the data and the formulas it contains. These items are what make your worksheet unique from all others and allow you to carry out specific tasks.

To begin to use a worksheet, you must first understand how to get data into the cells and how to revise what's already there. Although we touched upon many of these concepts in Chapter 6, we will now expand upon them and explain how to enter, edit, copy, move, and delete data. Tips for speeding up data entry, validating data, and correcting erroneous data will also be covered.

Adapted from *Mastering Excel 2000 Premium Edition*
by Mindy C. Martin, Steven M. Hansen, and Beth Klingher
ISBN 0-7821-2317-1   1328 pages $39.99

ENTERING INFORMATION

Data is entered in Excel by simply selecting a cell and then typing into it. When you do this, you will notice that a few things happen. As you type, the data will fill the formula bar and the active cell at the same time. In addition, two small buttons will appear to the left of the formula bar, one containing an X and the other a check mark.

The X is called the Cancel button and can be used to cancel the entry of the data you are in the process of entering. However, you must cancel the entry *before* you press the Enter key. It is equivalent to pressing Esc on your keyboard. The check mark is also called the Enter button and clicking it is equivalent to pressing the Enter key on your keyboard. The data is not considered to be entered into your worksheet until you press the Enter key or click the check mark.

TIP

Moving your cursor, either with the mouse or keyboard, will automatically cause the data to be entered and move the active cell to the new cell chosen.

When you press the Enter key, you may find that you are automatically moved one cell down on your worksheet. This can be helpful if you are entering columns of data, one cell after another. However, if you would prefer to either remain in the same cell, or move in another direction, you can change this on the Edit tab of the dialog box shown in Figure 7.1 and accessed from Tools ➢ Options. Notice that you can choose to have the active cell move in any direction or not at all.

When you choose a direction for Move Selection After Enter, you automatically create another keyboard shortcut for the opposite direction. To use this option, hold down the Shift key while you press Enter. The cursor will move one cell in the opposite direction. For example, if you have chosen the option to move the selection Down after entering, simply entering the data will move the cursor to the cell below. But, if you hold down the Shift key when you enter, the cursor will move in the *opposite* direction, to the cell above.

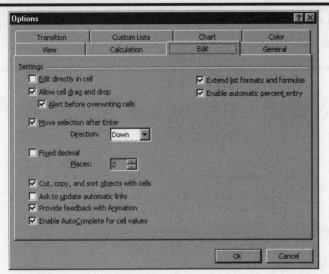

FIGURE 7.1: You can customize a number of editing options in the Options dialog box.

TIP

If you are entering data into a block of cells, it is often easier to select the entire range first and then use the Tab key to move throughout the range after each entry. The Tab key will move across a row to the end of the selected range and then jump down one row to the first column of the range.

How Excel Interprets Your Data

Although simple data entry may seem straightforward, there are a couple of important points to remember. Excel always attempts to interpret the data you are entering, either as a number or text. If Excel interprets the data as text, it will automatically left justify the data. If Excel assumes the data is a number, it will right-justify the data and may attempt to format the data with commas or decimals—or even convert the data to a date or time.

Numeric data can only include numbers 0 through 9 and the characters +, −, E, e, (,), $, % , and /. If any other character is included, Excel assumes that the data is text. The only exceptions to this are dates and times, which are interpreted by Excel as numbers.

In some cases, Excel's interpretation can result in erroneous data. Table 7.1 lists some of the characters that Excel may interpret incorrectly or display in an unexpected way.

TABLE 7.1: How Excel Interprets Data

CHARACTER	EXCEL'S INTERPRETATION	ENTRY	RESULT
Leading +	Ignores plus sign if followed by a number.	+5600	5600
	Converts to an equal sign if followed by a formula.	+75+$D$6	=75+$D$6
E or e	Assumes scientific notation if included with all numbers.	4.5e7	4.5E+07 or 45,000,000
Parenthesis	If around a number, interprets as a negative number.	(500)	-500
Percent Sign (%)	Interprets as percent of 100. (Divides number by 100.)	10%	0.10
Forward slash (/)	If surrounded by numbers, tries to interpret as a date.	11/4/57	4-Nov-1957
		5/20	20-May-Current Year
		3/99	1-Mar-1999
Minus sign (–)	If surrounded by numbers, tries to interpret as date.	8–02	1–Aug–2002
		1–00	1–Jan–2000
		11–02–33	2–Nov–1933
Leading 0	Ignores leading zero if followed by numbers.	06511	6511

Potential Problems with Date Formats

Excel's automatic interpretation of data can pose a problem, especially with fractions. If you enter 1/25, Excel will convert this to January 25th of the current year. If you really want to enter 1/25 or 0.04, either add an equal sign or plus sign to the front of the number, or include a zero as the primary digit (e.g., =1/25 or +1/25 or 0 1/25), as seen in Figure 7.2. The last option will also automatically format the cell as a fraction and display 1/25 rather than 0.04.

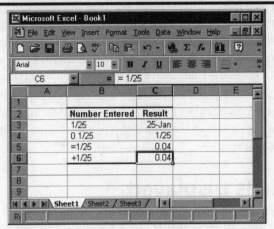

FIGURE 7.2:   Excel interprets numbers with fractions as dates. To enter a fraction, put an equal sign before the number.

Entering a Number as Text

There are also cases when Excel assumes that the data you enter is a number, although you really want it to be treated as text. This often occurs with special identification numbers that may need leading zeroes displayed, such as zip codes or product identification numbers. To force Excel to display the leading zero, you have a few choices. You can convert the data to text, which is simply done by preceding the number with a single quote such as '06511, shown in Figure 7.3. You can also format the cell as text by using the Format ➤ Cells command. Just choose Text on the Number tab. Once the data has been converted to text, it will automatically be left-justified. However, in many instnaces, you can still use the data in calculations, if you like, because Excel will attempt to convert the text to a value prior to performing most calculations.

	Product Number	Description	Color	Quantity in Stock
2				
3	01758	Patent Leather Hip Boots	Blue	25
4	01759	Patent	reen	36
5	01760	Patent	lack	11
6	01761	Patent	ed	0
7	14638	Sling	lack	44
8	14639	Sling	rown	44
9	14640	Sling Back Alligator	Tan	45
10	00456	Old Fashioned Mary Jane	Red	12
11	00457	Old Fashioned Mary Jane	Black	15

To enter a leading zero, precede the number with a single quote - '.

FIGURE 7.3:   Notice the single quote before the identification code. This tells Excel to interpret the number as text.

Part ii

Another option is to create a number format that will display all of the required digits in the format desired like 000-000. This format will force the display to show six digits with a hyphen in the middle, even if the leading digits are not entered. This technique is often useful for product numbers or account numbers that must be a certain number of digits.

The last option is to use one of Excel's Special formats, such as Zip Code format or Telephone Number format. These special formats, found in the Format Cells dialog box in the Number tab, will automatically format the data accordingly.

How Your Data Is Displayed

There is another important concept to understand in the way Excel stores and displays data. What is shown in a cell may be different from what is actually in the cell. This is obvious in the case of a formula, which displays the results of the formula in the cell but retains the actual formula to recalculate or edit. However, this also is true for a number of other types of data.

Excel stores up to a maximum of 15 digits per number, including integers and decimals. Numbers with more digits are converted to scientific notation. In General Number format, the number of decimals displayed depends on the column width. If you have a number with eight decimal numbers and you narrow the column, you may only see one or two. If you widen the column, all eight decimal places will be displayed. If you narrow the column so that the full numbers cannot be displayed, a series of pound signs (#) will be shown as seen in Figure 7.4. However, in all cases, editing the cell will display the entire number. It is also important to understand that any calculations will be based on the underlying number, not merely what is displayed.

TIP

If a cell displays a number of pound signs, ####, use Excel's Format ➣ Column ➣ AutoFit Selection or simply double-click the right border of the column heading to widen the column.

Excel also handles text in a unique way. Text that is too wide to fit in a cell will be displayed across a number of cells. However, if there is data in the cells to the right, the text will be truncated at the end of the cell, as seen in Figure 7.5. The text is still stored in the original cell, but it is not displayed.

	A	B	C	D	E	F	G
1							
2	Apple	3.1416	3.14159	3.1415927	3.1416	3.1	3.141592654
3	Cherry	13.142	13.1416	13.141593	13.142	13	13.14159265
4	Strawberry Rhubarb	113.14	113.142	113.14159	113.14	113	113.1415927
5	Peach	1113.1	1113.14	1113.1416	1113.1	###	1113.141593
6	Mincemeat	11113	11113.1	11113.142	11113	###	11113.14159
7	Pecan	111113	111113	111113.14	111113	###	111113.1416

FIGURE 7.4:   The same number is displayed in columns A through G. Note column F, which displays #### because the column is too narrow to display the number accurately.

	A	B
1		
2	Apple	3.141
3	Cherry	13.14
4	Strawberry Rh	113.1
5	Peach	1113.
6	Mincemeat	1111
7	Pecan	11111

FIGURE 7.5:   Text that is too wide for a specific cell will overlap the neighboring cells.

There are a number of options provided by Excel to handle text that is too wide for a particular column.

▶ You can widen the column to display all of the text.

▶ You can simply wrap the text within the cell.

▶ You can shrink the font so that it fits in the cell.

▶ You can merge the cells so that the text displays over a number of columns, if the cells to the right are empty.

▶ You can change the orientation of the text so that it displays on an angle.

NOTE

For more information on formatting cells, see Chapter 8.

Part ii

USING FIXED DECIMALS TO SPEED DATA ENTRY

Excel provides a feature that is helpful if you are entering large amounts of data with a fixed decimal point, such as dollars and cents. If you want to avoid entering the decimal point for all entries, choose Tools ➤ Options and, on the Edit tab, select Fixed Decimal. When you enter data, Excel will automatically place a decimal point at the correct position in the number. Keep in mind that you must enter zeroes to fill the decimal places in the event that you are entering a whole number. For example, $2.00 must be entered as 200 when using a fixed decimal of two places.

Mastering Data Entry Techniques

There are a number of techniques that can help you speed your data entry and ensure its accuracy when working with worksheets. Becoming familiar with the wealth of data entry techniques offered by Excel can save you a significant amount of time as you work. In the following sections we cover how to use the Data Fill and Custom Fill methods, as well as how to work with AutoCorrect, AutoComplete, and Data Validation.

Using Data Fill

You may often find it necessary to enter the same data and formulas across a number of columns or rows. Rather than use the copy and paste technique, Excel provides an easier method called Data Fill. Data Fill will copy the contents and format of the original cell but not the cell comments. The most common operation is either to fill down a column or to fill right across a row. However, you can also fill up or left by dragging the cursor in that direction.

WARNING

If you are filling up or left, the bottom-right cell will be the one copied to the other cells in the range.

To fill using the menus, first choose the entire range to be filled. The first cell in the range must be the cell whose contents will be filled down or right. Choose Edit ➤ Fill and then select the direction to fill the remaining cells.

If you are comfortable with the mouse, Excel's fill handle is much easier to use than the menu options. Simply select the cells to be copied and then move your cursor over the bottom-right corner of the bottom cell until the cursor changes to a small plus. Click and drag the data down, right, up, or left.

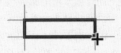

NOTE

If you drag the fill handle inside the selected range, the contents of the cell will be cleared.

If you are filling a group of cells alongside another range of data, like the one in Figure 7.6, you can also double-click on the fill handle to fill down. Simply select the cell to copy and then move your cursor over the fill handle until it changes to a small plus. Double-click the fill handle and the data is copied to extend to the same length as the range of data alongside it.

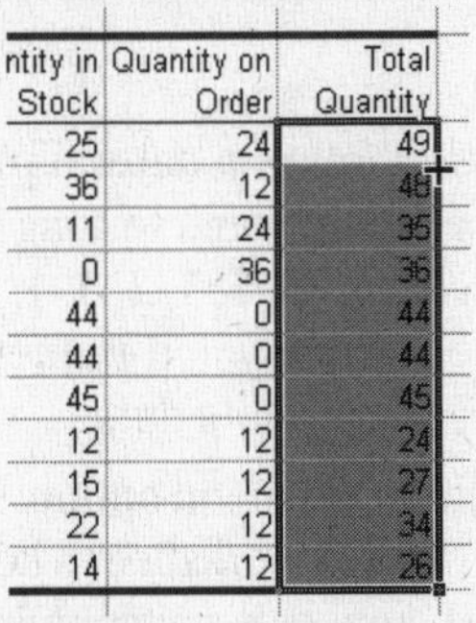

ntity in Stock	Quantity on Order	Total Quantity
25	24	49
36	12	48
11	24	35
0	36	36
44	0	44
44	0	44
45	0	45
12	12	24
15	12	27
22	12	34
14	12	26

FIGURE 7.6: You can double-click a fill handle to copy data alongside another range of data.

Part ii

TIP

Ctrl+D and Ctrl+R can also be used to fill data down or right in a selected range.

Copying across Worksheets

If you want to copy data or formulas across a number of worksheets, you can use the Fill Across Worksheets command. First, you must group the worksheets. To group a number of worksheets, select the first sheet and then hold down the Shift key and select the last sheet. You will see all of the selected sheets highlighted and the word Group will appear next to the workbook name. You will also notice that the option for Edit ➤ Fill ➤ Across Worksheets is no longer grayed out. You will be presented with the option to fill All, Contents, or Formats, as shown in Figure 7.7. Remember, the data selected on the active worksheet will be filled across all of the other worksheets in the group in the exact location on each worksheet.

FIGURE 7.7:   When you fill across worksheets, you can choose to fill Contents, Formats, or both.

Using Data Series

A data series is a series of numbers of items that follow a natural progression. The numbers are either related to each other in some way, as in 2, 4, 8, 16, 32, or because they follow a pattern such as 1, 2, 3, 1, 2, 3, 1, 2, 3. Excel can interpret both types of series, as well as many non-numerical series, and will automatically fill a range with any missing data.

The Series command is found under the Edit ➤ Fill menu option. Before you fill a series, you must first select the range on your worksheet where you want the series to be placed. This range can be blank, or it can contain the first entry or the first few entries in your series. Choose Edit ➤ Fill ➤ Series, and a dialog box will appear, as shown in Figure 7.8.

FIGURE 7.8: The Series dialog box lets you fill data to fit specific trend lines or growth patterns.

The Series dialog box offers the following options:

Series In: Rows or Columns   Excel will guess at the correct orientation, depending upon the range selected. If you have a single cell selected, you must indicate in which direction you want the series placed—across a row or down a column.

Type: Linear   This option creates a straight linear progression, starting at the current value of the cell and incrementing each cell in the range by the number entered in Step Value. If your first cell contains a 12 and the step value is 12, the numbers will increment by 12s—12, 24, 36, 48, and so on. (This is handy if you sell a product in quantities of a dozen.) You may notice that if you select a range with a few values already entered, the step value will be filled with Excel's best guess.

Type: Growth   This option will grow the data by the number entered in the Step Value box using simple multiplication. If you start with a value of 1 and grow the data by a step value of 2, the numbers will grow as follows: 1, 1*2, 2*2, 4*2, 8*2, and so on, or 1, 2, 4, 8, 16, 32, and so on.

Type: Date   Date allows you to enter a series of dates a specific number of days apart so that you can enter weekly dates, monthly dates, or other options. This option even lets you specify weekdays and is smart enough to determine the correct date for the end of each month. For instance, if you enter 8/31/01 in the first cell and choose Monthly, the data series will read 8/31/01, 9/30/01, 10/31/01, 11/30/01, and so on.

Type: AutoFill   This option allows you to enter a series of numbers and have Excel determine the relationship between them in order to fill the remaining cells in the series. For example, if you place a 15 in the first cell and a 25 in the next, Excel will fill the remaining cells with 35, 45, 55, and so on. AutoFill will also extend a series of text when the text has a numeric component that can be incremented. For example, Period 1 will be extended to Period 2, Period 3, and so on. Dates will also be automatically filled based upon the data originally entered in the cells.

To suppress AutoFill, hold down the Ctrl key as you drag. AutoFill is much easier to do with a mouse than with the keyboard. Simply select the cells that contain the beginning of the series and drag the fill handle to create an AutoFill.

NOTE

If you use AutoFill for a single cell, it is equivalent to copying the cell value a number of times. The exception to this is when filling a predefined list, such as the days of the week. (See Custom Fill for more information on predefined lists.) Excel will automatically increment these, as well as other text values that contain numbers, such as Product 1, Qtr 1, etc.

Trend   This checkbox is only available in conjunction with linear or growth series. In this case, Excel analyzes the data selected and determines what the trend line for the data should be, ignoring any step value and replacing the current values of the cells with a calculated series. The calculated series is based upon the trend of the original values. The Trend function for a linear series uses a simple least-squared algorithm, $y=mx+b$, which you probably remember as the basic calculation for a line. The growth trend line uses an exponential curve algorithm, $y=b*m^x$. Figure 7.9 illustrates the different types of trends that can be produced. The original data was entered into the worksheet as is, the second used the original data with a linear trend, and the third displayed the same data with a growth trend. Notice how the chart illustrates the different trend lines that are created.

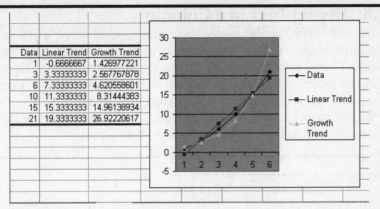

FIGURE 7.9:   An example of three data series created using the Trend option.

Step Value and **Stop Value**   The step value is used to determine the increment value for a linear series or date series, and the multiplication rate for a growth series. Stop Value is the maximum value for the series. Both Step Value and Stop Value are grayed out when you choose the Trend option.

Table 7.2 illustrates the different series created using the AutoFill option.

TABLE 7.2: Series Created by AutoFill

VALUES SELECTED	RESULTS
9:00	9:00, 10:00, 11:00, 12:00
11:00 , 11:30	11:00, 11:30, 12:00, 12:30, 13:00
Sunday	Sunday, Monday, Tuesday, Wednesday, Thursday
Monday, Wednesday	Monday, Wednesday, Friday, Sunday, Tuesday, Thursday
Mar, Jun	Mar, Jun, Sep, Dec, Mar
31-Jan, 28-Feb	31-Jan, 28-Feb, 31-Mar, 30-Apr, 31-May
Qtr1	Qtr1, Qtr2, Qtr3, Qtr4, Qtr1
1st	$1^{st}, 2^{nd}, 3^{rd}, 4^{th}, 5^{th}, 6^{th}$
10, 20	10, 20, 30, 40, 50, 60
3/4, 1 1/2	3/4, 1 1/2, 2 1/4, 3, 3 3/4, 4 1/2

Justifying Text in a Column

The Justify command that appears when you select Edit ➤ Fill is used to justify a block of text down a column of cells. For example, if you want to add a note or some commentary about a table, you could enter the data in a single cell to the right of the table, as shown in Figure 7.10. However, the data may scroll off the screen, making it difficult to read. Select the cell and choose Edit ➤ Fill ➤ Justify and the data will be divided up between cells so that the text flows down the column.

Data	Linear Trend	Growth Trend	
1	-0.6666667	1.426977221	Note the original data shows a slight
3	3.33333333	2.567767878	
6	7.33333333	4.620558601	
10	11.3333333	8.31444383	
15	15.3333333	14.96138934	
21	19.3333333	26.92220617	

Data	Linear Trend	Growth Trend	
1	-0.6666667	1.426977221	Note the original data
3	3.33333333	2.567767878	shows a slight growth
6	7.33333333	4.620558601	rate, but grows at a
10	11.3333333	8.31444383	slower pace than the
15	15.3333333	14.96138934	exponential rate.
21	19.3333333	26.92220617	

FIGURE 7.10:   A line of text before and after the use of the Justify command

Using the Fill Handle

The fill handle provides the easiest and quickest way to create a data series. Earlier we explained how to use the fill handle to fill a range of cells with the same value or formula. You can also use the fill handle to implement Excel's AutoFill. Select the range of cells containing the start of the series and drag the fill handle down, up, right, or left to select the range of cells to fill. The series will be extended in the same manner as described above under AutoFill. You will also notice that as you drag your mouse across a selection, a small note appears at the bottom right of the range indicating the current last value in the series. This is equivalent to the stop value.

TIP

Using the fill handle to fill down a single cell simply copies the cell if it contains a value. However, you can implement AutoFill by pressing the Ctrl key while you drag the fill handle. For example, using fill down on a single cell containing the value 10 copies the value, but using Ctrl with the fill handle results in a series starting with 10, 11, 12, and so forth.

You can also double-click the fill handle to implement AutoFill if the series happens to be next to another range of data.

Using the Right Mouse Button

The shortcut menu on the right mouse button provides additional control for the AutoFill function. Instead of using the left button, depress the right button before you drag the fill handle. When you have selected the appropriate range to fill, release the button and a shortcut menu, shown in Figure 7.11, will appear with the following choices:

▶ Copy Cells will AutoFill copies of the cell rather than creating a trend or series.

▶ Fill Series gives the same results as using AutoFill to fill a series.

▶ Fill Formats is similar to Edit ➤ Paste Special ➤ Formats. However, it also copies the formats in the same sequence as the original range so that formats like stripes or alternating borders are maintained.

▶ Fill Values copies the contents of the source cell or extends the series, but it does not extend the cell formatting.

▶ Fill Days, Weekdays, Months, and Years is only applicable if the data in the range is date based.

▶ Linear Trend, Growth Trend, and Series are also available. The latter will bring up the Series dialog box.

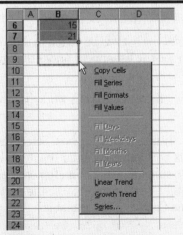

FIGURE 7.11: The shortcut menu is displayed when you use the fill handle with your *right* mouse button.

Part ii

Working with Custom Fill

The AutoFill feature can automatically extend a range of cells that contain days of the week, incrementing each of the days accordingly. For example, if you place the word Monday in a cell and then drag the fill handle across the row, the adjoining cells will contain the remaining days of the week—Tuesday, Wednesday, Thursday, and so on. This is a handy feature for entering frequently used lists such as the days of the week. There are probably many other lists of this type that you frequently enter in cells on the worksheet, either as headings, fields, or database items.

Excel provides a feature that allows you to create your own custom list of names or text. This list is then available in conjunction with Auto-Fill so that you can enter the first name on the list and simply drag the remaining names into your worksheet. To create a custom list, follow these steps:

1. Enter the list of names in a column on your worksheet. Be sure to enter the data in the desired order.

2. Select the range of cells containing the list and choose Tools ➤ Options. Select the Custom Lists tab.

3. Be sure that the first item in the Lists box, NEW LIST, is highlighted.

4. You will notice that the selected range appears in the box labeled Import List from Cells. If the range is incorrect, you can change it or select a new range.

5. Press the Import button and the list will be added to the List Entries box. You will also see the list appear under the Custom Lists box to the left.

6. Choose OK and the list will be added to your workspace, as shown in Figure 7.12.

You can also type a new list directly into the dialog box. Select the New List option in the Custom Lists box, and then enter the items in the List Entries box on the right. Be sure to press Enter after each entry to separate the items from one another. Once done, choose the Add button and your list will be added to the Custom Lists available.

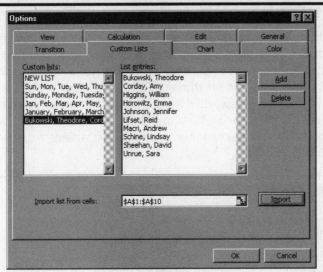

FIGURE 7.12: A custom list created for a list of frequently used names.

TIP

A custom list is limited to text or text and numbers, but it does not allow simple numeric entries. You can enter numbers in the List Entries box, but in order to use the list, the numbers must be entered as text. (To enter numbers as text, precede the number with a single quote or format the cell as text.)

You can edit a custom list in a similar manner by simply selecting the applicable list in the Custom Lists box and editing the entries. Again, be sure to hit Enter after each entry to separate them from one another.

NOTE

You cannot revise the custom lists that come with Excel for weekdays and months. You will notice that the entries for these lists are grayed out.

If you have more than one list that starts with the same item, Excel will use the last custom list created. However, if you want to use a different custom list, simply enter a few of the entries and then choose Auto-Fill. This will ensure that your list is unique, and Excel will match the correct list to your data and fill it accordingly.

Part ii

Getting It Right with AutoCorrect

Excel's AutoCorrect feature checks your spelling as you enter the data and automatically corrects commonly misspelled words as you type them. Frequently misspelled words can be added to the AutoCorrect dictionary in one of two ways. The first is through Excel's Spelling Checker, as seen in Figure 7.13. When a misspelled word is displayed, you are given the option to add the word to the AutoCorrect dictionary. Simply press the button marked AutoCorrect and the misspelled word along with its correct spelling will be saved.

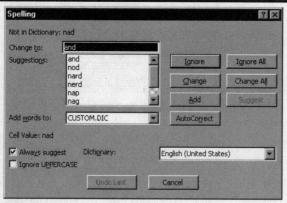

FIGURE 7.13: You can add words to AutoCorrect from the Spelling Checker.

You can enter frequently misspelled words directly into AutoCorrect. Choose Tools ➤ AutoCorrect and a dialog box will appear. Enter the misspelling in the Replace box and the correct spelling in the With box. Press the Add button to add this entry to your list.

AutoCorrect also allows you to speed data entry by abbreviating frequently used words or statements so that you only need type the abbreviation and the entire word or statement will be entered. This is very useful for company names, product names, or other frequently typed data. For example, to replace the name Willow Solutions, Inc., you could simply type **wsi**. Choose Tools ➤ AutoCorrect and enter the abbreviation in the Replace box, as shown in Figure 7.14. Enter the full name or statement in the With box. Click the Add button.

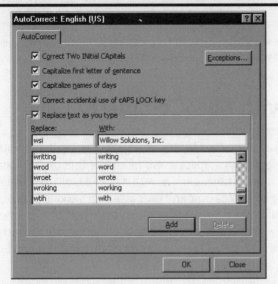

FIGURE 7.14:   You can enter misspelled words directly into the AutoCorrect dialog box.

You will also notice a number of checkboxes at the top of the Auto-Correct dialog box. These list common typing errors that can be automatically corrected as you type. The Exceptions button opens another dialog box that allows you to enter exceptions to these rules. For example, you may be in the habit of entering employee names with the first initial and last name together as TJones. This will be automatically corrected to Tjones unless you add it to the exceptions list, as seen in Figure 7.15.

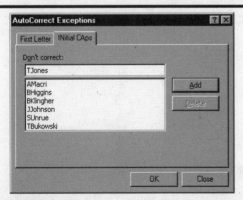

FIGURE 7.15:   The AutoCorrect Exceptions box can be used to enter words that may be erroneously corrected by AutoCorrect, but are okay as entered.

Part ii

NOTE

AutoCorrect is shared among all Office programs so the corrections you add to Excel will also apply to Word, Access, and PowerPoint.

Saving Time with AutoComplete

There are often circumstances when you find yourself entering the same data again and again. For example, in a check register, you might enter the name of the telephone company every month or that of your local grocery store a number of times each month. Or, you may need to enter employee or customer names over and over again for various projects. To save time and avoid misspellings, you can automate part of this process with AutoComplete. AutoComplete will attempt to complete an entry *as you type* it into a cell. Excel bases its guess on all other values previously typed into the column.

NOTE

You can turn AutoComplete on and off by selecting Tools ➢ Options. Choose the Edit tab and check the Enable AutoComplete for Cell Values to turn Auto-Complete on.

Figure 7.16 illustrates the concept behind AutoComplete. You will notice a list of product numbers, descriptions, and quantities on order for each. As you begin to type in a new product description, Excel will attempt to match it with one of the previous entries. You can simply press Enter to accept Excel's guess, or you can keep typing.

Product Number	Description	Color	Quantity in Stock	Quantity on Order	Q
01758	Patent Leather Hip Boots	Blue	25	24	
01759	Patent Leather Hip Boots	Green	36	12	
01760	Patent Leather Hip Boots	Black	11	24	
01761	Patent Leather Hip Boots	Red	0	36	
14638	Sling Back Alligator	Black	44	0	
14639	Sling Back Alligator	Brown	44	0	
14640	Sling Back Alligator	Tan	45	0	
00456	Old Fashioned Mary Jane	Red	12	12	
00457	Old Fashioned Mary Jane	Black	15	12	
00458	Old Fashioned Mary Jane	Green	22	12	
00459	Old Fashioned Mary Jane	Brown	14	12	
00460	Old Fashioned Mary Jane				

FIGURE 7.16:　As you type, AutoComplete will suggest a cell entry based upon the previous entries in the list.

Using Pick from List

Another option available from AutoComplete is the ability to pick an entry from a drop-down list of all the previous entries. To view this option, select the next cell in the list and click your right mouse button. Choose Pick from List and a list of the previous entries is displayed, as seen in Figure 7.17. Choose one and hit Enter. This feature is useful when you have numerous entries and prefer to choose from an existing entry rather than use Auto-Complete, which may require you to type out a large portion of the name.

Green	
Yellow	
Black	
Blue	
Brown	
Green	
Red	
Tan	
White	
Yellow	

FIGURE 7.17:   Pick from List displays a drop-down list of all previous entries in the column.

Setting Limits with Data Validation

In order to avoid entering incorrect data, you can use Excel's Data Validation feature to define certain criteria for data entry. This is useful if you are setting up a worksheet in which others will be entering data, as well as if you want to automatically check your own data entry for potential problems.

You can set up criteria that restricts data entry based upon the type of data, a specific range of data, or particular entries that you specify. When you attempt to enter data that does not meet the specified criteria, a message box appears, notifying you of the error. You can specify exactly what type of message box to display and the exact message in it. You can even display an input box *before* the data is entered, indicating the type of data acceptable for the range.

NOTE

Data validation only occurs when data is manually entered into a cell. Data that changes due to calculations or macro code is not validated.

Data validation is defined for a particular range on your worksheet and can be implemented by following these steps:

1. Select the range on your worksheet where you want to restrict the type of data entered.

2. Choose Data ➤ Validation and the Data Validation dialog box, shown in Figure 7.18, will be displayed.

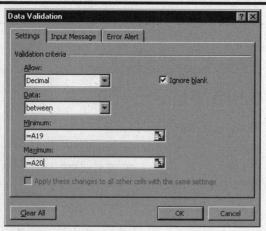

FIGURE 7.18:   The Data Validation dialog box with the Settings tab displayed

Using the Settings Tab

The Settings tab is where you enter the criteria for the data you want to allow. If you open the Allow drop-down list you will see a list of available options. You can restrict data to any of the following options:

Any Value   This option is equivalent to allowing any cell entry. This is made available so that you can include an input note to users, as defined on the second tab of this dialog box, without restricting data input.

Whole Number   Limits entry to integers.

Decimal   Allows both integers and decimals.

List   A predefined list of entries.

Date   Only allows dates or numbers that can be interpreted as dates.

Time   Only allows time values or numbers that can be interpreted as time.

Text Length   Limits data entry to text or numbers with a certain number of characters.

Custom   Restricts data entry to values that meet certain criteria based on a custom formula.

If you choose whole number, decimal, date, time, or text length, you will be prompted to enter a Data criteria, such as between, greater than, equal to, etc., and a maximum and minimum value. These can be a value or formula entered directly into the dialog box, or they can be a cell reference to the worksheet. The option to link the Minimum and Maximum to worksheet cells provides a great amount of flexibility and allows you to create powerful data input forms without code. For example, you could prohibit users from ordering a certain product before a specific date, you could only allow appointments to be scheduled during business hours, or you could prohibit the entry of checks that would deplete the account.

If you have chosen a list in the Allow box, you can either enter the list of acceptable values directly into the Source text box, separated by commas, or point to a range on the worksheet that contains the data. You will also notice a checkbox for an In-cell drop-down list, as seen in Figure 7.19. If you check this option, a drop-down box will appear in the selected cell providing a list of all of the choices available for data entry, as shown in Figure 7.20.

Part ii

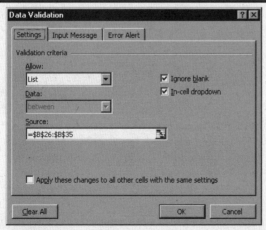

FIGURE 7.19:   The Settings tab of the Data Validation dialog box used to display a drop-down list.

Date	Expenses	Amount
23-Jun-02	Parking	$ 12.00
23-Jun-02	Hotel	$ 209.79
23-Jun-02		
	Travel: Bus	
	Travel: Train	
	Travel: Airplane	
	Auto Mileage	
	Tolls	
	Meals: Lunch	
	Meals: Dinner	
	Expenses	

FIGURE 7.20: Data Validation allows you to limit data entry to only specific items, automatically adding a drop-down list to each cell in the validation range.

The Custom option allows you to enter a true/false formula. When the formula evaluates to false, data entry is prohibited. For example, if you are entering a list of expenses for office supplies, you might want to limit the quantity ordered so that the total spent is below a budgeted amount. The example in Figure 7.21 shows a custom data validation where the custom formula is =TotalExpense<Budget.

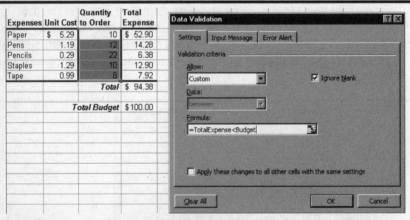

FIGURE 7.21: A custom formula validation in which data entry is restricted to cases where the total expense is less than the budgeted amount

TIP

Excel will calculate the worksheet before it validates the formula so that the data validation checks to see if the data would be valid if it were entered into the cell.

The Ignore Blank checkbox allows users to leave cells blank. If this box is unchecked, blank cells will be treated as a zero.

TIP

Custom formulas can only refer to data on the same worksheet as the data validation range. If you want to refer to cells on other worksheets or workbooks, create a cell link to the data from your current worksheet and then refer to that cell in the formula.

The Apply These Changes To All Other Cells With The Same Settings checkbox is useful for revising data validation. You need not select the entire range; you can select only one cell within that range. Check this checkbox and the entire range that shares the same data validation criteria will be selected.

Displaying an Input Message

You can choose to have an input message displayed whenever a cell in the data validation range is selected. Your message will appear as part of the Office Assistant, as shown in Figure 7.22. You can enter a title for the message and up to 255 characters of text.

FIGURE 7.22: The Input Message tab allows you to display a message whenever a cell in the data validation range is selected.

TIP

If you do not use the Office Assistant, the input message and error alert will appear as a small comment next to the selected cell.

Calling on Error Alert

The last tab on the Data Validation dialog box is for error and alert messages. These are the messages that appear when invalid data is entered. To display a message, check the box labeled Show Error Alert After Invalid Data Is Entered.

The Style option lets you designate the type of message to display, in some cases allowing invalid data to be entered after displaying a warning message:

> **Stop**   This option will prohibit the user from entering invalid data, as shown in Figure 7.23.

TIP

Although the Stop option prohibits you from entering data that does not meet the Data Validation criteria, you can get around this restriction by using Excel's copy and paste.

> **Warning**   This option will display a warning with an option to continue, allowing the user to override the message and enter the data. The options are displayed as Yes, No, and Cancel buttons.

> **Information**   With this option, an information message box will appear, allowing the user to enter the data by pressing an OK button, or to cancel data entry.

You can enter a title for the message box in the title text box. The error message allows you to enter up to 255 characters. We strongly recommend that this message provide the user with a clear explanation of which type of data is valid and which is invalid.

TIP

If you leave the Error Alert tab blank, Excel will provide a standard error message indicating that the value entered is not valid. We do not recommend using this message box as it does not provide any clues about why the data is invalid and can be quite frustrating for the user.

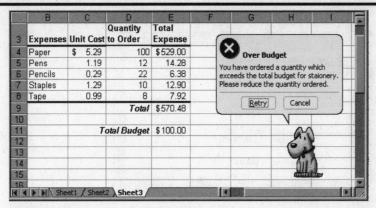

FIGURE 7.23: An error message is displayed when the data does not meet the criteria defined for the range.

EDITING YOUR DATA

Once you have entered a value or formula into a cell, you may need to change it. To do this, first select the cell. The value or formula will appear in the formula bar. Either click the formula bar or press F2 to edit the cell. A few things will happen:

▶ The word Edit will appear on the status bar to indicate that you are in Edit mode.

▶ A cursor will appear in your formula bar to allow you to move through the data and edit it, or if you have in-cell editing turned on, a cursor will also appear directly in the cell.

▶ If the cell contains cell references, those cells will be outlined and color coded to match the formula, as seen in Figure 7.24.

TIP

In-cell editing is enabled in the Tools ➢ Options dialog box on the Edit tab. Choose the Edit Directly in Cell option. If you have in-cell editing selected, you can also double-click the cell to edit the data. If you haven't chosen in-cell editing and there are cell references in a formula in the cell, double-clicking the cell will select each of the references.

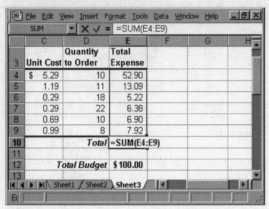

FIGURE 7.24:   In-cell editing allows you to edit the formula from within the cell, in addition to doing so from the formula bar.

Editing a cell is very similar to editing data in any program and much like using a simple word processor. You can use the arrow keys or mouse to move through the cell; the Backspace and Delete keys can be used to remove characters; and you can highlight text and over-write it. The Home and End keys can be used to move you to the beginning or end of the cell data. When you have finished editing the data, you can press Enter or click the Enter button in the Formula bar, in the same way you do when you enter data.

TIP

Data entered as an array formula cannot be simply edited and entered. You must press Ctrl+Alt+Enter to enter an array formula after it has been edited. Array formulas are covered in greater detail in Chapter 10.

Correcting Data

Like most other Windows programs, Excel provides an Undo command on the Edit menu. The Undo command on the menu usually lists exactly what action will be undone if you choose it. Pay attention to this information before choosing to undo the action. Since Excel supports multiple levels of Undo, each time an action is undone, the action previous to this will be displayed next to the Undo option on the Edit menu, as shown in Figure 7.25.

FIGURE 7.25:   The Undo command on the Edit menu displays the last command to be undone.

The Undo button on the Standard toolbar provides a button to undo your last action. In addition, it provides a list of your last 16 actions in a drop-down box and lets you choose one, a few, or all of these actions to undo. Figure 7.26 shows the items listed in the Undo drop-down box.

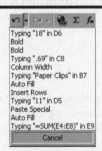

FIGURE 7.26:   The Undo button allows you to choose from among the last 16 actions to undo.

WARNING

There are a number of actions that cannot be undone. Two important examples are Delete Sheet and Insert Sheet. Changing the Tools ➢ Options settings is something that also cannot be undone.

Immediately below Undo on the Edit menu is the Redo command. This command allows you to redo an action that you mistakenly undid. You can also use it to repeat certain actions on a number of different cells, like changing a cell font to bold. Simply highlight a new cell and choose Edit ➤ Repeat Font.

A Redo button is also provided next to the Undo button on the Standard toolbar, providing you with a list of the last 16 actions to choose from to redo. You can also use the keyboard shortcuts Ctrl+Z and Ctrl+Y to Undo and Redo your last action.

TIP
You can repeat your last action with the F4 key.

Moving Data

Cutting, copying, and pasting data are probably the most frequently performed worksheet commands. As a result, Excel provides numerous ways to carry out these actions. Regardless of the method chosen, you should keep in mind that pasting the data will overwrite whatever is currently in the cell. Excel will warn you of this if you use drag and drop, but it will simply overwrite the data with no warning if any of the other methods are used.

WARNING
To receive a warning when cells are about to be overwritten, you must have this option selected on the Edit tab of the Tools ➤ Options dialog box. Be sure the Alert Before Overwriting Cells checkbox is checked.

Drag and Drop

One of the easiest ways to move data in Excel is to drag the data from one location to another using the mouse. This is done by first selecting the range of data that must be moved and then grabbing the border and moving the data to a new location. You will notice that Excel provides feedback as you drag the data across the worksheet to let you know the current cell references where the data will be dropped (see Figure 7.27).

FIGURE 7.27: When you drag and drop to move data, the small note below the
cursor defines the current drop range.

NOTE

Drag and drop is an optional setting that can be found on the Edit tab of the
dialog box that appears when you select Tools ➢ Options. If you do not see a
wide drag-and-drop border around the active range, you may need to revise
your settings.

You can copy data the same way by simply holding down the Ctrl key
before you drop the data. In Figure 7.28, notice the small plus sign that
appears above your cursor to indicate that you are copying the data
rather than cutting it.

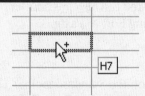

FIGURE 7.28: When using drag and drop to copy data, the small plus sign above
the cursor indicates a copy rather than a cut.

TIP

The Ctrl key is often used to indicate copy rather than cut. This is true for copying cells, worksheets, and files.

Keyboard Shortcuts

Keyboard shortcuts are standard in many Windows programs. Ctrl+C is used to copy data, Ctrl+X is used to cut data, and Ctrl+V is used to paste data. These keys were chosen because they are close to the Ctrl key at the bottom right of the keyboard and can easily be reached with the fingers of one hand. Rather than pressing Ctrl+V, you can also simply press Enter once the data has been copied to the Clipboard. These same keyboard shortcuts can be used in dialog boxes, to copy and paste data from one control to another, and in the formula bar, to cut and paste data within the formula.

TIP

Copied data can be pasted numerous times only if you paste the data using keyboard shortcut keys or toolbar or menu commands. If you paste the data using the Enter key, it is removed from the Clipboard.

From the Menu

Under the Edit menu there are options for Cut, Copy, and Paste. These options can also be found in the shortcut menu that is displayed when you right-click with the mouse over a cell. You can also press Enter once the data has been copied instead of selecting Edit ➤ Paste.

From the Standard Toolbar

There are buttons for cut, copy, and paste on the Standard toolbar. Using these buttons is identical to choosing the same options from the menu.

TIP

Drag and drop is good for moving or copying data in situations where you are working with short distances. The keyboard, menu, and toolbar options are the preferred method when you are copying data from one worksheet to another or from one workbook to another, or across a great number of columns and rows.

When to Cut and Paste

Cutting and pasting data moves your data and/or formats from one section of your worksheet to another section, from one worksheet to another, or from one workbook to a totally separate workbook. Although the terminology used refers to "cutting" a cell, only the contents of the cell are removed; the empty cell remains in place and reverts back to its original format. To actually cut the cell out of the worksheet, you need to delete it, a procedure that is discussed later in this chapter.

When you cut a cell or a range of cells, a moving dotted line surrounds the range, indicating that a copy of the data has been moved to your Clipboard. Excel does not actually cut the data from the old location until you have pasted it to a new one. Once pasted, the dotted lines disappear, the original data is deleted, and the formatting for the original range is restored to the default format.

TIP

When selecting where to paste a range of data, select a single cell at the left corner rather than the entire range. Excel will automatically select the correct number of columns and rows.

Data that is cut and pasted retains all of the same cell references, regardless of the absolute or relative nature of these references. For example, when you cut the formula =E8*D8 from cell F8 and paste it to cell H4, it still refers to cells E8 and D8.

TIP

You can only cut and paste data once. Copied data remains on the Clipboard and can be pasted numerous times, unless you do so using the Enter key.

When Copying Is a Better Option

Copying data is similar to cutting data except that the original copy of your data is left behind. A new copy is created and that copy can be pasted to a number of locations, one after another or at the same time.

When you copy a cell or a range of cells, a moving dotted line surrounds the range to indicate that a copy of the data has been moved to your Clipboard. You can then select a range on the worksheet where you want to paste the data. After the data has been pasted, you will notice that the moving dotted border still surrounds the original cells. This gives you the opportunity to paste another copy of the data to a new location. Simply select the new range and paste another copy of the data to your worksheet.

When you copy a formula with relative or mixed cell references, Excel evaluates the references and revises them to refer to the new area of the worksheet. Figure 7.29 illustrates the following example. If you copy the formula =(D4-B4)/D4 from cell F4 to cells F5 through F14, the new formula in cell F5 will read =(D5-B5)/D5 to reflect the new location.

	A	B	C	D	E	F	G
3	Product Number	Jan-00	Feb-00	Mar-00	Average Qtr 1	Growth Qtr 1	
4	01758	34,545	31,523	32,099	32,722	-8%	
5	01759	4,554	3,998	3,872	4,141	=(D5-B5)/D5	
6	01760	5,454	4,928	4,777	5,053	-14%	
7	01761	63	44	55	54	-15%	
8	14638	36	33	53	41	32%	
9	14639	346	243	255	281	-36%	
10	14640	224	234	238	232	6%	
11	00456	626	645	666	646	6%	

Sheet1 \ **Sheet2** / Sheet3

FIGURE 7.29: In this example of copying data from a single cell to a range of cells, notice that the relative references in the formula are automatically revised to refer to the correct cells.

TIP

Just like in a cut-and-paste operation, it is easier to select a single cell at the left corner of the range rather than selecting the entire range to paste. Excel will automatically select the correct number of columns and rows.

Pasting Your Data

The Paste command simply pastes whatever data is currently on your Clipboard to the selected area of your worksheet. If you have selected a single cell, paste will automatically highlight the range necessary to hold all of the data. You can also select the range yourself. If you do not select the proper size and shape, Excel will alert you with an error message, as shown in Figure 7.30.

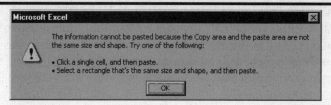

FIGURE 7.30: When the data copied and the paste area selected are different shapes, an error message will appear.

Pasting Multiple Copies

If you are copying a single cell and you select a multiple cell range to copy to, Excel will replicate your original data across all of the cells in the selected range. You can also use the Ctrl key to select a non-contiguous range in the worksheet in which to paste your data. First copy the data and then select the first range to paste the data to. Press the Ctrl key and select the second non-adjacent range, as shown in Figure 7.31. Continue selecting additional ranges while holding down the Ctrl key. When you have selected all of the target ranges, paste your data as you normally would.

Part ii

Description	Amount
Lunch with prospects - Familial Estates	$ 78.59
Train - Round trip Metro North	$ 14.75
Taxis from/to downtown	$ 18.56
Photocopying white papers	$ 23.27
Train - Round trip Metro North	
Train - Round trip Metro North	
Taxis - from/to west side	$ 6.50
Lunch with Clients - Fiber Brothers	$ 45.69
Train - Round trip Metro North	
Parking at train station	$ 22.00
Train - Round trip Metro North	

FIGURE 7.31: Pasting data to non-adjacent ranges

TIP

To enter the same data into multiple cells, first select all of the cells where you want to place the data. You can select non-contiguous ranges by pressing the Ctrl key after highlighting the first selection and then highlighting additional ranges on your worksheet. Once all the ranges have been selected, type the data into the formula bar and press Ctrl+Enter. The data will be entered into every selected cell.

Collecting and Pasting Multiple Items

Office 2000 introduces a new Clipboard toolbar that enables you to collect a number of items, including items that you have copied from within
any other Office program. The Clipboard retains the last 12 objects that
were copied from within Microsoft Office, including Word, Access, Power-
Point, Outlook, and Excel.

NOTE

The Office Clipboard is not the same as the Windows Clipboard, which copies
and pastes items between any Windows program. The Office Clipboard is limited
to copying and moving data between Office documents. When you use Excel's
Copy and Cut commands, data is automatically copied to *both* Clipboards.

To view the Office Clipboard, choose View ➤ Toolbars and then
choose Clipboard. You will notice icons for each of the items that are currently copied to the Clipboard. You can choose to paste any one of these
objects by first selecting the cell where the item is to be pasted and then
selecting the item. To see a small section of any of the text objects on the
Clipboard, pause your cursor over the item, and the first 50 characters
will appear, as shown in Figure 7.32.

FIGURE 7.32: The new Office Clipboard enables you to copy and paste multiple
items between Office documents.

You will notice that the Office Clipboard has a number of buttons
across the top. The first button allows you to copy data in a manner that
is identical to any other method of copying in Excel. The Paste All button
will paste all of the objects down a column on your worksheet. Clear will
clear out the Clipboard and make space available for more copies. Once
you have copied the maximum number of items, you will be prompted to
clear the oldest item from the Clipboard before you can make additional
copies.

TIP

Excel data is pasted from the Office Clipboard as values only, not formulas.

As you work within Excel, you may find that the Office Clipboard appears in your workspace. This will happen if you perform any of the following operations:

- ▶ Cut or copy two times in one Office program, without performing any other action in between.

- ▶ Copy, then paste, and then copy again.

- ▶ Copy a single object two times in a row.

If you don't want to view the Clipboard, simply click the Close button (X) at the top-right corner of the Clipboard.

Paste Special

Excel provides a more advanced pasting feature called Paste Special, which provides you with a number of pasting options, as shown in Figure 7.33:

- ▶ Paste All is a straightforward paste, identical to Edit ➢ Paste.

- ▶ Paste Formulas is very helpful when you want to copy or move a formula but do not want the associated cell formatting.

- ▶ Paste Values calculates the results of the formula and pastes only the resulting value—a useful feature when you no longer need the underlying calculations.

TIP

The Paste Special ➢ Values command is very often used to convert array formulas to numbers so that they can be manipulated.

- ▶ Paste Formats allows you to copy cell formatting only.

TIP

The Format Painter, an icon available on the Standard toolbar, is the same as using the Copy and Paste Special Formats.

▶ Paste Comments copies cell notes from one cell to another, but does not disturb the actual contents of the cell.

▶ Paste Validation copies the validation criteria. To learn more about data validation, see "Setting Limits with Data Validation" earlier in this chapter.

▶ Paste All Except Borders is a handy feature to ensure that the borders of the new range aren't disturbed when new data or formulas are copied over the cells.

NOTE

Paste Special only works with the Copy command. It cannot be used with data that is cut from the worksheet.

The Paste Special dialog box is shown in Figure 7.33.

FIGURE 7.33: The Paste Special dialog box displays a number of options to limit the type of data pasted.

The Operation section of the Paste Special dialog box contains options that refer to mathematical operations that can be applied to your data before it is pasted. For example, you may want to consolidate data for two regions and no longer need the separate data on your worksheet. Rather than creating a formula to add the two regions in an entirely new area of the worksheet, you can simply copy the data for one region. Then, choose the Paste Special command using the Operation Add to paste the data over the second region. This will add the two sets of numbers and place the new sums onto the worksheet. Keep in mind that once you paste this information using an Operation other than None, the old values you pasted over are lost and cannot be redivided.

TIP

When you apply operations to your pasted data, it is usually a good idea to paste values only, not formulas. Pasting formulas may create unexpected results. For example, if you are pasting formulas on pre-existing formulas and choose to Add the data, Excel will attempt to combine the two formulas. This may work fine in certain circumstances, but it may not always give the correct results.

Moving further down the Paste Special dialog box, Skip Blanks does not overwrite the existing data with blank cells. In other words, blank cells in the copied range don't overwrite filled cells in the paste range. Rather than copying each individual cell within a range, you can highlight the entire range of data, including the blank cells. Then when you paste the data, use Paste Special ➤ Skip Blanks. Only the cells with formulas or data in them will be copied. The other cells in the destination range will be unaffected.

Transpose is another very useful feature. It allows you to switch the orientation of your data, so that the information currently contained in columns will now be in rows and vice versa. When you begin to enter data into a table it is often difficult to determine which type of information should be placed in columns and which in rows. As you add more data to the table, you may find it is too wide to view on a screen or that there are not enough columns to hold all of the information required. In these cases, you can simply flip the table by first copying the data and then choosing Paste Special ➤ Transpose to move it to a new location. The orientation of the data in the table will be transposed, as seen in Figure 7.34.

	A	B	C	D	E	F
2		*Bukowski*	*Higgins*	*Sheehan*	*Unrue*	*Total*
3	April	$ 5,100.00	$ 9,166.50	$ 13,075.60	$ 4,555.20	$ 31,897.30
4	May	$ 5,324.40	$ 10,569.83	$ 11,650.93	$ 4,755.63	$ 32,300.78
5	June	$ 5,963.33	$ 11,838.21	$ 10,485.83	$ 4,280.07	$ 32,567.43
6						
7		*April*	*May*	*June*		
8	Bukowski	$ 5,100.00	$ 5,324.40	$ 5,963.33		
9	Higgins	$ 9,166.50	$ 10,569.83	$ 11,838.21		
10	Sheehan	$ 13,075.60	$ 11,650.93	$ 10,485.83		
11	Unrue	$ 4,555.20	$ 4,755.63	$ 4,280.07		
12	*Total*	$ 31,897.30	$ 32,300.78	$ 32,567.43		
13						

Sheet1 / Sheet2 / Sheet3 /

FIGURE 7.34: The result of copying a table and then pasting it using Paste Special ➤ Transpose

Part ii

NOTE

You cannot use Copy and Paste Special ➤ Transpose to paste the data over the original data. You must first copy the data and then select a new range before pasting the data. You must then go back to the original data and delete it.

The last option available on the Paste Special dialog box is Paste Link. This option is only available if you have chosen All or All Except Borders. It allows you to create a link between the two ranges so that as data changes in the copied area, it will be updated in the paste area. In essence, pasting a link is like creating a number of formulas that simply point to the original range.

Deleting Data

You have two choices for removing data from the worksheet. You can either clear the data in the cells, which is equivalent to erasing the data, or you can delete the actual cells, which removes the entire cell and shifts the cells underneath or to the right.

Clearing the Data in a Cell

To remove the data in a cell, you can do any of the following:

- ▶ Edit the cell and delete the actual values.
- ▶ Use the menu option Edit ➤ Clear ➤ All.

TIP

The Edit ➤ Clear menu has a number of choices. The most commonly used are All, which returns the cell to its original state, and Contents, which removes the value in the cell but retains all formatting. Clear ➤ Formats can also be very useful, especially if you have formatted a cell to display a date and it now contains a number.

- ▶ Right-click with the mouse and choose Clear Contents.
- ▶ Drag the fill handle up and to the left so that it covers the cell. You will notice that the status bar displays the message Drag Inside to Clear Cells.
- ▶ Use the Delete key on the keyboard.
- ▶ Press the Backspace key and then press Enter.
- ▶ Type new data into the cell to replace the current data.

WARNING

Never use the spacebar to overwrite a cell with a space to erase the contents. Not only does this use unnecessary memory and storage space, it can result in erroneous worksheet and database calculations.

Deleting Cells

Deleting cells requires some thought about how it may affect your worksheet. Unlike clearing a cell, which only affects the selected cell, deleting a cell will alter all of the cells below and to the right of the selected cell by shifting the data. Often it is easier to delete an entire column or row, rather than deleting individual cells. This keeps your tables intact and usually maintains relative references.

Deleting Entire Rows or Columns

To delete an entire row or column, first select the row or column by clicking its letter or number header. Then choose Edit ➣ Delete. The row or column is deleted and all of the rows below are shifted upward or the columns to the right are shifted left. Excel automatically revises all formulas that may have been affected by the deletion. This is illustrated in Figures 7.35 and 7.36, which show a worksheet before and after deleting a number of rows.

SUM		✕ ✓ =	=SUM(H3:H18)	
	F	**G**	**H**	
2	Quantity	Cost	Total Cost	
3	49	$ 46.89	$ 2,297.61	
4	48	46.89	2,250.72	
5	35	46.89	1,641.15	
6	36	46.89	1,688.04	
7	44	32.59	1,433.96	
8	44	32.59	1,433.96	
9	45	32.59	1,466.55	
10	24	29.99	719.76	
11	27	29.99	809.73	
12	34	29.99	1,019.66	
13	26	29.99	779.74	
14	64	29.99	1,919.36	
15	46	26.79	1,232.34	
16	64	26.79	1,714.56	
17	63	26.79	1,687.77	
18	55	26.00	1,430.00	
19	704	$ 33.85	=SUM(H3:H18)	
20				

Sheet1 / Sheet2

FIGURE 7.35: In this table rows have not yet been deleted and the formula in cell H19 totals the data in cells H3 through H18.

Part ii

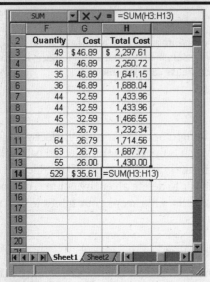

FIGURE 7.36: The formula automatically changes to adjust to the new range of data after rows 10 through 14 have been deleted.

Deleting a Specific Cell or a Cell Range

Deleting a specific cell or range of cells is similar to deleting an entire row or column except that you have to tell Excel how to shift the remaining data in the worksheet. Select the cells or range of cells to delete and choose Edit ➢ Delete. A dialog box will offer you a choice of shifting cells left or up, or deleting the entire row or column of your selection. Again, Excel will attempt to revise all formulas affected by the shift. In cases where the cells that were referenced have been deleted, the error #REF will be displayed, as seen in Figures 7.37 and 7.38. You will need to edit this formula to refer to new cells.

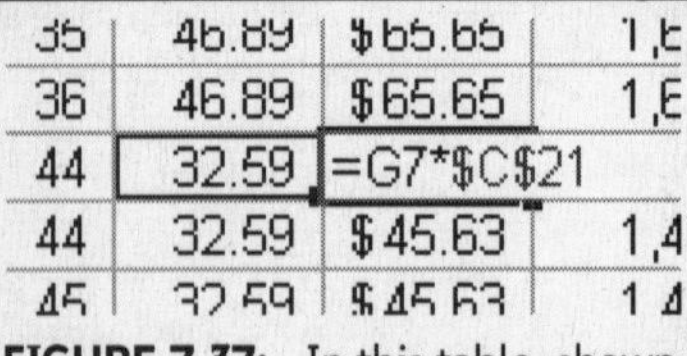

35	46.89	$65.65	1,6
36	46.89	$65.65	1,6
44	32.59	=G7*$C$21	
44	32.59	$45.63	1,4
45	32.59	$45.63	1,4

FIGURE 7.37: In this table, shown before a cell range is deleted, the formula refers to the data in cell C21.

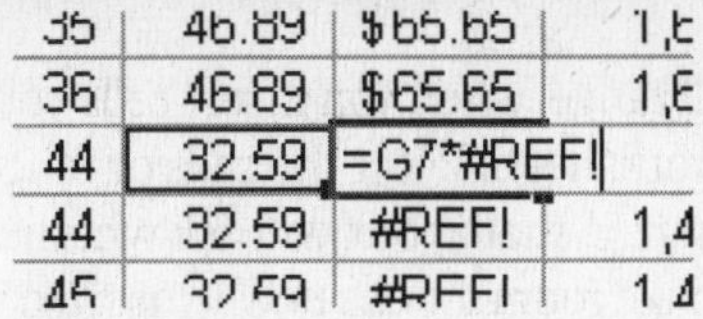

35	46.89	$65.65	1,6
36	46.89	$65.65	1,6
44	32.59	=G7*#REF!	
44	32.59	#REF!	1,4
45	32.59	#REF!	1,4

FIGURE 7.38: In the same table shown in Figure 7.37, after deleting row 21, the formula now displays a #REF.

Inserting Data

Inserting behaves in a similar fashion to deleting. You can insert entire columns and rows, or choose to insert specific cells or cell ranges. As in the case of deleting, using the entire row and column option is often simpler and less disruptive to the design of your worksheet.

Inserting Columns and Rows

To insert an entire row or column, first select the row or column by clicking its letter or number header. Then choose Edit ➢ Insert. A new row or column is inserted above or to the left of your selection. If the cells surrounding the new cells are formatted, Excel will assume that you want the new column or row similarly formatted. Excel will also automatically revise all formulas that may have been affected by the insertion, as illustrated in Figure 7.39.

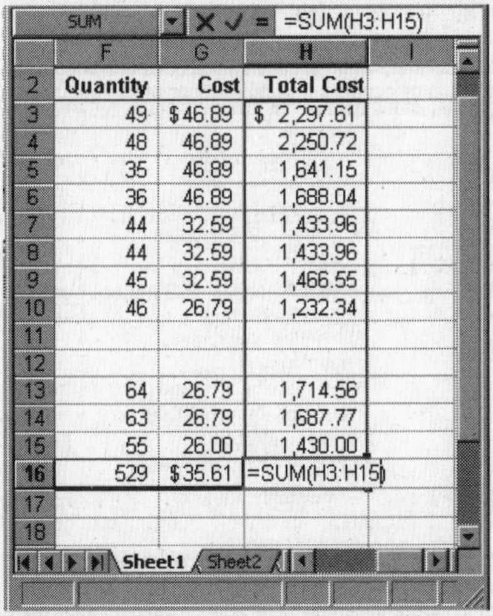

SUM		X ✓ =	=SUM(H3:H15)	
	F	**G**	**H**	**I**
2	**Quantity**	**Cost**	**Total Cost**	
3	49	$46.89	$ 2,297.61	
4	48	46.89	2,250.72	
5	35	46.89	1,641.15	
6	36	46.89	1,688.04	
7	44	32.59	1,433.96	
8	44	32.59	1,433.96	
9	45	32.59	1,466.55	
10	46	26.79	1,232.34	
11				
12				
13	64	26.79	1,714.56	
14	63	26.79	1,687.77	
15	55	26.00	1,430.00	
16	529	$35.61	=SUM(H3:H15)	
17				
18				

Sheet1 / Sheet2

FIGURE 7.39: Two new rows have been inserted and the formula has automatically adjusted to include the new rows.

Inserting Cells

Just like when you delete a cell or cell range, when you insert cells you are prompted to shift the data on your worksheet. Select the cells or range of cells to insert and choose Edit ➤ Insert. A dialog box will ask whether you want to shift cells right or down to make room for the newly inserted range.

You can also insert a new row or column. Again, Excel will attempt to revise all formulas affected by the shift. Figures 7.40 and 7.41 show a worksheet before and after inserting a range of cells. Notice that the data to the right of the table remains intact and only the data below the inserted cells is shifted.

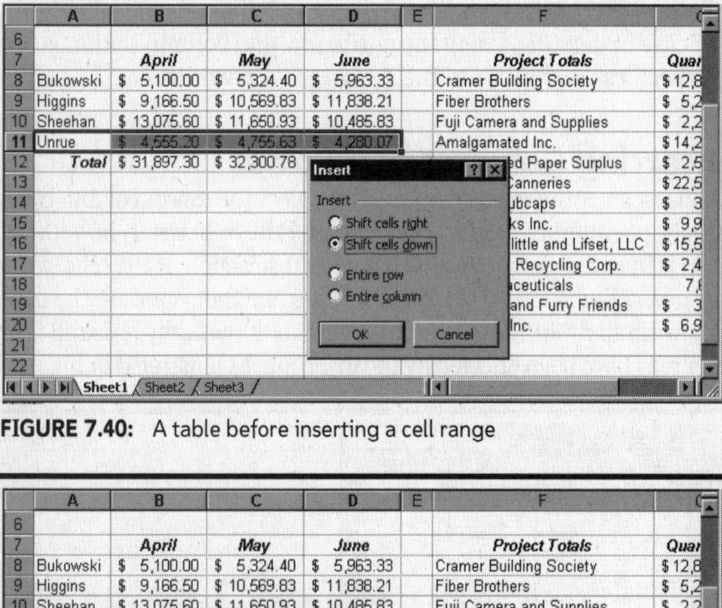

FIGURE 7.40: A table before inserting a cell range

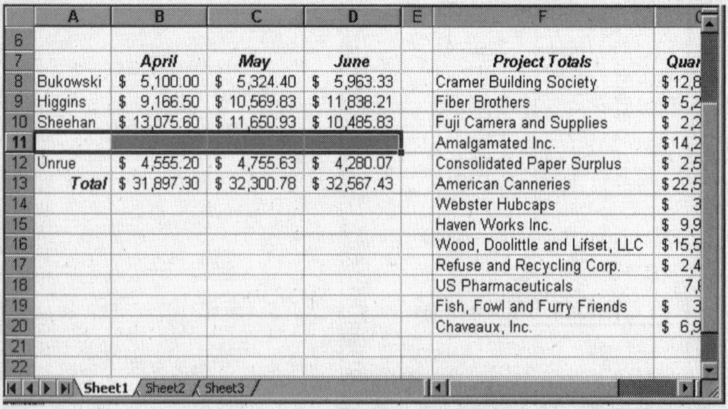

FIGURE 7.41: The table in Figure 7.40 is shown after a cell range has been inserted. Only the cells below the affected range have been shifted down.

TIP

If you frequently insert and delete data, you may find that it is useful to have buttons for these tasks placed on a custom toolbar. Excel provides a number of different buttons that, in addition to inserting and deleting data and/or cells, will eliminate the dialog box that asks you how to shift the data. Instead, Excel will attempt to guess the direction in which you want the data shifted, avoiding the interruption of the dialog box. These guesses are based on the shape of the current region.

Inserting Cut or Copied Cells

A common reason to insert cells is because you want to insert data copied from another area of the workbook or from a separate workbook. To speed these two tasks, Excel provides a combined task that allows you to cut or copy a range of cells and insert the range in one step. After you have cut or copied the cells, the option on the Insert menu will change to either Insert ➢ Cut Cells or Insert ➢ Copied Cells. Simply select the insertion point for your data and choose this option. Not only will the proper cells be inserted, but the cut or copied data will be written to the new range.

NOTE

The Cells option on the Insert menu is changed to Cut Cells or Copied Cells whenever you are in Cut or Copy mode. The status bar will display the message Select Destination and Press Enter or Choose Paste. To return to normal Edit mode simply press the Esc key.

Using the Right Mouse Button

The shortcut menu that appears when you click the right mouse button is often an extremely efficient way to perform specific tasks associated with the selected object. In the case of a cell, it offers you options that are specific to a cell or range of cells, such as Cut, Copy, Insert, Delete, Clear Contents, and more.

When there is data on the Clipboard, the menu choices change to include Paste, Paste Special, and Insert Copied Cells. Many users may not know that the shortcut menu provides entirely different choices when you are in the midst of dragging and dropping data. However, this menu

Part ii

is only available if you use your right mouse button to perform the drag and drop.

Select a range of cells you want to copy or move and begin to drag the data with your right mouse button rather than the left mouse button. When you reach the drop area, release the right mouse button. A new shortcut menu will appear, as shown in Figure 7.42. This menu will provide many options, such as Move Here, Copy Here, Copy Here as Values Only, Copy Here as Formats Only, Link Here, Create Hyperlink Here, Shift Down and Copy, Shift Right and Copy, Shift Down and Move, Shift Right and Move, and Cancel.

FIGURE 7.42:   Pressing the right mouse button displays a number of options for dragging and dropping data.

TIP

If you are not sure how to perform a particular task, always try to right-click the associated object to see if the task is available from the shortcut menu. Excel offers a number of commands on the shortcut menu that are tailored to specific tasks associated with a selected object.

Finding and Replacing Data

Even the best made plans change, often due to circumstances beyond your control. Perhaps the new product, code named "Nightingale," is being changed to "Eagle." Or maybe the new surfboard is no longer available in magenta but is now being offered in mauve and purple stripes. Your entire spreadsheet refers to this information and you need to change it, hopefully without manually searching through every cell and comment.

Excel provides a number of find and replace options to make this process relatively smooth and error free.

Finding

You can find almost any text string, whether located in a cell, formula, cell reference, or range name. Once it is found, you have the option of replacing the text on a case-by-case basis, or all at once using the Replace command.

You can choose to have Excel search for the text string within a specific range, or within the entire worksheet. To search the entire workbook, you must first group all of the worksheets together. To group the worksheets, select the first sheet and then hold the Shift key down before selecting the last sheet in the book.

To conduct a search, follow these steps:

1. To search the entire worksheet, select a single cell. To search a range of cells, select that range.

2. Choose Edit ➤ Find, or Ctrl+F, and the dialog box shown in Figure 7.43 will appear.

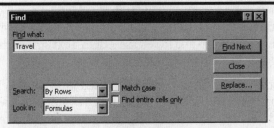

FIGURE 7.43: The Find dialog box

3. Enter the text string to find under Find What.

4. You can search by columns or rows, depending on how you would like to move through the worksheet. If you choose to do so by rows, Excel will begin searching in the current row and move across the entire row before dropping down to the next row. Choosing to search by columns will result in the entire column being searched before moving one column to the right. In either case, when the end of the worksheet is reached, Excel will continue searching from the beginning at cell A1 until it returns to the currently selected cell.

5. Set the Look In option. This is important and could result in not finding your string if set incorrectly. Your options are to look in:

Formulas   This means Excel will search cells that begin with an equal sign as well as any constant values. However, the results of the formula will not be searched.

Values   In this case, Excel uses the calculated value and searches the results as displayed, not the actual formula. Again, as in Formulas, constant values are also searched.

Comments   This checks cell comments only.

TIP

When Excel searches Values it looks at the displayed value, not the underlying value, so be specific about the exact number you are searching for. A search for 1.5 finds both "1.5" and an identical cell that's formatted as Currency, displayed as "$1.50." But a search for "$1.50" will only find the formatted cell "$1.50," not the value "1.5."

6. If you want to find an exact match, choose Match Case. This will require that the text string found be an exact match, with the same use of upper- and lowercase letters. Text strings that do not match exactly will be ignored.

7. To find the data in an entire cell, choose Find Entire Cells Only. This option will look at the entire cell contents and will only find a match if there are no other extraneous characters or numbers in the cell.

TIP

The wildcard characters * and ? can be used to expand the search. For example, to find all occurrences of the word total, use *total*. This will find Subtotal, Grand Total, and Totals.

8. Once Excel has located the text in question, it will highlight the cell containing the data. You can revise the text string by clicking the cell and editing the data directly, or you can use the replace button to replace the data with another text string. The dialog box will remain on the screen so that you

can search for additional occurrences of the text string or start a new search.

NOTE
You may need to move the dialog box to view the cell. Simply click the title bar and drag the box out of the way.

9. To continue to find additional occurrences of the text, choose the Find Next button.

10. Choose the Close button when you have found all occurrences of the data you need.

TIP
If you need to re-find data you were looking for and you have already closed the dialog box, press F4. This will repeat your last action and find the next occurrence of the text you were just searching for. You can also press Ctrl+F to redisplay the Find dialog box.

Replacing

Once you have located the text string with the Find command, you can choose to replace it by pressing the Replace button. Or, you can simply choose to Find and Replace with one action by choosing Edit ➢ Replace, or Ctrl+H, which will both find and replace text.

The upper portion of the Replace box is identical to the Find command with the exception that the Look In options are no longer available. Replace only finds and replaces text strings in formulas or constant values. It cannot find and replace the results of a calculation.

NOTE
You cannot use wildcards in the replaced text.

Replace allows you to replace the text string in the single selected cell, or you can replace the entire worksheet by using the Replace All button. You can continue finding and replacing text one cell at a time, or you can choose Replace All at any time. When Excel can no longer find any more occurrences of the text, it will alert you with a message. Choose Close to end your search.

WARNING

Be extremely careful with the Replace All button as it can have a significant effect on your worksheets, potentially replacing text that you may not want changed.

If you are only searching on a range within the worksheet and selected this range prior to invoking the Find and Replace command, then Replace All will only affect the selected range.

Using the Go To Special Dialog Box

When Editing a worksheet, you may find that you need to locate certain types of information, not just specific cell entries, such as error values, blank cells, or objects. This can be very helpful for debugging or auditing your worksheet once you have completed much of your data entry, or for reviewing a worksheet received from a colleague. Choose Edit ➢ Go To and then click the Special button. The dialog box shown in Figure 7.44 will appear.

FIGURE 7.44: The Go To Special dialog box allows you to select
cells based on specific criteria.

Just like many other Excel commands, the Go To Special command will apply to the entire worksheet if a single cell is selected, or to a specific range if only that range is selected prior to invoking the command.

The first few choices in the dialog box allow you to select specific types of cell entries, such as comments, constants, or formulas. You can further define the types of constants or formulas by selecting one or all of the checkboxes for Numbers, Text, Logicals, and Errors. Logicals refer to True/False values that may be the result of an IF statement in the cell formula. Selecting Errors can be very useful when debugging a worksheet in order to identify all cell formulas that evaluate to an error value.

Selecting blanks with the Go To Special command will highlight all of the empty cells within the active area of your worksheet. You can also select the current region or current array. Many Excel functions apply to the current region, such as Sort and AutoFilter. It is often useful to be able to select this area yourself to ensure that it is correct and does not contain adjoining cells. Choosing the current array can be useful because it is often difficult to determine exactly which cells share an array formula.

TIP

To move through the selected cells, use the Tab key or Shift+Tab to move backwards. You can also use the Enter and Shift+Enter keys. However, if you use the arrow keys or your mouse, the selection will be lost.

Selecting Objects in the Go To Special dialog box is useful for finding charts, pictures, or controls that have been added to the worksheet. These objects use a lot of memory and disk space and should be used only when needed. It is also easy to *lose* these objects when you are moving or resizing them, so the ability to select each of them can be a handy feature.

The Row Differences and Column Differences options in the Go To Special dialog box are extremely valuable for auditing your worksheet. They will highlight formulas that are different from other formulas in the same row or column. For example, if you have entered a formula to sum a cell range, Row Differences can highlight any of the cells in the row that may use the wrong range or may be erroneously entered as a value rather than a formula.

To select row or column differences:

1. First select the range that contains all of the formulas you want to compare.

2. Be sure the formula is correct in the active cell, choose Edit ➤ Go To, and click the Special button.

3. Then choose either Row Differences, if you are comparing across a row, or Column Differences, if you are comparing down the column.

4. Choose OK and Excel will highlight any cells that contain a different relative formula, perhaps referring to the wrong range or to a value rather than a formula.

The following figures illustrate how you might use the Row Differences option. In this example, the row containing the monthly sales totals for the department has been selected. After you choose the Special option in the Go To dialog box, the Special box is displayed, as shown in Figure 7.45. Row Differences is chosen in order to find any formulas in the totals row that may be incorrect. Figure 7.46 shows the results of this action. Notice that the cell selected does not contain a formula but shows a value instead. The Row Differences option has highlighted the fact that this cell differs from the formulas in the rest of the row and must be corrected.

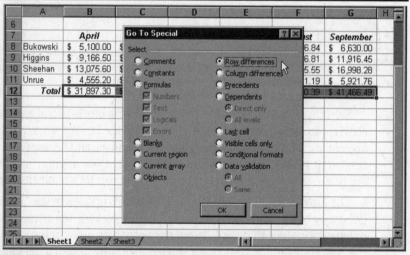

FIGURE 7.45: Row Differences has been chosen to determine if any of the cells in the row contain a formula that differs from the formula in the active cell.

		April						
9	Higgins	$ 9,166.50	$ 10,569.83	$ 11,838.21	$ 12,311.73	$ 11,626.81	$ 11,916.45	
10	Sheehan	$ 13,075.60	$ 11,650.93	$ 10,485.83	$ 10,905.27	$ 10,445.55	$ 16,998.28	
11	Unrue	$ 4,555.20	$ 4,755.63	$ 4,280.07	$ 4,451.27	$ 5,231.19	$ 5,921.76	
12	Total	$ 31,897.30	$ 32,300.78	$ 32,567.43	33870.13	$ 33,160.39	$ 41,466.49	
13								

FIGURE 7.46: The Row Differences option has identified a cell that contains a value rather than the correct formula.

The Precedents and Dependents options in the dialog box refer to other cells in your worksheet that are used as a component of the current formula, or that depend on the results of the current cell. This feature is valuable for auditing formulas to trace the related cells, either by being directly linked or indirectly linked to the current cell.

NOTE

For more information on cell precedents and dependents, see Chapter 8.

You can select the Last Cell option to determine the right-bottom corner of the worksheet. This option may be helpful in finding data that was entered off to the side and forgotten. Selecting Visible Cells Only permits you to format these ranges accordingly or copy only the visible cells to another range on the worksheet.

The last two options in the Go To Special dialog box allow you to select particular areas of your worksheet that contain conditional formatting or have specific validation criteria.

Many of the Go To Special options can be selected through keyboard shortcuts. Those shortcuts are listed in Table 7.3.

TABLE 7.3: Keyboard Shortcuts for Go To Special Options

GO TO SPECIAL OPTION	KEYBOARD SHORTCUT
Current Array	Ctrl+/
Current Region	Ctrl+*
Column Differences	Ctrl-Shift+I
Row Differences	Ctrl+\
Direct Precedents	Ctrl+[
Direct Dependents	Ctrl+]
All Precedents	Ctrl+Shift+{
All Dependents	Ctrl+Shift+}
Last Cell	Ctrl+End
Visible Cells	Alt+;

Part ii

Correcting Spelling Errors

We have already discussed Excel's AutoCorrect and AutoComplete features, which correct data as you enter it into your worksheet. Excel also provides a Spell Checker, which will check a specific word, entry, or your entire worksheet for misspelled words.

Excel provides access to the same spell checker available throughout all of the Microsoft Office programs. This Spell Checker is accessed through the Tools menu or a button on the Standard toolbar. Select a single cell to spell check the entire worksheet, or choose a range of cells to limit the area to be checked. If you choose to check the entire worksheet, Excel will spell check cell entries, cell comments, headers and footers, and other graphic objects, such as charts.

TIP

The keyboard shortcut for the Spell Checker is F7.

If you want to check the entire cell entry, choose Tools ➤ Spelling. You can also check the spelling of a single word or cell entry. In order to do this, you must be in Edit mode. Click the formula bar or press F2 to select Edit mode. To spell check a single word or phrase, you can select that word or phrase and choose Tools ➤ Spelling.

Figure 7.47 shows the Spelling dialog box. You will notice the original word displayed at the top of the dialog box and a list of suggestions below it. The suggestion that appears in the Change To text box is the most likely choice. To accept it, press the Change button or, to change this and all other occurrences of this misspelling in your worksheet, choose Change All. You can also select any of the other entries in the list by clicking them. You can revise the suggestion by typing directly into the textbox, or you may choose to ignore the misspelling and retain your original entry. To ignore only this instance, choose Ignore. To ignore all other identical entries in you worksheet, choose Ignore All and you will no longer be prompted for additional occurrences of this word.

If you use certain acronyms or pronouns that don't appear in your dictionary, it may make sense to add them. This will eliminate being prompted to correct the spelling each time you use the words. To add a specific word to your dictionary, press the Add key when you are in the Spell Checker. This will add the word to the dictionary displayed in the Add Words To textbox.

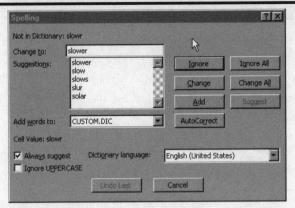

FIGURE 7.47: Excel's Spelling dialog box

The Spelling dialog box also allows you to add entries to AutoCorrect. If you find that you often misspell the same word, press the AutoCorrect button to add the misspelling to the AutoCorrect function. Whenever you type this word again, Excel will automatically correct it without interrupting you.

The other options in the Spelling box allow you to set certain preferences, such as always suggesting words when you spell check. When this option in unchecked, you will need to press the Suggest button to view a list of Excel's suggestions. Ignore UPPERCASE is helpful if you frequently enter uppercase acronyms and abbreviations, such as ID NO., SSN, or CUSIP, and don't want to be prompted to correct these entries. Excel will skip over all uppercase entries, assuming you have spelled them correctly.

WHAT'S NEXT

Chapter 8 will cover cells, ranges, and worksheets. We'll go over how to copy, move, clear, and delete cells, select a range, and manipulate rows and columns—basically manage your whole Excel document!

Chapter 8

WORKING WITH CELLS, RANGES, AND WORKSHEETS

Just about all your work in Excel will involve some piece of the workbook, such as a cell, a range, a column, a row, a sheet, or multiple sheets. This chapter shows you how to put these pieces together.

Adapted from *Excel 2000: No Experience Required*, by Gene Weisskopf.

ISBN 0-7821-2374-0   432 pages $19.99

EXCEL 2000
NO EXPERIENCE REQUIRED

SELECTING RANGES

A *range* is any combination of cells that you select, generally so that you can enter data or include the cells in a command or formula. In a broader sense, whenever you move about in the workbook, you are selecting a range, because the cell or range on which you stop is the selected, or active, cell.

In Excel, you can work with two types of ranges:

Single sheet or 2-D   A group of adjacent cells that are contiguous (within a rectangle) in a single worksheet, such as B5:D25. This is the type of range you work with most frequently.

Multisheet or 3-D   A range that spans multiple sheets, usually contiguous, in the workbook so that the same 2-D range is referenced on each sheet. For example, you could define a range on Sheet1 to Sheet4, which includes the cells in A5:F15 on each sheet. You refer to that range as Sheet1:Sheet4!A5:F15.

You can also work with a *noncontiguous* range, which consists of multiple ranges.

NOTE
Not all commands, such as Insert ≻ Rows, accept a noncontiguous range.

Selecting a Single-Sheet Range

Watch the Name box when selecting a range of cells; it displays the number of rows and columns you are selecting. When you are selecting entire rows and columns, a small window near the mouse pointer displays the number of rows or columns you are selecting. You'll also find that the row and column headings for a selected range take on the appearance of pressed buttons, which helps to define the extent of the range.

You can select a single-sheet (2-D) range in several ways:

▶ Click a corner cell of the range and then Shift+click the diagonally opposite corner.

▶ Click and drag over the range from corner to corner with your mouse.

- Choose Edit ➤ Go To (press F5 or Ctrl+G), and enter the range you want to select in the Go To dialog box. (See the "Selecting with Edit ➤ Go To" section, later in this chapter.)

- Select one corner of the range, hold down Shift, and then use the arrow keys to select the rest of the range.

- Click once within a column or a row heading to select an entire row or column.

- Click and drag over the headings or use Shift+click to select a range of rows or columns.

- To select data in a single column or row, select one cell at the top or bottom (or left or right if selecting a row) of the data. Then hold down Shift and double-click one side of the active cell (watch for the mouse pointer to turn into an arrow) to select all contiguous cells in that direction. With the keyboard, press Ctrl+Shift and an arrow key to select the contiguous cells in that direction.

- Select a range name from the Name box at the left of the Formula bar or by choosing Edit ➤ Go To. (Range names are discussed in the "Taking Advantage of Range Names" section, later in this chapter).

- To select the occupied range that surrounds the active cell, which is called the current region, press Ctrl+Shift+* (asterisk), or choose Edit ➤ Go To ➤ Special (which is discussed a little later). In Figure 8.1, I selected a cell within the range A1:D5 and then pressed Ctrl+Shift+*. The unoccupied columns and rows that surround the occupied range define the current region.

WARNING

When pressing Ctrl+Shift+*, you cannot use the asterisk on the numeric keypad.

Part ii

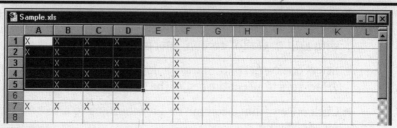

FIGURE 8.1: You can select the current block of data by pressing Ctrl+Shift+*.

Selecting a Multisheet Range

On occasion you might want to select a range that includes more than one sheet, for example, to include in a report. To select a multisheet (3-D) range on contiguous sheets, first select the 2-D range on the first worksheet of the range, such as A5:F15. Then hold down Shift and click the Sheet tab for the last sheet of the range, such as Sheet3.

TIP

Use the Ctrl+click method to select noncontiguous sheets.

In this example, the three Sheet tabs are highlighted, and the word *[Group]* appears next to the filename in the workbook's title bar. This indicates that you're now selecting the same range on a group of worksheets.

After you select multiple sheets, just about any action you take affects the same 2-D range on each sheet. For example, if you enter data in a cell in one sheet, the same data is entered in the same cell in all sheets in the group. Likewise, if you erase the contents of a cell, the contents of that cell are erased in all selected sheets.

To copy the cells from a 2-D range on the current sheet to the same range in all the other sheets in the group, choose Edit ➢ Fill ➢ Across Worksheets to open the Fill Across Worksheets dialog box, and then choose which cell components to copy:

All   Copies all aspects of a cell.

Contents   Copies only the contents of a cell.

Formats   Copies only the formatting of a cell, for example, alignment, number style, and so on.

When you want to dissolve the worksheet group, you can:

► Select a sheet that is not part of the group.

► Shift+click the active Sheet tab.

► Right-click one of the Sheet tabs in the group, and choose Ungroup Sheets from the shortcut menu.

WARNING

Don't forget to ungroup the sheets when you no longer want to affect them all. Otherwise, as you continue to work in what you think is only one worksheet, Excel assumes the group is still active and continues to duplicate your actions in all the other sheets. For example, if you delete a row in one sheet, it will be deleted in all the other sheets in the group.

Selecting a Noncontiguous Range

To select multiple noncontiguous ranges, select the first range, hold down Ctrl, and then select the next range. You can continue to select ranges as long as you hold down Ctrl. You can create noncontiguous 3-D ranges as well, just by clicking a Sheet tab while holding down Ctrl.

To type a reference to multiple ranges in a formula or a dialog box, include the sheet name, and separate each range with a comma. Here's an example:

```
=SUM(A1,D10:M30,Sheet2!A5:B10,Sheet2!M20:N20)
```

The result is the same whether you type the references or select them in the worksheet.

Selecting with Edit ➤ Go To

Choosing Edit ➤ Go To is a fast way to access any location in the workbook (see "Moving in Large Jumps" in Chapter 6). The range that you choose is selected after you click OK.

The Go To command also offers some powerful options, which you can access by clicking the Special button in the Go To dialog box. Figure 8.2 shows the options in the Go To Special dialog box.

FIGURE 8.2: The Go To Special dialog box sets the options for the Go To command.

For example, if you select the Constants option, only numbers or text is selected; cells that contain formulas will not be included. You can even fine-tune the Formulas option by selecting from its four options: Numbers, Text, Logicals, and Errors. For example, choose Numbers to select only formulas that produce numeric results.

You can select the Blanks option to select only blank cells within the occupied portion of the worksheet. The Current Region option is equivalent to the Ctrl+Shift+* combination that I mentioned earlier. Take some time to experiment with the other options for this very useful command.

COPYING AND MOVING CELLS

You can copy or move a cell or a range from its source to a destination (target) in many ways. Sometimes the method you choose is a function of convenience; at other times, you need to use a specific method to get the results you want.

When you copy or move a cell, everything associated with that cell ends up in the target cell, including the data within the source cell and any cell properties associated with it, such as a numeric format or color.

NOTE

When you copy or move cells, the target cells are overwritten by the incoming cells whether the source cells are empty or occupied. So use caution when you are shifting cells around the workbook, and don't forget that the Edit ≻ Undo command (Ctrl+Z) can undo many of the most recent changes you've made. See the "Using Edit ≻ Paste Special" section later in this chapter for ways to control which aspects of a source cell get put onto the target cell.

Copying and Moving with Drag and Drop

Sometimes the fastest way to perform a task in Excel is to use your mouse. *Drag and drop* refers to the process of dragging an object, such as a selected range, with the mouse and then dropping it elsewhere by releasing the mouse button.

If you find that your fingers and Excel don't work well together, you can disable the drag-and-drop feature. Choose Tools ≻ Options to open the Options dialog box, click the Edit tab, and clear the Allow Cell Drag and Drop check box.

Using the mouse to copy or move cells is efficient when the target range is within easy reach. But if you end up having to spend five minutes dragging around the worksheet looking for the destination cell, use Edit ≻ Copy and Paste and Edit ≻ Cut and Paste instead. These methods also enable you to paste the source cell(s) into multiple target cells, such as a single cell into an entire range of cells.

Doing the Drag and Drop

Whether you're copying or moving a single cell or a range, follow these steps:

1. Think about where the target area is in relation to the source cell(s) so that once you start it will be a straight shot to complete the job.

2. Select the source cell or cells.

3. To move a cell, point to any edge of the selection; the mouse pointer will change to an arrow, as shown here:

3		Jan	Feb
4	Insurance	51	51
5	Maintenance	48	48
6	Mortgage	925	925
7	Taxes	102	102

4. Hold down the mouse button and drag the range to the target location (see the next section for various mouse and key combinations). An outline of the range moves along with the mouse pointer as you drag, along with a helpful window that displays the cell that will be the target if you should release the mouse button. When you are dragging a range of cells, the target cell will be the upper-left cell of the range.

5. Position the source range over the range where you want it, and release the button.

NOTE

If data is already in the target range, Excel warns you that you are about to overwrite it. This may or may not be a problem, as long as you know that the existing data will be overwritten. If you're the confident type, you can turn off these warnings. Choose Tools ➢ Options to open the Options dialog box, click the Edit tab, and clear the Alert before Overwriting Cells check box.

Drag-and-Drop Methods

Let's look at some of the drag-and-drop techniques you can use to move or copy cells:

Copy Drag while holding down Ctrl to copy the source data to a new location; a small + will appear next to the mouse pointer to indicate that you are copying and not moving.

Move Drag the selection to move the source data to a new location.

Insert Drag while holding down Shift to move the source data into new cells inserted at the destination. The rectangle changes to a vertical or horizontal bar as you move the pointer to indicate whether the insertion will move rows down or columns to the right. If you want to copy and insert, hold down both the Shift and Ctrl keys while you drag.

Shortcut menu   Drag while holding down the *right* mouse button instead of the left one. When you release the button, you can choose the operation you want to perform from the shortcut menu.

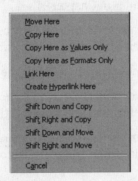

Worksheet   To copy or move data to another worksheet, hold down the Alt key and use any of the above methods. Then drag the selection to another worksheet tab to activate that sheet and drop the data in place.

Workbook   Dragging data to another Excel workbook is no different from moving or copying it within the same worksheet. As long as you can see both workbook windows on the screen, just drag from one to the other.

Other applications   You can use drag and drop to exchange data between Excel and other applications that use Windows *object linking and embedding*, or OLE. This timesaving technique is discussed later in this chapter in the section "Exchanging Data with Other Applications."

Knowing What Happens When You Move or Copy

Regardless of whether you move data or copy data, the resulting destination range looks exactly the same, because both moving and copying transfer everything from the source range to the destination range.

After a copy operation, the source range will still look exactly the same. After a move, however, the source cells will be empty, and their formatting will be set to the defaults for the worksheet.

Effects on Formulas

Moving and copying have different effects on other aspects of the workbook, especially on formulas (you can read about the effects of moving and copying formulas in Chapter 9):

- ► When you copy a formula cell, any cell references in the formula adjust to their new location in the worksheet.

- ► When you move a formula cell, none of its references changes.

- ► When you move cells that are referenced by a formula, the formula adjusts its references and "follows" the cells to their destination.

- ► When you copy cells that are referenced by a formula, the formula does not follow them; it still refers to the source cells.

Dangers of Moving

A formula will be "broken" and will refer to #REF! if you move another cell onto a cell it references, in effect "destroying" that reference. For example, the formula

```
=SUM(A1:A5)+B5/2
```

looks like this after you move another cell onto cell B5:

```
=SUM(A1:A5)+#REF!/2
```

The reference to cell B5 is now gone. To fix this problem you can, of course, resort to the Undo command. Or you can edit the formula and replace the reference to #REF!.

Copying and Moving with Edit ➤ Copy/Paste

When you want to copy or move cells to a distant location, or when the source range is too big to drag around the worksheet, you can use the commands on the Edit menu. The process is the same as in most Windows applications. To copy data, follow these steps:

1. Select the data you want to copy.

2. Choose Edit ➤ Copy (Ctrl+C) or click the Copy button on the Standard toolbar. You'll see a moving border around the source range, which is meant to remind you that a copy is in process and to show you what is being copied. If you are mo ving the data, chose Edit ➤ Cut (Ctrl+X) or click the Cut button on the Standard toolbar.

3. Select the target range (the next section discusses the different shapes and sizes of the source and target ranges).

4. Press Enter to paste the data one time; the moving border around the source range will disappear.

Choose Edit ➤ Paste (Ctrl+V) or click the Paste button on the Standard toolbar to paste the data while keeping the source range selected so that you can paste the selected range over and over. When you're finished pasting, press Esc to clear the moving border from the source range

If you want the pasted data to be inserted as new cells in the target range, choose Insert ➤ Copied (or Cut) Cells. The data already in the target range will be pushed aside and new cells inserted for the incoming data (this process is the same as using the Shift+drag method of copying or moving, which was discussed earlier).

TIP

You can also use the Copy/Cut and Paste method to copy or move portions of a cell's contents. While editing a cell (or by using the Formula bar), select the characters you want to copy—for example, by dragging over them—and choose Edit ➤ Copy (Ctrl+C). Then either paste the data into another part of the cell contents, or finish editing the current cell and then edit another cell and paste the data into it.

Using the Clipboard Toolbar

The Clipboard temporarily stores information such as text, values, and formatting. In the past, you could cut or copy to the Clipboard and then paste the information somewhere else. The only drawback was that the Clipboard could store only one piece of information at a time. The next time you copied or cut information, the previous Clipboard contents were replaced by the newest information.

In Excel 2000, the Clipboard can contain as many as 12 cut or copy operations, and you can select the operation(s) you want to paste from the Clipboard toolbar. The Clipboard toolbar displays after you copy more than one cell or range. You can also display the Clipboard toolbar by right-clicking a toolbar and selecting Clipboard from the shortcut menu. Pointing to an item on the Clipboard toolbar displays a ScreenTip that describes the contents.

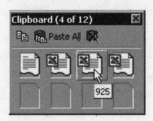

This new Clipboard is extremely handy when you need to copy multiple ranges of information. Before, this would have been a tedious process of selecting the information, moving to the new location, pasting the information, selecting the next piece of information, moving to the next location, pasting the information...you get the picture.

To see how the Clipboard works, follow these steps:

1. Create a list of 12 items in Column A.

2. Select the first four items, and choose Edit ➢ Copy to move the items to the Clipboard.

3. Select the next four items, choose Edit ➢ Copy, and repeat until all the items are on the Clipboard toolbar.

4. Click the Sheet2 tab, click cell A1, and click the first pasted object on the Clipboard toolbar. Repeat for all of the pasted objects, placing them in columns C and E.

5. Click Close to close the Clipboard toolbar.

You can also use the Clipboard toolbar to do the following:

▶ Copy a new cell or range.

▶ Paste all Clipboard items at once.

▶ Clear the contents of the Clipboard.

NOTE

If you don't use the clipboard by pasting an entry from it on three consecutive occasions, the clipboard will not display until selected. To display the Clipboard toolbar, right-click any toolbar and select Clipboard.

Copying Blocks of Various Dimensions

The shape and size of the source and destination blocks affect the results of the copy (or move) operation. When you choose Edit ➤ Copy or Edit ➤ Cut to place the source data onto the Clipboard, the target range can be:

- A single cell, which will serve as the upper-left cell of the pasted data
- A selected range, the same size and shape as the source range

If you choose Edit ➤ Copy but not Cut, the target can also be a selected range that can hold two or more of the source ranges. This option gives you the flexibility to copy a source range of one size to a target range of a larger size. Figure 8.3 shows how to do this. I copied the range A1:B3, which consists of 6 cells, to range F5:G13, which consists of 18 cells.

Part ii

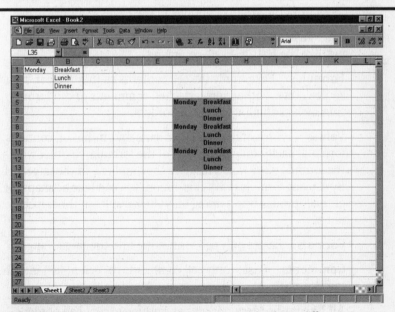

FIGURE 8.3: You can copy data to a target range that has a different size or shape than the source range.

Using Edit ➢ Paste Special

You use the Paste Special dialog box to select from several options that affect the paste operation. To open it, choose Edit ➢ Paste Special:

You can choose which components of the source cells to paste into the target cells from the group of options in the Paste section:

All   Pastes all aspects of a cell; this is the default and works just like the Edit ➢ Paste command.

Formulas   Pastes only the cell contents as they appear in the source range, without any attached comments or cell formatting such as shading, fonts, or borders.

Values   Pastes only the cell contents, but if the cell contains a formula, pastes only the results of the formula. In other words, the formula =2+3 would result in the number 5 in the target cell. By copying formulas with this option, you can take a "snapshot" of the formulas by retaining only their results in the target range.

Formats   Pastes only cell formatting into the target range.

Comments   Pastes only cell comments (or cell notes) into the target range.

All Except Borders   Pastes everything except cell borders.

The two options at the bottom of the dialog box affect the target range in this way:

Skip Blanks   Normally, a blank cell in the source range overwrites the target cell. Select this option to exclude empty cells in the source range from the paste operation.

Transpose   If you want to make a column of data into a row, or vice versa, select this option. If the source range is more than a single column or row and also contains formulas, you probably won't be happy with the result, because the formulas will no longer refer to the same data (see Chapter 9).

NOTE

The options in the Operation section in the Paste Special dialog box are discussed in Chapter 9, and the Paste Link button is also discussed in Chaper 9.

Exchanging Data with Other Applications

One of the nice things about Excel is that it gives you several ways to share data with other Windows applications. The method you use depends on what you plan to do with the data afterward.

Sharing Unlinked Data

You can copy or move data between Excel and another Windows program in the usual Windows way:

1. Select the source data and choose Edit ≻ Copy (or Cut to move the data).

2. Switch to the target program and select the location where the data should go.

3. Choose the target program's Edit ≻ Paste command. Windows pastes the data into the target program as editable text (when possible), and you can use the data as though you had created it there.

For example, when you copy a single cell from Excel to Microsoft Word, the result will either be the exact contents of the source cell or, if that cell is a formula, the result of the formula. When you copy a range of cells, Word creates a table of the same size.

You can also transfer a picture of the source data, which will show the source's formatting that is not otherwise supported in the target. You can't edit the data in the picture, however. To transfer a picture of the data source, follow these steps:

1. In Excel, select the data, and choose Edit ➤ Copy or Cut.

2. In the target application, choose Edit ➤ Paste Special. Figure 8.4 shows the Paste Special dialog box for Microsoft Word.

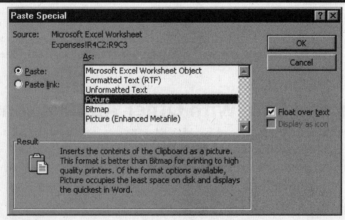

FIGURE 8.4:   Use the Paste Special dialog box in Microsoft Word to paste data from other applications in several formats.

3. Select the Paste option (Paste Link is discussed a little later), and choose Picture from the As list.

4. Click OK to paste the selection into the document in the other application.

Embedding Data

You can exchange objects, such as data, charts and pictures, between Excel and any other Windows program that supports OLE (object linking and embedding). The difference between *embedding* an object and simply pasting it, as discussed in the previous section, is that you can edit embedded data within the program in which it was created. For example, if you embed an Excel worksheet in a Word document, you can later edit that worksheet in Word, using the toolbars and menu items from Excel.

To embed an object in Excel, follow these steps:

1. Select the source data you want to embed in the other program.

2. Choose Edit ➢ Copy.

3. Select the target location in Excel.

4. Choose Edit ➢ Paste Special to open the Paste Special dialog box, and select Paste.

5. Choose one of the items in the As list that has the word *object* in it, such as *Microsoft Excel Worksheet Object*.

6. Click OK.

You can also embed an object by dragging it to the other application; hold down Ctrl if you want to copy and not move it.

The result of pasting an embedded object looks just like the Picture discussed in the previous section. However, there's a big difference in the way you edit each of the objects. You can modify an embedded object in two ways:

▶ Double-click it or right-click it, and choose Document Object ➢ Edit from the shortcut menu. This lets you edit the object within the current worksheet while using the menus and tools of the object's source application.

▶ Right-click the object, and choose Document Object ➢ Open, which opens this object's source application and loads the object into it; you can then edit it as usual. When you are finished, save the object, choose File ➢ Close and Return to *document,* and return to the first application. You'll see that your changes now appear in the object.

When you edit a picture, though, you use a drawing or painting program such as Windows Paint. You also work with an image of the source, and not the actual source document.

Linking Data

You can also exchange data between Excel and another program by creating a *link*. Any change you make in the data in the source document is reflected in the linked object in the target document.

The process of creating a link is much the same as creating an embedded object, as discussed above in "Sharing Unlinked Data." The only difference is that in the Paste Special dialog box you select the Paste Link option. Then, whichever format you choose in the As list is created with a link back to the source data.

Although both linked and embedded objects will be updated when the source document changes, there is one major difference between the two: the data for a linked object does not actually reside in the target document. Instead, a pointer to the data (the link) keeps track of the source data and displays it in the target.

Although you may not need to, you can edit a linked object just as you can edit an embedded object—double-click it, for example. In general, though, having a linked object in a program implies that you want to stay in touch with changes made to the source file for that object, without having to make those changes yourself.

NOTE
To view the sources for any linked objects in a workbook, choose Edit ➤ Links. This command is discussed in Chapter 9.

Finally, because pasting a link doesn't actually bring any data into the target document, you can't take that document off your computer and expect it to stay updated to the source of the link. If you need to be portable, embed the data.

CLEARING CELL CONTENTS, FORMATS, AND COMMENTS

Pencils will always have their erasers, hammers their claws, authors their editors, and computers their Delete and Backspace keys. Excel also gives you several ways to clean up after yourself.

To clear all or part of the selected cells without removing the cells from the worksheet, choose Edit ➤ Clear, and then choose one of the following commands:

All   Erases all aspects of a cell, including its contents, formatting, attached cell comment, and hyperlink.

Formats   Clears only the formats that have been applied to the cell (resets them to the worksheet defaults), but leaves the other cell attributes untouched.

TIP

Here's a quick way to clear only the cell formatting. Select a blank, unformatted cell and click the Format Painter button on the Standard toolbar (the little paintbrush). Then select the target cells, and their formats will be reset to those of the source cells—the worksheet default formats.

Contents   Erases only the contents of a cell (same as pressing the Delete key).

Comments   Clears only the cell comment, if one was attached to the cell.

Keep in mind that these commands work on any cells you've selected, which could be entire rows, columns, or all the cells in the worksheet. And don't forget the Edit ➤ Undo command.

EXPANDING AND CONTRACTING THE WORKBOOK

Even though your worksheets will always have precisely 65,536 rows and 256 columns, you are free to delete or insert rows and columns as your work progresses. Data will never be pushed off the edge of the worksheet when you insert new cells. Instead, Excel will alert you that it cannot shift occupied cells off the worksheet and cancels the procedure.

Deleting Cells from the Worksheet

When you choose Edit ➤ Delete, you can actually delete (remove) selected cells from the worksheet. The cells below move up to take their place, or the cells to the right move left to fill in the gap.

WARNING

When you delete a cell (such as A1) that a formula references (such as =A1), the formula will now display #REF!—indicating its reference has been broken. You'll have to edit the formula to fix or erase the reference. When you delete an entire row or column, be careful that you don't also lose unrelated data that occupies the same row or column, but is off the screen. You can avoid this problem by placing data on its own worksheet when possible.

The results of choosing Edit ➤ Delete depend on what you select before choosing it. For example, if you select one or more contiguous rows (or columns) by clicking in their headings, choosing Edit ➤ Delete removes them all without prompting you. The rows below move up (or the columns to the right move left) to take their place.

If you select one or more cells instead of entire rows or columns, Excel displays the Delete dialog box, which is shown below. If you choose Entire Row or Entire Column, the result will be as described above. To delete only the selected cells, you choose how you want the gap filled, either by having the cells below them move up or the cells to their right move left.

NOTE

The cells that take the place of the deleted ones are essentially moved to the new location. Formulas that had referenced them will now reference them in their new location. See Chapter 9 for more on this topic.

Inserting Cells in the Worksheet

To insert a row in the worksheet, you can either select the entire row by clicking the row heading or select any cell in that row. Then choose Insert ➤ Rows (or right-click any cell in that row and choose Insert from the shortcut menu). The new rows push all existing rows down to make room for themselves. You can also choose Insert ➤ Cells to open the Insert dialog box and choose Entire Row.

When you insert cells in the worksheet, they take on the formatting of the cells within which they were inserted. If you shift the cells down, they acquire the formatting of the cells above; if you shift the cells right, they acquire the formatting of the cells to the left. If that's not what you want, choose Edit ➤ Clear ➤ All or Edit ➤ Clear ➤ Formats immediately after the insertion to clear the inserted cells of their formatting.

For example, to insert seven new rows at row 10, select cells in rows 10 through 16 in any column in the worksheet, such as C10:C16. Then choose Insert ➤ Rows. Old row 10 becomes new row 17, and above it are seven new, blank rows.

If you choose Insert ➤ Columns, Excel inserts new columns and moves the selected columns to the right. The number of columns inserted depends on the number of columns you selected.

To insert a range of cells into the worksheet, select the cells where you want the new cells to appear, and choose Insert ➤ Cells to open the Insert dialog box:

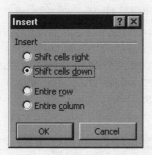

Choose whether you want to move the cells they replace down or to the right.

You can also take advantage of the AutoFill feature to insert new cells. Hold down Shift while you drag the fill handle; when you release the mouse button, new cells will be inserted into the worksheet.

As I mentioned earlier, when you choose Edit ➤ Copy (or Cut), the Insert ➤ Copied Cells (or Cut Cells) command is also available. This command, like the Insert ➤ Cells command, lets you choose how the cells inserted from the Clipboard will affect the surrounding cells in the worksheet.

Formulas Adjust to Changes

I will often mention in this book that one of the most helpful aspects of Excel is the work that it does for you. Applying your changes automatically is at the top of the list. In Chapter 9, you will read about referencing cells within formulas. For example, the formula

    =SUM(B5:B10)*C17

adds the values in cells B5 through B10 and multiplies that result by the value in C17.

When you expand or contract the worksheet, these formula references adjust automatically to the change. If you were to add three rows on or above row 5, for example, the formula shown above would look like this:

    =SUM(B8:B13)*C20

If you then deleted rows 9 and 10, the formula would look like this:

    =SUM(B8:B11)*C18

This effect is true for all defined ranges in the worksheet, such as the current print area or the rows or columns you have defined as print titles. Because Excel takes care of all this housekeeping, you're free to make changes to the worksheet without having to worry about the effects on any defined ranges.

Inserting and Deleting Worksheets

You can also expand and contract the workbook by inserting or deleting worksheets. There is no limit to the number of worksheets you can add to a workbook. Just as when you insert or delete cells, cell references in formulas will adjust to the change as needed.

Deleting Worksheets

To delete sheets from the workbook, select one or more sheets (such as by clicking the first sheet tab and Shift+clicking the last) and then either:

► Choose Edit ➤ Delete ➤ Sheet.

► Right-click one of the selected sheet tabs, and choose Delete from the shortcut menu.

WARNING

The Edit ➤ Undo command cannot undo the deletion of a worksheet. Therefore, it is always a good idea to save your workbook before making such a major change to it.

Just as when you delete cells, when you delete a worksheet, the existing sheets to its right move left to fill in the gap. Unlike cell addresses, however, the sheet names do not change. If you delete Sheet2, for example, the workbook no longer has a Sheet2.

Inserting New Worksheets

To add new sheets to the workbook, select one or more contiguous sheets and then either:

► Choose Insert ➤ Worksheet to insert a default worksheet, which will look the same as those in a new workbook.

► Right-click one of the selected sheet tabs, and select Insert from the shortcut menu.

The second method opens the Insert dialog box, as shown in Figure 8.5. You can select the type of sheet you want to insert from the available Excel template files, such as Worksheet and Chart.

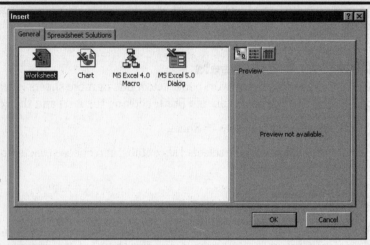

FIGURE 8.5: In the Insert dialog box, choose the type of sheet to insert in the workbook, based on the available templates.

TAKING ADVANTAGE OF RANGE NAMES

One of the problems with having millions of cells in a workbook is the ease with which you can lose track of the data and formulas you enter into them.

Every time you insert or delete a row or a column, all the addresses change for any data that are below that row or to the right of that column. So when it comes time to edit or print the data in a range, for example, you might not be sure where to find it. But there's a way to keep track of things that can simplify all your range relations in the workbook.

A *range name* is a name you create, such as MyData, that defines a range of cells, such as B10:H25. Once you've defined a name, you can refer to that range by its name instead of its cell coordinates. To add the contents of the cells in the range B10:H25, for example, you could write the formula like this:

    =SUM(MyData)

No matter how that range is moved, expanded, or contracted, the name will still refer to the correct range of cells, wherever they are.

The actual address no longer matters once a range is named. If you want to go to that range, for example, simply choose Edit ➤ Go To and specify the name MyData as the place to go. Better yet, just select the name from the list of range names in the Name box or in the Go To dialog box. It's that simple.

TIP

You can also name a worksheet and thereafter refer to it by that name. Double-click its sheet tab, and enter the new name. One difference between range and sheet names, however, is that a sheet name *replaces* its generic name. With a named range, you can refer to either the name or the address the name represents.

Defining a Name

You don't need to name every possible data area in the workbook, nor should you. In many cases, you can simply define new names as the need arises:

▶ If you find yourself regularly returning to a data area to update it.

▶ If you plan to print a range in future sessions with that workbook.

▶ If several formulas will refer to a cell that contains, for example, an interest rate—name the cell. Perhaps Interest would be a good choice for a name.

Here's how to name a range:

1. Select the range you want to name.

2. Choose Insert ➤ Name ➤ Define to open the Define Name dialog box shown in Figure 8.6.

3. Enter the new name, such as **MyCell**, in the Names in Workbook field.

4. Since you already selected the cells you want to name, you'll see their address displayed as a formula in the Refers To field. However, you can edit that address if you want to change it.

Part ii

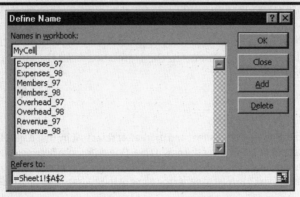

FIGURE 8.6: You define a new name, modify an existing name, or delete a name in the Define Name dialog box.

5. Click the Add button to add this name to the list—or click Close to cancel the operation.

6. Click OK to complete the job.

NOTE

You can also define a new name by selecting the cells you want to name, entering the name in the Name box to the left of the Formula bar, and then pressing Enter.

Here are a few rules of the road when it comes to naming cells:

▶ A name can be a maximum of 255 characters—but don't press your luck with excruciatingly long names.

▶ Excel does not allow spaces or most punctuation characters in a name.

▶ A name cannot look like a cell address, such as *GW1999*.

▶ You can make names more readable by separating words with an underline and by using uppercase and lowercase letters. Excel retains the case of the letters so that you can make a "one-word sentence" more readable, such as *Total_1999_Data*.

▶ Excel does not distinguish names by their case, however. If you create the name Sales and later create the name SALES, the new name definition will replace the earlier one.

▶ Names must be unique within a workbook.

Using Names in Formulas and Commands

Once you've created a name for a range, you'll generally want to use the name instead of the range address. Whenever the address is called for, such as in a dialog box or in a formula, you can enter the name instead.

It's easier to remember a name (such as MyData) than an address (such as B10:H25), and when you reference a name within a formula, the name appears in the formula and serves as a visual cue to the formula's purpose. For example,

```
=SUM(Sheet2!B1:S52)*Sheet1!B10
```

doesn't explain much. However, the formula is meaningful if the two addresses that are referenced are named appropriately:

```
=SUM(BudgetTotals99)*Inflation
```

Plus, when you reference a name, you are much less likely to refer to the wrong location.

Pasting a Name from the List

Here's a problem you may frequently encounter in Excel when you write a formula that references names: the formula results in #NAME?, and you may not realize why Excel didn't recognize one or more of the names. You probably just spelled a name wrong, which Excel lets you do on the assumption that you might create the name later on.

You don't have to type a name into a formula or dialog box, however. Instead, choose Insert ➤ Name ➤ Paste or press F3 to open the Paste Name dialog box and its alphabetized list of all the names in the workbook, which is shown below. Select the name you want and click OK to paste that name into the cell or dialog box as though you had typed it yourself.

Creating a List of Names

If Excel is in Ready mode when you display the Paste Name dialog box, it contains a Paste List button. Clicking Paste List creates a two-column list in the worksheet, starting at the active cell, of all the names in the workbook (in the first column) and the addresses they define (in the second column).

It's best if you do this in a blank worksheet to avoid the possibility of overwriting any data. This list is static; it does not update automatically as the names or their addresses change. You have to run the command again to update the list.

Having the list of names in a worksheet can be a handy piece of documentation for your workbook. Plus, if you have hundreds of names in a large workbook, you can choose Edit ➤ Find to search through the list for a specific name or address.

TIP

If you want to get a bird's-eye view of your worksheet and the named ranges in it, set the zoom factor to less than 40 percent (choose View ➤ Zoom). All named ranges in the worksheet will be outlined, and each one's name will appear within its outline. It's a great way to step back and take a look at the road map of your worksheet.

Applying Names to Existing Formulas

You don't have to create the names before you incorporate them in your formulas. If you create a name for an already-referenced range, you can have Excel substitute the name for the address within any formulas that use it.

Choose Insert ➤ Name ➤ Apply to open the Apply Names dialog box (see Figure 8.7), select the name or names from the list, and click OK. Excel finds all formulas that reference the name's address and replaces the address with the name.

WARNING

Incorporating a name into a formula with the Apply command is a one-way street; you can't go back to seeing the address in the formula. See the "For Users of Other Spreadsheets" section later in this chapter.

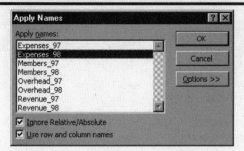

FIGURE 8.7: In the Apply Names dialog box, choose one or more range names that you want to substitute for their addresses in formulas in the worksheet.

As you'll learn in Chapter 9, a formula that references a name and not the address is always absolute. In the Apply Names dialog box, the Ignore Relative/Absolute option is selected by default so that a name will be pasted over its equivalent address in a formula, whether that address is absolute or relative. If you don't want that to happen, clear this option; the name will then be pasted only if it replaces an absolute reference.

You won't need to worry about the Use Row and Column Names option or the Options button until you become quite adept with range names.

Defining Multiple Names

Many cells in your worksheets will contain text entries that describe adjacent cells or that serve as titles for rows or columns. You can use these text entries to name cells in one operation.

Figure 8.8 shows a small worksheet with descriptive text labels in cells A1:A5. In this case, we want to name each cell to their right, B1:B5, according to each label.

To do so, select the two-column range A1:B5 and choose Insert ➤ Name ➤ Create. In the Create Names dialog box, which is also shown in Figure 8.8, click the Left Column check box and click OK.

Each cell in column B is now named after the label to its left so that B1 is named Principal and B2 is named Interest.

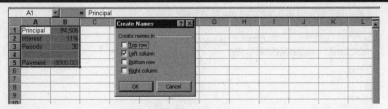

FIGURE 8.8: You can name cells from existing text in the worksheet by choosing Insert ➤Name ➤ Create.

Modifying or Deleting a Name

To change the address that a name defines, choose Insert ➤ Name ➤ Define. In the Define Name dialog box, select the name you want to change and edit its range address in the Refers To field. Click Add or OK to finish the job. Any formulas that reference that name will now refer to its new range.

NOTE

If you modify only the name itself, you create a new name that references the same range.

To delete a name, select it in the Define Name dialog box and click the Delete button. A formula that already references that name will result in #NAME?.

You can edit the formula and delete or change the now defunct name reference, or you can create the name again, and the formula will once more have a valid reference.

For Users of Other Spreadsheets

If you've worked with earlier DOS or Windows versions of Lotus 1-2-3 or Quattro Pro, you will find a few major differences in the way Excel handles range names:

▶ When you edit a formula that references a name in Excel, the name does *not* revert to its underlying address—the name remains the same.

- When you delete a name in Excel, formulas that reference that name do *not* revert to the underlying cell address; they continue to reference the name, but display #NAME? as their result.

- When you use a range name reference in a formula in Excel, it is always an absolute reference, whereas in Lotus 1-2-3 and Quattro Pro, the reference is relative unless you specifically make it absolute.

- When you define a new name for a range that a formula already references, the name does *not* appear in the formula automatically. You must choose Insert ➢ Name ➢ Apply to insert that name in a formula, as discussed earlier in this chapter.

NOTE

If you want Excel to treat range names closer to the manner of these other spreadsheet programs, choose Tools ➢ Options to open the Options dialog box, click the Transition tab, and then click the Transition Formula Entry check box. You can experiment to see if you prefer this mode, but in general, if you're using Excel, you should get used to the way it handles range names.

USING THE FIND AND REPLACE COMMANDS

You find and replace data in Excel in much the same way that you find and replace data in any Office application. To search for data in a workbook, choose Edit ➢ Find (or press Ctrl+F). To find and replace data, choose Edit ➢ Replace (or press Ctrl+H). A few aspects of the process are unique to Excel, however.

Before you begin a search, do one of the following:

- Select a single cell to look for the data throughout the current worksheet.

- Select a range to search only those cells.

- Select all the worksheets you want to search.

Finding Characters in Cells and Comments

To find characters in cells or comments, choose Edit ➣ Find to open the Find dialog box:

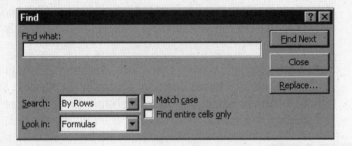

In the Find What field, you enter the characters you want to find. You can include wildcards to search for any characters (*) or any individual character (?), just as you can when specifying filenames.

The Look In drop-down list offers the following three choices, which determine what will be searched:

Formulas   All cells

Values   Only nonformula cells or the results of formulas

Comments   Only cell comments

You can make the search more specific by clicking the following check boxes:

Match Case   The case of characters must match exactly. For example, searching for *sum** finds "summary" but not "Summary" or "SUM."

Find Entire Cells Only   The complete contents of a cell must match the characters in the Find What field.

You can also set the direction of the search by choosing either By Rows (the default) or By Columns from the Search drop-down list.

TIP

To search in the opposite direction, hold down Shift when you click Find Next.

Replacing Characters That Are Found

If you want to replace the characters that are found, you can either click the Replace button in the Find dialog box or choose Edit ➤ Replace to open the Replace dialog box:

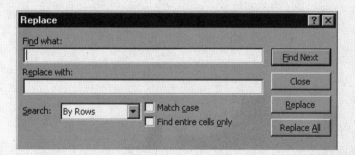

In the Replace With field, enter the characters that you want to appear in place of the characters that match the Find What field. Leave this field blank to erase the found characters.

You won't find the Look In list, because the Replace command essentially uses only the Formulas option to look inside cells, and it doesn't look in cell notes.

You can run the replace process in two ways:

▶ To find and replace cell-by-cell, click the Find Next button. As each cell is found, you can either click the Replace button to replace the characters in the cell or click Find Next to skip that cell and continue the search.

▶ Click the Replace All button to process all found cells in one step. Be sure of the results before you do this, and keep your mouse ready to jump to the Undo button.

WHAT'S NEXT

Now that you've learned how to work with cells and ranges, it's time to move on to what makes Excel truly excellent—formulas! You'll see how to build and reference formulas, copy and move formulas, create special calculations using the Paste Special command, and even link to workbooks to the Internet.

Chapter 9
WRITING FORMULAS

The rows and columns of an Excel worksheet are great for entering data, but it is Excel's powerful mathematical capabilities that bring your worksheets to life. This chapter shows you how to work with formulas in Excel and how to tap into its massive computing powers.

Adapted from *Excel 2000: No Experience Required* by Gene Weisskopf

ISBN 0-7821-2374-0   432 pages $19.99

Building a Formula

To begin a formula in Excel, always start with an equals sign (=). Then build the formula with any of the following pieces:

Value   Numeric (114.8) or string ("hello")

Cell Address   B10, A5:B10, Sheet2!B15, or a range name (My_Cell)

Function   SUM, AVERAGE, COUNT, LEFT, IF, LOOKUP, and so on

Operator   +, −, *, /, ^, >, =, and so on

Parentheses   To control the left to right order of precedence in the formula, such as =(A15+B3)*2

Filename   Such as [Sample.xls] to create a linking formula to that file

Spaces, tabs, or hard returns   Can be included to make your formulas more readable

When a cell contains a formula, you will see the result of the formula displayed for that cell. If you select the cell, you'll see the formula within the Formula bar.

TIP

If you enter a formula in a cell and see the formula instead of its result, be sure you prefaced the formula with an equals sign (=). Also, remember that you should never include an equals sign *within* a formula unless you are specifically creating a logical formula.

Including Values

You create a formula in Excel much as you would with a calculator. Simply build the formula from left to right, connecting values with operators. For example, you might want to add up the money you spent over several days on a trip:

```
=28.5+7.25+38.4+31.75
```

When you press Enter, the formula's result is displayed in that cell.

TIP

Most of your formulas will not (and should not) include numbers. Instead, they should refer to other cells that may contain numbers. These cells are often called *variables* because their contents can vary (change), while a formula's reference to them does not change (although the formula's result will change). This technique makes it easy to update the data in your worksheet without having to edit the formulas themselves.

When you want to include text within a formula, be sure to enclose the text within quotation marks. If cell A5 contains a number, such as 27.5, you could write the following formula in another cell:

```
="The amount in cell A5 is "&A5
```

The result would look like this:

```
The amount in cell A5 is 27.5
```

You use the ampersand (&) to concatenate, or join, text in a formula. In this case, the result of the formula is text, not a number. Excel decided, quite logically, that when you combine text and a number in this way, the result cannot be a valid number and must therefore be text.

Reliving Math 101: Operators and the Order of Precedence

Remember when you had to memorize the order of precedence for mathematical operators (such as + and −)? Well, the same concepts apply to the operators in Excel, which are the glue that joins the other components of a formula. When a formula includes multiple operators, Excel evaluates the formula from left to right. An order of precedence among the operators determines which operation between a pair occurs first. For example, the formula

```
=7+4*3
```

equals 19, not 33, because multiplication has precedence over addition.

NOTE

The rules of precedence are followed throughout the world of math and computers, although you may find slight differences for some of the less common operators, such as the ampersand.

Table 9.1 shows the operators you can use in Excel and their ranking in the order of precedence. An operator above another in the list is evaluated first. When two operators share the same ranking, such as multiplication and division, Excel evaluates them from left to right.

TABLE 9.1: Excel's Operators

Operator	Description
:	Reference operator (as in A1:C3)
,	Argument separator
–	Negation (as in –2)
%	Percent sign
^	Exponentiation
* and /	Multiplication and division
+ and –	Addition and subtraction
&	Text concatenation
>, <, > =, < =, < >	Comparison operators (greater than, less than, greater than or equal to, less than or equal to, not equal to)

Without an established order of precedence, you can find several answers for a formula, depending on the order in which you evaluate its operators. To see Excel's order of preference in action, open a blank worksheet and follow these steps:

1. In cell A1, type **=2+3^2**.

2. In cell A2, type **=1+4*3**.

3. In cell A3, type **=4+1*3**.

4. In cell A4, type **=10–8/2**.

Your formulas should have yielded the answers 11, 13, 7, and 6. You can circumvent the usual flow of calculations, however, with a pair of parentheses.

Using Parentheses to Change the Order of Precedence

When you enclose part of a formula within a pair of parentheses, Excel evaluates that part as an independent unit. The result it produces is used in the normal, left-to-right flow of calculations. Follow these steps to see how parentheses change the result of a formula:

1. In cell B1, type **=(2+3)^2**.

2. In cell B2, type **=(1+4)*3**.

3. In cell B3, type **=(4+1)*3**.

4. In cell B4, type **=(10−8)/2**.

This time, your formulas should have yielded the answers 25, 15, 15, and 1.

An opening parenthesis in a formula must always have a closing parenthesis. If not, Excel will catch the discrepancy and offer to fix the problem or let you complete the parentheses yourself. If you choose to fix it, Excel highlights a portion of the formula that may need a balancing parenthesis, as shown below (it's a bit of a guess on Excel's part though, because *you* are the one who must determine where they belong).

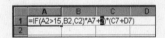

Excel can help you keep track of parentheses while you're working on a formula. As you enter a balancing parenthesis or move the insertion point through the formula and come to a parenthesis, Excel shows the pair of parentheses (briefly) in bold. Keep an eye out for this visual cue, and you're not likely to get out of balance.

Recognizing Error Results

Unfortunately, you can goof up a formula in lots of ways. Fortunately, Excel can warn you in a number of ways that you may be in trouble and can help you determine just what's wrong.

Here's a list of the common error results Excel returns when you enter a formula that Excel can't evaluate:

The column isn't wide enough to display the number; either widen the column, shrink the font, or change the numeric format.

#DIV/0!   Dividing by zero is invalid; note that a blank cell has a value of zero.

#N/A   Data is "not available," usually because your formula is referencing an NA function or value.

#NAME?   The formula references a name that is unknown to Excel.

#NUM!   The formula is using an invalid number, such as when the second argument is less than the first in the RAND-BETWEEN function.

#REF!   A cell reference is no longer valid; perhaps you deleted that cell or moved another cell onto it.

#VALUE!   The formula contains an invalid operator or argument; perhaps it is trying to add a text value to a numeric one.

NOTE

Choosing from the selections at Tools ➤ Auditing is a great way to track the source of a formula's error result.

Making Your Formulas More Readable

A formula can be a maximum of 1024 characters. I hope that your formulas never need to approach that length. Nevertheless, a complex formula can easily grow lengthy and become particularly difficult to write or, especially, to revise later. Here are some techniques you can use to make your formulas easier to create and interpret.

TIP

You can use Excel's built-in Range Finder to make your formulas more readable when they contain range references. We'll look at this in the "Referencing Cells in the Same Workbook" section, later in this chapter.

Use Parentheses to Clarify Your Intent

Even when a formula does not require parentheses, you may want to include them to clarify your intent. You can group sections of the formula within parentheses, which helps document the intended flow of calculations.

For example, the formula

```
=Sheet2!C15*D25+A25-A30-A35
```

is not all that long, but isn't it easier to read when it looks like this:

```
=(Sheet2!C15*D25)+(A25-A30-A35)
```

The added parentheses do *not* change the order of calculation here. They simply break the formula into more bite-sized pieces.

Include Spaces

You can place space characters within a formula, which might make it more readable, and doing so doesn't affect the formula.

```
=Sheet2!C15*D25  +A25-A30-A35
```

Split a Long Formula into Multiple Lines

To break a formula into several lines in its cell, press Alt+Enter to insert a linefeed. You could then make the formula from the example above look like this:

```
=Sheet2!C15*D25
+A25-A30-A35
```

Break a Long Formula into Multiple Cells

You can make a long formula much easier to handle if you break it into several cells. You can create components of the formula in separate cells and then tie them all together with another formula.

For example, you could split the formula used earlier into several cells in this way:

Cell A1   =Sheet2!C15*D25

Cell A2   =A25-A30-A35

Cell A3   A1+A2

You could use any cells for these components. The final formula that produces the desired result (cell A3) could be in some other part of the worksheet; it need not be right next to the cells it references.

Display Formulas, Not Their Results

When you are staring at a worksheet full of numbers, you really can't tell which are simply values and which are formulas. Here's a quick way to make the formulas stand out:

    1. Choose Tools ➤ Options to open the Options dialog box:

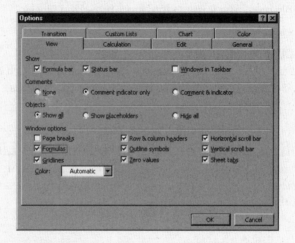

    2. Click the View tab.

    3. In the Window Options section, click the Formulas check box.

    4. Click OK.

Now the formulas, rather than their results, are displayed in the worksheet. Excel widens columns to show more of each formula, although some may still appear truncated. (But frequently that's all you'll need to get an idea of where the formulas are.)

You can choose either view as needed; press Ctrl+` (the grave accent found to the left of the 1 key, not an apostrophe) to switch between seeing the formula and seeing the result of the formula.

REFERENCING CELLS IN THE SAME WORKBOOK

Most of the formulas you write in Excel will refer to one or more of the millions of cells in the current workbook. A formula depends on the cells it references, and any changes you make to those cells affect the formula's result.

NOTE

Referenced cells are called *precedent* cells. You can trace the chain of precedents and dependents by choosing Tools ➤ Auditing.

Entering Cell References

You can refer to cells in a formula in several ways. To reference an individual cell, simply type the cell's address, as in this example:

```
=25+A3-B2+12
```

TIP

Excel automatically updates the addresses of all cell references in a formula when you insert or delete cells in the worksheet. In the above example, if you inserted two rows at row 1, the formula would reflect the change and now reference A5 and B4 instead of A3 and B2.

To reference a range of cells, define the range by specifying its upper-left and lower-right corners:

```
=SUM(B5:D9)
```

This formula sums the 15 cells in the rectangle whose corners are B5 and D9.

To reference multiple ranges, separate one from the next with a comma:

```
=SUM(B5:D9,F5:H9,I9,3.14)
```

This formula sums the three cell references and the number 3.14.

If the cell resides on another sheet in the same workbook, be sure to include that sheet's name in the address. To refer to cell B2 on Sheet3, the formula used above would look like this:

```
=25+A3-Sheet3!B2+12
```

The exclamation mark (!) at the end of the sheet name tells Excel that the cell being referenced is on a sheet other than the one that contains the formula. If the formula resides on the same sheet, the sheet name is understood.

If the sheet is named, be sure you reference that name. If the name has a space in it, you must enclose the name in single quotation marks:

```
=25+A3-'My Sheet'!B2+12
```

To reference the same range on multiple consecutive sheets—a *3-D range*—specify the first and last sheet, separated by a colon. The formula

```
=SUM(Sheet1:Sheet3!A1:B3)
```

adds the cells in the range A1:B3 on Sheet1, Sheet2, and Sheet3 (this assumes that those three sheets still have their default names, of course).

Pointing to a Cell or Range

In many cases, you may prefer to *point* to the cell or cells you want to reference in the formula instead of manually typing in the cell addresses. Pointing to and clicking the cell you want to reference displays its address in the formula, as though you had typed it there.

NOTE

In order to point to a cell, the insertion point must be positioned so that the formula can accept an address—for example, when the insertion point follows an operator.

For example, when you enter the formula =25+ in a cell and the insertion point is to the right of the plus sign, you can point to and click another cell to reference it within the formula. (Watch for the indicator on the left side of the status bar to display Point). You can then continue adding operators and references to the formula.

You can point to a range of cells by using the Shift+arrow key method. You can also reference noncontiguous ranges and 3-D ranges, as described in Chapter 8, and you can point to a cell or range of cells in another sheet.

Using the Range Finder

When a formula contains many cell references, it can look like nothing more than a long string of letters and numbers and give no clues as to what or where all the cells it references may be. Excel's immediate solution to this problem is the Range Finder. You'll see its effects when you edit a formula that contains references to cells or range names. To run the Range Finder, click the cell to display the formula in the Formula bar, and then click anywhere within the formula.

Figure 9.1 shows a formula being edited that contains three range references:

```
=25+SUM(A4:A8)+SUM(B10:D13)+15+10+MyCell
```

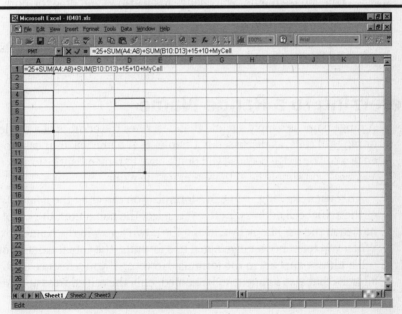

FIGURE 9.1:   Cell references within formulas come alive with the Range Finder.

The Range Finder performs two tasks when you change a formula:

▶ Each cell reference in the formula appears in a different color, so it's easy to discern one reference from another. Colors are repeated when there are more than a few references in one formula.

▶ The cells in the worksheet for each reference are surrounded by a border of the same color as the reference in the formula.

Suddenly the cell references seem to jump out of the formula and associate themselves with the actual ranges in the worksheet. Although Figure 9.1 doesn't show the actual colors, you can duplicate this formula in your worksheet to see the real thing (you'd also need to name a cell MyCell in order to mimic the formula).

The Range Finder not only helps you distinguish one reference from another, but it also lets you modify those references by changing the size or position of a range's border in the worksheet:

▶ To change the dimensions of a range reference, drag the handle in the lower-right corner of a range's border.

▶ To move a range reference, point to any edge of a range border (the mouse pointer will change to an arrow) and drag the border to a new position.

You can also edit the formula in the usual ways, such as by typing or pointing.

Referring to a Range Name

A range name is simply a name that describes the address of a single cell or range of cells, as discussed in Chapter 8. A name makes it easy to reference a cell or range because you don't have to remember the exact cell address—you simply need to remember the name.

To reference a range name in a formula, you can enter the name instead of the actual cell address. Better yet, select the name from the list of all names in the workbook by clicking the down arrow in the Name box. When you reference a range name in a formula, the actual name—not the cell address—appears in the formula. However, if you reference a cell address that also happens to be named, only the cell address appears in the formula. Either way, the formula produces the same result.

NOTE

Seeing the name in a formula can be an advantage. It helps you decipher the meaning of the formula (assuming the name for the range is somewhat relevant, of course) and also ensures that you're referencing the exact range you want. No matter how its address might change as you insert or delete cells in the workbook, the name will always follow the range and define the correct cells.

If you have formulas that reference addresses that are now named, such as

```
=C17*Y95
```

you can replace the addresses in the formulas with their names. Choose Insert ➢ Name ➢ Apply, as discussed in Chapter 8. The result is a more readable formula that might look like this:

```
=Pressure*Temperature
```

Here's a quick and easy way to name a range:

1. Highlight the range.

2. Click in the Name box, type a range name, and then press Enter.

Dealing with a Circular Reference

Suppose you write a formula in cell A6 that adds the cells above it in A1:A5, but you accidentally write the formula this way:

```
=SUM(A1:A6)
```

Because the formula refers to its own cell, you've created a *circular reference*, which Excel is unable to evaluate in its normal course of worksheet recalculation. Unless you are specifically designing a worksheet to include a circular reference, you can assume that any you encounter need to be fixed—either delete the circular cell reference or modify it so that it refers to another cell.

NOTE

A circular reference can be direct, as in this case where the formula actually refers to its own cell. It can also be indirect, where the formula refers to itself only by referencing another formula, which in turn refers to the circular one (possibly via many other formulas).

When you try to enter a formula that creates a circular reference, whether you do so intentionally or not, Excel immediately notifies you of the potential problem by displaying a warning dialog box. If you click OK, Excel will do the following:

▶ Enter the formula into the cell.

▶ Open the Help window to information about circular cell references. When you close or minimize the Help window, the Circular

Reference toolbar is displayed to help you track the source of the circular reference.

▶ Display the Circular indicator on the status bar, which shows the address of the offending formula.

▶ Not recalculate the formula, since the normal mode of recalculation has no way to deal with (resolve) the circular reference.

Figure 9.2 shows the worksheet that was described above, the Circular Reference toolbar, and the Circular indicator on the status bar.

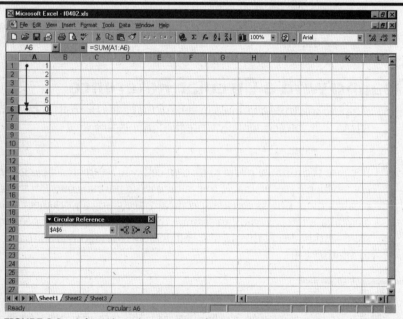

FIGURE 9.2: A formula with a circular reference, the Circular Reference toolbar, and the precedent and dependent arrows

You can also see a formula tracer arrow running from A1 to A6. This was created by clicking the Trace Precedents button on the Circular Reference toolbar while cell A6, the formula, was selected. The arrow runs through all the cells that the formula references.

The dot in cell A6 indicates that the formula is dependent on its own cell; hence, the circular reference.

REFERENCING CELLS IN NATURAL LANGUAGE FORMULAS

So far you've seen how you can write a formula that refers to other cell addresses, such as =A5*B16, and to range names, such as =A5*Interest. You can also reference cells in another way. Using *natural language formulas*, you can refer to row and column labels (text entries) within the worksheet instead of cell addresses or range names.

In Excel 2000, natural language formulas are not enabled by default. To turn on this feature, follow these steps:

1. Choose Tools ➤ Options to open the Options dialog box:

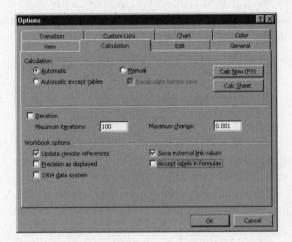

2. Click the Calculation tab, and check the Accept Labels in Formulas check box.

3. Click OK.

The worksheet in Figure 9.3, which is quite typical in its layout, is a perfect candidate for writing natural language formulas. You can use the column titles in row 3 and the row titles in column A to identify any of the data cells in the worksheet.

	A	B	C	D	E	F	G	H	I	J
1		Monthly Housing Expenses								
2										
3		Jan	Feb	Mar	Apr	May	Jun	Total		
4	Insurance	51	51	51	51	51	51	306		
5	Maintenance	48	48	48	48	48	48	288		
6	Mortgage	925	925	925	925	925	925	5,550		
7	Taxes	102	102	102	102	102	102	612		
8	Telephone	42	78	65	115	70	67	437		
9	Utilities	182	116	143	90	175	185	891		
10	Total	1,350	1,320	1,334	1,331	1,371	1,378	8,084		
11										

FIGURE 9.3: You can reference cells in formulas by referring to their row and column titles.

For example, the amount in January for Utilities is 182; the total of expenses for January is 1,350; the total for Utilities is 891; the difference between Utilities in January and in February is 66; and January's Utilities are about 20 percent of the Total Utilities. Here is how you would write natural language formulas for these:

```
=Jan Utilities

=Total Jan

=Total Utilities

=Jan Utilities-Feb Utilities

=Jan Utilities/Total Utilities
```

All it takes are unique column and row titles. In the formula, you separate one label from another with a space to define the intersection. If a row or column label consists of more than one word, you can enclose it in single quotation marks in the formula to make the reference more readable.

Here are a few other points to keep in mind when you work with natural language formulas:

▶ Ranges expand and contract as usual, so you can insert more rows without damaging any of the existing references.

▶ If you change a column or row title, formulas that reference those titles update accordingly.

▶ Be sure that column and row titles are unique, or you could run into trouble without even realizing it.

▶ When Excel finds more than one possible intersection for the titles you reference, it will prompt you to specify exactly which cell you mean.

▶ A formula cannot reference column and row titles that are on another worksheet.

▶ A natural language reference is a relative one; you can make it absolute by prefacing it with a dollar sign, just as you can with cell addresses in formulas (this topic is discussed in the next section).

To disable this feature, follow these steps:

1. Choose Tool ➤ Options to open the Options dialog box:

2. Click the Calculation tab, and clear the Accept Labels in Formulas check box.

3. Click OK.

COPYING FORMULAS AND MOVING PRECEDENT CELLS

When you copy a formula, such as with the Edit ➤ Copy and Paste commands, any cell references in the formula adjust their addresses to the copied formula's new location in the workbook. These addresses in the formula are called *relative* addresses.

Understanding How Relative References Adjust

You can think of a relative address as not really referring to a specific cell, but rather to that cell's position relative to the formula. For example, in this simple formula that resides in cell A1,

    =B3

the cell reference actually refers to the cell that is *one column to the right and two rows down.*

If you copy the formula from cell A1 to C15, the cell reference adjusts and still refers to the cell that is one column to the right and two rows down, so now it reads:

    =D17

A range address adjusts in the same way. Therefore, this formula in cell A1

    =SUM(B3:D10)

changes to

    =SUM(D17:F24)

when the formula is copied from cell A1 to C15.

Applying Absolute References That Do Not Adjust

You can also create an *absolute* cell reference in a formula, and it will not change when the formula is copied. To create an absolute reference, preface both its column and row with a dollar sign ($):

    =$B$3

You can copy this formula to any cell, and it will always reference cell B3.

NOTE

A reference to a range name is always absolute and never adjusts when the formula is copied. On the other hand, a natural language reference, as discussed in the previous section, is a relative one that you can make absolute with a preceding dollar sign.

A mixed reference contains both relative and absolute portions of the address:

    =$B3

When you copy this formula, only the row reference adjusts.

You can use F4 to create absolute or mixed references. When you are editing a formula and the insertion point is on an address, pressing F4 once makes the reference absolute. You can press F4 once or twice more to make a mixed reference:

Here are a few rules to keep in mind while copying or moving formulas to other worksheets:

- ▶ You can copy a formula with relative or absolute addresses to another worksheet.

- ▶ If you don't include a sheet address in a formula reference, Excel assumes that the sheet portion of the address is relative. If you copy the formula =$A$1 from Sheet1 to Sheet3, for example, the formula will refer to $A$1 on Sheet3.

▶ If you include the sheet name in the reference, however, Excel takes that as an absolute reference to that sheet. You don't need to, nor can you, preface the sheet name with a dollar sign.

▶ When you move a formula to a cell in the same or in another worksheet, its cell references will not change, no matter what type of reference was used.

Moving Precedent Cells

When you move a cell, such as by choosing Edit ➤ Cut and Paste, a formula that contains a reference to that cell "follows" the cell to its new location. It does not matter whether the reference was absolute or relative.

For example, the formula

```
=A1+$A$1
```

would look like this

```
=B5+$B$5
```

if you moved cell A1 to B5.

When you move a precedent cell to another worksheet, a formula that references it will follow it to that new sheet and update its reference accordingly.

Finally, when you *copy* a precedent cell, the formula that refers to it will still refer to the same cell afterward—the copy is ignored.

REFERENCING CELLS IN OTHER WORKBOOKS

Just as you can write a formula that refers to a cell on another worksheet, you can do the same with cells in another workbook. Writing this type of *external* reference in the *primary* workbook's formula creates a link to the cells in the *source* workbook.

By using workbook-linking formulas, you avoid having to duplicate data in one workbook that already exists in another. In fact, you can reference data in *many* workbooks; as a result, linking formulas vastly expand Excel's calculating abilities. Figure 9.4 shows an example of how you can take advantage of linking formulas. In the upper portion of the screen is the monthly housing expenses workbook from Figure 9.3, this time named *123 Main St.*

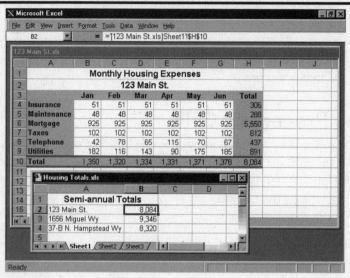

FIGURE 9.4: Linking formulas let you easily access data in other workbooks.

Imagine that you have several other housing workbooks and that you want quick access to their totals. Those files might be sent to you by others, for example, or reside elsewhere on your network or anywhere on the Internet.

The workbook in the lower portion of the screen in Figure 9.4 does the job. It simply lists the houses in column A; to the right of each one is a linking formula that references the cell containing the totals in the appropriate expenses workbook. For example, here is the formula in B2, which can also be seen in the Formula bar in Figure 9.4:

```
='[123 Main St.xls]Sheet1'!$H$10
```

NOTE

When you reference a range of cells in another workbook, such as with the SUM function, Excel actually stores all the values of that range in the primary workbook. Referencing a huge range could consume a lot of memory or disk space. That's when you might want to clear the Save External Link Values check box in the Calculation tab of the Options dialog box. Choose Tools ➢ Options to open the Options dialog box.

Specifying the Filename

A linking formula is essentially the same as any other formula, except that it includes a filename in a cell reference. The name is enclosed in square brackets, followed by the reference to the sheet (required) and cells in that file. For example, the linking formula in cell B2 in Figure 9.4 references cell H10 on Sheet1 in the source workbook 123 Main St. It doesn't matter if that file is open and in memory or only on disk.

If the source file is not open and does not reside in the same folder as the primary workbook, be sure to include the path to that file, such as =`'C:\Houses\[123 Main St.xls]Sheet1'!H10`. You must enclose the path and sheet reference within single quotation marks and enclose the filename in brackets. Even without the path, when the filename has a space in it, you must enclose it in single quotation marks.

Typing the Filename Link

To write a linking formula, you can begin the formula and then type the linking reference, although this can be tedious if you have to include the path to the file.

TIP

If you can't remember the file's name or location when you are typing a formula link to a file that is not open, enter an invalid filename in the formula and press Enter. You can then use the File Not Found dialog box to locate and select the correct filename.

Pointing to the File

If the workbook whose cells you want to reference is open, there's a much easier way to create the link. Simply point to the cells in the other workbook, just as you do when referencing cells in the active worksheet. Excel creates the linking reference for you in the formula.

Creating Links over the Internet

You can also create a linking formula that references a workbook residing on the Internet or your intranet, using the transfer protocols HTTP or FTP (as always, this assumes you already have a connection available). On a good day, you won't notice any difference when you link to a file on your local hard disk, on your network, or on the Internet. On a bad day, of course, a modem connection to a busy site on the Internet could really slow down a link to a large workbook.

You specify a Net link much as you would a local link, except that the path to the source file will be over the Internet, as in this example:

```
='http://www.domain.com/rentals/[123 Main St.xls]
Sheet1'!$H$10
```

You can either type in the full path and name or, if the source workbook is open, point to the cells you want to reference.

NOTE

When dealing with workbooks on the Internet, don't confuse linking formulas with hyperlinks. You can click a hyperlink to open the target workbook, whereas a linking formula simply brings in data from the target workbook for the formula to evaluate.

Keeping Links Current

When you open a workbook containing linking formulas to one or more workbooks that are not open, Excel will ask you if you want to update the results of those formulas with whatever data is in the other files. Generally you will want to click the Yes button and let Excel update the results of the linking formulas.

WARNING

If you change the data in the source workbook when the target workbook isn't open, the linking formulas won't be updated and your data won't be accurate.

However, if there are many links in the workbook or many links to sites on the Internet that could take a lot of time to access, you may not want to wait while the formulas are updated. If you're working on your portable computer away from your network connection, the source files may simply not be available.

In these cases, you can select No and not have the formulas updated. Just realize that the results displayed for any linking formulas will be from the last time they were updated and, therefore, may no longer be accurate.

NOTE

Formulas that link to open workbooks are evaluated during the normal course of formula recalculation, which by default is whenever you change any data to which the formulas refer.

You can update the results of linking formulas at any time by choosing Edit ➣ Links to open the Links dialog box (see Figure 9.5), which was mentioned in Chapter 8 in relation to creating object links between Excel and other Windows programs.

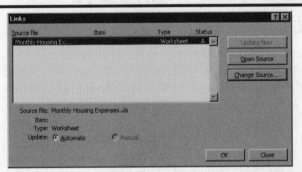

FIGURE 9.5: The Links dialog box lets you update, open, or change the source workbooks for linking formulas in the active workbook.

The Source File list shows the source files for all the linking formulas in the active workbook (as well as the source for object links to other programs). Its options include:

Update Now   Recalculates all formulas that link to the files you selected in the Source File list. This is called a manual update.

Open Source   Opens the selected source files.

Change Source   Lets you replace the selected source file-name with another filename, which you would do if the source file were moved or renamed.

Update   Is set by default to Automatic so that linking formulas are evaluated when you open the workbook. Choose Manual if you want Excel to update the links only when you click the Update Now button in this dialog box. To make this choice, you must first clear the Update Remote References check box on the Calculation tab in the Options dialog box.

TIP

Suppose that workbook A links to workbook B and that workbook B links to workbook C, and that all of them are closed. If you open C, update its data, save the file, and then open workbook A (but not B), the results in that workbook may not be accurate. You must first open workbook B, update its links to C, save it if it is not a local file, and then open workbook A and update its links.

RECALCULATING FORMULAS MANUALLY

By default, Excel recalculates formulas in all open workbooks whenever the data they reference change. This happens automatically, so under normal conditions your formulas are always up-to-date and correct.

When you have hundreds or thousands of formulas in open workbooks, the recalculation time may be longer than the blink of an eye that Excel usually requires. In that case, Excel displays the Calculate indicator on the status bar, and when you stop working for a moment, Excel takes that opportunity to recalculate the formulas. The presence of the Calculate indicator means that some formulas are not yet up-to-date.

You can turn off the automatic recalculation feature if it's too distracting or perhaps to avoid the stress on your less-than-state-of-the-art computer. To turn off the automatic recalculation feature, follow these steps:

1. Choose Tools ➤ Options to open the Options dialog box.

2. Click the Calculation tab.

3. In the Calculation section, click the Manual button.

4. Click OK to return to the worksheet.

Now when data changes, formulas will not automatically recalculate. The Calculate indicator on the status bar reminds you that not all formulas in the workbook are up-to-date.

NOTE

By default, when you select Manual, you also select the Recalculate before Save check box. This means that Excel will update all your formulas before it saves the workbook.

To recalculate formulas in all open workbooks while working in Manual mode, do either of the following:

▶ Choose Tools ➤ Options to open the Options dialog box, click the Calculation tab and then click the Calc Now button.

▶ From the worksheet, simply press F9.

To recalculate only the formulas on the active worksheet, do either of the following (doing this partial-workbook recalculation does not remove the Calculate indicator from the status bar):

▶ Choose Tools ➤ Options to open the Options dialog box, click the Calculation tab and then click the Calc Sheet button.

▶ From the worksheet, press Shift+F9.

Part ii

TIP

You can also press F9 while you're editing a formula to display the result of only that formula. If you want to keep only this result, you can press Enter; otherwise, press Esc to bring back the formula. You can also recalculate a piece of a formula by selecting that piece and pressing F9. Again, be sure to press Esc if you want to keep the formula and not its current result.

CALCULATING WITH EDIT ➤ PASTE SPECIAL

After you copy data to the Clipboard with the Edit ➤ Copy command, you can choose Edit ➤ Paste Special to perform arithmetic between the data you are pasting and data that are already in the worksheet.

Figure 9.6 shows the Paste Special dialog box. By default, the None option in the Operation section is selected. This means that no arithmetic is performed when the data are pasted, and the new data overwrite any data already in the worksheet.

NOTE

Along with the arithmetical options, you can also use the other options in the Paste Special dialog box, which were discussed in Chapter 8.

FIGURE 9.6: Choose Edit ➤ Paste Special, and use the Paste Special dialog box to perform arithmetic between the pasted data and the data already in the worksheet.

To perform arithmetic between each incoming (pasted) cell and the cell it overwrites, choose one of the other Operation options:

Add   Both data items are added together.

Subtract   The pasted data are subtracted from the cell data.

Multiply   Both data items are multiplied.

Divide   The cell data are divided by the pasted data.

This command is a handy way to perform arithmetic on existing data without having to create formulas elsewhere in the worksheet. Figure 9.7 shows a quick example using the housing expenses workbook used earlier in this book.

	A	B	C	D	E	F	G	H	I	J
	I2		=	1.04						
	A	B	C	D	E	F	G	H	I	J
1			Monthly Housing Expenses							
2									1.04	
3		Jan	Feb	Mar	Apr	May	Jun	Total		
4	Insurance	51	51	51	51	51	51	306		
5	Maintenance	48	48	48	48	48	48	288		
6	Mortgage	925	925	925	925	925	925	5,550		
7	Taxes	102	102	102	102	102	102	612		
8	Telephone	42	78	65	115	70	67	437		
9	Utilities	182	116	143	90	175	185	891		
10	Total	1,350	1,320	1,334	1,331	1,371	1,378	8,084		
11										
12										

FIGURE 9.7: Using the Paste Special dialog box, you can combine two groups of data with arithmetic.

You can also use the Paste Special dialog box as a fast way to replace a range of formulas with their results. For example, if you entered data via formulas, you could eliminate the formulas when you were done, leaving only their results. To do so, follow these steps:

1. Choose Edit ➤ Copy to copy the formula range to the Clipboard.

2. Select the first cell of that range.

3. Choose Edit ➤ Paste Special to open the Paste Special dialog box.

4. Click the Values option, and then click OK.

The formulas are overwritten by their results.

Suppose your housing expenses worksheet contained proposed or budgeted expenses for the coming year, but you realize that you forgot to factor in an expected 4 percent increase due to inflation. Follow these steps to use the Paste Special command to increase each data item by 4 percent in one operation.

1. Enter **1.04** into any blank cell in your worksheet, such as I2 in Figure 9.7. (This is just a temporary entry; we'll delete it after the task is done.)

2. Copy that cell to the Clipboard by choosing Edit ➤ Copy or clicking the Copy button on the Standard toolbar.

3. Select all the data cells in the worksheet (for example, B4:G9 in Figure 9.7).

4. Choose Edit ➤ Paste Special to open the Paste Special dialog box, and select the Multiply option.

5. Click OK.

You would not want to select any of the formula cells in this case, because they also would have been increased by the 1.04 value. For example, the formula in cell H4 in Figure 9.7, which adds the Insurance row for all months, looks like this before the Paste Special operation

```
=SUM(B4:G4)
```

and would look like this afterward:

```
=(SUM(B4:G4))*1.04
```

The result would be too large by 4 percent.

You need to change the format of the data to reflect that most of the numbers now include decimal places.

1. Select all the data and formulas (in Figure 9.8, cells B4:H10).

2. Click the Comma Style button on the Formatting toolbar to apply that numeric format to these cells.

3. With the cells containing data and formulas (B4:H10 in Figure 9.7) still selected, choose Format ➤ Column ➤ AutoFit Selection to expand the columns to accommodate the wider numbers.

4. Select the cell in which you entered 1.04 (for example, I2 in Figure 9.7), and press Del to remove that temporary value.

Your worksheet should look like the one in Figure 9.8. Each cell value was multiplied by the value in the Clipboard, 1.04.

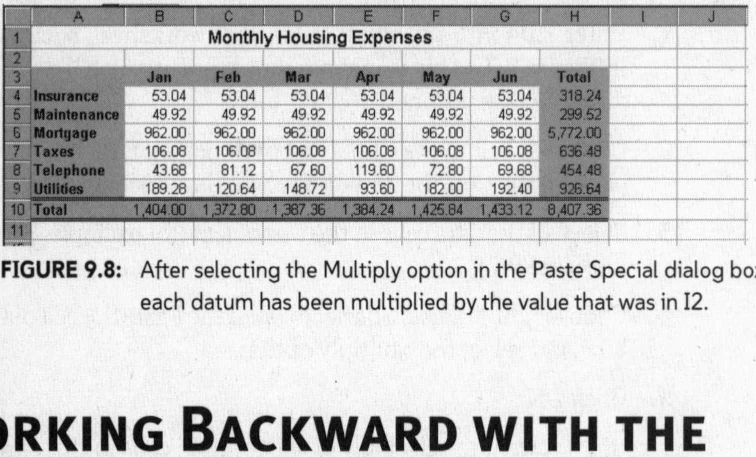

	A	B	C	D	E	F	G	H	I	J
1			Monthly Housing Expenses							
2										
3		Jan	Feb	Mar	Apr	May	Jun	Total		
4	Insurance	53.04	53.04	53.04	53.04	53.04	53.04	318.24		
5	Maintenance	49.92	49.92	49.92	49.92	49.92	49.92	299.52		
6	Mortgage	962.00	962.00	962.00	962.00	962.00	962.00	5,772.00		
7	Taxes	106.08	106.08	106.08	106.08	106.08	106.08	636.48		
8	Telephone	43.68	81.12	67.60	119.60	72.80	69.68	454.48		
9	Utilities	189.28	120.64	148.72	93.60	182.00	192.40	926.64		
10	Total	1,404.00	1,372.80	1,387.36	1,384.24	1,425.84	1,433.12	8,407.36		
11										

FIGURE 9.8:   After selecting the Multiply option in the Paste Special dialog box, each datum has been multiplied by the value that was in I2.

WORKING BACKWARD WITH THE GOAL SEEK COMMAND

The Tools ➤ Goal Seek command helps you solve a mathematical formula "backward," by finding a value that makes a formula result in an amount you specify. It's quite a powerful tool when you have a complex worksheet with many intertwined formulas.

Here's a typical example of how you can use Goal Seek. Suppose you want to buy a house and will be borrowing money at 9 percent annual interest. The bank that's loaning you the money believes that the maximum monthly payment you can afford is $900. How much house does that buy?

You can use the PMT function to find the payment amount on a loan. Its required arguments look like this:

```
=PMT(interest,periods,pv)
```

In our example, we know the interest rate is 9 percent, and we can assume the number of periods is 30 years. What we need to find is the present value of the money to be borrowed (the principal).

Figure 9.9 shows a small worksheet and the Goal Seek dialog box that will answer this question. The values needed for the PMT arguments have been entered in cells B1:B3. Here's the actual formula in B5:

```
=PMT(B2/12,B3*12,B1)
```

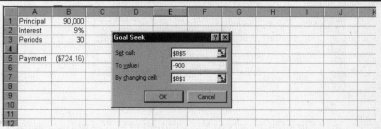

FIGURE 9.9: Use the Goal Seek tool to make a formula result in the amount you specify.

The principal amount in B1 is what we need to know. I entered a guess of $90,000, which returned a payment of $724.16 from the formula in B5. I could keep playing with the principal amount, increasing it or decreasing it until the formula produced a payment of exactly $900, but here's the easy way to do it.

1. Choose Tools ➤ Goal Seek to open the Goal Seek dialog box, as shown along with the worksheet in Figure 9.9.

2. In the Set Cell field, enter the address of the formula whose result you want to change—**$B$5** in this case.

3. In the To Value field, enter the result you want the formula to produce, which in this example is **–900**.

NOTE

You need to enter a negative value because the PMT function returns a negative value when calculating the payment for paying down a loan.

4. In the By Changing Cell field, enter the address of the principal—**$B$1** in this example.

5. Click OK and, in less than an instant, a suggested solution is displayed in the Goal Seek Status dialog box, and the number it offers has been placed in the cell containing the principal (B1 in this example).

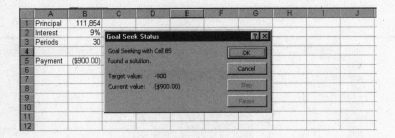

6. Click OK to accept the solution (111,854 in this example).

In many cases, there may be multiple solutions that would satisfy the criteria you specify for the Goal Seeker. Therefore, start with a value in the changing cell (B1 in this example) so that Goal Seek has a better guess at what result you expect to attain.

WHAT'S NEXT

Now you've completed your tour through the wacky wonderful world of Excel. Next stop is PowerPoint. In just three short chapters, you'll learn how to create vivid, professional-looking presentations for both your home and office.

PART iii
CREATING PRESENTATIONS
WITH POWERPOINT 2000

Chapter 10

THE QUICK AND EASY PRESENTATION

I f you, like many people, are responsible for putting together a presentation on short notice, you don't want to wade through lengthy academic descriptions of procedures you may never use just to find the few important pieces of information you need. Instead, this chapter is designed around a "ready, set, go!" approach. You'll learn only what you need to start up PowerPoint, to make some choices for starting your presentation, to add text and graphics, and to save, show, and print the file. The procedures described in this chapter will walk you through your first presentation in 30 minutes or less.

Adapted from *Mastering PowerPoint 2000*, by Katherine Murray
ISBN 0-7821- 2356-2   400 pages $29.99

NOTE

If you have not yet installed PowerPoint 2000, take the time to do it now. Appendix A tells you how to install the program.

Starting PowerPoint

You can start PowerPoint two ways. One way is to double-click the My Computer icon on your desktop, then navigate to the folder in which you installed PowerPoint 2000, and double-click the program icon, as shown in Figure 10.1.

FIGURE 10.1:   You can start PowerPoint by navigating to the program icon and double-clicking it.

The other way to start PowerPoint is via a menu command. Choose Start ➢ Programs ➢ Microsoft PowerPoint. (Figure 10.2 shows the submenu that appears after you open the Programs menu.)

With either approach, after you click Microsoft PowerPoint to start the program, you'll see the screen shown in Figure 10.3.

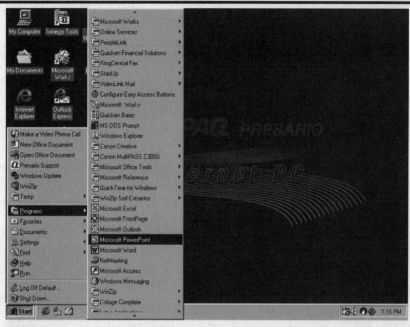

FIGURE 10.2: Choosing PowerPoint from the Programs menu

In the center of the PowerPoint work area, the PowerPoint dialog box appears. This dialog box gives you the choice of starting a new presentation (in several different ways) or opening an existing presentation. You can choose from the following options:

▶ AutoContent Wizard

▶ Design Template

▶ Blank Presentation

▶ Open an Existing Presentation

Choosing AutoContent Wizard takes you to an automated utility that helps you create the content of your presentation. You'll learn how to create a simple presentation using this feature in the next section. If you choose Template, you will be given the option of choosing a basic presentation design on which you can build your own presentation. Blank Presentation takes you to a blank presentation screen, where you can create all your own elements for your presentation. Finally, the Open an Existing Presentation option displays the Open dialog box so you can open a

PowerPoint file you have already created. After you make your choice, click OK to start working with PowerPoint.

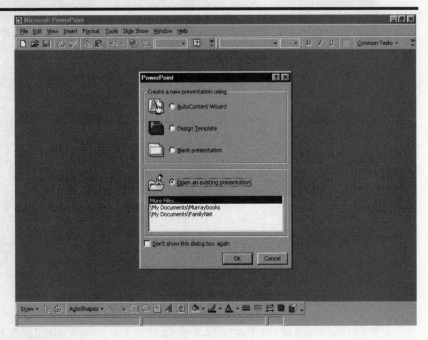

FIGURE 10.3:   The PowerPoint start-up screen

GETTING HELP

When you begin learning anything new, it's a good idea to know what tools are available to you in times of trouble. PowerPoint has a comprehensive help system that enables you to ask for and get help in whatever form is most comfortable for you. If you've worked with Windows programs before, you won't find any surprises in the PowerPoint help interface—the Help Topics dialog box enables you to search for help by topic or keyword, and the Answer Wizard enables you to enter plain-English questions and receive plain-English answers.

You'll also find help buttons in the upper right corner of dialog boxes (click on the small question mark and then on any option or setting you don't understand).

Working with the Office Assistant

Changes have been made in Office 2000 to the Office Assistant, an animated little fellow who pops up in the upper right corner of your work area when you seem to be struggling with a particular operation (see Figure 10.4).

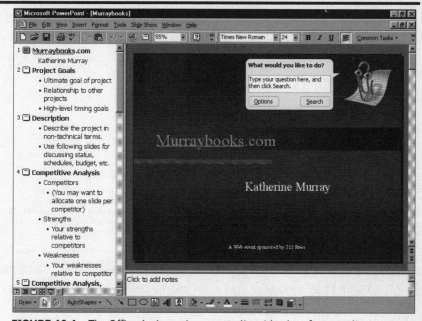

FIGURE 10.4: The Office Assistant is a paper clip with a lot of personality and perhaps just the procedures you need to get out of a confusing spot.

The purpose of the Office Assistant is to watch over your work and make suggestions when you seem to need it. You can also use the Assistant to help you search for information on specific PowerPoint topics. You can put the Office Assistant away if it annoys you, by right-clicking and choosing Hide. When you want its help again, simply open the Help menu and click Show the Office Assistant.

Microsoft on the Web

You can also get PowerPoint help surfing the World Wide Web. You'll find the Office on the Web option in the Help menu. After you click Connect and make the online connection, the Help menu lists the Office on the Web option, which you can click to move to the Microsoft Office Web site (see Figure 10.5).

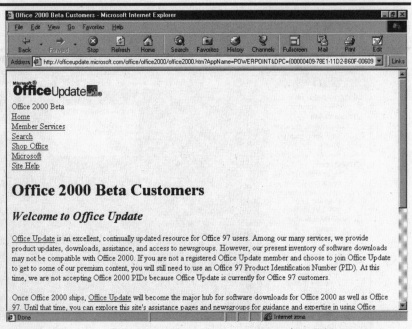

FIGURE 10.5: You can go right to the Web for Office information by choosing Help ➢ Office on the Web.

CREATING A SIMPLE PRESENTATION

With PowerPoint's predesigned templates and the AutoContent Wizard, you have everything you need to assemble an on-the-fly presentation. You just need to plug in your own ideas and present. In this section, we'll take you on a quick tour of the steps involved in creating a simple presentation. Specifically, you'll learn how to do the following things:

► Work with the AutoContent Wizard

► Choose a template

► Add text

► Add a title

- ▶ Move text areas
- ▶ Resize text boxes
- ▶ Add art
- ▶ Resize art objects
- ▶ Start a new slide
- ▶ Start a slide show
- ▶ Save the presentation
- ▶ Print slides

Working with Wizards and Templates

We learn most things in our lives through imitation. If we see an office design that appeals to us, we try to design our office in a similar way. If we run across a particularly successful advertising gimmick, we might try to use the same approach in selling our product. Imitation can be a great teacher.

PowerPoint gives you two different ways of learning by imitation. The AutoContent Wizard interactively leads you through the process of creating a presentation by asking you a series of questions. Similarly, templates give you the bare bones of a presentation upon which you build using text and graphics. In both cases, you learn the process and basic design concepts while using the time-saving tools PowerPoint provides.

Using the AutoContent Wizard

The AutoContent Wizard will lead you through a series of questions to help you construct the basic content of your presentation. From your answers, PowerPoint will assemble an outline to which you can add your own text, graphics, multimedia objects—whatever.

First, choose the AutoContent Wizard in the PowerPoint opening screen, which appears when you start PowerPoint (see Figure 10.6).

If you have been working in PowerPoint—that is, you're not just starting your work session—you can start a new presentation by opening the File menu and choosing New. The New Presentation dialog box, shown in Figure 10.7, appears.

Part iii

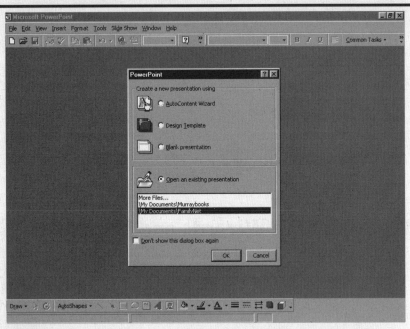

FIGURE 10.6:   Start the AutoContent Wizard from the PowerPoint dialog box.

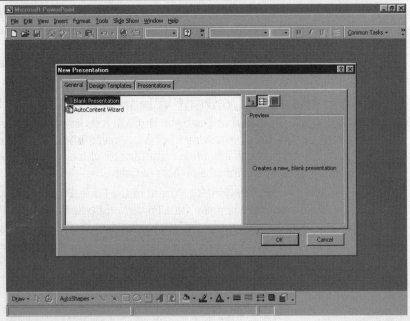

FIGURE 10.7:   The New Presentation dialog box

When the Presentations tab of the New Presentation dialog box is displayed, the AutoContent Wizard always appears in the upper-left corner of the window. To begin using the wizard, select it and click OK. The first screen of the wizard appears, as shown in Figure 10.8.

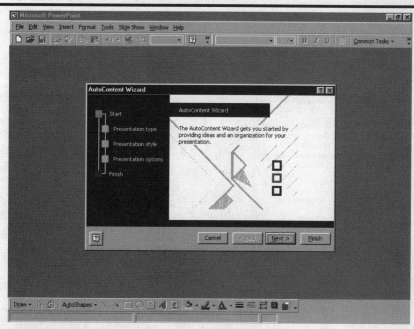

FIGURE 10.8: The opening screen of the AutoContent Wizard

First you need to choose the type of presentation you want to create. A number of different presentation types are listed, because the All button is selected by default. If you want to see what's available for a particular type of presentation, such as Corporate, click the button in the center of the dialog box. The list shows only those presentation types that correspond to the category you selected.

If you click the Carnegie Coach button in the bottom center portion of the dialog box, you'll get a list of various presentations on how to run a presentation meeting. These choices will help you produce a presentation that can be used to teach others how to hold meetings, prepare presentations, introduce speakers, and more. Click your choice in the right column; then click Next.

Next you need to tell PowerPoint how you will give the presentation. Are you planning an onscreen presentation? A Web presentation? Will you be creating 35mm slides? The options on this page list your choices; click the one that is appropriate for your needs and click Next. The next screen asks you for the presentation title and footer information. You can also elect to display the date and page number on slides. When you click Next on this page, the final screen tells you to click Finish to complete the process. After you do so, PowerPoint puts all the information together and displays the presentation in Normal view (see Figure 10.9).

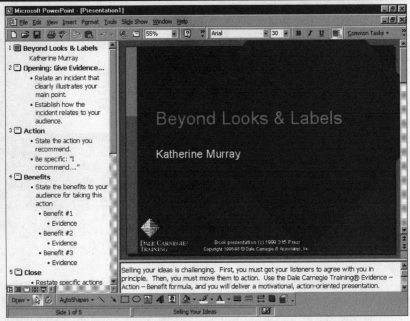

FIGURE 10.9:   The AutoContent Wizard completes the basic presentation and displays it in Normal view.

Now you need to add your own text, graphics, and multimedia objects. You can add text quickly here in Normal view. You just highlight the text you want to replace and type the new text. For more information about entering, editing, and enhancing text, see Chapter 11.

When you are ready to add graphics, charts, and multimedia objects, change to Slide view. To do that, click the Slide View button in the lower left corner of the work area. Figure 10.10 shows the presentation in Slide view.

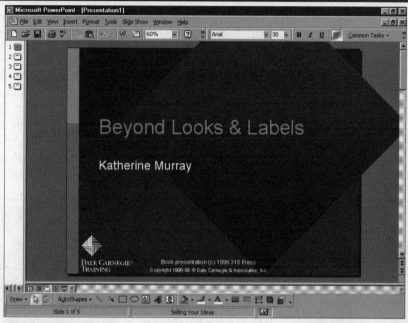

FIGURE 10.10: Display the AutoContent Wizard's creation in Slide view.

Using Design Templates

PowerPoint 2000 includes a number of new templates on which you can base your own presentations. Some include basic design elements for the background and text that are already set for you. Others include both these settings and sample text for your presentation.

To choose a template, either select the Design Template option in the PowerPoint dialog box that appears when you first start the program, or click the Presentations tab or the Design Templates tab in the New Presentation dialog box. Figure 10.11 shows the Presentations tab with the Reporting Progress or Status template selected. Notice that a preview of the template appears to the right of the icon area.

Part iii

Here are the distinctions between the Presentations and Design Templates:

▶ A Presentation is a sample presentation that includes text prompts suggesting the topics to cover in a specific order in your presentation. Figure 10.12 shows the Reporting Progress or Status presentation displayed in Normal view, so you can see the text that has already been entered.

▶ A presentation Design Template includes background color selections, text settings, formatting specifications, and background graphics, but no text. When you choose a Design Template and click OK, PowerPoint prompts you to choose a page layout and then displays the first page you choose in Normal view, as shown in Figure 10.13. Notice that there are no text entries in the Outline pane.

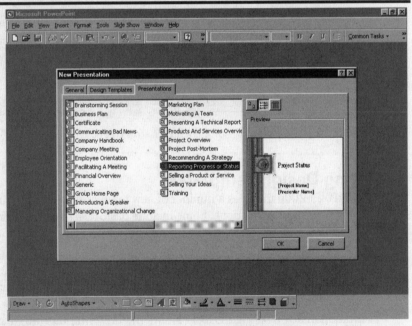

FIGURE 10.11: Choosing a predesigned presentation template

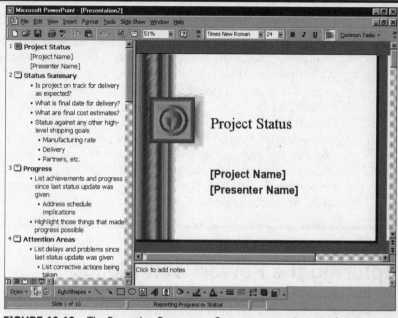

FIGURE 10.12: The Reporting Progress or Status presentation template in Normal view

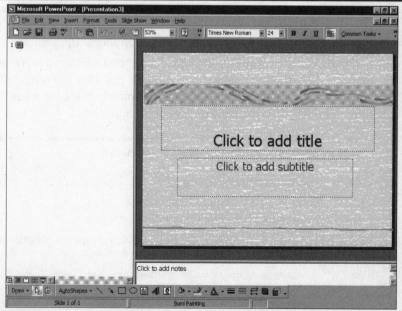

FIGURE 10.13: The first page of a presentation based on the Sumi Painting presentation design

MASTERING THE OPPORTUNITIES

If you're new to presentation graphics, starting out with either the AutoContent Wizard or a template is your best bet. The AutoContent Wizard will help you create the content of your presentation, depending on what message you are communicating. Templates — either in the form of Design Templates, which give you only the basic design of the presentation, or Presentations, which provide complete multipage presentations you can use and then add your own text and graphics — show you how the experts put together presentations. You'll be able to see how the different elements of the presentation work together most effectively while you learn the basics of the program.

Exploring the PowerPoint Menus

PowerPoint uses nine different menus to house the commands you'll work with throughout your PowerPoint experience. You can also select commands by clicking the icons in the toolbar, just below the PowerPoint menu bar. You have the option of adding different tools to the existing toolbar and creating your own custom toolbars. For more about creating your own toolbars, see the "Understanding Toolbars" section later in this chapter. But let's start with a basic understanding of the menus.

As you become more familiar with PowerPoint's features and commands, you'll discover where the commands you use most often are stored. Each menu includes a group of commands related to a specific function. Table 10.1 explains the menus in more detail.

TABLE 10.1: An Overview of PowerPoint Menus

Menu	Description
File	Provides commands for creating new files; opening, saving, and printing files; setting up pages; preparing a file for the road.
Edit	Enables you to copy, cut, and paste objects; undo operations; establish hyperlinks; delete slides; and find and replace words or phrases.
View	Allows you to select the different PowerPoint views. Choose Normal, Slide Sorter, Notes Pages, or Slide Show, or display the Masters for selected page types on which you can add repeating background elements. You can also control the display of on-screen items like the toolbars, rulers, and guides. You can also magnify the screen up to 400 percent.

TABLE 10.1 continued: An Overview of PowerPoint Menus

MENU	DESCRIPTION
Insert	Allows you to insert any of a number of elements into your slides and presentations. Specifically, you can insert a new slide, the date, time, or page number, slides from another file or outline, clip art, graphics, tables, graphs, or a sound clip or video piece. You can even insert an entire presentation into your presentation, if you like.
Format	Controls items like font, alignment, spacing, color, shadow, styles, and basic presentation characteristics such as layout, background, and color. You can also change the presentation design and replace fonts from this menu.
Tools	Provides add-on items that help you create effective presentations, including a spelling checker, AutoCorrect, a choice of transitions, and special effects. With the new Meeting Minder feature, you can take notes during a presentation or set up for presentation conferencing. Export allows you to prepare notes and slides you can use with Microsoft Word. Additionally, with commands in the Tools menu you can customize the displayed toolbar and control editing and general display options.
Slide Show	The commands in the Slide Show menu are concerned with displaying the show. You can choose to start the slide show, rehearse the timing of the show, create and set up animations, choose transitions, create custom shows, and more.
Window	Controls the look of your screen. New Window displays a new presentation window for you to work in; Arrange All tiles the slides on the screen; Fit to Page displays windows one at a time with no overlapping; and Cascade displays windows in overlapping style. Additionally, this menu shows you the names of any open presentation files.
Help	Includes commands for getting you out of tight places in PowerPoint. You can look through the Microsoft PowerPoint Help, show or hide the Office Assistant, use What's This? to find out about an object or item and get understandable answers and references, or go online with the Office on the Web option.

Part iii

Understanding Toolbars

PowerPoint includes a number of toolbars that you can use to streamline your work. For example, when working with graphics, you may want to display the drawing toolbars (there are two) on the screen. When adding special effects to objects, you may want to display the Animation Effects toolbar.

A toolbar is a graphical representation of commands that exist in the PowerPoint menus. While you are working, it is often easier to click a button than it is to find a particular command in one of PowerPoint's nine menus.

PowerPoint comes equipped with several toolbars, each containing tools related to a specific function. Table 10.2 explains the different toolbars available in PowerPoint.

TABLE 10.2: Understanding the Toolbars

TOOLBAR	DESCRIPTION
Standard	Includes tools for working with files and cutting, copying, pasting, and undoing operations.
Formatting	Contains the font, size, style, alignment, spacing, and bullet options.
Animation Effects	Includes several tools you can use to add motion and sound effects to objects in your presentation.
Clipboard	Shows the contents of items you've placed there in cut and copy operations.
Control Toolbox	A set of controls from Microsoft Access that will enable you to create forms that readers can use for data entry.
Drawing	Contains commands for working with text used as a graphic element (i.e., logos, oversized first letters, etc.) and drawing shapes with various colors and fill patterns.
Outlining	The Outlining toolbar displays buttons that enable you to rearrange the levels of text in your presentation.
Picture	Gives you a variety of options for importing and then editing images in PowerPoint.
Reviewing	The Reviewing toolbar is a palette of seven tools you can use when you are reviewing a presentation—five for comments, one for Outlook tasks, and one for sending mail.
Tables and Borders	Displays various tools for creating and modifying tables and borders.
Visual Basic	The Visual Basic toolbar includes tools that help you add programmability features to your presentation.
Web	Offers you standard browser buttons (like forward and back), the URL text box, and more.
WordArt	Displays a toolbar with the tool for creating WordArt and various tools for editing it.

You can display the available toolbars (and see which ones are enabled on your system) by choosing View ➤ Toolbars. When you place the pointer on Toolbars, the drop-down menu shown in Figure 10.14 appears.

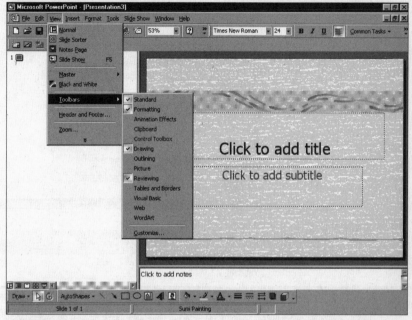

FIGURE 10.14: Displaying the available toolbars in the Toolbars cascading menu

If you like to use a specific set of tools, you can create a custom toolbar. To do this, display the Toolbars cascading menu, then select the Customize option. The Customize dialog box appears. Click the Toolbars tab. Click New. The New Toolbar dialog box appears, and you can enter the name for your new toolbar (see Figure 10.15). After you enter the name, click OK.

PowerPoint displays the new toolbar on top of the Customize dialog box. Click the Commands tab. In this tab, you will drag the commands you want to include in the new toolbar to the toolbar itself. As you add each tool, the toolbar grows. Figure 10.16 shows the Webtools toolbar after a number of tools have been added.

Part iii

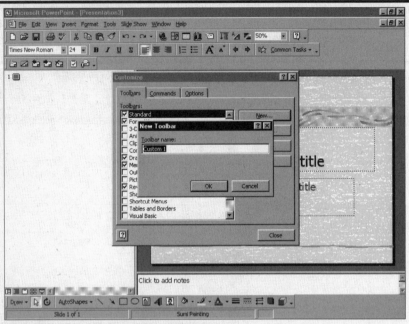

FIGURE 10.15:   Creating a custom toolbar

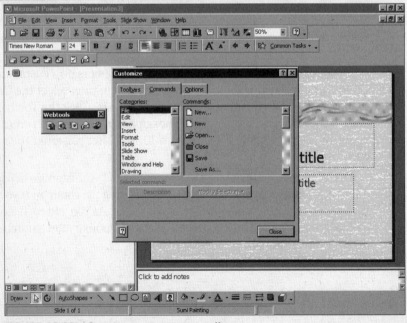

FIGURE 10.16:   Creating a new custom toolbar

To close the Customize dialog box, click Close. If you want to close the toolbar you've created, just click on the Close box in the upper right corner of the box.

TOOLBARS, TOOLBARS, EVERYWHERE

PowerPoint includes many different toolbars you can use for various tasks as you assemble your presentations. But what if your screen is cluttered with the multitude of toolbars you display? Chances are that you use only a few tools from each toolbar for the majority of your tasks. You can create a general toolbar that holds just the tools you want to use, which reduces the toolbar clutter on your screen.

Create the new toolbar using the procedure described in this section. Then, if you want to *move* tools from one toolbar to another, display the toolbar you want to move the tools from and drag the tools to the new toolbar. Notice that the tools are removed from the original toolbar. If you want to *copy* the tools from the original toolbar to the new toolbar, press and hold Ctrl while you drag the tools from one toolbar to another. When you're finished, click OK.

Adding Text

Thus far in the chapter, you've learned how to start a PowerPoint presentation with both the AutoContent Wizard and a template. Figure 10.17 shows the first page of a presentation based on the Bold Stripes design template displayed in Normal view.

As you can see, a PowerPoint Presentation doesn't leave any guesswork for you. Prompts on the screen tell you where to type the title and subtitle, and the color is already chosen. All you have to do is follow the instructions and enter your own text. We'll do this in the next few sections.

Adding a Title

To enter a title on the title page, position the mouse anywhere on the title box and click the mouse button to highlight the text box (see Figure 10.18).

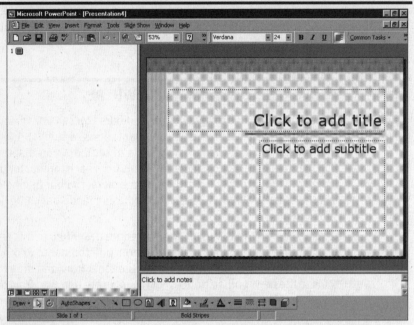

FIGURE 10.17:   The first screen of the new PowerPoint presentation design

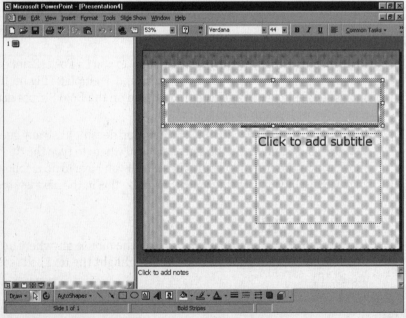

FIGURE 10.18:   Displaying the text box for text entry

Few things in life are as simple as this next step: Type whatever title you want, and PowerPoint formats the text in the font, style, color, and alignment of the template (see Figure 10.19).

When you click outside the text box, the edges of the text box disappear.

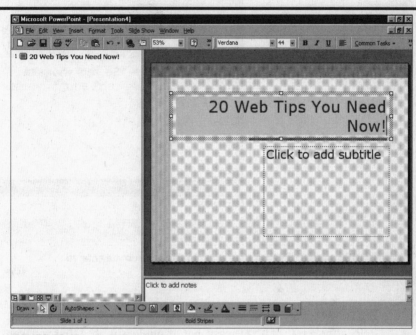

FIGURE 10.19: An entered title

TIP

After you add the title, you may decide that you want to change it. Simply click on the title. The text box will reappear and you can make your changes.

Adding a Subtitle

Adding a subtitle is just like adding a title, except that you click in the other text box and the text appears in a slightly different format, according to the template settings. Figure 10.20 shows the completed first slide.

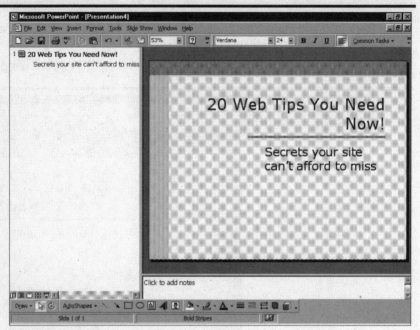

FIGURE 10.20:   The first slide with the title and subtitle entered

Moving Text Areas

Relocating a box of text is easy. For example, suppose that you want to move the subtitle down. Just move the pointer to the edge of the text box. When the pointer changes to an arrow, press and hold the mouse button while dragging the box downward. When the text box is where you want it, release the mouse button.

Resizing Text Boxes

It may be necessary to resize the text box so that it takes up less (or more) room on-screen. To do so, position the mouse pointer on the edge of the text box until you see a double-headed arrow, and then press the mouse button and drag the border, releasing the mouse button when the box is the size you want.

STARTING A NEW SLIDE

Now that you've mastered the first slide, you're ready to tackle a few more. Let's add another slide so we've got room to work. You can add a slide one of four ways:

- ▶ Click the New Slide button in the Standard toolbar
- ▶ Choose the New Slide button from the toolbar at the top of the screen
- ▶ Choose Insert ➤ New Slide
- ▶ Press Ctrl+M

Whichever you choose, the New Slide dialog box appears so you can choose the AutoLayout for the new slide (see Figure 10.21).

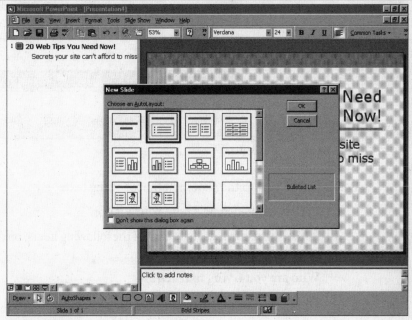

FIGURE 10.21: The New Slide dialog box

For example, select the layout in the bottom-left corner of the dialog box and then click OK. A new slide with areas blocked out for title text, bullet text, and clip art appears, as shown in Figure 10.22. Notice that the status area tells you which slide you are looking at.

If you are working with one of the Presentations that PowerPoint provides, you already have other slides created in your file. You can select one of those slides or add a new one using the procedures described previously.

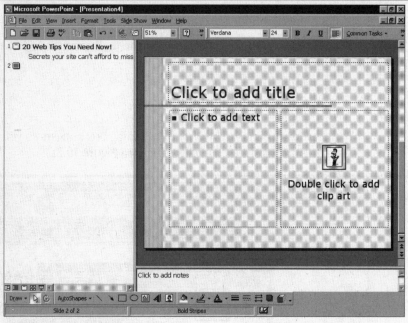

FIGURE 10.22: The new slide

Before you add art to the slide, add the following text:

1. In the title area, type **Know Your Visitor**

2. In the bullet text area, type each of the following items, pressing Enter after each phrase:

   Who are you trying to reach?

   How will they find your site?

   What are they looking for?

Adding Art

The slide we just added has a spot included for clip art. You can add clip art anywhere on a slide you want; however, the clip art boxes designed into your PowerPoint slide enable you to add clip art easily. Double-click the Double Click to Add Clip Art box, and the Microsoft Clip Gallery appears, as shown in Figure 10.23. You can move through the categories to display the different pieces of clip art and then choose the art you want from the Pictures box. After you've selected the art you want, click Insert, and PowerPoint adds the art to the slide.

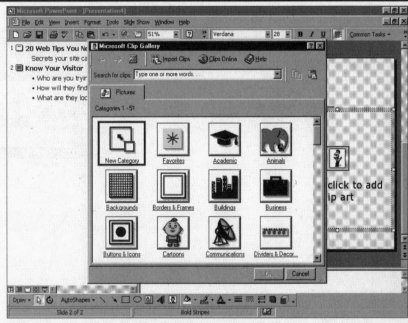

FIGURE 10.23: The Microsoft Clip Gallery dialog box

Resizing Art Objects

Resizing an art object in PowerPoint is the same basic process as resizing a text box. Click on the object you want to select, position the mouse pointer on one of the handles, and press and hold the mouse button while dragging the mouse in the direction you want to resize the object. When the object is the size you want, release the mouse button.

TIP

You can add a variety of other art special effects to your presentations, including custom-drawn objects and shapes or color schemes, shading, and patterns. Now, in PowerPoint, you can also animate shapes and art on your slides.

Changing Views

Thus far, you've been working on your presentation in Slide view. By changing to different views, you can see how the content of your presentation—in terms of both text and slide design—is shaping up.

Display the presentation in Outline view by clicking the Outline button in the bottom left corner of the window. Figure 10.24 shows the presentation created up to this point in Outline view.

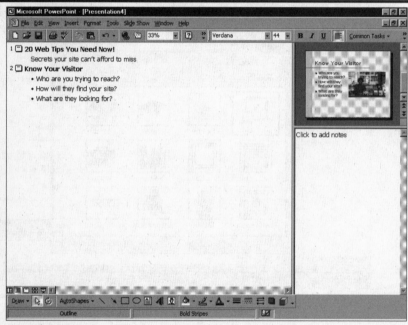

FIGURE 10.24:   The two-slide presentation in Outline view

Slide Sorter view is helpful when you have several different slides and want to be able to compare and/or reorder them. Change to Slide Sorter view by clicking the Page Sorter button, which also lies in the bottom left corner of the window. Figure 10.25 shows the presentation in Slide Sorter view.

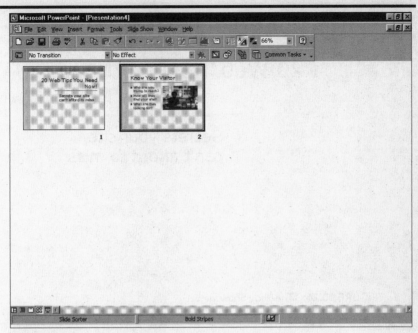

FIGURE 10.25: The presentation in Slide Sorter view

Starting a Slide Show

Although we're several pages short of what might be considered a real slide show, try out the slide show feature of PowerPoint. You can start a slide show four different ways:

- ▶ By clicking the Slide Show tool (the display-board icon to the right of the view buttons)

- ▶ By opening the View menu and choosing Slide Show

- ▶ By opening the Slide Show menu and choosing View Show

- ▶ By pressing F5

When you choose the Slide Show command, the show begins. The slides appear one at a time, taking up the entire screen (see Figure 10.26). When you are ready to advance to the next slide, press Enter or click the left mouse button. (To return to the previous view, press the Escape key.)

20 Web Tips You Need Now!

Secrets your site
can't afford to miss

FIGURE 10.26: The Slide Show view

Saving Presentations

Periodically save the presentation you're working on. For best results, save regularly—don't wait until you're finished with the file. You never know when a badly timed thunderstorm or a trip over the power cord will interrupt power to your computer. Most people save their files after each major step in the creation process. In other words, you might pause to save the file the first time after you select the template and add the first slide of text; then again after adding subsequent pages; then again after adding art, charts, and so on.

The process of saving files in PowerPoint is the same as that of saving files in any other Windows application—just open the File menu and choose Save, navigate to the disk and folder where you want to store the file, enter the filename you want, and click OK.

TIP

The next time you save the file by selecting the Save command you will not be asked to enter a filename; PowerPoint will use the name you specified in the initial save procedure. From this point on you can save the file by pressing Ctrl+S.

Printing the Presentation

PowerPoint makes it easy to print multiple copies of presentations, to print only selected pages, and to choose a number of different formats for printing (Slides, Notes Pages, Handouts, or Outline view). You can also specify print quality, print to a file, omit the background color, resize to fit the page, and change the print order (see Figure 10.27).

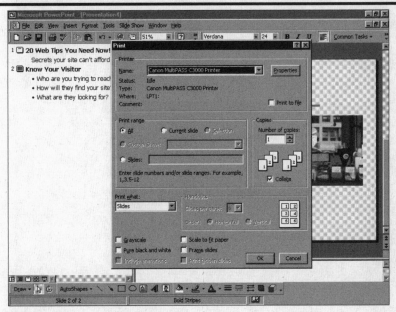

FIGURE 10.27: The Print dialog box

If you're having trouble getting pages to print, check to make sure you've got your printer set up to work with PowerPoint. (To do this, open the File menu, choose the Print command, and click the Printer button.)

WHAT'S NEXT

In this chapter, we've covered a lot of ground. From a basic understanding of the start-up procedure for PowerPoint, you explored selecting templates and wizards and investigating each of the PowerPoint menus. Additionally, you learned the basic tasks for creating a presentation, getting help, adding text and clip art, resizing objects, adding new slides, displaying a slide show, and printing the presentation. In Chapter 11, you'll learn how to enter, edit, and enhance text.

Chapter 11

ENTERING, EDITING, AND ENHANCING TEXT

The text of your presentation carries a lot of weight. Even though you'll be presenting, which means you'll have notes or a script to narrate from as you go through the slides, viewers are further clued in to your message and its meaning as they watch the story unfold on the slides. From the text you use—and the way you use it—your audience will understand:

- ▶ What's most important about your presentation
- ▶ What items you're covering
- ▶ Where they need to ask questions
- ▶ What response you hope to elicit

Adapted from *Mastering PowerPoint 2000*
by Katherine Murray
ISBN 0-7821- 2356-2   400 pages $29.99

In this chapter, you'll learn to use text to its best advantage. We won't waste time proselytizing about the power of the printed word—you already understand that. The power you're working with here is a combination of platforms—multimedia—and the trick lies in knowing what to put on-screen and what to say. Where will text help and where will it detract from your presentation? You'll learn to make those types of judgments in this chapter.

Once you get the basic content of your presentation down, take a good long look at it. Proofread it carefully. Watch the punctuation. A good presentation can be blown out of the water by bad grammar or incorrect punctuation. This chapter will help you get a handle on the editing aspect of your presentation.

Finally, you need to think about the way your text looks. Your text's appearance—although perhaps set by a wizard or a template—conveys quite a bit about your message. You may want to change the typeface, size, color, or other elements. Later in this chapter, you'll find out how to make these and other enhancements to your text.

TEXT RULES

This section gives you a few pointers for preparing the text content of your presentation. If writing is old hat to you, feel free to skip this section and move on to "Using the AutoContent Wizard," later in this chapter.

Too Much Is Too Much

The temptation may be very great to pack too much text into your slides, especially if you are preparing slides that will also be printed as handouts (which means that they will go back to the office or home with audience members and you want them to be able to remember what each slide was about). Fight it. Including too much text on a slide is overwhelming for audience members—they will read the first seven words of any bullet point or paragraph and then move on to the next item. Keep your blurbs succinct.

For example, consider this bullet entry, taken from a sample presentation:

▶ Before you can design an effective site, you need to think about who your audience is, how they will find you, and what they are looking for.

That sounds okay, but it's too long. By the time your audience gets to "effective" they've stopped reading. If you want to say clearly that you need to know your audience, you could rearrange the text (more succinctly and more powerfully, too) using the bullet points shown in Figure 11.1.

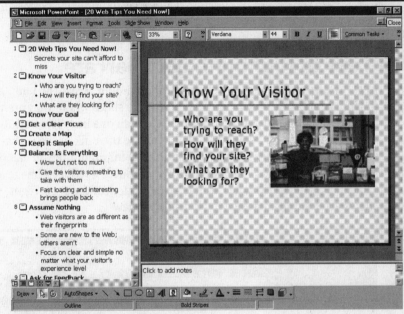

FIGURE 11.1: Using text sparingly but effectively

The Clearer, the Better

Whenever possible, be as specific as you can with the information you're presenting. Granted, being specific without being verbose is a difficult line to walk, but you should be as clear as possible about what's being shown. For example, although a slide titled "Projections vs. Actual Sales Results" sounds professional, your audience may better understand the content of the slide (and the charts on it) if the title is, "How Did We Do This Month?"

TIP

Tailor your presentation's tone to the audience you'll be speaking to. If conversational text won't fit their professional meeting, go with the flow and speak to them in a language they will understand.

Know Where You're Going

A presentation that wanders from topic to topic will seem disjointed and confusing to your audience. Make sure your text moves forward through a set series of topics—know where you want to go and then create the slides to get there. The sense of direction will help your audience better understand your presentation.

Use Text to Highlight, Not Narrate

Keep text to its essential, most powerful minimum: resist the temptation to write captions for your charts, add notes to slides where they aren't completely necessary, or use titles of more than one line. The narration of your presentation should be able to provide the bulk of the verbal communication. If you need to provide additional information, you can print handouts using Notes Pages view, which produces a reduced image of the slide plus any attached notes printed at the bottom of the page. Figure 11.2 shows an example of a page in Notes Pages view.

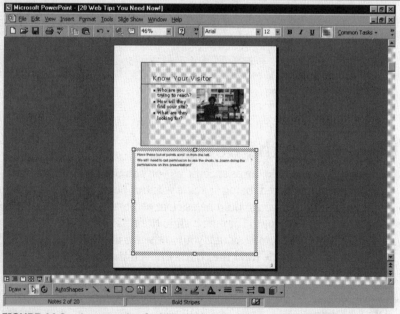

FIGURE 11.2: An example of additional text entered in Notes Pages view

Color and Contrast Are Important

Even though the color of the background and text may have been selected by the template you chose or the wizard you used, you may need to make changes based on where you'll be presenting and how large your audience is. Make sure that you've got enough color contrast for your text to show up on-screen. Before you give the presentation, test the color combinations on coworkers. Check to see whether or not they have any trouble reading the display under lighting that's similar to where you'll be presenting. Generally, light text on a darker background is easiest to see, but you may need to test different color combinations to see what works best for your particular circumstance. If you're in doubt about what to use, try white or yellow text on a dark background. This combination is very legible in most presentation situations.

Think about Your Audience

Before you begin composing the text, think about your audience. Who are they? Are they engineers, sales people, managers? Are they support personnel, students, or prospective employees? The "who" will help you determine the tone of your presentation. Remember to speak the language your audience will readily understand.

Timing Is Everything

Consider carefully the amount of time you'll need in order to discuss everything you need to discuss about a particular slide. You can either use Manual timing and advance the slides by clicking the mouse button when you're ready to move on, or use Automatic timing to have Power-Point advance the slides automatically after a preset period of time. Manual gives you more control, but Automatic helps you stay within a specified time frame.

Before You Add Text...

Assuming that you've selected your presentation's template and are ready to start entering text, take a minute to write down the key points of your presentation. This will help you create a basic game plan from which to work.

Experienced presenters and writers often prefer the question-and-answer approach to outlining ideas. In this method, you brainstorm about the basic questions your presentation should answer and then answer each one.

For example, if you are creating a presentation to promote a new service your company is offering, you might come up with these ideas:

▶ What is the name of our service?

▶ What does it offer?

▶ Whom does it appeal to?

▶ What benefits does it offer?

▶ How much does it cost?

▶ When does it start?

▶ How do I find out more?

Then, to flesh out the basic progression of the presentation, you'd answer each question in turn:

▶ AsDec On-Site Training

▶ Corporate, individual, and group training on the AsDec 400

▶ Corporations and small businesses who have recently purchased or upgraded to an AsDec 400

▶ Professional trainers; ongoing technical support; clear, useful manuals

▶ $1200 per three-day seminar, unlimited participants

▶ Seminars are scheduled on a bimonthly basis

▶ Call 1-800-55-ASDEC or write AsDec Industries, One Redfern Way, Sausalito, CA 94015

You can now build a presentation based on the answers you provided to your own questions. This gives you a basic plan for the presentation and makes sure that it moves logically from slide to slide.

ENTERING TEXT

In the previous chapter, you learned how to enter text quickly in the process of creating your first presentation. This section slows things down a bit and shows you the various ways you can enter and work with text in your presentation.

Once you've sketched out your ideas for the presentation, you're ready to get it on-screen. You can enter text in either Slide view or Outline view. The following sections explain how to do just that.

Adding Text in Slide View

When you first start PowerPoint and choose a page layout to begin a work session, the first slide of your presentation appears on the screen. The text entry sections are already blocked out on the screen. Whether you started your presentation by choosing a template or opting to start with a blank publication, prompts on your screen tell you where to enter text (see Figure 11.3).

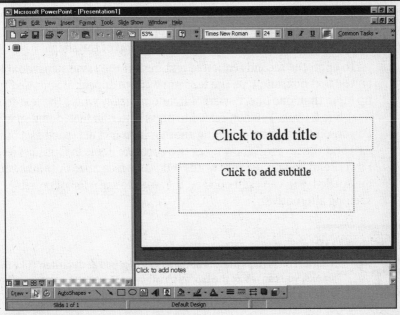

FIGURE 11.3: Text sections on a title page

TIP

Whether you've chosen to work with a template or start a file from scratch, PowerPoint applies certain default text settings to the words you type. You can change the text's typeface, size, style, and color at any time during your Power-Point work session. For more about changing the font and enhancing your text, see "Enhancing Text," later in this chapter.

TIP

What's a font? A *font* is a certain typeface in a particular size and style. For example, Times Roman 16-point italic is one font, and Times Roman 12-point bold is another.

To enter text, click on the text box you want to use. An entry box appears, as shown in Figure 11.4. Notice that your text cursor blinks in the center of the box. This happens because the alignment setting chosen by PowerPoint (another default) is centered. Type the title for the presentation in this top text box, assuming that you've displayed a Title page layout and haven't already entered the title in the AutoContent Wizard.

As you type, the letters appear in the text box. After you finish typing the title, click outside the text area. PowerPoint closes the text box and the text is displayed in the title area at the top of the slide.

To enter the second section of text, repeat the same steps: double-click on the text box, and type the text you want to appear. If your text takes up more than one line, PowerPoint automatically wraps the text to the next line for you. You don't need to press Enter; in fact, doing so will tell PowerPoint that you are adding another item in a list (such as a bulleted list) and the text will show up as two separate items in Outline view. Now PowerPoint will underscore words it doesn't recognize or thinks you have misspelled; you can right-click on the word to see a list of possible spelling alternatives.

TIP

If PowerPoint wraps the line automatically for you and you don't like the way it breaks, you can resize the box by positioning the mouse pointer on the corner and dragging the corner to reshape the box.

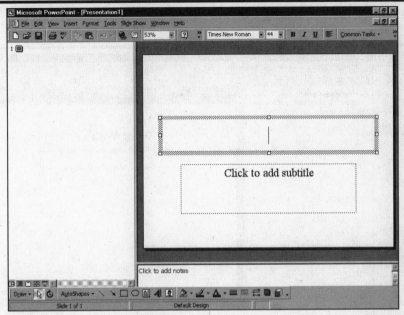

FIGURE 11.4: The text entry box

To add another item in the same text box, press Enter at the end of the first item and PowerPoint moves the cursor to the next line.

After you finish entering text, click outside the text box. Later, you can make any modifications you want by moving the text; changing the size of the text box; selecting a different font, size, or style; or even deleting the text at any time from Slide view.

Adding New Text Boxes

There will be times when you want to add more text than Slide view leaves room for. For example, suppose that on a particular slide, you want to add a line that shows the date the presentation was prepared.

Simply click the Text Box tool (it looks like a small document icon and lies in the center of the drawing tools row, just below the work area) and move the cursor to the point on the slide where you want to add the box. (If the Drawing toolbar is not displayed on your monitor, choose View ➤ Toolbars ➤ Drawing to display it.) Hold down the mouse button while dragging the mouse down and to the right, releasing it when the text box is the size you want. The data-entry area appears, as shown in Figure 11.5.

You can move the text box around just like the original text boxes—by dragging it.

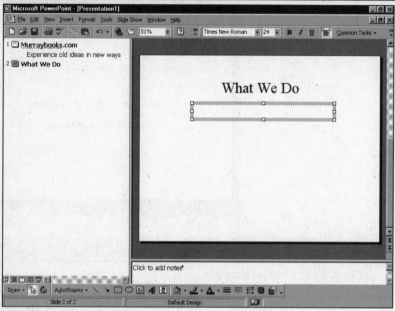

FIGURE 11.5:   Creating a new text box

Adding Text in Outline View

Outline view gives you another perspective from which to view your text. This view shows you only the text in your presentation, organized to show the indention levels, in standard outline format.

To display the presentation in Outline view, click the Outline View button in the lower-left corner of the screen or choose View ➤ Outline. You'll see any text you've entered in the presentation, as shown in Figure 11.6.

TIP

If you don't see the Outline toolbar along the left side of your work area, choose View ➤ Toolbars ➤ Outlining to display it.

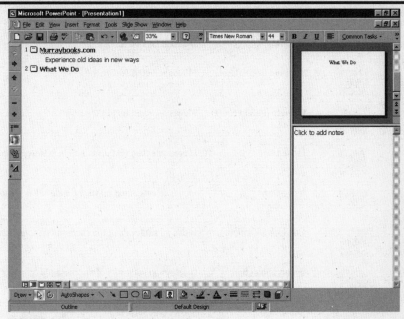

FIGURE 11.6:   Text displayed in Outline view

Outline Elements

The Outline screen looks quite a bit different from the Slide view screen. You see different tools along the left side of the window, and a different look in the work area itself. Table 11.1 explains each of the buttons in the Outline view toolbar.

NOTE

If your Outline toolbar does not appear automatically when you display Outline view, open the View menu, choose Toolbars, and click Outlining.

TABLE 11.1: Outline Buttons

BUTTON	NAME	DESCRIPTION
	Promote (Indent less)	Moves selected text to the left
	Demote (Indent more)	Moves selected text to the right
	Move Up	Moves selected text up one slide in the presentation
	Move Down	Moves selected text down one slide in the presentation
	Collapse Selection	Hides all sublevels of the currently selected slide
	Expand Selection	Displays all sublevels of the currently selected slide
	Show Titles	Shows only slide titles
	Show All	Displays all text in the presentation
	Summary Slide	Creates a summary slide based on the highlighted text
	Show Formatting	Works as a toggle to display text in the selected font and size; click again to disable formatting display and show text in uniform size and style

TIP

For more about working with the different tools in Outline view, see "Editing in Outline View," later in this chapter.

Adding, Indenting, and Outdenting Text on the Current Slide

To add text to the existing slide, use the arrow keys to move the cursor to the desired point. To begin a new line indented to the same point, simply press Enter, or press Tab to indent the line further. To "outdent" (that is, to move the insertion point to the left) the line, press Shift+Tab. Then type your text.

Creating a New Slide in the Outline View

To add a new slide, position the cursor in the slide where you want the new slide to follow. Then move the pointer to the New Slide button in the Standard toolbar and click the mouse button. Another number appears in the left column of the Outline view, indicating that you've started a new slide. The cursor is positioned so that you can add the title text for the slide (see Figure 11.7).

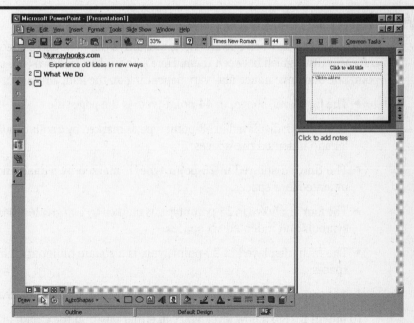

FIGURE 11.7: The added slide in Outline view

You can also add a new slide by pressing Enter after the preceding slide title or by "outdenting"; that is, press Shift+Tab to move the line of text out to the left margin as a new slide entry.

Inserting Text from Microsoft Word

If you've previously created an outline in Microsoft Word and want to use it directly in your PowerPoint presentation, you can use PowerPoint's drag-and-drop feature to use the text as is. Just minimize PowerPoint so that it appears only in the Taskbar; open the Windows Explorer, and locate the file containing the text you want to import.

Click on the file, and then, holding the mouse button down, drag the file to the PowerPoint tab in the Taskbar. After a moment, PowerPoint opens automatically, and you can drag the Word file's icon to the presentation. PowerPoint copies the information from the Word file directly into a new presentation file.

Working with Text Levels

Each of the text levels in PowerPoint is assigned a different text size so you can easily distinguish between them. Here's how it breaks down (the exact point size and appearance may vary depending on the template you use):

- ▶ The first level, shown in 44-point type, is the page title.
- ▶ The second, displayed in 32-point type, is marked by a square bullet and indented two spaces.
- ▶ The third, displayed in 28-point type, is marked by a dash and indented four spaces.
- ▶ The fourth, shown in 24-point type, is marked by two greater-than symbols and indented six spaces.
- ▶ The fifth, displayed in 20-point type, is a square bullet at eight spaces.
- ▶ The sixth, also displayed in 20-point type, is a dash at ten spaces.

To indent text to a new level, you can either position the cursor at the beginning of the text and press Tab, or click the Demote button (the right-pointing arrow in the text settings row).

Figure 11.8 shows the different levels of indention. Notice that all the text in the Outline pane is the same size, but the text as it appears in the Slide view pane reduces in size with each level.

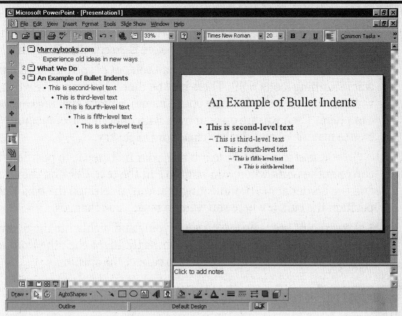

FIGURE 11.8: Outline view showing text indents

EDITING TEXT

Now that you've got some text to work with, you may be tempted to move things around a bit. Perhaps the text on page 3 would work better on page 5. What if you want to change the indent levels of text you've already entered or move a paragraph from one side of a slide to another?

This section explores the various aspects of editing your text. Editing includes many things: changing individual letters, replacing words, moving sentences or fragments, resizing text blocks, and running the spelling checker. We'll talk about enhancing text in the next section, but here, you'll make sure that the text is as accurate as possible.

Any program that lets you work with text must offer two different kinds of editing tasks: keystroke editing, in which you can correct a misspelling or a bad line break by typing a keystroke or two; and block editing, in which you mark a section of text as a block and move it, delete it, copy it, or paste it.

Simple Text Editing

Some typos don't even look like typos. How many times have you wondered how to spell the word "friend"? Is it I before E except after C, or what?

Luckily, the spelling checker can bail you out of spelling dead ends where nothing looks right. There may be times, however (like when you're trying to spell your new boss's name), when a spelling checker can't help. Then you are on your own, with only your own memory (or reference materials) and the backspace or Delete key.

To edit text in a specific text block, your first step is to position the cursor at the point where you want to edit the text. Click on the text box and the border appears, indicating that you've selected the box. Now position the cursor where you want to make your changes.

PowerPoint keeps an eye on your typing and highlights the text when it thinks you have entered a word incorrectly. Right-click the word to see suggestions for ways you may want to correct the spelling.

TIP

If you're having trouble seeing what you're doing, use the Zoom controls in the toolbar at the top of the screen to enlarge the display. Click the down-arrow beside 50% and choose from a larger percentage (100% is usually plenty). When you're finished with your up-close work, return to Normal view.

When you're finished making the text changes, click outside the box.

Selecting Text for Editing

Some editing procedures require that you mark the text you want to edit as a block. A text block can be as small as a single character or as large as the entire presentation—PowerPoint recognizes whatever you highlight as the current block. For example, before you can copy text, you need to tell PowerPoint what block of text you want to work with. To do this, you position the cursor and then highlight the block.

TIP

If you want to highlight all the text in your presentation, make sure the cursor is inside the outline and click Edit ➢ Select All. You might want to do this, for example, to make a global change such as changing the font, style, or color of all text in your presentation.

Click the mouse button when the pointer is placed at the beginning of the text you want to mark, then press the mouse button and drag the mouse over the section you want to highlight. If you're using the keyboard to highlight the text you want, move the cursor to the beginning of the text, and then press on the right-arrow key while holding down the Shift key.

TIP

If you've marked a block and want to remove the highlight (deselect it) press Esc or move the pointer outside the text area and click the mouse button.

Cutting and Pasting Text

PowerPoint includes all the basic editing procedures you'll find in other programs—and they are in the same place, too (the Edit menu). The Copy, Cut, and Paste commands all enable you to work with blocks of text in your presentation. These commands use a special new Office Clipboard as a temporary storage place for the information you're working with. This Clipboard holds up to 12 scraps and can be accessed from most Office applications, such as Word and PowerPoint (but not Outlook). To view the Clipboard, choose View ➤ Toolbars ➤ Clipboard. For example, if you're copying a block of text, PowerPoint puts the copy on the Clipboard. Then, when you paste the text somewhere else, Power-Point copies the text from the Clipboard to the cursor position.

TIP

PowerPoint gives you two different kinds of Paste commands: the regular Paste puts whatever is stored on the Clipboard at the cursor location, and Paste Special preserves the formatting style for the Clipboard contents you insert.

Drag-and-Drop Text

If you're working in Outline view, you can drag and drop text to move it from one place to another. This procedure allows you to bypass Copy and Paste from the Edit menu. Just highlight the text you want to move, position the pointer on the text, and drag the text to the new location. A bar cursor shows you where the text will be positioned as you drag the mouse. When the bar cursor is placed at the point you want the text to be inserted, release the mouse button.

Part iii

Undoing Editing Changes

For those times when you press a key and think, "I really wish I hadn't done that," PowerPoint includes the Undo feature. You can customize Undo to reverse up to 150 (!) of your most recent operations; the default is 20. To change the number of operations Undo will reverse, select Tools ➤ Options, and then select the Edit tab. Change the setting in Maximum number of undos by clicking the up-arrow or down-arrow to increase or decrease the number.

Using the Spelling Checker to Catch Spelling Errors

Consider how many times you will have read the text of your presentation by the time you finish it, and you can see how easy it is to become blind to errors. By then, you've read the text so many times that typos begin to look right.

PowerPoint reads through the presentation for you to ensure that all your words are spelled correctly. The spelling checker will check every word in your presentation, including additional material such as speaker notes and chart labels.

PowerPoint's spelling checker looks for three different kinds of possible errors:

- ▶ Any word not recognized in PowerPoint's dictionary
- ▶ Any word that includes numbers
- ▶ Any word that includes strange capitalization

Start the Spelling Checker one of three ways:

- ▶ Choose Tools ➤ Spelling.
- ▶ Press F7.
- ▶ Click the Spelling tool (sixth from the left, showing the letters ABC and a small checkmark) in the toolbar.

When PowerPoint finds a word that's not in the dictionary, it displays a screen giving you a number of options. You can skip the word, correct it, add it to a personal dictionary, or choose a different word from a list of alternatives.

Using AutoCorrect

PowerPoint includes a feature shared with other Microsoft products: AutoCorrect. If you are like most people, there are certain words you always misspell. You can "teach" AutoCorrect to watch for those words and correct them dynamically when you type them. Additionally, you can use AutoCorrect as a kind of shorthand interpreter—if you must type a long word or phrase repeatedly, you can teach AutoCorrect to find the phrase you type and substitute the long phrase for you. For example, you could type the letters *ref* and have AutoCorrect automatically substitute *Biographical Reference of American Sports Heroes*. AutoCorrect is available in the Tools menu.

Five options—Correct TWo INitial CApitals, Capitalize the first letter of a sentence, Capitalize names of days, Correct accidental use of the caps LOCK key, and Replace text as you type—are selected by default. You can disable each of those options by clicking the appropriate checkbox.

Enter the words you want to substitute in the Replace and With text boxes. Before doing so, use the down-arrow to scroll through the word list in the bottom of the dialog box to make sure the word isn't already entered.

Using the Style Checker to Catch Style Inconsistencies and Problems

In PowerPoint 2000, the Style Checker is integrated in the program. This automated utility goes through your presentation and checks its consistency, visual clarity, and style, taking the guesswork out of whether your presentation is ready to be presented. When it finds something it doesn't like, PowerPoint underlines the phrase with a green wavy line. You can then right-click the underlined phrase and choose the option you want to use to correct it. PowerPoint will make suggestions on how you can improve the section of the text stylistically.

You control the Style Checker options by clicking Tools ➤ Options. Click the Spelling and Style tab (see Figure 11.9).

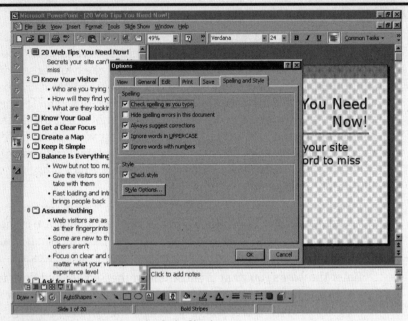

FIGURE 11.9: Turning on the Style Checker

If you want to turn off the Style Checker, click the checkbox to the right of the Check style option to remove the X.

Click the Style Options button. The Style Options dialog box appears, with the Case and End Punctuation tab showing (see Figure 11.10).

Case and End Punctuation enables you to choose the punctuation method of your text. You may want to add or remove periods for your text items or watch for incorrect punctuation characters that may inadvertently slip into your text. Make your selections and then click the Visual Clarity tab (see Figure 11.11).

Visual Clarity refers to the way your text looks on the slide. The options in the Visual Clarity tab provide you with a number of choices regarding the number and sizes of different fonts; in addition, you can double-check the legibility of your text by making sure that you don't have too many bullets or lines on a slide.

When you're finished reviewing the options, click OK to close the tab and then the dialog box.

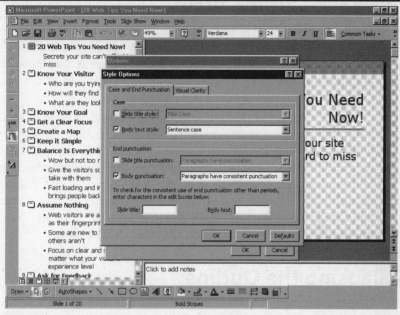

FIGURE 11.10:   Setting up Case and End Punctuation in the Style Options dialog box

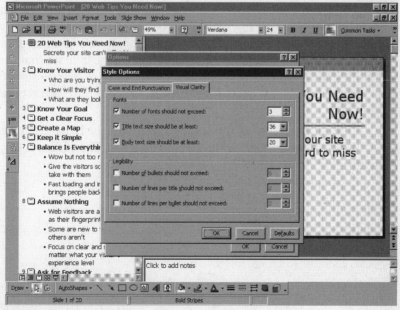

FIGURE 11.11:   Making sure your presentation is visually clear

Editing in Outline View

Up to this point, most of the editing tasks we've been talking about apply to both the Slide view and Outline view. You can do simple editing—like using the backspace or delete keys to make minor modifications—in Outline view; you can mark a text block and cut, copy, paste, or clear it, just as you can in Normal view.

You learned earlier that instead of using Cut and Paste to move a text block, you can use the drag-and-drop feature in the Outline view to move highlighted text from one point to another. But there are additional editing features available to you in Outline view that you *can't* accomplish in Slide view. In fact, an entirely new set of tools appears along the left edge of the outline, enabling you to collapse and expand outlines, check titles, and take a look at formatting changes. Earlier in this chapter, Table 11.1 provided a basic description of the different Outline tools.

Collapsing the Outline

PowerPoint gives you a way to determine easily whether your headings are parallel and your outline is balanced. The trick is known as collapsing the outline, and it turns the outline shown in Figure 11.12 into a simple list of headings.

To fully collapse the outline, click the Show Titles button (fourth from the bottom) from the row of Outline tools. All sublevels of information disappear. PowerPoint shows you which slides have additional information, however, by including a gray underline on those slides that contain hidden sublevels. Now you can compare the titles of your presentation to see whether they are parallel and present topics in the clearest possible manner.

To display all levels of the outline again, click the Expand All button (third from the bottom) in the Outline tools row. The outline is displayed with all sublevels intact.

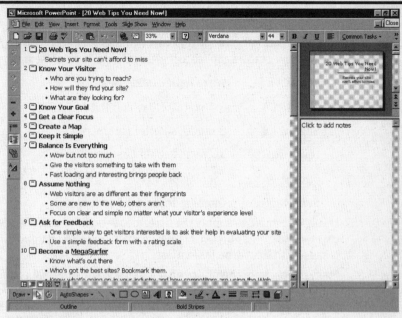

FIGURE 11.12: The outline before it is collapsed

CREATING A BALANCED OUTLINE

A significant part of creating a good presentation lies in making sure your concepts are organized in an orderly way. In fact, as an English teacher or two along the way has probably told you, there's a very definite process to creating a solid outline. PowerPoint won't make you stick to any particular rules when you're creating your outline, but you can make a good presentation better by making sure your outline works.

In a balanced outline, every A has a B, every 1 has a 2, etc.—there are at least two of everything. Here's an example of a balanced

CONTINUED ➡

Part iii

outline (on the left, you see the basic outline structure; on the right, you see how it can be applied to the AsDec 400 sample presentation):

Level One	We're AsDec Industries
Sublevel A	AsDec Yesterday and Today
Sublevel B	Building a Better Future
Level Two	We're a "People Company," offering
Sublevel A	Training Services
Sublevel B	Ongoing Technical Support

Levels One and Two supply the basic ideas—in this case, the slide titles—and the sublevels underneath supply the supporting ideas—in this case, bullet entries.

Many people find it helpful to go through and write the main points of their outlines first, before adding detail in the sublevels. As you become more experienced at writing and revising your own outlines, you'll learn what works best for you.

Collapsing and Expanding a Slide

In some cases, you may want to collapse only a single slide, rather than the entire outline. You can do this by positioning the cursor in the slide you want to collapse and clicking the Collapse Selection button (it resembles a minus sign). Only the collapsed slide's title will be displayed.

To expand a single slide, position the cursor in the title of the slide you want to expand and click the Expand Selection button (it looks like a plus sign).

Moving Text Items in Outline View

One additional feature available in Outline view that you won't find in Slide view is the ability to move a single line of text up or down through the presentation. Suppose, for example, that you want to move the fifth bullet item up to the third position. You would position the cursor on the line you want to move and then click the up-arrow (Move Up) button. The line exchanges places with the one above it. Click the Move Up button again, and the line is in the third position.

Similarly, you can move a line of text downward through the presentation by using the Move Down button. And you aren't limited to staying within the same slide; you can move text from slide to slide as necessary.

Creating a Summary Slide in Outline View

PowerPoint gives you the option of adding a summary slide—a slide that includes key points, slide titles, or important phrases—and enables you to show your audience at a glance what you plan to cover in your presentation.

You can create a summary slide from either Outline or Slide Sorter view by clicking the Summary Slide button. First highlight (in Outline view) or select (in Slide Sorter view) the slides you want to include on the summary slide (see Figure 11.13). Then click the Summary Slide button. The summary slide is then created for you (see Figure 11.14).

How will you use a summary slide? You might create a table of contents with hyperlinks that will take your audience—or individual users, if you're creating a self-directed presentation—to the slide covering the topic they select.

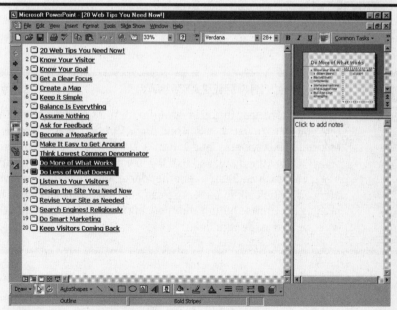

FIGURE 11.13:   Highlight the slides you want to summarize and click the Summary Slide button to create a summary slide.

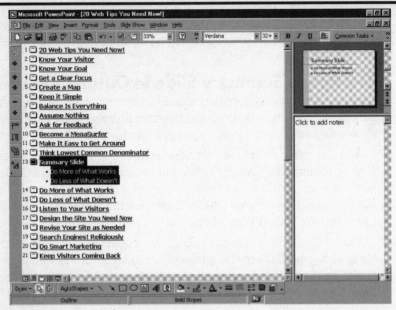

FIGURE 11.14:   The summary slide is created automatically from the text you select.

HYPERLINKING THE EASY WAY

Hyperlinks are easy to add in PowerPoint. You simply highlight the text you want to use as a link and press Ctrl+K. The Insert Hyperlink dialog box appears, and you enter the URL for the Web page or select it from the displayed list. If you want to link to an existing page, an e-mail address, or another document, click the appropriate icon in the Link To pane. You can also link to a specific file by clicking the Browse button and choosing the file you want. Click OK when you've made your link.

Editing in Slide Sorter View

Slide Sorter view, shown in Figure 11.15, doesn't look like a good place to edit text. After all, you can't see the text very well.

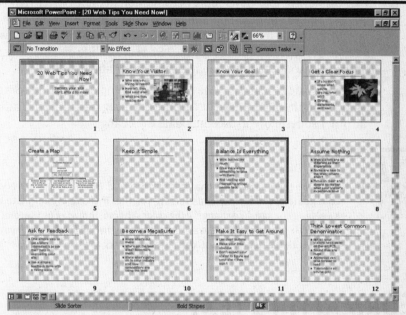

FIGURE 11.15: Displaying Slide Sorter view

But there is one major editing task you can perform in Slide Sorter view—a task that has a great deal to do with how your presentation will be received. While all your slides are displayed on one screen, you can visually scan through them and determine how the overall presentation is shaping up.

TIP

Don't remember how to get to Slide Sorter view? Go to the row of View buttons at the bottom of the screen (the row with five small icons) and click on the fourth button from the left, or choose View ➢ Slide Sorter.

Earlier you learned that the overall structure and clarity of your outline is important—you need balance and parallelism to help viewers know where you're going. Similarly, you need to make sure that the sequence of your slides makes sense.

By displaying your developing presentation in Slide Sorter view, you can keep an eye on the overall progression of your slides. Do they move logically from one to another? Are you missing a step? Should you vary the style of the slides you're creating? Slide after slide of bulleted text may present your idea, but it may also put your audience to sleep.

If you decide to rearrange the slides, it's a simple job in Slide Sorter. Just click on the slide you want to move and drag it to its new location. The other slides move to accommodate the change.

TIP

Remember to save your changes. After—and often before—every major change, take the few seconds to save the file. If you're preparing to make a sweeping change, like changing the color scheme, throwing out several slides, or selecting a set of off-the-wall fonts, back up the file first. Then, if you aren't happy with the new look, you can always go back to the original.

FORMATTING TEXT

What a presentation says—in words—is only part of its impact. How a presentation *looks* makes as loud a statement as the text itself. The way your text is positioned on a slide contributes to whether or not a viewer actually reads it. If the text is too small, in a font that's hard to read, or scrunched against other text, your audience may simply give up.

Once you get the text into your presentation, you may want to rearrange it and try it in different formats to see what's most effective. The way you go about making format changes depends on how far-reaching you want the changes to be. You can do simple changes yourself, like changing indents, moving tabs, and modifying line spacing. Or you can go all the way back to square one by letting PowerPoint apply a design template for you. This section describes the different ways in which you can change the format of your presentation:

▶ Applying a new design template to the entire presentation

▶ Choosing a new page layout for the current slide

▶ Using the ruler, tabs, indents, and alignment options to change the way elements are positioned on the slide

Applying a New Design

The simplest and quickest way to change the look of your presentation uses the Apply Design Template command in the Format menu.

When you choose this command, the Apply Design Template dialog box appears. Choose one of the different templates (these are the same templates displayed in the New Presentation dialog box when you first choose a presentation design) and then click Apply. The new design is automatically applied to all slides in your presentation.

Changing Format with a New Layout

One of the easiest ways to change the format is to select a different layout for the current slide. Suppose you're working on a standard bullet slide in Current Slide view. You can choose a different layout—but keep the same text—by clicking the Slide Layout button in the Common Tasks list in the Standard toolbar. That opens the Slide Layout dialog box, shown in Figure 11.16.

Click on the picture of the layout you want. Depending on the style you choose, you may have some additional work to do, however. For example, the new layout you choose may require that you add a chart or a table. When you click Reapply, the new layout is applied to the current slide.

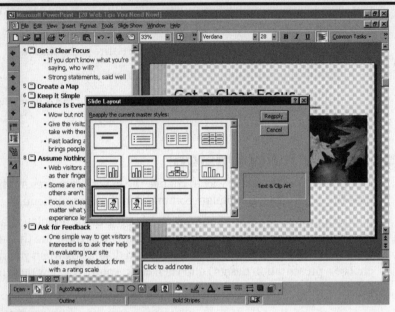

FIGURE 11.16: The Slide Layout box

TIP

If you changed the layout and don't like it, choose Edit ➤ Undo. Your old layout reappears, good as new.

Displaying the Ruler

Many hands-on formatting issues—such as setting indents and tabs—involve using the ruler. If your ruler is not already displayed, choose View ➤ Ruler to show the rulers along the top and left sides of the PowerPoint work area. Two rulers appear; one along the top of the slide area and one along the left edge (see Figure 11.17).

Notice that, unlike a typical ruler, the PowerPoint rulers show 0 (zero) as their center point. This enables you to measure from the vertical and horizontal center of the slide, which helps you position elements accurately.

When the ruler is displayed and you highlight text or click in a text box, the ruler changes (see Figure 11.18). Now the ruler reflects the width and height of the selected text box; the ruler is no longer vertically and horizontally centered to 0. Additionally, the white area narrows to show only the width and depth of the current text box.

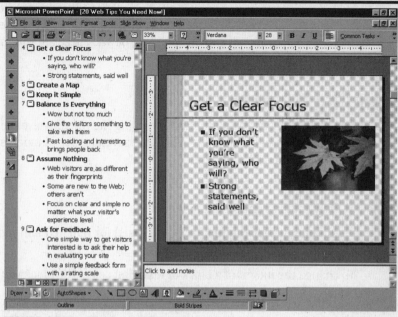

FIGURE 11.17: The PowerPoint rulers

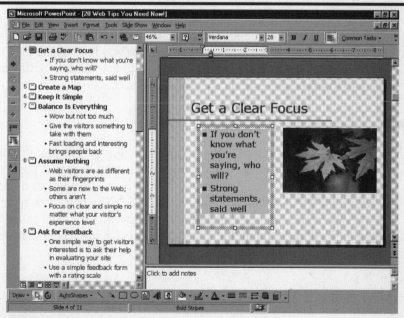

FIGURE 11.18: When you click in a text box, the ruler changes to show text box position

In the small square in the upper-left corner of the PowerPoint work area, you see a tab symbol. To the left of the horizontal ruler, you see two markers—one pointing up and one pointing down. These are your indent markers.

Changing Indents

One of the first tasks you might perform using the ruler involves changing the indention of specific text. There are several types of indents you could apply to presentation text:

- ▶ All lines of text indented evenly

- ▶ Only the first line of text indented

- ▶ All lines except the first indented (used for bulleted and numbered lists)

To change the indent of a block of text, first select the block you want to change, then move the pointer to the indent marker you want to move. The top marker on the ruler controls the first-line indent; the bottom marker controls the indent of subsequent lines. Drag the marker to the new position on the ruler.

To move both markers but maintain their relative distance from each other (for example, suppose that you've created a hanging indent for a bullet and want to move all the text—just the way it is—to the right), click on the small rectangle beneath the bottom indent marker. Both markers move together, preserving the space between them.

Working with Tabs

The primary function of a tab is to help you align text in your documents as painlessly as possible. The tab is a small marker that tells the text, "Stop here." PowerPoint gives you the option of choosing four different tab stops: left, right, center, and decimal tabs. (The first three types are pretty common; a decimal tab lines up the numeric values you enter according to the decimal point. It enables you to easily format columns of numbers in your presentations.)

Setting Tabs

You'll need the ruler and a selected text box to add tabs. After that, the steps are simple:

1. Choose the type of tab you want by clicking in the tab selection box at the left of the horizontal ruler until the tab type appears. Table 11.2 shows how the different tab icons appear.

2. Move the pointer to the ruler bar and click on the point at which you want to add the tab.

TABLE 11.2: PowerPoint Tab Types

BUTTON	TAB TYPE	DESCRIPTION
	Left tab	Left-aligns text at the tab
	Right tab	Right-aligns text at the tab
	Center tab	Centers text at the tab
	Decimal tab	Aligns text on decimal point

Part iii

Moving and Deleting Tabs

You can easily move or remove tabs you no longer need. First, you can simply slide them to a new location. Just move the pointer to the tab you want to move, press and hold the mouse button, and drag the tab to a new location.

Not good enough? Delete the tab by dragging it off the right end of the ruler. The tab just disappears, with no additional fanfare. Please note that Undo won't restore the tab.

Aligning Text

Another big part of formatting includes the position of the text on the slide. Depending on what other elements you include on the slide—such as a chart or other art items, or a table—you may want to experiment with different alignments. With PowerPoint, you can align your text in the following ways:

- ▶ Left aligned: the text is aligned with the left margin and is ragged along the right.

- ▶ Right aligned: the text is aligned with the right margin and is ragged along the left.

- ▶ Centered: the text is centered and ragged along both margins.

- ▶ Justified: the text is aligned with both the left and right margins.

How do you know which alignment to use? Table 11.3 provides ideas of when you might use the different alignment options.

TABLE 11.3: Alignment Ideas

ALIGNMENT	USE FOR
Left	Bullet text
	Single paragraphs
	Chart legends
	Paragraph-style bullets
Right	Figure captions
	Data labels
	Special text effects
	Aligning against a chart or graphic item
Center	Titles
	Subtitles
	Chart titles
Justified	Two-column bullet slides
	Text along a chart or graphic item
	Text notes on a chart

If you are choosing either left, right, or centered alignment, you can do so by simply clicking in the text box you want to change and then clicking the appropriate button in the toolbar (see Figure 11.19). The text automatically changes to reflect your selection.

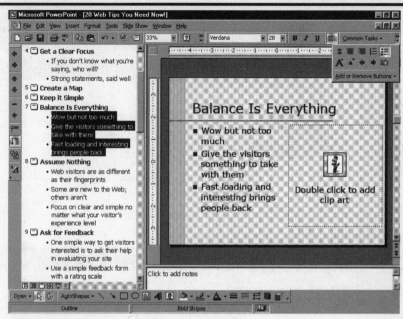

FIGURE 11.19: Choosing a different alignment

You can also change the alignment of text by opening the Format menu and choosing Alignment. A small pop-up box of different alignment choices appears.

Working with Line and Paragraph Spacing

PowerPoint takes care of the spacing of your text automatically. Type the text, and PowerPoint puts it where it needs to go. Sometimes, however, you may want to change the spacing PowerPoint has set for you. You might want to fit one more line of text on a slide, for example, or add space between lines.

You can modify the spacing between lines in your text box by choosing Format ➤ Line Spacing. The dialog box shown in Figure 11.20 appears.

In the Line Spacing area, you can choose the number of lines you want separating text lines. You can select either Lines or Points as the spacing measurement. To change the value, click either the up-arrow or down-arrow to increase or decrease the number.

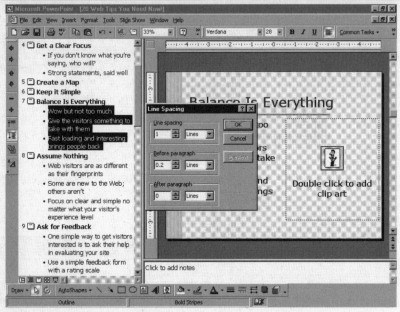

FIGURE 11.20: Choosing the Line Spacing for your presentation

TIP

A *point* is a standard typographical measurement, used in publishing and presentation projects. 72 points roughly equal one inch. This means that if you set your title to 72-point Helvetica font, the letters will be one inch tall.

You can change the spacing increment point by point or in .01 line increments. This gives you precise control over the way your lines are spaced. Use the Preview button to see how the change will look before you click OK to accept it.

Selecting Paragraph Spacing

Also in the Line Spacing dialog box are the Before Paragraph and After Paragraph settings, which, respectively, control the amount of space before and after the current paragraph.

The only trick to using the Before and After Paragraph settings is that you must highlight the text you want to work with before you choose the Line Spacing command to display the dialog box, so PowerPoint knows which text to adjust. If you're not sure how your changes will affect the text, use the Preview button to get a glimpse before you return to the slide.

Enhancing Text

Now that you know how to enter, edit, and format the text in your presentation, you need to know how to change its font, size, style, and color. PowerPoint also makes it easy for you to add your own unique bullets to the presentation. This section introduces each of these text enhancements.

Changing Text Font and Size

Unless you have time to study typography and graphic design, you're going to rely on your own instincts when it comes to choosing fonts for your presentation slides. In most cases, you won't have to do much choosing: PowerPoint chooses the typefaces, text styles, colors, and sizes for you when you use a Presentation or Presentation Design as the basis for your file.

The text font you choose for your presentation is an important choice. The text should reflect whatever tone you are projecting. Is it a serious presentation? Stick with conventional-looking text. Is it a brainstorming session? Go for a font that gives you a little more creative freedom.

TIP

When you're working with fonts, fight the temptation to overdo it—remember that *legibility* is your first goal.

To change the font, first select the text you want to change and then either:

- ▶ Click the down-arrow beside the font box in the text settings row (see Figure 11.21).

- ▶ Choose Format ➢ Font. The Font dialog box appears, as shown in Figure 11.22.

To choose a new font, select your font choice in the drop-down list. The text you selected appears in the new font.

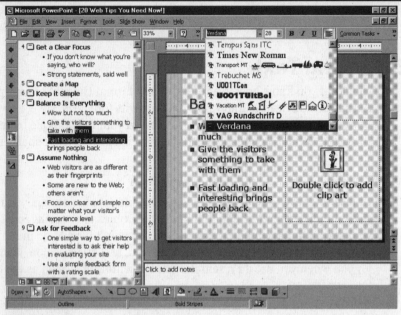

FIGURE 11.21: Displaying font options

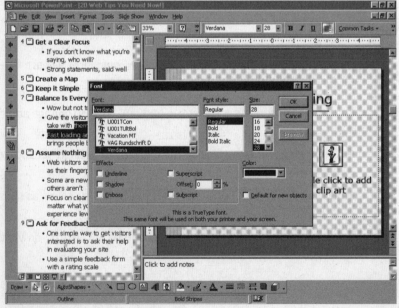

FIGURE 11.22: The Font dialog box

TIP

If you use one font in your presentation and then find something you like better, you can search for and replace the first font with another. Use the Replace Fonts command in the Format menu. Enter the name of the font to replace and the name of the font to replace it with. When you click OK, PowerPoint makes the change.

Changing the size of text is also a simple process. First highlight the text you want to change, then do one of the following:

- ▶ Click the down-arrow to the right of the Size button in the Formatting toolbar (see Figure 11.23).

- ▶ Click the Decrease Font Size or Increase Font Size button on the of the Formatting toolbar.

- ▶ Open the Format menu and choose Font; then select the size from the appropriate box.

Of these options, the easiest is to highlight the text and click the down-arrow beside the Size box in the Formatting toolbar.

TIP

Some fonts work better in larger sizes. For example, some of the specialty fonts, such as Mistral and Gradl, are barely readable until you enlarge them. Experiment with font sizes until you get what you want. And remember to consider the slide from your audience's perspective: will everyone be able to read the words from several feet away?

Setting the Style

The style of text allows you to call attention to individual words or phrases. For example, you might want to boldface a new product name or italicize the name of a report you're quoting. PowerPoint offers Regular, Bold, Italic, and Bold Italic text styles. After you highlight the text you want to change, you can choose a new style by clicking one or more of the buttons on the Formatting toolbar (see Figure 11.24). If you prefer, you can choose the style by selecting Fonts from the Format menu and clicking the style you want in the Font dialog box.

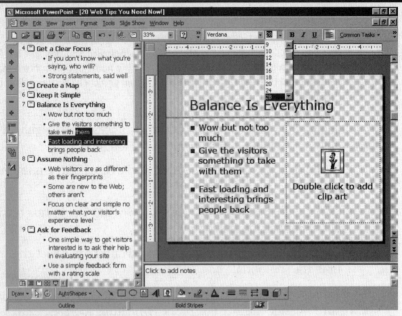

FIGURE 11.23: Selecting a new text size

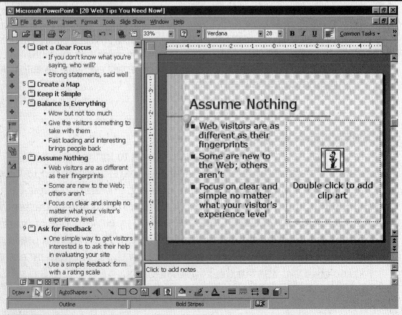

FIGURE 11.24: The style and effect buttons in the Formatting toolbar

To select more than one item in the text settings row, just click the buttons you want. For example, if you want to make a word bold and italic, just highlight the word, click the Bold button and then click the Italic button.

Selecting Text Effects

Text effects are slightly different than text styles. Styles affect the text's appearance: regular, bold, or italic. Effects, on the other hand, include underlining, shadowing, embossing, superscript, and subscript.

You can select these effects in the Font dialog box, available by choosing Format ➤ Font. You can also choose two of the five effects (Underline and Shadow) from the toolbar.

Changing Text Color

If you started your presentation using the Design Template, Presentation, or AutoContent Wizard, the colors of your background and text are already selected for you. The product designers at Microsoft put together effective color palettes that you can use as is or modify to suit your tastes.

To change the color of text on a particular slide, highlight the text, then click the Font Color button in the Drawing tools row at the bottom of the screen. (You can also use the Format/Font dialog box to set the color.) When you click the arrow beside the tool button, a small color pop-up box appears, as shown in Figure 11.25.

Click More Font Colors to see a larger palette of choices.

TIP

To change the text color for all similar slides in your presentation, change the slide's master, rather than the individual slides. For example, to change the color of all bullet text, choose View ➤ Master ➤ Slide Master to highlight the appropriate text level, and choose a different color.

PowerPoint shares a common palette with other Office applications. When you choose a color of blue in Word, you can be sure it's the same color blue when you copy the text to PowerPoint. This helps you create a consistent look among all your business applications.

Part iii

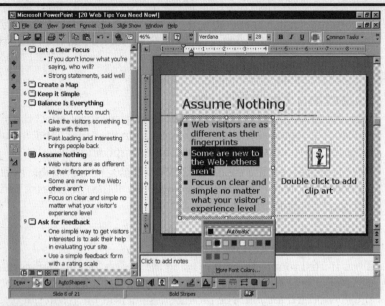

FIGURE 11.25: The color pop-up box

Using Bullets

Even a small change like the type of bullet you use can change the look of your presentation. PowerPoint gives you an incredible choice of bullets to use in your presentation.

PowerPoint 2000 knows you want to use customized images as bullets in your presentations. (You do, don't you? Oh come on—it's the latest thing.) Now you can use any graphical image as a bullet.

Before you start the process of selecting a different bullet character, highlight the bullet lines you want to change. If you want to change only one line, position the cursor in that line. Choose Format ➤ Bullets and Numbering, and the Bullets and Numbering dialog box appears, as shown in Figure 11.26.

To select a different bullet, click the Character button. You can select a different set of bullets by clicking the Bullets From down-arrow and choosing the font you want to work with. To choose a different bullet type, make sure the Use a Bullet checkbox is checked; then select the color, size, and the individual bullet character you want. When you click the bullet, the bullet enlarges so you can get a better look at it (see Figure 11.27).

When you click OK, PowerPoint applies the bullet to all highlighted bullet points.

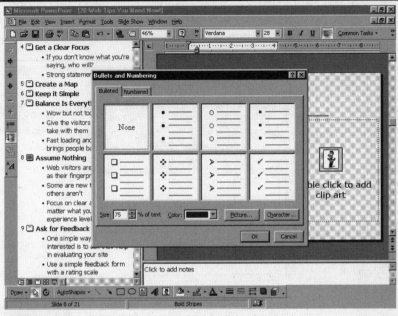

FIGURE 11.26: The Bullets and Numbering dialog box

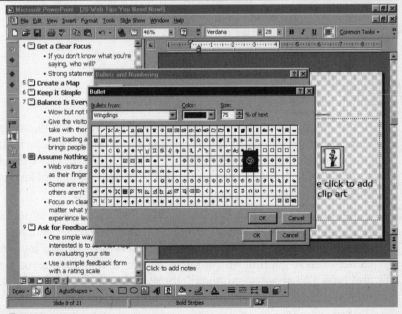

FIGURE 11.27: Getting a closer look at a bullet

If you want to use a picture as a bullet, click the Picture button. The Picture Bullet dialog box appears, as Figure 11.28 shows. Navigate to the bullet picture you want to use, click it, and click OK to add the bullet.

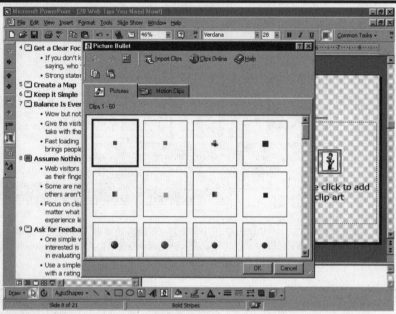

FIGURE 11.28:   Using a picture as a bullet

What's Next

In this chapter, you learned how to enter, edit, format, and enhance the text in your presentation. You now know how to plan the basic text in your presentation, create an outline, use the spelling and style checkers, work with the AutoCorrect feature, and perform a number of formatting and text-enhancement operations.

For the best results, take a few minutes and review your presentation after you've entered the basic text. Try printing the presentation in Outline view so you can show it to a few coworkers and get their input on the content you've got thus far. Making sure your text is the way you want it gives you a good basis for building the rest of your PowerPoint presentation. We'll start with the next step—creating and enhancing graphs—in the next chapter.

Chapter 12

CREATING AND ENHANCING GRAPHS

The text of your presentation is important, but it doesn't provide much in the way of visual instruction. You couldn't look at a printed page and know at a glance, for example, that sales in a particular area have increased dramatically or that your department has almost reached its productivity goal. A chart, or *graph,* can call attention to that information immediately, letting you skip over the read-and-figure-it-out stage and see immediately what point the presenter is trying to make.

Adapted from *Mastering PowerPoint 2000*
by Katherine Murray
ISBN 0-7821- 2356-2   400 pages $29.99

A Few Graph Ideas

How do you know what will work as a graph? Here are a few possibilities:

Comparisons   Graphs can help you illustrate relationships between data. For example, you can illustrate how the price reduction of an item increases or decreases sales, or show the hierarchy in your organization.

Processes   If you have several slides full of bullets, think about whether one could be converted into a graph. The change will break up the monotony of bullet lists and convey information in a new and interesting form.

Trends   When you need to show data trends, graphs can help you compare the progress of two data sets, whether those items are sales regions, products, or salaries.

TIP

Certain types of graphs are better than others for showing certain kinds of information. For example, if you want to compare two or more items, you can use bar charts, bar-line charts, and area charts to help readers visually identify the differences between the contrasted data series.

Is This PowerPoint or Microsoft Graph?

The graph capability of PowerPoint is not PowerPoint's own—it is actually Microsoft Graph 2000, an embedded graph utility you can use to create graph objects in your presentation. You won't notice any difference when you move between PowerPoint and Microsoft Graph—you'll simply use the Graph datasheet to enter the data for the graph and then use various Graph options to choose the graph type, set options, change the format, and enhance the graphs you create.

Using Excel Graphs in Your PowerPoint Presentations

If you, as an Office aficionado, have already created Excel graphs, you may not need to worry about creating any PowerPoint ones. Instead, you'll paste the Excel charts directly onto the slide. Microsoft Graph is also used to create Excel's charts, although Excel actually leads you through the process of creating the chart by using the ChartWizard.

NOTE
Excel's ChartWizard is much like PowerPoint's AutoContent Wizard, in that it leads you through the process of creating the item by asking you a series of questions.

To use an existing Excel graph in your PowerPoint presentation, you have several choices. You can:

▶ Copy the graph from Excel to PowerPoint.

▶ Use Edit ➤ Paste Special to paste the graph on the slide while maintaining the link to Excel.

▶ Tile both the Excel and PowerPoint windows side-by-side and drag-and-drop the graph from Excel to PowerPoint.

The process of linking an object—a graph is considered an object—enables you to make sure the object is updated whenever the original file changes. This means that whenever you change the data in your Excel spreadsheet, the changes will automatically be reflected in your PowerPoint file.

AN OVERVIEW OF GRAPH TYPES

When you're creating two-dimensional or three-dimensional graphs from scratch with PowerPoint, you've got a number of different graph types to choose from, including these:

▶ *Area graphs* show one or more data trends over time.

▶ *Bar graphs* show how data series "stack up" against each other.

▶ *Column graphs* are similar to a bar graph, except that the bars are stacked on top of each other instead of side-by-side.

▶ *Doughnut graphs* plot more than one data series as parts of a whole.

- *Line graphs* compare data series over time.

- *Pie graphs* show how individual data items relate to the whole.

- *Radar graphs* compare data series.

- *XY (scatter) graphs* plot data points according to x and y axes.

- *Surface graphs* show data trends in a two-dimensional view.

- *Bubble charts* compare three sets of data.

- *Stock charts* are actually high-low-close charts, which show three numeric values along each bar.

- *2-D and 3-D charts* offer cylinder, pyramid, and cone shapes.

Each type of graph includes a number of subtypes. In addition, each of these graph types is available in 3-D (which means that the Line graph category becomes 3-D Line graph).

Once you choose a basic chart type, you select individual options to create the kind of graph you want. You might start with a bar chart, for example, and then select options that enable you to create a *stacked* bar chart—with data ranges stacked one on top of another.

CREATING A GRAPH

First, you need a slide with a graph area. If your current slide doesn't have a graph area blocked out, click the New Slide button to display the New Slide dialog box (see Figure 12.1) and choose a slide with a graph area built in. When you've selected the file you want (click in the scroll bar to see more choices), click OK. The new slide appears on the screen with the graph area blocked out (see Figure 12.2).

Starting the Graph

When you double-click the graph area, PowerPoint churns away for a moment before displaying first a graph and then a datasheet. The datasheet already includes data, put there to provide an example of how PowerPoint's graphing capability works (see Figure 12.3). It is designed this way to prompt you to replace PowerPoint's data with your own, and choose the graph that best suits your needs.

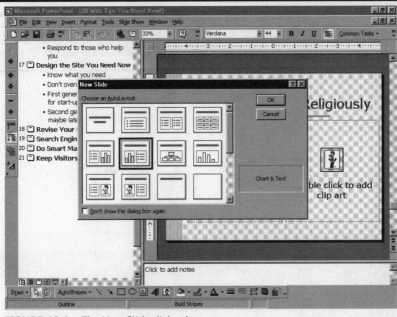

FIGURE 12.1:   The New Slide dialog box

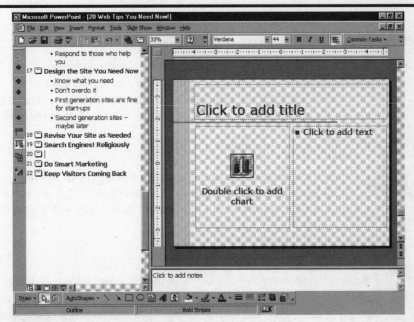

FIGURE 12.2:   The new slide with the graph area marked

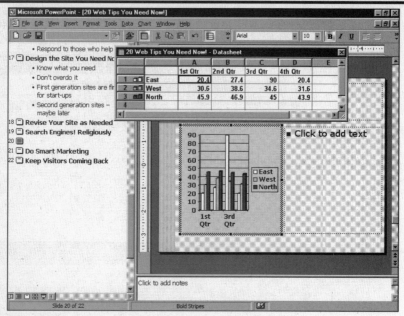

FIGURE 12.3: PowerPoint puts data in the datasheet for you.

Working with the Datasheet

The datasheet contains the data PowerPoint uses to build your graph. You enter the labels for the data you want to graph across the top and left rows of the datasheet. Each row represents a single data series and shows what type of symbol—in this case, a 3-D bar—represents the data in the series.

TIP

Before you can enter anything of your own, you need to get PowerPoint's fake data off the datasheet. First highlight the data; then use Edit ➣ Clear ➣ All to remove all information on the datasheet so you can start with a blank slate.

Entering Data Labels

Your first step is to replace the labels in the datasheet with your labels. The datasheet looks a little like an Excel spreadsheet, organized in a row and column fashion. The intersection of each column and row is called a *cell*.

Each row is a single data series, and each column shows the data values compared in each data series. For example, if you are comparing the sales of two products, the labels Product A and Product B might be listed in the label area of rows 1 and 2, and the column labels might list the months (see Figure 12.4).

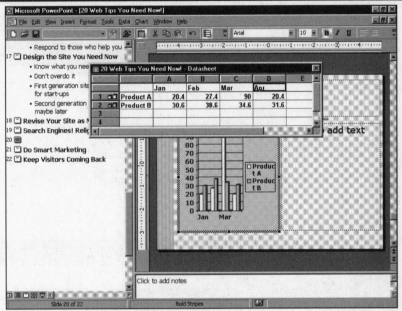

FIGURE 12.4: An example of row and column labels

Entering Data

To enter new information in the datasheet, click in the cell where you want the data to go and type. The new data replaces the old data. To move to another cell, use the arrow keys or move the mouse pointer to the new cell and click.

Editing the Datasheet

Once you enter the data for the graph, it's likely that you'll want to make some changes. To modify the data you entered, just click in the cell and retype the data. You can also copy, cut, or undo data, using the commands in the Edit menu.

Deleting Datasheet Rows and Columns

To delete entire columns or rows on the datasheet, click the label area for the row or column to highlight it as shown in Figure 12.5. Press Delete, and it's gone.

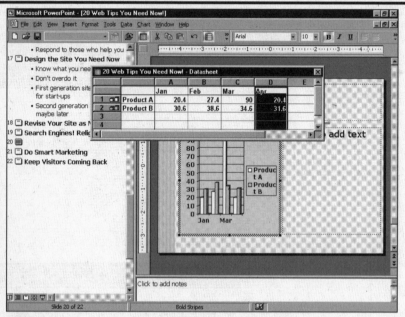

FIGURE 12.5:   Removing an entire column in the datasheet

Resizing Datasheet Columns

When the data you need to enter is too wide for the cells in the datasheet, you can widen the column to accommodate the data. Position the cursor on the dividing line between two column labels so that the cursor changes to a double arrow. To widen the column, drag the mouse in the direction you want and release the mouse button when the column is at the desired width. To have PowerPoint automatically adjust the column width to the text, double-click the dividing line. The column width will close to the widest data entry in the column.

Closing the Datasheet

After you've entered your own data labels and data, you are ready to close the datasheet and begin experimenting with graph types. Close the datasheet in one of these three ways:

- ▶ Double-click the control-menu box in the upper-left corner of the datasheet.

- ▶ Click the X in the upper-right corner of the datasheet. Click the View Datasheet tool.

- ▶ Select View ➤ Datasheet.

TIP

At some point, you may want to redisplay that datasheet to make additional changes. Click the View Datasheet button or choose View ➤ Datasheet to display the datasheet again.

CHOOSING THE GRAPH TYPE

Now that you've entered the data you're going to work with, the next step is to choose the type of chart you want. You can select a chart type in one of two different ways:

- ▶ Click the Chart Type button on the Standard toolbar to display the drop-down chart box (see Figure 12.6).

- ▶ Choose Chart ➤ Chart Type.

TIP

If you don't see a Chart Type command in your Chart menu, you haven't selected the graph.

Part iii

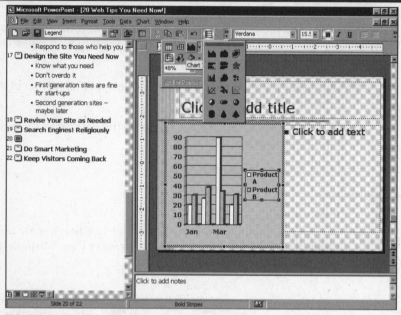

FIGURE 12.6: Choosing the type of graph you want

THE FOUR MOST EFFECTIVE GRAPHS

When you are displaying information visually, you want to show data in the clearest form possible. For that reason, if you have only a short amount of time to spend on each graph that you create, be sure to choose a graph type that will be recognized by your audience and will suit the type of data you are presenting.

One of the most common types of graphs is the *bar graph*. A bar graph is used to depict a particular data series. For example, suppose you are tracking the sales of four different regions. Each region would be represented by a bar on the graph. By looking at the height of the bars, audience members could easily tell which region had the highest sales, which had the lowest, etc. PowerPoint enables you to create both 2-D and 3-D bar graphs for different looks. You can enhance the appearance of bar graphs in other ways, too: for example, you can add a grid or labels and titles, or create a stacked bar graph where the data series are stacked one atop another.

CONTINUED ➡

A *pie graph* is another popular graph, used to show how portions of a data series relate to the whole. Suppose that you're doing a cost analysis of a recent project you've completed. What portion of your investment went to research and what portion went to development? What portion went to production? How much was spent on marketing and distribution? By plugging these numbers into the datasheet and then creating a pie graph based on the data, you can show what percentage of the total expenditure was allotted to each of these categories. Each of the categories are a data series, each getting one slice of the pie. Like bar graphs, you can enhance the appearance of a pie graph in many ways: you can make either 2-D or 3-D pies, create multiple pies, make pie slices explode out from the body of the pie, and add or change labels and titles.

Line graphs are popular for showing the progression of data over a specific period of time. You might be watching the development of a particular industry trend (How does the number of computers sold with CD-ROMs in 1994 compare to the number sold during each quarter of 1995?), tracking the expenses of a department (How much did Marketing spend on Federal Express charges over a 12-month period? How does that relate to the number of projects published?), or comparing projected and actual sales over a fiscal year. Again, line graphs can be flexible in appearance: you can choose 2-D or 3-D lines, change colors, add or remove gridlines, modify the legend, and more.

Another type of graph used to show a data progression is an *area graph*. An area graph allows you to compare two or more data series over time, representing the totals with a colored area assigned to the data series. For instance, if you are comparing how well two products sold over a quarter, you could show the different data series cumulatively in an area chart. One colored area represents the first product; the other colored area represents the second. At a glance, viewers can see the total amount sold of both products and tell which product fared the best in the marketplace.

If you choose the chart by selecting the one you want from the list, PowerPoint automatically changes the chart in the selected box. If you select a chart with the Chart Type command, the Chart Type dialog box appears (see Figure 12.7).

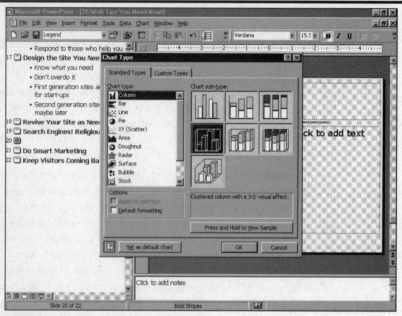

FIGURE 12.7: The Chart Type dialog box

The first set of options in the Chart Type dialog box allows you to specify the type of chart you want. The second set enables you to choose the chart subtype. When you make your choice of chart type, the subtypes you can select appear in the display area on the left side of the dialog box. Click the type you want and then click OK to return to the slide.

Choosing Custom Options   PowerPoint 2000 also gives you the option of creating custom charts. Click the Custom Types tab in the Chart Type dialog box to see additional choices (see Figure 12.8). Then click the type of chart in the column on the left side of the dialog box; subtypes appear on the right. You can now click the chart that best fits the type of data you're presenting. Click OK when you're through.

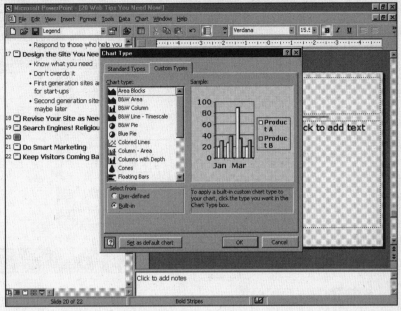

FIGURE 12.8: You can choose additional chart types by selecting the Custom Types tab.

Setting Chart Options   Once you've selected the chart type, you can modify chart options. Open the Chart menu and choose Chart Options. The dialog box shown in Figure 12.9 appears.

The dialog box includes as many as six different tabs, depending on the type of chart you've selected. Pie charts, for instance, will offer only three of the following tabs, but most of the others will show all six: Titles, Axes, Gridlines, Legend, Data Labels, and Data Table. The Titles tab gives you the space to enter chart titles and axis labels; the Axes tab lets you choose the measurement and type of the axes; the Gridlines tab controls where the gridlines are placed; the Legend tab enables you to choose the placement of the legend; the Data Labels tab lets you make selections about the data labels; and the Data Table tab helps you choose options for any data tables you display. In every tab, make your selections; when you are finished, click OK to close the dialog box.

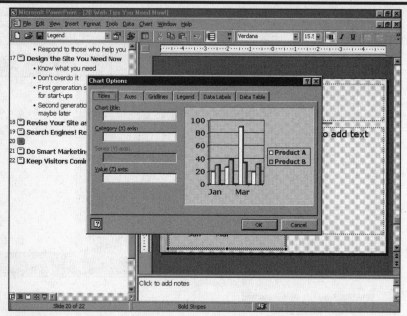

FIGURE 12.9: The Chart Options dialog box gives you up to six different tabs of choices.

Importing Chart Data

Microsoft Office is built on the enter-it-once, use-it-many-times concept. You can write an outline in Word, for example, and use it as the basis for a PowerPoint presentation. You can use a selected range from your Excel worksheet as the basis for your PowerPoint graph. You're not limited to importing from Microsoft products; PowerPoint lets you work with data from other applications as well. This section explores a few of the kinds of data you can use to create PowerPoint graphs.

WHAT DATA CAN YOU IMPORT?

In addition to Microsoft Excel files, PowerPoint directly supports several different text files and Lotus 1-2-3 files. If your spreadsheet filenames end with any of these extensions, your data can be imported into PowerPoint:

▶ XL* (Microsoft Excel)

▶ PRN, TXT, CSV (Standard text format)

▶ WK* (Lotus 1-2-3)

(In the preceding list, the asterisk character (*) is a wildcard, meaning that any character can be substituted for the asterisk. An acceptable Lotus 1-2-3 extension, for example, is WK1.)

If you use a spreadsheet program other than Excel or 1-2-3, you may still be able to use your data files with PowerPoint. Save the spreadsheet file in Excel or 1-2-3 format and then choose Edit ➢ Import Data to bring the information into PowerPoint. The instructions in your spreadsheet program should tell you how to save files in those formats.

TIP

If you're drawing data from a Windows application—perhaps Microsoft Works or another Windows program with spreadsheet capability—you should be able to copy data into the PowerPoint datasheet using Edit ➢ Copy in the other application and Edit ➢ Paste in PowerPoint.

Importing Files

To import data as the basis for your graph, you must first display and clear the datasheet. Select the area to clear, choose Edit ➢ Clear All to erase the information in the datasheet, and then enter any labels necessary to describe the data that you're importing.

Position the cursor in the upper left corner of the datasheet work area and choose Edit ➢ Import File. The Import File dialog box appears, as shown in Figure 12.10.

As a Windows user, you should be able to navigate this dialog box without any difficulty; it works much like File ➢ Open. Begin by navigating to the folder containing the file you want; then select it and click OK.

After you click OK, PowerPoint searches for the specified file, places the data in the datasheet, and updates the graph.

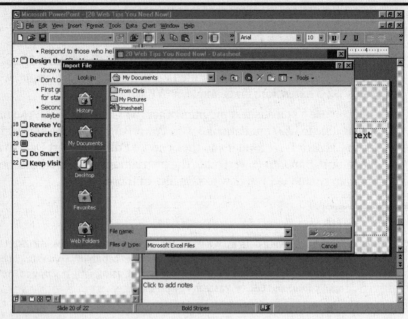

FIGURE 12.10:   The Import File dialog box

EDITING GRAPHS

You may not know exactly what you want in a graph until you see it drawn on the screen. Then your ideas on how to improve it ("What if I added a title? Would those bars stand out better if they were a different color?") can help you fine-tune the basic graph into something ready for presentation.

Basic Procedures: Cutting, Copying, Pasting, and Resizing Graphs

Working with a graph frame is like working with any frame in PowerPoint—you can easily resize, cut, copy, or paste graphs just as you would any other item. To perform these basic editing procedures, click the graph to select it. The graph frame appears, with handles around its outer edge.

To resize a graph: Click a handle and drag the graph to resize it horizontally or vertically.

To cut a graph: Make sure the graph is selected; then choose Edit ➣ Cut.

To delete a graph: Make sure the graph is selected; then press Delete or choose Edit ➣ Clear.

To copy a graph: Select the graph; then choose Edit ➣ Copy.

To paste a graph: Move to the slide on which you want to paste the graph and choose Edit ➣ Paste.

TIP

When resizing a graph, you can keep its original proportions by dragging the graph corner at a 45 degree angle inward or outward.

Modifying Graph Elements

When you double-click the graph to select it, several changes happen on the screen. First, the frame outline takes on a different look—instead of a thin outline with white handles, the outline becomes a thick white outline with black handles.

The toolbar also changes. Now a number of new tools appear, all having to do with importing, creating, displaying, and modifying graphs (see Figure 12.11). Table 12.1 shows the different tools in the Graph toolbar. In PowerPoint 2000, some of the tools are tucked away in a tools palette until you use them for the first time (see Figure 12.11 for an example). Click the small down-arrow button to display the tools palette and select more graph tools. When you use one of the tools in the palette, it will automatically be added to the toolbar so you can use it in the future without going all the way back to the palette.

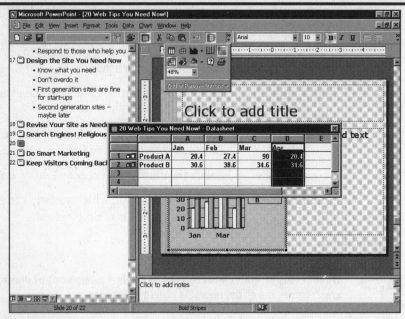

FIGURE 12.11:   When you select a graph for editing, the tools you need are displayed in the toolbar and the tools palette.

TABLE 12.1: Tools in the Graph Toolbar

Tool	Name	Description
Series "Jan" ▼	Chart Objects	Enables you to choose a chart element to modify
	Format	Displays the Format dialog box so you can change the way the selected element is displayed
	Import File	Imports an existing file from another application
	View Datasheet	Displays and hides datasheet

TABLE 12.1 continued: Tools in the Graph Toolbar

Tool	Name	Description
	Cut	Removes the selected item and places it on the Clipboard
	Copy	Copies the selected item to the Clipboard
	Paste	Pastes Clipboard contents to selected area
	Undo	Reverses last action
	By Row	Associates data row-wise
	By Column	Associates data column-wise
	Data Table	Turns the selected chart into a data table
	Chart Type	Allows you to choose the chart type you want
	Category Axis Gridlines	Adds or removes the vertical gridlines on the graph
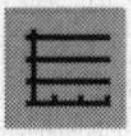	Value Axis Gridlines	Adds or removes the horizontal gridlines on the graph
	Legend	Displays or hides the legend

Part iii

TABLE 12.1 continued: Tools in the Graph Toolbar

Tool	Name	Description
	Drawing	Brings up the drawing tools
	Fill Color	Displays a color palette
	Office Assistant	Displays the Assistant so you can get help on the selected topic

TIP

If you plan on doing up-close work—like changing data values, adding labels, or changing markers and gridlines—you may want to Zoom the display so you can see what's going on. Click the Zoom down arrow to display the list of possible percentages; choose the display you want. You need to do this *before* you double-click the graph to display the graph toolbar and put the graph in editing mode.

Changing the Data Arrangement

There's a method to PowerPoint's madness when it comes to the way data is displayed in your graph. When you enter data in the datasheet, PowerPoint graphs the information first by row, then by column. This means that if you're working with the datasheet in Figure 12.12, Power-Point will show how Product A and Product B (rows) did over the first four months of the year (columns). The resulting chart is shown in an enlarged view in Figure 12.13.

You can change the way PowerPoint displays the data—that is, you can put the row data where the column data is and the column data where the row data is—to display your graph another way. That way, instead of showing how Products A and B did over four months, you show how the months look for each of those products.

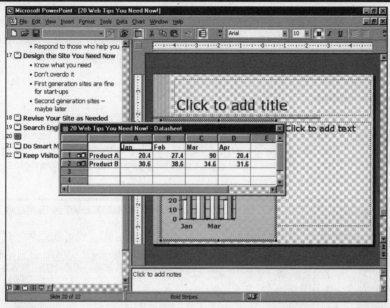

FIGURE 12.12: PowerPoint graphs the information in the datasheet first by row, then by column.

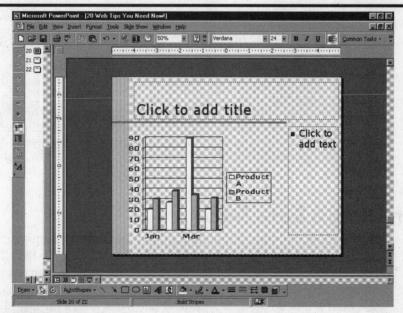

FIGURE 12.13: PowerPoint creates a default graph based on the values you enter in the datasheet.

For instance, you can change the way the data is arranged (this is also called the association of the data) by clicking the By Column button in the toolbar. When you click By Column, PowerPoint graphs Product A and Product B separately, with each bar in the graph associated with a particular month (see Figure 12.14).

TIP

If you're having trouble displaying your data just the way you want it, try switching the association of the data. If the By Row button is clicked, try using By Column, or vice versa. Sometimes data arranged differently makes more sense.

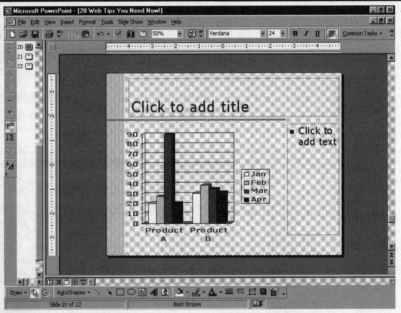

FIGURE 12.14:   Changing the data association to By Column

Creating a Data Table

Now you can easily turn a chart into a data table with the simple click of a button. When the chart is displayed on the screen, click the Data Table button, in the tools palette, unless you've used it before, and then it appears in the toolbar. The chart is redrawn as a data table (see Figure 12.15). If you want to change the data table back into a chart, click the Data Table button again.

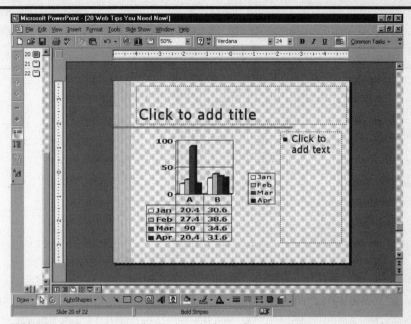

FIGURE 12.15: A data table displays the best of both worlds: graphical and numeric data.

Changing the Appearance of the X and Y Axes

You may want to change the way the axes of your graph are displayed. In some cases, you might want to change their color or thickness, or you may want to change the tick marks and the way they appear.

NOTE

The y axis extends vertically; the x axis is horizontal. Tick marks are the small lines that mark off increments on the axes.

To modify the axes on your graph, double-click on the axis you want to change. Figure 12.16 shows the Format Axis dialog box that appears when you do this.

Like other Windows 95/98 dialog boxes, this one is divided into tabs. First and foremost in the Format Axis dialog box are aesthetic concerns.

Part iii

What color do you want the axis to be? How do you want the tick marks to appear? A sample line at the bottom of the Patterns screen shows you your selections.

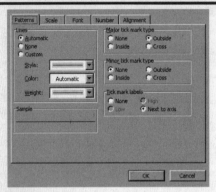

FIGURE 12.16:   The Format Axis dialog box

Other tabs behind Patterns include Scale, which allows you to set the increment values between tick marks; Font, which controls the font of the axis labels; Number, which controls the numeric format of values displayed; and Alignment, which allows you to choose the basic layout of text.

You can modify these settings at any time during your work with Power-Point. Simply make your selections and click OK to return to the graph.

ENHANCING GRAPHS

Your graph is done. You've added and edited its data and arranged it to your liking. The only problem? It's boring. What might you do to spruce up a chart? Maybe add some color. Tack on a text note. Add a title or data labels. You could even change a font or style. To round out our discussion of graphs, we'll talk about how you can enhance their appearance.

Changeable Chart Elements

You can select and change any of the following elements by double-clicking on them:

- ► Individual data series
- ► The plot area

- ► The x and y axes
- ► The legend
- ► The gridlines

TIP

In most cases, you can also change chart element settings by using a menu command or a tool. Use whichever method is most convenient for you.

Working with Graph Text

You can change the appearance of chart text (the axis labels) by double-clicking on the axis you want to change and then choosing Font from the displayed screen. There are other types of text you might want to consider working with and/or adding. This section explains how you can add a graph title and data labels and shows how to make basic graph text changes.

Adding a Title

This graph needs a title. Make sure the graph is selected and then choose Chart ➤ Chart Options. The dialog box shown in Figure 12.17 appears.

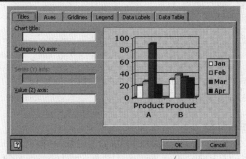

FIGURE 12.17: The Chart Options dialog box

If the Titles tab isn't already displayed, click it now. Type the text you want to use as the chart title and then click OK. A text box is added to the chart area where the title will go. Type the text for the title and click outside the Title box.

TIP

The best titles say it quickly and clearly. Make sure the graph title reflects in as few words as possible the basic concept of your graph. "December Sales Results" is much easier to understand than "Net Sales Based on December's Total Receipts."

Rotating Chart Text

PowerPoint makes it possible for you to rotate chart titles, axis titles, or data labels. To rotate chart text, begin by selecting the text item you want to change. Right-click and choose Format Axis Title. The Alignment tab is already displayed. This tab gives you the option of choosing the alignment for the text (see Figure 12.18). Either enter the angle you want in the Degrees box, or drag the small red diamond up or down on the arc to angle the text. When you're finished, click OK.

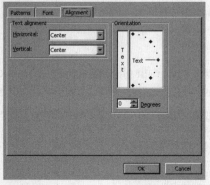

FIGURE 12.18: You can rotate chart text by typing a value or by dragging the marker.

Adding Data Labels

Depending on the type of data you are displaying, you may find it helpful to show the data values or labels on or beside the bars, lines, or columns themselves. To add data values or labels, choose Chart ➤ Chart Options; then click the Data Labels tab (see Figure 12.19).

You can add either values or labels. If you add values, the numeric values appear beside the data series items. If you add labels, the names of the data series appear beside the graph elements. Some items in your dialog box may appear dimmed, depending on the type of graph you're working with.

After you make your selection, click OK.

TIP

Once you add the data labels to the graph, things may look too crowded. You can drag one of the graph frame handles outward to enlarge the graph and make more room for all the elements inside.

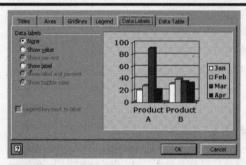

FIGURE 12.19: The Data Labels tab of the Chart Options dialog box

Changing Font, Size, and Style

The look of your text says a lot about your presentation. You may want to try using a different look—especially if you're worried about whether your data labels or graph titles will be legible to the people in the fourth row.

To change the font of something you've added, like a title or text note, click inside the text box and then open the Format menu in the menu bar. The first command there should reflect the item you've selected. So, if you've selected a chart title, the command is Selected Chart Title. (You can also double-click the item to display the dialog box.) If you've selected a legend, the command is Selected Legend. Click the command. The Format dialog box—either Format Legend or Format Title, depending on what you selected (see Figure 12.20)—will appear.

If you've been working with text in your PowerPoint slides, these options won't surprise you. In the Font screen, you choose the font, style, size, color, background, and effects of the text you've selected. The Sample box in the bottom of the screen shows you how your choices look. In the Alignment tab, you choose the alignment of text.

Part iii

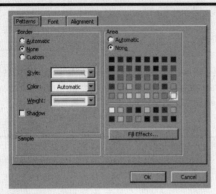

FIGURE 12.20:   The Format Title dialog box

TIP

If the x-axis labels on your graph bunch up and are difficult to read, you have three options: enlarge the graph, reduce the size of the label text, or change the orientation of the text so that the labels angle vertically instead of being spread horizontally below the graph.

Adding Gridlines

Gridlines can add a sense of proportion to the graphs in your presentation. If you've got a series of bar charts but no gridlines, it may be difficult for someone in the fourteenth row to tell how one data series compares to another. Gridlines help make it obvious which data series outreaches the other, even when it's a close call.

PowerPoint allows you to add two different kinds of gridlines: horizontal and vertical. The gridlines are tied to the major tick marks in the axes, so if you want to change the spacing of the gridlines, you'll need to make modifications on the x or y axis of your graph. Figure 12.21 shows how the chart looks with both vertical and horizontal gridlines.

To change the gridlines settings, open the Chart menu and select Chart Options; then click the Gridlines tab. The dialog box appears with the Gridlines tab showing, as shown in Figure 12.22. If you want to attach the gridlines to the minor gridlines—which means you'll have more of them in your graph—click Minor Gridlines. You might want to do this, for example, if you are graphing data series with data points close together;

the minor gridlines will help you read the placement of the data. When you've finished making changes, click OK.

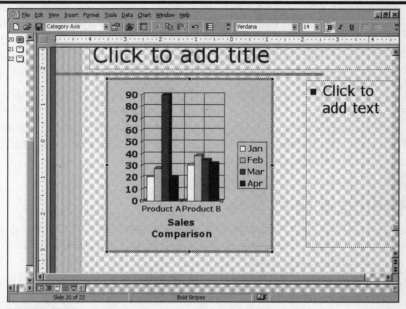

FIGURE 12.21: Adding horizontal and vertical gridlines

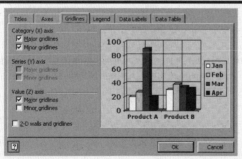

FIGURE 12.22: The Gridlines tab of the Chart Options dialog box

TIP

Remember that the actual tick marks and increments are part of the axis settings. To change the spacing between gridlines, double-click on the axis you want to change.

Hiding and Displaying the Legend

The legend of your graph is like the key to a map; it shows your viewers at a glance which data series is represented by which bar, color, line, or pie slice. By default, PowerPoint adds a legend to your graph. In some instances, you may want to remove the graph legend from the display, if only temporarily. This could give you more room for other items or save you from unnecessarily cluttering your slide when the data speaks for itself.

To hide the graph legend, display the Chart Options dialog box and click the Legend tab. Next click the Show Legend checkbox to remove the X. When you click OK to close the dialog box, the legend is gone. To redisplay the legend, open the Chart Options dialog box again and click the Show Legend checkbox.

Adding a Text Box

Another tool in the Graph toolbar allows you to add text to your graph. You might do this to call attention to a certain feature or add a note to the presentation slide.

To add a text box, click the Text Box tool in the toolbar at the bottom of the screen and use the mouse to draw the box in the graph editing area. The cursor is positioned in the upper-left corner of the new text box, ready to accept your text. Type the text for the note and click outside the box.

TIP

Once you add the text, you can change it easily: highlight the text and choose Format ➤ Font. Then make the necessary changes to font, style, color, size, and effect settings. Click OK when you're finished.

Specifying Color

Earlier you learned to choose the color of individual data items. Now you can use the Color tool to choose the background color of specific areas of your chart. For example, you might change the background color of the text note you just added.

Select the text box and then click the down-arrow beside the Fill Color tool in the More Buttons palette. A pop-up palette of colors appears below the toolbar (see Figure 12.23).

Click the color you want. Instantly, the palette disappears and the color is applied to the selected element—in this case, the text box.

PowerPoint gives you some additional choices for the way you fill the bars of your charts. Now, in addition to choosing the color for chart elements, you can add a custom touch to your chart by using pictures, textures, or gradient fill patterns for the chart items.

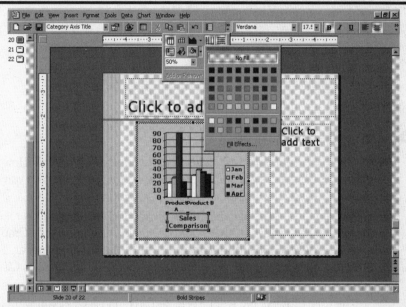

FIGURE 12.23: Selecting a different color for graph elements

Changing Patterns

Like color, pattern also affects the background of elements in your chart. After you select the item you want to change, you can choose from a variety of patterns by clicking the Fill Effects option in the color palette. This displays a dialog box that enables you to make more choices about the textures and patterns used in the chart. To see the available patterns, click the Pattern tab (see Figure 12.24). When you make your selection, the palette closes and the new setting is applied to the selected element.

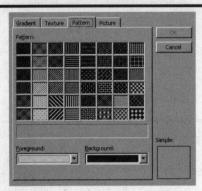

FIGURE 12.24:   Choosing a different pattern

Animating Charts

Trying to think of new ways to keep your audience interested? How about having charts grow right before their eyes? PowerPoint enables you to animate charts so they change and grow as your audience watches.

To animate a chart, begin with the chart displayed on your screen. Make sure the regular toolbar is displayed; you don't want the Graph toolbar displayed. Click the chart one time so the handles appear. Then open the Slide Show menu and choose Custom Animation. The Custom Animation dialog box appears, as shown in Figure 12.25.

The Chart Effects tab will be selected. To choose what you want animated, click the Introduce Chart Elements down-arrow and select the option for the way you want the elements introduced: All at Once, by Series, by Category, by Element in Series, or by Element in Category. Next, you can control the way the items appear and whether they are accompanied by a sound effect by choosing the options in the Entry Animation and Sound option boxes. Finally, if you want the element to be dimmed after it appears, you can set the After Animation option. Try out the effects you've selected by clicking Preview. When you are finished, click OK.

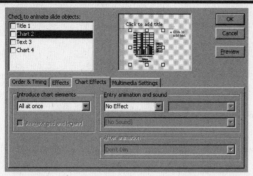

FIGURE 12.25: Animate a chart in the Custom Animation dialog box.

WHAT'S NEXT

This chapter rounds out the discussion of graphs in your PowerPoint presentation. In this chapter, you've learned to create, edit, and enhance the appearance of your graphs. You found out how to choose a graph type, edit data values, add titles, labels, and legends, and make a variety of other changes. Now it's time to move on to Access, where you'll learn how to use the most powerful database management tool on the market.

Part iii

PART IV
DATABASE CREATION
WITH ACCESS 2000

Chapter 13

ACCESS BASICS

I f you're planning to use Access 2000, chances are you already know what a database is. Just in case you're not sure, however, here's a super-brief definition before we get started.

In a nutshell, a *database* is a collection of data. Your phone book is a simple database and so is your checkbook. A history of a company's orders, invoices, and payments is an example of a more complicated database, as is a log of a salesperson's contacts with clients and any related follow-up plans.

Access is a flexible program that works for both simple and complex database projects. It's also a *relational database*, which means it lets you define relationships between different types of information (like customers and their orders) so you can use them together. But before you get buried in lots of database theory, let's get going and learn as we work.

Adapted from *Access 2000: No Experience Required* by Celeste Robinson

ISBN 0-7821-2485-2   608 pages $24.99

GET STARTED

To launch Access, click the Microsoft Access 2000 button on the Microsoft Office Shortcut Bar, or click the Start button and choose Programs ➤ Microsoft Access from the menu. When Access starts, you'll see a dialog box like the one in Figure 13.1. The names you see listed in the bottom half of the dialog box will vary depending on the database projects you've already started. At this point, you can:

- ▶ Create a database from scratch or with the Database Wizard

- ▶ Create a data access page for viewing Access data with Internet Explorer

- ▶ Create an Access project

- ▶ Open a database or project you've already created

FIGURE 13.1: Access' opening dialog box lets you create a new Access file or open one you've worked with before.

TIP

If you want to bring the Microsoft Office Shortcut Bar into view on the Windows Desktop, click the Start button and choose Programs ➤ Office Tools ➤ Microsoft Office Shortcut Bar from the menus. To hide the Shortcut Bar, double-click the Office icon in the blue section of the Shortcut Bar, or right-click the blue area and choose Exit.

Later in this chapter, you'll see how to create a new database using the Database Wizard. First, here's an overview of how an Access database is organized.

NOTE

An Access *project* is similar to an Access database, but it contains no data tables. Instead, it is connected to an SQL server that holds the tables for the project.

ELEMENTS OF AN ACCESS DATABASE

The heart of a database is the information it holds. But there are other important elements, usually referred to as *objects*, in an Access database. Here are the kinds of objects you'll be working with:

Tables hold information.

Queries let you ask questions about your data or make changes to data.

Forms are for viewing and editing information.

Pages are HTML (Hypertext Markup Language) files that let you view Access data with Internet Explorer.

Reports are for summarizing and printing data.

Macros perform one or more database actions automatically.

Modules are another type of Access object that you may or may not work with. A module is a program you write using VB (Visual Basic, the programming language included with Office 2000) to automate and customize database functions. In this section, you'll see how to create a customized database, but we'll do it all without programming.

NOTE

For more information on creating Access applications with VB, see the forthcoming *Access 2000 VBA Handbook* (Sybex, summer 1999).

Tables

Any information you enter in an Access database gets stored in a *table*. Figure 13.2 shows two tables from a Contact Management database created with the Database Wizard: a table called Contacts and another named Calls. These tables hold information about people and the calls made to them.

Fields

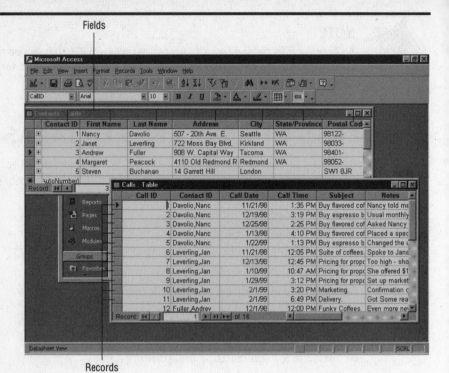

Records

FIGURE 13.2: Contacts and Calls are two of the tables included in the Contact Management database created by the Database Wizard. Each record in the Contacts table describes a person. The records in Calls describe the calls made to people in the Contacts table.

As you can see in Figure 13.2, a table consists of rows and columns of values. In database lingo, the rows are called *records*, and the columns are *fields*.

There are lots of different ways to create tables in Access. We'll explore the various options in Chapter 15.

Queries

Queries are most often used to ask questions about your data. You can formulate simple queries that look for records in a single table, or design complex queries that involve multiple tables and criteria. Here are some examples of the kinds of questions you can ask with a query:

▶ "Which customers have placed orders in the last three months?"

▶ "How many new leads did I contact last week?"

▶ "Show me my total sales for the last six months of 1998 broken down by product and month."

Select Queries

Figure 13.3 shows a fairly simple query that looks for all calls to Nancy in a table named Calls. This type of query is called a *Select* query. It finds any records that answer the question posed by the query and displays them when the query is run.

We won't get into a lot of detail about how to formulate a query at this point, but there are a few other things about the query in Figure 13.3 that may be interesting to you:

▶ The field names in the Field row, along with the check marks in the Show row, tell Access which fields to show when the query is run.

▶ "Nancy" in the FirstName column of the Criteria row tells Access to look only for records with Nancy in the FirstName field.

▶ If you check the top part of the Query window in the figure, you can see that the Calls table is linked to the Contacts table on the ContactID field. Access uses this link to gather information from both tables at the same time. (We'll talk more about relationships in Chapters 14 and 15.)

This line tells Access how to link the two tables involved in the query.

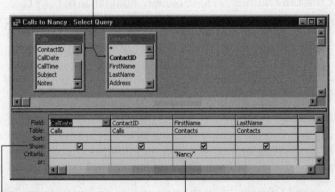

The check marks in the Show row tell Access what fields to show when the query is run.

This criteria tells Access to look for records with "Nancy" in the FirstName field.

FIGURE 13.3: A query that looks for calls to a person named Nancy

When you run a query, Access displays the results in *Datasheet view*, a simple arrangement of rows and columns of field values. (See Figure 13.4. Note that the tables in Figure 13.2 are also displayed in Datasheet view.) The query result in the figure includes only the calls made to Nancy and shows only the fields from the Calls and Contacts tables that were checked in Figure 13.3.

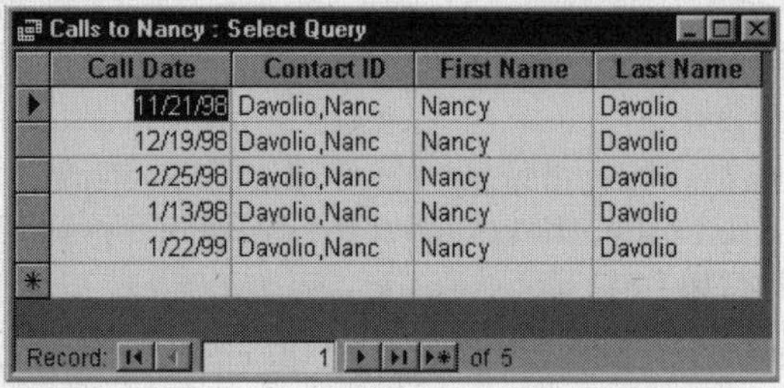

Calls to Nancy : Select Query

Call Date	Contact ID	First Name	Last Name
11/21/98	Davolio,Nanc	Nancy	Davolio
12/19/98	Davolio,Nanc	Nancy	Davolio
12/25/98	Davolio,Nanc	Nancy	Davolio
1/13/98	Davolio,Nanc	Nancy	Davolio
1/22/99	Davolio,Nanc	Nancy	Davolio

Record: 1 of 5

FIGURE 13.4: The result of the query in Figure 13.3 shown in a Datasheet view. Access automatically looks up and displays the names for each ContactID.

Other Types of Queries

Options in the Query Design window don't end with Select queries. Queries can be used to change data as well as look for it. You can use queries to crosstabulate data, create tables, delete records, or even add records to one table from another:

Crosstab Queries These queries summarize data by categories so you can answer questions like "What were my sales by product for each month last year?" There's a Crosstab Wizard to help you set up these queries.

Make-Table Queries When you turn a Select query into a Make-Table query, it writes the results to a completely new table.

Update Queries With Update queries, you can make global changes to a table (like changing all of a field's values to uppercase), do find-and-replace edits, or update one table against another.

Append Queries Use these queries to add information from one table to another.

Delete Queries   Instead of deleting records from a table one by one, you can use a Delete query to do quick deletes of entire groups of records.

Forms

When you open a table in Access, it gets presented in Datasheet view. Check the window called "Contacts : Table" in the background of Figure 13.5 to see an example of what Datasheet view looks like.

The same figure shows a record from the Contacts table presented in *Form view* in the window called Contacts. In Form view, you can see all the fields for Nancy Davolio's record at once. In contrast, Datasheet view displays a limited amount of fields at the same time, and you have to scroll sideways through the Table window to view a person's entire record. In most cases, using a form makes it easier to enter, edit, and view data.

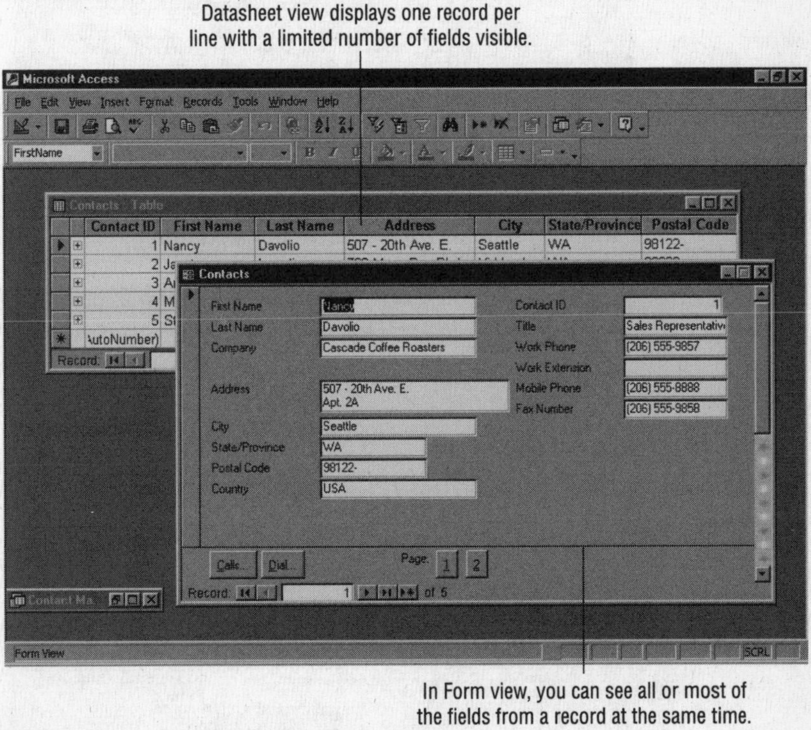

Datasheet view displays one record per line with a limited number of fields visible.

In Form view, you can see all or most of the fields from a record at the same time.

FIGURE 13.5:   Records from the Contacts table shown in both Datasheet view and Form view

Part iv

The Form Wizard and AutoForms

Putting together a database form from scratch is a tedious task, but thankfully there's plenty of help available. Access 2000 has a *Form Wizard* that will create a form after asking you a bunch of questions about what you want to see. The form we'll take a look at in the "Multi-table Forms" section was created with the Form Wizard.

If you want to go an even quicker route, you can use the AutoForm feature to create the following types of forms without providing any information other than the name of a table or a query:

Columnar   This type of AutoForm creates a form with one record per page and fields arranged in a column like this:

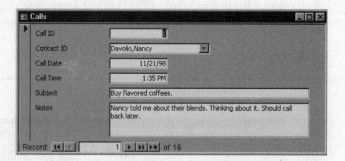

Tabular   This AutoForm arranges fields in a tabular format where they line up in rows rather than columns:

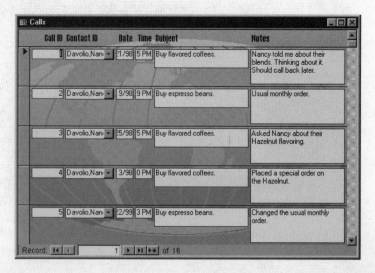

Datasheet   A form created with this AutoForm option shows multiple records in the Form window just like in a Table window:

CallID	ContactID	CallDate	CallTim	Subject	Notes
1	Davolio,Nancy	11/21/98	:35 PM	Buy flavored coffees.	Nancy told me about their
2	Davolio,Nancy	12/19/98	:19 PM	Buy espresso beans.	Usual monthly order.
3	Davolio,Nancy	12/25/98	:25 PM	Buy flavored coffees.	Asked Nancy about their H
4	Davolio,Nancy	1/13/98	:10 PM	Buy flavored coffees.	Placed a special order on
5	Davolio,Nancy	1/22/99	:13 PM	Buy espresso beans.	Changed the usual monthl
6	Leverling,Janet	11/21/98	:05 PM	Suite of coffees.	Spoke to Janet about NWi
7	Leverling,Janet	12/13/98	:45 PM	Pricing for proposed suite.	Too high - should wait and
8	Leverling,Janet	1/10/99	:47 AM	Pricing for proposed suite.	She offered $100 less per
9	Leverling,Janet	1/29/99	:12 PM	Pricing for proposed suite.	Set up marketing plans w/
10	Leverling,Janet	2/1/99	:20 PM	Marketing.	Confirmation of shipment.
11	Leverling,Janet	2/1/99	:49 PM	Delivery.	Got Some really odd new I
12	Fuller,Andrew	12/1/98	:00 PM	Funky Coffees.	Even more new blends.
13	Fuller,Andrew	1/29/99	:30 PM	Funky Coffees.	Ordered a sample.
14	Fuller,Andrew	2/1/99	:15 PM	Funky Coffees.	Ordered 1000 lbs. - good s
15	Peacock,Margaret	12/13/98	:00 AM	Usual order.	Shipment to Margaret was
16	Buchanan,Steven	1/1/99	:00 PM	Shipment went to wrong address.	Margaret's shipment went
*	(AutoNumber)				

Record: ◄◄ ◄ 1 ► ►I ►* of 16

Multi-table Forms

The forms we've looked at so far have included fields from only one table, but Access doesn't limit you to these simple views. You can show information from more than one table at the same time, like in Figure 13.6. The form in the figure shows the record for Nancy Davolio from the Contacts table at the top of the form window. Underneath Nancy's description is another form, called a *subform*, that shows all of Nancy's records in the Calls table. In this example, the call records are in Datasheet view, but they can appear in any of the formats listed in the last section.

Fields from Nancy's record in the Contacts table

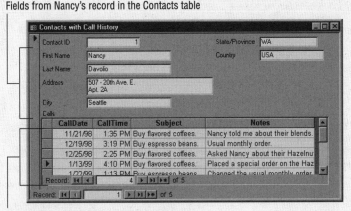

Records for calls to Nancy from the Calls table

FIGURE 13.6:   This multi-table form shows related information from the Contacts and Calls tables at the same time.

Part iv

NOTE

Forms can also include graphics, hyperlinks to Web sites or other data, OLE objects (links to other Windows programs), and other special purpose objects.

Pages

Pages, or *data access pages*, are a new feature of Access in Office 2000. These objects can be used to browse Access data with Internet Explorer, as well as with Access itself. Unlike forms and reports, which are stored as part of an Access database, pages are saved as HTML files that are separate from the database they are associated with.

Figure 13.7 shows a page that displays records from the Contacts tables in the Contact Management1 database. The same page is shown in Figure 13.8 viewed with Internet Explorer.

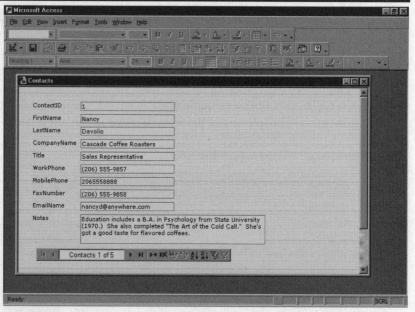

FIGURE 13.7: This data access page shows records from the Contacts table in the Contact Management1 database. The page is being viewed with Access.

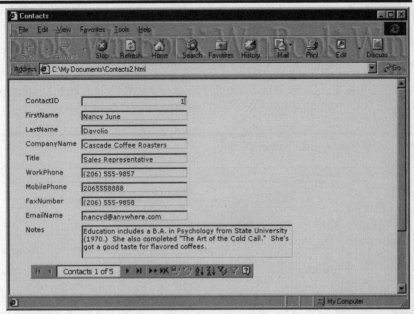

FIGURE 13.8: This is the same data access page shown in Figure 13.7, though it is viewed from Internet Explorer.

If you compare the record navigation controls at the bottom of the Contacts page (Figure 13.7) to those on the form in Figure 13.6, you'll see that they are somewhat different from each other. The Navigation toolbar at the bottom of the page in Figure 13.7 includes buttons for deleting records, undoing changes, and working with filters, as well as for moving between records and adding new records.

Reports

Reports are another type of object you can use in Access to view or print your data. Figure 13.9 shows a simple alphabetical listing of the people in the Contacts table that was printed using an Access report.

You can create reports from scratch with Access, but you will probably never need to with all the tools available to help you:

▶ The *Report Wizard* guides you through every step of designing a report, from selecting fields to choosing a style for the printed page.

▶ *AutoReport* can create a columnar or tabular report for you with one mouse click.

▶ The *Chart Wizard* assists you with creating all kinds of graphs from pie charts to 3-D bar graphs that show multiple series of data.

▶ The *Label Wizard* creates reports to print labels that fit standard formats (like Avery 5161) or layouts you design yourself.

Alphabetical Contact Listing

	Contact Name	Company Name	Title	Work Phone	Ext.	Fax Number
B						
	Buchanan, Steven	Health Food Store	Purchase Manager	(71) 555-2222		
D						
	Davolio, Nancy	Cascade Coffee Roasters	Sales Representative	(206) 555-9857		(206) 555-9858
F						
	Fuller, Andrew	Volcano Coffee Company	Sales Representative	(206) 555-9482		(206) 555-9483
L						
	Leverling, Janet	Northwind Traders	Vice President, New Produc	(206) 555-3412		(206) 555-3413
P						
	Peacock, Margaret	Fourth Coffee	Purchase Manager	(206) 555-8122		(206) 555-8123

FIGURE 13.9: This listing of people in the Contacts table was printed using an Access report.

Differences between Forms and Reports

Reports are similar to forms and, in fact, the Report Design window shares many of the features of the Form Design window. Yet there are some important differences between these two types of objects.

One difference is that forms are primarily used to edit or view data on your computer screen. When you move through a form, you usually navigate from one record to another, perhaps displaying related records from other tables as you do so. Reports can be previewed on the screen, as well, but their main purpose is to present information nicely on a printed page.

Another difference between forms and reports is that reports have special features to help you summarize data. For example, a report can group sales records by salesperson and month, and give you a summary of the total sales for each person by month. It's not possible to view this kind of summary information using a form unless you go through some hoops with queries first.

Multi-table Reports

Just as with forms, reports can present data from more than one table at the same time. These are called *multi-table reports*. The report in Figure 13.10 shows a list of the records in Calls for each person in the Contacts table.

Work Phone	Date	Time	Subject	Notes
(206) 555-9857				
	12/19/97	3:19 PM	Buy espresso beans.	Usual monthly order.
	12/25/97	2:25 PM	Buy flavored coffees.	Asked Nancy about their Hazelnut flavoring.
	1/13/97	4:10 PM	Buy flavored coffees.	Placed a special order on the Hazelnut.
	1/22/98	1:13 PM	Buy espresso beans.	Changed the usual monthly order.
	11/21/97	1:35 PM	Buy flavored coffees.	Nancy told me about their blends. Thinking about it. Should call back later.
(206) 555-3412				
	1/29/98	3:12 PM	Pricing for proposed suite.	Set up marketing plans w/ Janet.
	11/21/97	12:05 PM	Suite of coffees.	Spoke to Janet about NWIND carrying a coffee collection designed by us.
	1/10/98	10:47 AM	Pricing for proposed suite.	She offered $100 less per order (12 packages / order) - OK.
	2/1/98	3:20 PM	Marketing.	Confirmation of shipment.
	2/1/98	6:49 PM	Delivery.	Got Some really odd new blends.
	12/13/97	12:45 PM	Pricing for proposed suite.	Too high - should wait and see if Janet comes around.
(206) 555-9482				
	12/1/97	12:00 PM	Funky Coffees.	Even more new blends.
	1/29/98	2:30 PM	Funky Coffees.	Ordered a sample.
	2/1/98	3:15 PM	Funky Coffees.	Ordered 1000 lbs. - good stuff
(206) 555-8122				
	12/13/97	9:00 AM	Usual order.	Shipment to Margaret was late, oops.
(71) 555-2222				
	1/1/98	1:00 PM	Shipment went to wrong ac	Margaret's shipment went to Steven, oops.

FIGURE 13.10:   This multi-table report shows information from both the Contacts and Calls tables.

Macros

There's one more type of object we'll be using in the Database window: macros. A *macro* automatically executes one or more database commands when you run it. Macros are great for tasks that you do over and over again. If you spend the same time to set up a macro to do this kind of repetitive job, your investment will be paid back many times over.

Here are a few examples of database jobs you could automate with a macro:

▶ Print a bunch of month-end reports

▶ Add a new record to a table, date- and time-stamp it, and fill in your initials

▶ Import a data file, run some queries to format the new data, and add the resulting information to another table in your database

▶ Print letters for customers and make notes in the customers' records of when the letters were sent

▶ Copy data from one form to another

After a macro is set up, you can run it from the Database window or attach it to a *command button* on a form.

As mentioned earlier, a *module* is another type of object that can be part of an Access database. Modules hold programming code that works with objects like tables, queries, and forms.

NOTE

This section will focus on macros instead of modules since macros are easier to formulate and can be used to automate most database tasks, even if you're not a programmer.

A Database Plan

Even though you won't find a button for "Database Plan" in the Database window, this is probably the most important element of any database. Before you start creating any tables, forms, or reports, the first thing you need to do is figure out exactly *what* you need from your Access database.

Of course, it's impossible to devise a perfect plan when you might not yet have all the experience you need to make optimal choices. (Hopefully you'll have that experience by the time you're done with this book!) But it's still a good idea to devote some time considering these questions before you jump into a creating a database:

▶ Where is my data going to come from? Will I enter it myself or can I import it from another source? If the data already exists, can I link to it directly from Access? And do I need to share the data with other people?

- ▶ If the data I'm using is on an SQL server, should I use an Access database or a project file?
- ▶ What kind of standards do I want the data to conform to?
- ▶ How do I want to view information on the screen?
- ▶ Do I have to do any calculations or run through other kinds of processes with my data?
- ▶ What reports or charts do I need to print or send to other people?
- ▶ Does any of the data need to be accessed from the Web?
- ▶ What kinds of tasks will I need to do over and over again?
- ▶ Are other people going to be using my database? If so, what can I do to make it easier for them do their work?

We'll look at these questions in more detail in Chapter 14, with the intention of minimizing the work involved in getting a database up and running.

CREATE A NEW DATABASE WITH THE DATABASE WIZARD

Now that you are familiar with what a database is and what its components are, you're ready to put that knowledge to use. After you launch Access to begin work on a new application, the next step is to create a database or a project to hold your work. We'll use a database to illustrate the examples in the rest of this chapter, but many of the basic concepts that will be presented apply to projects as well. If you want to work with the examples on your own computer, follow these steps to create a new database using the Database Wizard:

1. In the opening dialog box shown in Figure 13.1, select Access Database Wizards, Pages, And Projects. Then click OK.

2. Click the Databases tab in the New dialog box.

3. Double-click the icon for Contact Management.

4. In the File New Database dialog box that opens, click Create. (You don't have to change the default name for the new database.)

5. In the first Database Wizard dialog box, click Next.

6. Select a style for the background of the forms in the new database and click Next.

7. Choose a style for your reports and click Next.

8. Enter a title for your database and click Next.

9. Click Finish to create the new database and open it.

After Access finishes its work, you'll see a window called Main Switchboard like the one in Figure 13.11. The Database Wizard includes *switchboards*, special-purpose forms that work like menus, in any new databases it creates. These switchboards have buttons you can click to choose tasks or leave the database. You can also add switchboards to databases or projects that you create without the help of the Database Wizard.

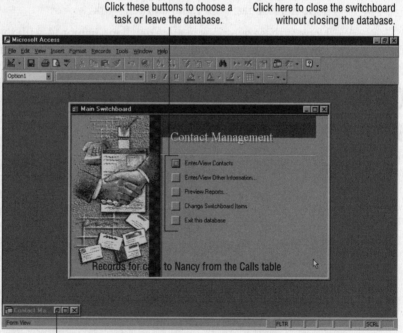

Click these buttons to choose a task or leave the database.

Click here to close the switchboard without closing the database.

Click this Restore button to open the Database window.

FIGURE 13.11: The Database Wizard includes switchboards in all new databases it creates. A switchboard has buttons you can click to easily navigate through a database.

We don't need to use the Main Switchboard now, so click its Close button and open the Database window by clicking the Restore button pointed out in Figure 13.11.

THE DATABASE WINDOW

Every Access database has a *Database window*. This window has an Objects bar with buttons for these types of objects: Tables, Queries, Forms, Reports, Pages, Macros, and Modules. It also has its own toolbar with buttons for the following actions:

Open   Use this button to open a database object so you can work with it.

Preview   (Reports only) Click this button to display a report in a Preview window.

Run   (Macros and Modules only) Use this button to run a macro or a module.

Design   Click this button to change the design of the selected object.

New   Use this button to create a new database object.

Figure 13.12 shows the Database window for a Contact Management database created by the Database Wizard.

NOTE

The Database window for a project has different buttons under Objects than those for a database.

Create a New Object

There's more than one way to create a new object when the Database window is open:

▶ Click the Database window button for the type of object you want to create and then click New.

▶ Click the drop-down arrow on the New Object toolbar button and select the type of object you want to create.

▶ Choose Insert from the Access menu bar and then select an object type.

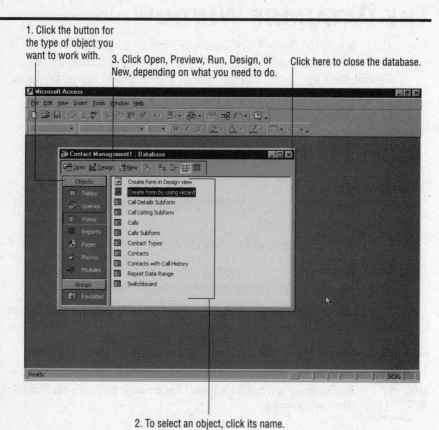

1. Click the button for the type of object you want to work with.

3. Click Open, Preview, Run, Design, or New, depending on what you need to do.

Click here to close the database.

2. To select an object, click its name.

FIGURE 13.12: The Database window for a Contact Management database. From this window, you can create new objects, revise their designs, or open them for viewing.

We won't get into the details of what to do next for specific types of objects. The important thing now is just to know how to use the Database window to start a new object.

Open an Object

To open an object:

1. In the Database window, click the button for the type of object you want to work with. (You can also click the Favorites button, or you can choose another group if you've added the object to a group as described a little later in this chapter.)

2. Highlight the object's name in the Database window.

3. Click Open.

TIP

To open a table, query, form, page, or report (or to run a macro or edit a module), double-click the object's name in the Database window. Alternatively, you can right-click the object and choose Open or Run from the shortcut menu.

Change an Object's Design

Once an object is created, you are free to change it in Design view. To open an object in Design view:

1. In the Database window, click the button for the type of object you want to work with (or click the name of any group the object may belong to).

2. Highlight the object's name in the Database window.

3. Click Design.

The tools you find in the Design view window vary depending on the type of object you are working with. You can do things like rearrange the data that's shown with the object; change the font, colors, and style of text; and add special elements like graphics and hyperlinks. You'll learn more about the Design view windows for tables, queries, forms, data access pages, reports, and macros later in this book.

TIP

To open an object in Design view, you can also right-click an object's name in the Database window and select Design from the shortcut menu.

View Objects by Group

When you click one of the buttons on the Objects bar in the Database window, Access changes the objects that are shown on the list in the middle of the window. For example, in Figure 13.12, the list in the Database window shows the names of all the forms in the Contact Management1 database. If you wanted to see a list of tables in the database, you would click the Tables button under Objects.

There is a new Access feature that lets you organize objects into groups as well as by type. One group is already set up for you: *Favorites*. When you click the Favorites button (under Groups in the Database window), Access shows the objects you have added to the Favorites group, regardless of the various objects' types. In other words, the Favorites group can include references to tables, forms, queries, reports, and other types of objects all in the same place.

To add an object to the Favorites group, right-click the object and choose Add To Group ➤ 1 Favorites from the shortcut menu.

To create a new group, right-click any button on the Objects bar or the Groups bar and choose New Group from the shortcut menu. Then enter a name for the new group and click OK.

To add an object to a new group, right-click the object, choose Add To Group from the shortcut menu, and select the group for the object.

TIP

You can create a new group and add an object to it at the same time by choosing Add To Group ➤ New Group from the object's shortcut menu.

Database Window Shortcuts

The Access 2000 Database window has its own shortcut menu, as do individual Access objects. Where you right-click in the Database window determines what you'll see on the shortcut menu that comes up.

Shortcut Menu for a Database

If you right-click the title bar or any gray area of the Database window, you'll see a shortcut menu for the database (or project) you are working with:

The Open command opens a dialog box from which you can select an Access database or project to open. (You can also open a few other types of files, like Web pages, from the Open dialog box.) We won't explore the other menu choices yet, but make a mental note that later on, you can probably use the shortcut menu for a database or a project to bypass menu commands.

Shortcut Menu for a Database Object

Each type of object in the Database window has its own shortcut menu. Figure 13.13 shows the shortcut menu for a form.

The form's shortcut menu includes Open, Design, Print..., Print Preview, Save As..., Export..., Send To, Add To Group, Delete, Rename, and other options. If you right-click a different type of object, like a report, you'll see a shortcut menu with slightly different choices than those that pop up for a form.

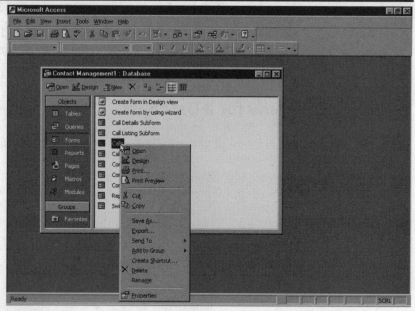

FIGURE 13.13: You can right-click an object's name in the Database window to see a shortcut menu of actions you can take with the object.

Shortcut Menu for the Database Window

The Database window has its own shortcut menu which differs from the shortcut menu for a database, a project, or a database object:

Some of the choices on this menu let you change the appearance of the Database window:

View   Use this selection to display database objects with Large Icons, Small Icons, as a List alone, or with Details like file descriptions, creation dates, and modification dates.

Arrange Icons   This choice lets you choose how icons are displayed in the Database window: By Name, By Type, By (Date) Created, or By (Date) Modified. If you are currently showing icons, the Auto Arrange choice is also available. Select (check) this choice to keep icons displayed in neat rows in the Database window.

Line Up Icons   When icons are displayed, this choice straightens icons into tidy columns.

NOTE

As with the shortcut menu for databases and projects, there are other choices on the Database window shortcut menu that we don't need to bother with yet. Relationships are covered in Chapter 15.

Opening a Database

To open a database, you have many different options:

▸ Choose File from the menu and make a choice from the list just above Exit. This list shows the databases you have used most recently.

▸ Double-click a database name in Windows Explorer.

 ▸ Click the Open button on the toolbar.

▸ Right-click the title bar or gray area of the Database window and select Open.

▸ Choose File ➢ Open from the menu.

▸ Press Ctrl+O.

All of these actions, except the first two, show an Open dialog box like the one in Figure 13.14 where you can select a database to work with. To choose a database from the list in the middle of the Open window, just double-click its name, or highlight it and click Open. Alternatively, use the drop-down list for File Name to select a file you opened recently.

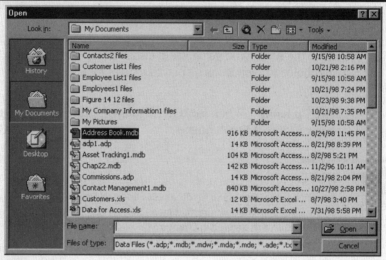

FIGURE 13.14:   The Open dialog box is where you select a database or project to work with.

NOTE

If you want to open a database and make sure no one else can use it at the same time, click the drop-down arrow on the Open button and select Open Exclusive.

Changing the Look In Folder

In the Open dialog box shown in Figure 13.14, you'll find icons and buttons that are common to many Windows Open dialog boxes. The Look In box shows the location of the folders and files shown in the main part of the Open window. You can use the Look In drop-down list or the Up One Level button to change the folder Access is looking in.

The group of buttons along the left side of the Open window is new to Access and other Office 2000 programs. By clicking these buttons, you can quickly change the location shown in the Look In box. Here's what each button does:

History shows the files in the Recent folder.

My Documents shows the files in the My Documents folder.

Desktop changes the Look In location to the Desktop and shows any shortcuts to databases.

Favorites shows the files in the Favorites folder.

Web Folders is for documents located on a Web server.

TIP

To add a database to your Favorites folder, select it in the Open dialog box. Then click the Tools drop-down arrow and select Add To Favorites.

Getting Help in the Open Dialog Box

To find out more about the various parts of the Open dialog box:

1. Press F1 while the Open dialog box is open to show the Office Assistant.

2. Type **open a database** in the text box and press Enter or click Search.

3. Click Open A Microsoft Access Database on the list of topics under "What would you like to do?"

You can also view brief descriptions of the various elements of the Open dialog box without going through the Office Assistant or opening Help. Click the Help button next to the Close button in the Open dialog box, and then click the button or other element you want to learn about. Or, right-click any element in the window and choose What's This? to see a brief description pop up.

TIP

By changing the Files Of Type setting in the Open dialog box, you can use Access to open Web pages, text files, Excel spreadsheets, and other types of files, as well as databases and projects. If you select a Web page (.HTM or .HTML file), Access opens the file as a Data Access Page. For text files and spreadsheets, Access creates a new database and starts the Link Text File or Link Spreadsheet Wizard.

Closing a Database

There are two ways to close a database:

- ▶ Click the Close button for the Database window.
- ▶ Choose File ➢ Close from the menu bar.

If you're working with a database you created with the Database Wizard, you also have the option of going to the Main Switchboard window and clicking Exit This Database.

WHAT'S IN A RELATIONSHIP?

At the beginning of this chapter, there was a brief allusion to the fact that Access is a *relational database*, allowing you to use different types of information together. We bypassed a theoretical discussion of what it means for a database to be relational, and we won't get into it too much now either. Instead, let's take a quick look at the benefits of a relational database, how Access relates tables, and what kinds of relationships can exist between tables.

What You Get from a Relational Database

To understand what's good about a relational database, let's first look at what goes on with a database that is *not* relational (called a "flat file" database). When you're working with a flat filer, you can only use one table of data at a time. For example, if you wanted to enter sales orders on your computer using a flat filer, you would have to create one table with fields for every possible bit of information that could be part of an order. You would have to include the details for order, customer, product, and tax information all in the same table. The structure of this table might look like the list of fields shown in Table 13.1.

TABLE 13.1: Fields for Orders File in a Flat File Database

Field Name
Order #
Order Date
Sales Rep
Customer #

TABLE 13.1 continued: Fields for Orders File in a Flat File Database

Name

Address

City

State

Zip

Product 1

Qty 1

Price 1

Product 2

Qty 2

Price 2

Product 3

Qty 3

Price 3

Sales Tax

Freight

It is assumed that the extended prices for each sales item and the order total can be calculated by the database software.

The disadvantages of having to store all this data in one table or file are quite obvious. For one thing, you would be limited to entering a fixed, maximum number of sale items for each order (three in the example in Table 13.1). Another disadvantage is that you would have to drag all this information around together, even if you only needed to work with part of the flat file. For example, if you wanted to create letters and labels to do a mailing to your customers, you would either have to create a separate file of customer information, or use the big Orders file and weed out the duplicates, since some customers may have placed more than one order.

In contrast, with a relational database, you could store Order Header details (like the order date and order #) in one table and Order details in another, allowing for a flexible number of sales items in each order. Customer, product, and tax fields would also all be stored in their own tables, as shown in Table 13.2.

TABLE 13.2: Fields and Tables for Orders in a Relational Database

ORDER HEADER FIELDS	ORDER DETAIL FIELDS	CUSTOMER FIELDS	PRODUCT FIELDS	TAX FIELDS
Order #	Order #	Customer #	Product #	State
Order Date	Product #	Name	Description	Tax Rate
Sales Rep	Qty	Address	Price	
Freight		City		
		State		
		Zip		

Again, it is assumed that the extended prices and order totals can be calculated by the database software.

The advantages of working with multiple related tables like the ones listed in Table 13.2 are that:

▶ You only have to enter information like customer names and addresses in one place, instead of in every order for the same customer. (The names and addresses in the Customer table can be linked as needed to the Order Header table.)

▶ An order can have a flexible number of sales items. This is possible since line items are stored in as many records as are needed in the Order Detail table, instead of in a set number of fields in one Orders table.

▶ Details like tax rates and product prices can be looked up from their own separate tables, eliminating the need to enter these values altogether.

▶ By keeping records for orders, customers, products, and other information in their own tables, it's easier to design forms and reports for different purposes.

NOTE

In Chapter 14 you'll find out how to analyze how your own information and decide how to divide it up into separate tables that can be related.

Relate Tables with Access

To show data in one table along with corresponding records in another table, Access has to be able to *relate* the tables. For tables to be related, they need to have fields with common values. For example, in the Contacts Management database that the Database Wizard created for us, both the Contacts and the Calls tables have a field for ContactID. In the Contacts table, ContactID serves as a unique identifier for each person's record, while in the Calls table, the ContactID indicates who each call record belongs to. This relationship is shown in the Relationships window in Figure 13.15. Using the linking ContactID field, Access can go to the Contacts table and look up the name of the person for each record in the Calls table.

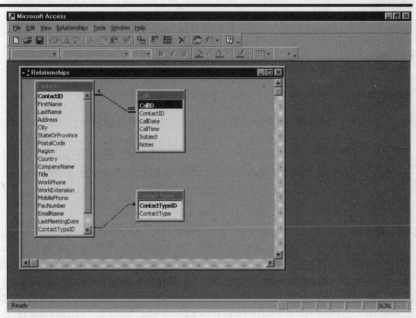

FIGURE 13.15: The Relationships window shows what fields are used to link the tables in a database. It also lets you add or change relationships.

NOTE

When you plan a database, be sure to include common fields in any tables you need to use together. We'll go over some examples of how to do this in Chapter 14.

Part iv

Types of Relationships

Relationships between human beings are never as simple as they appear, and this applies to databases, too. A *table relationship* exists between two tables when they are related (as described above) and always falls into one of these categories, depending on how many times the linking values can occur in each table:

One-To-One   This type of relationship exists when there is only one record on each side of the relationship for each linking value. For example, there is a one-to-one relationship from an Orders table to a Customer table when they are linked on the CustomerID field (only one customer for each order).

One-To-Many   When there can be more than one record for a linking value on one side of a relationship, you end up with a one-to-many relationship. The relationship between the Contacts and Calls tables is an example of a one-to-many relationship. There is only one record in the Contacts table for each person, but you can have many records in the Call table for each person.

Many-To-Many   This type of relationship describes the situation where linking values can appear in multiple records on both sides of a relationship. A table of Classes linked to a table of Club Members using a StudentID field would have a many-to-many relationship since a student could be in multiple classes and clubs.

In Access, the nature of a relationship between tables is determined by whether or not the linking fields are *key fields*. When a table is keyed, it means that one field, or a combination of fields, has been designated as the unique identifier for each of the table's records. Every record in a keyed table must have a unique value in the key field, or in the combination of key fields, if there is more than one. Because of this restriction, Access knows whether there can be only one possible record for a field value in a particular table. For example, if Access looks to a Customer table and finds that it is keyed on the CustomerID field, it knows that there can be only record for each CustomerID in the table.

NOTE

If key fields and relationships are still a mystery to you, don't worry. We'll talk about them more in Chapter 14.

You can check what kind of relationship exists between two tables in the Edit Relationships window as shown in Figure 13.16. Just right-click the line that links two tables, choose Edit Relationship, and check the Edit Relationships dialog box. In Chapter 15 you'll see how to create relationships between tables yourself and edit them in the Relationships window.

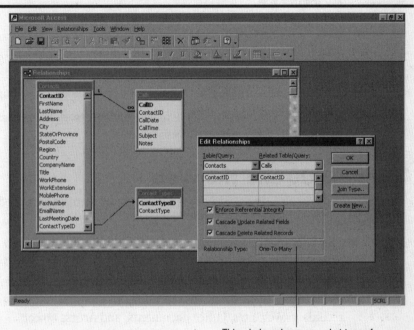

This window shows you what type of relationship exists between two tables.

FIGURE 13.16: The Edit Relationships dialog box shows you what field(s) link the tables in a relationship and what type of relationship exists.

ACCESS, OFFICE 2000, AND THE WEB

Access is certainly not a database unto itself. It has lots of features that make it easy to share data with other Office 2000 programs, and it's also quite Web-aware. You might want to glance through this section to get familiar with these features, even if you're not a big user of Office 2000 or the World Wide Web. You might see something that could be useful for one of your future Access databases or projects.

Part iv

Access and Office 2000

There are lots of ways you can expand the power of Access by calling on other Office 2000 applications from a database or project. You can:

 ▶ Click the OfficeLinks button on the Access toolbar to merge or publish data with Microsoft Word, or analyze a table with Microsoft Excel

▶ Link an Excel spreadsheet to an Access database

▶ Create a chart with MS Graph and show it on an Access form or report

▶ E-mail database information to someone via Microsoft Exchange

▶ Include objects like graphics, Excel spreadsheets, or Word documents in OLE fields in an Access table

Access 2000 and the Web

You may have already noticed several Web-related features sprinkled throughout Access:

▶ The Web toolbar has buttons for doing things like jumping to a Web site (when you have an active Internet connection), searching the Web, and adding sites to your Favorites list.

▶ You can use hyperlink fields in tables to jump from database records to Web sites, Office documents, and Access objects.

▶ With the Insert Hyperlink tool in the Form and Report Design windows, you can include links to the Web, as well as to other documents and database objects, right in your forms and reports.

▶ HTML files can be imported or linked to an Access database.

▶ Almost any database object can be saved as an HTML document.

▶ The new data access pages are HTML files that can be used to browse Access data with Access or Internet Explorer.

WHAT'S NEXT

Now that we've covered all the basic elements of Access, we can move on. It may be tempting to jump right in and start creating tables, forms, and reports right away, but spending a bit of time up front to lay a good database foundation will minimize the amount of time you have to spend revising your database later. Chapter 14 will cover how to use the Database Wizard, create a database yourself, plan your forms, reports, and queries, and much more!

Chapter 14

PLAN A DATABASE

F or some of us, it's hard to get started on a new task. If you fall into this group, just hearing the word "plan" may make you nervous, but this time you don't need to worry. The first decision you have to make when planning a database is actually pretty easy: whether you should use the Access Database Wizard to create the foundation for your database, or whether you should start from scratch. Once you know what the Database Wizard can do for you, it usually becomes obvious which way you should go. This section offers some guidelines on how to make a choice.

Adapted from *Access 2000: No Experience Required*
by Celeste Robinson
ISBN 0-7821-2485-2   608 pages $24.99

THE DATABASE WIZARD

The *Database Wizard* is a powerful tool that can build a foundation for many different types of databases. All you have to do is select the kind of database you need (asset tracking, contact management, donations, etc.), and the Wizard will create tables, forms, reports, queries, macros, and even switchboards for you. You get the chance to include optional fields for some tables and choose styles for forms and reports before the Database Wizard does its stuff, but otherwise the Wizard does its work unassisted.

The key question in determining whether the Database Wizard will save you time or not is this: What are the tables and fields that the Database Wizard will include in the database? There's no way to check out the structure of a database created by the Database Wizard other than to start the Wizard, choose a database, and examine the field list in the step that lets you choose fields for each table.

Start the Database Wizard

Here's how to start the Database Wizard:

1. Click the New icon on the toolbar, or press Ctrl+N.

2. Select the Databases tab in the New dialog box.

3. Scroll through the list of databases to see if any of them fit your project. If you don't find a good candidate, you might want to make a choice anyway and create a database, just to give you some ideas about what Access can do. Highlight the database you are interested in.

4. Click OK to open the File New Database dialog box.

5. Change the database name, if you like, and click Create to start the Wizard.

NOTE
You must have a printer installed in order for the Wizard to complete the Report portion of a new database setup.

Check the Tables and Fields in the Wizard's Database

To see what tables and fields are in the database the Wizard will create:

1. Click Next in the first Database Wizard dialog box.

2. To see the fields in each table, highlight a table name under Tables in the Database and check the list under Fields in the Table. You can scroll through the list to see what's included.

3. If you can see that the database you chose in the New dialog box is a hopeless candidate, click Cancel in any Database Wizard dialog box. Otherwise, continue on with the steps that follow to do more exploring

Figure 14.1 shows the tables in the Donations database the Wizard creates. In the figure, you can see some of the fields the Wizard includes in the Contributor Information table.

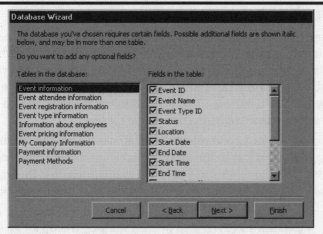

FIGURE 14.1: In this step of the Database Wizard, you can see the tables and fields that will be part of a new database. The Database Wizard is creating an Event Management database in this example.

Check for Optional Fields

Any field with a check mark in the Fields in the Table window is automatically included in the database. At the end of each field list, you may see unchecked fields with italicized names. These are optional fields that you can elect to add to the highlighted table. Just click an optional field's checkbox to include it in the database.

Choose Styles and Finish the Database

The next few steps of the Database Wizard are pretty self-explanatory:

1. Choose a style for forms and click Next.

2. Choose a style for reports and click Next.

3. Enter a title for the database, include a picture if you like, and click Next.

4. Click Finish to have the Database Wizard do its thing and open the new database.

Explore the Forms and Reports in the Database

It will take a little while for the Database Wizard to do its work. Once it's finished, it may ask you to enter some company information. Whether it asks for these details depends on the type of database you chose to create. Next the Database Wizard will display a switchboard that serves as a menu for the new database. Click the buttons on the switchboard to explore the forms and reports in the new database.

Why look at the forms and reports? Sometimes it's hard to visualize what a database does just by looking at its tables and fields. Reviewing the sample forms and reports will help you evaluate whether the Database Wizard will work for your project. It's a lot easier to see how tables work together when you're viewing them in a form or report.

Figure 14.2 shows a form created by the Database Wizard for an Event Management database. This form includes data from two tables in the database: Attendees and Registration. The top part of the form shows fields about an individual attendee, while the middle section of the form displays records for any events the attendee is registered for. This is an example of how related tables can be used together in one object. A field called AttendeeID links the tables behind the scenes but is not shown on the form.

Fields from the Attendees table   Fields from the Registration table

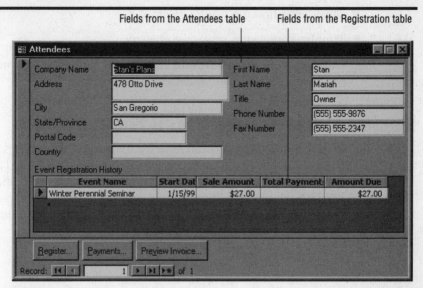

FIGURE 14.2: A form created by the Database Wizard for the Event Management
database

CREATE A DATABASE YOURSELF

As you look through a database created by the Wizard, check how closely
the Wizard's database structure matches what you need. If it looks like
you will have to make only a few changes (maybe delete a few fields, add a
couple of fields the Wizard didn't know you would need, and perhaps
change some field names), the Database Wizard is most likely a good
place to start. But, if it appears that you will end up spending lots of time
revising the Wizard's database to fit your project, it will most likely be
better to start from scratch.

If you decide to design a database yourself, it's best to spend some
time planning before you actually get started creating objects like tables,
forms, and reports. The rest of this chapter will give you some ideas for
things to consider as you go through the planning process. You'll find
information on:

- ▸ Choosing tables for your database
- ▸ Deciding on the fields for tables

- ▶ Considering how you want data entered

- ▶ Planning your forms, reports, and queries

- ▶ Thinking about how you can use hyperlinks, command buttons, and macros to automate your database

Decide What Tables You'll Need

As with many projects, you should work from the outside in when designing a database. Before you get engrossed in details like what should go where on a form and how a report should be sorted, which will be discussed later in this chapter, start by deciding what tables you will need. We'll go through a simple example to see what things you should think about in this phase of designing a database.

In brief, you will need to:

- ▶ Gather information on how your database will be used

- ▶ Look at the information to see what kind of records it describes (people, projects, orders, line items for orders, products, employees, etc.) and plan a table for each type of record

- ▶ List the details you will need to include in each type of record

- ▶ Make sure you don't have repeating details in a table

NOTE

In some situations, it's better to break this last rule than to force data in your tables into a theoretically proper structure. See "When to Break the Rules," later in this chapter, for examples of when you should ignore database theory and go with common sense instead.

Gather Information

The first step in designing any database involves gathering information about how the database will be used. You should make notes on:

- ▶ What information will go into the database

- ▶ How the data needs to be updated, summarized, or otherwise acted upon

- ▶ The reports or charts you will need to print or view

If you're lucky, you may have samples of the forms and reports now being used to do the tasks that will be managed with the database. You can use this information as a jumping-off point for your plan.

TIP

When you're gathering information for a database, be sure to consider what changes to your current system should be incorporated into the new database plan. Ask questions to find out if the current system tracks everything it should, or if it's lacking in some way. You may need to add fields that are not part of the forms and reports now being used.

Sample Notes

To see how all this theoretical planning works, let's create a plan for an Access database called Timekeeper that will track how much time people in a department are spending on various projects. Here's what our notes might look like after we go through the information gathering stage:

How Data Is Gathered

In the current system, each department member sends a spreadsheet to the boss that looks something like this:

	A	B	C	D	E	F	G
	Jan's Hours.xls						
1	**Jan's Hours**	**Week Ending 1/9/99**					
2							
3	**Project**	**Hours**		**Description**			
4							
5	Training	10		Update training guides for new hires			
6	Collections	6		Call "Over 90"s			
7	AR	20		Regular tasks			
8	Month End	8		Finish month end reports			
9							
10							
11							
12							
	Sheet1 / Sheet2 / Sheet3 /						

Even though there are rules for entering the data, each person ends up doing it a bit differently.

What Happens to the Data

The boss copies and pastes each person's spreadsheet into a master spreadsheet that has rows for each current project in the department. The spreadsheet has formulas that sum the hours by project and looks something like this:

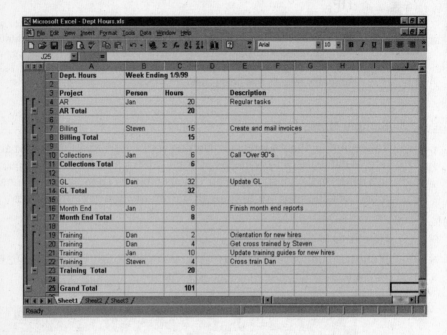

A copy of the spreadsheet is made and the records are rearranged to show totals by person. The totals for both summary spreadsheets are saved to a file of historical information.

Reports That Need to Be Printed

Two reports are currently printed each week:

▶ Total Hours by Project

▶ Total Hours by Person

Ideas for Changes

One problem with the current system is that it's not easy to keep a history of the records for each week. If too many records are left in the master spreadsheet, it becomes unwieldy. It's also difficult to report on the data for a selected week when there are records for more than one week in the file. Ideally, the new system should be able to easily handle an unlimited number of records.

Another desperately needed change involves data entry. It would be great to eliminate the need for the boss to consolidate everyone's spreadsheets. Each person should be able to enter their data in the same place.

It would also be nice to be able to print reports for user-specified time periods by project or person. That way summary information could be viewed by week, month, quarter, year, or whatever makes sense.

Review Your Research to Decide on Tables

When the information-gathering stage is complete, the next step is to decide which tables to use in the database. Look at all the information that will be recorded in the database to see what groups of records the data describes. Figure 14.3 shows the spreadsheet used to enter hours by project, with notes on how the pieces of data can be logically grouped.

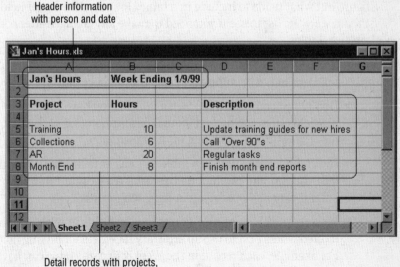

Header information
with person and date

Detail records with projects,
hours, and descriptions

FIGURE 14.3: The data-entry spreadsheet with the data grouped logically into two types of records

Looking at Figure 14.3, you can see that it makes sense to have at least two separate tables in Timekeeper:

▶ Weekly Records to hold records for each person/week-ending date combination

▶ Project Hours for the detail records for each weekly record: projects, hours, and descriptions

These two tables will be the backbone of the Timekeeper database plan. In the next section, you'll see how to set up these tables so they can be related and used together in forms and reports.

Decide on Fields

Once you decide on the tables you'll use in a database, you can move to the next level of work and choose fields for the tables. There's nothing difficult about this task, as long as you keep a few simple rules in mind.

Rules for Deciding on Fields

Usually you can just look at a sample of the data you will be entering to figure out what fields to include in a table. Jot down the list of fields and then review the list to see if you need to make any changes after considering these rules:

▶ If you want to sort on a value like Last Name, make it a distinct field instead of including it in a larger field like Name.

▶ Don't duplicate sets of fields in a table. If you have sets of repeating fields (like the project/hours/descriptions for each person/date), they probably belong in their own table.

▶ Avoid duplicating data in a table. It's easier to link in descriptive information like product names from a separate table than to enter it over and over again in repeated records.

▶ Be sure to include one or more common fields in related tables; it often works best to use an arbitrary ID # field for linking fields. For example, each record in the Weekly Records table can have a unique ID #. Then this field can be included in the Project Hours table to link detail records to a master weekly record.

Looking back at Figure 14.3, you can begin with these field lists for the Timekeeper database:

Fields for the Weekly Records Table	**Fields for the Project Hours Table**
WeeklyRecordID	Weekly Record ID (linking field)
Person	Project
WeekEndingDate	Hours
	Description

After looking at some of the other elements of database design, you may alter this structure a bit, but the basic layout here will serve well as a jumping-off point for the rest of the plan.

When to Break the Rules

As with most rules, there are times when it makes sense to throw out the rule book and go with what seems natural. Here's one example of when common sense should prevail over theory: If you have a small number of repeating fields, don't bother with a separate table.

For example, say you have an address book where you may need to enter multiple phone numbers for a person: a home phone, a work phone, a fax line, a cell phone, and a pager number. Based on the rule that says you should avoid duplicating fields for the same type of data in a table, you could decide to keep phone numbers in their own table and link them to a table of people records. The table structures might look like this:

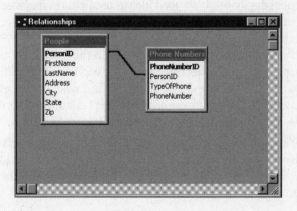

Is this worth the effort, though? When you break information down into separate, related tables, creating reports and queries gets more complicated. In this case, it might be more practical to create fields for three or four phone numbers and enter the rest in a catch-all field for notes. Even though more and more people can be contacted using many numbers, you may not want to make your phone book as complicated as their lives. You could keep it simple and use a structure like this:

Fields for a Simple Address Book Database

PersonID

FirstName

LastName

Address

City

State

Zip

HomePhone

WorkPhone

Fax

Notes (use this field for cell phone, pager, and so on when there are extra numbers)

Add Fields to Log Actions or Status

In most databases, it's a good idea to use fields to flag when certain actions occur or to note conditions like the status of an order. In our Timekeeper database, we could add a field called Entry Date to the Weekly Records table to show when each record was entered in the database. Don't worry about having to fill in another field—you can assign a default value of today's date to Entry Date to have Access fill in the field whenever a new record is added to the table. Default values are discussed later in this chapter in "Consider How You Want Data Entered," and in Chapter 15.)

Yes/No fields are good for any field that can have values of True or False. A Yes/No field automatically shows up as a checkbox in a table or a form, so it's a handy way to mark things like whether a letter has been sent.

Choose Field Types

After you choose fields for a table, the next step is to select *field types*. Field types determine what can be entered in a field, how the values can be formatted, and what can be done with the data.

Access Field Types Access has many field types. They are listed here with some notes on how each can be used:

AutoNumber Access automatically assigns a number to this field when a record is added to a table.

Currency This type of field is for money values.

Date/Time Dates, times, or date/time combinations go in Date/Time fields.

Hyperlink These fields hold hyperlink addresses that jump to Web sites, database objects, or other files.

Lookup Wizard A Lookup field starts a Wizard that places lookup constraints on a field; the lookup values can come from a list you enter, a table, or a query.

Memo This type of field holds an unlimited amount of text.

Number Numbers formatted in various ways can go in a Number field.

OLE Object Objects like pictures and Word documents go in OLE (Object Linking and Embedding) Object fields.

Text This type of field holds text: letters, numbers, and other characters.

Yes/No Values of True or False are stored in this kind of field; the values can be shown as Yes/No, True/False, Male/Female, etc.

You can see many of these field types in the form shown in Figure 14.4. Chapter 15 will show you how to include each one of these field types in a table.

Part iv

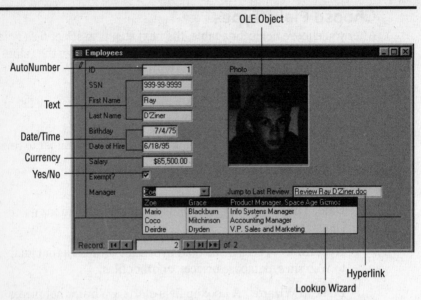

FIGURE 14.4: The table in this form includes many of the Access field types.

Field Types for the Timekeeper Database   Assign some field types to the Timekeeper database just for practice. You won't end up using all the field types yet; you'll add fields for some of the more exotic field types later.

Fields in Weekly Records Table	Field Type
WeeklyRecordID	AutoNumber
Person	Text
WeekEndingDate	Date/Time

Fields in Project Hours Table	Field Type
RecordID	AutoNumber
WeeklyRecord ID	Number (link to Weekly Records table)
Project	Text
Hours	Number
Description	Text (or Memo if you want to keep long notes)

Fields for Relationships

If tables are going to be related, they need to have one or more fields in common. For the Weekly Records and Project Hours tables, you already planned to link the tables using a WeeklyRecordID field. Figure 14.5 shows another example of two tables linked by a common field. In the figure, the Contributors and Pledges tables in the Donations database are linked by a field called ContributorID.

This line shows how the
ContributorID field links the
Contributors and Pledges tables.

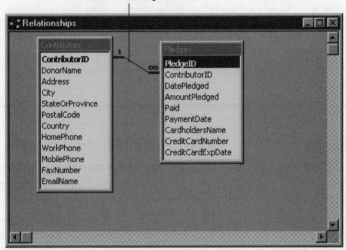

FIGURE 14.5:   The Relationships window for the Donations database shows how the Contributors and Pledges tables are linked by a common field called ContributorID.

Key Fields

A *key* consists of one or more fields whose values uniquely identify each record in a table. Key fields provide some special functions in a database:

- ▶ They are often used to link tables. They also determine the nature of a relationship. See Table 14.1 to see how key fields affect table relationships.

- ▶ Access automatically builds a *primary index* using any key fields in a table. This index makes it easier for Access to find key values and speeds up any searches or other operations that look for values in the key fields.

Part iv

In Figure 14.5, ContributorID is the key field, or *primary key*, for the Contributors table. This field is called a *foreign key* in the Pledges database. Because there can be only one record for each ContributorID in the Contributions table, but any number of records for the same ID in the Pledges table, a one-to-many relationship exists. The little symbols at either side of the line linking the tables in Figure 14.4 indicate the nature of the relationship.

In Chapter 15 you'll see how to specify key fields in a table.

TABLE 14.1: How Keys Fields Determine the Nature of a Relationship

LINKING FIELD KEYED IN...	RESULTS IN THIS TYPE OF RELATIONSHIP
Both tables	One-to-one
One table	One-to-many
Neither table	Many-to-many

Indexes

As mentioned just above, Access automatically builds a primary index for a table using the key fields in the table's structure. You can create additional indexes to speed up searches on other fields you think you will search frequently. For example, in the Donations database, the Database Wizard creates an index for the DonorName field in the Contributors table. This results in quicker searches by name than if the DonorName field was unindexed.

NOTE

When you create a database yourself, you can add indexes to tables in the Table Design view window. You'll see how to do this in Chapter 15.

One exception to this suggestion to create indexes applies when you are working with a small table. Adding an index to a non-key field in a table with hardly any records is probably not worth the effort it takes to set it up. If you are working in a table with lots of records, however, indexes will make a big difference in how long it takes to search non-key fields.

While you are planning a database, make a note of any fields you think you should index when you create your tables.

Consider How You Want Data Entered

The next task in planning a database involves defining rules for how you want data entered in your tables. It's important to enter data consistently for these reasons:

Linking Values Values in linking fields need to be controlled so you don't end up with orphan records. For example, Access won't match records where the Product ID is "a1234" in one table and "A 1234" in another.

Grouping and Sorting Records If values like names are entered differently in different records, Access won't be able to group or sort the records as you might expect. To Access, "Los Angeles" is a completely different value than "L.A." or "Hollywood."

Appearance When data is entered inconsistently, there's not too much you can do to make it look good on a form or in a report.

There are some tricks you can use to doctor data after it's entered in a table, but it's much easier to set up limits on field values ahead of time. Fortunately, Access has several features you can use to control data entry. Some of them are described next. The next chapter shows how to actually implement these features when you are creating tables.

Fill In Default Values

If a field will usually, but not always, hold the same value, you can assign a *default value* for it. When you plan a database, peruse your list of fields to see if using a default value for any of them would save data-entry time. For example, in the Project Hours table, you could assign a default value of "Regular work" to the Description field. You can also use Access Visual Basic functions for default values. If you use Date( ) as the default value for a field, Access will put today's date in that field in any new record. See Chapter 15 for some examples of handy default values.

Check Data against Input Masks

Input masks provide a couple of different kinds of data-entry checks. They can:

▶ Make sure a field value matches a pattern, such as 000-00-0000 for a social security number

Part iv

▶ Automatically fill in constant characters like dashes (-) or parentheses (())

▶ Optionally show placeholders to make data entry easier

▶ Store data with or without constants, depending on your preference

Adding an input mask to a field is easy because there's a Wizard to guide you through the process. Chapter 15 shows you how to add a predefined input mask, or one you define yourself, to a field.

Look Up a Value from a List or Table

To get good summary information from a database, some fields usually need to be limited to a certain set of values. For example, in the Timekeeper database, it would be a good idea to verify that a valid set of initials from a table of Employee records is entered in the Person field. You could also check that anything entered in the Project field has a matching entry in a table of Projects. There are a couple ways to do this with the Lookup Wizard when you are designing a table. You can:

▶ Limit a value to those that appear in a field in a table or query

▶ Check a value against a list of allowable entries that you define

Lookup fields have another benefit in addition to checking what's entered in a field against a set of values. When you create a lookup field that gets its possible values from a table, Access automatically defines a relationship between the main table and the lookup table. This makes it easy to include descriptive fields from the lookup table in forms and reports. For example, if you add a table for Projects to the Timekeeper database, you can include fields like Project Start Date, Project Manager, etc., in the new table. Then you can show these fields in any report for the Project Hours table, assuming the Projects and Projects Hours tables are linked on a common field like ProjectID.

TIP

When you are still in the planning phase, look to see which fields in your database should be checked using a lookup against a table, a query, or some other list of values. Chapter 15 explains how to use the Lookup Wizard to add these controls.

Validation Rules

There's another data-entry check you can apply to a field called a *validation rule*. A validation rule is a statement that checks whether data conforms to some rule after it is entered. When you set up a validation rule, you can also specify a message for Access to show when a value is entered that violates the rule. This section won't go into detail on how to use validation rules (they can be pretty tricky to set up), but you can look them up in Access Help if you think they would be useful for your database.

A Working Plan for Tables and Fields

With the previous information in mind, you can create a fairly detailed plan for the tables and fields that are needed in a database. Table 14.2 lists the fields for the Timekeeper database along with special properties, like indexes and lookups, the fields should have.

TABLE 14.2: Fields for the Timekeeper Database

Table	Field	Type	Key	Index	Default Value	Input Mask	Lookup
Weekly Records	WeeklyRecord ID	AutoNumber	Yes				
	Person	Text		Yes		LL?*	Employees table
	WeekEnding Date	Date/Time					
	EntryDate	Date/Time			Date()		
Project Hours	RecordID	AutoNumber	Yes				
	WeeklyRecordID	Number					Weekly Records table
	ProjectID	Number		Yes			Projects table
	Hours	Number					
	Description	Text (or Memo)			"Regular work"		
Employees	EmployeeID	Text	Yes			LL?*	
	FirstName	Text					
	LastName	Text					
Projects	ProjectID	AutoNumber	Yes				
	Name	Text					
	Start Date	Date/Time					
	Project Manager	Text					

*The input mask LL? allows for two or three letters to be entered in a field.

Part iv

PLAN YOUR FORMS AND REPORTS

Once you have a plan for your database tables, you can start on the forms and reports. First, gather any samples that are available to you and match the information on them to the fields in your tables to make sure you haven't forgotten a critical field or two. Also make notes on any calculated or summary fields that are needed on the forms or reports.

NOTE

If you need to show fields from more than one table on the same form or report, make sure that the tables have common fields. Then you can set up relationships between the tables. With the proper relationships in place, the Form and Report Wizards will let you include fields from multiple tables.

You don't have to answer the next couple of questions right away, but at some point you will have to consider them. You may want to wait until after you design your tables and start experimenting with the Form and Report Wizards, and the Form and Report Design windows.

Can the Wizards Do the Job?

You may be able to use the Form and Report Wizards to create many of your database objects. If you can't use the Wizard designs "as is," you will probably be able to use them as a foundation for your work instead of starting from scratch. (Designing a form or report from a blank design window can be a tedious, thankless task.)

NOTE

The key here is to select the right Wizard design as the basis for each form or report.

Do You Need to Show Selected Data?

Sometimes, maybe most times, you will have to show a form or print a report for selected records in your database. There's more than one way to do this. You can:

▶ Base a form or report on a query. (See Chapter 13 to find out what a query is, if you don't remember.)

- ▶ Include a filter in your form or report design. (Again, check Chapter 13 if you want to find out what a filter is.)

- ▶ Use a WHERE statement to limit the records that you see. (Check Access 2000 Help for details on WHERE statements. We won't cover them in this book.)

Review your list of forms and reports and make notes of how you want to limit the records that each document includes. Keep in mind that you can also prompt someone to enter criteria for a query.

NOTE

Remember: If you are using an Access project instead of a database, you will not be able to create queries from Access. You will have to set up SQL Server views to work with selected table records. You can create views with whatever SQL Server tools you are accustomed to working with, or using the Client Server Visual Design Tools that come with Access 2000.

Consider Whether You Need to Browse Data from the Web

If you want to let people browse the data in your Access database or project from the Web, you can use data access pages. (These objects were described briefly in Chapter 13.) Data access pages are similar to Access forms, but they let you browse Access data using Internet Explorer 5. These pages are stored in their own HTML files, but can be viewed from within Access as well as with Internet Explorer.

Think about Automation

This part of a database is really optional at this point, so you may want to move on to Chapter 15 and check back here when you are ready to add time-saving razzle-dazzle to your database. But if you have the patience to continue planning, read these sections now to get some ideas on how you can automate your database with hyperlinks, command buttons, and macros.

Use Hyperlinks to Create a Mini Info Highway

We briefly described hyperlinks in Chapter 13. To refresh your memory, you can use a hyperlink to do all these things:

- ▶ Jump to another object in the database you're working in

- ▶ Jump to an object in another database

- ▶ Open another Office file, like a Word document or an Excel spreadsheet

- ▶ Jump to a site on the Web

Even if you don't need to browse the Web from your database, you may want to use hyperlinks to create your own personal information highway. Look at how you will be working with your database to see if you will want to do things like open one form from another or view a report while you have a form open.

What Will You Be Doing Over and Over Again?

Some database tasks can get pretty boring when you do them repeatedly. Thankfully, you can automate many of these tedious jobs with *command buttons* and *macros*. As part of your database plan, make a list of the jobs you'd like to automate after all your tables, forms, queries, reports, and any data access pages are in place. You may want to use command buttons and macros to:

- ▶ Print a report while you're viewing a form

- ▶ Print an entire group of reports with one mouse click

- ▶ Print a report for selected records and note the action in each record

- ▶ Open a form and show a specific record

- ▶ Update a field value conditionally after another field changes

- ▶ Close a form and return to what you were doing

- ▶ Perform a series of calculations on records in one or more tables and then view the results in a report

- ▶ Close the database you're working with and leave Access

Actions like the last one seem pretty easy (just click the Close button!), so you may wonder why it would be worth the effort to set up a command button. The main reason is to make it easy for someone who's not familiar with Access to use the database. Clicking a command button labeled "Add record" is easier for a new Access user than hunting through the toolbar to find the built-in button that does the same job.

WHAT'S NEXT

Now that you've gone through a whirlwind tour of how to plan a database, you can really get started using Access. Get ready to do some hands-on work in Chapter 15.

Chapter 15

BUILD TABLES

After you create a new database and formulate a plan for the objects you think you'll need to work with, the next step is to make some tables to hold your information.

You'll find that Access 2000 offers many different ways to create tables: the Database, Table, and Import Wizards guide you through the process step-by-step, and the special Design and Datasheet views give you the flexibility to make customized tables to fit your needs.

Adapted from *Access 2000: No Experience Required* by Celeste Robinson

ISBN 0-7821-2485-2   608 pages $24.99

FIND YOUR STYLE FOR CREATING TABLES

There's more than one way to create a table. You can use:

The Database Wizard to create a database that includes tables, forms, reports, queries, macros, and switchboards.

The Table Wizard to select a table design from a set of business or personal table templates. You are free to select and rename fields, and the wizard helps you define relationships if there is more than one table in the database.

Design view to have complete freedom to create the fields, keys, indexes, lookups, and other data-entry checks you need in a table.

Datasheet view to enter data into a spreadsheet-type view and have Access make its best guess as to the data types for the fields (columns) of the new table.

The Import Wizards to get help bring data outside your database into Access tables.

With all these options, you may wonder which one is best for your project. Before exploring the primary skill covered in this chapter, using the Table Design window, take a quick look at each of these tools. See Table 15.1 for a summary of what these options have to offer.

TABLE 15.1: Comparing the Database Wizard, the Table Wizard, and the Table Design Window

CAN YOU ...	WITH THE DATABASE WIZARD	WITH THE TABLE WIZARD	WITH THE TABLE WINDOW
Choose fields	Optional fields only	Yes	Yes
Rename fields	No (you can do this later in Design view)	Yes	Yes
Move fields	No (you can do this later in Design view)	Yes	Yes
Create a key field	Automatically	Optionally	Manually
Relate tables	Automatically	Optionally	Manually

TABLE 15.1 continued: Comparing the Database Wizard, the Table Wizard, and the Table Design Window

Can You ...	With the Database Wizard	With the Table Wizard	With the Table Window
Add your own data-entry checks	No (you have to add them in Design view)	No (you have to add them in Design view)	Yes
Get forms, reports, switchboards	Yes	No (you have to create them yourself)	No (you have to create them yourself)

The Database Wizard

As we learned in Chapter 14, the Database Wizard can create an entire database for you, complete with tables, forms, reports, queries, switchboards, and even relationships defined behind the scenes. You do have to trade some flexibility, though, to get all this work done for you. The designs for the forms and reports created by the Database Wizard expect to find certain fields in the database tables. Because of this, you don't get a chance to rename or delete fields while the Database Wizard creates a new database for you.

You are free to add optional fields to some tables, but you can't alter the backbone of a table's design until the Database Wizard completes its work. Once a database is created by the Database Wizard, you can make changes to its tables using the Table Design window. If you opt to do this, though, be careful not to change any fields that are used to link tables. You can see which fields are linked in a database by using Tools ➤ Relationships.

The Database Wizard can create several different database projects for you. You can choose from these databases in the New dialog box shown in Figure 15.1.

Asset Tracking	Ledger
Contact Management	Order Entry
Event Management	Resource Scheduling
Expenses	Service Call Management
Inventory Control	Time and Billing

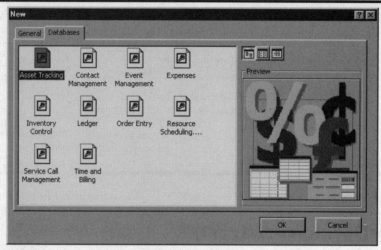

FIGURE 15.1: If you click the Databases tab in the New dialog box, you can select from several different projects.

NOTE

The process of creating a database with the Database Wizard was described in Chapter 14. If you need detailed instructions on using the Database Wizard, please refer back to Chapter 14. If you're still not sure whether the Database Wizard will work for you, refer back to Table 15.1 for a comparison of what you can do with the Database Wizard, the Table Wizard, and the Table Design window.

If the Database Wizard is too limiting for your needs, you can turn to the Table Wizard or go directly to the Table Design window to work on your own. The Table Wizard is discussed next.

The Table Wizard

The Table Wizard can be a great time-saver when you are creating tables. It lets you:

- ▶ Choose a table from lists of business or personal samples
- ▶ Select fields for a table
- ▶ Rename the fields and change their order
- ▶ Choose a key field

▶ Get help relating a table to other tables in the same database

Let's create a few tables with the Table Wizard to see how it works. To begin, create a new database called Timekeeper to hold your work:

1. Click New and choose File ➤ New from the menu, or press Ctrl+N.

2. Leave Database highlighted on the General tab in the New dialog box and click OK.

3. Enter **Timekeeper** in the File New Database dialog box and select Create.

Access will open a Database window:

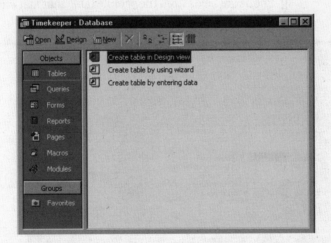

Create a Table with the Table Wizard
To start the Table Wizard, follow these steps:

1. Click the Tables button in the Database window.

2. Double-click Create Table By Using Wizard in the middle of the window. You'll see the opening dialog box of the Table Wizard.

3. Select Business or Personal to narrow down the Sample Tables list. For this example, leave it set to Business.

4. Highlight your choice on the Sample Tables list. This will change the selections on the Sample Fields list. Select Employees to create one of the tables we need for the Time-keeper database.

5. To add a field to the Fields In My New Table list, highlight its name on the Sample Fields list and click the > button. You can click the >> button to add the entire list of sample fields at once, if you think you want to use all or most of them. For the Employees table in the Timekeeper database, select the fields shown in Figure 15.2. There are a few extra fields that weren't in the plan you came up with in Chapter 14, but it's fine to add them at this point. Title, EmailName, and Work-Phone are fields from the sample table that may end up being useful in the Timekeeper reports.

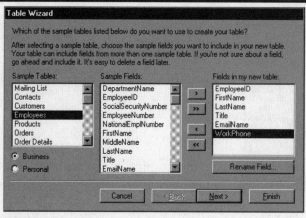

FIGURE 15.2: When you select a table in the first step of the Table Wizard, it changes the fields you can select on the Sample Fields list. This Table Wizard dialog box shows fields selected for a table called Employees.

6. If you want to rename a field, highlight the field on the Fields In My New Table list and click Rename Field. In the Rename Field dialog box, change the name as you like and click OK. (The rules for naming fields are discussed later in this chapter.)

7. Click Next after you complete the Fields In My New Table list.

8. Change the table name in the next step if you need to. For the Timekeeper example, leave it as Employees.

9. If you want to choose your own key field(s), select No, I'll Set The Primary Key. Otherwise, leave Yes, Set A Primary Key For Me selected. For the Employees table, let the Table Wizard make the choice for you.

10. Click Next.

11. In the last step, you can choose how you want to open the new table. Select:

    Modify the table design to open the table in Design view so you can make changes.

    Enter data directly into the table to open the table in Datasheet view so you can enter data.

    Enter data into the table using a form to have the Wizard create a basic form and open the table in Form view so you can enter data.

    For the Employees table in the Timekeeper database, select the last choice to create a new form.

12. Click Finish after choosing how you want the new table opened.

If you followed along with the example, you'll see a form window called Employees open on the Access Desktop. You don't need to enter data into this table yet, since there is more to learn about table design. So just click the form's Close button, select Yes, and choose OK to save the new form.

Relate Tables with the Table Wizard

As mentioned in Chapters 13 and 14, Access lets you create relationships between tables so you can use them together. The Table Wizard can assist you with this process. To see how this works, let's create another table called Weekly Records for the Timekeeper database with the Wizard's help. Because another table already exists in the database, the Table Wizard will give you a chance to relate the new table to the other one:

1. Click the Table button in the Database window if it's not already selected.

2. Double-click Create Table By Using Wizard, or click the New button and double-click Table Wizard in the New Table dialog box.

3. In the first Table Wizard step, leave Business selected and highlight Projects on the Sample Tables list.

4. Add these fields to the Fields In My New Table list and rename them as noted:

    ProjectID   Rename this field WeeklyRecordID.

    EmployeeID

    ProjectEndDate   Rename this field WeekEndDate.

You should end up with a dialog box that looks like this:

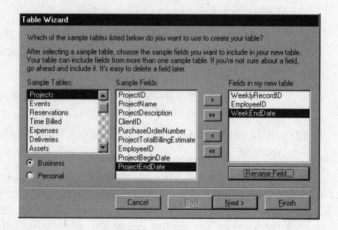

NOTE
You may have noticed that the field names being used here vary slightly from the plan in Chapter 14. This is fine, as it is helpful to work with the wizard's default names as much as possible.

5. Click Next.

6. Change the table name to Weekly Records and click Next.

7. This next step is where the Table Wizard helps you relate the new table to other tables in the database. Because the new table includes a field called EmployeeID, the Table Wizard

will automatically establish a relationship to the Employees tables you created earlier:

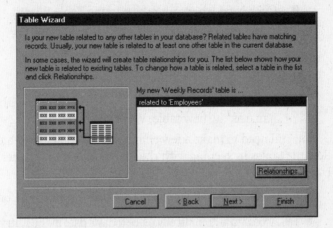

To see how the wizard has related the tables, click the Relationships button. Figure 15.3 shows that the Employees table has a one-to-many relationship to the new table. The Table Wizard comes to this conclusion because the EmployeeID field is keyed in the Employees table. This means that the Employees table can have only one record for each EmployeeID. However, there can be any number of records in the Weekly Records table for the same EmployeeID with different week-ending dates.

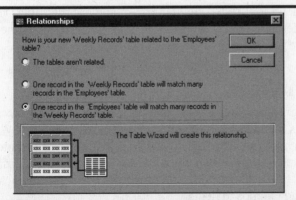

FIGURE 15.3: The Relationships dialog box, which you open from the Table Wizard, lets you change the way the wizard has chosen to relate tables.

8. Click OK when you are finished checking the Relationships dialog box.

9. Click Next when you return to the Table Wizard.

10. Select Enter Data Into The Table Using A Form... and click Finish.

11. Click the Close button for the new form.

12. Choose Yes and then OK to save the new form with the same name as the new table, Weekly Records.

You still need to make a few changes to the Employees and Weekly Records tables in keeping with the plan outlined in Chapter 14. In the Design window, you need to:

▶ Add a field called Entry Date to the Weekly Records table

▶ Tell Access to automatically place today's date in the Entry Date field

▶ Change the data type for the EmployeeID field to text and the length to 3, if the Table Wizard assigned AutoNumber or some other type that won't allow us to enter initials

▶ Add a data-entry check in the form of an input mask to the EmployeeID field to make sure that two or three uppercase letters are entered for the employee's initials

The "Use the Table Design View Window" section later in this chapter contains all the information you need to figure out how to make these changes yourself. If you want to follow along with the examples in the rest of this book on your own computer, you should use the Table Design view window (described next) to create the other tables for the Time-keeper database you planned in Chapter 14.

Table Design View

The Table Design view window is another place you can create new tables with Access. It's a completely different kind of tool than the Table Wizard. Instead of choosing fields from a predefined list, you enter whatever fields you like and select the data types for each field. The Table Design window is also the place where you add properties like default values, input masks, and lookups to fields.

Figure 15.4 shows the Table Design window for the Weekly Records table that was created with the Table Wizard in the last example.

TIP

No matter what method you use to create a table, you can always open it later in Table Design view to make changes or check its structure.

The Table Design view window will be used in another example to create a new table from scratch. You'll also see how to use it to make changes to a table's design.

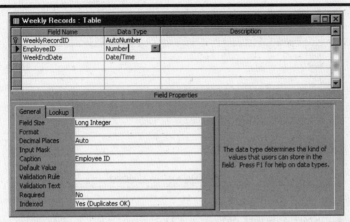

FIGURE 15.4: In Table Design view, you can create a new table or change a table's design. This window shows the design for the Weekly Records table created by the Table Wizard.

Before you get into all the features of the Table Design view window in "Use the Table Design View Window" later in this chapter, take a quick look at one other way to create tables in Access.

Datasheet View

When you open a table in Access, you see your data arranged in rows (records) and columns (fields). This is called *Datasheet view*. Access has a neat feature that lets you enter data directly into an empty Datasheet view window to create a new table. You can bypass the Database Wizard, the Table Wizard, and even the Table Design view window, if you're lucky. When you create a table this way, Access takes a look at the data you enter in the various columns of the Datasheet view window, and then makes its best guess as to what types of fields the new table should have.

To create a table in Datasheet view:

1. Select the Tables button in the Database window.

2. Double-click Create Table By Entering Data. (You can also click the New button and double-click Datasheet View in the New Table dialog box.)

3. Access will open an empty Datasheet view window that looks like this:

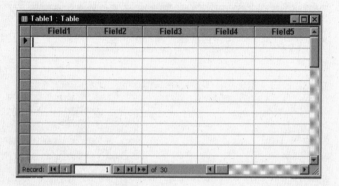

4. Start entering data in the Datasheet view, making sure you enter the values for each field in their own column. For example, to create the Weekly Records table for the Timekeeper database using this technique, enter initials for EmployeeIDs in Field1, WeekEndDates in Field2, and EntryDates in Field3. (Don't bother entering values for a WeeklyRecordID field. Access can add ID numbers for you, as you'll see in a minute.) You'll end up with a datasheet like this:

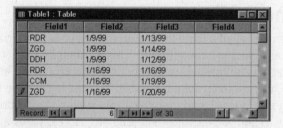

5. To give a column a more descriptive name than the default Field*n*, right-click the field header and choose Rename Column.

Edit the field name right in the field header area and press Enter. You can change the field names shown in the last step to EmployeeID, WeekEndDate, and EntryDate. The Datasheet view now has field names as shown here:

EmployeeID	WeekEndDate	EntryDate	Field4
RDR	1/9/99	1/13/99	
ZGD	1/9/99	1/14/99	
DDH	1/9/99	1/12/99	
RDR	1/16/99	1/16/99	
CCM	1/16/99	1/19/99	
ZGD	1/16/99	1/20/99	

Record: 1 of 30

6. To create the new table, click the Close button for the Datasheet view, choose Yes, enter a table name, and click OK.

7. Access will ask if you want to create a primary key. Click Yes to have Access add a key field called ID with the AutoNumber type.

Figure 15.5 shows the Table Design view window for a table created in Datasheet view using the field names shown in step 4 above. As you can see, Access has included a key field called ID. The EmployeeID field has the Text field type, and the WeekEndDate and EntryDate fields both have the Date/Time field type. Access was able to assign these field types by looking at what was entered in each column of the Datasheet view.

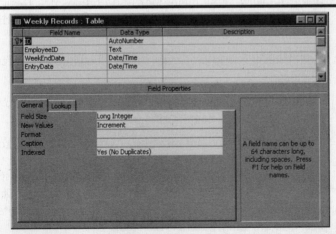

FIGURE 15.5: This table was created in Datasheet view. Access added the ID field automatically and assigned the Text and Date/Time field types to the other fields after looking at what was entered in each column.

USE THE TABLE DESIGN VIEW WINDOW

In the Table Design view window, you can create a new table or change a table's design. Next you'll see how to:

▶ Create a new table

▶ Add fields to a table, insert them, delete them, and move them

▶ Define key fields and remove them, in case you change your mind about the fields that should be keyed for a table

▶ Assign input masks, default values, or validation rules to fields

▶ Set up indexes

▶ Use the Lookup Wizard to make sure a field's values match those in another table or query (or in some list of values you enter)

Create a New Table in Design View

To create a new table with the Table Design view window, follow these steps:

1. Select the Tables button in the Database window.

2. Double-click Create Table In Design View(or click New to open the New Table dialog box and double-click Design View). You'll see an empty Table Design view window like the one in Figure 15.6.

3. Add fields and field properties as described in the next few sections.

4. Click the Close button for the Table Design view window, choose Yes, enter a name for the new table, and click OK.

5. If Access asks if you want to define a primary key, choose Yes to add an AutoNumber key field. Choose No if you want to create your own key field later or leave the table unkeyed. In either case, you will be returned to the Database window. The new table name will appear on the list of objects in the Database window when Tables is selected.

Choose "Lookup Wizard. . ." as the data type to
define a lookup with the Wizard's help.

Click here first and
then drag to move a field.

Click here to select a field.

Select your key field(s)
and click here to define a key.

Click here to open the Indexes dialog box.

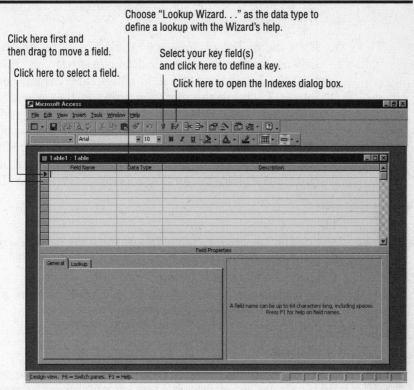

FIGURE 15.6: When you create a table using Design view, you will work in a
Table Design view window that looks like this.

Add a Field

The first thing you need to do in an empty Table Design view window is
add some fields. It's easy to do:

1. Enter a name in the first row under Field Name. A field name
    can be up to 64 characters long and can contain letters, num-
    bers, spaces, and other characters except for periods (.),
    exclamation points (!), accent graves (`), and brackets ([]).
    For other naming restrictions, see Access Help.

2. Move to the Data Type column and choose a data type for
    the field. You can enter a type yourself or choose it from the
    drop-down list of data types. (The arrow for this drop-down

list is visible only after you move the cursor to a box in the Data Type column.)

3. If you choose Text or Number for the data type, the field will have a Field Size property. The default length for Text fields is 50; the default Field Size setting for Number fields is Long Integer. To change this property, make sure the General tab is selected in the bottom half of the Table Design view window. Then, for a Text field, click the line after Field Size and change the size. For a Number field, click the Field Size line and use the drop-down arrow to choose a different setting (Byte, Integer, Long Integer, Single, Double, or Replication ID).

TIP

To change the default size for Text and Number fields, choose Tools ➢ Options, click the Tables/Queries tab, and change the settings for Default Field Sizes.

4. To add another field, move the cursor to the Field Name column in the next row and repeat steps 1–3.

WARNING

If you join a Number field to an AutoNumber field to relate two tables, leave the Field Size for the Number field set to Long Integer. Otherwise, Access will not be able to link the fields.

Move a Field

Once a field is added to a table's design, you are free to move it to a new location:

1. Click the row selector to the left of the field's name to select the field. (You can click and drag at this point to select multiple fields.)

2. Point your mouse to the selected field(s) and drag to a new spot. A small dotted rectangle will appear to the lower right of the mouse pointer while you are dragging, and you will see a thin horizontal line above the last selected field.

Insert a Field

To insert a field in the field list, instead of adding a field to the end of the list:

1. Click the row selector of the field that will appear below the inserted field.

2. Press Insert or click the Insert Rows button on the toolbar.

3. Enter a field name and data type for the new field in the blank row that is inserted.

TIP

You can also insert or delete fields in Datasheet view. See "Make Changes in Datasheet View" later in this chapter for details.

Delete a Field

It's easier to delete a field than to add one!

1. Select the field(s) you want to delete.

2. Press Delete or click the Delete Rows button on the toolbar.

If you make a mistake, you can use Edit ➤ Undo Delete right after you delete to get the fields back. If you make another change, however, you will not be able to use Undo to get the field back. The only way to recover the field, if the table was previously saved, is to close the Table Design view window and cancel all your changes to the table's design.

Add Key Fields

Key fields were covered in Chapter 14. In a nutshell, the *key* for a table must have a unique value for each record in the table. A key can consist of more than one field and is used to generate a *primary index* for the table. The primary index speeds up searches on the key field(s) and is used to determine the nature of a relationship when it is used to join tables (one-to-one or one-to-many).

With that speedy review out of the way, let's see how to actually key one or more fields in a table:

1. Click the row selector for the field you want to key. (Click and drag if you want to select contiguous fields for the key, or hold down the Ctrl key while you click fields that do not follow each other.)

2. Click the Primary Key button on the toolbar or choose Edit ➤ Primary Key.

When a field is keyed, it will have a small key in its row selector, as does the WeeklyRecordID field shown here:

Field Name	Data Type	Description
WeeklyRecordID	AutoNumber	
EmployeeID	Number	
WeekEndDate	Date/Time	

Weekly Records : Table

NOTE

When you use a query to append records into a table that has an AutoNumber key field, Access will automatically assign key values to the new records. However, if you append records to a table with another type of key field(s), you will have to make sure that each new record has a unique value in the key field(s). If there are records that don't have unique keys, Access will not append them.

Remove Key Fields

To remove a key field or fields:

1. Click the row selectors to select the key field(s).

2. Click the Primary Key button on the toolbar or choose Edit ➤ Primary Key.

The small key in the row selector(s) will disappear. The Primary Key button on the toolbar, just like the Edit ➤ Primary Key menu command, works as a toggle to turn key fields on or off.

Add Drop-Down Lists with the Lookup Wizard

If you want to use a drop-down list to limit what can be entered in a field, it's time to use the Lookup Wizard. The Lookup Wizard can help you create a drop-down list from values in a table or a query, or from a list of values you specify.

In addition to limiting the values that can be entered in a field, a drop-down list also offers these benefits:

▶ You don't have to remember the valid entries for a field since they are shown on the drop-down list.

▶ If you bypass the drop-down list and start typing, Access fills in the first value from the list that matches the character(s) you enter. As you continue typing, Access changes the value to reflect your changes. This saves data-entry time.

▶ You can type the first few characters of a value and then open the drop-down list to move to the first entry that matches what you type. This allows you to avoid scrolling through a lengthy list and is a convenient way to navigate through a long list of values that are sorted alphabetically.

▶ Using a drop-down list ensures that data gets entered in a uniform manner.

Let's use the Lookup Wizard to show the EmployeeID field in the Weekly Records table in the Timekeeper database as a drop-down list. The list will only show values that already exist in the EmployeeID field in the Employees table.

NOTE

Before following the next series of steps, make sure that you have created an Employees table like the one described in "Create a Table with the Table Wizard" earlier in this chapter. You will also have to open the table in Table Design view and change the data type of the EmployeeID field from AutoNumber to a Text field with a length of 3. Then open the Employees table and add records for any EmployeeIDs you have already entered in the Weekly Records table. Otherwise, Access will not allow the old records to remain in the Weekly Records table after the lookup is added to the EmployeeID field.

1. Open the Weekly Records table in Table Design view. (Right-click the table's name in the Database window and choose Design.)

2. Move to the Data Type for the EmployeeID field.

3. Select Lookup Wizard... from the list of Data Types to start the Wizard.

4. In the first step, make sure the first option, "I Want the Lookup Column to Look Up the Values in a Table or Query," is selected and click Next.

5. Select Employees on the list of tables in the next dialog box and click Next.

6. Highlight EmployeeID on the Available Fields list and click the > button to move this field over to the Selected Fields list. Add the FirstName and LastName fields, too, to show them on the drop-down list. Then click Next.

7. In the next dialog box, you can change the column widths that will show up on the drop-down list. (Drag the right border of a field's header to resize it or double-click the right border to have the column fit all its values.) You can also "unhide" the key field (the EmployeeID field) so it will appear on the drop-down list. If you want to see the EmployeeID, uncheck the Hide Key Column option and click Next.

8. If you unchecked Hide Key Column in the last step, you will be asked to select a field that uniquely identifies each record. Leave EmployeeID selected and click Next. If you don't see this step, don't worry.

9. Change the label for the lookup column, if you want, and click Finish in the last step of the Lookup Wizard.

10. Choose Yes when Access asks if you want to save changes to the table before it creates relationships.

To see how the new lookup works, click Datasheet View on the toolbar (assuming you are still in Design view) and move the cursor to the EmployeeID field. You will see a drop-down arrow appear at the right side of the field. Click this arrow to see a list of the records in the

Employees table. If you get an empty drop-down list, the Employees table has no records. Add some names to the Employees table and try the drop-down list for the Weekly Records table again. Figure 15.7 shows the EmployeeID drop-down list after it was opened in Datasheet view for the Weekly Records table.

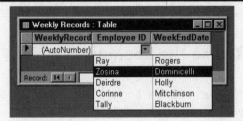

FIGURE 15.7:   This drop-down list for the EmployeeID field in the Weekly Records table was created with the Lookup Wizard. It draws its values from the EmployeeID, FirstName, and LastName fields in the Employees table.

Create Your Own Values for a Drop-Down List

In the first step of the Lookup Wizard, you can choose to create your own list of lookup values instead of using a table or query for the list. To create your own list, follow these steps:

1. In the Table Design view window, choose Lookup Wizard... as the data type for the field you want to add a lookup to.

2. In the first step of the Lookup Wizard, select "I Will Type in the Values that I Want" and click Next.

3. In the next step, enter the number of columns you want to see on the drop-down list (the default is 1). Then enter the values for the drop-down list in the columns shown in the dialog box. Click Next when you are finished.

4. If you used more than one column in step 3, choose the field that uniquely identifies each record on the lookup list and click Next.

5. Change the label for the drop-down list, if you like, and click Finish.

TIP

It's best to use this option when the number of lookup values is small and the values won't change frequently. If the lookup values for a field are likely to change, or you have a long list of possible values, you should probably take the time to enter them in a table before starting the Lookup Wizard. It's easier to edit a long list of lookup values in a table than in the Table Design view window.

If You Need to Revise the Lookup Wizard's Work

After you set up a drop-down list with the Lookup Wizard, you can revise the resulting list two ways. You can do either of the following:

▶ Open the table in Design view and rerun the Lookup Wizard

▶ Use the Lookup tab in the bottom of the Table Design view window and edit the various lookup properties

If you need to change the source of lookup values or the columns that are shown on the drop-down list, it's probably best to rerun the Lookup Wizard. To do this, just click the Data Type box for the field you want to change and select Lookup Wizard from the list of data types. Then follow the Wizard as described just above.

If you need to edit a list of values you supplied, or perhaps change the width of a column on the drop-down list, you can edit the Lookup properties directly:

1. Select the field with the lookup to make sure you are looking at the right stuff.

2. Click the Lookup tab in the bottom half of the Table Design view window.

You'll see some cryptic properties like Bound Column and other not-so-mysterious entries like Column Count and Column Widths. It's OK to edit these entries directly if you are cautious. Adjusting the column width property is not too dangerous, but be careful if you play with the others. You may have to start the Lookup Wizard over again if you end up with a mess!

Specify a Default Value for a Field

If you have a field that will hold the same value all the time, or most of the time, you can use the *Default Value* property to fill in the field automatically whenever a new record is added to a table.

To assign a default value to a field:

1. In the Table Design view window, click the field you want to define a default value for.

2. Select the General tab in the bottom half of the Table Design view window.

3. On the General tab, click the line for Default Value.

4. Enter the value you want to use for the default. You can use either a constant value or a Visual Basic function as explained below.

Figure 15.8 shows a default value in the Table Design view window for a field called Description. The Description field is selected in the top half of the window and "Regular work" is entered for the Default Value on the General tab.

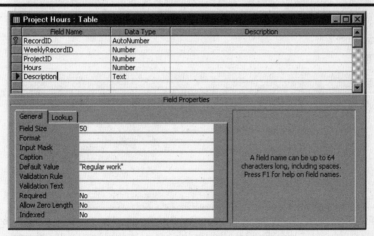

FIGURE 15.8:   In this Table Design view window for the Project Hours table, a default value of "Regular work" is assigned to the field Description.

Use a Constant for a Default Value

The default value for the Description field in Figure 15.8, "Regular work," is called a *constant*. A constant value always remains the same. To enter a constant in the Default Value box for a field, just type it in, unless it includes punctuation like periods or commas. If this is the case, you need to enclose the value in quotes as in "L.A." to make sure Access doesn't try to interpret it as a Visual Basic function. Otherwise, don't worry about the quotes. Access will add them to whatever value you enter as soon as you leave the Default Value box.

Use a Function to Derive a Default Value

You can also use a Visual Basic function for a default field value. A *function* is a bit of programming code that is designed to return a certain type of value. For example, the function Date() returns the current date from your computer's clock. The Now() function is similar to Date(), but it returns the current date and time. To automatically timestamp a Date/Time type field with today's date, just use Date() as the field's default value, as shown for the WeekEndDate field in Figure 15.9.

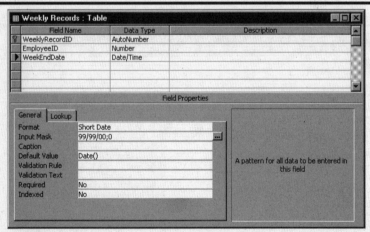

FIGURE 15.9:   The Visual Basic function Date() is used for the default value for the WeekEndDate field in this example. Whenever a new record is added to the Weekly Records table, Access places the current date in the WeekEndDate field.

Create Input Masks

Using an *input mask* is another way to limit what can be entered in a field. An input mask can do a couple of different things:

▶ It forces you to enter field values in a pattern such as 999-99-9999 or 415-555-5543.

▶ It can fill in constant characters like dashes (-) and slashes (/), and optionally store these characters as part of the field value so you don't have to enter them yourself.

Figure 15.9 (see above) shows an input mask for the WeekEndDate field that automatically fills in the slashes as dates are entered.

To add an input mask to a field:

1. In the Table Design view window, click the field that the input mask will belong to.

2. In the bottom half of the window, click the line for Input Mask.

3. You can enter an input mask yourself or click the "..." at the end of the Input Mask line to get help from the Input Mask Wizard for Text and Date/Time fields.

Use the Input Mask Wizard

The Input Mask Wizard lets you choose from a list of built-in masks that are included with Access. The list that the Wizard shows you depends on the type of field you are setting up a mask for. For a Text field, you'll see a list like this:

To use the Input Mask Wizard, follow these steps:

1. Start the Input Mask Wizard for a Text or Date/Time field as described in the last section.

2. Highlight the mask you want to use (e.g., Zip Code, Phone Number, etc.).

3. Click Next.

4. In the next dialog box, change the input mask and the place-holder character, if you need to. (The rules for creating input masks are outlined in the next section, "Create Your Own Input Masks.") Then click Next.

5. The next step asks whether you want Access to store constant characters like dashes and slashes with the field value. Make your choice and click Finish. (There's nothing else to do in the last step, so you may as well finish here.) See the Warning below for details on how your choice in this step can affect what happens when you look for data later.

WARNING

If you tell the Input Mask Wizard not to store constants with field values, you need to remember to leave out the constants when you do finds or queries. For example, if you have an input mask that automatically displays a zip code with a dash like this, *94002-0000*, but the dash is not stored in the Zip Code field, you have to enter *940020000* when you look for this zip code with a query or a find.

Create Your Own Input Masks

The built-in masks you can select using the Input Wizard are handy for zip codes, phone numbers, dates, and times. There's also a mask for entering hidden passwords. Beyond that, though, you're on your own. If you need to format other kinds of values (maybe product codes or tax codes), you'll have to create your own masks.

Creating an input mask is not difficult once you are familiar with the rules for setting one up. Basically, there are two things to be aware of:

▸ The three possible parts of a mask

▸ The way Access uses special characters in a mask to impose limits on what can be entered in a field

Check the sections below, "The Parts of an Input Mask" and "Input Mask Characters," if you need help formulating a mask.

The Parts of an Input Mask An input mask can have up to three parts, separated by semicolons (;):

▶ The first part is the mask itself.

▶ The second part tells Access whether to store any constant characters with the field values. A *0* tells Access to store constants; a *1* or blank says not to.

▶ The third part lets you change the placeholder from an underscore (_) to some other character.

Let's look at the parts of the input mask in Figure 15.9, *99/99/00;0*. The *99* tells Access to check that numbers, not other characters, are entered in the first two places of the Date field value. The *9*, as explained in the next section, also says that the entry of the character is optional. (In this case, because the input mask is for a Date field, this means you can omit either the first or second character before the slash (/), but not both since you need at least one character each for the month and for the day.) The slashes are shown automatically, and the *00* says that two numbers must be entered after the second slash. Finally, the *;0* after the input mask tells Access to store the slashes with the field values. Since there is no third part in this example, the default placeholder (_) is used.

That's a lot of words to explain how a short input mask works. The best way to see how an input mask affects data entry is to try it. In the first dialog box of the Input Mask Wizard, select any input mask, click the Try It box, and enter a value to see how it gets checked by the mask.

Input Mask Characters When you create an input mask, special characters tell Access how to limit the data that gets entered in a field. Table 15.2 lists the characters you can include in an input mask and describes their functions. To see some examples of how these characters work in a mask, check Table 15.3.

TABLE 15.2: Input Mask Characters

Use This Character…	To Check For …
0	Required number (0–9), no plus or minus signs
9	Optional number (0–9) or space, no plus or minus signs

TABLE 15.2 continued: Input Mask Characters

USE THIS CHARACTER...	TO CHECK FOR...
#	Optional number or space, plus and minus signs allowed
L	Required letter (A–Z)
?	Optional letter (A–Z)
A	Required letter or number
A	Optional letter or number
&	Required character or space
C	Optional character or space
. , : ; - /	Decimal placeholder, number, and date/time separators; characters used depend on Windows Control Panel settings
<	Character that gets converted to lowercase
>	Character that gets converted to uppercase
!	A mask that displays from right to left, characters always entered left to right
\	Next character in mask to display as a constant

TABLE 15.3: Sample Input Masks

THIS MASK...	ALLOWS THESE FIELD VALUES
(999)000-0000	(650)555-9999 ( )555-9999
>LL0000	AB0932
Aaa	123 12 AB1 AB 1a
00000-9999	94000-0000 94000-
000-00-0000	999-99-9999
>L<??????????	Melanie Benjamin

Enter Your Own Mask

Once you formulate an input mask, you can enter it two ways.

If you don't need the mask for other fields, just select the field the mask will belong to in the top half of the Table Design view window. Then, in the bottom half of the Table Design view window, click the General tab and type your mask on the Input Mask line on the General tab.

If you want to use the mask for other fields, add it to the Input Mask Wizard's list as described next.

Add a Mask to the Input Wizard's List

To add a mask you create to the Input Mask Wizard's list so you can use it for other fields in the future:

1. Start the Input Mask Wizard as described earlier.

2. In the first step of the Input Mask Wizard, click the Edit List button to show the Customize Input Mask Wizard dialog box:

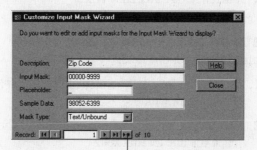

Click here to add a mask to the Input Mask Wizard list.

3. To add a new mask, click the New Record navigation button (the one with the asterisk at the bottom of the Customize Input Mask Wizard window). You'll see a blank record (except for Mask Type) where you can enter your input mask and a description.

4. Type in a description and the input mask. If you want to show placeholders in the field for the mask, enter an underscore or other character in the box labeled Placeholder. Whatever you enter in the box for Sample Data will be shown in the

Data Look column of the Input Mask Wizard dialog box. If you are creating a mask for a Date/Time field, change the setting for Mask Type to Date/Time. Otherwise, leave it set to Text/Unbound.

5. Click the Close button to return to the Input Mask Wizard dialog box.

When you return to the Input Mask Wizard dialog box, your new input mask will appear on the scrollable list in the middle of the window. You can then select it and try it out, just like one of the built-in masks.

Add Indexes to a Table

Access uses *indexes* to speed up finds and other operations where it has to look for data in one or more fields. Any table that is keyed automatically has a primary index created for its key field(s). You may want to create your own indexes for other fields that you search frequently to find records. Indexes are also good for non-key fields that you use to join tables or sort records. You can index using fields that have the Text, Number, Currency, or Date/Time type.

Create an Index Using One Field

To create an index for one field:

1. Select the field to be indexed in the top half of the Table Design view window.

2. In the bottom half of the window, select the General tab and click the line for Indexed.

3. Open the drop-down list for Indexed and select "Yes (Duplicates OK)" or "Yes (No Duplicates)," depending on whether there will be more than one record with the same value in the indexed field.

Create an Index with More Than One Field

You can create an index using up to ten fields. This type of multifield index is useful for queries or filters that search more than one field at the same time, and for tables that are joined on more than one field. To create a multifield index:

1. Click the Indexes button on the toolbar in the Table Design view window. You'll see an Indexes dialog box that looks something like this:

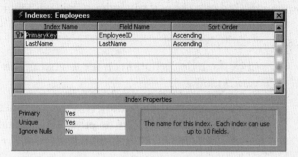

    The Index Names you see will depend on the table you are working with. This Indexes dialog box for the Employees table shows a primary index based on the EmployeeID field and another index called LastName for the field with the same name.

2. To add an index, enter a name on the next blank line in the Index Name column.

3. Move to the next column, Field Name, and select the first field for the index from the drop-down list of field names.

4. Move down a row in the Field Name column and choose the second field for the index. You don't need to enter anything under Index Name on this line; just leave it blank.

5. Repeat step 4 for each additional field you want to include in the index.

6. If you want to make sure that the index does not have duplicate values, change the setting for Unique to Yes in the bottom half of the Indexes window. If there will be lots of records with blanks in the indexed fields, change Ignore Nulls to Yes to save disk space.

7. Close the Indexes dialog box to return to the Table Design view window.

Delete an Index

If you have many indexes for a table, it may actually slow down certain operations (like append queries) because of the time it takes Access to maintain the indexes. Also, if you index a field with many repeated values, the index may not do you much good. To get rid of an index that doesn't appear to be useful:

1. Click the Indexes button on the toolbar in the Table Design view window.

2. Click the row selector to the left of the name of the index you want to delete. If you are deleting a multifield index, hold down Shift and click the first and last rows for the index.

3. Press Delete.

4. Close the Indexes dialog box.

Save a Table's Design

To save your work in the Table Design view window, you can do any of the following:

▸ Choose File ➤ Save from the menu and enter a table name if the table hasn't already been named.

▸ Press Ctrl+S.

▸ Close the Table Design view window, choose Yes when Access asks if you want to save your changes, and enter a table name if needed.

▸ Click the View button to switch to Datasheet view and choose Yes to save your changes.

CHANGE A TABLE'S DESIGN

Once you create a table, you are free to change its design. There are two different places you can make design changes:

Table Design view   Use this view for any kind of revision including field name changes, field moves, data type and length changes, field additions and deletions, and index changes.

Datasheet view Use this view to insert or delete fields, rename fields, or add lookup fields.

Make Changes in the Design Window

To change a table's design in the Table Design view window, right-click the table's name in the Database window and choose Design from the shortcut menu that pops up. Or:

1. Click the Tables button in the Database window.

2. Select the name of the table you want to change. (Click it to highlight it.)

3. Click Design.

 If you want to change a table that's already open in Datasheet view, just click the View button on the toolbar to switch to Design view.

Once you're in Design view, you can add, move, insert, or delete fields as described earlier in the "Use the Table Design View Window" section. You can also work with input masks, indexe, or any other table properties.

 WARNING

Access won't let you delete a field that is used to relate tables unless you delete the relationship first. (See "Define Relationships" later in this chapter for information on deleting and changing relationships between tables.)

Rename a Field in Design View

To rename a field, just click the field's name and make your changes.

 WARNING

Be careful about changing field names if you've already created forms, reports, and queries. Access won't recognize the renamed fields, and you'll have to do some repair work on your designs. To avoid this problem, turn on the new Auto-Correct feature before you make any changes to field names. Choose Tools ➤ Options, click the General tab, and click the boxes for Track Name AutoCorrect Info and Perform Name AutoCorrect under Name AutoCorrect. Then click OK to close the Options window.

Make Changes in Datasheet View

Some changes can be made to a table's design from a Datasheet view window. You can:

- ▶ Insert a field
- ▶ Delete a field
- ▶ Rename a field
- ▶ Insert a Lookup field

The quickest way to make these changes in Datasheet view is through the shortcut menu that comes up when you right-click a field header:

WARNING

When you make changes to a table's design in Datasheet view, you won't be able to cancel your changes when you close the window. Each change is saved as soon as you make it.

Insert a Field in Datasheet View

To add a field to a table while you are working with it in Datasheet view:

1. Right-click the header (field name) of the field that will follow the new field.

2. Choose Insert Column from the shortcut menu that comes up. Access will create a new field called *Field1* (or *Fieldn* where *n* is the next available number).

3. Right-click the header of the new column (field) and choose Rename Column from the shortcut menu, or double-click the field name. The field name will be highlighted and the cursor will appear to the left of the field name.

4. Type in the name you want to use for the new column and press Enter.

After you start entering data in the new field, Access will make its best guess as to what data type should be assigned to the field. You can check the data type, and change it if need be, in the Table Design view window.

Delete a Field In Datasheet View

You can bypass going to the Design view window if you want to delete a field while you're working in Datasheet view:

1. Right-click the header of the field you want to delete.

2. Choose Delete Column from the shortcut menu.

3. Choose Yes to delete the field and all the data it contains from the table.

Rename a Field in Datasheet View

It's easy to rename a field in Datasheet view. Just double-click the field name to highlight it and make your changes. Or you can:

1. Right-click the field name you want to change.

2. Choose Rename Column from the shortcut menu.

3. Click the field name if you want to edit it, or just start typing to replace the name completely.

Insert a Lookup Field in Datasheet View

You can start the Lookup Wizard to create a drop-down field right from Datasheet view:

1. Right-click the header of the field after the place you want to insert the lookup field.

2. Choose Lookup Column... from the shortcut menu.

3.   Follow along with the Lookup Wizard as described in "Add Drop-Down Lists with the Lookup Wizard" earlier in this chapter.

DEFINE RELATIONSHIPS

In Chapter 14's section on planning a database, you learned about table relationships and how Access uses them to link tables. You also learned about the types of relationships that can exist between tables (one-to-one, one-to-many, and many-to-many) and how they are determined by whether linking fields are keyed.

If you use the Database Wizard or the Table Wizard to create tables, you may not need to define any table relationships on your own. Also, when you use the Lookup Wizard to create a drop-down list that draws its values from a table, Access creates a relationship for you. Sometimes, though, you need to relate tables yourself. This task is performed in the Relationships window.

To open the Relationships window, choose Tools ➤ Relationships from the menu, or right-click anywhere in the Database window and select Relationships.

Figure 15.10 shows the Relationships window with two tables from the Timekeeper database used in some of the examples in this chapter: Employees and Weekly Records. The Table Wizard created this relationship between the Employees and Weekly Records tables using the EmployeeID field.

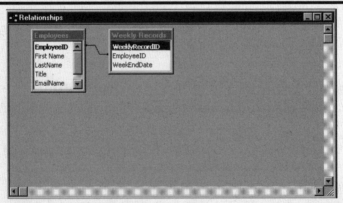

FIGURE 15.10:   In the Relationships window, you can see how tables are related as well as define relationships, change referential integrity rules, and join types.

Add a Relationship

Let's add another relationship to the window shown in Figure 15.10 to see how you can do this yourself. We'll relate the Project Hours table to the Weekly Records table.

1. Open the Relationships window as described in the last section.

2. Click the Show Table button on the toolbar.

3. In turn, double-click the names of the tables you want to work with if they are not already visible in the Relationships window.

4. When all the tables you need have been added to the window, click Close in the Show Table dialog box.

5. Click the linking field in one table and drag the mouse pointer to the linking field in the related table. When you release the mouse, you'll see an Edit Relationships dialog box like this:

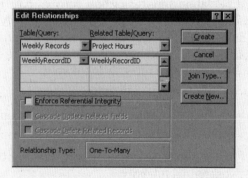

6. If you need to relate tables using more than one field, click the second row under Table/Query and choose the next field for the relationship from the drop-down list. Choose the linking field in the second row under Related Table/Query. Repeat this step for any additional pairs of fields you need to define the relationship.

7. Click Create to create the relationship. You'll see a line for the new relationship added to the Relationships window as in Figure 15.11.

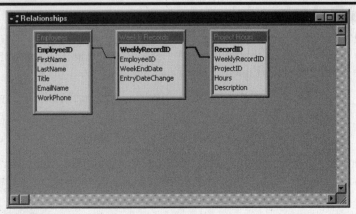

FIGURE 15.11: The line between the Weekly Records table and the Project Hours table shows that these tables are related on the WeeklyRecordID field.

Set Rules for Referential Integrity

In the Edit Relationships dialog box, you may have noticed a checkbox for Enforce Referential Integrity. *Referential integrity* is a way to protect data in linking fields so you don't end up with orphan records. You can turn this feature on or off in the Edit Relationships dialog box and set the rules for how referential integrity is enforced.

To turn referential integrity on:

1. Right-click the line that shows the relationship between two tables and choose Edit Relationship.

2. In the Edit Relationships dialog box, click the box for Enforce Referential Integrity.

3. Check any rules you want enforced:

   Cascade Update Related Fields changes the values in related records when the linking value in their master record is changed.

   Cascade Delete Related Fields deletes related records when the master record in a relationship is deleted.

4. Click OK to close the Edit Relationships dialog box.

TIP

If you have trouble getting a shortcut menu with the Edit Relationship choice, click the relationship line first to select it. It will appear as a bold line. Then right-click the line again. You should see a shortcut menu with the choices Edit Relationship and Delete.

Change the Join Type

When you do things like run queries to find records in related tables, by default Access looks for records that have matching values on both sides of the relationship. When records are matched up this way, it is referred to as an *inner join*. You can change the join type to an *outer join* so that Access includes all records from one side of the relationship, whether or not there are matching values in the linking fields on the other side of the relationship.

To change the join type:

1. Open the Edit Relationships dialog box as described earlier.

2. Click the Join Type button to show this dialog box:

3. Click 2 or 3, depending on which table you want to show all the records for.

4. Click OK to return to the Edit Relationships dialog box. Click OK again if you want to go back to the Relationships window.

Delete a Relationship

To delete a relationship:

1. In the Relationships window, right-click the line for the relationship you want to get rid of.

2. Choose Delete from the shortcut menu.

3. Choose Yes.

If you have trouble getting a shortcut menu with a selection for Delete, click the relationship line first to select it and right-click again.

Save Your Relationship Changes

To save any work you do in the Relationships window, just close the window and choose Yes.

WHAT'S NEXT

That's it for Access! Now it's on to Outlook, where you'll learn everything you need to know about using this application for managing contacts, sending and receiving e-mail, and scheduling your time.

PART V
MANAGING YOUR TIME
WITH OUTLOOK 2000

Chapter 16

MANAGING CONTACTS WITH OUTLOOK

Outlook is primarily a communication and organization tool and, as a result, your contacts form the foundation of your Outlook data. Contacts is the place to record name and address information, telephone numbers, e-mail addresses, Web page addresses, and a score of other information pertinent to the people with whom you communicate. If there is a piece of information you need to record about an individual, you can probably find a place for it in Contacts.

Adapted from *Mastering Microsoft Outlook 2000*
by Gini Courter and Annette Marquis
ISBN 0-7821-2472-0   816 pages $34.99

CREATING A CONTACT

In Outlook, a *contact* is an individual or organization you need to maintain information about. The information can be basic—a name and phone number—or include anniversary and birthday information, nicknames, and digital IDs. Outlook is, at its core, a contact management system. The other Outlook components are designed to work in conjunction with your contacts, so the more time you spend developing accurate and useful contact information, the easier it is to use Outlook to schedule meetings, send e-mail and faxes, and document time spent on the phone or visiting in person.

You probably have an existing address and phone list in a contact management system, such as a Day Runner, Franklin Planner, or Rolodex. When you start using Outlook, entering data from your current system as Outlook Contacts is the best way to begin. While Outlook is robust enough to help you easily manage business and professional contacts, don't forget to take time to add personal contacts like friends and family members so all your important names, e-mail addresses, phone numbers, and addresses are in one place.

You enter information about a contact in an Outlook Contact form. A blank form can be opened in several ways. If you're going to be entering a number of contacts, click the Contacts icon in the Outlook shortcut bar to open the Contacts component.

From the menu bar, choose File ➤ New ➤ Contact, or click the New Contact button on the toolbar to open a blank Contact form. If your hands are already on the keyboard, there's no need to grab the mouse: Press Ctrl+ Shift and the letter C to open a Contact form, shown in Figure 16.1.

If you're working in another component (for example, the Outlook Calendar), you don't need to switch to Contacts to open a Contact form. You can choose File ➤ New ➤ Contact from the menu bar in any module— you'll just need to look a bit further down the menu selections to find

Contact. The same list is attached to the toolbar; click the New Item button's drop-down arrow and select Contact from the menu.

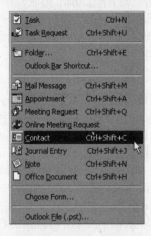

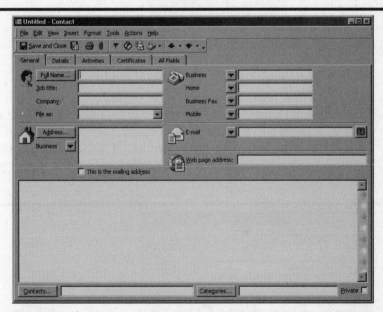

FIGURE 16.1:   Use Outlook Contact forms to collect and manage information about business and personal contacts.

The Contact form is a multi-page form, with tabs labeled General, Details, Activities, Certificates, and All Fields. The form opens with the General page displayed, as shown in Figure 16.1. (To move to another page, simply click the tab for the page.) You'll use the text boxes on the General page to enter the kinds of information usually stored in an address or telephone book.

Entering Names, Job Titles, and Companies

Begin by entering the contact's name in the first text box on the General page, next to the Full Name button. If you just want to enter the contact's first and last names, that's fine, but you can also include their title, middle name (or initial), and suffix. For example, "Mary Smith," "Dr. Mary Smith," and "Smith, III, Mr. Richard M." are all acceptable ways of entering names.

You don't have to fill all the fields; on the other hand, you can't use information you don't enter. For example, Outlook provides an easy way to quickly create a letter to be sent to a contact. If you might need to send formal correspondence to your friend Bill Jones, take the time to enter Bill's title when you create the Contact. You can always choose to omit the title on a specific piece of correspondence, but you can only include it easily if you've entered it in the Contact form.

When you've finished typing the contact's name, press Enter or Tab to move to the next field. Outlook will parse (separate) the name into parts for storing it. If Outlook can't determine how to separate the parts of the name, or if the name you entered is incomplete (perhaps you entered only a first name in the Full Name field), the Check Full Name dialog box, shown in Figure 16.2, opens so you can verify that Outlook is storing the name correctly.

FIGURE 16.2: The Check Full Name dialog box appears when you need to verify how a name should be stored in Outlook.

Outlook does a fairly good job of separating names appropriately. However, it doesn't handle some names and titles perfectly. If you enter the titles Dr., Miss, Mr., Mrs., Ms., or Prof., Outlook places them in the Title field. However, if you use other titles—for example, Rev. for a minister, The Honorable for a judge, or Fr. for a priest—Outlook will not recognize them as titles and places them in the First Name field. Names that are composed of two words, such as Jo Anne or von Neumann, may also not be separated correctly into first, middle, and last names. You can edit these fields manually by clicking the Full Name button to open the Check Names dialog box.

Full Name...

TIP

To instruct Outlook not to check incomplete or unclear names, clear the check box in the Check Full Name dialog box before clicking OK. To turn checking back on, open a Contact form, click the Full Name button to open the dialog box, turn the option back on, then click OK.

In the Job Title text box, enter the contact's complete job title. If you don't know the contact's job title, simply leave the field blank. Enter the name of the contact's company in the Company field. If you've already entered another contact from the same company, make sure you spell and punctuate the company name the same way. Later, you'll probably want to sort your contacts by company. Outlook views each unique spelling of a company name as a separate company. If some of your contacts work for *Sybex* and others for *Sybex, Inc.*, Outlook won't group them together.

In the File As field, either select an entry from the drop-down list or type a new entry to indicate how the contact should be filed.

Bonelli, Sherry
Sherry Bonelli
Sybex, Inc.
Bonelli, Sherry (Sybex, Inc.)
Sybex, Inc. (Bonelli, Sherry)

If you choose to file contacts with the first name first, you can still sort them by last name, so it's really a matter of personal preference. If you'll usually look up the company rather than the individual, it's a good idea to file contacts by company name. For example, ABC Graphics assigned

Jim as the sales representative to your account, but it might be more useful to file the contact as *ABC Graphics (Jim)* than as just *Jim*—particularly if you have trouble remembering Jim's name.

You aren't limited to the choices on the File As drop-down list. Select the text in the File As text box, then enter the File As text you'd like to use. This allows you to enter formal names for contacts, but store them in a way that makes them easy to retrieve; you can enter Dr. William Jones III as the contact name, but file your friend as Bill Jones so you can find him quickly.

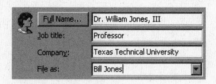

Entering Contact Addresses

Outlook allows you to store three addresses—Business, Home, and Other—for your contact and designate one of the three as the address you want to use as the contact's primary address. To choose the type of address you want to enter, click the drop-down arrow in the address section, and select the address type from the list. The address type will be displayed to the left of the arrow.

Click in the Address text box and type the address as you would write it on an envelope. Type the street address on the first or first and second lines, pressing Enter to move down a line. Type the city, state or province, country, and zip code or postal code on the last line. If you don't enter a country, Outlook uses the Windows default country.

NOTE
The Windows default country is set in the Windows Control Panel under Regional Settings.

When you press Tab to move to the next field, Outlook will check the address just as it did the contact name. If the address is unclear or incomplete, the Check Address dialog box opens, as shown in Figure 16.3. Make sure the information for each field is correct, and then click OK to close the dialog box.

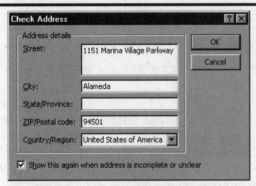

FIGURE 16.3:   The Check Address dialog box opens to allow you to verify an incomplete or unclear address.

In Outlook, the primary address for a contact is called the *mailing address*. The mailing address is the address displayed in most views, and is the address used when you merge a Word main document with your Outlook Contacts. By default, the first address you enter for a contact is set as the mailing address. To change the address used as the mailing address, make sure the address you want to use (Home, Business, or Other) is displayed in the Address text box; then click the This Is the Mailing Address check box to make the displayed address the mailing address.

Entering Contact Telephone Numbers

This is truly the age of connectivity. While three mail addresses are sufficient for nearly everyone you know, it isn't unusual to have five, six, or more telephone numbers to contact one person: home phones, work phones, home and work fax numbers, mobile phones, ISDN numbers, and pager numbers. With Outlook, you can enter up to nineteen different telephone numbers for a contact and display four numbers "at a glance" on the Contact form, as shown in Figure 16.4.

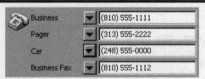

FIGURE 16.4:   The Contact form displays four of the nineteen numbers you can enter for a contact.

When you create a new contact, the four default phone number descriptions displayed are Business, Home, Business Fax, and Mobile. To enter a telephone number for one of those four descriptions, simply click in or tab to the appropriate text box and type in the telephone number. You don't need to enter parentheses around the area code, hyphens, or spaces—just enter the digits in the telephone number, as shown here.

NOTE

If you include letters in your telephone numbers (like 1-800-CALLME), you won't be able to use Outlook's automated dialing program to call this contact.

When you move out of the text box, Outlook will automatically format the digits, adding parentheses, spaces, and hyphens. If you enter a seven-digit telephone number, Outlook assumes the phone number is local and adds your area code to the number.

NOTE
International phone numbers get some rather convoluted treatment. Locate your contact, go to Actions ➤ Call Contact ➤ New Call, and click Dialing Properties. In the Dialing Properties dialog box, check the For Long Distance Calls, Use This Calling Card option and click the calling card button. Oddly enough, this does not mean you must have a calling card to make an international call—the default option is None (Direct Dial). Get your call information together and click the International Calls button. In the International Calls dialog box, you will be able to enter all of the information required to make a successful international connection.

Part V

To enter another type of telephone number, click the drop-down arrow for any of the four text boxes to open the menu of telephone number descriptions.

The telephone number descriptions with check marks are those you've already entered. From the menu, choose the description of the telephone number you wish to enter; then enter the number in the text box. When you've finished entering telephone numbers for the contact, the numbers that are displayed in the four text boxes may not be the numbers you use most frequently. That's not a problem—just open the menu next to each text box and, from the menu, select the descriptions for the numbers you want to display. In Figure 16.5, we've displayed the four numbers we use most frequently to reach Bill Jones.

FIGURE 16.5: You can choose to display any four telephone numbers in the Contact form.

Understanding E-mail Addresses

You can enter up to three e-mail addresses for a contact. The e-mail addresses are labeled E-mail, E-mail 2, and E-mail 3, rather than "Business" and "Home" like mail addresses and telephone numbers. You might think it would be easy to get a contact's home and work e-mail addresses confused, but the e-mail address itself usually contains the information you need.

Internet e-mail addresses have three parts: a username, followed by the "at" symbol (@), and a domain name. The domain name includes the *host name*, and may include a *subdomain name*.

Each e-mail account has its own *username*. In Windows NT, usernames include the owner's name, such as bjones, jonesb, or billjones. Many companies and e-mail providers also add a number to the usernames, so they look like bjones1, or they include the person's middle initial so that Bill Jones and Barbara Jones don't have to fight over who gets to be the "real" bjones.

The username and domain name are separated with the @ symbol. The *domain name* begins with the host name. The *host name* is the name of the server that handles the e-mail account. For example, in the address bjones@wompus.berkeley.edu, the host name is "wompus". (On one of the wompus server's hard drives, there's space for Bill Jones to keep his e-mail; the space is called his *mailbox*.) The *subdomain* is "berkeley"—the name or an abbreviated name of the organization that owns the server. The last part of the domain name, following the last period, is the *domain*, which describes the type of organization. Currently, there are six domains used in the United States, and seven additional domains may be added soon (if the politicians make some decisions). Table 16.1 lists the current domains.

TABLE 16.1: Current Domain Names

DOMAIN	TYPE	EXAMPLE
com	Commercial: for-profit organizations	sybex.com
edu	Educational: schools, colleges, and universities	berkeley.edu
gov	Governmental: federal, state, and local governmental units	michigan.gov
mil	Military: armed services	af.mil
net	Network: network access providers	att.net
org	Organization: non-profit businesses	uua.org

Outside of the United States, most domains are a two or three character abbreviation for the country: uk for the United Kingdom, ca for Canada, jp for Japan. An increasing number of educational organizations use us (United States) as their domain rather than edu; the domain name oak .goodrich.k12.mi.us describes a host at Oaktree Elementary in Goodrich Public Schools, a K-12 district in Michigan.

Entering E-mail Addresses

To enter an e-mail address, enter the entire address, including the username and the domain name. When you move out of the e-mail address text box, Outlook analyzes the address you entered to ensure that it resembles a valid e-mail address. Outlook does *not* check to make sure that the address is the correct e-mail address for this contact, or that the address exists. Outlook just looks for a username, the @ symbol, and a domain name. If all the parts aren't there, Outlook deletes the text you entered.

When you enter inappropriate characters, Outlook is a bit bolder in letting you know about it. Some addresses used within mail systems aren't compatible with the Internet. For example, many CompuServe addresses contain commas: 72557,1546. This is a valid e-mail address for a CompuServe member if you're a CompuServe member and stay within the CompuServe system, using the CompuServe Information Manager to send your e-mail. However, it's not a valid *Internet* e-mail address. The only punctuation used in Internet addresses are periods and the @ symbol. If you want to send e-mail to this CompuServe address from Outlook or any other Internet mail system, the address must be modified for use on the Internet. (For CompuServe addresses, change the comma to a period and add the CompuServe domain name: *72557.1546@compuserve.com*.)

If you mistakenly enter the CompuServe address as the e-mail address for your contact, Outlook thinks that it's two addresses, separated by a comma:

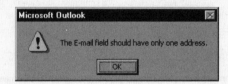

Outlook won't let you save this Contact until you either correct or delete the incorrect e-mail address.

All versions of Outlook support a file format called *Rich Text Format* (*RTF*). With RTF, you can format an e-mail message as you would a Word document, using boldface, italicized text, and different fonts and font colors to provide emphasis in the message. If you're using Outlook on a server at work, your colleagues running Outlook on the network will be able to open RTF messages and see your text in all its formatted glory.

However, not all e-mail services support RTF (and all of your colleagues may not be using Outlook). Services that don't support RTF support *plain text*. If your contact's e-mail service doesn't support RTF, the formatting of the message can make it harder to decipher the actual text of the message because it inserts funny codes. At best, the formatting doesn't appear, and you've spent time formatting for no good reason. If you know that your contact's e-mail service doesn't support RTF, check the Send Using Plain Text check box to send all messages to this contact in plain text. If you leave the check box disabled, messages will be sent in RTF if you choose RTF as your default e-mail format. (You'll find out how to select e-mail formats in Chapter 17.)

The Send Using Plain Text setting is for the Contact and affects all three of the contact's e-mail addresses. What happens when your contact's work e-mail service supports RTF, but their home service does not? In Outlook, you can change an individual e-mail message to plain text or RTF when you create the message. (See Chapter 17 for more information on e-mail options.) If one of the e-mail addresses you use for the contact doesn't support RTF, we suggest that you check the Send Using Plain Text check box.

Understanding URLs

When you're preparing for a visit, telephone call, or Internet meeting with a contact, you probably have a number of information sources you check. You'll look at your Calendar to see when you met last, check your Task list to ensure that all the tasks related to the contact are complete, and search online for recent news about the contact's organization. The contact's Web site is one of the places you'll want to search. Web sites often contain news about an organization, including recently announced products, promotions, legal actions, press releases, and other information of interest. By adding a *hyperlink* pointing to the URL of the General page on the Contact form, you can access the contact's Web site with one quick click of the mouse.

To find the contact's Web site, you must know the site's Internet address. An individual item you can find on the Internet is called a *resource*. Just as e-mail addresses are used to locate individuals, *Uniform Resource Locators*, or *URLs*, are Internet addresses that contain all the information needed to find a Web site or specific document.

The URL has two parts: the resource and a *protocol* that specifies the method used for retrieving the resource. The protocol for a page on the *World Wide Web* (*WWW*), the graphically based portion of the Internet, is *Hypertext Transfer Protocol* (*http*). Most of the URLs you'll see begin with http, but there are other protocols, including *file transfer protocol* (*ftp*), used on sites where you download files; *gopher*, a search and retrieve protocol used on university database sites; and *file*, used for files located on a local or network drive.

The protocol is followed by a colon and two slashes "*://*" and then the resource, including directions to the file you want to retrieve. The resource includes the host name and may also include a filename and path.

Assigning a Web URL to a Contact

When you enter a World Wide Web URL in the Web Page Address text box, you don't need to enter the protocol. Enter the resource name (for example, www.disney.com), and when you leave the text box, Outlook will automatically add http:// to the beginning of the URL. However, if you're entering an address for another type of protocol, such as gopher, telnet, or ftp, you must enter the entire URL, including the protocol and the resource. If you don't, Outlook will still add `http://` to the beginning of the URL, and it will be incorrect.

NOTE

If the URL you are pointing to includes standardized components, Outlook can handle things other than WWW links. For instance, `ftp.uunet.com` will become `ftp://ftp.uunet.com` and `gopher.ucla.edu` will become `gopher://gopher.ucla.edu`, which is nice if you need fast access to various different resources. However, if an FTP site begins with a WWW prefix (this is how most ISPs allow access to personal Web space), then it will still be interpreted as a Web address.

To visit the user's Web site, simply point to the URL, and the mouse pointer will change to the familiar browser-link hand shape. Double-click to launch your default browser and load the Web page. If the Contact form isn't open, select the contact in any view, and either choose Action ➤ Explore Web Page from the menu bar, or right-click the contact and select Explore Web Page from the shortcut menu.

Assigning a File URL

File URLs point to addresses on a local area network. A file URL begins with the `file://` protocol, followed by the file path and filename. For example, `file://k:\users\BillJones.doc` is a file on the K drive in the folder named "users". If there is a space anywhere in the filename or path, you must enclose the address in brackets, using the < and > symbols: for example, `<file://c:\My Documents\News About Bill Jones.doc>` is a valid URL. Without the < and > symbols, the URL is invalid. There are limitations to the usefulness of assigning URLs to files. You can only access files that you have network permissions for, and if another user moves or renames the files, the URL won't be correct.

Using Categories

A *category* is a key word or term that you assign to an item. Categories give you a way to sort, group, filter, and locate Contacts, Tasks, and other Outlook items. With the exception of e-mail messages, every type of Outlook item can be sorted and grouped by category. Outlook comes with 20 built-in categories, and you can delete categories or add other categories that reflect your work.

With categories, you can consistently organize items in all modules and use the categories as a way to relate items. If all the contacts, journal entries, tasks, and appointments related to Project XYZ are assigned to the Project XYZ category, you can use Advanced Find or the newly added Categories button located in many forms to locate and display them. You can sort and filter Outlook items based on category within a module. Thoughtful use of categories is a key to Outlook organization.

For example, you can create a category for each department in your organization and assign staff to the appropriate department category. Sorting by category results in a list sorted by department. Print the view, and you've got an employee directory.

To assign a category to a Contact, either type a category description in the Categories text box, or click the Categories button on the General page to open the Categories dialog box, shown in Figure 16.6.

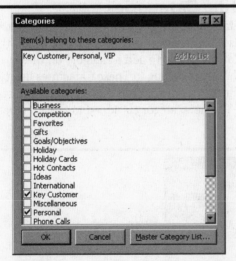

FIGURE 16.6: Assign, add, and delete Outlook categories in the Categories dialog box.

You can add as many categories as you wish to a Contact. Click the check box in front of each category that you wish to assign. Some of the categories, such as Holiday and Time & Expenses don't apply to Contacts. As you click the check boxes, the categories you select are listed in alphabetical order in the Items Belong to These Categories box at the top of the dialog box. When you close the dialog box, the categories are listed in the Categories text box on the General page.

Categories... | Key Customer, Personal, VIP

WARNING

While Outlook allows you to assign multiple categories to items, many Outlook-compatible personal data assistants (PDAs) are more limited. If you intend to synchronize your Outlook Contacts with a PDA, see the owner's manual both for the PDA and the synchronization software before assigning multiple categories to contacts.

Adding and Deleting Categories

There are two approaches to changing categories: you can add them one at a time, as you need to use them, or do a bit of planning and add them all at once in the Master Category List. To add a category on the fly, click after the last category in the Items Belong to These Categories list, type a comma and the name of the category, and then click the Add to List button, shown in Figure 16.7. The new category is added to the alphabetized category list.

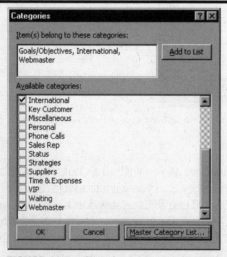

FIGURE 16.7:   Click the Add to List button to add a new category to the Master Category List.

While you can add categories on a whim, we suggest a more planned approach. If you've already entered a hundred Contacts, creating a new category or deleting existing categories often means you'll have to open existing contacts and change their categories. After you've looked at each of the Outlook components, but before you create too many Contacts, open the Categories dialog box and determine if the categories listed will meet your needs. Delete the categories you don't want to use and add the categories you require to the Master Category List.

To access the Master Category List from any Outlook form, click the form's Categories button to open the Categories dialog box. Then click the Master Category List button at the bottom of the Categories dialog box. The Master Category List dialog box, shown in Figure 16.8, opens.

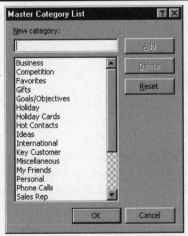

FIGURE 16.8:   Use the Master Category List dialog box to add or delete Outlook categories.

To remove a category from the list, select the category and click the Delete button. To add a category, type the category name in the New Category text box and click the Add button. If you click the Reset button, Outlook returns the Master Category List to the 20 default categories, most of which are visible in Figure 16.8.

Deleting a category from the Master Category List does not delete it from the Categories assigned to Contacts. In Figure 16.9, we've opened the Categories dialog box for a Contact after removing two categories, My

Friends and Sales Rep, from the Master Category List. The two categories are still assigned to this Contact, but probably won't be assigned to another Contact because they're no longer choices in the list.

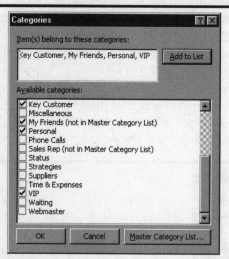

FIGURE 16.9:　Categories that have been deleted from the Master Category List are indicated in the Categories dialog box.

This presents a minor problem. When you sort your Contacts by category, every category that's used in a Contact shows up, even after you delete the category from the Master Category List. If you don't want to see Contacts grouped under categories you've deleted from the list, you'll need to open each Contact and delete the category from the Contact.

TIP

The same category list is used in all the Outlook components. So while it might not make sense to have a category for Phone Calls in Contacts, it can be very useful in categorizing Tasks. Create your category list with all the applications in mind.

Making a Contact Private

If you're using Outlook on a network, other users may have been given permission to share your Contacts folder, or you may place Contacts in a public folder. In the bottom-right corner of the General page, there's a check box marked Private. By enabling the Private setting, you prevent other users from seeing this Contact, even if they have access to your Contacts folder.

Entering Contact Comments

The large text box at the bottom of the General page is an open area for comments about the Contact: anything from quick phrases to eloquent paragraphs. For example, if the contact is your sales representative, you might put your account number in the comments text box. Or you might note hobbies and favorite ice cream flavors. If your company hands out t-shirts, it's a perfect location for shirt sizes.

You can't sort, group, or filter on comments, so don't put information here that you'll want to use to sort views. For example, one Outlook user wanted to be able to organize lists of employees who participated in the company softball league, so they entered the contact's team name as a comment. After entering over seventy team members, they realized the contacts couldn't be sorted by team. (This would have been a good use for categories.)

NOTE

You can use Find to locate text in comments, but it's a time-consuming process.

Adding Details

On the Details page, shown in Figure 16.10, you'll record less frequently used information about your contacts. Remember that you can sort and filter your contacts on these fields, so try to use standard entries. If, for example, you want to be able to find all the vice presidents in your Contacts folder, make sure you enter **vice president** the same way for each contact.

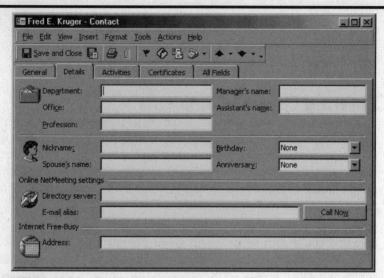

FIGURE 16.10: Use the Details page to record other additional information about your contact.

The Birthday and Anniversary fields have a drop-down arrow that opens a calendar. You can type dates in these fields using the *mm/dd/yy* format (3/8/57 for March 8, 1957), or you can select a date from the calendar. The Outlook calendar control is pretty nifty. Click the arrow, and the calendar opens, displaying the current month.

To choose the current date, click the Today button on the bottom of the calendar. To enter a different date in the current month, just click the date. Click the arrows in the calendar's header to scroll to the prior month or the next month. This is fairly tedious if you're entering a contact's birthday (unless he was born yesterday!). To scroll more rapidly, point to the name of the month in the header and hold down your mouse button to open a list of calendar pages. Scroll up or down through the list to select the calendar for the month and year you want to display; then select the date from the calendar.

Entering NetMeeting Addresses

Microsoft NetMeeting is Internet-based collaboration software included with Outlook. With NetMeeting, you can work with one or more contacts "face to face" over the Internet, using video and audio as you would in a video conference call. Some hardware is required to support NetMeeting's high-end video and audio functions.

Even if you don't use these functions, NetMeeting has a lot to offer. You can use NetMeeting to send files directly to a meeting attendee, have open chat sessions for brainstorming ideas about projects, diagram ideas on a Net whiteboard, and work with other attendees in real time in shared applications.

NetMeetings are held on an *Internet Locator Server* (*ILS*); each meeting participant must log on to the server, which maintains a list of users so that other participants can find out who is available for a meeting. On the Details page, you can enter two NetMeeting settings. Enter the ILS used for meetings with the contact in the Directory Server text box, and the contact's E-mail Alias (usually their e-mail address), as shown in Figure 16.11.

FIGURE 16.11: Enter the ILS and alias the contact uses for NetMeetings in the Details page.

Accessing Your Contact's Schedule on the Internet

Free/Busy refers to the times that a user is available (for meetings, including NetMeetings) or unavailable, according to their Outlook calendar. With Outlook, you can publish your free/busy times in two different ways: in Exchange Server on your local area network, or over the Internet using the iCalendar standard. With Exchange Server, the only people who can see your free/busy times are colleagues who can log on to your network. By publishing your free/busy times on an Internet Server, you make the schedule of free time available to people outside your network.

Before users can access your free/busy schedule, you need to tell them where the file that contains the schedule is located. The file can be stored on a server, FTP site, or Web page. If your contact has given you the URL for their free/busy schedule, enter it in the Internet Free/Busy text box on the Details page.

NOTE
Chapter 18 has more information on Internet Free/Busy.

Viewing Journal Entries

After you've entered a contact, Outlook's Journal component helps you track time spent working with or for the contact. Using the Journal, you can automatically record e-mail messages to a contact or manually record information during a phone call or after a meeting with the contact. The Activities page of the Contact form, shown in Figure 16.12, displays both automatic and manual entries related to the contact in a table.

The left column of the table has an icon for the type of entry, which is listed in the second column. The Start column is the start date of the entry; the Subject comes from the Subject line of the Activities form.

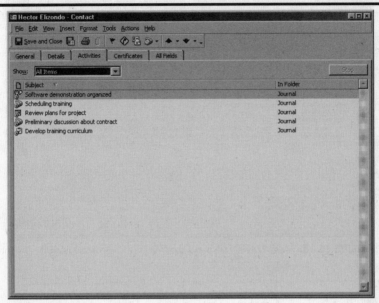

FIGURE 16.12:   On the Activities page of the Contact form, you can see all the entries related to the contact.

Previewing and Viewing Journal Entries

If you want to see more detail about each of the entries, right-click anywhere in the Journal window and select the AutoPreview option. The first three lines of the note in each entry will be displayed, as shown in Figure 16.13. It's easy to know if the preview shows all the text in the note, because the end of the note is marked <end>. If the note is longer than the preview, the preview ends with ellipses (...). To turn AutoPreview off, right-click and select AutoPreview again.

To see the entire entry, double-click the entry to open its Journal form.

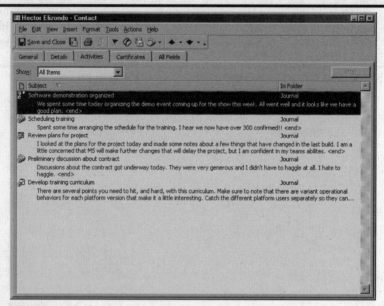

FIGURE 16.13: AutoPreview displays the first few lines of the note for the journal entry.

Sorting and Filtering Journal Entries

As with any Outlook view, you can click the heading of a column to sort the entries by the value in the column. For example, to arrange the entries by date and time, click the Start column heading. To filter the entries to show, for example, only phone calls, click the drop-down arrow in the Show control to open the list of types of journal entries, shown here.

Select a type of entry from the list, and Outlook will filter the list to only show the entry type you selected. In Figure 16.14, the journal entries in Figures 16.12 and 16.13 have been filtered so that only Word files are displayed, and they're sorted with the most recent Word file opened first.

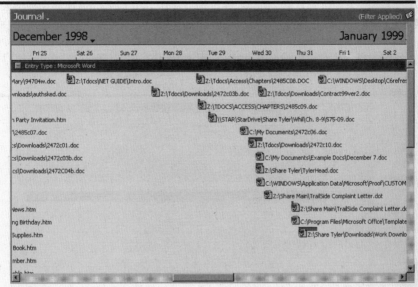

FIGURE 16.14: Use the Show drop-down list to filter entries by type.

Viewing Certificate Information

A *certificate*, or *Digital ID*, is used to verify the identity of the person who sent an e-mail message. Digital IDs have two parts: a *private key*, stored on the owner's computer, and a *public key* that others use to send messages to the owner and verify the authenticity of messages from the owner. The Certificates page of the Contact form shows Digital IDs that you've added for this contact. You can view the properties of the ID, and choose which ID should be used as the default for sending encrypted messages to this contact.

NOTE

See Chapter 17 for information on adding other users' IDs to their Contact forms and sending encrypted messages.

Viewing All Fields

In the Contact form's All Fields page, you can display groups of fields in a table format. The default display is User Defined Fields in this page. Unless someone has customized your Outlook forms and added fields, there won't be any fields displayed—but don't assume that this page is totally useless. Choose Phone Number Fields from the Select From drop-down list, and you'll see all the phone numbers associated with the contact, as shown in Figure 16.15. If you print the form now, you'll get the contact's name and a list of their phone numbers.

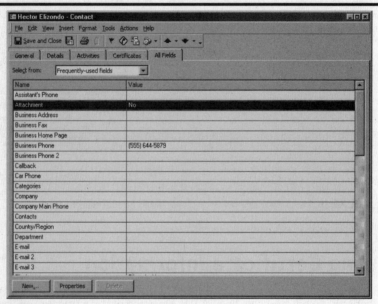

FIGURE 16.15: The All Fields page displays the Frequently Used Fields group of fields.

Saving a Contact

When you've finished entering information in the Contact form, click the Save and Close button, or choose File ➢ Save and Close to save this contact's information and close the form.

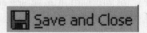

If you're going to be entering another contact immediately, it's faster to click the Save and New button, or choose File ➢ Save and New to save the current contact and open a blank form.

Adding a New Contact from the Same Company

Once you begin entering Contacts, you'll often have several contacts from the same organization. The contacts have the same business address, and the same or similar e-mail addresses and business telephone numbers. Outlook lets you create a Contact based on an existing contact, so you don't have to enter the business information again. When you've finished entering the first Contact, choose Actions ➢ New Contact from Same Company from the Outlook menu. The first Contact is saved, and the business information for the Contact is held over in the Contact form. Add the new contact's personal information, and edit the business information as required.

If you've already closed the original Contact, right-click the Contact in the Contact List and choose New Contact From Same Company from the shortcut menu to create a new Contact at the selected Contact's company. When you've entered the last Contact, click Save and Close to close the Contacts form.

Deleting a Contact

To delete a Contact, select the Contact or open the Contact form. Then choose Edit ➢ Delete from the menu, or right-click and choose Delete from the shortcut menu, or press Ctrl+D. You will not be prompted to confirm the deletion. However, if you immediately notice that you've deleted a Contact erroneously, you can choose Undo Delete from the Edit menu to restore the Contact.

USING PREDEFINED VIEWS

The Contacts component has seven predefined views: Address Cards, Detailed Address Cards, Phone List, By Category, By Company, By Location, and By Follow Up Flag. To switch to another view, choose View ➢ Current View on the menu bar, and select the view you want to apply.

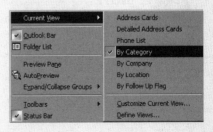

Card Views

The Address Card view, shown in Figure 16.16, displays basic information about the contact: File As name, mailing address, e-mail address, and telephone numbers. The Detailed Address Cards display additional data, including full name, job title, company name, and categories. Card views have a handy feature: an index on the right side that lets you quickly go to Contacts by the File By name. Clicking the *S*, for example, takes you to Contacts whose File By name begins with the letter *S*. Many users choose either Address Cards or Detailed Address Cards as their default view for Contacts.

List Views

The remaining predefined views are list views: Phone List, By Company, By Category, By Location, and By Follow Up Flag. All the list views look and function like Excel worksheets. Field names appear at the top of the column, with records below in rows. You use the horizontal and vertical scroll bars to move up and down and pan side to side through the list. The Phone List, shown in Figure 16.17, shows Full Name, Company Name, File As Name, and telephone numbers for each contact.

The By Category, By Company, By Location, and By Follow Up Flag views are all grouped views. When you open the By Company view, a dark bar with the company name separates Contacts from each company. You can expand or collapse the Contact detail for each company. Click the Collapse (minus) button on the company bar to hide the company's contacts and change the Collapse button to an Expand (plus) button. Click the Expand button to see all the Contacts for that company. If you work in a field where employees begin mailing out resumes the second week on the job, Outlook has a feature you'll appreciate. To move a Contact from one company to another, select the Contact and drag it into the new company, as shown in Figure 16.18.

NOTE

You can create your own views, adding and deleting fields and setting up custom grouping.

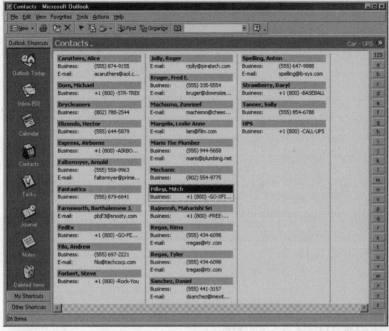

FIGURE 16.16: The Address Card view is the default Contacts view for many users.

			Full Name	Company	File As	Business Phone	Business Fax
			Click here to add a new C...				
				Ameritech Small ...	Ameritech Small Business Services	(800) 555-8959	
			Glenn Barton	Mission Health Care	Barton, Glenn	(810) 555-5659	
			Pamela Barton	Johnson' Electro...	Barton, Pamela	(508) 555-5656	
			Karla Browning	TRIAD Consultin...	Browning, Karla		(810) 555-2284
			Peggy Cartoni	Friend	Cartoni, Peggy	(810) 555-7845	
			Margaret Clinton	Carman-Ainswort...	Clinton, Margaret	(810) 555-8565	
			Amy Courter	Valassis Communi...	Courter, Amy	(800) 555-8959	(313) 555-8956
			Guy Courter	Flint Permanent ...	Courter, Guy	(810) 555-8959	
			Tom Crawford	Tom's Diner	Crawford, Tom	(800) 555-8956	(313) 555-8962
			Mary Rose Evans	PTR	Evans, Mary Rose	(248) 555-9856	
			Kent Fields	Sybex Books	Fields, Kent	(800) 555-5555	(510) 555-5555
			Jacklyn Flocker	Palatine Public S...	Flocker, Jacklyn	(517) 555-4141	
			Cindy Graystone	Church	Graystone, Cindy		
			Ingrid Guntner	Church	Guntner, Ingrid		
			Terrel F. Hatcher	Spring Valley Co...	Hatcher, Terrel F.	(616) 555-4151	(616) 555-4675
			David T. Holstein	Mission Communi...	Holstein, David T.	(616) 555-4545	(616) 555-1214
			Kimberly Mastersons	Mission Health Sy...	Mastersons, Kimberly	(549) 555-8959	(549) 555-5956
			Rosemary Walker		Walker, Rosemary		
			Gloria Wright	Genesee Interme...	Wright, Gloria	(810) 555-4545	(810) 555-7878

FIGURE 16.17: The Phone List shows contacts with their telephone numbers.

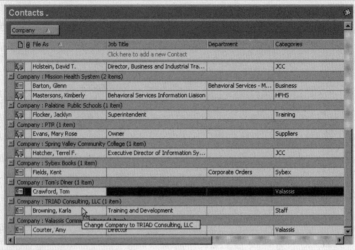

FIGURE 16.18:   In the By Company view, you can "transfer" employees from one company to another.

Locating a Contact

The easiest way to search through a long list of Contacts is by using Find, which can help you quickly locate items in any view. Click the Find button on the Standard toolbar to open the Find pane at the top of the list, as shown in Figure 16.19. If you're looking for a contact, enter all or part of their name, company name, or address in the Look For text box. To search all the fields in the contact, including the Comments field, leave Search All Text in the Contact check box enabled. Disabling the check box limits the search to the fields displayed at the left, and speeds up the search.

Click the Find Now button to find all the contacts that include the text you entered. Figure 16.20 shows the results obtained when searching for "Amy." When you find the contact you're looking for, just double-click on the contact to open the Contact form.

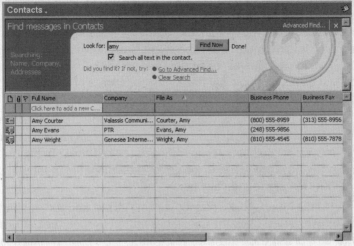

FIGURE 16.19: The Find pane opens at the top of the Contact list.

If you can't find the contact you're looking for in the Find pane, or if you're looking for text in specific fields or based on criteria other than text, consider using Advanced Find.

Advanced Find...

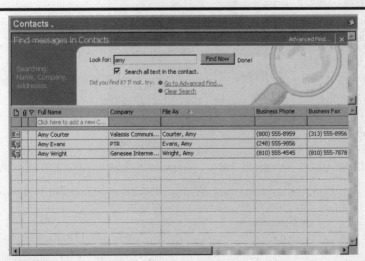

FIGURE 16.20: Use Find to locate a contact based on their name, address, or text anywhere in the Contact.

Click the Advanced Find button at the top of the Find pane to open the Advanced Find dialog box. On the Contact page of the dialog box, you can select the type of item, location, and fields to be searched. Open the topmost In drop-down list and select Name Fields Only, then click Find Now. Even if you just remember the person's first name or a part of their last name, Outlook will find every occurrence of those letters in the Name fields, without searching other fields.

Using the Time options, you can search for Contacts that were created or modified within a particular time frame. For example, you can find Contacts you created today or modified in the last week. In Figure 16.21, we're using Advanced Find to locate contacts modified in the last seven days with *Oak* in the company name.

Flip to the More Choices page by clicking its tab, and you can find Contacts by categories. Click the Categories button to open the Categories dialog box. Select the categories you want to search for. If you choose more than one category, Outlook treats the selection as a union and finds Contacts assigned to any of the categories you selected. Click OK to close the Categories dialog box, then click Find Now to find the contacts who are assigned to the categories you chose. Figure 16.22 shows a search for Contacts with the Business or Ideas categories.

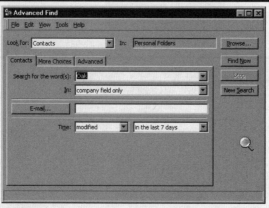

FIGURE 16.21: Advanced Find lets you search for contacts based on when they were created or modified.

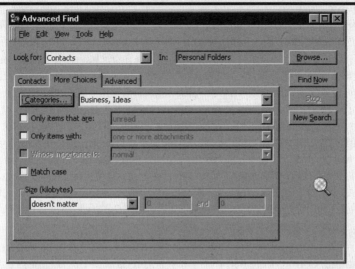

FIGURE 16.22: Use the More Choices page to search for contacts by category.

On the Advanced page of the Advanced Find dialog box, shown in Figure 16.23, you can enter multiple, specific search criteria based on the values in fields. To enter a search criterion, click the Field button to open a menu of Outlook field types. Choose a type (for example, All Contact Fields), and then select the field from the menu.

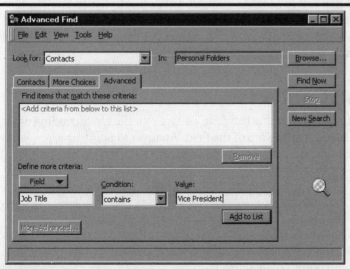

FIGURE 16.23: Use the Advanced page to find contacts based on one or more specific fields.

From the Condition text box, choose the appropriate operator. The operators in the list depend on the type of data that will be in the field you selected. For text fields, you'll choose between Contains, Is, Doesn't Contain, Is Empty, and Is Not Empty. Date fields have the same operators as the Time controls in the Contacts page: Anytime, Today, In the Last Seven Days, and so on. In the Value text box, enter the value you're looking for with Contains or Is, or not looking for if you use the Doesn't Contain operator. You don't have to enter a value for Is Empty or Is Not Empty. When you're finished building the criterion, click the Add to List button to add it to the Find Items list. To add another criterion, build it, and then add it to the list. When you've entered all the advanced criteria you need to conduct your search, click Find Now to find the contacts that match all the criteria you entered. In Figure 16.23, we're creating criteria to search for contacts with Vice President in their job title.

You can enter search criteria on more than one Find page and find, for example, Contacts created in the last seven days in the Business category. If you're finished with one search and want to search for other Contacts, click the New Search button to clear the criteria you entered from all three pages of the dialog box.

New Search

When you're finished with Advanced Find, choose File ➤ Close or click the close button on the dialog box title bar to close Advanced Find and return to Contacts. To close the Find pane, click the close button at the top of the pane, or switch to another view.

Sorting Contacts

Sorting is easy in any list view. To sort by a field in ascending order, click the heading at the top of the field. An upward pointing arrow is displayed in the field heading to remind you that it is sorted in ascending order.

Full Name   △

Click the heading again, and you sort the list in descending order. When the list is sorted in descending order, the heading arrow for the sort-by column points down.

Part V

PRINTING CONTACTS

If you've ever been asked to create an employee directory for your organization, you know the potential pitfalls. Someone (probably you) has to enter data, choose a layout for the directory, format all the data, add headings. By the time you actually send the directory to your printer, you've invested a lot of time in design issues. Outlook includes a number of printing options that will help you quickly and easily create directories, phone lists, and other print resources that formerly took hours or days to create.

When you choose File ➤ Page Setup from the Outlook menu bar, you are presented with a list of styles to choose from. The available styles are dependent on the current view, so before you print, select the view that most closely resembles the printed output you want. For a simple employee telephone list, choose one of the list views. For complete names and addresses, choose a card view. Table 16.2 identifies the Contact views and their corresponding print styles.

TABLE 16.2: Page Setup Styles

STYLE	VIEW	DEFAULT PRINTED OUTPUT
Table	Table	The view as it appears on the screen
Memo	Table	Data for the selected contact(s), printed in portrait view, with your name at the top of each entry
Phone Directory	Table	Two-column listing of names and phone numbers, with a heading for each letter of the alphabet (very slick)
Card	Card	A two-column listing of names and contact information
Small Booklet	Card	A multiple section listing of names and contact information prepared for two-sided printing
Medium Booklet	Card	A two-column listing of names and contact information prepared for two-sided printing

Before you print, it's a good idea to look at each of the styles. Choose File ➤ Page Setup and select the style from the menu.

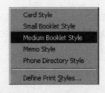

If you select the medium or small booklet style and your printer prints one-sided output, Outlook will ask if you wish to continue. Click OK to open the Page Setup dialog box, shown in Figure 16.24. The dialog box has three pages: Format, Paper, and Header/Footer.

In the Format page, choose the format options you would like to apply to the style:

> **Sections**   To have each letter of the alphabet begin on a new page, choose Start on a New Page.

> **Number of Columns**   As you increase the number of columns, Outlook decreases the font size.

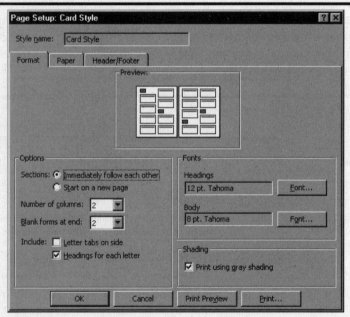

FIGURE 16.24:   Use the Page Setup dialog box to set printing options for the style you selected.

> **Blank Forms at End**   This option allows users to add new entries in the correct section.

> **Letter Tabs on Side**   This check box will generate an index, like the index used in Address Card view, with the section's letters highlighted.

Headings for Each Letter This feature gives you a high-lighted letter at the beginning of each alphabetic section.

Fonts These lists offer you choices of fonts for the letter headings and body.

Print Using Gray Shading This check box enables or disables gray shading in the letter tabs, letter headings, and contact names.

After you make a change, you can click the Print Preview button to see how the change affects your printed output. In Figure 16.25, we're previewing a booklet with letter tabs on the side and headings for each letter. Click anywhere in the preview to zoom in on the detail; click again to zoom out. To close Print Preview and return to the Page Setup dialog box, choose Page Setup. If you click Close, you close both Print Preview *and* Page Setup.

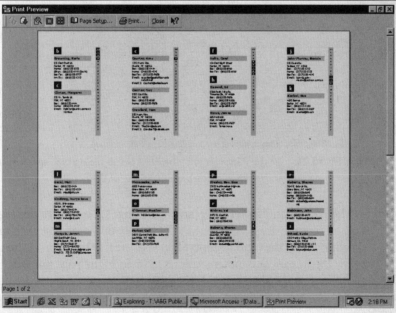

FIGURE 16.25: Use Print Preview to see how your format change affects the printed document.

On the Paper page of the Page Setup dialog box (see Figure 16.26), choose the settings that describe the dimensions of the paper you're going to use.

On the Header/Footer page, shown in Figure 16.27, you can create a header and footer that contain text and document information. Headers and footers appear on each page of the finished product. If you're creating a 1/4 page booklet, a header will appear four times on the printed sheet, so it will be at the top of each page after it is folded.

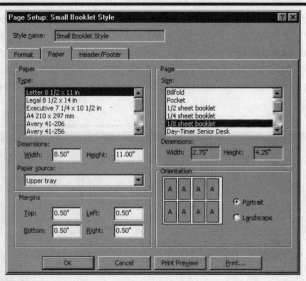

FIGURE 16.26: On the Paper page of the Print Setup dialog box, specify the size and location of the paper and size of the booklet.

The header and footer each have a left-aligned, centered, and right-aligned section. To include text in the header or footer, just click in the appropriate section and begin typing. Use the five buttons on the toolbar below the header and footer sections to include the page number, total number of pages, date printed, time printed, or username in the header or footer.

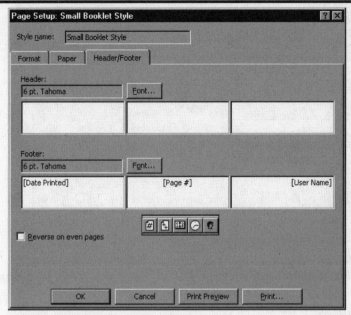

FIGURE 16.27: Create custom headers and footers in the Header/Footer page.

When you've finished setting print options, click the Print button to open the Print dialog box, shown in Figure 16.28. Select a printer from the Name list, the range of pages to print, and the number of copies. Click the OK button to send the job to the printer.

TIP

If you want to print a booklet with back to front pages and you have a one-sided printer, choose Odd in the Number of Pages drop-down list, and print all the odd-numbered pages first. Turn the sheets over and reinsert them into the printer. Choose Even to print the rest of the pages. Outlook will order the pages so they can be folded into a booklet when they're all printed.

The printing process is the same in all the Outlook components. Begin by selecting a view that supports the output you want. Preview the output in Print Preview. Change views, if necessary, and then adjust the Page Setup options to further define the final output. Finally, send the job to the printer, and think about how easy this was.

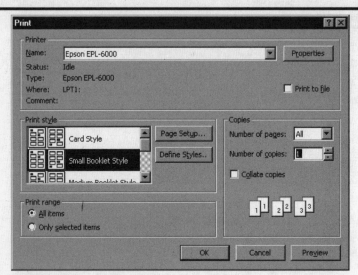

FIGURE 16.28: Change settings in the Print dialog box to specify the number of copies, range, and number of pages to print.

After you've entered your contacts into Outlook, and can locate the data you need, and print your Contact information successfully, you're ready to use Outlook's communication features to stay in touch.

WHAT'S NEXT

Chapter 17 will guide you through the world of e-mail communications.

Chapter 17

SENDING AND RECEIVING E-MAIL WITH OUTLOOK

In the 1970s and '80s, the telephone was the lifeblood of many organizations; if your phones weren't working, you weren't doing business. Today, electronic mail has taken center stage. If the phones aren't working, it's no big deal, but cut off e-mail for a few hours, and employees start wandering the halls aimlessly, wondering how to cope with the sudden loss of their primary means of communication. Well, this might be a bit of an exaggeration, but it's not far off the mark. Business depends on e-mail, and the dependence is growing every day.

Adapted from *Mastering Microsoft Outlook 2000* by Gini Courter and Annette Marquis

ISBN 0-7821-2472-0   816 pages $34.99

Outlook was designed first and foremost as an e-mail communication tool, and it offers features that go beyond those of most e-mail software, such as flagging and automatic message decryption. With Outlook, you can work collaboratively, using e-mail messages to distribute documents or to vote on important issues in your company, and you can use Outlook's mail management features to flag and prioritize incoming messages so that these vital communiqués don't get lost in the shuffle. This chapter will get you started with all the daily e-mail functions.

QUICK START: CREATING AND SENDING AN E-MAIL MESSAGE

If you have experience using another e-mail program or sending faxes in Outlook, you'll have no problem creating and sending e-mail messages in Outlook. This chapter covers all the numerous options for creating and sending e-mail, but to get started quickly, you can create and send a message by following the five simple steps listed here.

1. Choose File ➤ New ➤ Mail Message from the menu bar.

2. Enter the recipient's name(s) or e-mail addresses in the To, Cc, and Bcc text boxes, or click the To, Cc, or Bcc button and select recipients in the Select Names dialog box.

3. Type the subject of the message in the Subject text box.

4. Enter the text of the message in the open text area.

5. Click the Send button to send the message to the recipients.

For detailed information about these steps and other e-mail features in Outlook, read on.

OUTLOOK CONFIGURATIONS AND E-MAIL

There are three ways to send and receive mail, depending on how Outlook is configured on your PC:

▶ If Outlook was installed for Corporate/Workgroup use and you are connected to your organization's network, mail from within your organization is delivered directly to your Inbox. Internet mail may also be delivered directly, depending on your organization's connection to the Internet; if it is not, you use a separate dial-up connection to send and receive Internet mail.

▶ If you have the Corporate/Workgroup setup and are not connected to your company's network (for example, when you are working out of the office with your laptop computer), mail is only delivered on demand when you connect to your organization's server with a dial-up connection.

▶ If you chose the Internet Only mail option when Outlook was installed, you always need to tell Outlook to send and receive mail, either by changing the Mail Delivery options to automatically connect to your Internet service provider (ISP) at specified intervals, or by telling Outlook to connect to your ISP each time you wish to send and receive mail.

In this chapter we'll focus on the first and third options. Other mail settings are determined by your Outlook configuration; we'll point out the differences between the two configurations throughout the rest of this chapter.

NOTE

New to Outlook 2000 is a much easier way to change your Outlook mail configuration. Microsoft got smart and added this function to the Options dialog box. Simply go to Tools ➢ Options ➢ Mail Delivery, and click the Reconfigure Mail Support button at the bottom of the dialog box. Select your new configuration and click OK (if you select Corporate/Workgroup, make sure you can support it with either a local copy of Microsoft Mail or information on how to connect to your Exchange server). Under certain circumstances, the Outlook installer will ask you to insert your CD. When all is said and done, you'll be able to support new features and you won't even have to restart your computer.

CREATING AND ADDRESSING E-MAIL

To create a message, choose File ➢ New ➢ Mail Message from the menu bar, or open the menu on the New Item button and choose Mail Message to open a Message form, shown in Figure 17.1.

Part V

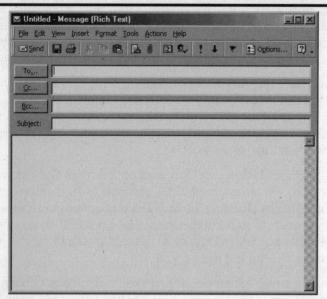

FIGURE 17.1:   Open a Message form to create an e-mail message.

TIP

There is a fourth installation option besides those listed above: No E-mail. If Mail Message is not a choice on the File ➢ New menu, e-mail has not been installed, and you must install it before you can send messages in Outlook. Choose Tools ➢ Accounts ➢ Mail, and then click the Add button to launch the Internet Connection Wizard and add an e-mail service to Outlook.

There are two view options that determine which text boxes are displayed in a message form: Message Header and Bcc Field. With both turned off, only the To text box is displayed at the top of the form. Enabling the Message Header (choose View ➢ Message Header from the form's menu) also displays the Cc and Subject text boxes. This is Outlook's default setting. With the Message Header displayed, choosing View ➢ Bcc Field from the form menu displays the Bcc text box, as shown in Figure 17.1.

Entering E-Mail Addresses

There are three ways to enter e-mail addresses: from your address books, by typing the address manually, or by searching for the person's e-mail address with a directory service, such as Four11 or WhoWhere?. Enter the recipient's name or e-mail addresses in the To text box, or click the To button to open the Select Names dialog box, shown in Figure 17.2. When you open the Select Names dialog box, the choices are based on the type of communication you're creating: To and Cc (courtesy copy) for letters; To, Cc, and Bcc (blind courtesy copy) for e-mail messages and faxes. To and Cc recipients are listed in the header of the message, while recipients of blind courtesy copies are not. Therefore, recipients of the original message and courtesy copies won't know that the message was also sent to the Bcc recipients.

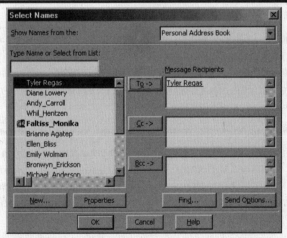

FIGURE 17.2: Select message recipients using the To, Cc, and Bcc buttons in the Select Names dialog box.

ABOUT ADDRESS BOOKS

An *address book* is a list of names that you can select addresses from. You may have only one address book (with the Internet Only configuration), three address books (with the Corporate/Workgroup configuration), or some other number of address books, depending on the services installed to handle mail messaging on your computer. The major address books are:

Personal Address Book   This address book can contain personal distribution lists (groups), and is located on your PC. This is the best place to keep your frequently used addresses.

Global Address Book   An address book for members of your organization, stored on a server; also called a Postoffice Address List. This address book can contain global distribution lists.

Outlook Address Book   The Outlook Address Book automatically contains the entries in your Contacts folder in the Corporate/Workgroup configuration. It only includes contacts that have an e-mail address or fax number listed.

Contacts   In the Internet Only configuration, this is your personal address book, and includes all your contacts, whether or not they have an e-mail address or fax number.

If you have installed other mail services, such as CompuServe, you may have additional address books.

In the Internet Only configuration, you select your recipient from the Contacts folder. With the Corporate/Workgroup configuration, as shown in Figure 17.2, you will have more than one address book, so begin by choosing an address book from the drop-down list in the Select Names dialog box.

Either scroll to the person's name, or begin entering the name in the Find text box and Outlook will find the name in the list. With the contact's name selected in the left pane, click the To, Cc, or Bcc button to add the name to the list of recipients. Or, right-click on the name and select To, Cc, or Bcc from the shortcut menu. You can hold Shift or Ctrl and click, to select a contiguous list of names or multiple names before clicking the To, Cc, or Bcc buttons.

The Contacts list is different in the two installation configurations. If you have Internet Only mail, each contact is listed only once. When you choose an address from the list, Outlook uses the contact's default e-mail address (the first address you entered). In the Corporate/Workgroup configuration, each electronic address is listed separately. For example, if Mary Smith has a fax number and two e-mail addresses, she will be listed three times: Mary Smith [Business Fax], Mary Smith [E-mail], and Mary Smith [E-mail2], so you can select either e-mail address.

TIP

You can use all of a contact's e-mail addresses in either configuration—it just takes a bit of planning. Instead of beginning with a blank message form, right-click on the contact in the Contacts folder and choose New Message to Contact from the shortcut menu. If the contact has more than one e-mail address, Outlook adds them all to the message and reminds you to delete those you don't wish to use.

After you've added all the recipients, click OK to close the Select Names dialog box and return to the message form. If the intended recipient isn't included in any of your Contacts folders, you can enter the e-mail address directly in the To, Cc, or Bcc text boxes in the message form, and then create a new entry from that information. For more information about adding contacts using e-mail addresses, see "Adding Addresses on the Fly" later in this chapter.

WARNING

In the Internet Only configuration, Outlook will let you address e-mail to any contact, even if they don't have an e-mail address. To see if the contact has an address, use the horizontal scroll bar below the list of names to scroll to the second column, e-mail address. If it is blank, there are no e-mail addresses listed for the contact.

Entering Addresses Manually

You may want to enter e-mail addresses or contact names directly in the message form for two reasons: to send mail to addresses that aren't in the address book, or to save time. Typing an address directly lets you send a message to a contact's temporary e-mail address, for example, or to any address that you may not want to enter into your address book. Typing a contact's name saves the time required to open the Select Names dialog box and locate the name; you need only type enough of the contact's name for Outlook to find the recipient. If you enter an e-mail address, you must enter the entire address.

When you enter text in the To, Cc, or Bcc text boxes, Outlook automatically checks the text against the names in the address books. If Outlook determines that the text is a valid e-mail address, it underlines it.

▶ If you enter an e-mail address for a contact, Outlook converts the e-mail address to the user's name and underlines it. For example, suppose Bill Jones is in your Contacts folder and the address `bjones@abc.com` is listed in his contact information. If you type **bjones@abc.com** in the To text box, Outlook will change the address in the message header to Bill Jones.

▶ If you enter an e-mail address that is not listed in one of your address books, Outlook checks the syntax of the address. If the text you entered has the proper format for an e-mail address, Outlook underlines the address. For example, if Bill was not in an address book, or his e-mail address was not listed in his contact information, Outlook would simply underline the address you entered: bjones@abc.com.

If you enter a name that is not an exact match for a name in an address book, Outlook underlines the name with a wavy red line (just as Word marks a spelling error). Right-click on the name, and select the recipient from the shortcut menu. For example, if you type **John** in the To text box, Outlook will underline the name in red. Right-click on the name and the menu will include all the entries in the address books that include the text:

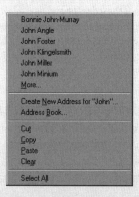

From the menu, select the person you want to send the message to. If you don't identify the recipient before sending the message, Outlook will open a dialog box so that you can select a name.

The next time you enter John as a recipient name, Outlook will automatically select the name you chose from the menu this time. However, the name will have a green, dashed underline so that you know there are other Johns in the address book:

John Minium

To choose a different John, right-click and select the appropriate recipient from the shortcut menu (who will become the new "default John").

 After you've typed the names in the To, Cc, and Bcc text boxes, choose Tools ➤ Check Names from the menu, or click the Check Names button on the message form toolbar.

Outlook's automatic name-checking option is on by default. To turn it off (or back on again) follow these steps:

1. Choose Tools ➤ Options from the Outlook menu bar.

2. Click the Preferences tab in the Options dialog box.

3. Click the E-mail Options button to open the E-mail Options dialog box.

4. Click the Advanced E-mail Options button to open the Advanced E-mail Options dialog box.

5. Enable or disable the Automatic Name Checking check box.

6. Click OK to close each of the three dialog boxes.

NOTE

Keep in mind that turning off Automatic Name Checking is just that, turning off the Automatic component. You can still check names manually, but, until you turn it back on, you will not have names checked automatically.

Using Directory Services

A *directory service* is an address book maintained in an LDAP directory. *LDAP* (*Lightweight Directory Access Protocol*), developed at the University of Michigan, is an emerging Internet/Intranet standard, that defines a common format for electronic directories and is used in many networking programs. The directory could be on a local network server running Microsoft Exchange or on a public directory service you access via the Internet, such as Four11 or Bigfoot. You use directory services when you know a person's name but don't have their e-mail address.

NOTE

Public directory services are automatically enabled in the Internet Only configuration. In the Workplace/Corporate configuration, LDAP directories are created or enabled by your network administrator. If clicking the Find button doesn't open a Find People dialog box, you don't have access to directory services.

To find an address using a directory service, open the Select Names dialog box, and then click its Find button to open the Find People dialog box, shown in Figure 17.3.

FIGURE 17.3:   The Find People dialog box provides easy access to your Contacts list and public directory services.

Click the arrow in the Look In text box to open a list of folders and directory services you can search to locate the person you're looking for.

If you're searching a folder that contains Outlook contacts, you can search by name, e-mail address, address, any of the phone numbers listed for the contact, or other information entered in the Contact form, as shown in Figure 17.3. For the directory services, you can usually search only by name or e-mail address.

When you're addressing mail, you'll enter a name and search for an e-mail address. If you receive unsolicited anonymous e-mail, you can use the Find People dialog box to search by the address and find out who sent the e-mail. Figure 17.4 shows the available search fields in the Find People dialog box with the Four11 public directory service selected.

FIGURE 17.4: Public directory services allow you to search by name or e-mail address.

Each of the directory services maintains its own list and provides other types of services on its Web site. Choose a service to search based on the type of information you're looking for:

Directory Service	Features
Bigfoot	Free e-mail aliasing and Internet services
Four11 and Yahoo! People Search	The most comprehensive lists of individuals; search for telephone numbers on the home page
InfoSpace and InfoSpace Business	Directories of e-mail users, community information, apartment locator, shopping info
Switchboard	The "people and business directory," with good lists of companies' e-mail addresses
Verisign	People with registered Digital IDs only
WhoWhere	Free e-mail and Internet services

Enter the name of the person whose e-mail address you want to find, and then click the Find Now button. Outlook will connect to the Internet, search the directory service you selected, and find individuals who match the Name text you entered, as shown in Figure 17.5.

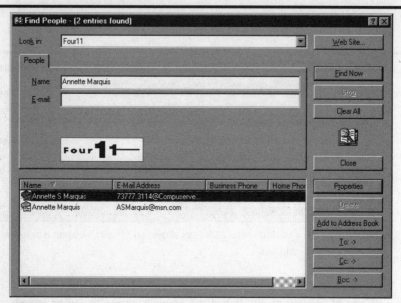

FIGURE 17.5:   Possible matches from the directory service are displayed in the Find People dialog box.

If the name is fairly common, you may see many entries in the list. How do you know which of them, if any, is the person you're looking for? Check the domain for the address. If the person you're looking for works for a company, look for the company's name followed by .com. Do the same for students or employees of educational institutions (.edu), governmental units (.gov), non-profit organizations (.org), and the military (.mil). With addresses from Internet service providers (.net) and the commercial online services (for example, aol.com, msn.com, and compuserve.com) there's no easy way to tell.

TROUBLESHOOTING DIRECTORY SERVICES

If the person you're looking for doesn't appear on the list (or if no potential matches were found), try the following:

▶   Select a different directory service and repeat the search.

CONTINUED ➡

> ▶ Enter the person's first initial rather than first name and search again.
>
> ▶ If the person uses both a nickname and their given first name, search both names.
>
> It's possible that the person you're looking for doesn't have e-mail, or that their e-mail address isn't listed in a public directory. Individual accounts with Internet Service Providers typically are not listed unless the person has taken the step of signing up with a directory service. Employees of public institutions in .edu and .gov domains are more likely to be listed than employees of private organizations. Many private institutions keep their e-mail lists private, so employees don't appear in public directories unless they've created an individual listing.

If you find the person you're looking for in a directory service, you can click the To, Cc, or Bcc buttons to add their e-mail address to your message and close the Find People dialog box.

However, if you plan to use this e-mail address again, first click the Add to Address Book button to open the Properties dialog box. The person's name and e-mail address are automatically copied to the appropriate text boxes on the Personal page, as shown in Figure 17.6.

Add to Address Book

Fill in any other information about the person on the other pages of the Properties dialog box. When you click OK, Outlook closes the Properties dialog box, adds the individual's entry to the currently selected address book, and automatically adds the name to the originally chosen field. To add existing contacts to the recipient list, click the To, Cc, or Bcc button to open the Add Recipient dialog box, select the name of the new recipient, and click the To, Cc, or Bcc button to add the person as a recipient for the current message.

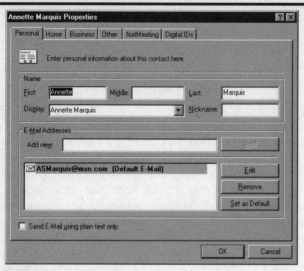

FIGURE 17.6:   Adding an entry to the address book from the Find People dialog box

Adding Addresses on the Fly

You can quickly create a contact from any e-mail address you enter in a message. Right-click on the address in the To, Cc, or Bcc text box, and choose Add to Contacts from the shortcut menu. Outlook will open a blank Contact form with the e-mail address in both the Name and E-mail text boxes. Correct the name, enter any additional information you wish, and then click Save and Close to close the form and return to your e-mail message. In the Corporate/Workgroup configuration, you can add the address to your Personal Address Book; the person will appear in your address book, but not in the Outlook Contacts list.

MASTERING ADDRESS BOOK ICONS

In the address book, different icons are used to identify the source for e-mail addresses.

The contact card icon identifies names from your global or personal address book.

CONTINUED ➡

When you include an address from a directory service, the remote address icon is displayed. If you add the person to your address book or Contacts, Outlook changes to the contact card icon.

Names of groups (distribution lists) are preceded by the group icon.

Creating and Using Distribution Lists (Groups)

When you work with a team or are a member of a committee or task force, you'll find yourself addressing e-mail to the same group of people: the other members of your team or committee. In the infancy of e-mail, you had to address your messages individually to each person on the team. *Distribution lists* streamline this process. With a distribution list, you create a named list in your personal address book and then add all the members of your team or committee to the group. When you address your next e-mail message, you can send it to the distribution list (and all its members) rather than adding each of the members as individual recipients.

In the Internet Only configuration, you create *groups* rather than distribution lists. Groups and distribution lists work the same way, but you create them in a slightly different fashion.

Creating a Group (Internet Only Users)   Creating a group is easy. Select Tools ➤ Address Book from the Outlook menu to open the Address Book dialog box. Click the New Group button to open the Group Properties dialog box, shown in Figure 17.7. Type a name for the group in the Group Name text box. Group names can include spaces, hyphens, and other punctuation you would include in a Windows filename. As you enter the name, the dialog box caption in the title bar changes to include the group name before the word *Properties*.

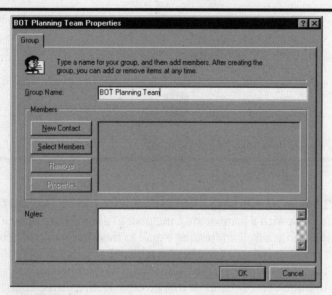

FIGURE 17.7:   Create distribution lists in the Group Properties dialog box.

There's a Notes area in the dialog box where you can enter any comments you have about the group. For example, you might note when you created the group; its purpose; and the names of associated groups.

Group members must be included in your address book. If the person you want to add to the group isn't already in the address book, click the New Contact button to open a Properties dialog box. Enter the person's information (including, of course, an e-mail address), and then click OK to create the new contact, close the dialog box, and add the person to the group.

To add a group member from the address book, click the Select Members button to open the Select Group Members dialog box, which looks much like the Select Names dialog box. Select the entry for the person you want to add in the left pane, and then click the Select button to add the person to the group in the right pane. You can hold Ctrl and click on more than one entry to add multiple addresses to the group at once, as shown in Figure 17.8.

Select Members

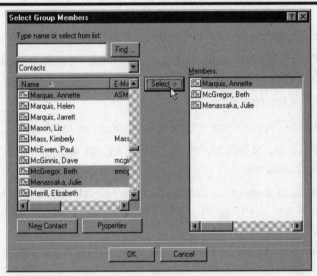

FIGURE 17.8:   Use the Select Group Members dialog box to add one or more contacts to the distribution list.

You can also add new contacts in the Select Group Members dialog box, using the New Contact button mentioned previously. After you've added the person as a contact, click Select to add them to the group. Click the Find button to open the Find People dialog box to add group members from a directory service (see "Using Directory Services" earlier in this chapter). When you've added all the group members, click OK to close the Select Group Members dialog box. If you've added any group members from a directory service, Outlook will prompt you to add the person to the address book:

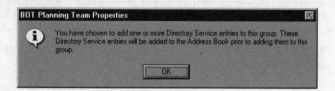

Click OK to close the dialog box. Outlook will open a Properties dialog box for the new contact. Add any other information for the person, and then click OK to add the individual to the address book and the distribution list.

In summary, to create a group in the Internet Only configuration:

1. Choose Tools ➤ Address Book to open the Address Book dialog box.

2. Click the New Group button.

3. In the Group Name text box, type the name for the group.

4. Click the Select Members button to add names from the address book.

5. Select a name in the list and click the Select button to add the address to the group. Hold Ctrl to select multiple names before clicking the Select button.

6. To add people to the distribution list that aren't in your address book, click the New Contact button and create a new contact.

7. Click OK to close the Select Group Members dialog box. Click OK again to close the Group Properties dialog box.

Creating a Distribution List (Corporate/Workgroup Users)   In the Corporate/Workgroup configuration, you create distribution lists in your Personal Address Book.

Choose Tools ➤ Address Book to open the Address Book dialog box, and select the Personal Address Book in the Select Names From drop-down list. Then choose File ➤ New Entry from the Address Book menu to open the New Entry dialog box, shown here:

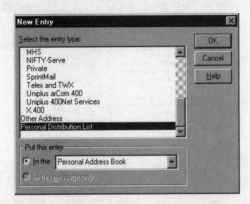

Scroll to the bottom of the Select the Entry Type list, and choose Personal Distribution List. Make sure that Personal Address Book is selected as the location for the entry, and click OK to open the New Personal Distribution List Properties dialog box, shown here:

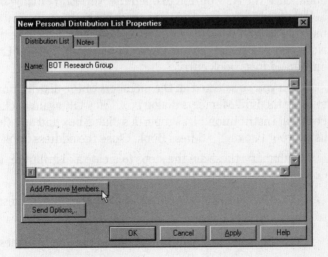

Enter a name for the list, and then click the Add/Remove Members button to open the Edit Members dialog box, shown here:

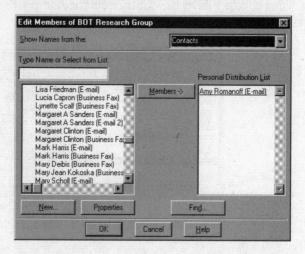

Choose the address book that contains the first member you wish to add. Select the member, and then click the Members button to add the member to the distribution list. To add a member who isn't in an address book, click the New button to open the New Entry dialog box again. Select an address type, and then choose whether you want to add the member to your Personal Address Book, or just to this distribution list. Note that you cannot create a new contact with the New Entry button—only an address book entry.

When you've selected all the members of the distribution list, click OK to close the Edit Members dialog box. Click OK again to close the New Personal Distribution List Properties dialog box and add the distribution list to your Personal Address Book. Close the address book.

In summary, these are the steps to create a distribution list in the Corporate/Workgroup configuration:

1. Choose Tools ➤ Address Book to open the Address Book dialog box.

2. Select Personal Address Book in the Select Names From list.

3. Choose File ➤ New Entry from the Address Book dialog box to open the New Entry dialog box.

4. Choose Personal Distribution List from the list of entry types. Make sure the Personal Address Book is selected under Put This Entry, and click OK to open the New Personal Distribution List dialog box.

5. Enter a name for the Distribution List in the Name text box.

6. Click the Add/Remove Members button to open the Edit Members dialog box.

7. Choose the address book with the member's name in the Show Names from The drop-down list.

8. Select the member's name from the entries in the left pane.

9. Click the Members button to add the selected address to the list. Hold Ctrl to select multiple names before clicking the Members button.

10. To add people who aren't in your address book to the distribution list, click the New Contact button to open the New Entry dialog box. Create a new entry in your Personal Address Book or just in this distribution list.

11. After selecting all members, click OK to close the Edit Members dialog box. Click OK again to close the Group Properties dialog box and add the distribution list to your Personal Address Book.

Addressing Mail to a Group or Distribution List   To send mail to all members of a group or distribution list, type the group name in the To, Cc, or Bcc text box on the message form, or click one of the three buttons to open the Select Names dialog box.

Group names are bold in the Select Names dialog box and address books, and they are preceded by the group icon. Select the group name and click the To, Cc, or Bcc button to add the group's members as message recipients. The group name will be bold in the To, Cc, or Bcc text box on the message form.

If you need to check the membership of a group, right-click on the group name in the message's address boxes or in the Select Names dialog box and choose Properties to open the group's properties sheet.

Adding or Removing a Name from a Group or Distribution List

The membership of a team or committee can change as members leave the team and new members are added. You can add and remove names from a group in the address book. Choose Tools ➤ Address Book from the menu, and select the address book that contains the group. Double-click the name of the group you want to change, or right-click on a group name and choose Properties to open the group's Properties dialog box.

If you have Internet Only mail, click the Select Members button to add new group members. To remove a member from a group, select the name you want to delete and click the Remove button in the Group Properties dialog box.

In a Workgroup or Corporate setting, click the Add/Remove Members button in the Properties dialog box to open the Edit Members dialog box. Use the Members button to add names to the group. To remove names, select the names in the right pane of the dialog box, and then press the Delete key on your keyboard. When you've finished adding and removing members, click OK to close the Select Names dialog box, and OK again to close the group Properties dialog box.

Delete a Group or Distribution List   When a team's work is complete or a committee is disbanded, you probably won't need the group or distribution list any more. You'll keep it for a while so you can send congratulatory messages or commiserate about the group's involuntary dissolution, but eventually you'll be finished with it. To remove a group list, open the address book (Tools ➤ Address Book) and select the group you want to remove.

In the Internet Only configuration, click the Delete button to remove the group. The entries for the individuals included in the group list will not be deleted. With Corporate/Workgroup settings, right-click on the name of the distribution list and choose Delete from the shortcut menu. When you delete the distribution list, any addresses that only existed in the list are also deleted.

MASTERING GROUPS AND DISTRIBUTION LISTS

When you address mail to a group (or distribution list), all the members of the group receive the original, or a courtesy copy, or a blind courtesy copy. With some projects, you'll want to create more than

CONTINUED ➡

one group so you can quickly send messages and copies to the appropriate people. For example, Beth, Jean, and Margaret are members of your planning team, but Denny and John, the team's supervisors, need to be kept "in the loop" as your team makes decisions and implements strategies. By creating two groups—Planning Team (Beth, Jean, and Margaret) and Planning CC (Denny and John)—you can send messages to the team and courtesy copies to Denny and John with two simple clicks. Reports of the team's progress can be sent to Planning Team, with courtesy copies to the Planning CC.

Entering Message Text

Type the text of your message in the open text area. Text automatically wraps at the end of the line, so you don't need to press Enter unless you are ready to end one paragraph and begin typing another. Use the Edit menu commands or the shortcut menu to cut, copy, paste, find, and select text in the body of the message. To check spelling in a message, choose Tools ➤ Spelling from the menu. Or, you can wait; by default, Outlook will automatically check spelling before sending your message.

E-mail is, in some ways, less formal than traditional correspondence. You don't need a date or internal address—the mail program provides them—and it isn't unusual for messages to end without a closing. When you're entering the body of your message, however, don't mistake casual for less formal. Use appropriate business language in business correspondence and save casual language for e-mail to friends and family. Also, remember that e-mail is read, not heard. Irony and sarcasm are prone to misinterpretation when the audience can't see your facial expression or hear your tone of voice.

ATTACHING ITEMS AND FILES TO MESSAGES

You can *attach* a file or an Outlook item to an e-mail message, using the message as you would use an envelope as a container for a letter. It doesn't matter which e-mail editor you use; you can attach items and files to messages in any format. Files and items can be inserted in a message as attachments, as shortcuts, or as text.

Attachment   Inserts a copy of the file or item as a separate file alongside the message. Use attachments when the recipient needs to work with a copy of the file or item in its original file format. For example, you could send a colleague a number of Contact items, which they could then use in Outlook, or an Excel worksheet, which they could open in Excel. Note that the attachment is a copy, so changes your colleague makes will not be reflected in the original file.

Shortcut   Inserts an icon in the message, which points to the original file. Insert a file or item as a shortcut when you and the recipient both have access to the file. For example, if the Excel worksheet is stored on your departmental server, you could send a shortcut so that your colleague could find the file and both of you could work with the original file.

Text Only   Inserts the text of the file in the body of the message. Use this option to send the contents of a file when the recipient doesn't have access to the creating program. For example, send a WordPad file as Text Only to a recipient who doesn't have access to WordPad, or information from a Contact form to a friend who doesn't use Outlook.

NOTE

When you send messages with categories like Ideas or Hot Contact as attachments, the categories you used are automatically added to the recipients' categories. Unless you and your recipient use exactly the same categories, you should consider deleting the categories from the attached item before sending the message.

 To attach a file to a message, choose Insert ➤ Item from the message menu to open the Insert Item dialog box, shown in Figure 17.9. Select the file, and then choose Text Only, Attachment, or Shortcut from the Insert As option group. Click OK to insert the file.

If you insert the file as an attachment or shortcut, an icon representing the file or file location appears in the message. Text (or something similar) appears for a file inserted as Text Only. In Figure 17.10, an Internet Explorer file has been inserted as a shortcut, a graphics (TIF) file as an attachment, and an executable batch file as text only. When the recipient clicks on the files, the Internet Explorer file will open in Internet Explorer; the TIF will be opened in the recipient's default graphics editor; and the batch file will open in the default text editor. If your recipient doesn't have the program needed to open a file, they can't view it.

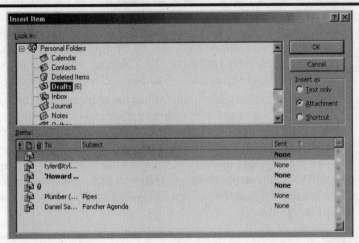

FIGURE 17.9:   In the Insert Item dialog box, select the file and choose how it should be inserted in the message.

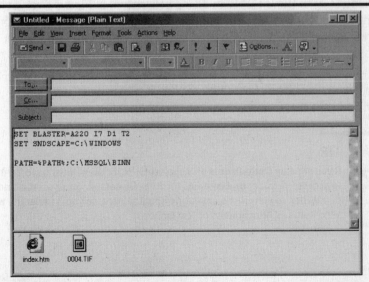

FIGURE 17.10:   Mail message with an attachment, a shortcut, and text inserted from a file.

TROUBLESHOOTING FILE ATTACHMENTS

Only a few file types can be successfully inserted as Text Only. Files created in plain text editors like Notepad and Rich Text editors such as WordPad insert well; these programs create files with extensions like `.txt`, `.bat`, and `.rtf`. Other files contain formatting that can't be translated as text. For example, Microsoft Word files begin and end with embedded codes that specify the document's properties. If you insert a Word file as Text Only in a plain text or RTF message, it will begin and end with symbols—hundreds or thousands of symbols.

If your intended recipient doesn't have the application to open an attachment, you can send the text of the document in the message without attaching it. For a Word document, for example, open the document in Word, select the text, and copy it to the Clipboard. Open the message in Outlook, position the insertion point, and paste the text into the message. You can also save the Word document using the Text Only or Text Only with Line Breaks format, and then attach the file.

To attach an Outlook item to a message, place the insertion point in the body of the message and choose Insert ➢ Item from the message menu to open the Insert Item dialog box, shown in Figure 17.11. Select the folder that contains the item you want to attach, then choose the item in the Items pane. You can use Ctrl or Shift and click to select multiple items.

If your recipient uses Outlook, send the item as an attachment. For recipients who don't have Outlook, insert the item as Text Only. Outlook will add the text from the selected item to the message.

TIP

If you send an Outlook item as a shortcut, the recipient must have permission to access the folder that contains the item. By default, other users do not have permission to view items in your personal folders, so you'll generally want to send items as Attachments or Text Only.

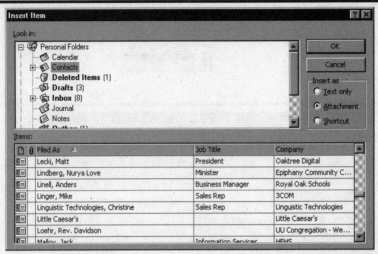

FIGURE 17.11: Use the Insert Item dialog box to select Outlook items to attach to an e-mail message.

SENDING YOUR MESSAGE

You've selected an e-mail editor, addressed your message, added text, and inserted attachments, and you're ready to send your message to the recipients. But first, take a moment and examine Outlook's message handling options to make sure your message is delivered and received with the same care you took while creating it.

Setting Message Options

Message Options are available for each message, and you can set them depending on your needs. Some of these options allow you to insert voting buttons or to receive a validation message confirming that a message you sent was received. Some of these options are only available for particular Mail Support configurations. Message options are set for the individual message you're creating now, not for all new messages.

Click the Options button in the message form's toolbar to open the Message Options dialog box. The Corporate/Workgroup Message Options

Part v

dialog box is shown in Figure 17.12; the Internet Only version of the dialog box does not include Voting and Tracking Options.

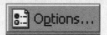

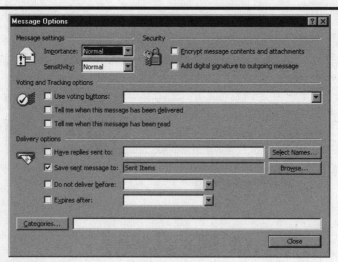

FIGURE 17.12:   Message options are set for a specific message.

Setting Importance and Sensitivity

Both the importance and sensitivity of a message can be set at High, Normal, or Low. Most e-mail programs have a way of marking the importance of incoming messages, so you can use the Importance setting to help the recipient prioritize incoming messages. If you set Importance at High, the recipient will know that the message is not routine; Low says "get to this when you have some free time," and it is generally used for messages you would mark FYI (For Your Information) if they were sent on paper.

The default Importance setting for a new message is Normal. To mark a message with Low or High Importance, choose Low or High from the Importance drop-down list in the Mail Options dialog box. Or you can click the Low Importance (down arrow) or High Importance (exclamation mark) button on the message toolbar.

There are four sensitivity settings: Confidential, Private, Personal, and Normal. You set sensitivity by selecting a setting from the Sensitivity drop-down list in the Mail Options dialog box. This setting is used to help a delegated person handling the recipient's mail know how to deal with incoming items, or route messages to delegates in the recipient's absence. When you use Outlook on a network running Microsoft Exchange, you can give other users permission to view and respond to your messages while you're out of the office. You can base your rules for how the delegates should handle your messages on the Importance and Sensitivity settings of the messages. Table 17.1 summarizes the settings for messages with different types of content.

TABLE 17.1: Message Importance and Sensitivity

IMPORTANCE	SENSITIVITY	MESSAGE CONTENT
Low	All	Routine information that doesn't require a response, to be reviewed as time permits.
Normal	Normal	"Regular" messages that may or may not require a response.
High	Normal	Messages that require immediate action or response, or time-value material the sender feels you need to know.
All	Personal	Messages that are not work-related.
All	Private	Work-related messages that are to be read only by the recipient; private messages cannot be altered after they have been sent.
All	Confidential	Messages that should only be opened by the recipient, but which can be altered.

MASTERING E-MAIL PRIVACY

E-mail can give you a false sense of privacy. You're sitting alone at your computer, creating a message that the recipient will read, alone at their computer. What could be more private, right? Wrong. No message is truly private or confidential. Your e-mail is vulnerable to anyone with high-level permissions on your network or the recipient's network.

CONTINUED ➡

Deleting a compromising message isn't enough; a message has a life of its own long after you delete it. Employers regularly back up data, including e-mail messages stored on a server; and backups of messages that defendants deleted from their desktop computers have been used in court as evidence. Employees have been fired for the content of messages sent to coworkers and supervisors. One individual was fired for forwarding sexist and sexually explicit jokes from the Internet to his male coworkers because it created a hostile environment in the workplace. The employer had discovered the messages on the company server.

If a message is marked as Personal, Private, or Confidential, the message may still be opened accidentally by your recipient's assistant if their mail service doesn't note it as private. Some e-mail systems recognize sensitivity settings, but others do not. For home users, anyone with access to the recipient's e-mail account can open the message, regardless of its sensitivity setting.

As an employee, your privacy rights vary in each state, and progressive companies generally have e-mail policies that you can review. But don't get lulled into believing that your messages are confidential or personal; if you wouldn't write it on a paper memo, don't communicate it in an e-mail message.

You can set the default importance and sensitivity for all new messages in the Options dialog box. Choose Tools ➢ Options ➢ Preferences, and then click the E-mail Options button to open the E-mail Options dialog box. In the E-mail Options dialog box, click the Advanced E-mail Options button to open the dialog box shown in Figure 17.13. Choose the default settings in the Set Importance and Set Sensitivity drop-down lists, and then close the open dialog boxes.

Directing Message Replies to a Third Party

There are times when you'll want the recipients of your message to reply to another address: your assistant, the person in charge of the help desk or the Habitat for Humanity sign-up sheet, or an alternate e-mail address that you use. You can put "please send replies directly to Mary Smith" in your message, but most people click the Reply button as a matter of habit. You can make sure that all the replies end up in the right place by using the Have Replies Sent To option:

1. Click the Options button on the Message toolbar to open the Message Options dialog box.

2. Enable the Have Replies Sent To check box (see Figure 17.12).

3. Type the name or e-mail address that replies should be sent to, or click the Select Names button to open the Select Names dialog box and choose a recipient for replies.

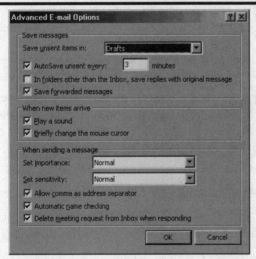

FIGURE 17.13: Set default importance and sensitivity in the Advanced E-mail Options dialog box.

You can't choose or enter the group name for a distribution list; you can only have replies sent to an address for an individual.

Saving a Copy of the Message

By default, copies of all messages are kept in the Sent Items folder. If you don't want to save a copy of the message, disable the Save Sent Message To check box in the Message Options dialog box (see Figure 17.12). To save a copy of the message in a different folder, click the Browse button and choose the folder in the Select Folder dialog box.

Don't save sent items in any of the regular Outlook folders except Sent Items unless you like being confused. The assumption is that you've created a new folder to hold certain types of sent items. If you're the point person on a new project, for example, you might want to save the messages you generate in a separate folder so you can easily find the messages related to the project.

Setting a Time Frame for Message Delivery

The Do Not Deliver Before and Expires After settings in the Message Options dialog box allow you to delay mail delivery or stop attempting to deliver a message after a certain date and time (see Figure 17.12). You might delay mail if, for example, you need to send an important announcement to all employees next Monday, and you won't be in the office. Setting an expiration time means that a client who is on vacation this week won't return next week to read about an offer that expires this Friday.

The Do Not Deliver Before and Expires After text boxes both open a calendar control, which you can use to set the delay or expiration date. If you want to include a time as well as a date (other than the default of 5:00 P.M.), choose the date, and then edit the time in the text box.

These are the steps for setting delay and expiration dates:

1. Click the Options button on the Message toolbar to open the Options dialog box.

2. Enable the Do Not Deliver Before and/or Expires After check boxes.

3. Use the calendar controls to set delay and expiration dates. If necessary, edit the time.

4. Click OK to close the Options dialog box.

Choosing a Delivery Service

If you have more than one e-mail account in the Internet Only configuration, you can select the account you want to use to deliver this message. This may be important, because when a recipient clicks the Reply button, the message is sent to the account that the original message came from. Choose an account from the Send Message Using drop-down list in the Message Options dialog box. This is not an option in the Corporate/Workgroup configuration.

Using E-Mail as a Voting Tool

You're a team player, and you want to know what the other members of your team think about a proposed course of action. You could call them all and keep a tally of their feedback. Or, you could send an e-mail message to each member of the team, wait for their replies, and then open and tabulate them. The Corporate/Workgroup configuration of Outlook has a built-in tool to help you gather opinions and feedback for solid decision-making that will automatically log and tally each team member's vote.

To turn a message into a ballot, open the Options dialog box for the message. In the Voting and Tracking Options section, enable the Use Voting Buttons check box, and then select the voting buttons you want to include in the message from the drop-down list. The choices are:

▶ Approve; Reject

▶ Yes; No

▶ Yes; No; Maybe

If none of these choices meet your needs, you can enter your own button choices, with semicolons between each item. In Figure 17.14, we're asking recipients to vote on a location for a meeting. Replies will be sent to the person in charge of the meeting.

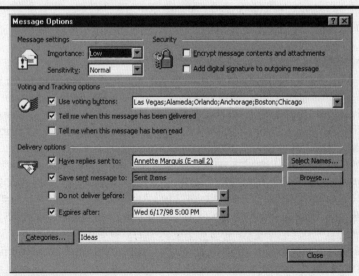

FIGURE 17.14:   Choose or enter button options to use a message as a voting tool.

Part v

As the recipients vote by clicking one of the buttons on their messages, Outlook sends the replies to the person designated in the message options. Outlook also attaches a tracking form to the original message (in the Sent Items folder) that tallies the responses, as shown in Figure 17.15. You can easily find the original message among the Sent Items; the message icon includes an information symbol.

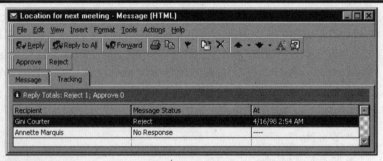

FIGURE 17.15: Votes are automatically tallied when replies are received.

NOTE

Voting only works for users in your workgroup or company; you can't use voting as an e-mail tool over the Internet.

Setting Tracking Options

The Corporate/Workgroup configuration also supports tracking for individual messages. Tracking notifies you when your message has been delivered to your recipient; this notification is called a *delivery receipt*. When the recipient opens your message, you are notified with a *read receipt*. The delivery and read receipts are sent by the recipient's mail server; not all mail servers send receipts, so asking for a receipt doesn't guarantee that you'll get one. Another thing to consider: "read receipt" is a bit of a misnomer. The server can't tell you that a message has been read, only that it has been opened. If your recipient opens the message and deletes it without reading it, you'll still receive a read receipt.

The system may be imperfect, but it's still very useful when you need to know, for example, that

▶ your message to Nancy about Saturday's emergency board meeting was delivered on Friday

- ▶ Nancy didn't open it until Monday

- ▶ which explains why she didn't come to the meeting.

To turn on tracking for a message, enable the Tell Me When This Message Has Been Delivered and/or Tell Me When This Message Has Been Read check boxes (see Figure 17.14).

NOTE
You can't set tracking options in the Internet Only configuration, but you can track specified messages using the Rules Wizard.

Mail Security Options

Outlook includes features that allow you to securely send and receive e-mail messages. There are two ways to secure a message: with a digital signature and with encryption. A digital signature provides corroboration that a message did, indeed, come from you, and has not been altered before the recipient opened it. Encryption uses a mathematical algorithm to scramble the message. Only the recipient can unscramble and read the message. Outlook uses S/MIME to secure Internet e-mail messages.

Adding a Digital Signature to a Message

To send messages with a digital signature, you need a certificate, also called a *Digital ID*. If you do not have a Digital ID registered on your PC, the Security Message Options will be disabled. When the Security options are enabled, as shown in Figure 17.16, you can add a digital signature to your messages.

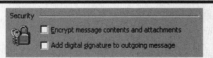

FIGURE 17.16:   The Security options are enabled if you have a registered Digital ID.

To add a digital signature to your message, open the Message Options dialog box, enable the Add Digital Signature to Outgoing Message check box, and then click OK to close the Message Options dialog box. If some of your recipients may not be able to decode messages with digital IDs, choose File ➤ Properties from the message menu to open the Properties dialog box, shown in Figure 17.17. Make sure the Send Clear Text Signed Message check box is enabled. If a recipient's mail system doesn't support S/MIME, they'll still get your message, but it won't include a digital signature.

TIP

The security options set in a message's Properties always override defaults set in Outlook's Options dialog box.

To summarize, these are the steps for adding a digital signature to a message:

1. Click the Options button on the message toolbar to open the Message Options dialog box.

2. Enable the Add Digital Signature to Outgoing Message check box.

3. Click OK to close the Message Options dialog box.

To add a digital signature to all new messages, choose Tools ➤ Options from the Outlook menu to open the Message Options dialog box, and then click the Security tab. Enable the Add Digital Signature to Outgoing Messages check box.

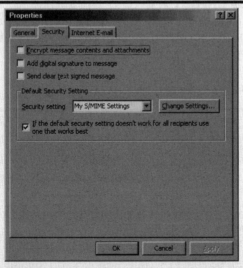

FIGURE 17.17: Open the message Properties dialog box to modify the security settings.

Encrypting a Message

Before you can send an encrypted e-mail message to someone, you must have a copy of that person's digital ID in your contact list. Ask the person to send you an e-mail message that includes their digital signature. Open the message and right-click on the sender's address in the message's From field. Choose Add to Contacts from the shortcut menu. The new contact will include the digital ID. To encrypt a message:

1. Click the Options button on the message toolbar to open the Message Options dialog box.

2. Enable the Encrypt Message Contents and Attachments check box.

3. Click OK.

To encrypt all new messages you send, choose Tools ≻ Options on the Outlook menu, and then click the Security tab. Enable the Encrypt Message Contents and Attachments for Outgoing Messages check box. If you want to send an unencrypted message, choose File ≻ Properties in the message menu and change the settings for the individual message (see Figure 17.17).

Sending Mail Messages

You're ready to send your message to its recipients. Click the Send button on the message toolbar, or choose File ≻ Send Using and select a service from the menu to place the message in the Outlook Outbox.

You may be wondering how long the message will hang around in the Outbox. The answer: it depends. There are three possible scenarios:

▶ In a Corporate/Workgroup installation where you are connected to a network, options are usually set to send messages immediately and your outgoing message will spend very little time in the Outbox.

▶ In an Internet Only or Corporate/Workgroup installation, you can establish automated Internet mail delivery at specified intervals. Outlook connects to the Internet every N minutes or hours, and delivers and receives messages.

▶ On the other hand, you may be using Outlook with the Internet Only configuration without automated mail delivery (the default for Internet Only) or you might be working offline in a Corporate/Workgroup configuration. In that case, mail waits in your Outbox until you instruct Outlook to send and retrieve messages.

To move the message out of the Outbox and into the Internet or local mail server, do one of the following:

▶ Choose Tools ➤ Send from the Outlook menu to send, but not receive, messages from your mail server.

▶ Choose Tools ➤ Send and Receive ➤ All Accounts (or a specific account) to both send and receive messages.

If you access your mail server with a dial-up connection, a dialog box opens while Outlook is connecting to your server. When connecting to an ISP or company server, Corporate/Workgroup users see the following message box:

This dialog box remains open while messages are being sent and received. Once Outlook has established a dial-up connection, you can move the dialog box to a less central location.

Internet Only users see a different dialog box. When you click the Details button, the dialog box expands to show connection information, as shown in Figure 17.18.

You'll still be able to keep track of Outlook's progress, even with the dialog box hidden. Check the right side of the status bar to see reports as Outlook sends and receives your messages.

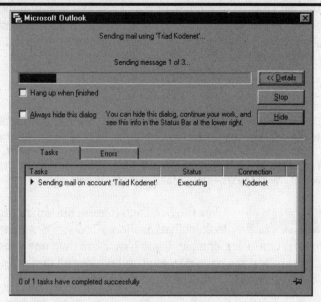

FIGURE 17.18: Click the Details button to watch Outlook send and receive mail.

If you need to cancel message sending or delivering, click on the arrow at the right end of the status bar and choose Cancel Mail Delivery from the menu. To redisplay the Details dialog box, choose Details from the menu. After each message has been sent, Outlook moves it from the Outbox to the Sent Items folder, or to another folder you specified in the message options.

RECEIVING MAIL

 One of the best parts of working on a network is automatic mail delivery. You're sitting at your desk typing a short memo, when a bell rings and a small envelope appears in the Windows taskbar tray. You've got mail! Double-click the mail icon in the taskbar, and you're automatically moved to the Inbox so you can see your new messages. If your company has an Internet mail gateway, messages from outside the company will also be automatically delivered. Of course, you must have Outlook running to receive messages. If you close Outlook, messages remain on your company's mail server until you start Outlook.

In the Internet Only configuration or the Corporate/Workgroup configuration without an established Internet mail account with automatic retrieval scheduled, you have to tell Outlook to retrieve Internet mail messages.

TIP

In either configuration, you can have Outlook display a message box (in addition to playing the sound effect and displaying the envelope icon) when new mail appears. Choose Tools ➢ Options to open the Options dialog box. On the Preferences page, click the E-mail Options button and enable the Display a Notification Message When New Mail Arrives check box.

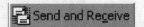   Click the Send and Receive button on the Outlook toolbar, or choose Tools ➢ Send and Receive from the Outlook menu bar. If you have more than one e-mail service or account, you can choose to send and retrieve all messages from the menu, or just messages from one account or service.

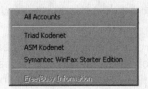

In the Internet Only configuration, a large dialog box appears to let you know that Outlook is connecting to your Internet server. You have the option to hide the dialog box or view more details. In the Corporate/Workgroup configuration, you'll see the smaller Deliver Messages message box. With either configuration, you need to wait until Outlook has made the connection and the mail server has verified your password, but then you can continue working in Outlook while messages are retrieved in the background.

PREVIEWING MAIL MESSAGES

When you look at folders like the Inbox icon in the Folder List, the number of unread messages appears in parentheses after the folder name. (If the folder list is not visible, choose View ➢ Folder List to display it.) In the table view of the messages, unread messages are in boldface, so they are easy to spot (see Figure 17.19).

Select a message, and the beginning of the message appears in the preview pane below the messages. If the preview pane is not open, choose View ➢ Preview Pane from the Outlook menu to display it. You can adjust the size of the preview pane by adjusting the bar at the top of the preview pane up or down with the mouse pointer.

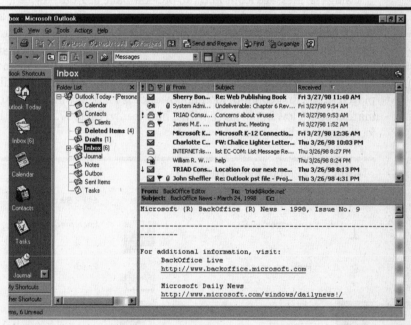

FIGURE 17.19:   Unread messages are boldface in the Inbox.

TIP

You cannot preview encrypted messages.

Right-click in the message list area and select AutoPreview from the contextual menu to display the first three lines of every message. Selecting AutoPreview again turns AutoPreview off.

Using the message icons and the preview pane or AutoPreview, you can quickly decide which messages need your immediate attention and which can wait. The previews usually let you see enough of a message to gauge its urgency. The first four columns of the default Inbox view show the message's Importance, Message Icon, Flag Status, and Attachment information. If the sender set the importance of the message, it is displayed in the first column; high importance is marked with a red exclamation point, low importance with a blue arrow. Table 17.2 shows the icons used in the Inbox.

TABLE 17.2: Inbox Message Icons

Icon	Message	Icon	Message
↓	Low importance		Encrypted message
!	High importance		Read
	Unread		Forwarded
	Meeting request		Replied to
	Flagged for follow-up		Rejected by server; can be re-sent

TABLE 17.2 continued: Inbox Message Icons

ICON	MESSAGE	ICON	MESSAGE
	Flagged; follow-up completed		Includes an attachment
	Attached Outlook item (task request, journal entry)		

REPLYING TO MAIL

After you read a message, you'll often want to reply to it immediately. You can reply to the sender, or to everyone who received the message and courtesy copies of the message. Select or open the message you wish to reply to, and then click the Reply button to address a reply only to the sender, or the Reply to All button to send a reply to the sender and all the other recipients of the message you received. Outlook opens a message form and enters the recipients' addresses in the To text box. You can add other recipients using the To, Cc, and Bcc buttons on the message form.

The text of the message you're replying to is at the bottom of the open text area of the form; this is called *quoted text*. Each line of quoted text begins with the > symbol so it doesn't get confused with the text of your reply. Enter the text of your reply, and then click Send to send the reply to your Outbox.

TIP

When you click the Reply or Reply to All button, Outlook opens and addresses the form, but the original message remains open. To have Outlook automatically close the original message when you click Reply, Reply to All, or Forward, enable the Close Original Message on Reply or Forward check box in the Options dialog box (Tools ➢ Options ➢ Preferences ➢ E-mail Options).

Changing Options for Quoted Text

Quoted text preceded by the > symbol is the norm for replies to plain text messages. If you're exchanging a lot of e-mail messages, or when a number of people are involved in a conversation, it's easy to get lost in the thread of the conversation. When Bob writes "Yes," which of the three proposals was he agreeing to?

You can change the format of quoted text, omit it entirely, omit or change the preceding symbol, or have your reply text preceded with your name. To change the format for replies, choose Tools ➢ Options to open the Options dialog box. On the Preferences page, click the E-mail Options button to open the E-mail Options dialog box, shown in Figure 17.20.

There are five options for quoted text in the When Replying to a Message drop-down list:

- ▶ Do Not Include Original Message
- ▶ Attach Original Message
- ▶ Include Original Message Text
- ▶ Include and Indent Original Message Text
- ▶ Prefix Each Line of the Original Message (default)

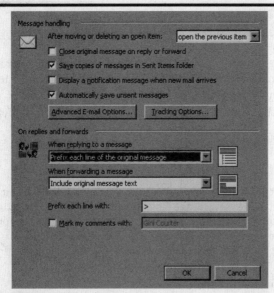

FIGURE 17.20:   Change options for message replies in the E-mail Options dialog box.

Prefixing each line of the original message is the default because all mail programs support text, so the prefix is handled just like any other character. Some older programs will remove indenting, or replace it with a symbol. If you prefix each line, Outlook uses the symbol in the Prefix Each Line With text box. The downside of prefixing quoted text is that Outlook's spell check treats it as newly entered text, and checks the spelling of the original messages, as well as the reply text you enter.

There is a trend away from quoted text in business correspondence. If the original text is lengthy, recipients appreciate it if you don't include the full text of the message. Each reply adds another header, and as the conversation continues with replies to replies, you can quickly acquire pages of original text with multiple headers. (It's considered good manners to delete all but the relevant portion of the quoted text.)

When replying to a complex message, comments may provide the best solution. With comments, your name or other custom text appears in brackets to the right of comments you make in the original text. This option won't work if you choose Word as your e-mail editor. Figure 17.21 shows a message reply with comments interspersed in the original text.

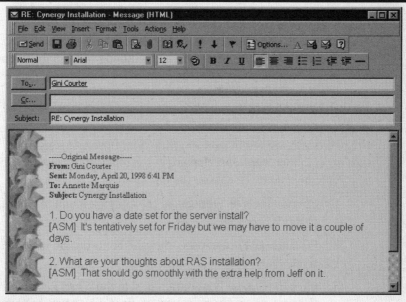

FIGURE 17.21: Comments clearly identify your replies within the original text.

If you want to change how quoted text is handled in your messages, modify the e-mail options for quoted text:

1. Choose Tools ➣ Options on the Outlook menu to open the Options dialog box.

2. On the Preferences page, click the E-mail Options button to open the E-mail Options dialog box.

3. Choose a format from the When Replying to a Message drop-down list.

4. If you choose the Prefix format, enter a prefix symbol or leave the default symbol (>) in the Prefix Each Line With text box.

5. To add comments to replies and forwarded messages, enable the Mark My Comments With check box, and enter your name or other text in the text box.

6. Click OK to close the E-mail Options dialog box.

7. Click OK to close the Options dialog box.

Changing the Font for Replies

When you reply to a message, Outlook uses the same format as the original message. If the message is plain text, Outlook will use the plain text font you selected for your reply text. However, if the original message was created with an HTML, Word, or Rich Text Format editor, you can use another font for the text you enter in your reply. The same font will be used for text you enter in forwarded messages.

Quoted text will retain its formatting from the original message. As with other Outlook options, changes in the reply font take effect on the next reply you create. To change the reply font:

1. Choose Tools ➣ Options on the Outlook menu to open the Options dialog box.

2. On the Mail Format page, click the Fonts button to open the Fonts dialog box.

3. Click the Choose Font button next to the When Replying and Forwarding text box to open the Font dialog box.

4. Set font options, and then click OK to close the Font dialog box.

5. Click OK to close the Fonts dialog box.

6. Click OK to close the Options dialog box.

FORWARDING MESSAGES

Forwarding a message sends the entire message, and any text you add, to another recipient. To forward an open message, click the Forward button or choose Actions ➤ Forward from the message menu. If the message is not open, right-click the message in the view list, and choose Forward from the shortcut menu.

As with a reply, the original message is copied into a new message form; you simply need to choose recipients and enter your text before clicking the Send button.

To indicate how the original text and text you add should appear in the forwarded message, open the E-mail Options dialog box. The options for the original message text are:

▶ Attach Original Message

▶ Include Original Message Text (default)

▶ Include and Indent Original Message Text

▶ Prefix Each Line of the Original Message

If comments are enabled for replies, they are also enabled for forwarded messages. To change options for what's included with forwarded messages:

1. Choose Tools ➤ Options on the Outlook menu to open the Options dialog box.

2. On the Preferences page, click the E-mail Options button to open the E-mail Options dialog box.

3. Choose a format from the When Forwarding a Message drop-down list.

4. To add comments to replies and forwarded messages, enable the Mark My Comments With check box, and enter your name or other text in the text box.

5. Click OK to close the E-mail Options dialog box.

6. Click OK to close the Options dialog box.

TO FORWARD OR NOT TO FORWARD?

Forwarding a message is even easier than replying to a message; all you need to do is pass it on. Forwarding has other implications, however; it's essentially the same as handing a colleague a memo you received or sharing the information from a phone conversation with a third party. Make sure you have the author's permission before forwarding the message.

Some people don't realize that e-mail correspondence is intended to be read by the addressees only, and they forward mail indiscriminately. To lessen the odds of your messages being forwarded without your knowledge, create a custom signature stating that the contents of the message are not to be forwarded without your express written consent. In many companies, this type of signature is required for all messages sent to recipients outside the company.

Changing the Font for Forwarded Messages

When you forward a message, Outlook uses the same format as the original message. If the message is plain text, Outlook will use the plain text font you selected to display forwarded text. However, if the original message was created with an HTML, Word, or Rich Text format editor, you can use another font for the text you enter in the forwarded message. This font will also be used for text you enter in replies. You can change the font used in forwarded messages by following these steps:

1. Choose Tools ➤ Options on the Outlook menu to open the Options dialog box.

2. On the Mail Format page, click the Fonts button to open the Fonts dialog box.

3. Click the Choose Font button next to the When Replying and Forwarding text box to open the Font dialog box.

4. Set font options.

5. Click OK to close the Fonts dialog box.

6. Click OK to close the Options dialog box.

WHAT'S NEXT

Now that you are well versed in the sending and receiving of e-mail, you may want to explore Outlook 2000's scheduling capabilities. In Chapter 18, you'll find out how to use the calendar feature to schedule appointments and organize your life!

Part V

Chapter 18

SCHEDULING YOUR TIME WITH OUTLOOK

Timing is everything, and controlling your scheduling often makes the difference between success and failure in this fast-paced world. Whether you keep your own calendar or have an assistant keep it for you, it can be a challenge to schedule your time wisely. Every fall, millions of people search through office supply stores and catalogs looking for the perfect calendar that will keep them organized in the coming year. If you are among them, Outlook's Calendar is for you. Not sure whether to choose a calendar with a daily view or a weekly view? With Outlook you can have both. In fact, you can view your calendar by the day, multiple days, workweek, calendar week, month, and a variety of other ways.

The real power of using an electronic calendar lies in being able to schedule recurring appointments and, if you are on a network, schedule appointments with other people. In this chapter, you'll learn how to make your calendar work for you instead of becoming a slave to it.

Adapted from *Mastering Microsoft Outlook 2000* by Gini Courter and Annette Marquis

ISBN 0-7821-2472-0   816 pages $34.99

VIEWING AND NAVIGATING THE CALENDAR

When you first enter the Calendar, either by clicking the Calendar icon on the Outlook bar or by choosing View ➤ Go To ➤ Calendar from the menu, you are shown the Day/Week/Month view, shown in Figure 18.1.

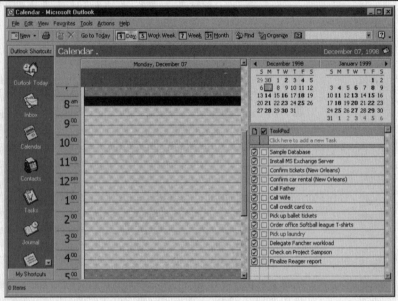

FIGURE 18.1:   The Calendar's Day/Week/Month view

The Day/Week/Month view is actually a combination of a daily calendar; a monthly calendar, called the date navigator; and a list of active tasks on the TaskPad. So why, you may be asking, is this called the Day/Week/Month view when there is no week visible? It's because you can easily switch from Day view to Week view to Month view using buttons on the Standard toolbar, as shown in Figure 18.2.

FIGURE 18.2: The Standard toolbar with the Day button selected

The Day button shows the default view. The next button, Work Week, displays a workweek of five days. If your workweek is made up of different days, you can customize the week, using the Calendar options. (See "Configuring the Calendar" later in this chapter.)

The Week button shows all seven days of the week in the typical week-at-a-glance format, shown in Figure 18.3, which you may be used to from your paper-based calendar.

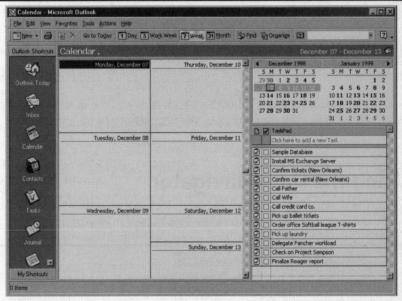

FIGURE 18.3: The typical seven-day week view

The Month button displays a month at a time, alternating gray and white backgrounds to differentiate the months, as shown in Figure 18.4.

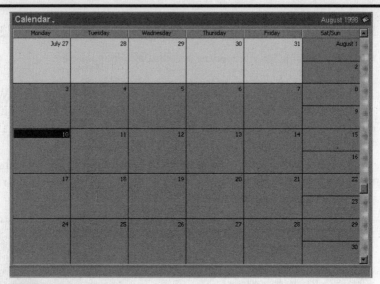

FIGURE 18.4: The Month view

Personal preference dictates which view you use most frequently. Choose the view that gives you the best sense of where you have to be and what you have to do.

Using the Date Navigator

The date navigator, shown in Figure 18.5, not only shows you the monthly calendar, but also lets you select days to view in the Calendar itself.

◀	August 1998						September 1998						▶
S	M	T	W	T	F	S	S	M	T	W	T	F	S
26	27	28	29	30	31	1			1	2	3	4	5
2	3	4	5	6	7	8	6	7	8	9	10	11	12
9	10	11	12	13	14	15	13	14	15	16	17	18	19
16	17	18	19	20	21	22	20	21	22	23	24	25	26
23	24	25	26	27	28	29	27	28	29	30	1	2	3
30	31						4	5	6	7	8	9	10

FIGURE 18.5: The date navigator

Click any date in the date navigator, and that date becomes visible in the Information Viewer.

Click the left and right arrows next to the month headings to select a different month.

To select an entire week, move your pointer to the left side of the date navigator. The pointer changes position and points toward the date navigator. Click your mouse to select the week. To select multiple weeks, hold your mouse button down and drag, as shown in Figure 18.6.

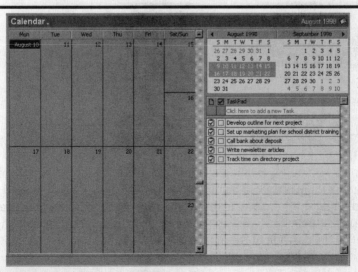

FIGURE 18.6: Selecting multiple weeks

It's also easy to compare nonconsecutive days. Click a day and hold the Ctrl key down before selecting the next day, as shown in Figure 18.7.

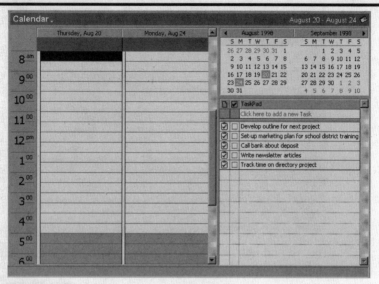

FIGURE 18.7:   Selecting nonconsecutive days

To move quickly to a different month, click on the month name and select another month from the list.

Using this month-selection feature can be a little bit tricky if the month you want is not immediately visible among the months displayed. Pretend there is a scroll bar and hold your mouse button down and drag. You'll find that you have to drag outside of the list in order to activate the scroll feature. Figure 18.8 shows an example of scrolling the month list. Notice the position of the mouse pointer.

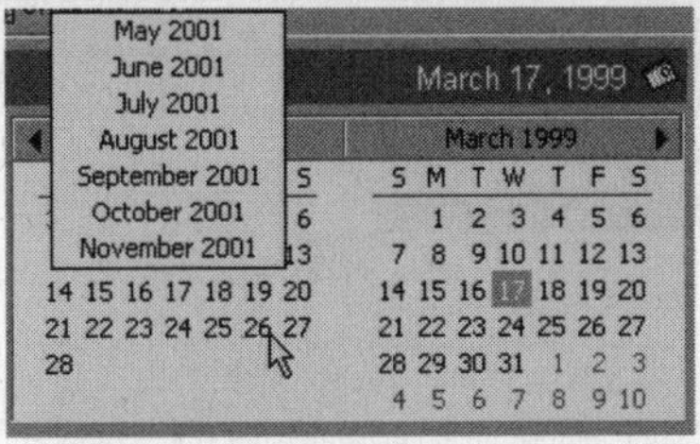

FIGURE 18.8: Scrolling the Month list

Moving the mouse pointer farther away from the list will increase the speed of the scroll. To slow down the scroll rate, move the mouse pointer closer to the list. To move to a previous month, position the mouse pointer above the list, as shown in Figure 18.9.

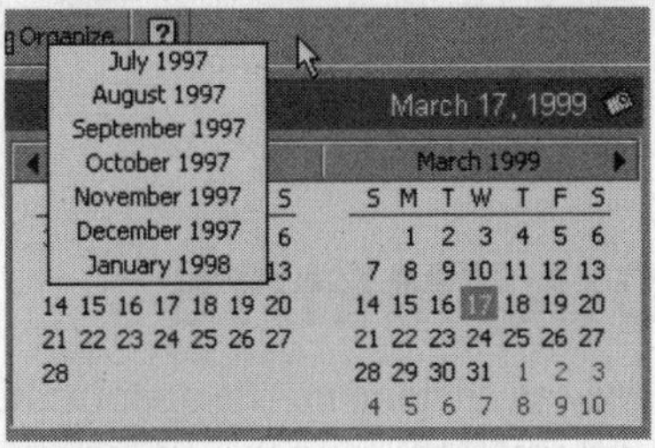

FIGURE 18.9: Scrolling to a previous month

Any time you want to move quickly back to today, click the Go to Today button on the Standard toolbar.

If you prefer to display only one month in the date navigator, move your mouse pointer to the left side of the date navigator—the pointer will change to a resize arrow. Drag the border of the date navigator to the right until only one month is visible, as shown in Figure 18.10.

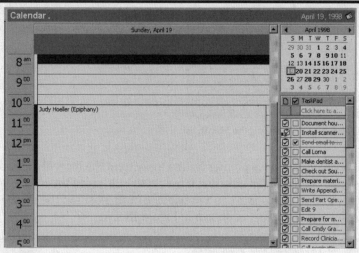

FIGURE 18.10:   Displaying only one month in the date navigator

SCHEDULING APPOINTMENTS

Scheduling an appointment is as easy as clicking on the appointment slot in the Day view and typing in the information, as shown in Figure 18.11.

FIGURE 18.11:   Entering an appointment in the Calendar

Once you have typed in the entry, point to the lower border of the appointment slot and, with the two-headed arrow pointer, drag down to identify the end time of the appointment. Drop the blue line just above the desired end time.

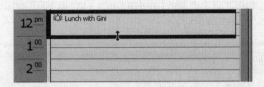

To change the start time of the appointment, drag the blue line above the appointment slot. If you want to maintain the length of the appointment but alter the start and end times, point to the blue line on the left side of the appointment and, with the four-headed arrow, drag the entire appointment to a new time.

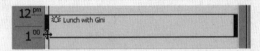

Once you begin dragging, the four-headed arrow will change shape to a pointer with a move box.

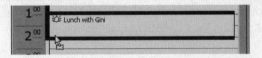

To change the appointment to a different day, it's necessary to first make the new date visible in the date navigator. Switch to the desired month in the date navigator, and drag the appointment to the new date using the four-headed arrow/move box.

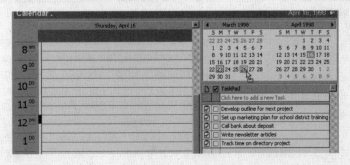

Entering an Appointment in the Appointment Form

When you want to enter more details about an appointment, double-click the appointment in the Information Viewer to open the Appointment form (see Figure 18.12).

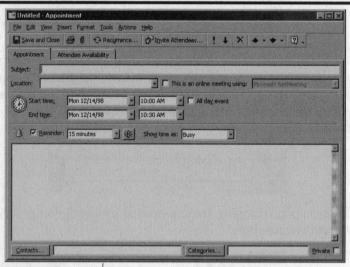

FIGURE 18.12: The Calendar's Appointment form

In addition to the Subject and Start Time and End Time, the Appointment form allows you to enter a location, to set a reminder, and to enter other notes about the appointment.

APPOINTMENTS VERSUS EVENTS

Outlook's Calendar feature distinguishes between appointments and events. An *appointment* has a start and end time and may last for less than one day or may span multiple days. An *event*, on the other hand, encompasses an entire day or perhaps several days but does not have a specific start and end time. For example, a holiday, a birthday, or a vacation is designated as an event. To change an appointment to an event, click the All Day Event check box to the right of the Start Time on an Appointment form. The Start Time and

CONTINUED ➡

End Time fields are removed from the form. Because an event does not automatically impact your schedule, the Show Time As field is set to Free. Events appear as a banner in the Day view of the Calendar. See "Scheduling Events" later in this chapter for more information about events.

Click the This Is an Online Meeting check box if the meeting will occur over the Internet.

To set the Start Time and End Time in an Appointment form, click the down arrow to the right of the Start Time and End Time fields. The first arrow opens a calendar from which you can select the date for the appointment. Use the left and right arrows next to the month name to select from a different month.

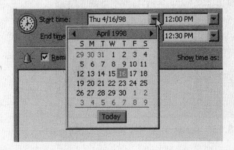

The arrow to the right of the second field opens a list of times on a 24-hour clock. Be careful to select the correct A.M. or P.M. time, or you may be expected to have lunch some day at midnight.

TIP

Outlook has incorporated the use of natural language for dates. Rather than typing a date in traditional format or selecting the date from the calendar, you can type in text to describe the date. For example, rather than locating the date for next Friday, you can simply type in the words **next Friday** and Outlook will translate the text to the correct date.

Setting a Reminder

One of the biggest advantages of using an electronic calendar is that it can automatically remind you when it's time to go to your appointments. Assuming that most of your appointments are held in your office, the default reminder is set for 15 minutes prior to a scheduled appointment. For a meeting that occurs out of the office, you can set this reminder from 0 minutes to up to 2 days by selecting a different choice from the drop-down list. As a matter of fact, you can type in a reminder that extends even beyond the two days that are included in the list. To turn off the reminder, click the check box to the left of the Reminder field.

When a reminder is scheduled, it will appear as a small dialog box in whatever application is running at the time (as long as Outlook is at least running in the background). Figure 18.13 is an example of an appointment reminder.

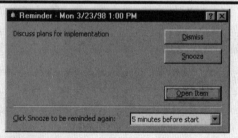

FIGURE 18.13: A reminder for an appointment

When you receive a reminder, you have several options. You can:

▶ Dismiss the reminder (click Dismiss), in which case Outlook assumes you are on your way and won't bother you again.

▶ Choose to be reminded again in a designated amount of time by selecting time interval from the Click Snooze to Be Reminded Again drop-down list and clicking Snooze.

▶ Open the Appointment form so you can review the appointment or make changes to it.

When the reminder dialog box opens, clicking anywhere outside of the dialog box will move it to the Windows taskbar. You are then free to open it at any time to respond to the reminder.

By default, an appointment reminder is accompanied by a short ding (actually it's the Windows default ding). You can choose to turn the ding off or choose a more dramatic sound to accompany the reminder.

 To change the sound options, click the speaker icon next to the Reminder text box. This opens the Reminder Sound dialog box.

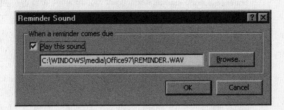

To turn off the sound so that the reminder appears silently on your screen, simply click the Play This Sound check box to clear it. To designate a different sound file, either type the path to the sound file or click the Browse button to access your file list. The file must be a .wav file—the reminder cannot play a MIDI or other type of sound file.

TIP

You can record your own reminder sound using the Windows Sound Recorder and play that sound file (.wav) when it's time to go to an appointment. You'll find the Windows Sound Recorder in the Accessories program group on the Programs menu.

When you have set the Sound Reminder options, click OK to return to the Appointment form.

Scheduling Recurring Appointments

You probably have a number of appointments that occur on a regular basis—for example, a weekly staff meeting, a daily project review meeting, or a monthly district sales meeting. With Outlook's Calendar, you can set up a meeting once and it will automatically recur in your calendar.

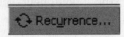

To access the recurrence features, set up the appointment in the Appointment form, and then click the Recurrence button on the Standard toolbar of the Appointment form. This opens the Appointment Recurrence dialog box.

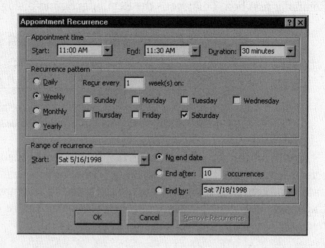

Use the Start, End, and Duration fields to designate the typical time for the recurring appointment. You only have to set two of these three fields—Outlook will calculate the third. For example, if the start time is noon and the duration is three hours, Outlook will automatically set the end time to 3:00 P.M.

Choose the recurrence pattern that most closely matches the recurring appointment's schedule. Each of the four options—Daily, Weekly, Monthly, and Yearly—offer different choices for setting up the pattern. If, for example, the meeting occurs every day, choose Daily as the recurrence pattern and click the Every Weekday check box. If, however, the appointment occurs on the fourth Monday of every other month, set the recurrence pattern to Monthly and enter the fourth Monday of every two months, as shown in Figure 18.14.

After establishing the recurrence pattern, you'll want to identify the range of recurrence. This tells Outlook when to schedule the first meeting and how many times the appointment will recur. Enter the date of the first meeting in the Start field and choose among the following three options to indicate how many times to add the appointment to your calendar:

No End Date Use this option if it appears that the meeting will occur from now until the end of time.

End after *N* Occurrences With this option you can designate exactly how many times to add the meeting to your calendar.

End By This option allows you to designate a specific end date. The meeting will be scheduled only between the designated start and end dates.

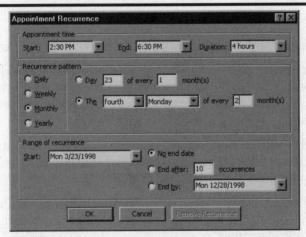

FIGURE 18.14: This meeting occurs the fourth Monday of every second month.

When you have set the recurrence options, click the OK button to assign the recurrence pattern to the appointment. You'll notice that the recurrence pattern is listed on the Appointment form.

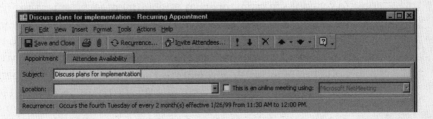

You don't have to have the Appointment form open to recognize a recurring appointment. A recurring appointment is displayed in the Information Viewer with an icon composed of two circular arrows.

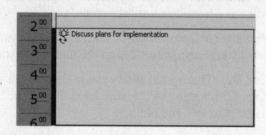

To set a recurrence pattern, then, follow these steps:

1. Open an Appointment form and click the Recurrence button.

2. Choose the frequency of the recurrence (daily, weekly, monthly, or yearly), and then specify the day on which the meeting will occur; for example, the first Friday of every month.

3. Identify the range of recurrence, that is, how far in the future these meetings will continue to be held: until the end of time, for three weeks, from now until December 31, 2001, etc.

4. Click OK to save the recurrence pattern. A recurring appointment is designated in the Information Viewer by an icon with two circular arrows.

Scheduling Events

As indicated earlier in this chapter, an event that has no start and end times, such as a holiday, anniversary, or any other day that you want to note. To schedule an event, open an Appointment form, enter the Subject and date information, and click the All Day Event check box. This removes the Start Time and End Time fields from the Appointment form. You can set a reminder for an event and set a Recurrence Pattern just as you would for any other appointment. So when you find out the date of your best friend's birthday, enter it as an event and set the recurrence pattern to yearly. To make sure you have time to buy a gift, set a reminder for one or two days before the birthday. Your friend will be shocked when you actually remember the all-important day.

Outlook assumes that an event does not occupy your time, so it shows your time as Free. However, you may want to change this if, for example, the event you are entering is your vacation. In this case, you could set the Show Time As field to Out of the Office.

Because there are no times associated with an event, events are displayed differently from regular appointments in the Information Viewer. In the Day view, an event appears at the top of the day's schedule. In the Week and Month views, events are displayed in bordered boxes, such as the one in Figure 18.15.

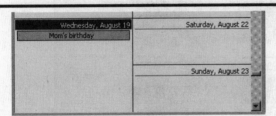

FIGURE 18.15: An event in Month view

TIP

Outlook gives you the option of loading a variety of different holidays into your Outlook Calendar. For example, you can load United States holidays and Christian, Jewish, and Islamic religious holidays. See "Configuring the Calendar" later in this chapter for more information about how to add these holidays to your calendar automatically.

Scheduling a Multi-day Event

Multi-day events are scheduled activities that have no set start and end times and span several days. To enter a multi-day event, open the Appointment form and set the start and end time dates to coincide with the dates of the event.

Scheduling Time to Complete a Task

In an effort to help you manage your time more effectively, Outlook displays the TaskPad as part of the default Calendar view. This is not only so you get a sense of tasks that you have to accomplish; it's so you can actually schedule time to work on individual tasks.

To schedule time to work on a task, display the day and select the time in the Information Viewer. Drag the task that you want to work on from the TaskPad to the designated time. Outlook will create an appointment based on the task and will open an Appointment form with the contents of the task already included in it, as shown in Figure 18.16. Set the other options just as you would for any other appointment—the only difference is that this is an appointment with yourself.

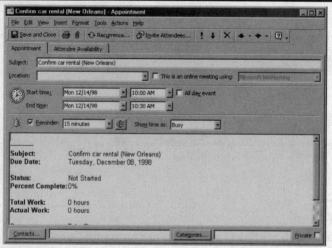

FIGURE 18.16:   An appointment created from a task

When you complete the task, mark it complete on your Task list just as you would any other task. You'll be surprised at how much easier it is to check off items on your Task list when you schedule time in your daily calendar to complete them.

Creating a Shortcut to a Task

If you'd rather an appointment were created with only a shortcut to the corresponding task, drag the appointment onto the Calendar using the right mouse button. When you release the mouse button, you will be given options to do the following:

▶ Copy the task as an appointment with text

▶ Copy the task as an appointment with a shortcut

▶ Copy the task as an appointment with an attachment

▶ Move the task as an appointment with an attachment

When you copy the task as an appointment with a shortcut, the contents of the task do not occur in both the Calendar and the Task list. When you open an Appointment form, you'll find an icon representing the task. Double-click the icon to open the task in the Task list. This option saves space on your hard drive and reduces the size of your Personal Information Store. The two other options, involving attachments, create copies of the task, which you would also access by double-clicking the icon within the Appointment form. Use one of the attachment options if you plan to share this appointment with someone else using Outlook (see "Using the Calendar in a Workgroup" later in this chapter).

CONFIGURING THE CALENDAR

Because people work very different schedules these days, Outlook has included a number of options that let you define the days you work, the hours that you want to display in your calendar, and which day is the first in your week. To change the Calendar options, click the Tools menu on the Standard toolbar and choose Options. This opens the Options dialog box, shown in Figure 18.17.

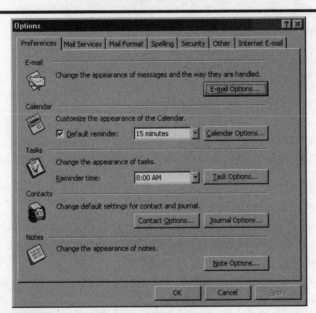

FIGURE 18.17: The Options dialog box

This is your gateway to the options for each of the Outlook components. You can adjust the Calendar option for the Default Reminder time from this initial dialog box. Just choose a different time from the choices available in the drop-down list.

To access additional options, click the Calendar Options button. This button takes you to more specific Calendar options, as shown in Figure 18.18.

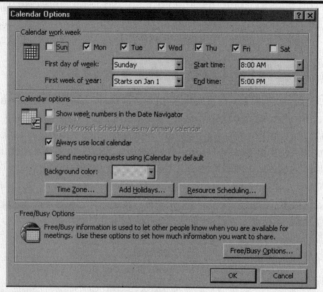

FIGURE 18.18: The Calendar Options dialog box

The first set of options relates to your default workweek. Click the check boxes in front of the days of the week to designate the days that make up your workweek. If you would prefer the Calendar to display Monday or any other day as the first day of the week, select the day from the First Day of the Week field.

The Day view of the Calendar is set to display the typical workday. If your workday differs from this, set the start and end times of your typical day using the Start Time and End Time fields.

To keep your calendar in line with your staff schedules, you may want to start your calendar year on a date other than January 1. Perhaps yours starts on the first four-day week or first full week of the year. Choose one of these options from the drop-down list.

The second set of options relates specifically to the Calendar. For many companies it is important to know the week number in order to calculate payroll and benefits for employees. Outlook will let you display the week number in the date navigator, as shown in Figure 18.19, by clicking the Show Week Numbers in the Date Navigator check box.

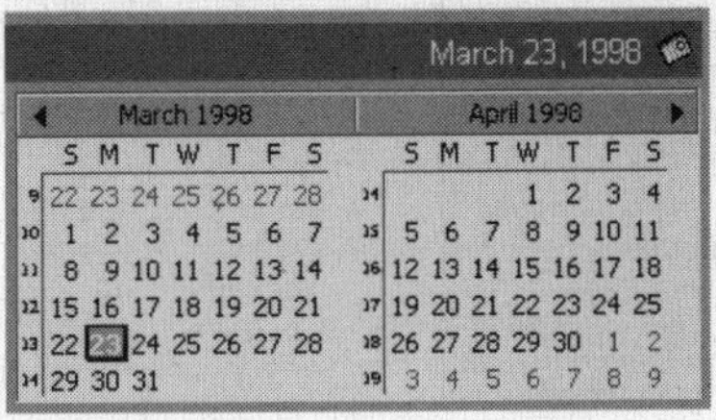

FIGURE 18.19: The week numbers can be displayed in the date navigator.

Showing Two Time Zones

If you are someone who travels frequently across different time zones or has regular phone conferences with people in different time zones, it's helpful to know what time it is in another place. You can choose to show more than one time zone in the Day view of the Information Viewer. Click the Time Zone button to set up an additional time zone or to make adjustments to your current time zone, such as adjusting for daylight savings time.

To set up an additional time zone in the Time Zone dialog box, shown in Figure 18.20, start by giving the time zone a label. This will identify the time zone in the Day view of the Calendar. Select the desired time zone from the Time Zone drop-down list. Indicate if you would like Outlook to automatically adjust for daylight saving time by making sure there is a check in the Adjust for Daylight Saving Time check box. Outlook will display the current date and time based on the Windows Date/Time Properties. If you find that the date or time is wrong, double-click the time in the Windows taskbar and adjust the settings there.

When you would like to display an additional time zone, click the Show an Additional Time Zone check box. This activates the second set of fields so you can enter a label and choose a new time zone. To display both time zones, click OK to close the dialog box. Click OK again to close the Calendar Options, and click OK a third time to close the Options dialog box. The two time zones will be displayed side-by-side, as shown in Figure 18.21.

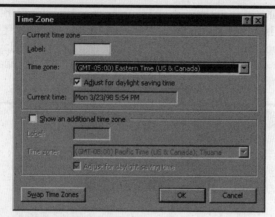

FIGURE 18.20:   The Time Zone dialog box

FIGURE 18.21:   Displaying two time zones

TIP

If you'd prefer to only display one time zone at a time but frequently move between the two, re-open the Time Zone dialog box (Tools ➢ Options ➢ Calendar Options ➢ Time Zone) and click the Swap Time Zones button. You can then clear the Show an Additional Time Zone check box to display only the secondary time zone.

Loading Holidays

We find it a lot easier to remember the date of some holidays than to remember others—the Fourth of July and Christmas are easy ones. However, many holidays are not content to occur on the same day every year; they are constantly moving around the calendar. Outlook makes it easy to load these dates into your permanent calendar. In fact, you have to be careful to not load too many holidays, or your calendar will be overrun with them. To load holidays into your calendar, follow these steps:

1. Select Tools ➢ Options ➢ Calendar Options ➢ Add Holidays.

2. Select from the list of national holidays (from such countries as the United States, Australia, and Canada) and religious holidays (such as those of Christianity, Judaism, and Islam).

3. Click OK three times to close all the option dialog boxes.

Holidays appear on your calendar as events, so they are displayed in the banner at the top of each day. If you've chosen holidays from a particular country or religious group, that group's name will appear in parentheses after the holiday, as shown in Figure 18.22.

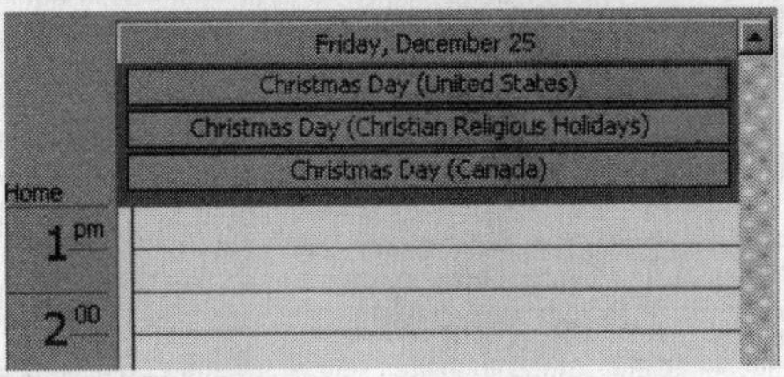

Friday, December 25
Christmas Day (United States)
Christmas Day (Christian Religious Holidays)
Christmas Day (Canada)
Home
1 pm
2 00

FIGURE 18.22: The source of each holiday is displayed next to the holiday name.

WARNING

Many holidays are repeated from country to country and between countries in religious groups. For example, Christmas Day is shared by Christians and people in the United States, Ireland, and numerous other countries. If you choose to add all of these holidays to your calendar, you will have multiple occurrences of these shared holidays on your calendar. Be selective when choosing which groups of holidays to add. There is no way to have Outlook remove the holidays once you've added them, except by selecting and deleting them each individually.

The other Calendar options available from the Options dialog box are specific to using Calendar on a network. For information about the network applications of Calendar, see "Using the Calendar in a Workgroup," later in this chapter.

PRINTING THE CALENDAR

Recognizing that it may be difficult at first to part with your paper-based planner, Outlook has set up a wide variety of printing options that allow you to print your calendar so it fits right into your planner. Until you are able to develop a system that no longer depends on carrying around that book, you can rest assured that your Outlook calendar can still go with you.

Before you can print your calendar, you need to decide what style you want to use. If you go directly to Print Preview, you'll see that whatever view is visible on your screen is the view that will print. For example, if you are in Day view, you'll see all your appointments for that day, as shown in Figure 18.23. If you are in the Week or Month views, you will get a weekly or monthly view of your calendar.

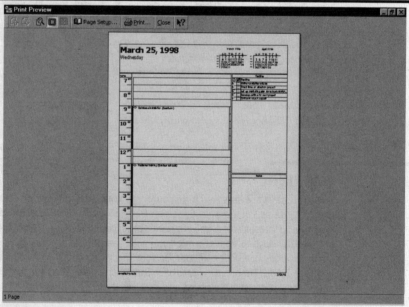

FIGURE 18.23: Print Preview of the Day view

Have you ever struggled over which paper-based planner best meets your needs? Now you can choose whichever style you want whenever you want it. You can print out your calendar in all three views if that will make your life easier.

If you are more particular about your calendar's layout, click the File menu and choose Page Setup to have a world of options available to you. Before a dialog box even opens, you are presented with a list of choices.

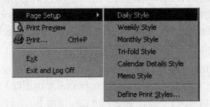

Choose the primary layout that you want for your calendar. Depending on which style you choose, you are presented with different page setup options. The page setup options for the Weekly view are displayed in Figure 18.24.

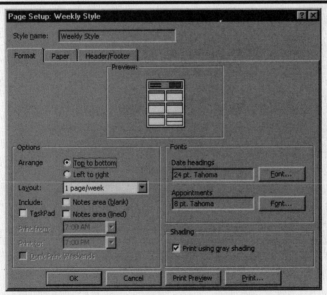

FIGURE 18.24:　Page Setup dialog box for the Weekly style

The first page of the Page Setup dialog box presents the Format options. Here you can indicate what sections you want to appear on the page. You can even include a lined or unlined notes area for your handwritten notes. At any point in the Page Setup process you can click the Print Preview button to see how your printed document will appear. If you are satisfied, click the Print button; if it needs more work, click Page Setup and you're brought right back here.

The second page of the Page Setup dialog box, shown in Figure 18.25, is the Paper page. This page is especially critical if you plan to print your calendar on paper other than a standard 8½×11 sheet. On this page you can set the paper type, size, dimensions, orientation, and margins, and you can identify what tray of the printer the paper will be in.

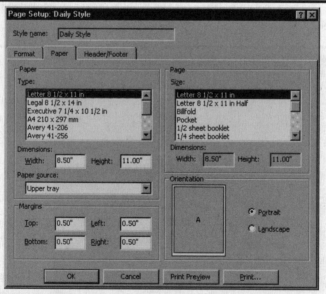

FIGURE 18.25: The Paper page of the Page Setup dialog box

TIP

If you are using a planner from the big three: Day-Timer, Day Runner, or Franklin, take special note of the Page Size list. Your planner is probably listed, so you'll be able to select an exact match.

Headers and Footers

The Header-Footers page of the Page Setup dialog box, shown in Figure 18.26, closely resembles the Header-Footer feature of Microsoft Excel. If you're familiar with Excel, this will be a snap. If you are not an Excel user, don't let it scare you—it's easier than it looks.

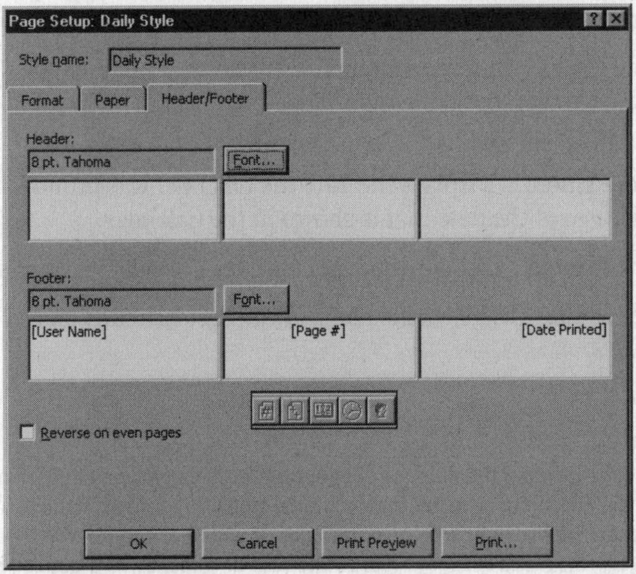

FIGURE 18.26: The Header/Footer page of Page Setup

A header appears at the top of every page of your document, which in this case is the Calendar. A footer appears at the bottom of every page. Typically, you'll find the title and subtitle in the header. By default, Outlook includes the User Name (that's generally you), the Page Number, and the Date Printed in the footer. You are not bound by this convention, however. You are free to put any information anywhere you want it.

The header and footer sections are each divided into three subsections: left, center, and right. Click in any of the six text boxes to enter text in that section.

Outlook provides you with placeholders for five variable fields that you can insert in either the header or the footer. To insert a placeholder, click in the section of the header or footer where you want the placeholder to appear, and then click the placeholder button. The following list identifies the function of each of these placeholders, from left to right:

Page Number   Inserts the actual page number of the document.

Total Pages   Can be combined with the page number placeholder to create the expression "Page 1 of 4" (Page [*Page Number*] of [*Total Pages*]).

Date Printed   Displays the date the Calendar was printed, regardless of the date that is shown in the Calendar.

Time Printed   Displays the actual time the Calendar was printed.

User Name   Displays the name of the user currently logged in to Outlook.

TIP

If you're printing the Calendar in booklet form, you may want to reverse the header and footer on pages that face each other. For example, if the date printed appears on the right side on odd pages, it would appear on the left on even pages. This touch can make it look like your document was produced by a professional printer.

When you have finished setting up the Page Setup options, click the Print button to print your calendar.

Creating a Style for Printing Your Calendar

After you've gone through changing all of the Page Setup options a few weeks in a row, you may find that it's easier to define a Page Setup style you can reuse every time you want to print your calendar. This is a great way to save time and still be able to use a consistent format for your calendar from week to week. Follow the steps below to define your own print style, which will appear in the Page Setup menu list.

1. Select File ➤ Page Setup ➤ Define Print Styles.

2. Choose to edit an existing style or to create a new style by copying an existing style.

3. If you choose to copy an existing style, enter a name for the new style in the Style Name text box at the top of the Page Setup dialog box.

4. Create your custom style using the Page Setup options.

5. Click OK to save your changes.

6. Select your newly created style from the Page Setup menu.

If you want to delete a custom style, choose Define Print Styles, select the style you want to delete, and click the Delete button.

TIP

If you are editing an existing style, the original style will no longer be available. However, you can reset the original style by choosing Define Print Styles from the Page Setup menu, selecting the style, and clicking the Reset button.

USING THE CALENDAR IN A WORKGROUP

If you've ever worked in an office that holds lots of meetings, then you know firsthand how much time is spent scheduling and rescheduling meetings. Some office studies have found that nearly 30 percent of secretarial time is spent scheduling meetings for managers and administrators. One of the fastest-growing software markets today is the group scheduling market. Companies all over the globe are recognizing the need to simplify the process of scheduling meetings.

Outlook is ready to address this challenge. With Outlook, you can schedule a meeting with people on your network or over the Internet (using either vCalendar or iCalendar, depending on your compatibility needs). For now, let's look at appointments with people who are part of your internal network.

Planning a Meeting with Others

Outlook offers several ways to invite others to attend a meeting. The simplest way is to click the down arrow on the New button and choose Meeting Request from the list of choices. This opens the e-mail message form, shown in Figure 18.27, but you may notice that there are some differences between this and the standard message form.

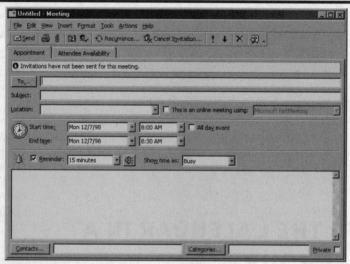

FIGURE 18.27:   A Meeting message form

First, there is an informational message telling you that invitations for this meeting have not yet been sent. Of course, you already knew that in this case, but you can always find the status of an invitation here even after you send it.

Second, in addition to the To and Subject fields, there is a Location field for you to identify where the meeting will take place. Clicking the To button will take you to a special version of your Contacts address book, shown in Figure 18.28. Here you can identify those people whose attendance at the meeting is Required, those whose attendance is Optional, and the Resources, such as meeting rooms and AV equipment, that are required for the meeting (for more about scheduling meeting rooms and equipment, see the sidebar "Scheduling Meeting Rooms and Equipment" later in this chapter). Click OK once you have identified all the attendees.

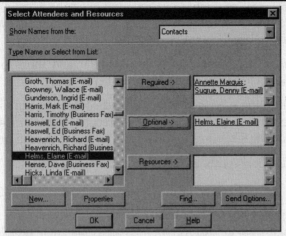

FIGURE 18.28: The Select Attendees and Resources dialog box

The other fields on the Meeting request form are similar to the standard Meeting form. To create a meeting request on your own, follow these steps:

1. Click the down arrow on the New button and choose Meeting Request.

2. Click the To button to open the Select Attendees and Resources dialog box.

3. Double-click the names of those people whose attendance at the meeting is required.

4. If a person's attendance is optional, click their name and click the Optional button.

5. If you have meeting rooms and other resources set up with their own mailboxes, select the resource you want to assign to the meeting and click the Resources button.

6. If the person you want to invite to a meeting is not in your Address book, click the New button and, in the Properties dialog box that opens, enter information about the contact. Click OK to add this person to your Address book.

7. Click OK to close the Select Attendees and Resources dialog box and return to the Meeting request form.

8. Enter the Subject and Location, and click the This Is an Online Meeting check box if it is an online meeting that you are scheduling.

9. Fill in the Start Time, End Time, Reminder, and Show Time As fields, just as you would for any other meeting.

10. If the meeting is going to be regularly scheduled, you can click the Recurrence button and set up the recurrence pattern (see "Scheduling Recurring Appointments" earlier in the chapter).

11. Click the Send button to send out the meeting requests.

Responding to a Meeting Request

Each person you invited to the meeting will receive an e-mail message labeled *Meeting*. When they open the message, they will be able to read the information about the meeting. Once they've made a determination about whether or not they can attend, they can click one of the Accept, Decline, or Tentative buttons at the top of the Meeting form, shown in Figure 18.29.

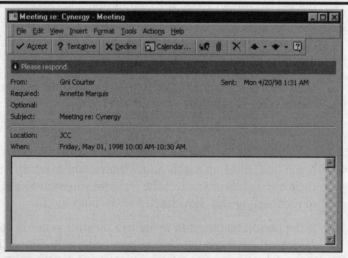

FIGURE 18.29: Meeting request response buttons

Clicking one of these three buttons generates an e-mail message back to you, the meeting request originator, which indicates to you whether or not this person will attend. If the person accepted the meeting request, it's automatically placed on their calendar. In addition, all of the responses are automatically tabulated for you, so there is no need for you to keep a manual count. It really couldn't be easier. All you have to do is open the appointment in your calendar and click the Attendee Availability tab to see the list of attendees and their responses to date, as shown in Figure 18.30.

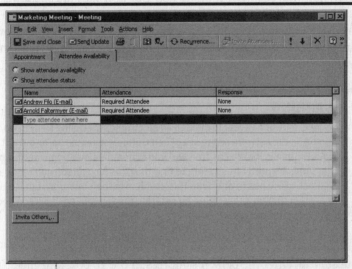

FIGURE 18.30: Attendee Availability page of the Meeting form after a meeting has been scheduled

If, after seeing who has accepted your invitation, you decide that you want to invite other people to this thrilling meeting, click the Invite Others button on the Attendee Availability page. You'll then be able to generate new e-mail meeting requests.

That's all there is to it. Never again will you have to make 25 phone calls to get 4 people to attend a meeting. Now you'll actually have time to get some real work done.

Checking Your Coworkers' Schedules

Even the steps outlined previously for requesting a meeting could backfire, though, if you find that the majority of the people you need at your meeting can't attend at the time you requested. It might be easier to check individual schedules first and schedule the meeting at a time when all of your key people can attend.

A lot of people get nervous when you talk about making their schedules available for other people to see. Outlook has found how to give you
the best of both worlds. It allows you to look at what is referred to as the
individual's free/busy information. In other words, you can see when an
individual is free, busy, out of the office, or tentatively scheduled. You
cannot, however, see what they are doing or how they are spending their
time (unless the other person has given you permission to do so). This
seems to relieve most people's anxiety about Big Brother looking over
their shoulders and still allows for the greatest success in scheduling
meetings with the first request.

WARNING

There is only one caveat to making an electronic scheduling system work: Each
person on the network has to keep their Outlook schedule up-to-date. If an individual's time is marked as free and you schedule a meeting with them during
that time, it's pretty frustrating to find that this key person can't make it after
all. Each office has to deal with this problem in their own way, but it's critically
important that an expectation be set from the top that each person keep their
schedule current.

To check to see when someone is available to meet, open a Meeting
Request form, enter the person's address in the To box, and click the
Attendee Availability tab. The Attendee Availability page, shown in Figure 18.31, lists all attendees in the left column. When you first open this
page, Outlook automatically goes out to the network to gather the most
current free/busy information. The grid on the right side of the page
shows each individual's free/busy status.

If an individual is free, their time is not marked in the grid. If they are
out of the office, a maroon-colored bar extends across the grid to mark
the time they will be gone. If they are busy, you'll see a blue-colored bar,
and if they are tentatively scheduled, you'll see a light blue bar.

The white vertical bar represents the duration of the meeting. The
green border on the left indicates the start time, and the brown border
represents the end time of the meeting.

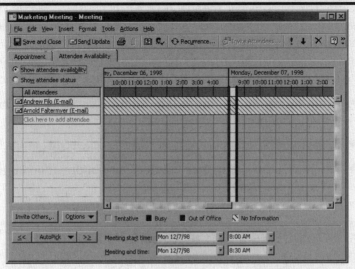

Part v

FIGURE 18.31:   The Attendee Availability page of the Meeting form

TIP

If you're still uncomfortable releasing your free/busy information because you don't want someone booking up your schedule for the next month while you're still working on booking your own appointments, go to Tools ➤ Options ➤ Calendar Options and click the Free/Busy Options button. You can indicate there how many months of your free/busy information you want to make available at one time. You can also indicate how often you would like your free/busy information to be updated on the server. Increasing the frequency will reduce the likelihood that someone might schedule a meeting during a time that you just booked for yourself.

The key to working with the Attendee Availability grid is to start by manually setting your preferred meeting time in the Meeting Start Time and Meeting End Time text boxes. Even if the desired attendees are not available at this time, this action sets a beginning date and the duration of the meeting. Click the AutoPick button to locate the first time when all attendees are available. Notice that the Meeting Start Time and Meeting End Time text boxes change to correspond to the time indicated by the grid. When you find an agreeable time, click the Send button at the top of the form. This will generate the attendees' e-mail messages. Because you've already checked their schedules, you should be pretty confident that the attendees will accept the meeting request.

If you decide to invite others to the meeting, click the Invite Others button. Click the Options button to access the following three options:

▶ To show only work hours in the Calendar, choose Show Only Working Hours.

▶ To see more dates at once, choose Show Zoomed Out.

▶ To force Outlook to update the free/busy information on the server, choose Update Free/Busy.

SCHEDULING MEETING ROOMS AND EQUIPMENT

One of the most common scheduling needs in an office setting is the need to schedule meeting rooms and AV equipment. It's not unusual to spend hours setting up a meeting only to discover that there's no available room for it. Or maybe you get the meeting room scheduled, only to find out there's no way to show your PowerPoint presentation because someone just took the last LCD projector out of the building. Outlook provides a way for you to schedule meeting resources at the same time you schedule people to attend a meeting. To do this, the Microsoft Exchange network administrator needs to set up mailboxes for each of the rooms and each of the pieces of equipment. These can be kept in a separate address book that is made available to all the users on the network. The people or person responsible for maintaining the schedule of resources needs to have access to each of these mailboxes.

When you schedule a meeting, you can then select the meeting room and other resources from the address list in the Select Attendees and Resources dialog box. Now when you check for attendee availability, the availability of the room and required resources will also be considered.

So, you may ask, who's supposed to handle all the e-mail generated by meeting requests? You can have Outlook handle these requests automatically by carefully setting the Calendar options for the resources. To set the options for a resource, you first have to log in to Outlook as that particular resource. For example, if you

CONTINUED ➡

want to set the options for Meeting Room A, you would log into Outlook under the username Meeting Room A. (If it's your job to maintain the schedule of resources, check with your network administrator to find out the usernames that were set up for the company's resources.) Then go to Tools ➢ Options ➢ Calendar Options and click the Resource Scheduling button. Here you're given three options regarding a resource's mailbox:

Automatically Accept Meeting Requests and Process Cancellations   This option gives anyone the freedom to schedule any room or other resource as long as it's available.

Automatically Decline Conflicting Meeting Requests With this option turned on, no one can schedule a resource if it's already tied up.

Automatically Decline Recurring Meeting Requests You may have a policy that recurring meetings must be scheduled in person with the meeting coordinator. This option restricts users from booking a room or other resource for regular meeting time every week or every month.

After you have set these options, scheduling meeting rooms and other resources can happen behind the scenes with very little personal maintenance.

Canceling a Meeting

After a meeting has been scheduled and everyone has gotten back to you with their enthusiastic confirmations, a situation may arise that requires you to cancel a meeting you've already arranged. Don't despair; you don't have to make a slew of phone calls. Open the meeting in your calendar and click the Cancel Invitations button on the Meeting form's toolbar. This will generate an e-mail to all attendees, indicating that the meeting has been canceled. You'll be given an opportunity to explain why you are canceling the meeting. You can then follow it up with another invitation to the meeting at the new date and time. What used to take hours is now handled in just a few minutes. Everybody's notified, everyone's calendar is updated, and no one had to be interrupted from their work to make it happen.

What's Next

Maintaining your scheduled appointments in Outlook gives you the peace of mind of knowing that you'll be reminded where you're supposed to be and that other people you've invited have been properly notified. Chapter 19 will take you on to the next step in the Office 2000 suite: Publisher. You'll get started on creating the perfect publication.

PART VI
USING PUBLISHER 2000

Chapter 19

CREATING ELECTRIFYING PUBLICATIONS

So you've just been handed the company newsletter to produce? Or perhaps it's the human resources employee manual. You have a project that requires that "extra-professional" touch, and you want it to look like it came off a printing press. When working with complex documents containing many graphic elements and text boxes, Publisher is the Office tool of choice.

Publisher is designed to handle multiple elements on a page. The focus, as you might expect, is on the overall appearance of the publication. Of course, you certainly can't ignore the formatting and content details of your document, and Publisher allows you to work well on that level, too; but the real power comes from the ease with which you arrange components on the page.

Adapted from *Mastering Microsoft Office 2000 Professional Edition* by Gini Courter and Annette Marquis

ISBN 0-7821-2313-9   1200 pages $39.99

Flyers, newsletters, calendars, brochures, directories, and countless other publications will glide off your printer in no time. Let's take a look at just how easy it can be.

ELEMENTS OF PUBLISHER

If you are used to working in Word or another word processing program, you may have to learn to think differently about how to put together a document for publication. With this program you will quickly discover that it's not as simple as typing text on a page and letting it wrap at the margin. Before you place anything in a Publisher document, it needs to have space reserved for it.

The Object-Oriented Model

Publisher works from an object-oriented model. This simply means that everything on a page is an object of some kind and has to be in a frame. You can't just type text anywhere; you need a text box to house it.

Graphics such as ClipArt and WordArt behave much the same as they do in a Word document. However, you'll find that text is treated somewhat differently in Publisher. You can move an entire block of text (in a text box) anywhere on the page by clicking and dragging. It won't take you long to get used to the object-oriented model. Later in this chapter you will learn how to create text boxes using the text frame tool. In Chapter 20 we will explore other object tools so you can decide which to choose to create the type of object you need.

THE RIGHT TOOL FOR THE JOB

Should you use Word or Publisher? The answer to that question depends largely on how comfortable you are with each tool and the design of the document you want to produce. There aren't many features available in one program that are unavailable in the other. So the question to ask yourself is this: "How easy is it to carry out the commands necessary to produce this document?"

CONTINUED ➡

The simpler the document, the more likely it becomes that Word is the better tool. No need for frames and fancy formatting if all you are producing is a one-page cover letter to accompany a sales brochure. But the brochure is likely to be a more complex document with an emphasis on graphics. In this case, you might want to switch to Publisher.

A related question is whether you expect readers to follow a single path through the document, as in a personal letter or a novel, or plan to provide multiple entry points, as in a magazine or Web site. If readers will have a choice about where to begin, you'll need to focus their attention on the main topic areas; and that implies a more complex, graphically rich document, for which Publisher is the better tool.

In the best of worlds, you make use of both tools to produce one publication. Since you can type text faster in Word (no need to create frames first), why not compose and edit at the text level in Word? You might even have someone else create the Word text you will eventually use. Design and create frames to house the text in Publisher; arrange graphic objects here as well, and import the text into the existing frames when you're ready for it.

Part vi

THE PUBLISHER INTERFACE

Unlike the Office 2000 applications that combine buttons from the Standard and Formatting toolbars into a single "personal" toolbar, Publisher shows the Standard toolbar by default. You can always recognize the Standard toolbar because its first button is the New button, shown at left. Buttons for common commands such as print and save also appear on this toolbar.

The Formatting toolbar is also on by default. However, you won't see it until you have created and selected an object. In Publisher 2000, the Formatting toolbar is dynamic. That is, it changes depending on what type of

object is selected. If you have selected a graphic object, the Formatting toolbar displays the tools for wrapping, rotating, cropping, and flipping, among others. Selecting a text box causes the toolbar to display text-formatting tools: italics, alignment, and font size, to name a few.

It's the Object toolbar, however, where you will find yourself clicking each time you need to add another element to a page. Here is where you will begin. Using the Object toolbar, you will choose the tools to build text and graphics that give your publication that professional look.

Boundaries and Guides

Publisher equips you with everything you need to place and align objects precisely. You can choose to view the nonprinting boundaries and guides when needed and hide them when you're through.

The red outer line shows page margins, which default to 1" all around. The blue line appears 1/8" inside the outer margin boundary. Use the blue line as a guide to keep from placing objects directly on the margin.

NOTE

The term *boundary* implies that the program somehow prohibits you from working outside the designated area. This is not the case at all. There is nothing to prevent you from placing objects on Publisher's margin boundaries, or even outside them. Rely on your own judgement and design skills for proper object placement.

Adjust boundaries by choosing Layout Guides from the Arrange menu. Use the spin boxes or select and overtype the existing numbers to adjust left, right, top, and bottom margin boundaries. You may find it helpful to lay out your page in quadrants or other informal divisions. Use the grid guides for columns and rows to visually section off your publication as a professional layout artist might do.

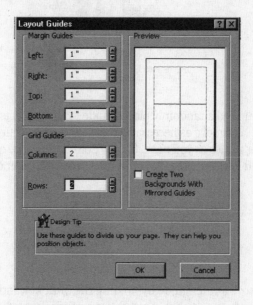

Rulers and Ruler Guides

The horizontal and vertical rulers are turned on by default in Publisher. Choosing View ➤ Rulers from the menu turns them off if you prefer. It is quite likely, however, that you will need rulers fairly frequently when creating documents with multiple objects. Click and drag either ruler to bring it onto the page of your document. Click the box at the intersection of the two rulers, as shown here, to drag both rulers at once. Measure distances from clip art to boundaries; measure text boxes and other objects to ensure design consistency. Simply drag the rulers away when you're through.

If you need a randomly placed guide to align objects, ruler guides are easy to place and move as necessary. You can insert as many horizontal and vertical ruler guides as you need. Simply point to the edge of either ruler, hold the Shift key, and drag the green ruler guide into your document.

Remove a ruler guide by holding the Shift key and dragging it back to the ruler from which it came. Since boundaries and guides can be distracting at times, you may wish to hide them by choosing View ➢ Hide Boundaries And Guides from the menu. Display them again by clicking View ➢ Show Boundaries And Guides.

TIP

Ctrl+Shift+O also hides and displays nonprinting boundaries and guides.

The Scratch Area

Think of the Publisher program window as a large table where you can place blank pages along with the text and objects that you will eventually display on them. When you are working at a table with all your text and art scattered about, you might arrange a picture in a particular location and then change your mind and place it on another page altogether. Later, you might decide you really want this picture on a page at the end of the document and set it aside for now.

In Publisher your table is the gray space surrounding the displayed page(s), called the scratch area. Use it to hold objects while you decide where to place them. If you're working on Page 3 and come across a piece of clip art you think you might need later, grab it now! Items you place in the scratch area are saved along with your publication.

Viewing Your Publication

Since the default zoom setting for blank documents is often too small to view text easily, you will find that you frequently need to enlarge text to proof it. When working with graphics, you'll probably want to zoom back out to determine whether the object is properly placed on the page. Zoom buttons really get a workout in Publisher. Click the plus sign to move closer to your document (that is, to enlarge it); click the minus (repeatedly, if necessary) to view from a distance.

Navigating between pages in Publisher 2000 is easier than ever. Page navigation buttons are displayed at the bottom left of the scratch area. Just click the page you wish to view. Adjacent pages may display two at a time. Zoom in as necessary to work more closely with one page or the other. You can also use the View menu to toggle on or off the two-page display and to zoom in or out.

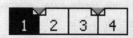

Part vi

STARTING A PUBLICATION FROM SCRATCH

When you launch Publisher you will see the Catalog dialog box, shown in Figure 19.1. There are essentially three different ways you can begin creating a new publication: Publications By Wizard, Publications By Design, or Blank Publications.

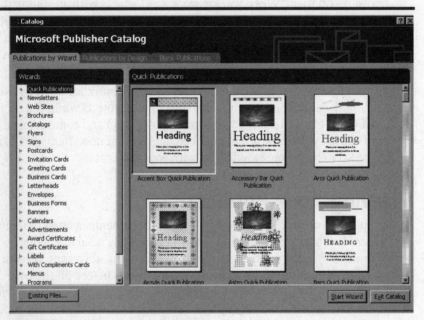

FIGURE 19.1: The Catalog dialog box

You might be tempted to start your first publication using one of the many Quick Publication Wizards that walk you through steps to create cards, calendars, invitations, resumes, and other documents. If you are happy with the results after the wizard finishes, this may not be a bad way to start. However, if you plan to edit any of the elements generated by the wizard, you'll need to recognize the different components used in a Publisher document and know what to do with them. That's why it is helpful to start from scratch when you are learning Publisher. Once you have built a document by placing, resizing, and formatting different objects, one at a time, it becomes easy to recognize and edit the various components produced by wizards.

From the Publisher Catalog dialog box select the Blank Publications tab. Several choices are available to you, as shown in Figure 19.2. You can select from the list on the left or scroll through the gallery on the right to see visual representations of the list items. Click the Custom Page button to enter specific page dimensions if you don't see a style that suits your needs. Click the Custom Web Page button if you are designing for the World Wide Web.

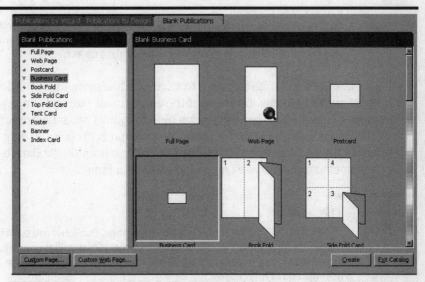

FIGURE 19.2: Use the Blank Publications tab of the Catalog dialog box to start creating a publication from scratch.

Choose one of the blank publication styles and click the Create button at the lower-right corner of the window. Your blank page will be displayed along with the Quick Publications Wizard on the left. To allow more working space, click the button to hide this wizard. Arrange boundaries and guides as desired, and you are ready to go!

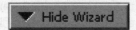

Part vi

Entering Text

Since Publisher operates from an object-oriented model, you won't just start typing on the blank page. Instead, you will use the text frame tool to create a space to house your text.

TIP

It's easy to forget about text frames and just start typing on a page. When you do this, Publisher will create one big text frame that fills the page. If you have only typed a word or two in the frame when you catch your error, you can quickly remove it and start again by clicking Edit ➤ Delete Object.

Click the text frame tool once to select it. Then move into your document and drag to create a frame of the approximate size and shape you need. Keep in mind that creating an object requires two separate actions. The first is to click the tool of choice; the second is to click and drag inside the document. Avoid dragging the button from the toolbar to your document since this won't allow you to create a frame.

TIP

If you forget to drag and only click the blank page, Publisher will create a text frame that measures 2" × 3". If Single Click Object Creation has been disabled, forgetting to drag creates nothing. (Publisher Options are discussed at length near the end of this chapter.)

Release your mouse button when you have dragged a text frame of the size and shape you want, and begin typing. The insertion point starts at the top-left corner of the frame, effectively left-aligning your text by default.

Resizing and Repositioning a Frame

RESIZE

At some point you will decide to change the size and/or position of your text frame. Select the object you wish to resize with a single click anywhere inside the frame. Then position your mouse over one of the resize handles until you see the resize pointer. Click and drag larger or smaller.

TIP

To resize an object and still maintain its original proportions, hold the Shift key while resizing.

Move an object by placing the mouse on the gray outline that frames it. When the mouse pointer changes to the moving van icon, click and drag to a new position.

Formatting Text in a Text Frame

Like Microsoft Word, Publisher offers two general types of text formatting: character and paragraph. Frequently, you can perform paragraph-editing functions by selecting just the text frame. To format characters, you usually have to select the text itself, rather than the frame that houses it. Figure 19.3 illustrates the difference between selecting a text frame and selecting text within a frame.

Part vi

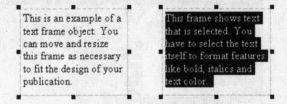

FIGURE 19.3:   Selecting a text frame (left) is very different from selecting text within a frame (right).

Formatting Characters and Words

Select a word, sentence, or paragraph within a text box and click the buttons on the Formatting toolbar to make them bold, italic, and/or underline. Basic text formatting works the same way as it does in Word. Change fonts and font sizes from the toolbar drop-down lists, or choose Format ➤ Font from the menu. Use the toolbar buttons to increase and decrease font size by one point.

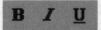

Select text and click the Text Color button on the Formatting toolbar to see available color choices. Publisher 2000 provides built-in schemes to lend consistency to your creations. If you like the default scheme, simply click one of the color choices currently displayed to apply it to your text.

Click the More Color Schemes button to see additional scheme options. The More Colors choice takes you to the Colors dialog box where you can blend different colors to produce the exact shade you're looking for. Choose Fill Effects to explore different tints of a base color.

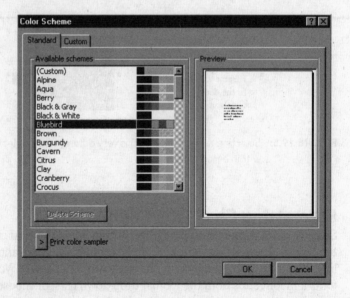

Paragraph Formatting

To apply formatting in a text box that contains one paragraph, you are only required to select the text frame before clicking the appropriate button. If the text box contains more than one paragraph, select all the text so formatting is applied to each paragraph within the frame. Use the alignment buttons on the Formatting toolbar to change from left-aligned to centered, right-aligned, or fully justified.

Increase the indent of the paragraph with the toolbar button to move and align all the text in the frame one tab to the right. Decrease indent to move and align the text one tab to the left.

Bulleted and Numbered Lists   Bullets and numbering now work much the same way they do in Word. Select the list of items you wish to bullet or number and click the appropriate toolbar button. The most recently used bullet or number format will be applied. If you wish to choose a custom format, select the list text and choose Indents and Lists from the Format menu.

In the Indent Settings area, choose either Bulleted List or Numbered List, and the other options in the dialog box will reflect your choice. For a bulleted list, the most recently used bullet characters will be displayed. Click the one you like and change its size, if desired. (The size of the bullet character defaults to match the size of the text it precedes.) If you increase the number in the Indent List By field, the text moves farther away from the bullet character. Change the way the list aligns within its frame by selecting a different option from the Alignment drop-down list in this dialog box. Use the Line Spacing button to increase or decrease the space between your list items. Click the New Bullet button to see other choices for bullet characters.

If you choose the Numbered List option, there are three new settings to consider. First, choose a number or letter format from the list of available choices. Then choose the separator you prefer to use. Finally, adjust the Start At number if you are continuing from a previous list. You have the same options for changing the indent distance, alignment, and line spacing as you have with bulleted lists.

Drop Caps   Newsletter and magazine articles frequently begin with a *drop cap* to draw readers into the first paragraph:

rop Caps can create dramatic effects at the beginning of a paragraph.

Publisher offers numerous options for creating this eye-catching effect. Select the character you wish to format as a drop cap. Click Format ➤ Drop Cap from the menu. Scroll through the available drop caps, click the one you like, and click OK to apply it in your publication. If you don't see a drop cap style you like, try the Custom Drop Cap tab of this dialog box to choose the number of lines above and below the drop, as well as the the font, font style, and color of the drop cap.

Change your mind later? Select the text frame with the drop cap you wish to remove. Click Format ➤ Change Drop Cap from the menu, and click the Remove button.

Inserting Pages

When it is time to place another page into your document, choose Page from the Insert menu to open the Insert Page dialog box. Choose where to insert the page and select whether you want a new page with one large text frame, duplicated background objects, or just a blank page. If you choose Insert Blank Pages, each page you add will have the layout guides you have already set.

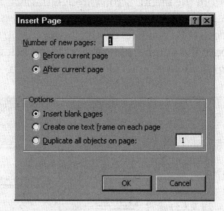

Importing Text from Other Sources

When creating complex documents, it's best to separate the design process from the writing process. One way to do this is to compose and type the text for your publication in another program, most likely a word processor. As long as Publisher's converters are installed, you shouldn't have any problem bringing in text produced in another Windows-based program. There are essentially two ways to make this work.

Using the Clipboard to Bring in Text

Create an empty text frame in your Publisher document to house the text you wish to bring in. Open the text document in its native application and select the desired text. Click the Copy button to place the selected text on the Clipboard. (Use Ctrl+C on the keyboard if the application doesn't have a Copy button.) Switch back to the Publisher window, select the empty text frame, and click the Paste button or press Ctrl+V. Depending on the program used to create the pasted text, it may or may not retain its original formatting. If you have created a text frame that is too small to house the text you are pasting, Publisher will prompt you with a warning and options to create additional frames. Clicking Yes to these options will bring the text into a series of connected frames. (For more on this, see the section "Managing Text Frame Overflow.")

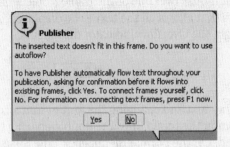

Using the Import Option

Create an empty text frame in Publisher, and make sure it is selected as you choose Insert ➢ Text File from the menu. The Insert Text dialog box opens to allow you to locate and select the desired file. Click OK. Publisher will import (and convert file formats, if necessary) to the selected text frame. You will see text overflow warnings if the receiving text frame is too small for the text you are importing.

NOTE

If Publisher's converters are not installed and you attempt to import a file that requires them, you will be prompted to install this feature.

Managing Text Frame Overflow

When Publisher warns you about text frame overflow, you may want to ignore those warnings (click No to the overflow warning) and handle the problem manually. This method gives you better control over the placement and sizing of the text frames your additional text will flow into.

Resizing the Frame

It is quite possible you won't want your imported text in multiple frames. And there may be times when you accidentally resize an existing frame too small to fit the text it contains. Any time you select a text frame that is too small to display its contents in total, the Text In Overflow Indicator appears at the bottom-right of the selected frame. One way to fix it is to place your mouse over one of the frame's object handles and drag to a larger size that allows all the text to be displayed. As soon as the frame is big enough, the Overflow Indicator disappears.

Selecting text and changing the font or font size might also give you more room in the frame. If you're double-spacing the text, consider using 1.5 instead. On the Format menu, click Line Spacing. Type the number of lines you want in the Between Lines field.

AutoFit Text

In Publisher, you can use automatic copyfitting to resize text to fit into a designated amount of space. For example, if a title is too big to fit on one line, you can use copyfitting to reduce the font size of the text until it does fit.

Automatic copyfitting adjusts the text whenever you type or delete text, change formatting, or resize a frame. Using the copyfitting feature does not prohibit you from making manual adjustments, however. Try a little of both when creating and formatting your next publication.

Turn on automatic copyfitting using Format ➤ AutoFit Text. The Best Fit choice shrinks or expands text to fit in the text frame when you resize it. To reduce the font size of text until it no longer overflows, choose Shrink Text On Overflow.

To turn off automatic copyfitting, point to AutoFit Text on the Format menu and then click None. Now the font size will remain the same when you resize a text frame or insert additional text.

Connecting to Another Frame

Magazines, newspapers, and newsletters generally require layouts where articles begin on one page and continue on another. You can arrange and size the empty frames, and then bring in the text so that it automatically flows from frame to frame.

Create, size, and place the appropriate number of text frames where you want the text to appear in your publication. Type or import text into the first frame. If you are importing and Publisher prompts you to use AutoFlow, you can click Yes as long as the frames you want to use are the *only* empty ones in your document. Publisher will give you the option to automatically create additional frames if you haven't designated enough space for the text file you are importing. Give it a try in most cases. The worst that will happen is that you will have to resize or reset the properties on the new frames. (More on frame properties in Chapter 20.)

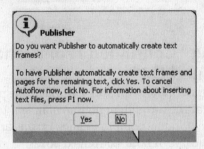

Text imports gone awry can be fixed with a simple click of the Undo button. In Publisher 2000, you can now undo (and redo) multiple operations as in the other Office applications.

As an alternative to AutoFlow, when the Text In Overflow indicator appears, you can choose Tools ➤ Connect Text Frames to turn on the Connect Frames toolbar. Click the Connect Text Frames button and move the mouse back into your document.

The mouse icon now looks like a pitcher. When you place this icon inside any empty text frame, the pitcher tips to the right. Navigate to the text frame you want to use for your continued text and click once inside the frame to "pour" overflow contents. If the second frame overflows, click the Connect Text Frames button again and pour the overflow into another empty frame.

Follow your text forward and backward through a series of linked frames using the frame-navigation buttons. If you later wish to disconnect linked frames, select any of them and click the second button on the Connect Frames toolbar. You will disconnect all linked frames that follow the selected frame.

Inserting "Continued From" and "Continued On"

Help your readers follow an article through the publication with Continued notices at the top and/or bottom of linked text frames. Right-click a connected text frame, point to Change Frame, and click Text Frame Properties. Enable one or both Continued boxes.

By default, Continued messages appear in Times New Roman Italic in a font size somewhat smaller than the text in the frame. To change the appearance of one of these messages, select it and format as desired. You can change font, font size, alignment, and font color, and you can even reword the "continued" language, if you like. Rather than repeating this procedure multiple times, you can save all of your changes as a new or redefined style by choosing Text Style from the Format menu.

You can remove Continued notices by right-clicking the linked text frame and choosing Change Frame ➢ Text Frame Properties. Disable one or both Continued boxes and repeat this procedure for each linked frame in the series.

SAVING YOUR WORK

The Open and Save dialog boxes in Publisher now match those found in the other Office applications. When opening files, you can choose to bring them in for editing or as read-only. The Save and Save As commands function as you would expect. You also have other options for storing publications.

Save Options

Click the File menu to see the choices you have for saving Publisher documents. In addition to the usual Save and Save As commands, you have the option to Save The Current Publication As A Web Site or Use Pack And Go to prepare a document for use on another computer or with a commercial printing service.

Since the program only allows you to open one publication at a time, there's never a question of which document gets saved—it's always the one being displayed.

AutoConvert

Publisher 2000 allows users to convert content from existing publications into additional publications. That means you can use the text and graphics in your company's trifold brochure to create a Web site. And you can do it with only a couple of mouse clicks, without importing the content into another Publisher file. AutoConvert is a feature you can access when you create documents using wizards.

SETTING PUBLISHER OPTIONS

You can have as much or as little help from Publisher as you wish. Enable the settings that allow you to work most efficiently by choosing Options from the Tools menu.

General

The General tab of the Options dialog box offers miscellaneous options. You can change the default starting page number if you typically create a cover page in another application (PowerPoint, for example). In this case your Publisher documents should start page numbering with 2.

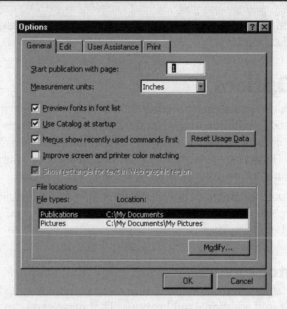

Select from the Measurement Units list to display other units of measurement on the rulers. If the Preview Fonts In Font List feature is enabled, the list of fonts on the Formatting toolbar and in the Format dialog box shows the name of the font in the typestyle of that font. In the case of symbol fonts, the list displays samples from that symbol set. If you prefer to load Publisher directly to a blank page, disable the Use Catalog At Startup feature. Improve Screen And Printer Color Matching allows you to get a better idea of how your colors will appear on the printed page. Ever wonder why your documents come off the printer in a lighter shade than they appear on screen? Try enabling this feature to see a more accurate screen view.

You can change the default locations for opening existing documents and inserting pictures by clicking the Modify button and selecting the folder you wish to default to. At any point if you decide to change the settings back to system defaults, click the Reset Usage Data button.

Editing

The Edit tab of the Options dialog box allows you to enable or disable Drag-And-Drop Text Editing. If you tend to accidentally drag your mouse over selected text, you might want to turn this off. Automatic selection of the entire word means that you can't select part of a word for formatting. Enabling this feature helps prevent you from accidentally missing parts of your text when you use the Format Painter.

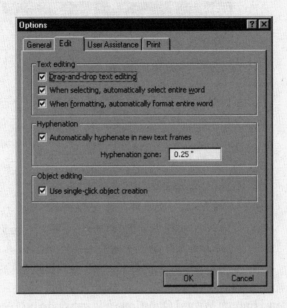

You will like the feature that allows you to automatically format the entire word where the insertion point currently rests. This means you don't have to double-click before you italicize a word in a sentence. Make sure the insertion point is somewhere in the word you wish to format and click the toolbar button(s) to apply desired changes. The Hyphenation Zone is the distance from the frame's right boundary within which Publisher will hyphenate words. You can change this distance or disable this option if you prefer not to hyphenate at all. Single-Click Object Creation allows you to click an object tool and click once in your document to create a 2″ × 3″ text frame, but you can still drag to create frames of other sizes.

User Assistance

The User Assistance tab of the Options dialog box offers you some control over how certain wizards behave. The Quick Publications Wizard is on by default when you select a blank page to begin. You can disable it here if you don't use it often.

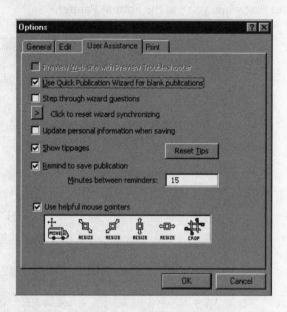

Step Through Wizard Questions allows you to proceed through a series of dialog boxes to produce a publication, rather than clicking the steps from a list. You can re-enable smart coloring (covered at length in Chapter 20) by resetting wizard synchronization here. Disable tippages (a form of context-specific user assistance about Publisher's features) and save reminders if you prefer not to see these messages while you work. Helpful mouse pointers include the moving truck and arrows that say "Resize." Disabling these gives you a more typical set of pointer shapes.

Print Options

The Print options that are available to you depend on the type of printer(s) you have installed on your system. Enable the Print Troubleshooter to assist you with problems arising after you send publications to the printer. Enabling the Print Line-By-Line option may help if your DeskJet printer consistently mishandles objects and upside-down text. If you are connected to a printer designated for envelope printing, you'll see options for automatic formatting and print feed.

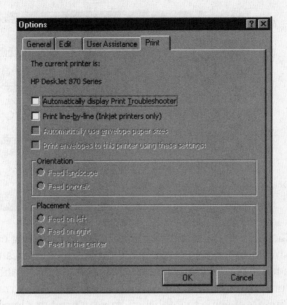

PRINTING YOUR PUBLICATIONS

Before you even begin creating your publication, you should give serious thought to how you are going to print the final product. Will you use your own printer or a commercial printing service? What type of paper will you print on? What color paper? Will you duplex? Staple? Fold? Collate?

It's a good idea to set up your publication for the type of printing you want before you place objects on the page. Otherwise you may be forced to make design changes just before the final printing.

Desktop Printing

If you are printing from a desktop printer, click File ➤ Print Setup for printer options. Select the size and location of the paper you will be using. (In Tray is the most common location; however, some printers have a sheet feeder as well.) Click the Properties button to set properties specific to your printer. Look for features like reverse order printing and collating. If your printer supports duplexing, booklet or banner printing, or stapling, you will also find these options under Properties.

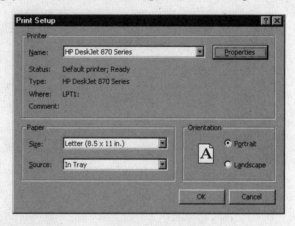

Click File ➤ Print to set options in the Print dialog box. Most options are similar to those in other Office applications: you can choose a printer, set a range of pages and a number of copies to print, and print to a file (for printing or further processing elsewhere). The Advanced Printing options are specific to Publisher. You can print at a lower resolution (it's a good idea to do this on drafts) and choose whether to let your printer substitute fonts. You can also choose to print crop marks and bleed marks. Bleeds are text and images that go beyond the trim edge of your publication (like those used in this book). If you want to print bleed marks, you have to select a paper size 1" larger than your document.

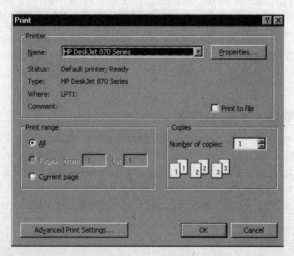

Working with a Commercial Printing Service

If you plan to print your final publication at a printing service, it is a good idea to set up your publication to do this right from the start. First you need to decide which type of printing service you will use: black-and-white printing, process color printing, or spot color printing. For either type of color printing, you also have the option of using the industry-standard Pantone Matching System.

NOTE

If you're taking your publication in Publisher format to your printing service, use Pack And Go to save all the files your printing service will need.

Black-and-White Printing

In black-and-white printing, the printer uses only one color of ink (usually black, but most commercial printers will allow you to choose a different color if you want). Black-and-white printing uses grayscale to distinguish light and dark areas of your publication. Text and graphics can still produce dramatic effects in black-and-white. If you absolutely must have color and budget is a concern, considering printing on colored paper.

To set up for black-and-white printing, click Tools ➤ Commercial Printing Tools ➤ Color Printing to open the Color Printing dialog box shown in Figure 19.4.

Part vi

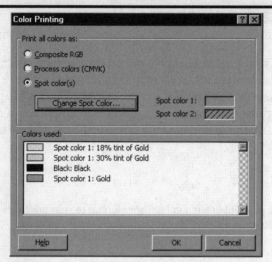

FIGURE 19.4:   The Color Printing dialog box

Choose Spot Color(s) from the available options, and then click Change Spot Color. In the Choose Spot Color dialog box, click Black And White Only. Click OK twice to close both dialog boxes.

Process Color Printing

Use process color printing when your publication contains high-quality color photos or if you need to print a wide range of colors. As you might expect, process color printing costs more than other types because of the number of different colors you use. If budget is a consideration, you might want to look at the other two commercial printing options. To set up for process color printing, click the Tools menu, point to Commercial Printing Tools, and click Color Printing to open the dialog box shown in Figure 19.4. Click Process colors (CMYK) from the list of options. Selecting the Cyan Magenta Yellow Black (CMYK) color model for a commercially printed publication is important because not all colors you see on your monitor, which uses the Red Green Blue (RGB) color model, can be printed using CMYK. To ensure that your printing service can match the colors on your screen, choose CMYK and then review the publication for color changes. If you see color changes you don't like, select the object and recolor it in the publication.

Spot Color Printing

Spot color printing allows you to use color for lines and accents in your publication. You can match up to two colors in a company logo or other artwork. Your publication prints primarily in black, but you can choose up to two spot colors. Tints of the spot colors can be used throughout the publication as well. Spot color printing is a nice budget compromise between complete black-and-white and the more expensive process color printing.

Click Tools➤ Commercial Printing Services ➤ Color Printing. Select Spot Colors and click Change Spot Color. Select one or two spot colors and click OK.

TIP

If you choose black plus one spot color, all colors except black are converted to tints of the spot color.

Switching to Another Type of Printing

Change your mind about which type of printing to use? Click Tools ➤ Commercial Printing Tools ➤ Color Printing. Choose Composite RGB to switch back to desktop printing. Choose Process Colors or Spot Colors or, if you want to switch to black-and-white, click Spot Colors ➤ Change Spot Color and select the Black And White Only option.

Pantone Color Matching

When you work with a commercial printer, colors on your computer screen may not exactly match the colors that get printed in your publication. The colors in your Publisher file only tell your printing service *where* the color goes, not *what* the exact color will be.

Printing services support a number of different color-matching systems. It is best to ask your printer which colors and paper types would work best, before you design your publication. Most likely they will give you some numbered color swatches and suggestions for paper types. You can choose Publisher colors from process color-matching systems that your printing service supports and then specify colors from the swatches for use in your publication. Publisher provides the Pantone Matching System (PMS), which you can use to specify colors for a commercial printing service. Before you can use this color matching system, you have to decide whether to use spot color printing or process color printing.

Regardless of which type of printing you choose, navigate to the Color Printing dialog box shown earlier, in Figure 19.4. Choose the Spot Color Option and click Change Spot Color. Select More Colors from the Spot Color 1 drop-down list and click All Colors. Under Color Model, select Pantone from the list.

For spot color printing, make sure you are on the Pantone Solid tab. If you're opting for process color printing, use the Pantone Process tab. Under Color Type, choose whether your publication will be printed on Coated or Uncoated Paper. If you know the PMS number for the color you want, type it in the Find Color Name box and press Enter, or scroll to the color you want. Click OK four times to close all the dialog boxes.

You might design process color publications (like brochures or sales materials) that include spot color objects (like a company logo). In this case you need to convert each object's Pantone solid color to a process color that matches. Select the spot color object. Click Format ➤ Fill Color ➤ More Colors. Choose All Colors if it is not already selected. Under Color Model, choose Pantone. Make sure you select the Pantone Solid tab of the dialog box and choose Convert To Process under Color Type. Select the color and click OK twice to close both dialog boxes.

Font Embedding

Any time you plan to print your publication from a computer other than the one you used to create it, you should consider font embedding. Embedded fonts show up in printed material just as they appeared on your screen.

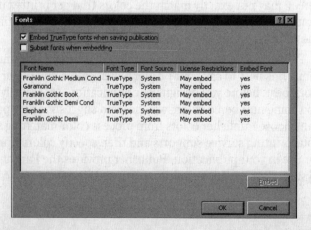

Click Tools ➤ Commercial Printing Tools ➤ Fonts to open the Fonts dialog box. If you choose Embed TrueType Fonts When Saving Publication, your fonts will appear as expected on most any computer and you will have the ability to edit using your own fonts whether the other machine has them installed or not. Choosing this first option causes your Publisher file to be larger because it saves the font sets along with it. The Subset option also embeds fonts but only saves the actual characters you've used in your publication. If the printing service needs to edit, they will be limited to those characters you have already included.

WHAT'S NEXT

As soon as you are comfortable creating and formatting text frames, you will want to look at the other object tools in Publisher. Pictures, ClipArt, WordArt, borders, shapes, and a myriad of other design elements are at your fingertips. In Chapter 20, you'll learn about placement, formatting, and editing of graphics.

Part vi

Chapter 20

WORKING WITH GRAPHIC OBJECTS IN PUBLISHER

Text frames can be put together in ways that create very professional-looking documents, as you saw in the last chapter. But certain types of business publications rely on exceptional graphics to interest the reader. What's a marketing brochure without illustrations? How can you sell products from a catalog without displaying pictures? Even text-heavy documents can benefit from the occasional sidebar (another type of graphic element).

In this chapter you will learn how to create, format, edit, and align different types of graphics for maximum "Wow!" factor.

Adapted from *Mastering Microsoft Office 2000 Professional Edition* by Gini Courter and Annette Marquis

ISBN 0-7821-2313-9   1200 pages $39.99

INSERTING PUBLISHER GRAPHIC OBJECTS

There are so many object choices available in Publisher that it can be difficult to know where to begin. Some of the objects, like clip art, WordArt, and tables, may be familiar from other Office applications and are covered in greater depth elsewhere in the book. You will find that certain objects (like pictures and clip art) are easy to select and insert, while others (like WordArt) require that you spend some time on formatting. That's not to say you won't ever spend lots of time on the select-and-insert variety. Once you bring an object into your publication, you may decide to recolor, rotate, flip, or otherwise edit the piece. Your starting point for working with graphic objects is the Object toolbar:

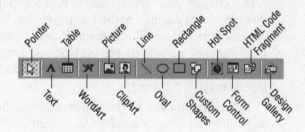

These Publisher frame tools work the same, in concept, as the text frame tool. One click on the object tool selects it. A click and drag in your document creates a space to house the object while you format and edit it. If Single-Click Object Creation is left enabled, you can create a 2" × 3" object frame with two clicks: one on the object tool and one in the document. As you would expect, you can move or resize an object at any time.

Tables

You may have heard it said that if you press Tab more than once on the same line, you should be working in a table. Use the Table frame tool to display data in columns and rows. By design, tables allow text to wrap within a cell so that there is a minimal amount of reformatting when text is inserted or deleted. Figure 20.1 shows an example of a publication that includes a table.

Ten Minute Trainer

Continuing computer education for students and former students of

Triad Consulting, LLC

Volume 1, Issue 1   February, 1999

TRIAD at a Glance

As a manager in today's business world, you know that having all of the information needed to make quality decisions is no easy task. Running an organization requires efficient and accurate data from a variety of sources. Computer technology makes collecting and communicating data easier-- but only for those who know how to use technology effectively. TRIAD Consulting can provide you with the knowledge you need to bring your organization into the information age. Whether it is designing data systems, training your employees, or helping you evaluate hardware and software to meet your needs, TRIAD can make technology work for you.

Installing powerful computers in your workplace will not make your organization more efficient unless your employees know how to make the best use of them. TRIAD offers customized training programs that are designed around the way your employees work and your organization's needs so employees can put what they learn into practice immediately when they return to their desks.
We provide training in Windows 3.1, Windows 95, NT Workstation, and Microsoft Office products: versions 4.2, 95, and 97. Our training teams also design and deliver specialized training your employees need, such as:

- Visual Basic for Applications
- Programming in Excel
- Impromptu (4 GL)
- Database theory

With the thousands of new computer products on the market today, deciding which ones will best meet your company's needs requires a dedicated information professional. TRIAD will research and answer your information management questions so you can decide how to make the most of your computer

Upcoming Training Classes

Class	Dates	Times
Beginning Word	12/5 and 12/10	4– 7 PM
Beginning Excel	12/7 and 12/14	8– 11 AM
NT Server	12/1– 12/4	2– 7 PM
Intermediate Word	12/11 and 12/18	4– 7 PM

Quick System Maintenance

Illegal Operation Errors? Keyboard and Mouse freezing? Complete crashes without saving your documents? Yes, it can happen to you if you are not running proper system maintenance. Who would

(Continued on page 3)

1

FIGURE 20.1: This publication shows several graphic design elements: WordArt, company logo, barbell design, drawn lines, and a table.

As soon as you finish dragging the Table tool, the Create Table dialog box opens.

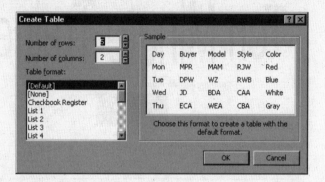

Enter the number of rows and columns for your table and choose a table format from the list on the left. Use the Sample window to view the borders, shading and special text formatting included with each design. Select the one that's closest to what you have in mind; you can always modify formatting manually. When you click OK, Publisher throws a formatted empty grid onto your page.

Enter text and/or numbers into each cell, pressing Tab to move one cell to the right. You can also use the mouse or arrow keys to position your insertion point in a cell. Apply or remove formatting as you would in a Word table. Select rows or columns by clicking the gray header box (your pointer changes to a hand).

Class	Dates	Times
Beginning Word	12/3 and 12/10	4—7 PM
Beginning Excel	12/7 and 12/14	8—11 AM
NT Server	12/1—12/4	2—7 PM
Intermediate Word	12/11 and 12/18	4—7 PM

Select Cells

Select multiple rows or columns by dragging the headers. Select the entire table by clicking the gray box at the upper left of the table, where row and column headers intersect. Adjust column width and row height by dragging the Adjust tool between headers.

WordArt

Use the WordArt Frame tool to create dramatic shapes and patterns out of text. In Figure 20.1, the publication title and company logo are examples of WordArt. You can create letters that cascade up, ripple down, or wave like a flag, and you can add borders to the letters, fill them with patterns, or rotate them for different effects.

When you work in WordArt, the Publisher tools are not available to you. The toolbar displays only the WordArt tools, but you can get back to Publisher by clicking away from the object. Double-click an existing WordArt Object to edit it. Use the WordArt tool on the Object toolbar only when you want to create a new WordArt object.

You won't see ToolTips on the buttons in the WordArt toolbar, so you may have to experiment a bit at first. Or you can choose to edit using the Format menu from within WordArt. Choosing Format ➤ Border allows you to add or edit how your letters are outlined. Format ➤ Shading allows you to fill the interiors of letters with solid colors or patterns. If you want to shadow letters, choose a style and color by clicking Format ➤ Shadow. You can rotate a WordArt object or "slide" the letters horizontally by choosing Format ➤ Rotation And Effects.

TIP

Publisher 2000 uses a different version of WordArt than the other Office tools. To open the more robust WordArt through Microsoft Draw, click Insert ➤ Object. From the Insert dialog box, click Microsoft Draw 98 Drawing, and then click OK. Use the WordArt button on the Microsoft Drawing toolbar to create a new WordArt object.

Pictures and Clip Art

You will find frame tools for pictures and clip art on Publisher's Object toolbar. Publisher treats clip art and pictures much the same. Pictures usually look more like photographs while clip art has the flavor of a cartoon drawing. While it is true that you can insert clip art into a picture frame or insert a picture into a clip art frame, it's more efficient to start with the type of frame you need to produce the type of graphic you prefer.

When you drag a space using the Picture tool, a blank frame appears in your document. Insert a picture by double-clicking the empty frame (you can also select the frame and choose Insert ➤ Picture ➤ From File) to go to the Insert File dialog box. Navigate to the drive and folder where the picture is stored, select it, and click Insert. Double-click this object if you want to return to the Insert Picture dialog box and select a different picture to replace it.

The ClipArt tool behaves slightly differently. After you drag to create a space using the ClipArt frame tool, Publisher automatically takes you to the ClipArt Gallery, where you can browse the available art. Select one of the gallery objects to insert or, if you don't see one you like, you can cancel out of the gallery and insert a picture instead. Make sure the frame is selected and choose Insert ➢ Picture ➢ From File to select a picture stored on your local drive, a network drive, or a floppy disk.

Shapes

Publisher gives you the ability to draw lines of various weights and colors. You can also create ovals, rectangles, and a host of custom shapes like arrows, cubes, and triangles. The most commonly used shapes—lines, ovals, and rectangles—have their own buttons on the Object toolbar. Click a button to select the shape you like and drag the size you want in your document.

Select the frame that contains the shape and use the Fill button to select a color for its interior. The Border button allows you to select a plain black line to outline the frame, or you can click More Styles to select an alternate weight and color for the outline. If you want a border that is wider than 10 points, type the size you want in the field at the bottom-left of the Border dialog box.

The Custom Shapes tool allows you to create hearts, stars, lightning bolts, triangles, and more. Once you have created a shape, Publisher 2000 gives you the ability to resize one or both object dimensions. The arrow shown below has been resized two ways: the width of the base has been narrowed, and the height of the tip has been shortened. To resize one dimension, place your pointer on the gray diamond and drag the Adjust tool. You still have the ability to resize the entire object using the regular handles.

Web Tools

There are three Web tools on the Object toolbar: Hot Spot, Form Control, and HTML Fragment.

Design Gallery Objects

The Design Gallery contains roughly twenty categories of objects, such as mastheads, linear accents, calendars, and logos that you can add to your publication. You even have the ability to store objects that you create in a publication on a special tab of the Design Gallery dialog box. That means you can store your company logo in the Design Gallery and easily use it again and again.

To display the Design Gallery, choose Insert ➤ Design Gallery Object. Figure 20.2 shows the Objects By Category tab of the Design Gallery.

If you prefer, you can select a Design Gallery object based on a design set. Click the Objects By Design tab, shown in Figure 20.3, and select from the list on the left. You will see different types of objects with certain design elements in common. Using objects from the same set gives a consistent look and feel to your publication.

Part vi

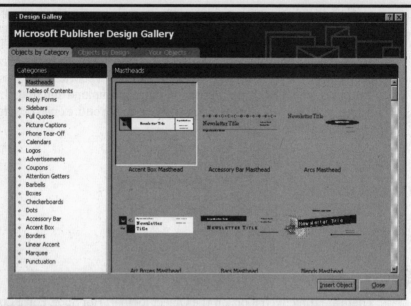

FIGURE 20.2:   The Design Gallery contains many categories of objects ready to be inserted into your publication.

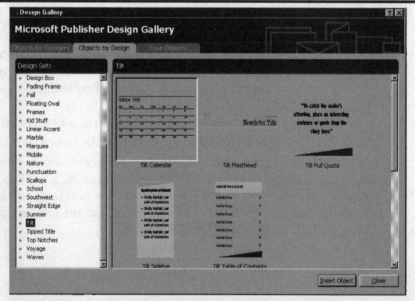

FIGURE 20.3:   The Objects By Design tab with the Tilt set selected

You can store the objects from your current publication on the Your Objects tab of the Design Gallery. (This is particularly helpful if you have edited or recolored objects and want to have them readily available for use in other publications.) When you first create a publication, its design set on the Your Objects tab is empty. You create a design set for your publication by creating categories and adding objects to the categories. Select the object you want to add and open the Design Gallery from the Objects toolbar.

Choose the Your Objects tab and click the Options button in the lower-left corner. Click the Add Selection To Design Gallery menu option to open the Add Object dialog box. Under Object Name, type a name for the object; under Category enter a new category or select a category that you have already created. Click OK and then Close to return to your document. Changes that you make to the Design Gallery are saved when you save your publication.

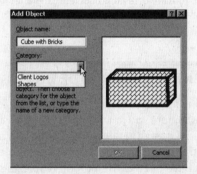

You can add, rename, and delete categories in your design set by choosing Options ➤ Edit Categories at the bottom of the Your Objects tab of the Design Gallery. Choose the category you wish to edit and click the Rename button. Type the new category name and click OK. To remove a category, select it in the Edit Categories dialog box and click the Delete button. Click the Add button and type a name for the new category to add it to your design set.

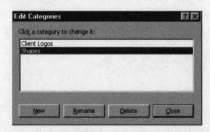

Delete an object from your design set by selecting it and choosing the Your Objects tab of the dialog box. Then click Options ➤ Delete This Object. Once again, these changes to the Design Gallery are saved when you save your publication.

The categories and objects you add are specific to the publication you added them from. However, if you want to insert an object from a design set you (or someone else) created in another publication, click Options on the Your Objects tab of the Design Gallery and choose Browse from the menu. Select the publication that has the object you want and click OK. The Your Objects tab now displays the design set for the publication you just selected. Choose the object you want and click Insert Object.

NOTE

You can only rename and delete categories from the design set in the active publication. You cannot rename or delete categories from another publication's design set, and you cannot rename or delete Publisher's built-in object categories.

ESSENTIALS OF GOOD DESIGN

Knowing how to use Publisher's object tools won't guarantee good results. Before you put your first frame on a page, you should have an overall design in mind. And before you come up with your overall design, you should know the essentials of good design. Entire books have been written on this topic, and you would be wise to keep one handy for reference. At the absolute minimum, consider three elements when creating publications: simplicity, consistency, and contrast.

Simplicity means just that: Keep it simple! Use no more than two font families per publication. Use a sans serif font for headings and a serif font for body text. Avoid the tendency to include too many graphic objects. It should be obvious where you want your audience to glance when they first look at a page. Too many graphics can cause the reader's eye to wander all over the page with the likely result that they end up seeing nothing.

CONTINUED ➡

When a publication follows the consistency rule, every element seems to naturally belong there. The idea is to create a "personality" for your document. You may find this is easier to do with lengthy publications, but keep the rule in mind when you're designing a one-page flyer as well. Internally, use the same heading format for each section of your document. Choose a bullet character and stick with it throughout. Page numbers should appear in the same location on each page. Use an overall color scheme to create a unified look throughout. Work with the Objects By Design tab of the Design Gallery.

If you publish your document periodically, there are external consistency considerations as well. Certain graphic objects (borders, banners, and logos, for example) should remain the same from issue to issue. Illustrative graphics such as photographs will be different each time you publish, but text formatting and page setup should be consistent. Radical design changes between issues require notice to the reader, or they may not recognize your publication the next time they see it.

It is possible to overwhelm your audience with too much on a page. Be sure to incorporate contrast into your work. Leave plenty of white space around and between your objects. (It's called *white space* even if you print on blue paper.) The blank areas of your document are just as important as text and other objects in determining whether someone will want to pick up and read your publication.

Part vi

WORKING WITH MULTIPLE OBJECTS

Chapter 19 introduced Publisher's object-oriented model, in which every element of your publication is a separate object. Suppose you have a picture that goes with a particular section of your employee manual. If you change the placement of the section, you would want the picture to move with it, right? Or suppose you have two pieces of clip art that need to overlap slightly. Wouldn't you like to choose which piece is on top? Finally, suppose you're placing three objects at the left margin of your newsletter cover. You most certainly want them to line up, right?

These are some of the issues that come up when you work with many objects on a page.

Grouping Objects

If a particular graphic will always appear next to a certain piece of text, it makes sense to group the two objects. Two or more objects with fixed positions relative to each other should be grouped, since grouped objects can be moved and resized as one unit. As shown here, a title should be grouped with the text or other object it describes so the two never become separated. Drag one and you're dragging the other as well:

To group objects, select the first with a click. Hold Shift and click each additional object you wish to group. Click the Object Grouping icon at the bottom of the frame surrounding the selected objects. These objects are now "hooked" together so you can move and resize them as a group. Click the icon again to ungroup the objects. Now you can move and resize them separately—just click the one you want.

Layering Objects

There are times when you will want to place one object on top of another. The Bring To Front and Send To Back buttons make it easy to do that. Here is an example of a text box displayed on top of a piece of clip art. The objects are layered—clip art on the bottom, text on the top.

Insert and arrange the two objects you wish to layer. If you can't see the object that's currently on the bottom, select the one on the top and click the Send To Back button. If you can see at least part of the object that is underneath, select it and click the Bring To Front button.

Lining Up Objects

You can align selected objects to each other or a margin. The Snap To feature lets you easily align objects to a ruler guide as well. Select all objects to be aligned and click the Arrange menu. Then choose Align Objects to open the dialog box. (You can also right-click selected objects and choose Align from the shortcut menu.)

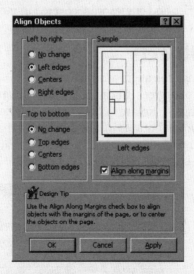

The titles of the option groups in this dialog box refer to the object frames themselves, so use the Left To Right options if you are aligning objects vertically. Use the options under Top To Bottom if you want to line up your objects horizontally across a page.

TIP

To center selected objects between the left and right margins, enable the Align Along Margins feature and then choose Left To Right Centers.

Snap To

The Snap To option makes it easy to align objects precisely. It creates an invisible grid on your page; objects are pulled to the imaginary grid lines or to nearby boundaries and ruler guides. You can also have objects snap to other objects.

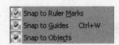

You'll find the Snap To options on the Tools menu. Turn on Snap To Boundaries, and each time you drag an object near a boundary, it will "jump" to the edge of the boundary. Snap To Ruler Guides works the same way. If the boundaries and guides are hidden, objects will still Snap To. (Boundaries and guides were covered in more detail in Chapter 19.)

Rotating Objects

You can change the angle at which an object is displayed by rotating it any number of degrees. Click the Rotate tool on the Standard toolbar (or choose Arrange ➢ Rotate or Flip ➢ Custom Rotate) to open the dialog box. The rotation buttons in this dialog will change the display angle by 5 degrees per click. For larger rotations, you can simply type the degrees in the Angle box and click OK.

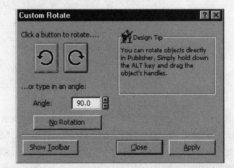

Click Show Toolbar to see the Measurement toolbar. You can change the size, spacing, display angle, or position of a selected object using the spin boxes shown here.

To rotate by 90 degrees, use the buttons on the toolbar or click Arrange ➤ Rotate or Flip ➤ Rotate Right (or Left).

TIP

If you prefer working directly in Publisher, you can rotate any object by pressing Alt and dragging an object handle.

Flipping Objects

Publisher 2000 gives you the ability to "flip" a graphic from the Clip Gallery vertically or horizontally. Select the object and click the appropriate toolbar button. You can also choose Arrange ➤ Rotate or Flip ➤ Flip Horizontal (or Vertical).

RECOLORING OBJECTS

Frequently you will find a piece of clip art that looks great except for its color. Choose and insert it anyway because you have several options for changing object color(s) with a few clicks of the mouse. You can change all the colors in a picture to different shades of one color and leave the black lines untouched. Or you may prefer to have the black lines change with the new color as well. If these options don't work for you, you can bring the picture into Paint or Microsoft Draw and edit colors there.

Part vi

TIP

For an easy way to recolor clip art, copy the art into PowerPoint and click the Recolor button on the Picture toolbar. When you're finished, copy and paste back into your Publisher document.

To change all the colors in a picture to a single color, shade, or tint, select the picture and click Format ➤ Recolor Picture. You can also right-click the object and choose Change Object ➤ Recolor from the shortcut menu. Select a color from the drop-down list and choose whether to recolor the entire picture or leave the black lines as is. Unfortunately, recoloring an object using two or more colors is a much less efficient process in Publisher. The only easy way to do that is to automatically recolor clip art by applying a color scheme to the entire publication. Publisher will select colors for your objects that fit the scheme you select.

If you choose fill effects from the Color drop-down list, you have options for formatting tints and shades as well as gradients and patterns. *Tints* are a base color mixed with white; *shades* are a base color mixed with black. Tints and shades can be part of a custom color scheme.

TIP

To create a watermark, recolor pictures using tints or shades of a base color.

Patterns are simple repeating designs, and gradients use tints and shades to create vertical, horizontal, and other shading patterns. Here you can see the difference between a pattern and a gradient.

TIP

If you are planning to use a commercial printing service, it's probably best not to use patterns in your publication. Patterns can slow down the imaging time, thus increasing your costs.

MODIFYING FRAME PROPERTIES

Part VI

The shortcut menus for both text and graphic object frames give you access to properties you can modify for various purposes. For example, you can add a border so that the frame itself prints. You can add color, patterns, or other effects to an object's background. Changing frame properties also allows you to display text in multiple columns.

Text Frames

Right-click any text frame and point to Change Frame on the shortcut menu. Choose Fill Color to see a multitude of possibilities for background colors, with the current scheme's colors shown first. Choose More Schemes to choose another scheme of colors, or More Colors to see an entire palette. Fill Effects offers you options for tints, shades, patterns, and gradients.

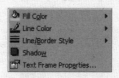

The Line Color choice on the shortcut menu is unavailable if you have not previously applied a border to the frame. Use the Line/Border Style choice to apply a border of your chosen point size and color. The next time you wish to edit this object's border, you can do so under Line Color. Shadow Effects creates a gray shadow on the right and bottom borders of the text frame. Shadows look great with or without a border. Choosing

Text Frame Properties from this shortcut menu brings you to a dialog box where you can adjust margins and change column settings.

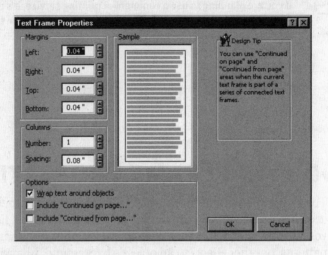

Change the distance from the text to the frame using the spin boxes for margin adjustment. Format text for two or more columns using the spin box on the Columns control. The spacing control adjusts space between columns.

Enable the Wrap Text Around Objects feature if you plan to place objects in the middle of text. The template shown here includes a text frame formatted for two columns with Text Wrapping enabled. The object and its caption are in two separate frames that have been grouped.

Graphic Frames

Select the object for which you wish to modify frame properties. Right-click and choose Change Frame or click the Format menu to see the same choices you get on the shortcut menu. You can format borders and add fills just as you would for a text frame. The Picture Frame Properties dialog box offers options for how closely you want text to wrap around the art. The margin controls in this dialog box control the distance from the picture to the frame.

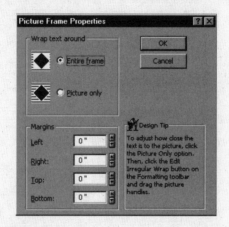

CROPPING ART

You can use just part of a picture or other graphic by selecting it and dragging the Crop tool over one of the resize handles. As you drag the frame border, instead of making the entire picture smaller, it removes the areas of the picture you drag over, leaving only the parts that remain inside the frame. Drag the Crop tool over as many of the resize handles as you need to use until your art is perfectly positioned. Click the Crop tool again to turn it off, or click anywhere else in your publication.

Part vi

MODIFYING PAGE SETUP OPTIONS

If you are printing on paper that is a different size than your publication, you may need to modify Page Setup. On the File Menu, click Page Setup. In the bottom-left corner of the dialog are settings for Portrait and Landscape. Choose the correct setting for your publication.

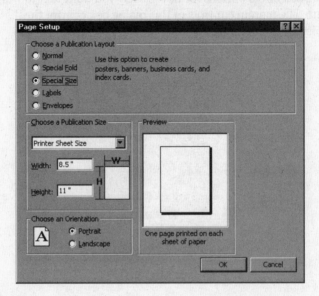

From the Publication Layout options, choose Normal if you want one printed page on each sheet of paper; choose this if you are duplexing on a manual-feed printer as well. The Special Fold option is for printing folded documents like cards or small booklets with two pages on a sheet. The Special Size option supports banners, index cards, and poster printing. The Special Fold, Special Size, Labels, and Envelopes options each display a list where you'll need to make further selections.

Margins

Publisher doesn't use page margins in the usual sense of the word. Instead, you get boundary lines that show a 1" margin by default. (Chapter 19 shows how to set up these lines the way you want them.) The boundary lines don't act like margins in Word; you can place objects on or outside them without having to adjust them. You can set margins for frames (see "Modifying Frame Properties" earlier in this chapter). Frame margins act more like the traditional margins you may be used to. They determine how far text or art appears from the edge of the frame.

Headers and Footers

Publisher also treats headers and footers differently than Word. Text and objects that appear on every page in a Publisher document are placed on a "background" layer. To display this layer, click View ➤ Go To Background. Any objects you may have already placed in the foreground become invisible as you work on the background, and the View menu now displays Go To Foreground as a choice.

Create a header by placing and formatting text and/or object frames outside the top margin boundary. Footers go just outside of the bottom boundary. Click the View menu and choose Go To Foreground to return to your regular document. You should still be able to see your background text and objects.

To hide a header or footer on the first page of your document, navigate to the first page of your publication. Hide all background objects using View ➤ Ignore Background. If there are other background objects besides the header or footer that you don't want to hide, drag a new text frame to cover just the header and/or footer. When you print, you won't see the empty text frame.

There may be times when you want to mirror header and footer setup. Booklets are a great example of when you might want to do this. Go to the background and create the header or footer as you normally would, but make sure you set it up to appear on every *right* page of your publication. Click Arrange ➤ Layout Guides. Enable the Create Two Backgrounds With Mirrored Guides feature and click OK. Switch back to the foreground and continue working.

WHAT'S NEXT

Part VII is next, and you're in for a treat. We'll get into that amazing thing known as the Internet, and you'll be surfing and e-mailing in no time.

Part vi

PART vii
EXPLORING THE
INTERNET

Chapter 21

GETTING ON THE INTERNET

So what exactly does it mean to be "on the Internet"? Generally, if someone asks you, "Are you on the Net?" it means something like, "Do you have an Internet e-mail address?" That is, do you have e-mail and can your e-mail account be reached over the Internet? With the popularity of the Web being what it is, another common interpretation of what it means to be on the Net is, "Do you have the ability to browse the World Wide Web?" Often these two features—Internet e-mail and Web access—go hand in hand, but not always. In a short while, the concept of "being on the Internet" will likely include having your own home page, a "place" on the Web where information about you is stored and where you can be found. This is also sometimes known as having a "presence" online or on the Web.

THE INTERNET

Adapted from *The Internet: No Experience Required*
by Christian Crumlish
ISBN 0-7821-2385-6   496 pages $19.99

CRUISING THE NET AT WORK

More and more companies these days (as well as schools and other organizations) are installing internal networks and relying on e-mail to share information. E-mail messages are starting to replace interoffice memos, at least for some types of announcements, questions, and scheduling purposes. The logical next step for most of these organizations is to connect their internal network to the Internet through a gateway. When this happens, you may suddenly be on the Net. This doesn't mean that anything will necessarily change on your desktop. You'll probably still use the same e-mail program and still send and receive mail within your office in the same way you always have.

WARNING

Some companies use Internet-usage monitoring programs that tell them how long employees have been using the Internet and what type of sites they are visiting. Use good judgment when you surf the Internet at work and try to explore only those sites that have potentially important work-related information.

What will change at this point is that you'll be able to send e-mail to people on the Internet outside of your office, as long as you type the right kind of Internet address. (Generally, this means adding @ and a series of words separated by periods to the username portion of an address, but I'll explain more about addresses at the end of this lesson.) Similarly, people out there in the great beyond will be able to send e-mail to you as well.

Depending on the type of Internet connection your company has, e-mail may be all you get. Then again, it might also be possible for you to run a Web browser on your computer and visit Internet sites while sitting at your desk. Of course, your company will only want you to do this if it's relevant to your job, but it works the same way whether you're researching a product your company uses or reading cartoons at the Dilbert site.

NOTE

Your ability to find information your company needs on the Internet will become a highly prized career asset, especially as more and more organizations contribute to the growth of the Internet.

CRUISING THE NET AT HOME

If you're interested in exploring the Internet as a form of entertainment or for personal research and communication, then a work account is not really the way to do it. (An account minimally consists of a username and an e-mail inbox; it may also provide storage space on a computer or access to a Web server.) You'll need your own personal account to really explore the Internet on your own time, without looking over your shoulder to make sure nobody's watching.

TIP

If your office is sophisticated, you may actually be able to dial in to a company network from home via a modem to check your e-mail messages or even browse the Web; but again, unless it's work-related surfing or research, this might not be an appropriate use of your boss's resources.

Your best bet is to sign up for an account from a commercial online service or a direct-access Internet service provider. What's the difference between those two choices? Well, an *online service* (such as CompuServe, America Online, Prodigy, Microsoft Network, and so on) is first and foremost a private, proprietary network offering its own content and access to other network members, generally combined with Internet access. An *Internet service provider* (also called an *ISP*) just offers access to the Internet and no proprietary content (or only limited local information and discussion groups). Figure 21.1 will help illustrate this distinction.

A few years ago, online services began to offer full Internet access as a normal part of the service. Because they are trying to do two things at once (sell you their own content *and* connect you to the Internet), they are generally more expensive than local ISPs. On the other hand, they tend to offer a single, simplified interface. I often recommend that people who just want to get their feet wet sign up for a free trial account at one of the online services.

In the long run, you may decide you can save money by switching to a direct-access Internet service provider.

ISPs can be cheaper than online services, especially if you can find one that offers a flat rate—a monthly charge that doesn't vary no matter how much time you spend connected to the Net. They also don't try to compete with the Internet by offering their own content and sponsors. Instead, they function as a gateway, getting you onto the Internet and letting you go wherever you want.

Part vii

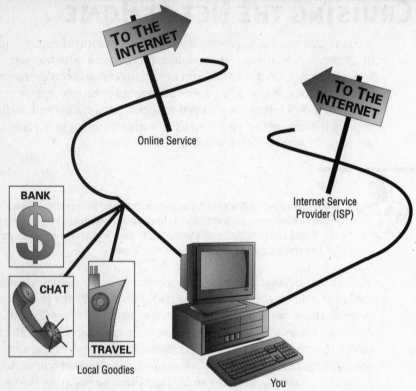

FIGURE 21.1: Online services connect you to the Internet but encourage you to explore their own offerings, whereas ISPs just connect you to the Internet and let you fend for yourself.

What Kinds of ISP Accounts Are There?

An ISP account generally includes (along with the e-mail address) storage space on a computer somewhere on the Net. You will be billed monthly, and depending on the provider, there may be a surcharge based on the amount of time you spent connected that month or the amount of space you used on their hard drive (over a usually ample quota, often something like 5 megabytes of storage).

But how do you use an account? Well, you need a computer with a modem, and you need software that knows how to use that modem to call up (dial up) your provider and that allows you to log in to your account. Fortunately, most modems come with their own software.

TIP

You don't necessarily need a computer to connect to the Net. Another approach is to sign up for WebTV, a service that works with a television and a phone line.

Your ISP will take care of all the technical details for you and will probably supply you with a setup disk and easy-to-use software for connecting to the Internet. Once you're set up, you won't have to think much about whether you have a PPP, SLIP, or any other kind of account, but I want to introduce the terminology now so you'll know what I'm talking about when I mention it again. If you want more than a connection to a Unix command-line and a plain-text account (and I suspect that you do), then you need something called a *PPP* or *SLIP account*. (The other kind is usually called a *shell account* or sometimes a *Unix shell account*.)

A PPP (or SLIP) account lets your computer behave like it's connected directly to another computer on the Internet—when it's really connected over a phone line whenever you dial up—and it enables you to run software, such as a graphical Web browser like Microsoft Internet Explorer, that functions in your computer's native environment (for example, Windows or the Macintosh operating system) instead of forcing you to deal with options-limited programs like the text-only browsers Lynx and Unix (see Figure 21.2).

PPP-Type
Internet Connection

Unix-Shell Type
Internet Connection

FIGURE 21.2: If you can get a PPP (or SLIP) account, then your connection to the Internet will be more seamlessly integrated into your computer's normal environment (and much easier to use!).

WARNING

By the way, the speed of your modem—and that of the modem at the other end of the dial-up line (that is, your provider's modem)—determines the speed of your Internet connection, and even the fastest modems these days are still slower than a direct network connection to the Net, such as you might enjoy at your office.

THE ANATOMY OF AN INTERNET ADDRESS

One of the confusing things to Internet newbies is that the word "address" is used to mean at least three different things on the Internet. The most basic meaning—but the one used least often—is the name of a computer, also called a *host* or *site*, on the Internet in the form `something` `.something.something` (to really use the lingo properly you have to pronounce the periods as "dot"—you'll get used to it and it saves a lot of time over the long haul). For example, I publish a magazine (or 'zine) on the Internet called *Enterzone*; it's stored on a machine in San Francisco that is part of a collective. The address of that machine is

`ezone.org`

Reading from right to left, you first have the *domain,* `org`, which stands for (nonprofit) organization. Next you have a *subdomain,* `ezone`. Finally you sometimes have a *hostname* (often, but not always, `www`), which is the name (or *a* name) of the specific computer the magazine is stored on.

Another type of address is an e-mail address. An e-mail address consists of a *username* (also called a *login,* a *log-on name,* a *userID,* an *account name,* and so on), followed by an "at sign" (@) and then an Internet address of the type just described. So, for example, say you want to send e-mail to me in my capacity as editor of *Enterzone*. You could address that e-mail message to a special username created for that job (it will stay the same even if someone else takes over in the future):

`editor@ezone.org`

The third type of address is the kind you see everywhere these days, on billboards, on TV commercials, in the newspaper, and so on—a Web address, also called a *URL* (*Uniform Resource Locator*). The Web address of that magazine I told you about is

```
http://ezone.org/ez/
```

TIP

You can leave out the `http://` portion of the address when using certain Web browsers.

Fortunately, you often can avoid typing in Web addresses yourself and can zip around the Web just by clicking pre-established *links*. Links are highlighted words or images that, when clicked or selected, take you directly to a new document, another part of the current document, or some other type of file entirely. Figure 21.3 shows Yahoo, one of many Web sites on which to surf the Web via links.

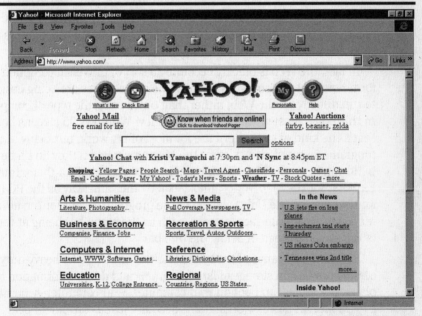

Part VII

FIGURE 21.3: Yahoo, a Web Directory, is one of the most popular sites on the entire World Wide Web. Users can select categories of pre-established links to aid them in finding those sites which are of interest to them or in searching for information.

NOTE

The InterNIC registration service assigns and maintains most of the domain names you see. These include .org for nonprofit organizations, .com for commercial users, .net for service providers, .edu for 4-year educational institutions, .mil which is reserved for the military, and .gov for government agencies.

GETTING ON THE NET WITH MAC, WINDOWS, OR UNIX

One of the nice things about the Internet is that it makes some of the seemingly important distinctions between types of computers a lot less important. Sure, if you use a Macintosh, you have to run Macintosh software, and if you use Windows 95 or Windows 98, you have to run Windows software. The information on the Internet, the public discussion areas, and the World Wide Web, however, look and act more or less the same no matter what kind of computer you use.

In fact, the Web is quickly becoming a sort of universal computer platform now that certain types of programs and services are being designed to run directly on the Web, rather than on one specific type of computer. In this book, most of the screen shots show Windows 95 screens because that's the kind of computer I use for most of my work, but many of the programs featured also exist for the Macintosh; when they do I'll be sure to fill you in on the Macintosh versions and where to find them. Internet Explorer for the Mac works almost exactly the same way as the PC (and, for that matter, the Unix) version of the program, except for the normal Macintosh user-interface features, such as the menu bar being at the top of the screen instead of below the title bar.

Part of the elegance of the Internet is that much of the heavy-duty processing power and storage of large programs and dense information takes place "out there," and not on your computer. Your computer—whether it's a PC, a Mac, or a Unix workstation—becomes just a convenient beanstalk to climb up to the land of the Internet giants. You'll sometimes refer to this common structure of Internet facilities as *client-server* (sorry for the jargon). In this scenario, you are the client (or your computer or the program running on it is) and the information source, World Wide Web site, or e-mail–handling program is the server. Servers are centralized repositories of information or specialized handlers of certain kinds of traffic. All you (as a client) have to do is connect to the right server and a wealth of goodies is within your reach—without overloading your machine. This is a major reason why it doesn't matter what kind of computer you prefer.

WHAT'S NEXT

Now that you know Web basics, you can get down to what it's all about: browsing the Internet. The next chapter will detail how Internet Explorer 5 will help you get the most out of that vast place known as the Web.

Chapter 22

AN INTRODUCTION TO INTERNET EXPLORER

This chapter will give you a broad overview of the way you work with Internet Explorer. We'll start at the beginning and show you the different ways you can start the program.

Later in the chapter, you'll learn about Internet Explorer's various tools, commands, and program features that help you navigate the Web and your local computer. You'll also find extensive material on the types of files that Internet Explorer can display, and we'll tell you how you can specify the way it should handle the ones that it can't display.

Adapted from *Mastering Microsoft Internet Explorer 4*, by Gene Weisskopf and Pat Coleman

ISBN 0-7821-2133-0   960 pages $44.99

This material has been updated for Internet Explorer 5.

STARTING INTERNET EXPLORER

Like just about all Windows programs, Internet Explorer can be started in many ways. You can also run more than one copy of Internet Explorer at a time, which allows you to view multiple documents or different sections of the same document.

To start Internet Explorer at any time, simply choose it from the Windows Start menu. In a standard installation, choose Start ➤ Programs ➤ Internet Explorer ➤ Internet Explorer. The program will start and open its *start page*, which is the page Internet Explorer displays first whenever you start it in this way.

If the start page is available on a local or networked drive on your computer or if you are already connected to the Internet, Internet Explorer opens that page immediately and displays it.

If you use a modem to connect to the Internet, however, and the start page resides there but you're not currently connected, Internet Explorer opens your Dial-Up Networking connector to make the connection to the Internet.

Dialing In to the Internet

If you normally use a network connection to access the Internet, any program can connect to the Internet as needed. That's not so when you link to the Internet through a modem and a telephone line. In that case, whenever Internet Explorer (or any other Windows application) needs access to the Internet (such as to open its start page) but does not yet have it, someone has to make that phone call to get connected.

That someone is Dial-Up Networking, which makes the call and gets connected to your Internet service provider (ISP). For example, Figure 22.1 shows the Dial-Up Settings dialog box, in which you can revise or verify the user name, password, and telephone number that will be needed to make the connection.

TIP

If you want your password saved to your local disk so that you won't have to enter it the next time you connect to the Internet, select the Save Password option (the password is encrypted on your local disk).

Click the Connect button in the Connect To dialog box to make the call. You'll see status messages as the call and connection are being made. In about 20 or 30 seconds, the connection will be completed and you'll see the Dial-Up Networking icon displayed on the status bar (as shown here). Internet Explorer can now open its start page, and this connection to the Internet is also available to any Windows program that needs access to it, such as your e-mail program, an FTP client, and so on.

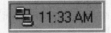

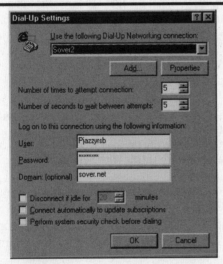

FIGURE 22.1:   When a program needs a connection to the Internet, the Windows Dial-Up Networking connector makes the call over your modem.

Note that you'll see this dialog box only when you have enabled the Prompt For Information Before Dialing option, which you'll find when you open the Dial-Up Networking folder and choose Connections ➤ Settings. If you have disabled this option, the call will be made as soon as the dialog box opens.

Starting from Your Start Page

The start page serves as a "home base" while you are working in Internet Explorer. You begin your leaps and bounds through the Web from the links on your start page. If you ever want to return to your start page (to return home, so to speak) during a session with Internet Explorer, click the Home button on the toolbar.

NOTE

You'll sometimes hear the start page referred to as the *home page*. Even the button on the Internet Explorer toolbar that opens your start page is labeled *Home* and displays a picture of a house. Nonetheless, you should stick with start page, the more commonly used term, to avoid any confusion with the *home page* of a Web site.

When your start page is open, you can navigate to any other page you choose. For example, you can click a hyperlink to open that link's target file, or you can choose an item from Internet Explorer's Favorites menu to go to that site.

TIP

You can specify any page to serve as the start page. You'll find this setting on the General tab in the Internet Options dialog box when you choose Tools ➢ Internet Options in Internet Explorer. You can also access the Internet Options dialog box by clicking the Internet icon in the Windows Control Panel.

If Internet Explorer cannot find your start page, such as when you cannot connect to the Internet, it displays a local page that offers a few tips for dealing with the problem. At this point, you can use your Favorites menu to go to a site, or you can enter a URL directly into the Address toolbar.

The start page is just like any other Web page you can open in Internet Explorer. The only thing special about it is that you see it each time you begin a session in Internet Explorer. A start page typically serves its purpose by containing one or both of the following types of content:

▶ Hyperlinks to one or more sites that you usually go to in each session with Internet Explorer

▶ Updated information that you want to see each time you start Internet Explorer, such as news, weather, stock market reports, sports scores, and so on

Starting Internet Explorer from a Hyperlink

Many programs besides Web browsers can display either text hyperlinks (which may be in a different color and underlined) or image hyperlinks; clicking the text or image opens the target file of that link. In a standard Windows installation, when you click a link whose target is an HTML Web page, you'll find that the target will be opened in Internet Explorer.

For example, suppose someone sends you an e-mail suggesting that you check out a site on the WWW, and the text of the message includes the URL of that site. In Outlook Express Mail (and in most other e-mail programs), the text that makes up the URL is displayed in color and underlined, just as it would be in a browser. If you click the URL, Internet Explorer opens, and then it opens that site.

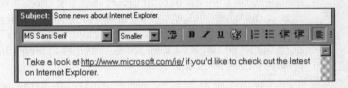

Opening an Existing Document

When you open an HTML file (one with an .HTM or .HTML file name extension) in Windows Explorer, that file opens in Internet Explorer (assuming Internet Explorer is the default browser on your computer.

NOTE

Quick reminder: When we refer to *Windows* Explorer, we're referring to the Explorer configuration you'll see when you're browsing your local disk drives or network drives. The *Internet* Explorer is the configuration you see when browsing Web pages.

While you're in Internet Explorer, you can choose File ➢ Open to open a specific file, either by typing the path and name of the file or by clicking the Browse button to find the file on your local or networked disk. Once you've found the file, choose OK to open it.

You can also open a file by simply dragging it from Windows Explorer or a folder window into Internet Explorer. Among the files you can open are HTML Web pages and GIF or JPEG image files (see "Viewing Various File Types" later in this chapter).

Part vii

MAKING INTERNET EXPLORER YOUR DEFAULT BROWSER

If you have installed another browser since installing Internet Explorer, Internet Explorer may not be set as your default browser, and that other browser will be called upon to open any Web pages you request. If you want to make Internet Explorer your default browser and keep it that way, here's how to do it.

In Internet Explorer, choose Tools ➤ Internet Options. On the Programs tab, you'll find an option called "Internet Explorer should check to see whether it is the default browser." Select this option, and close the Internet Options dialog box.

Now whenever you start Internet Explorer, it will check to see if it is still the default browser. If it finds that it isn't, it will ask if you want it to become the new default browser. If you choose Yes, it will change the Windows settings to make it the default. Now when you open an HTML file—for example, by clicking a hyperlink in a Word document that targets a Web page—Internet Explorer will be the program that opens it.

If you later install another browser that makes itself the default, the next time you start Internet Explorer, it will check to see if it is the default and prompt you accordingly.

Closing Internet Explorer

To close Internet Explorer, choose File ➤ Close, or click the Close button on the far right side of its title bar. Remember, Web browsers such as Internet Explorer are used only for viewing documents, so you never need to save anything before exiting the program.

WARNING

Even though there are normally no documents to save in Internet Explorer, you might still lose data if you exit the program prematurely. For example, when you are filling out a form in a Web page, you must click that form's Submit button to send your responses to the server. If you were to close Internet Explorer before doing so, any information you had entered into the form would be lost. Plus, if you open an OLE-compliant document, such as one from Microsoft Word, and you have its associated program installed on your system, you'll actually be editing that document in Internet Explorer. In this case, closing Internet Explorer would have the same effect as closing Microsoft Word when a document is open.

Closing Your Dial-Up Networking Connection

When you started Internet Explorer, it may have caused Dial-Up Networking to make the telephone call over your modem to connect to the Internet. In that case, when you later exit Internet Explorer, you will be asked if you want to disconnect from the Internet.

You can choose to disconnect if you're through working on the Internet for now. Doing so will close the connection so that your telephone line can receive other calls. Otherwise, you can choose to stay online and maintain the connection. You could then open your e-mail program, for example, and send or receive mail on the Internet. Or you might open Internet Explorer again, and the connection would be waiting for it.

If you do leave the connection open, don't forget to disconnect later. To do so, double-click the Dial-Up Networking icon in the System Tray on the right side of the Windows taskbar, then click the Disconnect button in the dialog box. Or right-click the icon in the taskbar and choose Disconnect from the shortcut menu.

A QUICK TOUR WITH INTERNET EXPLORER

Now that you've read about starting and closing Internet Explorer, let's take it on a short test ride to experience the thrill of the wind in our hair as we travel to new lands on the World Wide Web.

1. From the Windows Start menu, choose Programs ➤ Internet Explorer ➤ Internet Explorer.

2. If you connect to the Internet via a modem, Dial-Up Networking should open, dial your Internet service provider, give your user name and password, and complete the connection to the Internet.

3. Once connected, Internet Explorer opens its start page. If you installed Internet Explorer from a Microsoft source, for example, by downloading it from Microsoft's Web page, it opens the page at `home.microsoft.com`. The page you see in Internet Explorer will look something like the one shown in Figure 22.2.

Part vii

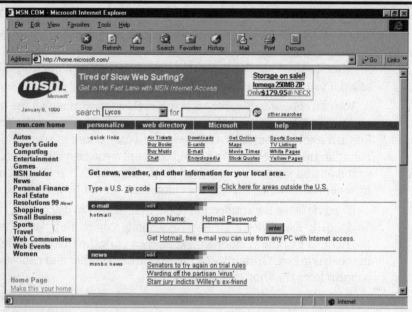

FIGURE 22.2:   Internet Explorer opens your start page, where you can begin your travels on the World Wide Web.

4. At this point, you're free to click any of the hyperlinks in the current page to open a new page. Simply click a link, and off you go. Continue to click your way through several pages and see where you end up.

NOTE

When you point to a text or an image hyperlink, the mouse pointer changes to a small hand, and the address of the link's target is displayed on the status bar. Text hyperlinks are underlined and displayed in blue by default.

5. Now that you've traveled through several pages by following hyperlinks, go back through the pages you've followed by clicking the Back button on the toolbar. Each click takes you to the page you visited before the current one. Eventually you'll reach your start page.

6. Now let's go to a specific address on the Web, one of our own choosing. Either click within the Internet Explorer Address

toolbar, or choose File ➤ Open. (If the Address toolbar isn't displayed, choose View ➤ Toolbars ➤ Address Bar.)

7. Enter the following URL:

    www.census.gov/datamap/www/

    and press Enter, or the Go button to the right of the Address bar, to open that page.

8. In the blink of an eye (perhaps longer if it's a busy time of the day on the Web), we've opened the Map Stats page on the Web site of the U.S. Census Bureau, as shown in Figure 22.3.

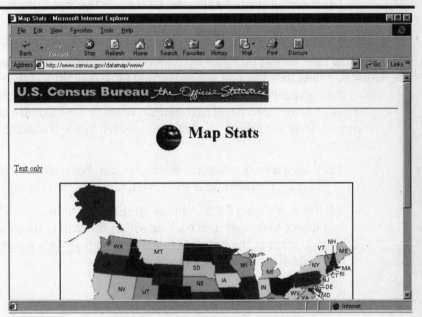

FIGURE 22.3:   On the Map Stats page of the U.S. Census Bureau, you can access a wealth of information about any region in the country.

9. Just in case you'd like to return to this page at another time, you should add it to your Favorites menu. Choose Favorites ➤ Add to Favorites, and then click OK.

Part vii

NOTE

When you want to return to this site, simply select it from your Favorites menu, which you'll find not only in every Explorer window, but also on your Windows 95 Start menu. You can also move this new item to another submenu on the Favorites menu.

10. Click your home state, which will open a map of that state. Let's save this picture of your state to your local disk.

11. Right-click anywhere within the map, and choose Save Picture As from the shortcut menu.

12. Specify a location and name for the new file, and click OK to save it.

You now have a GIF image file of that map on your local disk, which you can later import into your word processor or any other program that handles GIF files. Just remember that most content you retrieve from the Web cannot be used for commercial purposes without specific permission from the owner of that content. When in doubt, drop a note asking whoever runs the Web site for permission to use the image or content.

13. Click a county within the state map, and then click the Tiger Map link, which opens an interactive map of that county.

14. Try magnifying the map by selecting the Zoom In option (as shown here) and then clicking within the map at the point you want at the center of the magnified map. In a few seconds, the new map will be displayed.

Click on the image to:
⊙ Zoom in, factor: 2
○ Zoom out, factor: 2
○ Move to new center
○ Download this map as a GIF file

15. If you'd like to print this page, choose File ➤ Print, or click the Print button on the toolbar. In the Print dialog box, click the OK button.

SECURITY ALERT

When you click within the map to change its magnification, you may see a Security Alert dialog box warning you that you are about to send information over the Internet that could be seen by others. This is simply a not-so-gentle reminder that the Internet is not a private network. When you make a choice on a Web page and then click a Submit or Send Now button (or simply click within the map to make your choice in this case), you are sending some information over the Internet that could be viewed by others. Once you're familiar with these situations and no longer need the constant reminder, you can turn off this message in the future by selecting its "In the future, do not show this warning" option.

Now let's use Internet Explorer in a somewhat different way, to view a page from your local disk.

16. Using the Address toolbar or the File ➢ Open command, enter the drive and path to the folder where you stored the map image file you saved earlier in step 12. Press Enter when finished.

17. Internet Explorer will open that folder and display its contents; you should see the GIF file you saved earlier.

18. To go back to the previous page you were viewing, simply click the Back button on the toolbar. Or perhaps you might choose the Map Stats site from your Favorites menu to go back to that site.

We could play on this site for another dozen pages of this book, but it's time to wrap up this tour.

Don't ever worry about getting lost, because that concept just doesn't apply to your travels in Internet Explorer. Sure, you can easily forget how you reached the current page, but that's what the Back and Favorites buttons are for.

Whatever happens, you can always jump back to your start page at any time by clicking the Home button on the toolbar. Although there's nothing magical about your start page (it's just another page you can display in Internet Explorer), it's a familiar place that will have familiar content and links.

Part vii

Otherwise, you can simply close Internet Explorer by choosing File ➤ Close and call it a day. If you are connected to the Internet via a Dial-Up Networking connection, you should be asked whether you want to disconnect; choose Yes to hang up.

INSIDE INTERNET EXPLORER

Now we'll look at the components that make up Internet Explorer. You'll find that Internet Explorer has many similarities to other Windows programs you have used, especially to those in Microsoft Office (Word, Excel, Access, and so on). Figure 22.4 shows Internet Explorer while displaying a Web page. As you can see, the Internet Explorer window contains many of the usual Windows components.

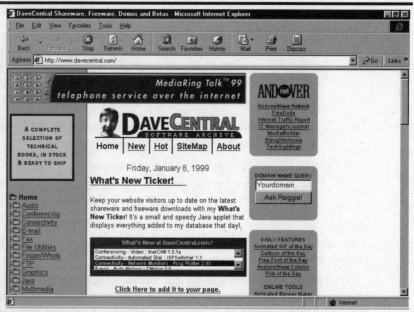

FIGURE 22.4:   The Internet Explorer program window contains many components that are common to other Windows programs.

NOTE

A company or an Internet service provider (ISP) can customize Internet Explorer to make it look and act as though it were their own browser and then distribute it to employees or customers. So if your ISP or your employer gives you a copy of Internet Explorer, it may not look exactly like the one shown in Figure 22.4.

When you want to show as much of the Web page as possible, try the View ➤ Full Screen command, or click the Full Screen button on the toolbar. Internet Explorer will be maximized to occupy the entire screen, it will lose its title bar, status bar, two of its toolbars, and even its menu bar. (You can right-click a toolbar and choose Menu Bar to display it again.)

You can switch back to the normal view by choosing the Full Screen command again. The full-screen mode is the default when you open a channel from the desktop, when it's formally called the Channel Viewer.

The Components of Internet Explorer

Let's discuss the parts that make up the Internet Explorer window. Keep in mind that if a tool or an object looks similar to one you've seen in another Windows program, it most likely performs the same task in both.

Title Bar

At the top of the window is the usual title bar. It displays either the title of the Web page you are viewing (*Dave Central Shareware, Freeware, Demos and Betas Page* in Figure 22.4) or the document's filename if it is not a Web page. On the right side of the title bar are the Minimize, Maximize/ Restore, and Close buttons; on the left side is the System menu. As usual, you can double-click the title bar to maximize the window (or restore it to its previous size if it was already maximized), or you can drag Internet Explorer by its title bar to move the window on the screen (assuming the window is not maximized).

Program Window

Internet Explorer's program window is shown full-screen in Figure 22.4. If it is smaller than full-screen, you can resize it by dragging any of its corners or sides. You'll find that the paragraphs in a Web page generally adjust their width to the size of the browser window. As you change the dimensions of Internet Explorer, the page reformats to fit the new size.

Menu Bar

Beneath the title bar is the menu bar, which contains almost all the commands you'll need in Internet Explorer. If a command has a keyboard shortcut, you'll see the keystroke displayed next to the command on the menu. For example, you can use the shortcut Ctrl+O (hold down Ctrl and press O) instead of choosing the File ➤ Open command, or you can press function key F5 instead of choosing View ➤ Refresh.

Toolbars

By default, the toolbars appear beneath the menu bar in Internet Explorer and contain buttons and other tools that help you navigate the Web. The three toolbars are Standard, Links, and Address (top, middle, and bottom in Figure 22.4). We discuss these a little later in "Using the Toolbars." The Internet Explorer logo to the right of the toolbar is animated when the program is accessing data.

Document Window

Beneath the menu and toolbars is the main document window, which occupies the majority of your screen. The current document, such as a Web page or an image, is displayed here. You cannot display multiple document windows in Internet Explorer. Instead, you can view multiple documents by opening multiple instances of Internet Explorer (choose File ➤ New ➤ Window). Each instance of Internet Explorer is independent of the others.

Explorer Bar

When you click the Search, Favorites, History, or Channels button on the Internet Explorer toolbar (or choose one of those commands from the View ➤ Explorer Bar menu), the Explorer bar will appear as a separate pane on the left side of the window. It displays the contents for the button you clicked, such as the search options shown in Figure 22.5.

With the window split into two separate panes, you can make choices in the Explorer bar on the left and watch the results appear in the pane on the right. For example, in Figure 22.5, you can specify what you want to search for in the Explorer bar, and the results of the search appear in that same pane as a list of links you can click. When you click one of the result links, the target of the link appears in the right pane, while leaving the Explorer bar unchanged. You can select another result link to try that target and continue through as many as you like.

To close the Explorer bar, choose View ➤ Explorer Bar ➤ None, or click the appropriate button a second time, such as the Search button to close the Explorer bar in Figure 22.5.

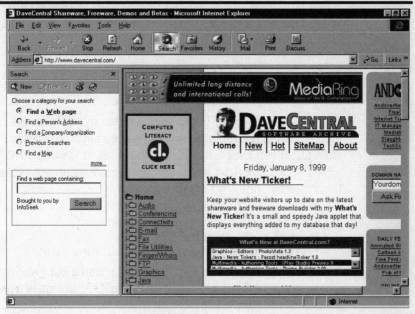

FIGURE 22.5:   When you click the Search, Favorites, History, or Channels button on the toolbar, the Explorer bar opens as a separate pane on the left side of the window, where you can make choices and see the results appear in the right pane.

Scroll Bars

The horizontal scroll bar is at the bottom of the document window, and the vertical scroll bar is on the right side of the document window. When a document is too large to be displayed within the window, you can use the scroll bars to scroll the window over other parts of the document.

Watch That Status Bar

At the bottom of the Internet Explorer window is the status bar. It displays helpful information about the current state of Internet Explorer, so keep an eye on it.

▶ When you are selecting a command from the menu bar, a description of the currently highlighted command appears on the status bar.

Searches the current window for text

▶ When you point to a hyperlink on the page (either text or an image), the mouse pointer changes to a hand, and the target URL of the hyperlink is displayed on the status bar.

> http://www.sybex.com/books.html

▶ When you click a hyperlink to open another page, the status bar indicates what is happening with a progression of messages. For example, if you click a hyperlink whose target is `www.sample` `.com/somepage.htm` you might see the following messages on the status bar, one after another:

```
Finding site: www.sample.com
Web site found. Waiting for reply
Opening page: somepage.htm
(7 items remaining) Downloading picture http://. . .
```

▶ Icons that appear on the right side of the status bar give you a status report at a glance. For example, you'll see an icon of a padlock when you have made a secure connection to a Web site, and you'll see a network wire with an X across it when you're working offline.

TIP

You can use the Toolbar and Status Bar commands on the View menu to toggle on or off the display of the toolbars and status bar. You might want to hide these otherwise useful features to give yourself a little more screen real estate for displaying pages. If you want as much room as possible, try the View ➢ Full Screen command.

Getting Help

Internet Explorer offers the usual variety of program help, with a few touches of its own. When you choose Help ➢ Contents and Index, what you get is not quite the standard Windows help viewer. Internet Explorer uses a new help system that is built with HTML, just like a Web page. Nonetheless, it behaves very much like the more traditional help system. You can browse through the topics in the Contents tab, look up a specific word or phrase in the Index tab, or find all references to a word or phrase on the Search tab.

NOTE

Clicking the E icon in the upper-right corner of the program takes you to Microsoft's ever-so-humble home page. You can catch up on the latest Microsoft news, read corporate press releases, and get information for stockholders.

To see if there is a newer version of any of the Internet Explorer software components, choose Tools ➢ Windows Update. This is the best way to keep your software current—immediately and online.

NOTE

To work through a basic online tutorial about browsing the Web, choose Help ➢ Web Tutorial. Internet Explorer goes online to a Microsoft Web site and opens the tutorial page, where you can click your way through the lessons. To find answers to your questions or problems, choose Help ➢ Online Support. This will open Microsoft's online support page for Internet Explorer. It's packed with tips, troubleshooting guides, answers to common questions, and much more. It's a great place to go for up-to-the-minute solutions and fixes.

The other items under Help should prove to be quite valuable. Each takes you online to the Internet:

Tip of the Day   This option gives you extra hints about the latest version of Internet Explorer. To close the tips windows, simply click the Close button in the upper-left corner.

For Netscape Users   Are you new to Internet Explorer after using Netscape for awhile? If so, this page is designed to make the transition smoother for you. Discover the terminology differences and tips on importing your bookmarks into your Internet Explorer Favorites.

Send Feedback   Do you have a comment about Internet Explorer for Microsoft? Would you like to report a bug or send in a request for a special feature you'd like to see in the program? Use this command to go to the feedback page, where you can tell Microsoft what you think.

Repair...   Clicking this will enable you to choose the option of allowing Internet Explorer to detect and repair problems within itself. Keep in mind though, you'll have to restart your computer in the event changes are made to your software.

Part vii

About Internet Explorer   This windows contains your current Internet Explorer software's version number, Product ID code, and Microsoft's copyright information.

NOTE

The Microsoft Home Page command is *not* the same as the Go ➤ Home Page command (or the Home button on the Toolbar), which opens your own start page.

You can often learn something about an object on screen from its Tool-Tip. Internet Explorer displays ToolTips when you point to some of its components, such as when you point to an icon on the status bar (shown here), a hyperlink within the page, or a button on the toolbar (when the button descriptions are not displayed). Here's what a ToolTip looks like:

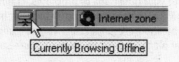

Another way to find out about an object in the current document, such as a picture or video clip, is to right-click it and choose Properties from the shortcut menu.

AT THE HELM IN INTERNET EXPLORER

The simplest way to navigate within Internet Explorer is to click a hyperlink to open another file (the target of the link). That's probably how you'll spend most of your time while browsing, but there are plenty of commands available that can help you explore the Web, save information to your local disk, and so on.

In Internet Explorer, you can perform an action in three main ways:

- ▶ Using the menus and shortcut menus
- ▶ Using the toolbars
- ▶ Using the keyboard and shortcut keys

Using the Menus and Shortcut Menus

In Internet Explorer, you can perform just about any action by choosing commands on its menus. Many components also have shortcut menus that you access with a right-click of the mouse.

Let's take a quick look at the commands on the menu bar (you can breeze over these just to familiarize yourself with them; you won't be tested on any of this):

File Open the current page in a new Internet Explorer window; open a file by specifying a name and URL or location; save the current page to disk; print the current page; send the current page or its URL in an e-mail message or create a shortcut to it on your desktop; edit the page in FrontPage; import or export bookmarks/favorites and cookies; view the properties of the current page; choose to browse without being online (data is opened from your Internet Explorer cache on your local disk); close Internet Explorer.

Edit Select the contents of the entire page; copy selected data from Internet Explorer to another program; find characters or words on the current page.

View Hide or display the toolbars and status bar; change the size of the fonts used in Internet Explorer; cancel the downloading of the current page; refresh the contents of the page by downloading it again; view the HTML source code for the current page in Notepad; explore history and favorites; go backward or forward through URLs you've already visited; open your start page; change the text size on the Web page you're viewing; switch to full-screen mode to show as much of the page as possible.

Favorites Open a site that you have previously saved as a shortcut on the Favorites menu; add the current URL to the Favorites menu; open one of the channels you have subscribed to; open a URL from your Links toolbar; open the Favorites folder so you can rename, revise, delete, or otherwise organize its contents; create a subscription for the current page or any item already in the Favorites menu; manage your existing subscriptions.

Tools View and send Mail or News; update all offline content; check for Microsoft software updates; view or change your Internet Options.

Part vii

Help   Access the help system for Internet Explorer; take the Internet Explorer Web tutorial; open a Microsoft site on the WWW to learn about Internet Explorer.

You can also invoke many of these commands from the toolbars or with shortcut keys, as well as with shortcut menus.

To access a shortcut menu for an object in Internet Explorer, point to the object and click the *right* mouse button. The choices on the shortcut menu depend on the object you click.

▶ Right-click anywhere on the page outside a hyperlink or an image, and the shortcut menu includes choices relevant to the page. You can open the next or previous page, add this page to your Favorites menu, show the properties dialog box for this page, print the page, and so on. If the page uses a background image, you can choose to save that image to a file or make it your Windows desktop wallpaper.

▶ Right-click a hyperlink, and the shortcut menu lets you open the target of that link, copy the link to the Windows Clipboard, or add the target of the link to your Favorites menu.

▶ Right-click an image, and the shortcut menu lets you save the image to a file, make that image your Windows desktop wallpaper, or copy the image to the Clipboard.

▶ Right-click selected text, and you can choose to print that text or copy it to the Clipboard.

Using the Toolbars

The toolbars in Internet Explorer (shown below) can appear in every Explorer window, whether you're viewing a Web page, folders and files on your disk, the Windows Control Panel, and so on. Two of them are also available from the Windows taskbar. They go by the names Standard, Links, and Address. You can rearrange the layout of the toolbars at any time, as discussed a little later in "Moving and Resizing the Toolbars."

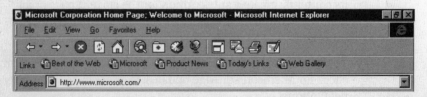

TIP

Even the menu bar now behaves as a toolbar, in that you can place other tool-bars on its row or move it to one of the other rows of toolbars. When you're work-ing in Full Screen mode (choose View ➤ Full Screen), you can even hide the menu bar.

Standard Toolbar

You'll regularly use the buttons on the first row of the toolbar, as shown above. All are shortcuts for commands on the menus. As you'll see shortly, you can choose to hide the row of descriptive text below the buttons. Table 22.1 describes each button.

TABLE 22.1: The Buttons on the Standard Toolbar

BUTTON	COMMAND	DESCRIPTION
Back	View ➤ Go ➤ Back	Displays the page you were viewing before the current page.
Forward	View ➤ Go ➤ Forward	Displays the page you were viewing before you went back to the current page.
Stop	View ➤ Stop	Cancels the downloading of the content for the current page.
Refresh	View ➤ Refresh	Updates the content of the current page by downloading it again.
Home	View ➤ Go ➤ Home Page	Opens your start page, the one you see when you first start Internet Explorer.
Search	View ➤ Explorer Bar ➤ Search	Opens the Explorer Bar on the left side of the screen and displays the search options there.
Favorites	View ➤ Explorer Bar ➤ Favorites	Opens the Explorer bar and displays your Favorites menu there.
History	View ➤ Explorer Bar ➤ History	Opens the Explorer bar and displays your browsing history there.
Channels	View ➤ Favorites ➤ Channels	Displays your channels.
Mail	File ➤ Send; Tools ➤ Mail & News	Opens your e-mail program, sends new e-mail, or opens your news reader.

Part vii

TABLE 22.1 continued: The Buttons on the Standard Toolbar

BUTTON	COMMAND	DESCRIPTION
Print	File ➤ Print	Prints the current page.
Discuss	View ➤ Explorer Bar ➤ Discuss	Opens your news reader.
		The Internet Explorer logo is animated when you are sending or receiving data. Click the logo to open Microsoft's home page.

Links Toolbar

Each of the buttons on the Links toolbar is a hyperlink to a URL (you can also access these links from the Links command on the Favorites menu). In the version we're using to write this chapter, by default, they all target Microsoft Web sites that serve as gateways to a wealth of information on the WWW (if you received a customized version of Internet Explorer, these hyperlinks may point to other locations). Microsoft updates these sites frequently, so their content will likely be fresh each time you visit.

Best of the Web   A useful collection of links to reference-related Web sites, where you might look up a company's phone number, find an e-mail address of a long-lost relative, or find sites that will help you with travel arrangements or personal finance.

Channel Guide   The home page of Microsoft's Web Events site, where you'll find news and other events to see and hear using multimedia applications.

Internet Explorer News   Valuable information about Microsoft Internet Explorer and its related applications (Mail and News, NetMeeting, and so on).

Internet Start   This is yet another way to get back to your start page.

Remember, the buttons on the Links toolbar are just hyperlinks to pages on the Web. Feel free to try them out and see what's there.

Once you've tried these buttons and have a feeling for the content on each of the sites, you may decide to revise the buttons so they point to other sites that you want to access with a click or to new buttons that point to other sites.

To add a new button, simply drag a link from a Web page onto the Links toolbar. To delete a button, right-click it and choose Delete from the shortcut menu. To move a button, drag it to another location on the Links toolbar.

The best way to revise a button's name or target URL is to use the Favorites ➤ Organize Favorites command. Open the Links folder, and you'll find the shortcuts that make up the buttons on the Links toolbar. You can rename a shortcut, and its new name will appear on the button. Right-click a shortcut, choose Properties from the shortcut menu, and you can revise the link's target URL. You can also right-click a button on the Links toolbar to access the Properties command on the shortcut menu.

Address Toolbar

This toolbar shows the address of the file currently displayed in Internet Explorer, which might be a URL on the Internet or a location on your local disk. You enter a URL or the path to a file and press Enter to open that file.

NOTE

When you are entering a URL that you have entered once before, Internet Explorer's AutoComplete feature recognizes the URL and finishes the typing for you. You can either accept the URL or continue to type a new one. Or right-click in the Address toolbar, choose Completions from the shortcut menu, and then select one of the possibilities from the menu.

To revise the URL, click within the Address toolbar and use the normal Windows editing keys. For example, press Home or End to go to the beginning or end of the address. Drag over any of its text to select it, or hold down the Shift key and use the keyboard arrow keys to select text. When you're finished entering the new address, press Enter to have Internet Explorer open the file.

The arrow on the right side of the Address toolbar opens a drop-down list of addresses. Select one, and Internet Explorer will open that site. You visited these sites before by entering the address in the Address toolbar and pressing Enter. They're listed in the order you visited them.

Moving and Resizing the Toolbars

The toolbars in Internet Explorer are quite flexible. You can change the size or position of each one in the trio, or you can choose not to display them at all. In fact, the menu bar is also quite flexible and can be moved below one or more toolbars, or share the same row with them.

▶ To hide a toolbar, choose View ➤ Toolbars and select one from the menu; to display that toolbar, choose that command again. Or right-click any of the toolbars or menu bar and select a toolbar from the shortcut menu.

▶ To hide the descriptive text below the Standard toolbar buttons, choose View ➤ Toolbars ➤ Customize, then No Text Labels in the Text Options pull-down menu, or right-click a toolbar and choose Customize, then No Text Labels in the Text Options pull-down menu. To display the text, repeat these steps choosing Show Text Labels.

▶ To change the number of rows that the toolbars use, point to the bottom edge of the bottom toolbar; the mouse pointer will change to a double-headed arrow. You can then drag the edge up to reduce the number of rows or drag it down to expand them.

▶ To move a toolbar, drag it by its left edge. For example, drag the Address toolbar onto the same row as the Links toolbar.

▶ When two or more toolbars or the menu bar share the same row, you can change the width of one (not the left-hand one) by dragging its left edge. In the arrangement shown below, the Address and Links toolbars are sharing the same row. You could drag the left edge of the Links toolbar to the right or left to make it narrower or wider.

▶ To expand a toolbar to display all its buttons or to make the Address toolbar as wide as possible, double-click its name on the left side of the toolbar. Double-click the name again to shrink that toolbar.

NOTE

Remember, these three toolbars are common to both Windows Explorer and Internet Explorer (the new single Explorer in Windows); the Address and Links toolbars are also available on the Windows taskbar.

Using Your Keyboard

In a world of pure browsing, you would rarely need the keyboard. In the real world, however, you might be using the keyboard quite a bit. For example, you'll frequently encounter online forms on which you will want to enter information: a feedback form for your comments; a survey form for your opinions; or a registration form that will give you access to an online newspaper.

As discussed earlier, you'll also be using the keyboard when you want to type a URL into the Address toolbar so you can open the file at that address. Many commands have keyboard shortcuts. Those that you may find useful on a regular basis are shown in Table 22.2.

TABLE 22.2: Useful Keyboard Shortcuts

KEY	COMMAND	DESCRIPTION
Esc	View ➤ Stop	Cancels the downloading of the content for the current page. (You can also click the Stop button on the toolbar.)
F5	View ➤ Refresh	Updates the content of the current page by downloading it again. (You can also click the Refresh button on the toolbar.)
Tab		Selects the next hyperlink on the page; press Shift+Tab to select the previous hyperlink.
Enter		Activates the selected hyperlink, as though you had clicked it with your mouse.
Home/End		Moves to the beginning or end of the document.
Arrow keys		Use ↓ or ↑ to scroll toward the bottom or the top of the document. When the document is too wide for the Internet Explorer window (as evidenced by the display of a horizontal scroll bar beneath the document), use → or ← to scroll toward the right or left edge of the document.
PgDn/PgUp		Scrolls toward the bottom or top of the current document, moving approximately one screen at a time (the height of Internet Explorer's document window).
Alt+←	Go ➤ Back	Displays the page you were viewing before the current page. (The Back button on the toolbar also does this.)

Part vii

TABLE 22.2 continued: Useful Keyboard Shortcuts

Key	Command	Description
Alt+→	Go ➤ Forward	Displays the page you were viewing before you went back to the current page. (The Forward button on the toolbar also does this.)

Accessing Outlook Express Mail and News

Internet Explorer and the Office 2000 software suite of components contain an integrated package of Internet or intranet tools. While browsing in Internet Explorer, you can access Outlook Express directly from the toolbar.

NOTE

This discussion assumes that either Microsoft Outlook or Outlook Express is your primary e-mail and newsreader program. If you have not installed Outlook Express, you may not be able to perform these tasks in your own e-mail and newsreader programs.

You can send mail in several ways while working within Internet Explorer. You'll find the following commands by clicking the Mail button on Internet Explorer's toolbar:

Read Mail opens Outlook Express Mail and displays the contents of your Inbox (you can also choose Tools ➤ Mail & News ➤ Read Mail in Internet Explorer). You're free to continue working in Outlook Express as you normally would. You can return to Internet Explorer at any time in the usual ways, such as by pressing Alt+Tab.

New Message creates a new Outlook Express Mail message, as though you had clicked the Compose Message button in that program. You can also choose File ➤ New ➤ Message or Tools ➤ Mail & News ➤ New Message in Internet Explorer.

Send a Link creates a new Outlook Express Mail message that includes an attached file—a shortcut to the page that is currently displayed in Internet Explorer. The icon or the name of the attachment appears in the pane beneath the message pane. The recipient of the message can then treat the shortcut as any other shortcut, so that opening the icon will open the target page.

You can also use Internet Explorer's equivalent commands File ➤ Send ➤ Link by Email or Tools ➤ Mail & News ➤ Send a Link.

Send Page creates a new Outlook Express Mail message (see Figure 22.6) that consists only of the page that you're currently viewing in Internet Explorer. The recipient can view the page in Outlook Express Mail or click a link to open its target in Internet Explorer. You can also use the commands File ➤ Send ➤ Page by Email or Tools ➤ Mail & News ➤ Send Page.

Read News opens Outlook Express News in the usual way (or you can choose Go ➤ News or Tools ➤ Mail & News ➤ Read News).

NOTE

You can access your Windows Address Book from within Internet Explorer with the File ➤ New ➤ Contact command.

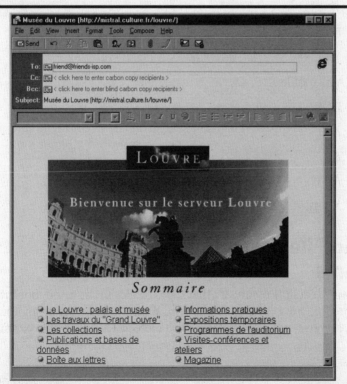

FIGURE 22.6:   The Send Page command creates an Outlook Express Mail message that contains the page currently open in Internet Explorer.

Viewing Various File Types

Internet Explorer is a browser, which means that its primary purpose is to display files, not to edit or create them. Internet Explorer can display several types of files on its own, and it can display other files with the aid of other programs. When it encounters any other type of file, you can choose to save the file to disk or let Internet Explorer attempt to open the file by passing it to the appropriate program.

Viewing Standard Web Files

When you browse, you'll encounter several types of files at virtually every Web site you visit. Internet Explorer can display all the following file types:

- .HTML
- .GIF
- .JPEG
- .PNG
- .TXT
- ActiveX files
- .DOC
- .ART
- .AU
- .AIFF
- .XBM

Viewing Files with the Help of Other Programs

There are certainly plenty of other types of files in the world, but Internet Explorer can't display them on its own. With a little help from another program, however, Internet Explorer can handle just about any file you might encounter. This ancillary program can normally expand the file-handling abilities of Internet Explorer in two ways:

Helper or Add-On   With a helper or an add-on program, Internet Explorer does not open the new file type directly; it hands the file over to the helper program. The helper may appear as a separate window of its own or as a new component within the Internet Explorer window.

Plug-In   A plug-in program allows Internet Explorer to open a new file type within the Internet Explorer window; the relationship between the two programs is almost seamless, as though the other program has been "plugged in" to Internet Explorer.

Any individual or company can create a helper or plug-in program to extend the capabilities of Internet Explorer. Most of these applications are available free for the downloading.

What happens if Internet Explorer encounters a file type that neither it nor any of its associated programs can open? That's when your Windows file associations come into play, as discussed next.

Dealing with Unknown File Types

When you click a link or otherwise open a file, Internet Explorer verifies that the file type is one it recognizes. It has two ways of recognizing files:

▶ By the file's MIME type

▶ By the file's extension

Before a server sends the file to Internet Explorer, the server first sends the file's MIME type. This acronym stands for Multipurpose Internet Mail Extensions and is a standard method on the Internet for identifying file types. If Internet Explorer recognizes the MIME type, it will know what to do with the file, such as displaying the file itself or passing it along to another program on your system.

CRIPES! MIME TYPES YIPES!

Danger Will Robinson! I wouldn't go looking for MIME types in Internet Explorer if I were you. Why? You won't find them there. In fact, you might just drive yourself nuts trying to. Let us hearken back to the days of Windows 3.1x and marvel at the thrill of Associations and we begin to see the light where MIME is concerned. If you are unfamiliar with earlier versions of Windows then you'll need an explanation of MIME and Associations. Try these:

Association: /n/, (ass•ohsh•ee•ay•shun), A sort of roadmap that tells Windows which applications to use for which filename extensions. i.e., document.doc = Word 97, picture.psd = PhotoShop, write.wri = Windows Write, and so on and so forth.

MIME: /n/, (my•mm), 1) An energetic individual that uses familiar motions to mimic reality, 2) also referred to as Multipurpose Internet Mail Extensions, MIME helps client applications, like e-mail or Web browsers, determine which application to use for a file it cannot handle (i.e., RealAudio or RealVideo, QuickTime, or PDF...)

Do you feel as if you need to make some modifications to your MIME types or just curious what they look like? Here, do this:

► Go the the Desktop, making the My Computer (or whatever you have changed it to) icon visible.

► Open My Computer and go to View ➢ Folder Options.

► Click on the File Types tab in the resultant dialog box to make the tab active

You'll note that there is a large list of items, some familiar, some alien. Most of these items are not even related to the Internet at all, but there are some important ones. The key to the kaboodle is the x-text/html MIME type that allows your browser to see Web pages in the first place. Nifty, huh?

WARNING

It's not nice to mess with Mother MIME! Unless you are very familiar with MIME or are tops at reading complex documentation, we do not suggest you modify MIME types. Doing so can cause you to lose the nifty gizmos you added in the first place.

Many MIME types and file name extensions are already associated with the appropriate programs on your computer (as discussed in the next section). For example, an HTML document has the MIME type *text/html*, a GIF image file has the type *image/gif*, and a JPEG image file has the type *image/jpeg*. You can view or revise the MIME types and program associations for files on your system, which is discussed in the next section.

When you click a link to a file, several outcomes are possible, depending on the file's MIME type and extension:

▶ If Internet Explorer recognizes its MIME type as one that already has an association in Windows, it will automatically open that file from the server. Internet Explorer will display the file if it can (such as with an HTML or a text file) or pass it along to the program with which that MIME type is associated in Windows.

▶ If Internet Explorer does not recognize the file's MIME type, it will look at the file's extension. If a program in Windows is associated with that file type, Internet Explorer will then make the following determination.

▶ If the Confirm Open After Download option in the Edit File Type dialog box for this association (discussed in the next section) is not selected, Internet Explorer will open the file immediately, using the program defined for this file in the file's association.

▶ If the Confirm After Download option is selected, Internet Explorer will display a dialog box, asking if you want to open the file or save it to disk. When in doubt, you're better off leaving that option selected so that you'll have the opportunity to decide what to do when you encounter that file type.

▶ If the file has no association in Windows, Internet Explorer will display the dialog box shown in Figure 22.7 and let you decide how to proceed. If you decide to open the file from the Internet, you'll then have to choose the program that should be used.

Part vii

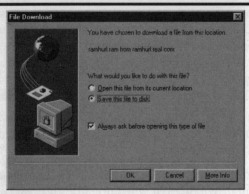

FIGURE 22.7:   When Internet Explorer encounters a file that it cannot handle, you can either open the file in its associated program (if there is one) or save the file to disk.

> ▶ If the file is a viewable file for which you do not have the proper viewer software or plug-in (say, an Audio or Video file) Internet Explorer will display a dialog box and let you know what software you need and where to get it from. You will also be prompted to decide if you want to go get it right then. See Figure 22.8 for an illustration.

FIGURE 22.8:   When Internet Explorer encounters a file for which you do not have the proper software or plug-in to display, it will prompt you with this dialog box.

When you are presented with the File Download dialog box, you can choose either to open the file in its associated program (if it has one) or simply save the file to disk. For several reasons, the latter choice is often the prudent one.

First, downloading a file from the Internet puts your computer at risk of being infected with a virus—who knows where that file has been lurking? When you save the file to disk, you can later run your virus-checking program on it to see if it gets a clean bill of health.

Another reason to save a file instead of opening it is to avoid the possible chaos of having too many things happening at the same time. While you're online browsing a Web site, an incoming program file that you opened might be setting up a new game on your computer, and the resulting clash might make a messy electronic battleground.

NOTE

You may often go to a Web site specifically to download a file, such as a program update for software you own. When you click on the link to the file, Internet Explorer displays the dialog box and asks you what you want to do with the file. Unless the site tells you to do otherwise, choose to save the file to disk.

Saving a file to disk is a neat trick because you can then deal with it later. You can still install that game or patch that software, but you'll do it when the time is right. Plus, with the file safely on disk, you can make a backup copy of it, if necessary, or pass it on to a friend or coworker.

As you can see, the way in which Internet Explorer handles a file depends on whether the file has an association under Windows and whether that association is by its MIME type or by its file name extension. The next section shows how you can view, create, revise, or delete a file association.

Setting File Associations

In Windows, when you choose to open a file outside the program that created it, such as by double-clicking the file in Windows Explorer, Windows must check to see which program is associated with that file type.

Windows makes the determination based on the file's extension (only Internet Explorer looks at a file's MIME type when you're connected to the Web or your intranet), which is the characters after the period in the filename (after the final period if there is more than one). Here are some

Part vii

common filename extensions that you may recognize and the file types that Windows assigns them:

.BAT	MS-DOS Batch File
.BMP	Bitmap Image
.EXE	Application
.HLP	Help File
.INI	Configuration Settings
.TTF	TrueType Font file
.WRI	Write Document

The extensions listed above are generic to Windows, in that those types are defined in a brand-new Windows installation. If you encounter one of these files in Internet Explorer and choose to open it, Windows takes over and performs the appropriate action.

For example, when you double-click a program file with a BAT or EXE extension, Windows simply runs the file. It opens an HLP file in the standard help viewer in Windows, as though you chose a command from a program's Help menu. In Windows 95, a WRI file opens in WordPad, and in Windows 3.1 that file opens in Write.

When you install new programs under Windows, the installation routine may add new file-type definitions to Windows. For example, when you install Microsoft Office, the following file types are defined (and there will be many more, as well):

.DOC	Microsoft Word Document
.WKB	Microsoft Word Backup Document
.XLS	Microsoft Excel Worksheet
.XLT	Microsoft Excel Template

NOTE

In this case, with the help of its ActiveX abilities, Internet Explorer can view Word (DOC) and Excel (XLS) documents. Therefore, if you have Word and Excel installed on your computer, you won't even be offered the Open/Save dialog box when you click a link to one of these files. Internet Explorer will open it.

The point to remember is this: Any file that can't be viewed within Internet Explorer is handled by the program with which its extension is associated in Windows (unless it has a MIME-type association, which will be used first). For example, when you attempt to open a file with a WKB file name extension, Windows tells Word to open that file.

You can also create your own file associations or revise existing ones. While viewing a folder (not a Web page) in any Explorer window, choose View ➤ Folder Options and select the File Types tab. You'll see the list of file types, similar to the one shown in Figure 22.9.

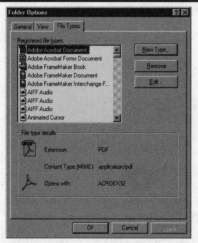

FIGURE 22.9:   You can view or revise file associations or create new ones in the File Types tab.

Part vii

DON'T ASK ME WHAT PROGRAM TO USE, JUST OPEN THE FILE!

How many times have you tried to open a file in Windows Explorer, only to be presented with the Open With dialog box (shown here), asking you to choose a program to use to open that file? The problem is that the file you want to open has no program associated with it under Windows, so Windows is stymied and now must wait for you to decide how to proceed. You'll also see this dialog box when

CONTINUED ➡

you choose to open a file in Internet Explorer and that file has no association.

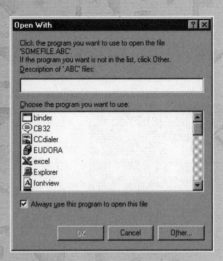

At this point, you can either choose a program from the list of associated programs already in Windows or click the Other button and select a program name from your disk drive.

For example, suppose in Internet Explorer you saved the file SOMEFILE .ABC, and in Windows Explorer you double-click the file to open it. Unless Windows on your computer has the file name extension ABC already associated with some program, you'll get the Open With dialog box.

If you know that this ABC file is, for example, a text file, you could choose Notepad from the list as the program to use to open it. If you're going to be working with more ABC files in the future, you could also select the Always Use This Program To Open This File option to establish an association between any ABC files and Notepad.

If the item named Internet Document (HTML) is selected in the list of file types, then beneath the list of file types you can see that:

▶ The file name extension recognized for this type of file is HTM or HTML.

▶ The MIME type for this type of file is *text/html*.

The name of the associated program that will be used to open this type of file is Explorer. You can revise this definition by clicking the Edit button, which displays the Edit File Type dialog box (where you'll find the Confirm Open After Download option, which was discussed in the previous section). For example, you could specify that FrontPage Express be associated with the editing of this file type so that when you right-click the file name and choose Edit, the file would open in that program. To create a completely new file association, click the New Type button.

NOTE

There are no laws establishing sole rights to a file name extension! Therefore, the name and associated program for any given file type could vary on different computers. For example, the DOC extension might be used by some other program. In fact, if you were to install that program on a computer that already has Microsoft Word installed, a new association would be established for DOC files. When you later double-click a DOC file, the other program, not Word, would be the one to open it.

WHAT'S NEXT

Gene Weisskopf and Pat Coleman took you on a whirlwind tour of Internet Explorer in this chapter and introduced you to the ways you can start the program; use its menus, toolbars, and keyboard shortcuts; and view different types of files. In the next chapter, they will teach you how to use your browser to find stuff on the Web.

Part vii

Chapter 23

SEARCHING THE WEB

T he concept of browsing the Web is a great one; clicking from link to link is a wonderful way to gather information. But the aspect that makes this process truly astounding is the seemingly endless extent of the Web. From our own perspective as users, the Web appears to be infinite in scope. No matter how many pages you could click through in one day, there would be many more new pages the next day! This chapter will help you to take advantage of this fabulous resource by introducing the basics of Web browsing.

Adapted from *Mastering Microsoft Internet Explorer 4* by Gene Weisskopf and Pat Coleman
ISBN 0-7821-2133-0   960 pages $44.99
This material has been updated for Internet Explorer 5.

The trick to using the Web is often just being able to find what you want, and that's what we're going to talk about in this chapter. There are many ways to find information on the Web, and you can use any number of them to corral material. The process of searching the Web can be as simple as:

1. Click the Search button on the toolbar.

2. In the Explorer bar on the left side of the window (discussed later in this chapter), select the search site you want to use.

3. Enter some keywords to describe what you want.

4. Click the Go button (it may be labeled Submit, Seek, or Search, depending on which search site you're using), and wait a few seconds while the results appear.

5. Click any of the links that were found to open that site, and see if that site contains what you want.

You can follow many paths while making a search, as you'll see in the sections that follow.

Performing a Search in Your Browser

You can initiate a search in several ways. Each of them can end up taking you to the same site, so feel free to experiment with them all to find the method that seems the most convenient.

You'll find that there are generally two ways to search the Web:

By keyword   Search for all pages that contain the keywords you specify. If you query with the keywords *bicycle* and *tours*, you'll find any pages that contain either one or both of those words, even if the mention is only a short "We do not conduct bicycle tours."

By topic   Browse through categories of topics until you find the category that interests you. You might start at the Leisure category, continue through the Travel subcategory, then on to a Bicycling subcategory, and finally into a Touring category for links to Web sites that relate to bicycle touring.

ENDLESSLY INDEXING THE WEB

The ability to search the Web for specific sites or files relies on one tiny factor: the existence of searching and indexing sites that you can access to perform the search. These sites are often known as Web spiders, crawlers, or robots, because they endlessly and automatically search the Web and index the content they find.

Search sites literally create huge databases of all the words in all the pages they index, and you can search those databases simply by entering the keywords you want to find. Despite the size of this vast store of information, they can usually return the results to you in a second or two. This is definitely a Herculean task with Sisyphean overtones (sorry about the mixed myths), because the Web is huge and continues to grow with no end in sight. Plus, a search engine must regularly return to pages it's already indexed because those pages may have changed and will need to be indexed again. Don't forget that many pages are removed from the Web each day and that a search engine must at some point remove those now invalid URLs from its database.

We'll be looking at some of the more popular search sites on the Web in this chapter. To give you an idea of just how big a job it is to search and index the Web, the AltaVista search site at www .altavista.com recently reported that its Web index as of that day covered 140 million pages from 1,158,000 host names on 627,000 servers. AltaVista also had indexed 15 million articles from 14,000 newsgroups. On top of that, this search site is accessed more than 36 million times each day.

Keeping track of what's on the Web is definitely a job for that infinite number of monkeys we've always heard about.

Part vii

Searching with the Explorer Bar

When you want to perform a search of the Web in Internet Explorer, you begin with the Explorer bar, which you can open by selecting View ➤ Explorer Bar ➤ Search, or clicking the Search button on the toolbar. Internet Explorer opens its Explorer bar, the separate pane on the left side of its window, while the page you had been viewing is displayed in the right pane. Figure 23.1 shows Internet Explorer with its window split into the two panes.

FIGURE 23.1: The Explorer bar allows you to perform a search in one pane and then sample its results while keeping those results on the screen.

TIP

You can close the search bar by choosing View ➢ Explorer Bar ➢ Search, clicking the Search button on the toolbar, or clicking the Close button at the top of the Explorer bar. In this way, you can toggle the search bar open or closed while still retaining the results of the last search you performed.

Once the Explorer bar is open, performing the search is as easy as entering the keywords you want to search for and selecting a search site from the list. For example, in Figure 23.1, I entered the search criteria **Form 1040** in the text-entry field (see "Searching the Web by Keywords" for tips on using quotes and logical operators when you create your query), and I selected the site named Infoseek. To perform the search, simply click the Search button.

In a second or two (or more if the Internet or the search site you chose is having a busy day), the results of the search will appear in the Explorer bar, as shown in Figure 23.2. In this example, only the first 10 results are displayed in the search bar. You can click a link at the bottom of the results to view the next 10.

NOTE

If none of the results looks right, you can create an entirely new search by entering new keywords into the text-entry field and clicking the Search button, or by selecting a different search site and starting from that one.

Each result is a link to the page that was found to contain the keywords you entered. The Infoseek search site, like most others, arranges the resulting links in order of their likelihood of matching your query. If you point to one of the links with your mouse, a ToolTip displays information about it, usually a short description of the target page, or the first few lines of text found on that page.

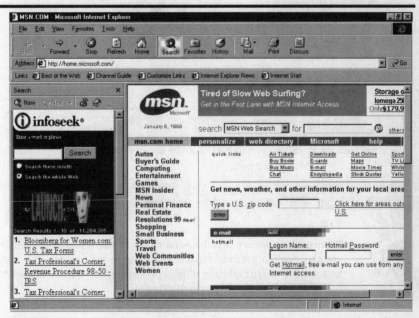

FIGURE 23.2: After you click the Search button in Internet Explorer, the results of the search will appear as links in the search bar.

In Internet Explorer, you can click a link in the search bar to open its target in the right pane. Figure 23.3 shows Internet Explorer after one of the links in the Explorer bar was clicked. The target page appears on the right, where you're free to work in it as you would with any other page. In fact, if this looks like a page you'll want to spend some time with, click the Search button to close the Explorer bar so you'll have the entire screen for the target page.

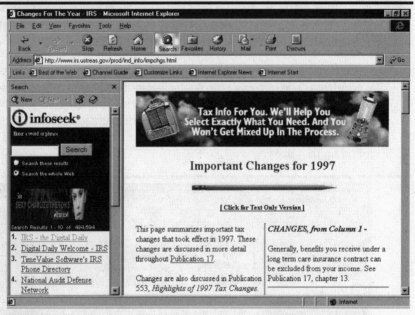

FIGURE 23.3:   When you click a link in the Explorer bar, its target is opened in the right pane.

TIP

When you're viewing one of the resulting pages from a search and you like what you see, don't forget to add that page to your Favorites menu. That way you'll be able to return to that page without performing another search. See "Saving the Results of a Search" later in this chapter.

Later in this chapter, you'll read about creating more complex queries on some of the other search sites. Now let's look another way to perform searches, using Microsoft's own aggregate search page.

Searching with Microsoft's Best of the Web Pages

You can perform a variety of searches through Microsoft's Best of the Web pages:

Best of the Web Click the Best of the Web button on the Links toolbar, or choose that command from the Favorites ➢ Links menu.

NOTE

If you don't have the button mentioned above on your links toolbar, and would like to use the page discussed in this section, you can check out Best of the Web at http://home.microsoft.com/exploring/exploring.asp. Make sure you drag the address to the links toolbar so you can access these pages easier later.

Best of the Web

This page, which is also called the Start Exploring page, offers links to a variety of topics such as Business and Finance, Computers and Technology, Living, and News. Each link takes you to another page where you'll find more links to sites within that category. See Figure 23.4. (Most of these best of the Web sites are generally solid, well-established sites but only "best" according to someone at Microsoft.)

The links you'll find here are updated frequently, so when you have a spare moment, you may want to stop by and see what's new.

TIP

When you have a results page open with its list of result links, such as at Info-seek, you don't have to leave that page in order to follow one of those links. Simply right-click a link and choose Open in New Window from the shortcut menu. The target will be displayed in a new browser window, leaving the search page available in the other window. Press Alt+Tab or click the taskbar to switch back to the search page as needed.

Part vii

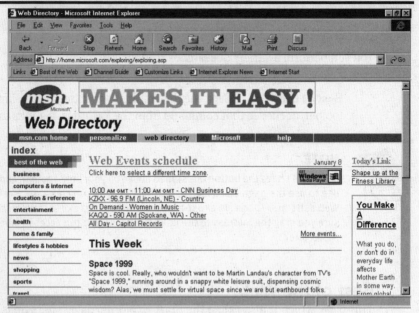

FIGURE 23.4:   The Best of the Web page lets you browse and search from a variety of topics.

Searching with the Address Toolbar

You can also perform a search right from the Address toolbar in your browser. Begin a query in the Address toolbar with the word Go or Find or with a question mark. Follow that with the topic you're interested in, for example, you might try any of the following three searches:

```
go weather Honolulu
find "border collie"
? "12-meter yacht"
```

SAVING THE RESULTS OF A SEARCH

When you perform a search that returns a list of pages, don't forget that you might want to save some of those pages so that you can return to them in the future. You can save the results of a search in several ways:

▶ Choose File ➢ Save As and save the page that displays the list of search results to your local disk, so you can open that file at any time to access those links.

CONTINUED ➡

> ▶ Right-click a link in the search results list, or open that page and add that page to your Favorites menu (your Bookmarks menu in Netscape).
>
> ▶ Open a page and save it to your local disk.
>
> ▶ Copy selected text or images from a page to another document.

SEARCHING THE WEB BY KEYWORDS

The most common way to search the Web is by entering keywords: Show me all pages that contain the words "cooking" and "French." In not much more than an instant, you'll be presented with a list of links to pages that contain those words. At many sites you can search the Web or newsgroups by keywords, and with most you go through the following steps:

1. Select the search site you want in your browser window or open the home page for that site.

2. Enter the keywords you're searching for in a data-entry field.

3. Click the Go or Search button.

4. Wait a second or two while the search site scans through its database and displays a page of results. For most search sites, each result includes a title for the page (based on the page's HTML title), which is actually a link right to that page, and a short description of the page.

5. Click one of the result links to open that page.

TIP

When you open a page via a result link from a search page, that page will contain the words you were searching for. But there's no guarantee that those words will be used in a context that's meaningful to you. Therefore, you might want to the Edit ➢ Find (Ctrl+F) command to find your keywords on that page and see whether they are relevant.

Part vii

The differences between the various keyword search sites are minor compared with the tremendous job any one of them can do for you. After all, how would you like to sift through a few dozen *million* pages trying to find those that contain a few specific words?

Some of the more popular keyword search sites include:

Search Engine	URL
AltaVista	www.altavista.com
Infoseek	www.infoseek.com
WebCrawler	www.webcrawler.com
Lycos	www.lycos.com
HotBot	www.hotbot.com

Performing a search by keyword can really be quite simple, but it can also be somewhat of an art. You'll get a glimmer of this the first time a search site finds several million pages that contain your keywords.

WARNING

Searching the Web is one time that you might run into a Web site whose content you find inappropriate or just plain disgusting. No matter what your tastes or moral standards might be, there's bound to be a site somewhere that flies off the scale of your Taste-o-Meter. So use caution when browsing through the list of results from a search, and realize that although all of them contain some or all the words or phrases you were searching for, some of these topics may not be what you wanted at all.

The search process will vary somewhat between the search sites, so you may need to use a somewhat different syntax to perform the same search at different sites. Nonetheless, some concepts apply to all of them, and you can generally follow some rules with success.

Although every keyword-search site claims to search the entire Web, performing the same query at different search sites will produce different results. This phenomenon might only have to do with how recently each site updated the pages that happened to be contained in your results. It might also have to do with how well the various sites carry on their searches and index their results. Whatever the differences, if a search is an important one that will have a limited number of results, taking that search to several sites will ensure that you're covering the possibilities.

Searching for a Simple Series of Words

The easiest way to perform a keyword search is to simply enter the words and hit the Go button. Let's try out a simple search at the AltaVista search site (www.altavista.com).

If you're interested in bicycling in the Pacific Northwest, simply enter **bicycling in the Pacific Northwest** in the search field and click the Search button. In an instant or two, the results will be displayed on the page, as shown in Figure 23.5.

TIP

According to the folks who know at AltaVista, about 75 percent of all Web pages are in English, which can make it difficult when you'd like to search for pages in another language. AltaVista has thought about that, and implemented multi-langage searches. Just select a language from the drop-down menu before you click the Search button.

Notice that AltaVista tells you how many pages (documents) were found in its index; in this case it's 596,030 (see Figure 23.5). Only the first 10 are shown; you access the rest via links at the bottom of the page.

Result Pages: 1 2 3 4 5 6 7 8 9 10 11 12 13 14 15 16 17 18 19 20   [Next >>]

At the bottom of the page, you'll also see how many occurrences were found for *each* of the words you specified: 108,048 for *bicycling*, and about 100,000 for *Pacific Northwest*. If you think that's a lot, notice also that the words *in* and *the* were found hundreds of millions of times but, thankfully, were ignored.

TIP

Even though the relevance of the results may range far and wide, they are ranked so that the pages with the most likely matches are at or near the top of the list. AltaVista assigns the highest rank to pages on which the keywords appear closest to the beginning of the page, such as in its title. Below that in ranking are pages on which the keywords appear close to one another. Finally, pages are ranked by the number of your keywords that appear within them (but not the number of times they might appear in a page).

AltaVista looks for pages that contain any of the words you specify, which is an OR relationship—find pages that contain this word *or* this word *or* this word, and so on. Some sites, such as HotBot, by default do the opposite with your simple search and will only find pages that contain all the words you specify. This is an AND relationship—find pages that contain this word *and* this word *and* this word, and so on.

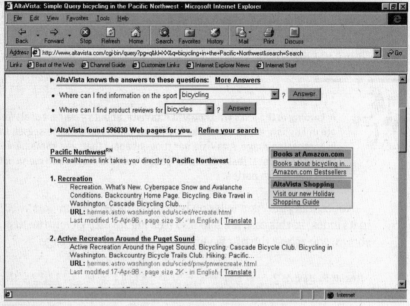

FIGURE 23.5:   Performing a simple search at AltaVista produces a wide range of relevant pages.

Keep this issue in mind when you try out a new search site, because the difference between the two styles is astronomical in scope. Including more words in an AltaVista search broadens the scope of the search, whereas doing so in a HotBot search narrows the scope. With either search site, however, you're assured that the most likely result pages will appear at the top of the list.

Now let's look at the different ways you can narrow your search so that the results more closely match what you really want.

TIP

AltaVista and several other search sites let you create a customized search page, just as you can do with customized start pages at other sites.

Searching for a Phrase

Although the previous example, where you typed **bicycling in the Pacific Northwest**, seemed like a reasonably specific query, the AltaVista search site included all pages that contained any of those words, producing the broadest possible list of results.

To really enter a specific phrase as your query, enclose the text in double quotation marks and type **"bicycling in the Pacific Northwest"**.

When you enter keywords in this way, most search sites will look only for this exact phrase and will ignore all pages that might contain only a word or two. For example, the results of searching for *sled dogs* would return thousands of pages that happen to include the word *sled* or *dogs* anywhere in the page, and not just those pages that contain both words in the context of dogs that pull sleds. This would be the time to enclose the phrase in quotes and type **"sled dogs"**. Doing so would return only pages that include that specific phrase and would shorten the list of results drastically.

Unfortunately, in the bicycling example, the phrase we used might be a little too specific. Only that exact string of text will be looked for, which could easily eliminate some good bicycling pages that might not happen to include it. What might work better is to limit the search only to those pages that contain all these words.

Requiring That a Word Must or Must Not Exist

To require that a word in your query be found in the resulting pages, precede the word with a plus sign. Using our bicycling example, in AltaVista you could search only for pages that include both the word, "bicycling" and the phrase, "Pacific Northwest" and eliminate pages that contain only one of those (about 99 percent of the pages found in the first search!). To do so, type **+bicycling +"Pacific Northwest"**.

To exclude a word or a phrase from a search, precede it with a minus sign. For example, when searching for information about a mouse for your computer, you could eliminate some obvious mouse references to shorten the list of results, by typing **+mouse +computer –Mickey –rodent –rat –pet**.

NOTE

Use only lowercase letters in a query unless you want the search to be case-sensitive. In other words, searching for "president" will find all instances of that word, whereas searching for "President" will only find those instances in which the first letter is capitalized. However, be sure to capitalize words when you only want that specific spelling. For example, when searching for a restaurant named *The Brown Cow*, spell it exactly that way to avoid all pages that simply refer to brown cows.

Using Logical Operators

All the search sites have some method for you to specify the logical operators AND and OR in your queries (at the AltaVista site, you can use these operators when you choose their Advanced search option). You use OR to require that two words or phrases can appear separately in a page; you use AND to require that both appear together somewhere in that page. In the previous section, you saw how preceding a keyword with the plus sign makes that a required word in the query. If you precede two words with a plus sign, such as by typing **+mouse +computer** you are creating an AND relationship. You are looking for *mouse* and *computer* in the same document. If you did not use both plus signs, you would be creating an OR relationship.

At the HotBot site, you can select the relationship from a drop-down menu. Choosing "all the words" creates an AND relationship between the words or phrases you enter in the query. If you choose "any of the words", it's an OR relationship between them all.

At the WebCrawler site, you can literally include the words AND and OR in your queries (the case of the words doesn't matter) by typing, for example, **mouse and computer**.

NOTE

Because AltaVista ranks a result higher if that page contains more of your query words, there's less reason for you to worry about creating a logical relationship between the query terms.

You can create an OR relationship in an AltaVista query to include words that might relate to the subject you're interested in, such as by typing **bike biking bicycle bicycling + "Pacific Northwest"**.

By including multiple variations of a word, you may be able to find more pages that are on your topic of interest. The next section shows how you can widen or narrow a search by using wildcards.

Broadening a Search with Wildcards

You can use the asterisk (*) in an AltaVista query to search for any and all characters in place of the asterisk, so that typing **bicycl*** will help you find *bicycle*, *bicycles*, and *bicycling*, and typing **bicycl*s** will help you find only *bicycles*.

WARNING

The asterisk is truly a wildcard, in that it will find all the words that include the text you've entered before or after it, not only those words you might expect to find. In other words, the examples above would also find all occurrences of *bicyclette* or *bicyclettes* on a French Web site.

Another reason to try to include wildcards whenever you can is that, although computers never make mistakes, people just love to! While working with these queries on AltaVista, I mistakenly entered the query **bicyl***, which returned 700 pages in the results! In fact, the first few dozen results contained that misspelling in their page titles, which is the key ranking factor for AltaVista.

Granted, those pages undoubtedly also contained many instances of the correct spelling of bicycle, so they would have been found had we spelled the word correctly. Nonetheless, experiment with the use of wildcards or with variant spellings if the word you are searching for:

▶ Might only be included once or twice in a page, so that you would miss it if the spelling did not match yours precisely.

▶ Is often misspelled, such as *lazer* for *laser*, or *Laser Jet* for *LaserJet*.

▶ Has accepted variations in its spelling, such as *CD ROM* and *CD-ROM* or *floppy disc* and *floppy disk*.

Searching through Page Elements

At most of the search sites, you can limit your search to specific elements of the Web page. For example, at AltaVista you preface what you're looking for with the name of the page component and a colon. At other search sites, look at the Help page to see how you should format a query.

Part vii

To search for the word *bicycle* only in page titles in AltaVista, type **title:bicycle**. Only the titles of the pages in this Web index will be searched, and all other portions of the page will be ignored. Some of the other page components you can search include:

text Searches only the normal text in the page that you would see were you viewing the page in Internet Explorer.

link Searches only within HTML anchor tags in a page, allowing you to find all pages that contain a link to whitehouse.gov, for example (see the next section).

image Searches only within HTML image tags, allowing you to find references to specific image files, such as monalisa.jpg.

domain Searches only within pages from the domain you specify, allowing you to limit a search only to URLs that are in the *gov* (U.S. government) or *uk* (United Kingdom) domains, for example.

You can combine these constraints to find, for example, pages that have *bicycle* in their title, the word *touring* in the normal text on the page, and are only in the British domain:

```
title:bicycle text:touring domain:uk
```

At AltaVista, enter these page component keywords in lowercase, don't forget the colon, and don't include a space on either side of the colon.

Finding Who Links to Whom

If you have a Web site of your own, you'd probably like to know what other sites on the Web contain links to your site's URL. Several search sites make it easy for you to perform this type of search by using the *link* keyword mentioned in the previous section.

At the AltaVista and Infoseek sites, enter the query in this way: **link: http://www.sample.com**.

At the HotBot search site, enter the URL and set the search options so you are searching on *the Web* for *Links to this URL*.

SEARCHING THE WEB BY CATEGORY

So far in this chapter we've looked at how you can search the Web for all pages that contain one or more keywords or phrases that you specify. As mentioned at the beginning, searching the Web in this way is much like looking up a word in the index of a book, where you will find the page numbers of all references to that word in the book. If you think of the Web as the book and URLs as page numbers, you've got the idea.

Now we're going to look at another way to search the Web that isn't quite so literal. With this method, you go to the search site and browse through a category of topics. This method of searching the Web is more like browsing through the table of contents of a book, where the book is broken down by categories (chapters or sections). You can turn to a chapter that seems to relate to the topic you're interested in, but there's no way to tell just what you'll find there. You might be disappointed, or you might be quite surprised to find other topics that mesh quite nicely with the one you wanted.

NOTE

Most of the concept search sites can also perform a literal, keyword search of the Web, so you can attack your query from either direction.

Some of the more popular concept search sites include:

Search Engine	URL
Yahoo	www.yahoo.com
Excite	www.excite.com
Magellan	www.mckinley.com

Yahoo is probably the most well-known site, no doubt because it was the first. The Magellan site is owned by the company that owns the Excite search site, and it uses the same database of Web sites. But Magellan is notable because it has a team of editors who actually visit thousands of sites, rating them and writing short reviews of them. Magellan also has a special category of *Green Light sites* that contain no material that would be unsuitable for children (according to the standards in effect at Magellan).

When you access the Yahoo site, you'll be presented with the page shown in Figure 23.6. As you can see, there is a familiar search field at the top of the page, but beneath that are two columns of categories. You can click one of the categories to open a page of subcategory links, and you can continue to click until you narrow the search to a page that contains links to actual Web sites in the chosen subcategory.

TIP

Some Yahoo categories have an [Xtra] link tacked onto them. Each of these opens a page of current news headlines about the topic. For example, click the [Xtra] link on the Health category to see headlines relating to issues in health.

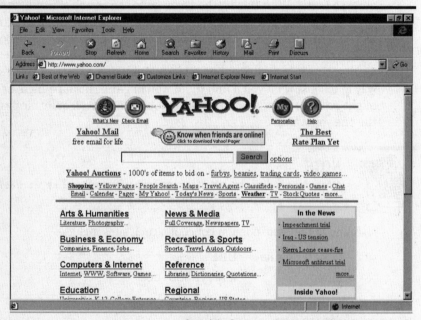

FIGURE 23.6:   At the Yahoo search site, you can click your way through categories of topics to find the one that interests you.

Choosing the Right Path

Before you can even begin a search through the categories of Yahoo, you need to have an idea not only of what you're looking for but also of *why* you're looking for it! For example, suppose you want to find sites that relate to bicycling. Sounds simple, but realize that categories can overlap. Many categories could include some aspect of bicycling.

Are you interested in bicycling from a rider's standpoint? If so, you might start with the Recreation and Sports category. If you're looking for a list of bike stores on the Web, you might start with the Business and Economy category. If laws relating to bicycles in your state are your primary interest, you could start with the Regional category.

Some topics are more easily categorized and will be easier to find. For example, if you want to learn about creating Web pages, you could click your way through the following links (in Yahoo syntax, categories are separated from subcategories with a colon):

```
Computers and Internet: Internet: World Wide Web: Authoring
```

Sometimes following a minor interest by browsing through Yahoo can produce impressive results. For example, while you were on your way to the Authoring page in Yahoo, you might take a sidetrack through the categories

```
Computers and Internet: Information and Documentation: Data
Formats: HTML
```

You would find a wealth of information that is only slightly off the subject you were intending to find, but surrounds it, overlaps it, and expands upon it.

Clicking through the Yahoo Categories

Let's attack the bicycling topic from a rider's point of view and say that we want to know about bicycling in the Pacific Northwest, which we searched for earlier with a keyword search.

Start by clicking the Recreation and Sports link on the Yahoo home page. This opens another page that lists the main subcategories for Recreation and Sports, including Amusement and Theme Parks, Automotive, Dance, Drugs, Motorcycles, and Travel. There are no specific links to bicycles, so we're still feeling our way along at our current location:

```
Recreation:
```

We could try the Travel link to branch out in a travel-related direction, but let's click the Sports link to head in a more bicycle-specific direction. The Sports link opens a page of sports-related links, one of which is called Cycling (no, not Bicycling; you have to keep your wits about you when you're looking for subjects of interest).

TIPS FOR NAVIGATING YAHOO

Each main category on the home page has several popular subcategories listed below it. If one of those subcategories looks relevant, click it to go directly to that topic's page.

To the right of many subcategory links in Yahoo, enclosed in parentheses, is the number of Web sites that will be found within this category. For example, if you see

```
Baseball (2778)
```

this means that a total of 2,778 Web sites are listed within the Baseball category. This doesn't mean that all those sites are listed on the next page. Rather, it means that the Baseball link will lead you to that many sites beneath it.

When a subcategory is followed by an at symbol, such as

```
Recreation: Sports: Art@
```

this category is not in a direct path from your current location. In this case, the Art category actually belongs in

```
Arts: Thematic: Sports
```

In other words, the Art link is one instance in which categories overlap.

Keep in mind that Yahoo places the links to Web sites (if there are any) beneath the category links on the page, so be sure to check down below, as there just might be a site that you will want to investigate.

As shown here, at the top of each Yahoo category page, you'll find the path that you've taken to reach the current category, as well as a search field. The path gives you a quick frame of reference for your current location. You can use the search field as you would a literal keyword search site, and you can choose whether to search all of Yahoo or only those sites that fall within the current category (Sports in this case).

Top:Recreation:Sports:Cycling

[   ] Search Options

⊙ Search all of Yahoo ○ Search only in **Cycling**

TIP

The larger Yahoo categories will have a Sub Category Listing link near the top of the page, which you can click to see the entire list of subcategories for a topic. The topics will be arranged in an indented, outline format. These lists can be *very* long, however, so don't bother opening one unless you're going to be searching for a variety of subcategories within that topic.

Clicking the Cycling link is an obvious choice at this point. It opens a page that contains not just more subcategory links, but some actual links to Web sites that fall into this category (remember to look below the category links for the site links). Eureka! We're getting down to the details.

You can look at any of the site links that seem interesting, but if none do the trick, you should still be happy that the category links on this page

```
Recreation: Sports: Cycling
```

are much more relevant. In fact, just about any one of them might lead to topics that relate to bicycling in the Pacific Northwest. This is actually a hurdle of sorts because it leaves too many options open. But it is also an opportunity to explore other aspects of bicycling that might end up showing you much more than you expected to find.

For our search, clicking the Tours and Events link seems like a good choice. In fact, right at the top of its target page at

```
Recreation: Sports: Cycling: Tours and Events
```

is the category link Tour Operators@, which steps outside of our current category and points to

```
Business and Economy: Companies: Sports: Cycling: Tour
Operators
```

Before you follow that tempting link, however, take a look on the current page at the links to Web sites, as shown in Figure 23.7. All of them relate to companies or organizations that conduct bicycle tours, many of which operate in the Pacific Northwest.

Where to go from here? You can see that finding sites via categories is a subjective and variable undertaking. If you were to repeat a search a day or two later, you might take a completely different route through the categories.

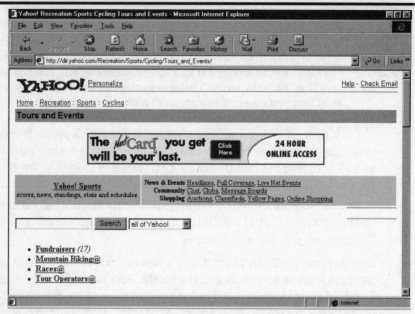

FIGURE 23.7:   As you narrow your search through the Yahoo categories, you'll find Web site links outnumbering the category links.

FINDING PEOPLE ON THE INTERNET

Some search sites specialize in finding people, and you'll be amazed at how fast you can locate that high school chum you used to hang out with or a dozen people who all go by your name.

Of course, you can use any of the search sites we've discussed so far in this chapter to find people's names when they appear in Web pages. Simply search for the person's name, but be sure to enclose it in quotes to get only that name.

With the people-finding search sites, you can find an individual's e-mail address, telephone number, or mailing address. If you want to find out where that person is right now, well, you'll have to wait a few years for that.

All these people-finding sites are quite simple to use, and you'll know soon enough if the results are helpful or not.

Let's try the WhoWhere site as an example. You can access it either from Microsoft's Search the Web page or at the URL www.whowhere .lycos.com. Figure 23.8 shows the WhoWhere home page.

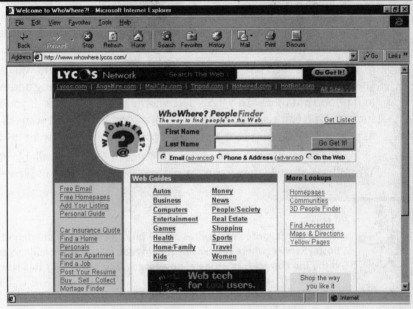

FIGURE 23.8: You can search for people through search sites such as the WhoWhere site.

You can search for a person's e-mail address from this page or for his or her phone number and mailing address. For example, to find an e-mail address, simply enter the person's name in the Name field (quotes aren't required), and in the Domain field enter their e-mail server domain name, such as att.net or aol.com.

TIP

If the person's name is reasonably unique, you can try entering only his or her name. You might get lucky and find only the person you're looking for or perhaps just a few people with that same name. With any luck, you'll be able to decide which one is most likely the one you're looking for.

Click the Go Get It button, and in a second or two the list of results will be displayed. Each result is a *mailto* link to that person's e-mail address, so clicking a name creates a new message to that person in your e-mail program.

To find a person's mailing address and phone number, enter as much as you know about that person in the Last Name (required), First Name, City, and State fields, and then click the Find button. The results won't be a link this time, but will be the information you might find in that person's local phone book.

If you want to ensure that someone else will be able to find you through this site, you can register your own name, e-mail and mailing addresses, and phone number with WhoWhere via the Get Listed link. If you're so inclined, you can also add more personal information about yourself, such as your hobbies, your place of employment, and where you went to school.

You'll also want to check out the other search features available at the WhoWhere site, which you can see in the left-hand column in Figure 23.8.

TIP

One of our favorite search sites on the Internet is that of the United States Postal Service, where you can find the zip code for any street address and also verify the correct formatting of an address. You can access this site at www .usps.gov/postofc/.

SEARCHING THROUGH NEWSGROUPS

Newsgroups are the place to go to exchange information with people of similar interests. You can use Outlook Express News to access Usenet (the User Network) and its tens of thousands of newsgroups. You can read articles (messages) that were posted by other people, respond to those that interest you or for which you have an answer, post your own questions, and generally just browse about to see what looks good.

Usenet has a mountain of information but, just like the Web, finding what's relevant is the hard part. Fortunately, most of the Web search sites also let you search newsgroups. Creating a query is much the same as when you search the Web. However, the results will often range far and wide in relevance, because a newsgroup article is simply one person sending a message that happens to contain the words or phrases you were searching for.

Searching through Newsgroups at AltaVista

To search through newsgroups at the AltaVista search site, choose Usenet in the Specialty Searches links under the main search area. Then enter your query as you would when searching the Web, and click the Search button when you're finished.

For example, to find all newsgroup articles that mention bicycling and the Pacific Northwest, you could try typing **+bicycling +"Pacific Northwest"**. Figure 23.9 shows the results from this query.

NOTE

Don't forget that a message that includes your search keywords doesn't necessarily relate at all to the act of bicycling in the Pacific Northwest. The mention of your search terms could be as irrelevant as "my friend John likes bicycling to work . . . doesn't Microsoft have a subsidiary called the Pacific Northwest?"

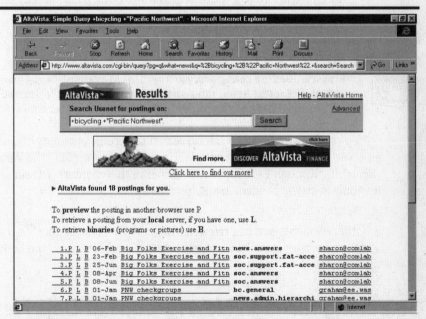

FIGURE 23.9:   When you search through newsgroups at AltaVista, you can read the articles in the results list or send e-mail to an article's author.

Looking from left to right in Figure 23.9, each item in the AltaVista results list contains the following:

▶ The item number and a small icon; click either one to open this article in a new browser window.

▶ The L link, which you can click to open the article in your newsreader program.

▶ The B link, which you can click to download the article as a plain text file. This would allow you to convert any binary files that are attached to the article, such as an image file.

▶ The date the article was posted.

▶ The article header (title), in which the author describes the subject of the article; click the header to open the article in your browser.

▶ The newsgroup to which the article was posted.

▶ The e-mail address of the article's author (which may or may not be the author's actual address).

NOTE

To post articles to a newsgroup, you'll need to use a newsreader program such as Outlook Express News, although the Web site Deja News (discussed next) allows you to read and write to newsgroups through your Web browser.

You can narrow your newsgroup search to specific elements of a newsgroup article, just as you can with Web pages when searching the Web (see "Searching through Page Elements" earlier in this chapter). To search the text only in article headers, use *subject,* as in:

```
subject:bicycling
```

Other elements you can reference include *from* (the sender's e-mail address), *newsgroups* (the newsgroup name), and *summary* (the body of the article).

Searching through Newsgroups at Deja News

Perhaps the premier site for newsgroup-related information is Deja News at www.dejanews.com. Its search engine not only indexes all the articles that pass through thousands and thousands of newsgroups, but also archives them so that they'll always be available (Deja News claims to have upwards of 100 million articles). Most newsgroup servers regularly delete articles after a few days or weeks to make room for newer ones, so Deja News is the place to go when you're searching for in-depth information or when you want to recover articles you saw in a newsgroup months earlier.

You can also search for newsgroups by topic. Instead of getting a list of articles in the results, you get a list of newsgroups that are ranked by the number of times your query keywords are contained in their articles. This not only gives you a quick look at which newsgroups might be of interest to you, but you can also click one of the results to display a list of headers from all the articles in that newsgroup that contain your query keywords. You can then click one of the articles to open it in Internet Explorer.

With the Power Search feature in Deja News, you can perform a very detailed search of newsgroup articles, both in their current index of newsgroups (compiled from articles during the previous two or three months) or in their archived index of newsgroups. Figure 23.10 shows the Power Search form where you specify any or all of the criteria for the search.

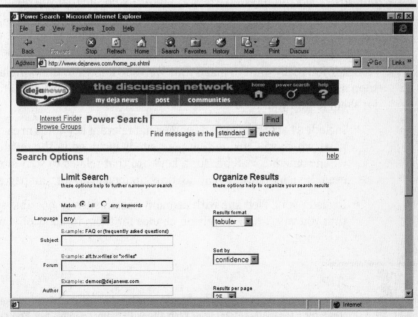

FIGURE 23.10: With the Deja News Power Search, you can easily fine-tune the scope of a Usenet search.

To increase the power of a Power Search, you can create a Search Filter. The filter lets you narrow the scope of the search by limiting it to a range of dates, newsgroups, authors, or subjects. Plus, when you've applied a Search Filter, your search automatically looks through both the current and archived set of newsgroup articles.

NOTE

When you are creating a new newsgroup message (article) in Outlook Express News (or any other newsreader), you can specify that newsgroup search spiders exclude your article from their indexes. Simply include the text *X-no-archive: yes* in the message's first line, or look in your newsreader for a command that puts this flag in the message header. Realize that your message will still appear publicly in that newsgroup, but most spiders will respect your request and not index your article.

BEING FOUND ON THE WEB

It's important to be able to find things on the Web, but it's just as important *to be found* on the Web when you have a Web site that you don't want the world overlooking. Of course, without your doing anything at all, the pages in your site will probably be found soon enough by one or more of the search sites, as they blast through the Web, indexing all that they find.

But if you really want to make your Web site known to the world as soon as possible, you'll want to go to the search sites instead of waiting for them to find you:

- ▶ Include a list of relevant and somewhat relevant keywords in each page, which will ensure that your site is included in the results when someone searches for a keyword that relates to your site, even though that word may not be contained in any of your pages.

- ▶ Register your Web site with as many search sites as possible so that you won't have to rely on chance for them to know of your existence.

TIP

If you want to cover the most ground in the least amount of time, use services that, for a fee, will register your Web site with many search sites. You can find a list of these services in the Yahoo category Computers and Internet: Internet: World Wide Web: Announcement Services.

Of course, being found on the Web is usually the whole point, but you can also work to exclude your Web site or some of its pages from the various search sites, as you'll see later in this section.

Including Keywords in Your Pages

A Web author can take advantage of the fact that just about all search sites recognize the HTML <META> tag when they are indexing a Web page. This tag allows the author to specify the description of the page, as well as a list of keywords. Both types of information are critical to the likelihood of your site being found through a query in a search site.

By supplying relevant keywords, your site is more likely to be included in the results of a relevant query, and the description ensures that a person reading those results will have a clear understanding of your site's purpose. The keywords you supply for a page are a supplement to the normal indexing of the page, not a substitution for it.

The <META> tag is an informational tag for Web servers and browsers, not for the person reading the page. You can use two of these tags to provide a description and keywords for Web robots that visit your site, using the format:

```
<META NAME="description" CONTENT="This is a description of
the page">
<META NAME="keywords" CONTENT="keyword1, keyword2, keyword3">
```

NOTE

If you don't provide the description in this way, a search site's indexing engine will most likely use the first few lines of text in the page, without making any value judgements about whether that text is a helpful description.

For example, if you run the Superman Fans Web site, you might include the following tags at the beginning of its home page (they're shown on multiple lines for clarity):

```
<TITLE>Superman Fans Home Page</TITLE>
<META NAME="description" CONTENT=
"Looking for the Man of Steel? We have a complete list of
every Superman comic, and lots more.">
<META NAME="keywords" CONTENT="comic, comic book, clark kent,
krypton, kryptonite, daily planet">
```

When someone searches for *Superman* at AltaVista, the results would look something like the following:

Superman Fans Home Page

Looking for the Man of Steel? We have a complete list of every Superman comic, and lots more.

http://www.sample.com/ - size 15K - 28 Jan 99

AltaVista allows a maximum of 1024 characters in the description and list of keywords and ensures that the words in both those items will be included in its index. Infoseek uses a maximum of 200 characters in the description and 1000 characters in the keywords. Before you include the <META> tag in pages in your Web site, check with a few other search sites to get their current rules.

WARNING

In years past, search sites employed a less sophisticated algorithm when indexing Web pages. If a word you were searching for appeared many times in a page, that page would show up at the top of the list of results. This encouraged some Web authors to include a few hundred repetitions of a keyword in their pages, simply to get a higher ranking in a list of search results. This practice, often known as *spamming*, is not only frowned upon, but is also no longer effective with today's search sites. In fact, most search sites will either ignore repeated occurrences of a word or actually exclude that page from their index.

Registering with a Search Site

Most search sites let you send your Web site's URL to them so the pages in your site can be included in their indexes. This process of registering is an informal one, in that it costs nothing and requires little more than sending them your URL.

At the AltaVista search site, you can register a URL by clicking the Add a Page URL link that you'll find at the bottom of the home page. On the Adding a New URL page that is opened, you simply enter the URL of your Web site (which must begin with HTTP) and click the Submit URL button. That's really all there is to it.

AltaVista asks that you send just one URL for your entire site, which might as well be the home page for that site. A new URL is usually added to their index within one day. Their searching program will snoop throughout your site and find and index all the other pages.

The Infoseek search site has a similar registration process, but that site does not tell you to submit just one page from the site. You can either register each page individually or create a list of pages and submit them all in one e-mail.

The easiest way to register your site at Yahoo is to locate the category within which you think your site belongs and then click the Add URL button, which you'll find at the top of the page. This opens the registration page, where you enter the URL of your site and a title and description for its listing in Yahoo. You can also enter secondary categories and regional information. The more you provide, the easier it will be to find your site on Yahoo. Be sure to take note of the three or four rules pertaining to registering business sites, personal Web pages, and the like.

Removing Pages from a Search Site

Most search sites also provide a way for you to unregister (remove) a page that's already in their index. This is actually quite important, because you won't attract many visitors to your site through searching if people have to fight their way through a dozen old and now invalid URLs.

The AltaVista search site and most others will automatically remove any page whose URL can no longer be found (the infamous "error 404" message). Therefore, you can remove a page from their index immediately simply by registering the page's now invalid URL. This will cause the Web robot to check this URL, which it will find to be invalid and will therefore remove it from the index.

Excluding Pages from Search Robots

You can also exclude a page or an entire Web site from the prying robots of search sites, although you will find that there is not yet just one accepted way to do so. One method that is used by several search sites, and may yet become an accepted standard, requires that you place a special text file called ROBOTS.TXT in the root folder of the Web server. The file includes instructions to search robots that visit the site about what can be searched and what should be excluded from the search.

Part vii

NOTE

The ROBOTS.TXT file does not prevent a search robot from requesting one or more pages from the site; it only asks the robots to exclude them. In other words, it's a voluntary system that allows search sites to index the Web without getting a bad reputation from Web site administrators who either don't want the extra traffic caused by robots or want to keep some pages out of the search indexes.

Here's a ROBOTS file that asks that the entire Web site be excluded by all search robots:

```
User-agent: *
Disallow: /
```

The asterisk is the wildcard that represents any and all search robots, and the slash represents the root folder of the server and, therefore, all files and folders within it.

You can also specify individual search robots and selective folders. For example, if you want to exclude the entire site from AltaVista, and you want to exclude the folders /users and /logs from every other site, the following would do the job:

```
User-agent: altavista
Disallow: /

User-agent: *
Disallow: /users

User-agent: *
Disallow: /logs
```

You can read more about using a ROBOTS file to mitigate the effect of search robots at the WebCrawler site:

```
info.webcrawler.com/mak/projects/robots/faq.html
```

You can also ask Web robots to exclude an individual page from their search, as well as all the pages that are targeted by its links, by including a <META> tag in the page:

```
<META NAME="ROBOTS" CONTENT="NOINDEX, NOFOLLOW">
```

Again, this is not yet an accepted standard, but it is respected by several of the major search sites.

WHAT'S NEXT

Your tour of the Internet has come to a close. You've learned the basics of Web usage and seen how to use Internet Explorer to effectively search the Web. Now it's time to take this to another level. Part 8 will throw you into the world of Web publishing. You'll get a look at how Web pages are made, and run through a crash course in using Microsoft FrontPage.

PART viii
INTRODUCTION TO WEB PUBLISHING

Chapter 24

Introducing Web Pages and HTML

This chapter introduces you to the way in which Web documents are built with the *Hypertext Markup Language* (HTML). You'll learn about the features of the language you'll encounter within the pages you browse in Internet Explorer.

There is no need to consider this chapter required reading if you just want to browse the Web (see Chapter 23 for that!). You can certainly use the Web without any knowledge of the HTML code that lies beneath all Web pages. But your browsing experience on the Web will be greatly enhanced if you do take the time to become familiar with the basic concepts of HTML.

Recognizing the common elements in virtually all Web pages will help you feel more at home on the Web. And if you're ready to build your own Web pages, this chapter will give you a solid background in the process.

Adapted from *Mastering Microsoft Internet Explorer 4*, by Gene Weisskopf and Pat Coleman

ISBN 0-7821-2133-0   960 pages $44.99

This material has been updated for Internet Explorer 5.

An Overview of HTML

You create Web pages with the Hypertext Markup Language, or HTML. In keeping with the original and ongoing theme of the Internet—openness and portability—the pages you create with HTML are just plain text. You can create, edit, or view the HTML code for a Web page in any text editor on any computer platform, such as Windows Notepad.

Although creating simple Web pages in a text editor is easy, it can quickly turn into a grueling and mind-numbing task. That's why there are Web-authoring tools, such as FrontPage, which let you create HTML Web pages in the same way you create documents in your word processor.

Viewing HTML Pages

When you open a Web page in Internet Explorer (or any other Web browser), you don't see the HTML code that creates the page. Instead, Internet Explorer interprets the HTML code and displays the page appropriately on the screen. If you're creating a Web page in a text editor and want to view the file you're working on, save your work and open the file in your browser. You can then continue to edit, save your work, and view the results, switching back and forth between the text editor and the browser to see the effects of your edits.

The original intent of the HTML specification was to allow Web authors to describe the structure of a page without spending too much time worrying about the look of a page—that part of the job was left to the browsers. Traditionally, each browser had its own way of interpreting the look of the page, and Web authors had to live with the fact that pages they created might appear somewhat differently in different browsers. Authors merely shrugged their shoulders and were happy that their pages could be viewed so easily from anywhere on the planet.

Here's an example of the inherent flexibility that was designed into the HTML specification: Later in this chapter, you'll read about the six HTML codes you can use for creating six levels of headings in a Web page. You as an author can specify that a paragraph of text be defined as one of the six heading levels, but the HTML heading code does *not* describe what that heading should look like. It merely says something to the effect that "I'm a level two heading." It's up to the Web browser to differentiate each type of heading from the others. One browser might display the first-level heading in a large font that is centered on the page, while another browser might display it in italics and left-aligned on the page. That's why authors try to test their pages in several of the more popular browsers.

Speaking of popular browsers, the good news is that the browser market has been consolidating and standardizing. You'll find few differences in the way Internet Explorer and other browsers display the widely accepted HTML features in a page. Of course, new HTML features are being promoted all the time. Web authors must decide whether to include a new feature in a page, when that feature may not be well interpreted by some browsers.

HTML Elements and Tags

A Web page is made up of *elements*, each of which is defined by an HTML code, or *tag*. A tag is always enclosed in angle brackets, and most tags come in pairs, with an opening and a closing tag. The closing tag is the same as the opening tag, but starts with a forward slash.

For example, to define text as a first-level heading in HTML, you use the <H1> tag, as in:

```
<H1>This Is a Main Heading</H1>
```

A browser interprets these tags and displays the text within the tags appropriately (as shown below). But the tags themselves are not displayed within a browser, unless there is a problem with a tag, such as if one of the angle brackets was mistakenly left out (although most browsers will ignore any codes within angle brackets that they do not recognize).

This Is a Main Heading

And this is Internet Explorer's normal text.

Some tags have optional or required attributes. An *attribute* is usually a keyword that takes one of several possible values (you define each value by enclosing it in quotes). For example, the heading tag can take an optional alignment attribute:

```
<H1 ALIGN="CENTER">This is a main heading that is
centered</H1>
```

NOTE

You can create a tag in either upper- or lowercase; it doesn't matter to a browser. For example, the two tags <H1> and <h1> are equivalent to a browser. In this chapter, we're using all uppercase for consistency and clarity.

The Essentials of a Web Page

Every Web page must include a few tags that define the page as a whole so that when a browser receives the page it will recognize it as such. For example, the following HTML code will produce the page that is shown in Internet Explorer in Figure 24.1 (it could also be viewed in any other browser):

```
<HTML>
<HEAD>
<TITLE>Greetings from the Web</TITLE>
</HEAD>
<BODY>
<P>Hello, world!</P>
</BODY>
</HTML>
```

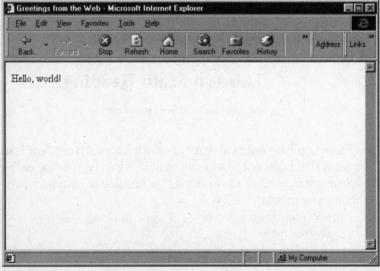

FIGURE 24.1:   A sample page displayed in Internet Explorer

Remember, this code is just a text file, plain and simple. Table 24.1 lists the tags that should be included in every page so that any browser can view it:

TABLE 24.1: Essential HTML Tags for a Page

TAG	PURPOSE
<HTML>	Declares that the text that follows defines an HTML Web page that can be viewed in a Web browser. The closing </HTML> tag ends the page.
<HEAD>	Defines the header area of a page, which is not displayed within the page itself in the browser. The closing </HEAD> tag ends the header area.
<TITLE>	The text between this tag and the closing </TITLE> tag is the title of the Web page and is displayed in the title bar in Internet Explorer, as shown in Figure 24.1. The title should be descriptive, as it is frequently used by Web indexing and searching programs to name your Web page. In Internet Explorer, a page's title serves as the default name when you save the page as a favorite location.
<BODY>	Delineates the actual content of the Web page that will be displayed in Internet Explorer. In the example above, only the words *Hello, world!* will appear within the browser. Most of the other HTML features that we will discuss in this chapter always appear within the <BODY> and </BODY> tags in a Web page. There are several optional attributes for this tag. One of them is BACKGROUND, with which you can specify a background graphical image for the page.
<P>	Use the paragraph tag to mark the beginning of a new paragraph; the ending tag, </P>, is optional but should be included for clarity (whenever you or someone else needs to inspect or revise this code). You can include the ALIGN attribute to specify whether the paragraph should be centered or right-aligned in the page (left-aligned is the default).

There are dozens and dozens of other HTML tags you can incorporate into a Web page. The ones you use and how you use them depends only on your design, capabilities, and imagination.

NOTE

There is one important tag whose effects you won't notice in Internet Explorer, but you will appreciate when you're editing or viewing the HTML code for a page. You use the <COMMENT> tag to create descriptive comments within the code, which will be ignored by a browser. You can also use this combination of symbols to create a comment: <!- This text is a comment. ->

ADDING SPACES AND BLANK LINES FOR READABILITY

You can include extra spaces and blank lines in HTML code to make the code easier for you or others to read and interpret. When Internet Explorer (or any other browser) opens a Web page, it ignores multiple spaces within the code and displays them as a single space. It also ignores all hard returns within the code, such as when you press Enter at the end of a line of text you're editing in Notepad. Therefore, any blank lines you create in the code by pressing Enter a few times will not be displayed in Internet Explorer.

There is one HTML tag in which spaces and hard returns in the HTML code *do* count, and that is the preformatted tag, <PRE>. It instructs a browser to display the text in a monospaced font that allows you to align text precisely, such as you would when showing a program listing.

Learning HTML

As more and more of the world's documents end up as Web pages, we will all be viewing, creating, and modifying them as part of our daily routine. Learning about HTML will give you an understanding of how it works and how it looks in use, which will prove invaluable to your Web-browsing experience. But please rest assured that in this book we have absolutely no intention of molding you into a code cruncher!

With the proliferation of elegant HTML editors such as FrontPage, it is unlikely that a text editor will be your first tool of choice for creating Web pages. Unless you really take off in the science and art of Web-page authoring, you will probably never have to become an HTML jockey, and you will forego the pleasure of wrangling your way through screenfuls of angle brackets, slashes, and esoteric codes.

NOTE

Creating a successful Web page requires a good deal from both sides of your brain—the logical side that helps you write computer programs, and the artistic side that helps you compose a tasteful, inviting document. That's why it's important to have several people test and critique your Web efforts, since few of us can lay full claim to both sides of our brains!

You can learn about HTML in many ways without specifically studying it. Perhaps the most important method is already staring you in the face when you're browsing the Web in Internet Explorer—the pages themselves. All Web pages are built from the same text-based HTML language, so when you're viewing a page in Internet Explorer that strikes your interest, stop and take a look at that page's underlying code. You can do so in two ways:

- ▶ Choose View ➤ Source to display the current page's HTML code within Notepad. You can then view the code to your heart's content or save it to disk for later use.

- ▶ If you know you'll want to spend some time with the HTML code later on, you can save the current page to your local disk from within Internet Explorer by choosing File ➤ Save As. The resulting HTML file is the HTML code from which the page was built (but it will not include any of the graphic images from the page).

By viewing the HTML code for a page, you can get a feeling for how the page was created.

If you want to learn more about encoding Web pages, you can find countless books and even more Web sites devoted to that subject. A great place to start is Microsoft's Site Builder Network:

    www.microsoft.com/sitebuilder/

It is designed primarily for "Web professionals," but the complexity and depth of the material on the site ranges far and wide. It has thousands and thousands of pages, hundreds of megabytes of downloadable software, and great links to other Web-related resources. You'll also find countless examples of what you can build in your Web site, especially when you are using Microsoft's Web technology.

Anyone interested in building or browsing Web sites will find something of value here. If you want to access the entire site, you'll need to register as a member of the Site Builder Network, which is free for a basic membership.

Another site related to the Site Builder Network is the Site Builder Workshop:

    www.microsoft.com/workshop/

You could easily spend days browsing through this huge collection of information (all of which is current) about designing, building, and running Internet and intranet Web sites.

Another site that we found via the Microsoft site is the Web Design Workgroup. This informal association of Web-page designers was founded to help other designers create truly portable Web pages that could be viewed by any browser on any computer platform:

    www.htmlhelp.com

Part viii

To find Web-related sites elsewhere on the Web, take a look at the following Yahoo category:

```
Computers and Internet: Internet: World Wide Web: Information
and Documentation
```

A STANDARD MAY NOT ALWAYS BE ONE

The language of HTML is constantly evolving. Enthusiastic Web authors may happily include brand new and improved tags within their Web pages to produce dazzling new effects. But unfortunately, those effects may be lost on most visitors to that Web site because their browser software does not recognize those HTML features.

Officially, it's up to the World Wide Web Consortium (W3C) at the Massachusetts Institute of Technology (MIT) to define and establish new versions of HTML. Unofficially, leaders in the rush to the WWW, such as Microsoft and Netscape, regularly come up with their own extensions to official HTML in the hopes of improving the language. Eventually, many of these new codes are, indeed, included in the official HTML specification.

Skip the Programming: Use FrontPage

Microsoft FrontPage 2000 is one of the components in the Microsoft Office 2000 suite. It is essentially an easy-to-use word processor for creating HTML documents. Unlike a text editor such as Notepad, FrontPage is a WYSIWYG environment, in which "what you see is what you get." In other words, what you see in your document in FrontPage is pretty much what you'll see when you view the resulting HTML file on the Web in Internet Explorer. FrontPage has two important virtues:

- ▶ It is designed specifically to create HTML pages, so you won't find any unrelated commands or features on its menus. You don't have to think about how those options work; you simply choose them from the menu.

- ▶ When you create a page in FrontPage, you are assured that the HTML tags in that page (even though you might never see them) will be correct, with no missing angle brackets, misspelled tags, and so on.

If you're not sure what the big deal is about creating Web pages in FrontPage versus encoding them with HTML in a text editor, here's a simple but telling example. Shown below is some HTML code that you could create in Notepad and save to disk as an HTML file:

```
<HTML><HEAD><TITLE>Sample HTML Page</TITLE></HEAD>
<BODY>
<H1>This Is the Main Heading</H1>
<P>Here's a bulleted list:</P>
<HR>
<UL>
<LI>Item 1</LI>
<LI>Item 2<UL>
    <LI>Item 2A</LI>
    <LI>Item 2B</LI>
  </UL></LI>
<LI>Item 3</LI>
<LI>Item 4</LI>
</UL>
<HR>
<P>...and the page continues...</P>
```

Now look at Figure 24.2 to see how you could create that page in the WYSIWYG environment of FrontPage. The HTML code stays hidden beneath the page you create, which appears much the way it will when viewed in Internet Explorer.

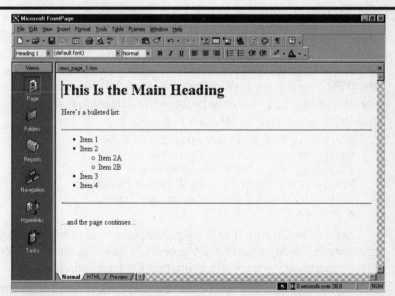

FIGURE 24.2:   When you create Web pages in a WYSIWYG HTML editor such as FrontPage 2000, "what you see is what you get" when that page is later viewed in a browser.

ADDING SOME STRUCTURE TO A PAGE

Just about any Web page you create will benefit if you impose some sort of structure on it. For example, think about how you would put your company's procedures manual up on the Web:

- ► If the manual is divided into chapters, you could make each one a separate Web page.

- ► You could easily re-create the manual's table of contents by making each section reference a hyperlink to that part of the manual. The reader could simply click on a section in the table of contents to open that file.

- ► Each chapter in the manual might have several levels of headings, which you could emulate perfectly with the heading tags in HTML.

- ► The body of the document would, of course, be divided into individual paragraphs.

You'll find that HTML offers several elements that let you create this type of structure in a Web page.

Using Paragraphs or Line Breaks

You create a paragraph by enclosing text within the paragraph codes <P> and </P>. Remember that Internet Explorer and other browsers will ignore any "paragraphs" you create by pressing Enter while working on the HTML code in a text editor (such as Notepad). You must specifically define a paragraph in the code by using the paragraph tag. Consider the text in the six lines of HTML code that follow:

```
<P>This is the first paragraph; its code
continues over several lines, but will be
displayed as a single paragraph in a
browser.</P><P>And this is a second paragraph
that will also be displayed as such in
a browser.</P>
```

This code would appear as two separate paragraphs in Internet Explorer, as shown in the upper portion of Figure 24.3. Note that the length of each line is determined by the width of Internet Explorer's window.

Internet Explorer and most other browsers insert some extra space between paragraphs, so in some instances, you will not want to use the

<P> tag. For example, when you display your name and address in a page, you would not want extra space between each line of the address.

In those cases, use the line break tag, <BR>. It tells the browser to wrap the text that follows onto a new line, without inserting any extra space between the lines. Here is an address within HTML code:

```
John and Joan Doe<BR>The Hanford Corp.<BR>123 S Proton
Dr<BR>Hanford, WA 98765
```

You can see how this is displayed in Internet Explorer in the lower portion of Figure 24.3.

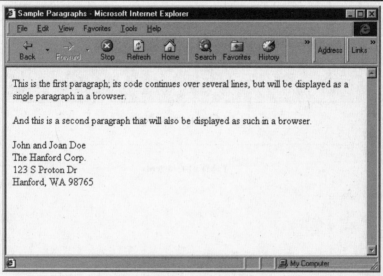

FIGURE 24.3:   You use the <P> tag to define a paragraph and the <BR> tag to create a line break.

Dividing Sections with a Horizontal Line

A simple and effective way to separate sections within a Web page is to insert a horizontal line, <HR>, also called a horizontal rule. By default, the line stretches from one side of the page to the other.

For example, if your page has a banner across the top with your company name, you could insert a horizontal line beneath it. This would separate it from a table of contents showing links to other pages, beneath which you could insert another line, followed by the main body of the page. At the bottom of the page, you could have another line, and beneath that line would be the important page identifiers, such as its URL, the date the page was last modified, a link back to a home page, and so on. An example is shown in Figure 24.4.

The <HR> tag takes several optional attributes. For example, you can specify the line's thickness (the default is one or two pixels in most browsers) and how much of the browser's window it should span (as a percentage or in pixels), such as:

```
<HR SIZE="6" WIDTH="60%">
```

which displays a line six pixels thick that spans 60 percent of the browser's window (the default is to center it in the window).

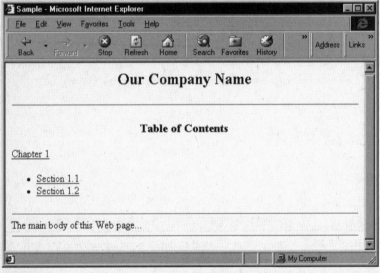

FIGURE 24.4:   You can use the horizontal rule, <HR>, to divide a page into sections.

Creating a Hierarchy with Headings

A common way to add structure to a Web page is through the use of headings. This book, for example, uses headings to divide each chapter into logical chunks. Its table of contents reveals the various levels of headings, where each chapter is divided into several main headings, each of which may contain several subheadings, and those subheadings may contain their own subheadings.

A Web page can have a maximum of six levels of headings, the HTML codes for which are conveniently named <H1>, <H2>, <H3>, and so on:

```
<H1>This is a two-line<BR>first-level heading</H1>
```

As mentioned earlier, no style is inherent in the headings—different Web browsers might interpret the look of a heading in slightly different ways. Structurally, however, all browsers will display headings so that a third-level heading looks subordinate to a second-level heading, a second-level heading looks subordinate to a first-level heading, and so on.

In Internet Explorer, a first-level heading is displayed in a larger, bolder font than a lower-level heading. Shown here is a sample of the six headings within Internet Explorer.

Heading 1   Heading 2
Heading 3   Heading 4
Heading 5   Heading 6

You are free to use the HTML headings in any goofy order you prefer, but it makes good sense to use them as you would in an outline. The first-level heading, <H1>, is the highest level, and the sixth level, <H6>, is the lowest or most subordinate.

When you are structuring a page with headings, the first heading you use should generally be the highest level that will occur on the page. But this doesn't mean that it must be the <H1> heading. You might start with <H2> because you want a heading that appears in a smaller font than <H1>. In this case, then, the level two heading would be the primary level, and you would not use <H1> on this page.

FORMATTING TEXT AND PAGES

Because the World Wide Web was originally conceived to be open to all, the designers of HTML avoided using literal descriptions of Web pages as much as possible. For example, the following tag would not have been appropriate:

```
<FONT FACE="TIMES ROMAN" SIZE="5" COLOR="#ff0000">
```

This tag requires a browser to have a specific, named font available that can be displayed in various sizes and requires that the browser's computer be connected to a color monitor.

Part viii

But the days of trying to write to the least common denominator are waning quickly, and, in fact, the tag shown above is now a part of the official HTML specification. The <FONT> tag also illustrates two types of HTML tag attributes:

Absolute (literal) The font type Times Roman is specified by name, and the color is specified by a hexadecimal RGB color value. There can be no doubt about how the author wanted this to look.

Relative (logical) The font size 5, however, does not refer to an actual point size. It is a size that is relative to the browser's default font size (which is size 2 in Internet Explorer) and gives the browser a little more flexibility in how it displays the font. The author wanted the font to be larger than the browser's default, but was willing to let the browser assign the actual size.

Formatting Text

Table 24.2 shows a few of the many HTML character-formatting tags. All of them require both an opening and closing tag.

TABLE 24.2: Basic HTML Character-Formatting Tags

Tag	Purpose
<ADDRESS>	To display a Web page's author information, such as the page URL, author name, date of last revision, and so on, in italics in Internet Explorer.
<I>	To italicize text.
<EM>	To emphasize text, which Internet Explorer displays in italics; this is a relative tag compared to the more specific <I> tag.
<PRE>	To display text in a monospaced (fixed-width) font, where multiple spaces, tabs, and hard returns within the HTML code are also displayed. Use this tag when the position of characters within each line is important, such as program listings and columnar lists.
<B>	To boldface text.
<STRONG>	To give text strong emphasis, which Internet Explorer displays in bold. This is a relative tag compared with the more specific <B> tag.
<S>	To display strike-through text.
<U>	To underline text. You should generally avoid underlining text since that is how browsers indicate hypertext links in Web pages.

You can insert these tags where they are needed in a paragraph, and you can combine some tags. The browser in Figure 24.5 shows an example of HTML text formatting. That page was built from the following HTML code:

```
<HTML><HEAD><TITLE>HTML Formatting
Tags</TITLE></HEAD><BODY><P>With HTML formatting tags, you
can make text <STRONG>bold</STRONG>, <EM>emphasized</EM>, or
<EM><STRONG>bold and emphasized</STRONG></EM>. You can also
<STRIKE>strike-out text</STRIKE> or make it
<U>underlined</U>.</P>
<P>If you don't use the Preformatted tag, Internet Explorer
displays text in a proportional font, where different charac-
ters take up different amounts of space.</P>
<P>Here are two lines of 10 letters, i and M, where each line
of the HTML code also had five spaces entered between the
fifth and sixth letters:</P>
<P>iiiii     iiiii<BR>
MMMMM     MMMMM</P>
<P>Here are those letters and spaces within the Preformatted
tags:</P>
<PRE>iiiii     iiiii<BR>
MMMMM     MMMMM</PRE>
</BODY></HTML>
```

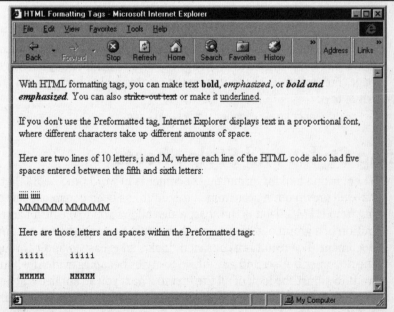

FIGURE 24.5: HTML formatting tags change the look of text in a Web page.

Formatting Pages

You can use a variety of tags to change the look of an entire Web page. You've already read about the <TITLE> tag, with which you create a title for a page. Internet Explorer displays that title in its title bar.

You can change the color of the page's background with the optional attribute BGCOLOR for the <BODY> tag. For example, the tag

```
<BODY BGCOLOR="#0000FF">
```

creates a blue background for the page.

NOTE

As with many tags, if you don't specify a color for a page, a browser that is displaying that page will use its own default color. Internet Explorer uses your Windows colors, by default, which are normally a white background with black text.

You can specify a picture instead of a color for a page's background. You don't need a large, page-sized picture, however, because Internet Explorer (and other browsers) tile the picture to fill the entire background. This allows you to use a small image file that will download quickly. You include the BACKGROUND attribute in the <BODY> tag to specify a background picture:

```
<BODY BACKGROUND="smallpic.gif">
```

If you choose a fairly dark background color or picture, you may need to use the TEXT attribute to change the default color of any text on the page. For example, the following tag creates a blue background with white text:

```
<BODY BGCOLOR="#0000FF" TEXT="#FFFFFF">
```

Using Styles and Style Sheets

There is one tool for formatting documents in word processors that we have all grown quite accustomed to, but it has been conspicuously missing from HTML. That is the *style*, which allows you to create a named definition of a group of formats and then apply that style to any text in the document. The result is a consistent look that is easy to apply throughout the document. A second advantage to styles becomes evident when you want to adjust the look of all the text to which you've applied a style. You simply redefine the style, and that change is immediately reflected throughout the document.

In the past, HTML contained no mechanism for performing this simple, automated formatting task. But that's about to change with the acceptance of styles and style sheets in the HTML specification.

NOTE

The style sheets now implemented within the HTML specification are recognized by Internet Explorer 5 and, to some extent, by Internet Explorer 4 (and even back in Internet Explorer 3). In fact, FrontPage 2000 now supports styles, so you can use the program to create your own. However, because styles are still new in the HTML specification, few sites have yet to take advantage of them. Once styles become a more accepted part of the standard, you will undoubtedly find them in greater use throughout the Web.

Just as you would use styles in a word processor, a Web author can incorporate styles into a Web page. This can be done in several ways; the following is the simplest.

Within the <HEAD> tags for a page, you can specify style elements for various tags that will affect those tags throughout the page. For example, you could use styles to:

▶ Create a light gray background for the page

▶ Center all <H2> headings and display their text in white

▶ Indent the first line of all paragraphs

Here is the HTML code that creates these effects. Figure 24.6 shows the page as it appears in Internet Explorer (with added text):

```
<HTML><HEAD><TITLE>Sample Style</TITLE>
<STYLE>
  BODY {BACKGROUND: silver}
  H2   {TEXT-ALIGN:"center"; COLOR:"white"}
  P    {TEXT-INDENT:"+10%"}
</STYLE>
</HEAD><BODY>
<H2>This Heading Is Centered</H2>
<P>This is a normal paragraph...</P>
</BODY></HTML>
```

You could use this method to create many Web pages that all use the same styles, but there's a much more efficient way to use styles. The term *style sheet* refers to a single file that contains multiple style definitions. You can reference that file in any HTML Web page to apply those styles to that page.

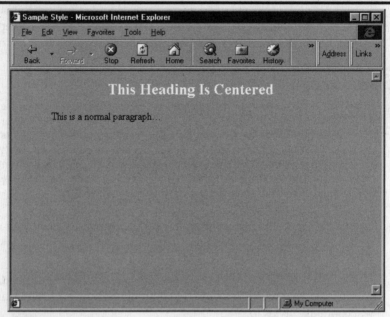

FIGURE 24.6: You can create a more consistent look in a page with much less effort when you use styles to set the formatting of HTML elements.

Here are the contents of a style sheet (they're plain text files with a CSS filename extension) that emulates the styles shown in the previous example:

```
BODY {BACKGROUND: silver}
H2   {TEXT-ALIGN:"center"; COLOR:"white"}
P    {TEXT-INDENT:"+10%"}
```

If you save that style sheet file in a Web site (under the name NORMALPG .CSS in this example), you can reference it in any Web page with the following code. This code is the same as that used in the previous example; however, here the <LINK> tag replaces all the code within the opening and closing <STYLE> tags:

```
<HTML><HEAD><TITLE>Sample Style</TITLE>
<LINK REL=StyleSheet HREF="normalpg.css" TYPE="text/css"
</HEAD><BODY>
<H2>This Heading Is Centered</H2>
<P>This is a normal paragraph...</P>
```

The resulting page would look exactly the same as the one in the earlier example in Figure 24.6. As you can see from these quick examples, styles and style sheets have a great potential for easing the job of creating and, especially, maintaining a Web site. When many pages reference the same style sheet, you can simply modify the style sheet to have the changes appear in all the pages.

NOTE

If you'd like to learn more about style sheets, you'll find a great guide from the Web Design Group at www.htmlhelp.com/reference/css/.

LINKING PAGES TO THE WORLD

The little feature that creates the Web for countless computers and networks is the hyperlink. When you're reading a Web page in Internet Explorer, you can click a link to jump to a new resource (open it). That resource can be another HTML page, a graphic image, a sound or video file, or something else, and it might be located on the browser's local hard disk, on an intranet site, or on a site anywhere on the World Wide Web.

Creating a Text or Image Hyperlink

The HTML anchor tag, <A>, defines a hyperlink within a Web page and at the minimum contains two components:

- ▶ The text or image that you click to activate the link
- ▶ The URL of the link's target that will open when you click the link

Here is the HTML code for a text hyperlink (it's shown here on two lines, but remember that a browser ignores any line breaks in the HTML code):

```
<P>There's <A HREF="http://www.sample.com/helpindex.htm">
online help</A> when you need it.</P>
```

The text *online help* is the clickable link, and in Internet Explorer that text is underlined and displayed in blue, as shown in the top of Figure 24.7. The target of this link is the file HELPINDEX.HTM.

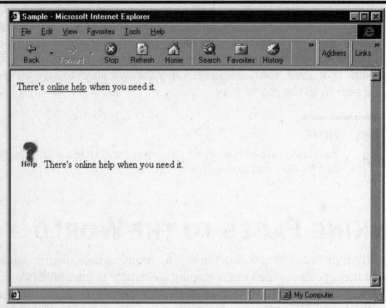

FIGURE 24.7:   You can create a hyperlink from an image or from text, which is displayed in blue and underlined in Internet Explorer.

An image can also serve as a hyperlink; clicking the image activates the link. The bottom of Figure 24.7 shows an image hyperlink. In this case, the text that is next to the image serves to describe the link, but cannot be clicked to activate the link. Here's the HTML code (shown on three lines) for this link and the text to its right:

```
<P><A HREF="http://www.sample.com/helpindex.htm">
<IMG SRC="help.gif" border="0" width="46" height="51"></A>
There's online help when you need it.</P>
```

This example has the same target file as the previous example, HELPINDEX .HTM, but the clickable portion of the hyperlink is the image file HELP.GIF. The reference to that image file falls within the anchor tags <A> and </A>, and the sentence describing the link, *There's online help when you need it*, is outside those tags.

RELATIVE VERSUS ABSOLUTE REFERENCES

When an author creates a reference in a Web page to another file, such as the target of a hyperlink, the reference can be defined as either relative or absolute.

In the two examples above, an *absolute* reference was made to the target file HELPINDEX.HTM. The reference contained the target's complete URL that defined the exact location of the file. It starts with the protocol and includes the usual host, domain, and filename, like this:

```
http://www.sample.com/helpindex.htm
```

With an absolute reference, the location of the target is "written in stone" and always points to the same file in the same location. However, this is not an advantage or even a requirement when the target of the link is stored in a location that is *relative* to the page that contains the link.

For example, if the reference to the target contained only the target file's name, such as

```
helpindex.htm
```

it would be assumed that this file resides in the same folder as the page that contains the link. Its location is, therefore, relative to the link-containing file.

Another relative reference to a target might look like this:

```
help/helpindex.htm
```

In this case, the target file resides in a folder named HELP, which resides in the same folder as the page that contains the link. The complete (absolute) URL to that file would look like this:

```
http://www.sample.com/help/helpindex.htm
```

Because the administrator of a Web site may need to change the location and directory (folder) structure of the site, a Web author will always try to use a relative reference whenever possible. In that way, if a Web site is moved to another folder on the same server or to a completely new server, all the relative references to files within that site continue to work.

Specifying Other Link Targets

You'll often find that the target of a link is another Web page, but there are other types of targets. Here are some you may encounter:

Named target   When the target of a link is a Web page, you can specify a named location within that page. That location, not the top of the page, is displayed when the page is opened in a browser. You use the anchor tag to create the name for the location, and you reference that name in the anchor tag for the link.

Frame   Later in this chapter, you'll read about the frameset, which is a Web page that you divide into multiple frames, each of which can open and display a separate Web page. When a link resides in one frame of a frameset, you can have the target for that link displayed in any of the frames in that frameset. You do so by including the TARGET attribute in the link's anchor tag, along with the name of the frame that should receive the target of the link.

Other file types   The target of a link can be any type of file. Internet Explorer can open several types of files on its own, including Web pages, text files, and GIF or JPEG image files. For other file types, it must rely on Windows 95/98 and request that the appropriate program handle that file. For example, sound files (WAV or AU) and movie files (MOV, MPG, or MPEG) would be played by the appropriate sound and movie player.

E-mail address   The target for a link can use an Internet protocol other than HTTP, such as the *mailto* protocol that defines an e-mail address. When the reader of the page clicks the link, the reader's e-mail program should open with a new message displayed and already addressed to the address specified in the link. The reader can create the body of the message and send it to the target address in the usual way.

Creating a Clickable Image Map

A variation of the image hyperlink discussed in the previous section is the *image map*, which is a single image that contains multiple hyperlinks. Each hyperlink is associated with a defined area of the image called a *hotspot*, which, when clicked, activates that link. In Internet Explorer, you see only the image; there is no indication that it has clickable hotspots.

You've undoubtedly encountered image maps in many, many pages on the Web. They can be informative, attractive, and intuitive and can also transcend language, which is an important consideration on the World Wide Web.

TIP

Even though images can convey information without language, an image is nonetheless open to a variety of interpretations. Images may not even be seen when visitors to a site have turned off the display of images in their browsers to speed things up. Therefore, good Web design often means including corresponding text hyperlinks next to an image map so that a visitor to that page can either click within the image map or click one of the text links.

A typical use of an image map is literally in the form of a map: You can click on a city, state, or region to display information about that region. An image map built from a map of the United States works well when the hotspots are defined around the large, regularly shaped western states. But the plan doesn't work so well for the smaller, irregularly shaped eastern states.

In such a case, the image map would work better with a regional map of the United States. Clicking in the east would display an enlarged map of just that region of the country, and clicking in the west would display the western states, as shown in Figure 24.8.

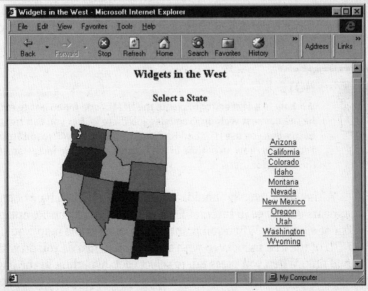

FIGURE 24.8:   A geographic map can be a practical way to implement an image map.

Part viii

A Web-page author can create an image map from an image in two ways:

A server-side image map is the traditional type. When you click within an image map, Internet Explorer sends the coordinates of the click (relative to the image) to the server of that Web site. The server looks up those coordinates in a table of hotspots for that image map and processes the appropriate hyperlink target. Different servers may use different systems for storing the coordinates and targets for an image map.

A client-side image map obviates any server interaction, because the hotspot coordinates are included in the HTML definition for the image map that is sent to Internet Explorer. When you click within the client-side image map, Internet Explorer looks to see which target is associated with those coordinates and then opens that target.

Here is a sample of the HTML code for a client-side image map:

```
<AREA SHAPE="RECT" COORDS="308,32 380,72" HREF="choice1.htm"
<AREA SHAPE="RECT" COORDS="223,174 365,246"
HREF="choice2.htm"
<AREA SHAPE="RECT" COORDS="7,177 179,246" HREF="choice3.htm"
```

When you click within the image, Internet Explorer determines the coordinates of the point on which you clicked and finds the corresponding target for that portion of the image map, as though you had clicked a normal text or image hyperlink.

NOTE

Working in a text editor to create the HTML code for an image map just might be the nastiest Web-programming job there is. But you can create them with ease when you use HTML editors such as the one in Microsoft FrontPage 2000. You simply draw an outline of the hotspot within the image and then specify the target for that link.

Although it usually shouldn't matter to you which type of image map appears on a page in Internet Explorer, you'll find one advantage with a client-side map. When you point to a hotspot in the map, you'll see the URL of the link associated with that hotspot, just as you do with a normal link. When you press tab to select each hyperlink in the page, you also select each hotspot in an image map. Pointing at a hotspot not only conveniently tells you where you'll go, it also tells you that this image is, indeed, an image map and not just a pretty picture.

Finally, because all the links are processed within the browser, a client-side image map reduces the processing burden on the server. It also is more flexible than a server-side image map, because it is guaranteed to work no matter which server is hosting the page that contains the image map.

INCLUDING PICTURES IN A PAGE

You can include images (pictures or other nontext objects) in any Web page to provide information or to make the page more attractive. An image that you include in a Web page is called an *inline image*, as opposed to an image that is viewed separately in Internet Explorer, such as when the image file is the target of a link. You reference the inline image in this way:

```
There's more <IMG SRC="Images/arrow-rt.gif"> if you're
interested.
```

In this case, the image file ARROW-RT.GIF (from the folder Images) is displayed within the text that surrounds it and might look like the one shown here.

There's more 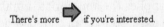 if you're interested.

NOTE
The two most common graphic file formats you'll find on the Web are GIF and JPEG. The data is compressed in both types of files, so images can be transmitted much faster over a network.

Let's take a look at some of the attributes for the <IMG> tag for an inline image; all are optional:

Alternate text   When a browser cannot display graphic images, perhaps because the image file cannot be found or because the browser's image-loading capabilities have been turned off to save download time, you can include the ALT attribute in an image tag to have text displayed in place of the image.

Sizing the image   By default, Internet Explorer loads an image from the top down and displays the image in as large a box as needed. You can choose to specify an exact size for the image by including the WIDTH and HEIGHT attributes within the HTML tag (see the inline image example earlier in this chapter in "Creating a Text or Image Hyperlink").

Aligning the image   You can use the ALIGN attribute with the LEFT, CENTER, or RIGHT options to position the image either flush-left, centered, or flush-right in the browser window. You can also use the TOP, BOTTOM, or MIDDLE attributes to align text with the top, bottom, or middle of the image.

CREATING LISTS

Using HTML, you can arrange items in lists in several ways. The two most useful ones are:

Bulleted   Or *unordered* lists, in which each item (paragraph) in the list is prefaced with a bullet; the <UL> tag begins the list.

Numbered   Or *ordered* lists, in which each item in the list is prefaced with a number; the <OL> tag begins the list. Internet Explorer applies the appropriate number to each line when it opens the page, so you can add to or delete items from the list while you create the page and not have to worry about updating the numbering.

You define each item within either type of list with the <LI> tag. The following unordered list:

```
<P>Chapter I</P>
<UL>
<LI>Section 1</LI>
<LI>Section 2</LI>
<LI>Section 3</LI></UL>
```

Chapter I

- Section 1
- Section 2
- Section 3

looks like the example at left in a browser. The bulleted or numbered list is a fast, easy way to apply some structure to a Web page, and you'll no doubt use it frequently. As always, the way a browser formats the list, such as the amount of indention and the style of the bullets, could vary from browser to browser.

You can nest one list within another simply by beginning the new list with the appropriate list tag. This allows you to create outlines, for example, or tables of contents that have subheadings indented in their own lists. Here's the list from the example above with a second list within it:

```
<P>Chapter I</P>
<UL>
<LI>Section 1</LI>
<LI>Section 2<UL>
<LI>Part A</LI>
<LI>Part B</LI>
<LI>Part C</LI>
</UL></LI>
<LI>Section 3</LI></UL>
```

In Internet Explorer, the secondary list is indented from the primary list and displays a different type of bullet. Again, in other browsers these lists may look somewhat different. Here is the indented list from above shown in Internet Explorer (on the left) and another browser.

Chapter I

- Section 1
- Section 2
  - o Part A
  - o Part B
  - o Part C
- Section 3

Chapter I

- Section 1
- Section 2
  - ☐ Part A
  - ☐ Part B
  - ☐ Part C
- Section 3

ARRANGING ITEMS WITHIN TABLES

Another and even more powerful way to structure data within a Web page is the table. Like the tables you can create in your word processor or spreadsheet, an HTML table consists of rows, columns, and cells.

You can place just about anything you want within a cell in a table; there are few restrictions. Because of the flexibility of HTML tables, you'll find them used in countless ways in Web pages.

Sometimes a table will look like a table, with border lines dividing its rows, columns, and cells. In other cases, though, the structure of the table will be used, but its borders won't be displayed. The table serves as a convenient way to organize elements on the page without making them appear within the confines of an actual table.

Part viii

Like image maps, tables are HTML elements that are best created in a dedicated HTML editor, such as FrontPage. You can still build a small table "manually" in a text editor, such as the table shown in the next example, but for anything more complex, you'll want to move to a more powerful editing tool.

Table 24.3 shows the basic tags with which you define a table:

TABLE 24.3: Basic HTML Table-Building Tags

TAG	PURPOSE
<TABLE>	Begins the table definition.
<TR>	Defines a new row in the table.
<TD>	Defines a single cell within the table.

Shown below is the code for a simple, six-cell table:

```
<TABLE>
  <TR>
    <TD>Cell A1</TD>  <TD>Cell B1</TD>
  </TR>
  <TR>
    <TD>Cell A2</TD>  <TD>Cell B2</TD>
  </TR>
  <TR>
    <TD>Cell A3</TD>  <TD>Cell B3</TD>
  </TR>
</TABLE>
```

The result is a table that has three rows and two columns; the text within the <TD> and </TD> tags appears in each cell. By default, as in this example, the table has no borders. You must specifically include them by specifying the width of their lines (in pixels) with the BORDER attribute for the <TABLE> tag, so that this tag:

```
<TABLE BORDER="1">
```

would enclose all the cells in the table with a border that is one pixel wide. Shown next is the first table, on the left, and the same table with a border, on the right.

Cell A1 Cell B1	Cell A1	Cell B1
Cell A2 Cell B2	Cell A2	Cell B2
Cell A3 Cell B3	Cell A3	Cell B3

You can include the <CAPTION> tag once in a table. Any text between this tag and its closing tag is displayed as the table's caption, which by default is centered just above the table.

You use the table header tag, <TH>, instead of the <TD> tag to create a header cell for the table. Internet Explorer displays the text between the opening and closing header tags boldfaced and centered within the cell. You will often use these table headers as titles in the first row or column of a table.

By default, a table will only be as wide as the longest entries in its cells. You can specify an exact width in the <TABLE> tag with the WIDTH attribute, either in pixels or as a percentage of the browser's window. For example, this tag:

```
<TABLE WIDTH="320">
```

creates a table exactly 320 pixels wide. If you want a table to be exactly half the width of the browser's window, no matter what width that might be, use the following tag:

```
<TABLE WIDTH="50%">
```

If a table is less than the full width of a browser's window, it is aligned with the left edge of the window. You can include the ALIGN attribute in the <TABLE> tag and specify Left, Center, or Right alignment within the browser's window.

If you specify an exact width for the table, you might also want to set the width of each column with the WIDTH attribute within the <TD> tag for a cell. You can specify the width either in pixels or as a percentage of the table (not of the browser's window).

As you'll see when you create a table in FrontPage, you can include many other tags and attributes, such as a background color or image for the table or any of its cells, the color of its borders, and which of its borders should be displayed.

GETTING FEEDBACK WITH FORMS

So far in this chapter, all the HTML elements we've discussed have been display-oriented, in that they affect the way a page appears within a browser. Now we'll look at the HTML form, an element that not only affects the display but also allows the reader to send information back to the server.

Those two issues, display and send, are the primary pieces of a Web-based form:

▶ The form controls that you create on a Web page are displayed in a browser and can be used by the visitor to enter data, select checkboxes or radio buttons, select items from a list, and so on.

▶ Once the visitor enters data into the form, he or she must have a mechanism for sending the data back to your server. Once the server receives the data, it must have another mechanism for storing or manipulating that data.

Designing a Form

Designing a form for a Web page isn't especially difficult if, as with tables, you do the job in an HTML editor such as FrontPage. The forms you create for the Web look and behave much like any other computer-generated forms you may have come across. For example, an HTML form can have a one-line data-entry field (sometimes called an edit field), in which the reader can type, for example, an e-mail address.

E-mail address: `myname@xyz.com`

You use the <FORM> tag to begin the form definition. As part of that definition, you specify where the data should be returned (a URL) using the ACTION attribute. The destination might be the server for the form's Web page, or it could be some other server that will accept the data. You also specify how the data should be returned, using the METHOD attribute. The POST method is a common way to handle the job.

Within the opening and closing <FORM> tags, you lay out the controls of the form. You can include any other HTML elements, as well, which will appear in the page along with the form controls. Some of the more common form control tags are shown in Table 24.4 and Figure 24.9.

TABLE 24.4: Common HTML Form Control Tags

Tag	Form Control	Description
`<INPUT TYPE="TEXT">`	Data-entry field	A one-line data-entry field
`<INPUT TYPE="PASSWORD">`	Password field	A one-line data-entry field in which the characters you type are displayed as asterisks to hide them
`<TEXTAREA>`	Multiple-line data-entry field	Enter a paragraph or more of text
`<INPUT TYPE="CHECKBOX">`	checkbox	Select an item by clicking its checkbox
`<INPUT TYPE="RADIO">`	Radio button	Select one of a group of radio buttons
`<SELECT>`	List	Select one or more items from a list
`<INPUT TYPE="SUBMIT">`	Button	When clicked, sends the form's data to the server
`<INPUT TYPE="RESET">`	Button	When clicked, resets all form controls to their defaults

The definition for each control (other than the Submit and Reset buttons) must include a name for the control, which is sent to and used by the server to identify the data that was returned from that control. Each control can have several other attributes that define how it behaves. For example, the single-line data-entry field has the following attributes:

Size   The displayed width of the field in the form.

Maxlength   The maximum number of characters that can be entered into the field.

Value   The characters that appear within the field when its page is first opened or when the Reset button is clicked. You might use *(none)* as this default value, so that when the data is returned to the server, this entry indicates that the visitor has entered no data in this field.

Here is an example of the code for a data-entry field:

```
<INPUT TYPE="TEXT" NAME="COMPANY" SIZE="25" MAXLENGTH="100"
VALUE="(none)">
```

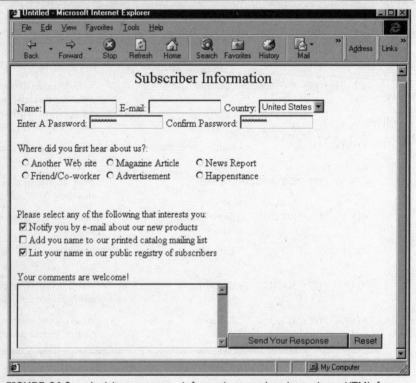

FIGURE 24.9:   A visitor can enter information or select items in an HTML form.

As the visitor enters information into a form, that data is still on the visitor's local computer—it has not reached the server yet.

Getting the Data Back to You

In a form such as the one shown in Figure 24.9, the visitor clicks on the Submit button (labeled *Send your responses* in the figure) to send the data back to the server. The browser collects at least two pieces of information about each control in the form:

- ▶ The name of the control
- ▶ Its current value

For example, if a visitor has entered *Pat Coleman* in the Name field, Internet Explorer sends back the following information:

```
NAME="Pat Coleman"
```

By naming each datum, the server can identify each piece of information it receives. Radio buttons are organized into named groups so that a visitor can select only one button in a group. It is the value of the selected button that is returned for the named group.

When the server receives the data, the possibilities are wide open. Web servers usually have built-in form-handling tools that let you choose how incoming data should be manipulated:

▶ Format the data into a standard HTML page and display it to the visitor for confirmation of what he or she has entered.

▶ Write the data to a database file in any of several file formats.

▶ Send the data to an e-mail address.

▶ Let the data trigger the display of another Web page, such as the home page of a company catalog that the visitor selected in the form.

Beyond using a server's built-in tools to handle the incoming data, programming work will be needed to create the necessary script or program to manipulate the data.

SPLITTING A PAGE INTO FRAMES

With the HTML feature called *frames*, you can create and display multiple Web pages within a single page. In the traditional way of browsing a Web, if you click a link in one page, a new page opens and replaces the first page in the browser.

For example, when you click a link in a page that serves as a table of contents of other pages, the target page opens, but the table of contents page is removed from the browser. By splitting a page into two frames, such as in the page shown in Figure 24.10, the table of contents page can be displayed in a frame on the left, for example, while the target of the selected link is displayed in the other frame on the right side of the browser's window. In this way, the table of contents is always available so that the reader can make another selection.

The concept of frames is neat and simple:

▶ Create a single Web page as a *frameset*, which contains no content other than the frameset definition.

▶ Specify how the frameset should be divided into frames.

▶ Assign a Web page to each frame.

You use the <FRAMESET> tag instead of the usual <BODY> tag to begin the frameset definition in the page. For example, this tag

```
<FRAMESET COLS="33%,67%">
```

creates a frameset page that consists of two frames arranged as columns. The first frame will be in a column on the left side of the browser's window; that frame's width will be one-third of the browser's window. The second frame will be a column to the right of the first one and will take up two-thirds of the browser's window.

You specify the source Web page to be opened in each frame with the <FRAME> tag, as in

```
<FRAME SRC="CONTENTS.HTM">
<FRAME SRC="INSTRUCT.HTM">
```

In this case, when the frameset is opened in a browser, the frame on the left displays the page CONTENTS.HTM, and the frame on the right displays INSTRUCT.HTM. You now have two Web pages sharing the same browser window.

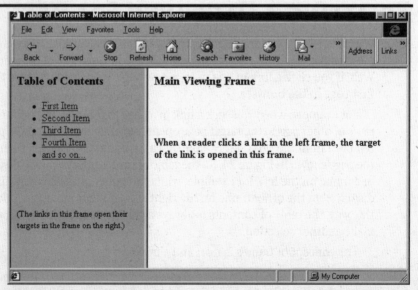

FIGURE 24.10:   By splitting a page into frames, you can have a table of contents displayed in one frame, while the target of each link is displayed in the other frame.

Let's revisit the example from the beginning of this section. If the frame on the left contains an index of links, you can have each of those links display its target in the frame on the right. You do so by including the TARGET attribute in the anchor tag for the link and specifying the name of the frame (as mentioned earlier in this chapter in "Specifying Other Link Targets").

To specify a target frame, you must first name the frame. You do so with the NAME attribute in the <FRAME> tag. In the previous example, you could name the tags in this way:

```
<FRAME SRC="CONTENTS.HTM">
<FRAME SRC="INSTRUCT.HTM" NAME="RIGHT">
```

which gives the name RIGHT to the frame on the right. With that frame named, you can define each link in the index page so that its target resource appears in the named frame, such as:

```
<A HREF="SOMEFILE.HTM" TARGET="RIGHT">
```

In this way, your index remains in the frame on the left, while the target of each link is displayed in the frame on the right.

Finally, since frames are relatively new features of HTML, not all browsers yet support them. You can include the <NOFRAMES> tag within the frameset to provide a message to a browser that cannot display frames. Here's an example:

```
<NOFRAMES><BODY>
<P>Sorry, but this page uses frames, which your browser does
not support.</P>
</BODY></NOFRAMES>
```

As you can see, the <NOFRAMES> tag includes the <BODY> tag, which is not used in defining a frameset but would be recognized by a frames-unaware browser. Anything within the <BODY> tags would then be displayed in the browser.

WHAT'S NEXT

In the next chapter, you'll learn about the design considerations involved in creating a Web page with FrontPage 2000.

Part viii

Chapter 25

CREATING A WEB AND WEB PAGES

FrontPage is your web navigation center, the place where you start and finish your work on a web. This chapter shows you how to create a web and use the Page view to design exciting web pages. The overview of the editing process and the features presented in this chapter will help you to create you own presence on the World Wide Web.

Adapted from *Microsoft FrontPage 2000: No Experience Required* by Gene Weisskopf

ISBN 0-7821-2482-8   432 pages $19.99

The Standard toolbar (shown below) contains many of the tools you'll use to manage and edit your web.

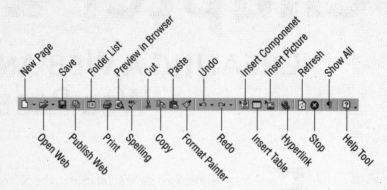

CREATING A NEW WEB

We'll call the web you are viewing or modifying in FrontPage the *current* or *active* web. When you create and save individual pages for that web using FrontPage's built-in editor, they become part of the active web unless you specify otherwise.

Because creating or revising web pages is probably the job you'll perform most often in FrontPage, when you start the program you'll normally see just two panes: the Views bar and the Page view with a blank web page, ready for editing. You can instead open an existing page or an entire FrontPage web, or create a brand new FrontPage web.

TIP

You can also choose to have the last web you worked on open automatically when you start FrontPage. Choose Tools ➢ Options, and select Open Last Web Automatically from the General tab in the Options dialog box.

There are two primary steps required to create a new web: select the type of web you want to create, and specify a location for it. First choose File ➢ New ➢ Web, or select Web from the drop-down list in the New Page button (on the Standard toolbar). This opens the New dialog box, which is shown in Figure 25.1.

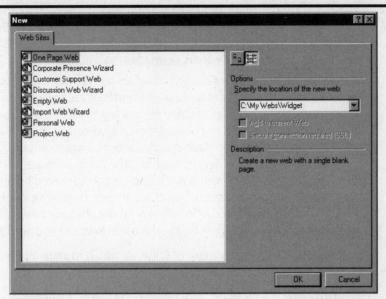

FIGURE 25.1: The New dialog box lets you create a new FrontPage web from a web template or wizard.

In this dialog box, select one of the web templates or wizards listed on the Web Sites tab. For example, if you are new to FrontPage, you may want to start out by creating just a one-page web from the template of that name. This way you can get comfortable working with web pages before moving on to more complex projects.

You also specify a name and location for the new web in the New dialog box. You can give your web any name you want using spaces, upper- and lowercase letters, numbers, and any other characters that are acceptable in filenames.

WARNING

You may want to avoid spaces in your web names, because some Web servers won't accept them. You should also stick with just lowercase letters, because some servers are case-sensitive and will distinguish between the file or folder name "my web site" and "My Web Site." It's easier for visitors to enter all lowercase letters in their browsers to access your site, and not have to remember the case of the name exactly.

When you are creating a local web (as opposed to a web on a server), the default location for your web is generally the My Webs folder. When you are ready to publish your web for all the world to see, you can transfer the web from your local drive to its permanent location.

A FrontPage web contains not only the files you create, but several other folders and files that are created by FrontPage and used to manage and run your web. The names of these folders begin with an underscore, such as _borders, and are not normally displayed within the Folders List in FrontPage because they are strictly for FrontPage's own use. You can, however, view these folders by enabling the Show Documents in Hidden Directories option, which you'll find on the Advanced tab for the Tools ➤ Web Settings command. You can also view them within Windows Explorer, although you definitely should not change or delete them. There are two FrontPage folders that you are free to use as you need them:

images   This is a convenient folder in which to store image files, such as GIF and JPEG files.

_private   This folder is not visible to browsers when your FrontPage web is hosted by a FrontPage-aware server, so any files in it are invisible as well. Once your site is up and running under a server for the public to see, this might be a place to keep pages that are under construction, reference files, and other documents you want to be available for your use only. Unlike the other FrontPage folders that begin with the under-score character, the contents of this folder are visible to you while you're working in FrontPage.

When you create a new web, it is ready for you to enhance and expand it.

NOTE

One bonus of FrontPage is that you don't have to worry about periodically saving your web. When you make changes, such as renaming pages or importing new files, those changes are saved automatically. When you are editing pages, however, there is a File ➤ Save command for you to use, just as you would in any word processor.

Opening an Existing Web

 To open an existing FrontPage web that you've recently worked on, use the File ➤ Recent Webs command, which lists the webs you've opened in the recent past. Otherwise, use File ➤ Open Web, or click the Open Web button on the Standard toolbar. (If that button is displayed as the Open button, for opening a file not a web, click the down arrow next to it and select Open Web).

The Open Web dialog box is similar to a typical files dialog box, except in this case you are not selecting a file but an entire folder—the folder that contains a FrontPage web. Select the one you want and click OK to open that web. If you already had a web open in FrontPage, a new FrontPage program window will be started for the web you're opening. You will then have two FrontPage windows open, each displaying a different web.

NOTE

If the web you open has security controls placed on it, you may have to enter your username and password before you can open the web.

To open a different web in the same window, choose File ➤ Close Web first. You can choose File ➤ Exit at any time to close FrontPage. If you have been editing one or more web pages and have not saved your work, you will first be asked if you wish to do so. Note that if you have multiple FrontPage windows running, each displaying a separate web, you can close any of them while leaving the others open.

Creating, Opening, and Saving Web Pages

You normally use the Page view's built-in HTML editor to create and revise web pages. If you are familiar with an earlier version of FrontPage, you'll most likely be pleased that the HTML editor is now an integral part of FrontPage, and not a separate application. You don't need to switch back and forth between the page you are editing and your web in FrontPage.

Creating a New Page

To create a new blank web page, simply click the New Page button on the Standard toolbar, and the new page will appear in the right-hand pane. You can have multiple pages open at the same time, switching between them as needed by choosing one from the Windows menu.

You can also create a new page from a FrontPage template, which is a ready-built page that serves as the basis for the new page. You choose a template when you use the File ➢ New ➢ Page command (Ctrl+N), or you can right-click a folder in the Folders List and choose New Page from the shortcut menu. The Normal Page template is the standard blank page that opens when you click the New Page button.

To close the active document, choose File ➢ Close. If you have not saved the document since making changes to it, you will be prompted to save it to avoid losing that work.

Opening an Existing Page

 There are several ways to open an existing page for editing in FrontPage. You can use File ➢ Open (Ctrl+O) and choose a file from the Open File dialog box, or click the Open button on the Standard toolbar. You can also double-click a page name or icon from the Folders List or the Hyperlinks view, or right-click the filename or icon and choose Open from the shortcut menu.

Saving Your Work

 Just as in your word processor, you must save your work to keep it. Normally, you will save a web page within the active web in FrontPage, but you can choose to save it elsewhere as a separate file, independent of your web. Use the File ➢ Save command (Ctrl+S), or click the Save button on the Standard toolbar. If the page is a new one that you have not yet saved, you will see the Save As dialog box, shown in Figure 25.2, which will always be displayed when you choose File ➢ Save As.

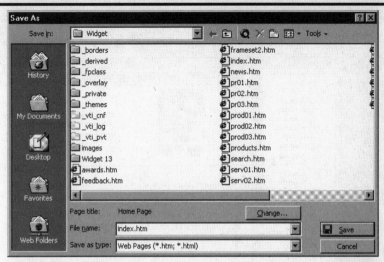

FIGURE 25.2: The first time you save a web page, or when you choose File ➤ Save As, you specify the filename, location, and page title in the Save As dialog box.

In the Save As dialog box, you pick a location for the file (normally one of the folders in your web), enter a name for the file and, optionally, click the Change button and specify a page title (you can also specify a title while editing the page).

TIP

You can create folders in your FrontPage web to organize its files. For example, you can save or move files to them, just as you do with the normal folders and documents you create on your computer. When you insert a hyperlink into a page in your web, the location of its target is automatically specified in the link.

ENTERING AND EDITING TEXT

Editing a page in the Page view is very much like working in a typical WYSIWYG word processor, where "what you see is what you get." In this case, what you see is pretty much what the rest of the world sees in their Web browsers when they view that page on your Web site (see Figure 25.3).

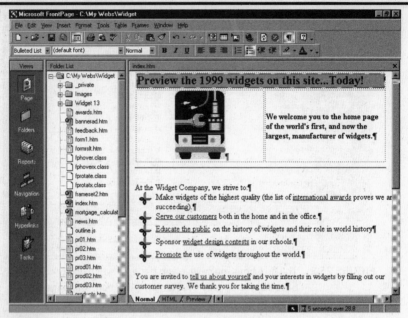

FIGURE 25.3:   You create pages in FrontPage in much the same way that you create documents in a word processor.

If you are a Microsoft Word user, you may notice that the process of editing an HTML document in FrontPage looks suspiciously similar to Word. The similarities are not accidental. Microsoft has worked very hard to have all its Office products—Word, Excel, PowerPoint, and FrontPage—share the same look and even the same program resources. For example, you'll find the same toolbar buttons for commands such as New, Open, Save, Cut, and Paste. Those commands also appear in the same menus, so if you're already familiar with Microsoft Word, you won't have any trouble getting started in FrontPage.

TIP

Paste Special is also available, so you can insert text with or without formatting that copied from within FrontPage or from other applications. For example, when you copy a paragraph from a Word document, FrontPage will convert the formatting into an equivalent look in HTML (as best it can). If you want the text without any formatting, choose Paste Special ➢ Normal Paragraphs.

Let's take a quick look at some of the features of the Page view in Figure 25.3:

► At the top of the screen, beneath the title bar, is the menu bar, the Standard toolbar, and the Formatting toolbar. Several other toolbars are available as well. You can turn the display of a toolbar on or off by selecting it from the View ➤ Toolbars menu.

► At the bottom of the screen is the status bar, which displays useful information as you work on your web page. For example, the left side of the status bar displays the target address of a hyperlink when you point to a link in the page.

► Just above the status bar are three tabs that switch you between views of your document: Normal, HTML, and Preview (more about those later).

► The web page you're editing appears in the window beneath the toolbars and to the right of the Views bar and Folder List (unless you have closed those panes to provide more room for the page you're editing). You can open multiple web pages and switch between them with the Windows menu.

► The horizontal and vertical scroll bars offer one way to scroll through your document; you can also use the usual keyboard keys, such as PgUp and PgDn. If your mouse has a scrolling wheel, such as Microsoft's IntelliMouse, you can use the wheel to scroll up or down through the page.

Basic Editing Procedures

The best way to familiarize yourself with the process of editing pages in the Page view is to start typing. Most of the basic procedures you've already learned in your word processor are applicable in FrontPage:

► You can have multiple documents open at the same time, but only one is active. The active page receives the text you enter and is the target of any commands you issue.

► In the active document, enter text just as you would in your word processor; FrontPage wraps text automatically, so press Enter only to create a new paragraph.

► Press Del to delete the character to the right of the insertion point; press Backspace to delete the character to its left. Press

Ctrl+Del to delete the word to the right of the insertion point, and press Ctrl+Backspace to delete the word to its left.

▶ Press Home to go to the beginning of the current line and End to go to its end. Press Ctrl+Home to go to the top of the document and Ctrl+End to go to the bottom.

▶ When you have opened multiple documents, their windows are stacked one on top of the other in the Page view pane; you can't reduce their size or minimize them.

▶ Select text by dragging over it with your mouse or by pressing the Shift key while you use a keyboard arrow key to select the material.

▶ Once you select a portion of the document, you can act on the selection by making choices from the menu, a toolbar, or a shortcut menu. For example, choose Edit ➢ Cut from the menu, click the Cut button on the toolbar, or right-click and choose Cut from the shortcut menu to remove the selection from the document and send it to the Windows Clipboard.

▶ You can transfer text or images between FrontPage and other programs in the usual ways by using Copy or Cut and Paste with the Clipboard.

▶ Choose Edit ➢ Undo from the menu, click the Undo button on the Standard toolbar, or press Ctrl+Z to undo your most recent action in the document. You can "undo an undo" by choosing Edit ➢ Redo or by clicking the Redo button.

You can add comments in a page by selecting Insert ➢ Comment from the menu. The text you enter is displayed in the page you're editing, but not when the page is viewed in a browser. A comment can explain an area in the page or serve as a reminder to you or another author.

Inserting Paragraphs and Line Breaks

When you want to create a new paragraph in a document, simply press Enter, just as you would in your word processor. Behind the scenes, this inserts new <P> and </P> opening and closing tags in the underlying HTML code, defining the beginning and end of the new paragraph.

A new paragraph not only begins on a new line, it also has its own formatting, just as in Word. For example, if you press Enter at the end of a left-aligned paragraph (the default alignment), you can center the new paragraph, right align it, or add other paragraph formatting without changing the formatting for the previous line.

NOTE

When you press Enter but do not enter any text in the new paragraph, FrontPage places the HTML code for a non-breaking space (Ctrl+Shift+ Space) between the two paragraph tags, so the code created looks like this: <P> </P>. The non-breaking space on a line by itself forces a browser to display a blank line, where it might otherwise ignore the "empty" paragraph.

You can force a line to break without creating a new paragraph by pressing Shift+Enter instead of Enter. This inserts the line break tag,
 (you can also choose Normal Line Break from the dialog box of the Insert ➤ Break command). The text that follows the line break appears on a new line, but is otherwise still a part of the current paragraph and carries all of its formatting.

Most browsers insert some extra space between two paragraphs of text, so there are instances when you'd rather use the <BR> tag than the <P> tag to create a new line. For example, when you display your name and address in a page, you don't want extra space between each line of the address.

The next graphic shows two addresses in a table in a page being edited in FrontPage. In the address on the left, Enter was pressed at the end of each line to insert a line break. In the address on the right, Shift+Enter was pressed.

John and Joan Doe¶	John and Joan Doe ↵
	Widgets, Inc. ↵
Widgets, Inc.¶	123 S Proton Dr ↵
	Hanford, WA 98765 ¶
123 S Proton Dr ¶	
Hanford, WA 98765 ¶	

Notice that FrontPage displays a right-angle arrow for the line break and a paragraph mark between regular paragraphs. You can turn the display of line breaks and some other on-screen marks on or off by clicking the Show All button on the Standard toolbar.

Inserting Special Characters

Your computer's keyboard is limited to a standard set of letters, numbers, and punctuation. But there are a lot of other characters that simply are not included on your keyboard. For example, there's the degree symbol (100°), the copyright symbol (©1999), and the fraction symbol for one-half ($^1/_2$).

In FrontPage, you insert symbols into your page just as you do in Word: with the Insert ➤ Symbol command, which displays the Symbol dialog box (see Figure 25.4). Select the symbol you want and click the Insert button to place that symbol into your document at the insertion point. You can continue to select other symbols in the dialog box and click the Insert button. When you are finished, click the Close button.

FIGURE 25.4: The Insert ➤ Symbol command lets you pick a symbol to include in your page.

HTML and Browsers—The Start and End of Your Work

All of the pages that you edit are built from HTML code. However, FrontPage does such a good job of displaying the page and letting you manipulate it that you often just work along without even thinking about the underlying code that is being created.

Nonetheless, HTML is there and waiting if you need it, and the more you work with web pages, the more often you may want to take a peek at the HTML code. The Page view gives you several ways to interact with a page's HTML code:

▶ You can view the code at any time, making changes to it as though you're working on the page in a text editor.

> ▶ You can display the HTML tags within your document while still viewing your document in the WYSIWYG format.

> ▶ You can insert HTML tags that FrontPage doesn't support.

> ▶ You can view your page in any available Web browser, so you can see exactly how the HTML in the page will be interpreted by various browsers.

Seeing the HTML Source Code

When you want to see the HTML code behind the active page, click the HTML tab on the bottom left of the editing pane. The display switches to show the actual HTML code for your page—the same code that is saved on disk when you save your page.

Figure 25.5 shows the HTML view for the page that was displayed in Figure 25.3. If you're just viewing the code and do not want to make any changes to it, you can return to the page by clicking the Normal tab.

The HTML view is just another way to display your web page. Use caution when making changes to the HTML code, as they're reflected in the page when you return to Normal view. If, for example, you accidentally delete one of the angle brackets for an HTML tag, you'll see the result reflected on the page when you switch back to Normal view.

NOTE

Many, but not all, of the menu choices are available while you are in HTML view. For example, you can use Cut, Copy, and Paste to move or copy text; insert a horizontal line or graphic image; and create a data-entry form.

HTML view not only displays the underlying HTML for the active page, it also helps you interpret it by color-coding it. For example, text you enter is shown in the normal black, while HTML tags are shown in blue. To adjust the colors that are used, choose Tools ➤ Page Options and the Color Coding tab in the dialog box.

The different colors make it a lot easier to make sense of the code as you scroll through it. Viewing the underlying code is always a good exercise to help you get a feel for the ins and outs of HTML.

Part viii

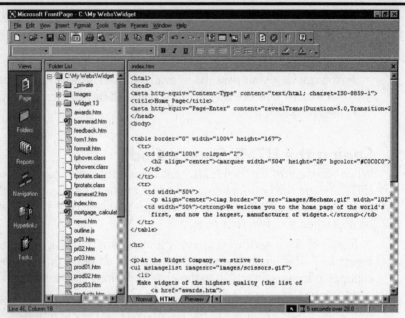

FIGURE 25.5:   Clicking the HTML tab lets you view or edit the underlying HTML code for a page.

Displaying HTML Tags in Your Document

Another way to get a sense of the HTML code that makes up a page is to display just the tags—choose View ➤ Reveal Tags (choose it again to turn off the display of the tags). Your page will still be shown in the Normal view, but the HTML tags for paragraphs and text will be displayed as well. Figure 25.6 shows the same page from Figure 25.3 after the Reveal Tags option was turned on.

The tags can help you differentiate between the various codes, and you can delete a tag to eliminate that code from your document. Point to a tag and its definition will be displayed in a pop-up screen tip. On the other hand, the tags tend to clutter the screen and slow down screen scrolling, so you will generally want to leave them turned off.

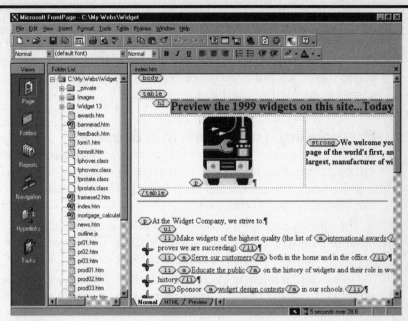

FIGURE 25.6: Choosing View ➤ Reveal Tags displays the basic HTML paragraph and text formatting tags within your WYSIWYG page.

Inserting Unsupported HTML Code

The fast-paced development of HTML means that there will always be some tags that some browsers accept even though those tags have not been incorporated into the official HTML specification.

Even if it is not supported by FrontPage, you can still add HTML code to your web pages by using the Insert ➤ Advanced ➤ HTML command. This displays the HTML Markup dialog box, in which you enter the HTML code you want to include in the page.

WARNING

FrontPage basically ignores the HTML code you enter in the HTML Markup dialog box, and does not check it for accuracy. So it's up to you to enter the code with no mistakes and ensure that it will be interpreted correctly by a browser.

When you click OK to close the HTML Markup dialog box, you'll see a small icon in your page (as shown here) that represents the code you added. Even though you won't be able to see how the page lays out around this new material in Page view, the code you added will be interpreted and displayed (assuming you entered it correctly) when you preview the page in a browser, as discussed in the next section.

Previewing Your Work in a Browser

The ultimate outcome for a page is to be viewed within a Web browser. Although FrontPage does a very good job of showing you how a page will appear within a browser, it can never offer the final and absolutely definitive view of a page. No editor can.

The primary reason for this is that HTML is designed to be very flexible in the way its pages are formatted. The same HTML code can be interpreted somewhat differently in different browsers.

On top of that inherent flexibility is the fact there are just too many variables that affect the ultimate appearance of a page within a browser. For example, a browser running within a screen resolution of 800 × 600 pixels displays over 50 percent more of a page than a browser running within a screen resolution of 640 × 480.

The only way to be sure how your web looks is to view it within a browser or, preferably, in several of the more popular browsers. You can also view a single page, right from within FrontPage, to see how that page looks in Internet Explorer. Click the Preview tab at the bottom of the editing pane to view the page. (This requires that you have Microsoft Internet Explorer 3.0 or higher installed on your system. If you do not, you won't have a Preview tab.)

To open Microsoft Internet Explorer, choose File ➢ Preview in Browser. The Preview in Browser dialog box, shown in Figure 25.7, opens so you can choose which browser you want to use.

When you initially install FrontPage, it searches for browsers on your computer and automatically adds installed browsers to the list in the Preview in Browser dialog box. If you add other browsers after you install FrontPage, you can add them to the list by clicking the Add button. You enter a name for the browser, which appears in the list of browsers, then enter the command that opens that browser. Use the Browse button to select the program from a typical Windows files dialog box.

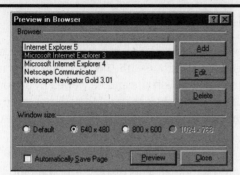

FIGURE 25.7:   The Preview in Browser dialog box lets you choose a browser to view your page.

Once the new browser appears in the list, you can select it to preview the page you're editing. Use the Edit or Delete buttons in the Preview in Browser dialog box to revise the settings for a browser or to remove a browser from the list.

If you have not saved the page you want to view, click the Automatically Save Page check box. (If you don't, you'll be told that you can't view the page until you save it.) FrontPage opens a Save As dialog box if you haven't saved the page. If you've previously saved the page, it just goes ahead and saves it again before displaying it in the browser.

Before clicking the Preview button, select a size for the browser's window in the Window Size group of options. For example, if your monitor's resolution is 800×600 or higher, you can choose the 640×480 option to see how the page looks in a browser that has been maximized to full-screen size on a monitor whose screen resolution is only 640×480. Choose the Default option to open the browser without specifying a size.

Now you're ready to click the Preview button. If you've already saved your page, this action takes you directly to the browser you selected.

When the page opens in the designated browser, you can see how your page actually looks when others view it on the Web. Review how the page looks when displayed within the specified window size and how the features within the page compare to the way they appear in FrontPage. When you're ready to go back to work on the page, switch back to Front-Page in one of the usual Windows ways: Alt+Tab, click its icon on the Taskbar, minimize the browser, or close the browser completely. When you are ready to view the page again in the same browser, all you have to do is click the Preview in Browser button on the toolbar.

Part viii

PRINTING YOUR PAGE

You can print the active page of the Page view in the same way you print a document in your word processor. Of course, the need to print rarely arises, since a page is meant to reside on a Web site and be viewed by a browser. Nonetheless, you may wish to print pages to proof them for accuracy, hang them on your refrigerator, or show them to others when you can't access a computer.

 To print the active page using the current print settings, choose File ➤ Print or click the Print button on the toolbar. This displays the standard Print dialog box, in which you can specify the number of copies to print, the range of pages to print, and the printer to which the job should be sent.

Previewing the Printout

Before you print a page, take a few seconds to preview what your printout will look like on paper by choosing File ➤ Print Preview. The buttons on the Preview toolbar perform the following tasks:

Print   Closes the preview but opens the Print dialog box, where you can print as usual to a printer.

Next Page   Displays the next page of a multipage printout; you can also use PgDn. The left side of the status bar shows the current page number.

Previous Page   Displays the previous page; you can also use PgUp.

Two Page/One Page   Toggles between displaying a single page or two pages of the printout.

Zoom In   Magnifies the preview so you can see more detail on the page, but less of the entire page.

Zoom Out   Shows you more of the page but shrinks the size of the characters on it.

TIP

Here's a fast way to zoom in on a specific portion of the page without having to hunt for it after the screen is magnified. Just point to the portion of the preview you want to see and click. Click again to zoom out again.

Close Closes the preview and returns to the active page; you can also press Esc.

Again, your pages are meant to be viewed within your Web site by a browser, so you'll probably print pages only if you're developing the web and want input from others, or if you want to lay it all out and see how the pages fit together.

SPELL-CHECKING

When you create a web, you should make sure that all the text is spelled correctly in each page. After you publish the web, you still need to provide periodic maintenance as new pages are added and existing pages require editing. It's all too easy to introduce a misspelling, even if you only spend 30 seconds on a page.

You probably use the spell-checker in your word processor every day as a quick and easy way to check the spelling of all the words in a document. FrontPage offers you the same tool, and it's even more powerful than you might suspect, because you can check the spelling in every page of your entire web in one operation. This is yet another example of how FrontPage condenses huge web management tasks into simple, one-step operations.

NOTE

FrontPage only checks the spelling of text that you can edit from the Normal tab of the Page view. Generally, that's the text that a visitor to your site will see. FrontPage doesn't check the underlying HTML code, such as the page title or hyperlink target names, nor the text in any included pages in the active page. These are pages that appear as the result of the Include Page component. You must open these pages separately to check their spelling.

Spell-Checking the Active Page

 To check the spelling of the active page in the Page view, choose Tools ➢ Spelling (F7), or click the Spelling button on the Standard toolbar. If you have experience with any of the applications in Microsoft Office, this routine is quite familiar.

If the spell-checker finds no misspelled words in the page, a dialog box notifies you of the success. If it finds a misspelled word (or rather, a word not in the spelling dictionary), you see the Spelling dialog box (shown in Figure 25.8) with the suspect word displayed in the Not in Dictionary field.

TIP

FrontPage can check your spelling while you work and underline those words that it can't find in the spelling dictionary. To turn this feature off or on, choose Tools ➢ Page Options, select the Spelling tab, and select or deselect the Check Spelling As You Type option.

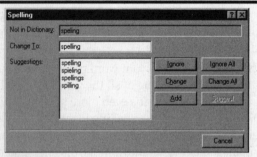

FIGURE 25.8: The Spelling dialog box displays a suspected misspelled word and offers a list of suggested replacements.

If the Word Is Spelled Correctly

The spell-checker flags many words that are actually correct, especially proper names and technical or medical terms. When the suspect word is correct, you can do any of the following:

- ▶ Click the Ignore button to bypass this word and continue to check the spelling; if the suspect word appears again, it's flagged again.

- ▶ Click the Ignore All button, bypassing all occurrences of the suspect word during this spell-checking session.

- ▶ Click the Add button to add this word to the custom dictionary. In the future, FrontPage will recognize that the word is spelled correctly.

If the Word Is Misspelled

If the word in question is not correct, you can either type the correct spelling into the Change To field or select one of the words from the Suggestions list (which then appears in the Change To field). At this point you have some options:

▶ Click the Change button to replace the misspelled word with the word in the Change To field.

▶ Click Change All to change all occurrences of the misspelled word in the active page.

You can also click the Cancel button at any time to end the spell-checking session.

Spell-Checking an Entire Web

To check the spelling of all or selected pages in the active web, first save all open web pages in the Page view to ensure that they are up to date on disk. Then display your web in Folders view, Navigation view, or Hyperlinks view. If you want to check the spelling of only some files, select the files in the Folders view. Then choose Tools ➢ Spelling (F7), or click the Spelling button. This displays the web-wide Spelling dialog box, shown in Figure 25.9, which offers two options for web-wide spell-checking:

▶ Choose to check all pages in the web or just those you had selected.

▶ Choose whether to fix misspellings immediately, or simply to add a task to the Tasks view for each filename that contains misspelled words so you can return at your convenience to correct the misspellings.

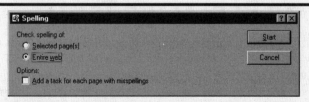

FIGURE 25.9: The Spelling dialog box allows you to check the spelling in selected pages or the entire web.

Part viii

When you click the Start button to begin the spellcheck, the dialog box expands to list all the pages in which misspelled words have been found, as shown in Figure 25.10. You can click the Cancel button at any time to stop the spell-checking.

When the process is finished, you can double-click a page to open it, at which point the spell-checking continues as described earlier for a single page. When you're finished with one page, you're given the option to open the next one and continue.

You can also choose to return to a page later by selecting the page in the list and clicking the Add Task button. A new task will be added to the Tasks list that reminds you to check the spelling on that page.

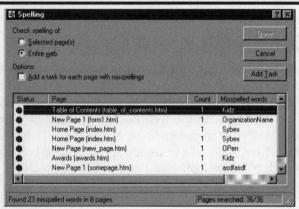

FIGURE 25.10: Each page that contains a suspected misspelling is listed in the Spelling dialog box; you can either fix each one immediately or add a task so you can fix it later on.

FINDING OR REPLACING TEXT

Suppose the Widget Company decides to change its business focus and create a new image, including changing its name to the Technical Tools Company. Even though you redesign the web to reflect the company's new image, you also want to make sure that the company's online presence is maintained through the transition so that visitors to the online aren't disappointed. You need to find every occurrence of *Widget* in every page in the Web, and replace it with *Technical Tools*.

Once again, FrontPage can come to your assistance by providing another set of tools that you undoubtedly already use on a regular basis in your word processor—the Find and Replace commands. You use these commands to seek out a word, sentence, or just a few characters in the document, and to replace text with other text. Like the spell-checker in FrontPage, the Find and Replace commands can act on the active page of the Page view or on every page in your entire web.

Finding or Replacing Text in the Active Page

Select Edit ➤ Find to find all occurrences of text you specify in either the active page or in all pages in your web (that procedure will be discussed a little later). Enter the characters you want to find in the Find What field of the Find dialog box (shown in Figure 25.11). There are several options you can use to refine your search:

▶ You can find those characters in the current page or in all pages in the web.

▶ You can select the Find Whole Word Only option to specify that the characters should be found only when they are a complete word.

▶ You can select the Match Case option to specify that the case (UPPER or lower) exactly matches the case of the text you entered.

▶ You can also choose to search up or down the page, starting from the insertion point.

▶ When you're displaying a page in the HTML view, you can use the Find in HTML option to search through all the HTML code that underlies your page, allowing you to find, for example, all occurrences of a <B> or <HR> tag.

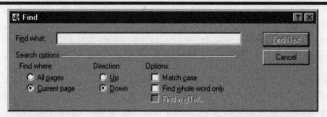

FIGURE 25.11: While in Page view, the Find dialog box lets you search for text in the current page or in all pages in the web.

To begin the search in the active page, click the Find Next button. The first occurrence of the specified text is selected in the page. At this point you can:

- ▶ Click Find Next to find the next occurrence.

- ▶ Click Cancel to close the Find dialog box.

- ▶ Click on the page so you can continue to work in it, perhaps to edit the text that was found. The Find dialog box remains open.

Select Edit ➤ Replace command to specify the text to search for as well as the text with which to replace it. If you leave the Replace With field empty, the text that is found is deleted. You perform the Replace operation with three buttons in the Replace dialog box:

- ▶ Click Find Next to find the next occurrence of the specified text.

- ▶ Click Replace to replace the current occurrence, then move on to find the next occurrence.

- ▶ Click Replace All to replace every occurrence of the text.

TIP

Practice safe computing by saving the page before using the Replace All command on the entire page.

When you're finished finding and replacing text, you can click on the page to leave the dialog box open and continue working on the page, or click the Cancel button to close the dialog box and return to the page.

Finding or Replacing Text in the Entire Web

The process of finding or replacing text in all or selected pages is very much like the spell-checking process described earlier in "Spell-Checking an Entire Web." If you want to check just a few pages, first select them in Folders view. Then choose Edit ➤ Find or Edit ➤ Replace, and choose either the Selected Pages or All Pages option.

This time, instead of seeing the matching text that is found, you'll see a list of all the pages that contain that text. As with the web-wide spell-checking (look back at Figure 25.10), you have two options. You can double-click a page to open it and then decide whether or not to replace each occurrence of the text in that file, or click the Add Task button to create a reminder task for a page so you can return to it later on.

NOTE

When you double-click a page to replace text within it, the Replace command does not automatically replace the text it finds; you can verify each change within the page itself so you can confirm the changes.

WHAT'S NEXT

Your official tour of the Office 2000 suite has almost come to an end. You've mastered the basics of Word, Excel, PowerPoint, Access, Outlook, and FrontPage, and you know how all the Office applications work together. You also have a good understanding of HTML and the Internet. Now, it's time to take care of some loose ends: Chapter 26 discusses the special features and commands available in Windows 98, and Appendix A describes how to install Office 2000.

PART ix
DISCOVER WINDOWS 98

Chapter 26

WINDOWS 98 COMMAND AND FEATURE REFERENCE

Adapted from *Windows 98 Instant Reference* by Peter Dyson

ISBN 0-7821-2191-8   352 pages $14.99

ACTIVE DESKTOP

 In Windows 98, you can use a conventional Windows interface similar to that in earlier versions of Windows, or you can use the Active Desktop. The Active Desktop brings the world of the Web right to the Windows 98 Desktop, allowing you to replace the static Windows wallpaper with a fully configurable, full-screen Web page. The Active Desktop can contain other Web pages, dynamic HTML, even Java components such as stock tickers and ActiveX controls, and you can add these elements to the Taskbar or to a folder.

> **NOTE**
> You can combine the Active Desktop and Internet Explorer's subscription capabilities to create your own personal push-content client, displaying data on your Desktop from whatever sources interest you. For example, you can display a continuously updating stock ticker or sports results right on your Desktop; assuming of course that you have continuous Internet access.

To set up your Active Desktop, choose Start ➤ Settings ➤ Active Desktop, and you will see three options: View As Web Page, Customize My Desktop, and Update Now. You can also right-click the Desktop and select Active Desktop from the menu.

View As Web Page

Turns on the Active Desktop interface. Selecting this option a second time removes the checkmark and turns the Active Desktop off again.

Customize My Desktop

Opens the Display Properties dialog box. You can also right-click the Desktop and select Properties, or if you prefer, choose Start ➤ Settings ➤ Control Panel and select the Display icon. The Display Properties dialog box contains six tabs, but we are only concerned with the following two:

Background   Lets you choose an HTML document or a picture to use as your Desktop background. In the Wallpaper box, select the background you want to use, or click Pattern to choose or modify the background pattern. You can also click the Browse button to locate a file or to go directly to a Web site to find the

HTML document you are interested in using as a background. To cover your entire Desktop with a small wallpaper image, select Tile from the Display box, or choose Center if you prefer to see the image centered. Click the Apply button to see the effect of your changes before you exit the Display Properties dialog box, or click OK to accept the changes and close the dialog box.

TIP

You can also right-click any Web page graphic that takes your fancy and then click Set As Wallpaper.

Web   Lets you select and organize Active Desktop elements. At the top of the tab, you will see a representation of your Desktop, indicating the location of any Active Desktop elements. These same elements are listed in the box below. To add a new element such as a stock ticker or a weather map, click New to open the New Active Desktop Item dialog box. If you want to browse through Microsoft's Active Desktop Gallery on Microsoft's Web site for a component to add, click Yes. To select a different Web site, click No, and then enter the address or URL for the Web site, or click the Browse button to locate it. Be sure that the View my Active Desktop as a Web page box is checked if you want your Desktop to look like a Web page.

NOTE

You can also right-click any link on a Web page, drag it to your Desktop, and then click Create Active Desktop Item Here.

Update Now

Updates the Desktop contents right now to display any changes you have made.

ADD NEW HARDWARE

Guides you through the process of adding new hardware to your system using the New Hardware Wizard. This Wizard automatically makes the appropriate changes to the Registry and to the configuration files so that Windows 98 can recognize and support your new hardware. Be sure you have installed or connected your new hardware before you go any further.

ADD/REMOVE PROGRAMS

Installs or uninstalls individual elements of the Windows 98 operating system itself or certain application programs. Installing or removing application or system software components in this way enables Windows 98 to modify all the appropriate system and configuration files automatically so that the information in them stays current and correct.

To start Add/Remove Programs, choose Start ➤ Settings ➤ Control Panel, and then click the Add/Remove Programs icon to open the Add/Remove Programs Properties dialog box. This dialog box contains four tabs if you are connected to a local area network; otherwise, it contains three tabs.

Install/Uninstall Tab

To install a new program using the Add/Remove Programs applet, follow these steps:

1. Select the Install/Uninstall tab if it isn't already selected, and then click the Install button.

2. Put the application program CD or floppy disk in the appropriate drive, and click the Next button to display a setup or install message, describing the program to be installed.

3. To continue with the installation process, click the Finish button. To make any changes, click Back and repeat the procedure.

To uninstall a program previously installed under Windows 98, you must follow a different process. The programs that have uninstall capability (not all of them do) will be listed in the display box of the Install/Uninstall tab. Click the program you want to uninstall, and then click the Add/Remove button. You may see a warning message about removing the application. You will be to told when the uninstall is finished.

NOTE

Once you remove an application using Add/Remove Programs, you will have to reinstall it from the original program disks or CD if you decide to use it again.

Windows Setup Tab

Some components of the Windows 98 operating system are optional, and you can install or uninstall them as you wish; the Windows Clipboard Viewer is an example. Select the Windows Setup tab to display a list of such components with checkboxes on the left. If the box has a checkmark in it, the component is currently installed. If the checkbox is gray, only some elements of that component are installed; to see what is included in a component, click the Details button. Follow these steps to add a Windows 98 component:

1. Click the appropriate checkbox.

2. If the component consists of several elements, click the Details button to display a list of them, and check the boxes you want to install.

3. Click OK to display the Windows Setup tab.

4. Click the Apply button, and then click OK.

To remove a Windows 98 component from your system, follow these steps:

1. Click the Details button to see a complete list of the individual elements in the component you want to uninstall.

2. Clear the checkmark from the checkboxes of the elements you want to uninstall, and then click OK to open the Windows Setup tab.

3. Click the Apply button, and then click OK.

Startup Disk Tab

A startup disk is a floppy disk with which you can start, or "boot," your computer if something happens to your hard drive. When you originally installed Windows 98, you were asked if you wanted to create a startup disk. If you didn't do it at that time or if the disk you created then is not usable, you can create one now. Simply insert a disk with at least 1.2MB capacity in the appropriate drive, click Create Disk, and follow the instructions on the screen.

Network Install Tab

In some cases, you can also install a program directly from a network using the Network Install tab. If the Network Install tab is not present in the Add/Remove Programs Properties dialog box, this feature may not have been enabled on your computer or on your network; see your system administrator for more details.

If the Install/Uninstall tab is selected, your system is currently connected to the network, and you can click Install followed by Next to find the setup program for your network.

If the Network Install tab is selected, follow the instructions on the screen.

ADDRESS BOOK

Manages your e-mail addresses, as well as your voice, fax, modem, and cellular phone numbers. Once you enter an e-mail address in your Address Book, you can select it from a list rather than type it in every time. To open the Address Book, choose Start ≻ Programs ≻ Internet Explorer ≻ Address Book, or click the Address Book icon on the Outlook Express toolbar.

Importing an Existing Address Book

Address Book can import information from an existing address book in any of the following formats:

- ▸ Windows Address Book
- ▸ Microsoft Exchange Personal Address Book
- ▸ Microsoft Internet Mail for Windows 3.1 Address Book
- ▸ Netscape Address Book
- ▸ Netscape Communicator Address Book
- ▸ Eudora Pro or Lite Address Book

▶ Lightweight Directory Access Protocol (LDAP)

▶ Comma-separated text file

To import information from one of these address books, follow these steps:

1. Choose Start ➤ Programs ➤ Internet Explorer ➤ Address Book, or click the Address Book icon on the Outlook Express toolbar.

2. Choose File ➤ Import ➤ Address Book to open the Address Book Import Tool dialog box.

3. Select the file you want to import, and click Import.

Creating a New Address Book Entry

To add a new entry to your Address Book, click the New Contact button on the Address Book toolbar or choose File ➤ New Contact to open the Properties dialog box. This dialog box has six tabs:

Personal   Lets you enter personal information including the person's first, middle, and last names, a nickname, and an e-mail address. If the person has more than one e-mail address, click Add and continue entering addresses.

Home   Allows you to enter additional information about this contact; enter as much or as little information as makes sense here.

Business   Allows you to enter business-related information; again, enter as much or as little information as makes sense.

Other   Offers a chance to store additional information about this contact as a set of text notes.

NetMeeting   Lets you enter NetMeeting information such as a person's conferencing e-mail address and server name. If Net-Meeting is not installed on your system, this tab will be called Conferencing.

Digital IDs   Allows you to specify a digital certificate for use with an e-mail address.

Setting Up a New Group

You can create groups of e-mail addresses to make it easy to send a message to all the members of the group. You can group people any way you like—by job title, musical taste, or sports team allegiance. When you want to send e-mail to everyone in the group, simply use the group name instead of selecting each e-mail address individually. To begin creating a new group, click the New Group icon on the Address Book toolbar or choose File ➤ New Group to open the Group Properties dialog box.

ADDRESS TOOLBAR

Shows the location of the page currently displayed in the main window; this may be a URL on the Internet or an intranet, or it may be a file or folder stored on your hard disk.

To go to another page, click the arrow at the right end of the Address toolbar to select the appropriate entry, or simply type a new location. When you start to type an address that you have previously entered, the Auto-Complete feature recognizes the address and completes the entry for you.

The Address toolbar is available in most Windows 98 applications, including the Explorer, Internet Explorer, My Computer, the Control Panel, and others.

BACKUP

Creates an archive copy of one or more files and folders on your hard disk and then restores them to your hard disk in the event of a disk or controller failure or some other unforeseen event.

BROWSE

The Browse button is available in many common dialog boxes when you have to choose or enter a file name, find a folder, or specify a Web address or URL. Clicking the Browse button or the Find File button opens the Browse dialog box.

You can look through folders on any disk on any shared computer on the network to find the file you want. When you find the file, folder, computer, or Web site, double-click it to open, import, or enter it in a text box.

CD Player

Allows you to play audio compact discs on your CD-ROM drive. Choose Start > Programs > Accessories > Multimedia > CD Player to open the CD Player dialog box.

Chat

→ *See* NetMeeting

Clipboard

A temporary storage place for data. You can use the Cut and Copy commands as well as the Windows screen capture commands to place data on the Clipboard. The Paste command then copies the data from the Clipboard to a receiving document, perhaps in another application. You cannot edit the Clipboard contents; however, you can view and save the information stored in the Clipboard by using the Clipboard Viewer, or you can paste the contents of the Clipboard into Notepad.

WARNING

The Clipboard only holds one piece of information at a time, so cutting or copying onto the Clipboard overwrites any existing contents.

Closing Windows

Closing an application program window terminates the operations of that program. In Windows 98, you can close windows in a number of ways:

▶ Click the Close button in the upper-right corner of the program title bar. ☒

▶ Choose Control ➤ Close (identified by the icon to the left of the program name in the title bar) or simply double-click the Control Menu icon.

▶ Choose File ➤ Close or File ➤ Exit within the application.

▶ If the application is minimized on the Taskbar, right-click the application's icon and choose Close or press Alt+F4.

CONNECTION WIZARD

Walks you through the steps of setting up your Internet connection. All you need is an account with an ISP (Internet Service Provider), and you're all set. You can start the Connection Wizard in several ways:

▶ Choose Start ➤ Programs ➤ Internet Explorer ➤ Connection Wizard.

▶ From the Windows 98 Help system, choose the Using the Internet Connection Wizard topic.

▶ Choose Start ➤ Settings ➤ Control Panel ➤ Internet to open the Internet Properties dialog box, and then select the Connection tab and click the Connect button.

▶ In Internet Explorer, choose View ➤ Internet Options to open the Internet Options dialog box, and then select the Connection tab and click the Connect button.

No matter which method you use, you first see the Welcome screen; click the Next button to continue. The Setup Options dialog box gives you three choices:

▶ Open a new account with an ISP. Select the first option if you do not have an account. The Wizard takes you through the steps of finding an ISP and starting an account and sets up the dial-up link for you.

▶ Establish a connection to an existing Internet account. Select the second option to set up a connection to your existing Internet account or to revise the settings for your current account.

▶ Make no change to your existing account. If you choose this option and click the Next button, the Wizard closes because there is nothing for it to do.

Creating a New Connection to the Internet

To create a new dial-up connection to the Internet, start the Connection Wizard, click Next at the Welcome screen, and then follow these steps:

1. In the Setup Options dialog box, choose the first option to select an ISP and set up a new Internet account, and then click Next.

2. The Connection Wizard now begins the automatic part of the setup by loading programs from your original Windows 98 CD. You may be asked to restart your computer; the Wizard will resume automatically. Be sure you complete all the steps; otherwise, the Wizard may not be able to set up your connection properly.

3. If you have a modem, the Wizard attempts to locate an ISP in your area and sets up the appropriate Dial-Up Networking software on your system. Follow the prompts on the screen to complete the setup.

Modifying an Existing Connection to the Internet

You can modify your existing Internet account settings at any time. Start the Connection Wizard, click Next at the Welcome screen, and then follow these steps:

1. In the Setup Options dialog box, select the second option to set up a new connection to an existing Internet account.

2. Choose the method you use to connect to the Internet, either by phone line or through your local area network, and click Next.

3. In the Dial-Up Connection dialog box, check the Use an Existing Dial-Up Connection box, select the connection from the list box, and click the Next button.

4. You'll then be asked if you want to modify the settings for this connection. Click Yes, and then click Next to open the Phone Number dialog box where you can enter the phone number to dial to make the connection.

5. In the next dialog box, enter your user name and password information, and click Next.

6. In the Advanced settings dialog box you are asked if you want to change any of the advanced settings for this connection, such as connection type, logon script filename, and IP address. You should only change these settings when your ISP or system administrator tells you to and provides the new information to use. Click Next.

7. You'll then be asked if you want to set up an Internet e-mail account; click Yes and then Next to specify whether you want to use an existing account or create a new one. If you opt to continue using an existing account, you will be asked to confirm your e-mail account settings; if you establish a new account, you will have to enter this information from scratch. Click Next.

8. Next, you'll be asked if you want to set up an Internet news account; follow the instructions on the screen.

9. Finally, click the Finish button to complete the configuration and close the Wizard.

CONTROL PANEL

Provides a way to establish settings and defaults for all sorts of important Windows features. To access the Control Panel, choose Start ➤ Settings ➤ Control Panel.

If you are using the conventional Windows interface, you will see a window that looks like this:

To open an applet, double-click it, or click once on its icon to select it and then choose File ➤ Open.

If you are using the Active Desktop and you have View As Web Page turned on, you will see a much different Control Panel:

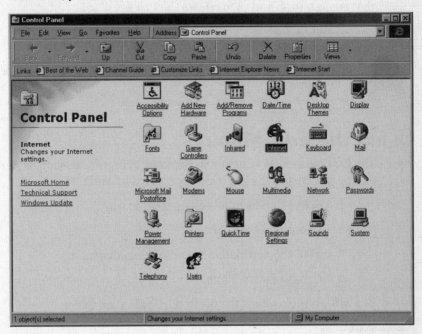

The Control Panel now looks and works like a Web page displayed in a browser. All the names of the applets are underlined, and the mouse pointer turns into a hand when you move the cursor over an icon. You will also see a short description of what each Control Panel applet does on the left side of the window. More important, it now takes only a single mouse-click to open an applet.

COPYING FILES AND FOLDERS

When you copy a file or a folder, you duplicate it in another location and leave the original in place. In Windows, you can copy files and folders in three ways. Let's take a look.

Using Drag-and-Drop

To use the drag-and-drop method, both the source and the destination folders must be open on the Desktop. Press and hold the Ctrl key while holding down the left mouse button, and drag the file or folder from one location to another. When the file or folder is in the correct place, release the mouse button and then release the Ctrl key.

WARNING

Be sure to hold down Ctrl. If you do not, the file or folder will be moved rather than copied.

Using the Edit Menu

The Edit menu in My Computer, Explorer, or any folder window provides a Copy and Paste feature. Follow these steps to use it:

1. Select the file or folder you want to copy.

2. Choose Edit ➤ Copy.

3. Find the destination file or folder and open it.

4. Choose Edit ➤ Paste.

You will see the name of the file in the destination folder.

TIP

You can select multiple files or folders to be copied by holding down Ctrl and clicking them. If the files are contiguous, you can also use Shift to select files.

Using the Right Mouse Button

Right-clicking a file or a folder opens a pop-up menu that you can use to perform a number of functions, including copying. To copy using the right mouse button, follow these steps:

1. Locate the file or folder you want to copy, and right-click to open the pop-up menu. Select Copy.

2. Open the destination folder, click the right mouse button, and select Paste.

You will see the name of the file in the destination folder.

CREATING NEW FOLDERS

Sooner or later you will want to add a new folder to a disk or to another folder, and you can do so in Explorer. Follow these steps:

1. In Explorer, select the disk or folder in which you want to place a new folder.

2. Choose File ➤ New ➤ Folder.

A new folder is added to the disk or the folder you indicated with the name "New Folder" highlighted.

3. Type a new folder name, something that will act as a reminder as to the files it contains, and press Enter.

You can also right-click in the blank part of the Windows Explorer file pane to open a pop-up menu from which you can choose New ➤ Folder.

TIP

If you would rather bypass Explorer altogether, you can create a new folder on the Desktop by clicking My Documents and then choosing File ➤ New ➤ Folder. Give the folder a new name, and then drag it to the Desktop.

DATE/TIME

The clock that appears in the right corner of the Taskbar displays the system clock, which not only tells you the time, but also indicates the time and date associated with any files you create or modify. At any time, you can place the mouse pointer on the time in the Taskbar to display the complete date. To vary the format of the date and time displayed in the Taskbar, select the Regional Settings applet in the Control Panel.

To set the clock, follow these steps:

1. Double-click the time in the Taskbar, or choose Start ➤ Settings ➤ Control Panel ➤Date/Time to open the Date/Time Properties dialog box.

2. Select the Date & Time tab to set the day, month, year, or current time.

3. To change the time, either drag across the numbers you want to change beneath the clock and type the new time, or highlight the numbers and click the up and down arrows to increase or decrease the values.

4. To change the date, click the drop-down arrow to select the month, use the up and down arrows to change the year, and click the appropriate day of the month.

DELETING FILES AND FOLDERS

You can delete a file or a folder in several ways. First, select the file or folder you want in My Computer or Windows Explorer, and then do one of the following:

▶ Choose File ≻ Delete. After you confirm that you want to delete the file or folder, Windows sends it to the Recycle Bin.

▶ Press the Delete key on the keyboard and verify that you want to delete the selected file or folder; Windows then sends it to the Recycle Bin.

▶ Right-click the file or folder to open the pop-up menu. Select Delete and then verify that you want to delete the selected file or folder. Off it goes to the Recycle Bin.

▶ Position the My Computer or Explorer window so that you can also see the Recycle Bin on the Desktop; then simply drag the selected file or folder to the Recycle Bin.

NOTE

If you accidentally delete a file or folder, you can choose Edit ≻ Undo Delete or retrieve the file or folder manually from the Recycle Bin. You cannot retrieve a deleted file or folder if the Recycle Bin has been emptied since your last deletion.

TIP

To delete a file without placing it in the Recycle Bin, select the file and then press Shift+Delete. You cannot recover the file if you do this. You will be asked to confirm the deletion.

DESKTOP

What you see on the screen when you first open Windows. If you are not using any of the Web-like features of the Active Desktop, you see the conventional Windows Desktop. Initially, it contains a set of icons arranged on the left, plus the Taskbar with the Start button across the bottom. As you work with Windows and load application programs, other objects such as dialog boxes and messages boxes are placed on the Desktop.

You can also change the appearance of the Desktop by right-clicking it and selecting Properties. This allows you to change display properties for the Desktop background and screen savers. You can also change the monitor type, as well as font types, sizes, and colors for objects on the screen.

DISK CLEANUP

A quick and convenient way to make more space available on your hard disk. Choose Start ➤ Programs ➤ Accessories ➤ System Tools ➤ Disk Cleanup to open the Disk Cleanup dialog box.

Alternatively, you can open Explorer or My Computer, right-click the disk you want to work with, and then choose Properties from the pop-up menu. On the General tab, click the Disk Cleanup button.

DISK SPACE

To find out how much disk space a file or folder occupies, select it (hold down the Ctrl key to select more than one) in My Computer or Explorer. The window's status bar will display the number of objects selected and the amount of disk space they occupy.

Alternately, you can choose File ➤ Properties or right-click a file or folder and select Properties. The General tab displays the amount of disk space or, in the case of a folder, its size plus the number of files or other folders it contains.

To see how much disk space remains on the entire disk, select the disk name in My Computer or Explorer and then choose File ➤ Properties or right-click and choose Properties. The Properties dialog box displays both the amount of used and the amount of free space. The status bar of My Computer also displays the free space and capacity of a disk drive.

DISPLAY

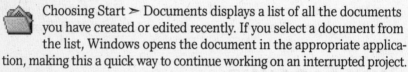 Controls how the objects on you screen—patterns, colors, fonts, sizes, and other elements—look. Choose Start ➤ Settings ➤ Control Panel ➤ Display (or simply right-click the Desktop and select properties) to open the Display Properties dialog box. It has six tabs: Background, Screen Saver, Appearance, Effects, Web, and Settings.

DOCUMENTS

Choosing Start ➤ Documents displays a list of all the documents you have created or edited recently. If you select a document from the list, Windows opens the document in the appropriate application, making this a quick way to continue working on an interrupted project.

Windows maintains this list of documents and preserves it between Windows sessions even if you shut down and restart your computer. The last 15 documents are preserved in this list, but some of them may look more like applications or folders than documents.

To clear the list of documents and start the list over, choose Start ➤ Settings ➤ Taskbar & Start Menu. Select the Start Menu Programs tab and click the Clear button. Once you do this, only one entry will remain in the list, the shortcut to the My Documents folder.

DRAG-AND-DROP

You can use drag-and-drop to move, copy, activate, or dispose of files and folders on the Desktop and in many accessory and application windows. Place the mouse pointer on a file, press the left button, and drag the file or folder to another disk or folder. Position the pointer over the destination and release the mouse button. The result depends on the file or folder being dragged and the destination:

- ▶ Dragging a file or folder to another folder on the same disk moves it (hold down the Ctrl key if you want to copy the file or folder).

- ▶ Dragging a file or folder to another disk copies it.

- ▶ Dragging a file to a shortcut printer icon on the Desktop prints the document.

- ▶ Dragging a file or folder to the Recycle Bin disposes of it.

ENTERTAINMENT

Menu used to access the Windows multimedia applications. Choose Start ➤ Programs ➤ Accessories ➤ Entertainment. This menu includes CD Player, Media Player, Sound Recorder, TV Viewer, and others.

EXPLORER

The Windows Explorer (to use its full name) is *the* place to go when working with files and folders in Windows 98. The Explorer lets you look at your disks, folders, and files, in a variety of ways and helps you perform such tasks as copying, moving, renaming, and deleting files and folders, formatting floppy disks, and so on.

Explorer Menus

To access Explorer, choose Start ➤ Programs ➤ Windows Explorer, or right-click the Start button and choose Explore. You may want to create a shortcut for it on the Desktop or in the Start menu itself since it is used so often.

The Explorer menus give you access to all common functions. However, for some menu selections to work, you may first have to select an appropriate object in the main Explorer window, and the type of object you select determines the available options. You may, therefore, not see all these options on any given menu, and you may see some options not listed here. You will also find similar menus in My Computer, the Recycle Bin, and Network Neighborhood.

File Menu

Displays basic file-management options. It allows you to do the following:

▶ Open a folder or file

▶ Explore the contents of a selected computer, disk, or folder

▶ Print a file or get a Quick View of the contents of a file (not shown on the menu unless it is available)

▶ Set parameters for sharing a folder with other users

▶ Send a file to a floppy disk, to an e-mail or fax correspondent (using Windows Messaging), to My Briefcase, or to another destination

▶ Create a new folder or a shortcut

▶ Make a shortcut to a file or folder

▶ Delete or rename a file or folder

▶ Display a file's properties

▶ Close a file or a folder

If you are working with the Printers folder, you will also see options to Capture Printer Port and to End Capture.

Edit Menu

Allows you to work with the contents of a folder or file. It allows you to do the following:

▶ Undo the previous action

▶ Cut, copy, and paste folders or files

▶ Paste a shortcut within a folder

▶ Select all files and folders

▶ Select all files except those already selected, which become deselected

View Menu

Allows you to change the window to include or exclude the toolbars, Status bar, and Explorer bar. You can choose how the files and folders are displayed:

▶ As a Web page

▶ With large icons or small icons

▶ In a list

▶ With details, describing the size and type of a file and the date modified

You can arrange icons by name, type of file or folder, size, or date created or last modified. You can also arrange icons into columns and rows. Refresh redisplays your screen. Folder Options lets you set defaults for how information is displayed in the main Explorer window, and Customize This Folder lets you change the appearance of the folder.

Go Menu

Lets you go back, forward, or up one level and gives fast access to certain Web sites and other Windows elements such as Mail, News, My Computer, Address Book, and Internet Call.

Favorites Menu

The Favorites menu is divided into two parts. You use the first part to manage your favorite Web sites with Add to Favorites and Organize Favorites, as well as those Web sites to which you subscribe with Manage Subscriptions and Update All Subscriptions. You use the second part for fast access to groups of Web sites with Channels, Links, and Software Updates.

Tools Menu

Gives you quick access to Find so that you can find Files or Folders, Computer, On the Internet, or People. You can also map a networked drive and disconnect a networked drive.

Help Menu

Provides access to the Windows Help system.

TIP

Some functions available from the Explorer menus are also available as buttons on the toolbar.

Explorer Toolbar

The following buttons are available on the standard Explorer toolbar:

Back   Displays the item you last displayed. Click the small down arrow just to the right of this button to see a list of all the items you have displayed in this Explorer session and click an item to go to it directly.

Forward   Displays the item you were viewing before you went back to the current item. Click the small down arrow just to the right of this button to display a list of items. Click an item to go to it directly.

Up   Moves up the directory tree in the left Explorer window, changing the contents displayed in the right window as it goes.

Cut   Moves the selected items to the Clipboard.

Copy   Duplicates selected items, placing their content on the Clipboard.

Paste   Transfers the contents of the Clipboard to a file or folder. A destination folder must already exist and must be selected.

 Undo   Cancels the previous action. The label changes depending on what you did last—for example, Undo Delete or Undo Copy.

Delete   Places the selected file or folder in the Recycle Bin.

 Properties   Opens the Properties dialog box for the selected disk, file, or folder.

Views   Changes the way information is displayed in the right-hand Explorer window. Click the small down arrow just to the right of this button to display a menu you can use to select the various displays. Alternatively, each time you click the Views button, the display cycles through these four views:

> **Large Icons**   Displays larger-sized icons representing the contents of the selected folder or disk.
>
> **Small Icons**   Displays smaller-sized icons in a horizontal, columnar list representing the contents of the selected folder or disk.
>
> **List**   Displays the contents as small icons, except in a vertical rather than horizontal orientation.
>
> **Details**   Displays the contents in a detailed list with additional information about the file size, file type, and modification date.

The Explorer also contains two other toolbars:

Address   Displays the location of the item currently displayed by the Explorer. The arrow at the right end of the Address toolbar opens a drop-down list of items; select one to open it.

Links   Displays a set of hyperlinks to various parts of Microsoft's Web site; you can also access these links from the Links selection in the Favorites menu.

You will also see a single status line across the bottom of the main Explorer window; it displays messages about your actions and lists information on disk storage space, including the number of items in a folder and the occupied and free disk space.

Explorer Window

When you run the Explorer, all items that make up your computer are listed in the left pane. Some objects have a plus sign (+) next to them, indicating that the object contains other objects that are not currently visible. To display the contents of such an item in the right pane, click the item, not the plus sign.

When you click the plus sign associated with an object, you display all the subelements, usually folders, in the left window, where they become part of the overall tree structure. The plus sign becomes a minus sign (−) if an object's contents are expanded. This tree structure is a graphical representation of how the files and folders on your system are related; the name of each folder appears just after its icon.

Customizing a Folder

Choose View ➤ Customize This Folder to open the Customize This Folder Wizard with these options:

Create or Edit an HTML Document   Lets you create an HTML (Hypertext Markup Language) document in three steps:

1.   Open the editor and create the HTML document.

2.   Save the document.

3.   Close the editor.

Choose a Background Picture   Lets you select a picture that will be displayed as wallpaper when you open this folder.

Remove Customization   Lets you return this folder to its original look and feel.

Selecting a Drive and Choosing a File or a Folder

When you open the Explorer, all the disks and folders available on your computer are displayed in the left pane. The right pane displays the contents of the disk or folder you selected on the left. Follow these steps to find a file or a folder:

1. Scroll up and down using the left scroll bar. On the left, you can see all the disks on your computer, plus those that are shared on your network, and all the folders within each disk. On the right, you will see all the folders and files within the selected disk or folder.

2. If the drive you want is not visible, you may have to expand the My Computer icon by clicking its plus sign. Normally, you will be able to see a floppy disk and at least one hard disk.

3. Click a disk or folder in the left pane to display its contents in the right pane; when a folder is selected, its icon changes from a closed folder to an open one.

4. Once you find the file or folder you want, open it and get to work.

FAVORITES

Contains selections you can use to track your favorite Web sites. You can open your favorite Web sites from many places within Windows 98. You can choose Start ➢ Favorites, or you can use the Favorites menu in Windows Explorer, My Computer, Internet Explorer, Network Neighborhood, and Control Panel; even the Recycle Bin has a Favorites menu.

Add to Favorites

Choose Favorites ➤ Add to Favorites to bookmark a Web site so that you can find it again quickly and easily. Once you place the address, or URL, for the site in this list, you can revisit the site simply by selecting it from the Favorites menu; the result is the same as if you had typed the whole URL into the Address toolbar and pressed Enter. You can also display your Favorites menu from the Explorer Bar; choose View ➤ Explorer Bar ➤ Favorites.

Organize Favorites

Choose Favorites ➤ Organize Favorites to group your Web sites into an arrangement that makes sense to you; a single long list is certainly not the most efficient organization.

Subscribing to a Web Site

In addition to visiting Web sites in the normal way with Internet Explorer, you can also subscribe to a Web site. A subscription is a mechanism that Internet Explorer uses to check for new or updated content on a Web site without your involvement.

Fax

 Sends and receives faxes between computers or fax machines. You can send a fax in several ways:

▶ Drag a text or graphics file to the Microsoft Fax icon in the Printers folder.

▶ Right-click an icon and select the Send to Fax Recipient command.

▶ Select Microsoft Fax as the printer in any application program.

▶ Use Windows Messaging.

▶ Choose Start ➤ Programs ➤ Accessories ➤ Fax ➤ Compose New Fax.

No matter which of these techniques you use, the Compose New Fax Wizard will guide you through creating and sending a fax. Once you have a suitable profile set up under Start ➤ Programs ➤ Windows Messaging, the rest is a breeze.

TIP

To install Fax, you must have Microsoft Exchange, Windows Messaging, or Outlook already installed on your system.

Compose New Fax

Follow these steps to compose a new fax message:

1. Open the Compose New Fax dialog box using one of the techniques discussed earlier.

2. If you are using a laptop (and therefore may not always be calling from the same location), click Dialing Properties and review the methods used to dial an outside line. If you are not using a portable computer, you can click *I'm not using a portable computer, so don't show this to me again.* Click Next.

3. Complete the information on the person to whom you want to send the fax. Type a name, country, fax number, and a recipient list, if applicable.

4. Select whether to send a cover page and its type. Click Options to open the Send Options for This Message dialog box.

5. Specify the following settings for this fax:

   Time to Send   Specifies when the fax will actually be transmitted. Choose from As Soon as Possible, Discount Rates (click Set to specify the times when discount rates take effect), or a Specific Time (which you set using the up and down arrows).

   Message Format   Specifies whether the recipient can edit the fax message. You can send a message that is Editable, if Possible (the fax will be sent in the binary editable format; the recipient must also have Microsoft Fax to be able to edit the fax), Editable Only (Microsoft

Fax will try to send the fax as binary files and will refuse to send the message if the receiving system cannot accept that format), or Not Editable (the fax is sent as a bitmap).

Paper   Establishes the paper specifications, including size, orientation (landscape or portrait), and image quality—choose from Draft (200 × 100 dpi), Fine (200 × 200 dpi), 300dpi, or Best Available.

Cover Page   Confirms your choice of cover page.

Dialing   Specifies how fax numbers are dialed, how many times you want to retry a busy or unavailable number, and the waiting period between such retries. Click Dialing Properties to set the default location you normally dial from, the dialing prefix, and credit card information. Click Toll Prefixes to identify phone-number prefixes that are inside your default area code but which require you to use the area code.

Security   Specifies the security method to use with this fax. You can choose from None, Key-Encrypted (which uses a public-key encryption technique), and Password-Protected (the recipient must enter the same password you used when creating the fax to read the message).

6. When you have made your selections, click OK to return to the Compose New Fax dialog box. Click Next.

7. Type the subject of the fax, and in the Note box, type the contents of your fax message. Check the checkbox if you want the Note contents to be part of the cover page. Click Next.

8. If you want to send a file with this fax, click Add File to open the Open a File to Attach dialog box. Locate the file, and then click Open. The name will appear in the Files to Send text box. Click Next.

9. Your fax is now complete, and all you have to do to send it is click the Finish button. You will see two icons in the notification area of the Taskbar for the fax and dialing actions.

Request a Fax

You can also use Fax to call a remote computer, information service, or fax machine to retrieve a specific document; and you can retrieve all the documents available. Once the call is complete, the documents are placed in your Inbox. Follow these steps:

1. Choose Start ➢ Programs ➢ Accessories ➢ Fax ➢ Request a Fax to open the Request a Fax dialog box.

2. To retrieve all faxes stored at the remote site, click Retrieve Whatever Is Available. To retrieve one particular document, click Retrieve a Specific Document, and then type the name of the document and its password (if there is one) in the two boxes in the lower part of the dialog box. Click Next.

3. Type the name of the person to whom the retrieved fax will be routed in the To box. To retrieve a name from the Address Book, click that button, select a name, and then click Add. Verify the country, and type the fax number. Click Next.

4. To specify when you want to call, select from As Soon As Possible, When Phone Rates Are Discounted, or A Specific Time. Click Next.

5. Click Finish to complete the request.

TIP

To review the list of faxes scheduled to be sent, open Inbox and choose Tools ➢ Microsoft Fax Tools ➢ Show Outgoing Faxes to open the Outgoing Faxes dialog box. You'll see the sender, subject, size, recipients, and time to send.

FIND

Windows 98 adds several powerful items to the Find menu, which now includes options for finding files and folders, a computer, information on the Internet, or people. Choose Start ➢ Find and select an option, or choose Tools ➢ Find in Explorer.

Find Files or Folders

To find a file or folder, you can either use My Computer or Explorer to scan the disks yourself, or you can use the Find command to have

Windows 98 conduct the search for you. To use the Find command, choose Start ➤ Find ➤ Files or Folders, or in Explorer, choose Tools ➤ Find ➤ Files or Folders.

In the Find: All Files dialog box, you will see three tabs: Name & Location, Date Modified, and Advanced.

Name & Location Tab

Contains the following options:

Named   Displays the name of the file or folder for which you're searching. Click the down arrow to display a list of your most recent searches.

Containing Text   Lets you specify any text that you want to locate.

Look In   Tells Windows to search a specific path for the file or folder. Click the down arrow to display a list of the disks and folders on your computer.

Browse   Lets you look through the available disks and folders to find the one you want.

Include Subfolders   Searches sublevels of folders as well as the level you specified.

Date Tab

Contains the following options:

All Files   Searches all files in the specified path for the desired file or folder.

Find All Files   Restricts the search to files created, last accessed, or modified between two specified dates, during the previous number of months, or during the previous number of days.

Advanced Tab

Contains the following options:

Of Type   Searches for a specific type of file. Click the down arrow to display a list of registered types.

Size Is Restricts the search for files to At Least or At Most (selected by the first down arrow) the number of kilobytes specified (typed or entered using the arrow keys).

Enter the Find specifications you want, and then select one of the following buttons:

Find Now Starts the search.

Stop Ends the search.

New Search Allows you to enter new search criteria.

To save a search, including its parameters, choose File ➤ Save Search. To save the results of a search, choose Options ➤ Save Results. To make a search case-sensitive, choose Options ➤ Case Sensitive.

Find a Computer

To locate a computer on your network using the Find command in either the Start menu or Explorer, follow these steps:

1. Chose Start ➤ Find ➤ Computer, or in Explorer, choose Tools ➤ Find ➤ Computer to open the Find Computer dialog box.

2. Enter the computer name or select it from a list of previous searches by clicking the Named down arrow.

3. Click Find Now to activate the search. Stop terminates the search, and New Search allows you to enter the criteria for a new computer search.

Find on the Internet

The Find menu's On the Internet option uses Internet Explorer to connect to the Web site at home.microsoft.com/search/search.asp This site gives you access to some of the most powerful and popular search engines on the Internet, including Infoseek, AOL NetFind, Lycos, Excite, and Yahoo.

You can also use one of the other sites in the categories of General Search, Guides, White Pages, Newsgroups, Chat Guides, Specialty, or International. If you can't find what you are looking for using one of these search engines, what you are looking for doesn't want to be found.

Find People

The Find menu's People option lets you searches public LDAP (Lightweight Directory Access Protocol) directories on the Internet such as Bigfoot (www.bigfoot.com), Four11 (www.four11.com), and WhoWhere? (www.whowhere.com) for particular information. Here are the steps:

1. Choose Start ➤ Find ➤People, or in Explorer, choose Tools ➤ Find ➤People to open the Find People dialog box.

2. In the Look In list, select the name of the directory service you want to use

3. Type the information on the person you are looking for, usually just the first name followed by the last name, and then click Find Now.

The results of a search may vary depending on which of the services you use, but you will normally see a long list of names with different e-mail addresses. It is then up to you to decide which of those names is actually the person you want to contact.

FOLDER OPTIONS

In Explorer, choose View ➤ Folder Options (or Start ➤ Settings ➤ Folder Options) to open the Folder Options dialog box, in which you specify how your folders will look and work. The Folder Options dialog box contains three tabs: General, View, and File Types. When you open the Folder Options dialog box in My Computer, Network Neighborhood, and the Recycle Bin, you will see two tabs: General and View.

General Tab

Defines how the following systemwide settings work on your computer:

Web Style   Specifies that your folders work with a single click just like the Web. Icon names will be underlined, and the normal arrow-shaped mouse pointer will turn into a hand as it passes over the icon.

Classic Style   Specifies that your folders behave in the traditional Windows way. Click once to select an item; double-click to open or run an item.

Custom, Based on Settings You Choose   Specifies that you want to choose your own configuration. Click the Settings button to set these preferences.

View Tab

Controls advanced settings for files and folders. The Folder Views box contains two options you can use to make all the folders on your system look and work in the same way:

Like Current Folder   Uses the current settings in effect in the View menu (except for the toolbar settings) on all folders on your computer.

Reset All Folders   Uses the original View menu settings in effect when the program was first installed.

The Advanced Settings box contains a set of checkboxes for certain display options, such as how to treat hidden files, whether file attributes are shown in the Details view, and so on. Click the Restore Defaults button to put everything back into its original state.

File Types Tab

Displays all the file types currently registered with Windows; this is how Windows knows which program to use to open specific data files. When you select a file type in the list, the File Type Details box displays a short summary of which file name extension belongs to that type, its MIME content type, and the name of the program used to open it.

To change or delete one of the existing types, select it in the Registered File Types box, and then choose Edit or Remove. Click the New Type button to register a new file type with Windows. Here are the steps:

1. Click the New Type button to open the Add New File Type dialog box.

2. In the Description of Type field, enter a short text description along the lines of the other entries used, such as Active Streaming File Format.

3. Type the file name extension in the Associated Extension field.

4. Select an existing MIME Content_Type from the drop-down list, or enter a new MIME type.

5. Click the New button, and in the Actions field, enter the operation you want to perform; common operations are Open (to open the file) and Print. Then, in the Application Used to Perform Action field, enter the full path and file name of the application you want to associate with this file type. Click OK when you are done.

6. Click OK to return to the File Types tab in the Folder options dialog box.

Fonts

The styles of type used when Windows displays or prints text. Windows maintains a library of fonts that all applications that run under it use. Choose Start ➣ Settings ➣ Control Panel ➣ Fonts to open the Fonts folder, which displays all the fonts installed on your computer. Windows applications primarily use two types of fonts:

▶ TrueType fonts (represented by a pair of *T*s in the icon)

▶ Adobe fonts (represented by an *A* in the icon), which are bitmapped or vector fonts

The View menu of the Fonts folder offers two unique and quite useful views for fonts: List Fonts by Similarity, which groups fonts that are reasonably alike; and View ➣ Hide Variations, which hides bold, italics, and other variant forms of a typeface.

Fonts Used in Windows 98

The defaults for the size and type of fonts used in the Windows 98 windows and dialog boxes are set in the Display Properties dialog box. You can vary the font and size for text objects and in menus, message boxes, and title bars.

Right-click the Desktop and choose Properties from the pop-up menu to open the Display Properties dialog box, or choose Start ➣ Settings ➣ Control Panel ➣ Display. You use the Appearance and Settings tabs to control the size of fonts on the screen and the size and typeface of fonts for selected objects on the screen.

Adding a New Font to Your Computer

If you have acquired some new fonts, you can add them to those that come with Windows 98 by following these steps:

1. Choose Start ➤ Settings ➤ Control Panel ➤ Fonts to open the Fonts folder.

2. Choose File ➤ Install New Font to open the Add Fonts dialog box.

3. Select the drive and then select the folder that contains the new font.

4. Click the font you want to add. Hold down the Ctrl key and then click to select more than one font.

Displaying and Printing Font Samples

Once you have collected a large number of fonts, remembering what each one looks like can be difficult. Fortunately, the Windows 98 Font Viewer can help. To use it, follow these steps:

1. Open the Font folder.

2. Select any icon in the folder to open that font in the Font Viewer. Open additional Font Viewer windows if you want to compare two or more fonts.

3. To print an example of the font, click the Print button in the Font Viewer; alternatively, right-click the font in the Font folder and select Print from the pop-up menu.

FORMATTING DISKS

| Format... | Unless you purchase formatted disks, you must format a floppy disk before you can use it the first time. Formatting a new disk places information on the disk that Windows needs to be able to read and write files and folders to and from the disk. Formatting a used disk erases all the original information it contained and turns it into a blank disk, so be sure that you are formatting the right disk.

FRONTPAGE EXPRESS

A quick-and-easy Web-page editor you can use to create or customize your own Web pages without having to learn the details of Hypertext Markup Language (HTML). You can edit Web-page elements by selecting them in the main FrontPage Express window and then using a toolbar button or menu selection to apply formatting and alignment.

GAMES

Windows 98 includes four games: FreeCell, Hearts, Minesweeper, and that addictive time-waster, Solitaire. You can play Hearts over the network with other players. To get to the games, choose Start ➢ Programs ➢ Accessories ➢ Games, and then click the game you want to play. If you get stuck, click Help for instructions on how to play.

HELP

Windows 98 contains an extensive help system that provides you with online assistance at almost any time. You can use the main Windows 98 Help System to gain access to a huge amount of information, you can use Windows 98 Troubleshooters to diagnose and isolate a problem relating to specific hardware or software, and you can use Web Help to connect directly to Microsoft's Web site to look for program updates.

Windows Help System

Choose Start ➢ Help to open the main Windows 98 Help System dialog box, which has three tabs:

Contents   Lists the main categories in the Help system itself and a general overview of Windows 98.

Index   Lists all the subjects in the Help system in one giant alphabetic list. Type the first few letters of the word you're looking for in the text box at the top of this tab, and the list box will automatically scroll to the subject closest in spelling to what you have typed. Or you can scroll to it yourself by using the scroll bars on the right of the display box. When you get to the subject you want, select it and click Display.

Search   Allows you to find specific words or phrases contained within a Help topic. To do this, Windows 98 must create a database containing words used throughout the Help system. When you click the Search tab for the first time, the Search Setup Wizard creates this database. You can then use the Search tab to find the specific word or phrase you want.

When a Windows 98 Help topic is displayed, you may see a link icon. Click it to open the specific application, dialog box, or other element under discussion. When you close the application, you return to the same place in the Help system.

Using the Built-In Troubleshooters

Windows 98 extends the usual concepts of the Help system to include a set of built-in technical support troubleshooters you can use to help diagnose and isolate certain problems. There are two ways to find the right Troubleshooter and start it running on your system:

▶ You can choose Start ➤ Help to open the Windows 98 Help System. Select the Contents tab, select the Troubleshooting topic, and then open Windows 98 Troubleshooters. Choose the appropriate Troubleshooter from the list and follow the directions on the screen.

▶ Alternatively, you can start a Troubleshooter directly from a page of Help information. As you read through the information the page contains, you will come across a link to a Troubleshooter; click the link to start the Troubleshooter.

Once the Troubleshooter starts, click the Hide button on the Help toolbar to close the left pane. Be sure to follow all the steps the Troubleshooter suggests.

Troubleshooters are available for problems encountered with networking, printing, startup and shutdown, hardware such as modems, and procedures such as dial-up networking and connecting to the Microsoft Network.

Getting Web Help

Click the Web Help button on the Help System toolbar to connect to a Microsoft site to look for updated versions of programs and device drivers. You then select what you want to install; perhaps more important, you can also uninstall a program or a device driver that is causing you problems.

Help in a Dialog Box

Context-sensitive Help is also available in certain dialog boxes and on some property sheets in Windows 98. You may see a Help button on a dialog box; click it to see information specific to that dialog box.

Other dialog boxes and many of the Windows 98 property sheets have a Help button in the upper-right corner (look for the button with a question mark on it) next to the Close button. Click this Help button and the question mark jumps onto the cursor; move the cursor to the entry on the property sheet that you want help with and click again. A small window containing the help text opens; click the mouse to close this window when you are done.

INTERNET

 In Windows 98, you can view or change the configuration options relating to the Internet in two ways:

▶ Via your connection to the Internet

▶ In Internet Explorer

To open the Internet Options dialog box, choose Start ➤ Connections ➤ Control Panel ➤ Internet, or open Internet Explorer and choose View ➤ Internet Options. The Internet Options dialog box has six tabs.

General Tab

The General tab contains these groups of settings:

Home Page   Lets you choose which Web page opens each time you connect to the Internet. The home page is the first Web page you see when you start Internet Explorer.

Temporary Internet Files   Lets you manage those Web pages that are stored on your hard disk for fast offline access.

History   Contains a list of the links you have visited so that you can return to them quickly and easily. You can specify the number of days you want to keep pages in the History folder.

Colors   Lets you choose which colors are used as background, links, and text on those Web pages for which the original author did not specify colors. By default, the Use Windows Colors option is selected.

Fonts   Lets you specify the font style and text size to use on those Web pages for which the original author did not make a specification.

Languages   Lets you choose the character set to use on those Web pages that offer content in more than one language.

Accessibility   Lets you choose how certain information is displayed in Internet Explorer, including font styles, colors, and text size. You can also specify that your own style sheet is used.

Security Tab

Lets you specify the overall security level for each of four zones. Each zone has its own default security restrictions that tell Internet Explorer how to manage dynamic Web-page content such as ActiveX controls and Java applets. The zones are:

Local Intranet   Sites you can access on your corporate intranet; security is set to medium.

Trusted Sites   Web sites you have a high degree of confidence will not send you potentially damaging content; security is set to low.

Internet   Sites you visit that are not in one of the other categories; security is set to medium.

Restricted Sites   Sites that you visit but do not trust; security is set to high.

To change the current security level of a zone, select it from the list box, and then click the new security level you want to use:

High   Excludes any content capable of damaging your system. This is the most secure setting.

Medium   Opens a warning dialog box in Internet Explorer before running ActiveX or Java applets on your system. This is a moderately-secure setting that is good for everyday use.

Low   Does not issue any warning but runs the ActiveX or Java applet automatically. This is the least secure setting.

Custom   Lets you create your own security settings. To look at or change these advanced settings, click the Settings button to open the Security Setting dialog box. You can individually configure how you want to manage certain categories, such as ActiveX controls and plug-ins, Java applets, scripting, file and font downloads, and user authentication.

Content Tab

Contains settings you can use to restrict access to sites and specify how you want to manage digital certificates:

Content Adviser   Lets you control access to certain sites on the Internet and is particularly useful if children have access to the computer. Click Settings to establish a password, and then click OK to open the Content Advisor dialog box. Use the tabs in this dialog box to establish the level of content you will allow users to view:

> **Ratings**   Lets you use a set of ratings developed by the Recreational Software Advisory Council (RSAC) for language, nudity, sex, and violence. Select one of these categories, and then adjust the slider to specify the level of content you will allow.

> **General**   Specifies whether people using this computer can view material that has not been rated; users may see some objectionable material if the Web site has not used the RSAC rating system.

> **Advanced**   Lets you look at or modify the list of organizations providing ratings services.

Certificates   Lets you manage digital certificates used with certain client authentication servers. Click Personal to view the personal digital certificates installed on this system, click Authorities to list the security certificates installed on your system, or click

Publishers to designate a particular software publisher as a trustworthy publisher. This means that Windows 98 applications can download, install, and use software from these agencies without asking for your permission first.

Personal Information   Lets you look at or change your own personal profile; this information is sent to any Web sites that request information when you visit their site. Click Edit Profile to review the current information.

Click Reset Sharing to clear the list of sites you previously allowed to access your personal information without asking your permission first. Microsoft Wallet gives you a secure place to store credit card and other information you might need for Internet shopping.

Connection Tab

Allows you to specify how your system connects to the Internet:

Connection   Lets you specify whether your system will connect to the Internet via your corporate network or by modem. Click the Connect button to run the Connection Wizard and set up a connection to an Internet Service Provider (ISP). If you use a modem, click the Settings button to open the Dial-Up Settings dialog box where you can specify all aspects of the phone connection to your ISP.

Proxy Server   Lets you access the Internet via a proxy server system connected to your corporate intranet. A proxy server is a security system designed to monitor and control the flow of information between your intranet and the Internet.

Automatic Configuration   Lets you network system administrator configure your copy of Internet Explorer automatically.

Programs Tab

Lets you set your default program choices for e-mail, newsgroup reader, and so on and specify whether Internet Explorer should check to see if it is configured as the default browser:

Messaging   Lets you choose which application programs are used for mail, news, and Internet calls.

Personal Information   Lets you choose which application programs are used for calendar functions and for your contact list.

Finally, you can specify that Internet Explorer check to see if it is configured as the default browser on your system each time it starts running.

Advanced Tab

Lets you look at or change a number of settings that control much of Internet Explorer's behavior, including accessibility, browsing, multimedia, security, the Java environment, printing and searching, and the Internet Explorer toolbar and how HTTP 1.1 settings are interpreted.

Changes you make here stay in effect until you change them again, until you download an automatic configuration file, or until you click the Restore Defaults button, which returns the settings on the Advanced tab to their original values.

INTERNET EXPLORER

The application that displays Web pages from the Internet or from your corporate intranet. In many ways, Internet Explorer resembles Windows Explorer; it is a *viewer* that presents information in a structured way. Internet Explorer is an easy-to-use program that hides a large part of the complexity of the Internet and Internet operations.

Help Menu

Gives you access to the Internet Explorer Help system through Contents and Index, lets you check for a newer version of Internet Explorer available through Product Updates, guides you through an online tutorial with Web Tutorial, and helps locate information on technical problems with Online Support.

When you choose Help ➤ Microsoft on the Web, the items on the submenu are actually links to different parts of the Microsoft Web site, including:

Free Stuff   Locates Internet Explorer program updates, free stuff, and add-on programs.

Get Faster Internet Access   Displays information about ISDN (Integrated Services Digital Network) service.

Frequently Asked Questions   Answers the most commonly asked questions about Internet Explorer.

Internet Start Page   Opens your home page.

Send Feedback   Lets you send your opinions right to Microsoft.

Best of the Web   Opens Microsoft's Exploring page, which contains a variety of links to useful and interesting sites. This is equivalent to clicking the Best of the Web button on the Internet Explorer Links toolbar.

Search the Web   Opens the same Web site as choosing Go ➤ Search the Web.

Microsoft Home Page   Opens Microsoft's Web site.

Configuring Internet Explorer

To view or set the many configuration options for Internet Explorer, choose View ➤ Internet Options to open the Internet Options dialog box. Or you can choose Start ➤ Connections ➤ Control Panel ➤ Internet. The Internet Options dialog box has six tabs. For a complete discussion of all the settings on these tabs, see the Internet entry earlier in this appendix.

Browsing Offline

You can browse the Web with Internet Explorer without being connected to the Internet. This is because many of the files that you open while browsing the Web are stored in the Temporary Internet Files folder on your hard disk. Choose File ➤ Work Offline, and Internet Explorer will not attempt to connect to the Internet when you select a resource, but will display the copy in the Temporary Internet Files folder instead. To go back to online browsing, choose File ➤ Work Offline a second time.

Speeding Up Internet Explorer

The text component of a Web page downloads quickly, but some of the other common elements, such as graphics, sound files, and animation clips, can take quite a long time to download.

Of course, there is nothing you can do to change the way a Web site is constructed, but you can stop certain types of files from being downloaded to Internet Explorer. You can essentially tell Internet Explorer to ignore all graphics files or all video clips and just collect the text. Here are the steps:

1. In Control Panel, click Internet, or choose View ➤ Internet Options within Internet Explorer to open the Internet Options dialog box.

2. Select the Advanced tab.

3. Scroll down the list box until you see the Multimedia settings, all of which are selected by default.

4. Deselect all the items you want to exclude from the Web pages you download to your system.

5. Click OK to close the Internet Options dialog box.

Remember that these options stay in effect for all subsequent Internet Explorer sessions until you turn them back on.

Installing Applications

You can install applications from floppy disks and CD-ROMs using the Add/Remove Programs applet in the Windows 98 Control Panel. You can also choose Start ➤ Run to invoke an individual Install or Setup program.

Keyboard

 The Keyboard applet in the Control Panel allows you to set several important defaults for keyboard properties, such as the language displayed and at what speed a key must be pressed to be recognized as a repeat key.

To look at or change the keyboard properties, choose Start ➤ Settings ➤ Control Panel ➤ Keyboard to open the Keyboard Properties dialog box. It has two tabs: Speed and Language. The Speed tab contains the following options:

Repeat Delay   Sets the length of time you must hold down a key before the repeat feature kicks in.

Repeat Rate   Sets the speed at which a character is repeated while a key is held down.

Click Here and Hold Down a Key to Test Repeat Rate Tests the repeat delay and repeat rate speeds that you have chosen.

Cursor Blink Rate Sets the rate at which the cursor blinks, making the cursor easier to spot in some instances.

The Language tab contains the following options:

Language and Layout Displays the language and keyboard layout loaded into memory when the computer is first started. Double-click the highlighted language or layout to open the Language Properties dialog box and select another keyboard layout.

Add Adds a language and keyboard layout to those loaded into memory when the computer is booted.

Properties Allows you to change the keyboard layout default.

Remove Deletes the selected language and keyboard layout. It will no longer be loaded into memory when you boot the computer.

Set As Default with More Than One Language Installed
Makes the currently selected language and keyboard layout the default to be used when the computer is started.

Switch Languages Switches between two or more language and layout settings, as listed above. Click the key combination you want to use to switch the default.

Enable Indicator on Taskbar Displays a language on the right of the Taskbar. Click this indicator to open a dialog box in which you can switch language defaults quickly.

LOG OFF

Windows 98 maintains a set of user profiles, each containing a different user name, password, Desktop preferences, and accessibility options. When you log on to Windows 98, your profile ensures that your Desktop settings—including elements such as your own desktop icons, background image, and other settings—are automatically available to you.

Windows 98 contains an option you can use to log off and log on again as another user quickly and easily. Click the Start button, and then click

Log Off *username*. In the Log Off Windows dialog box, click Yes. This closes all your programs, disconnects your system from the network, and prepares the system for use by other users.

Log On

When you log on to Windows 98 and are prompted to enter your user name and password, your user profile is loaded to ensure that your Desktop settings—including elements such as your own desktop icons, background image, and other settings—are automatically available to you.

Unfortunately, you can also press the Esc key to bypass this logon screen and completely circumvent all aspects of Windows logon security. This makes Windows 98 a particularly unsecure system.

If you are connected to a local area network and Windows 98 is configured for that network, you will also be prompted to enter your network password.

Maximize/Minimize Buttons

Allows you to change the size of an application window.

The Maximize button is in the upper-right corner of an application window, and when you click it, the window expands to full-screen size. Once the window has expanded, the Maximize button changes to the Restore button, which you can then use to shrink the window back to its original starting size.

You can also place the mouse pointer on the window border, and when the two-headed arrow appears, drag the border in the direction in which you want to change its size.

Use the Minimize button to place an open application on the Taskbar; click the Taskbar icon when you are ready to work with the application again.

Media Player

Allows you to play multimedia files, such as video, animation, and sound clips, depending on the hardware installed on your computer system.

Modems

 Allows you to look at or change the settings Windows uses with your modem. Choose Start ➤ Settings ➤ Control Panel ➤ Modems to open the Modem Properties dialog box.

Mouse

Changes your mouse settings. Choose Start ➤ Settings ➤ Control Panel ➤ Mouse to open the Mouse Properties dialog box, which contains three tabs. If you make changes to the settings in any of these tabs, click the Apply button to make sure your changes are implemented and then click OK.

Buttons Tab

Sets the mouse button configuration and speed with these options:

Button Configuration   Allows you to switch functions from the default right-handed use of the mouse buttons to left-handed.

Double-Click Speed   Allows you to set and then test the speed at which a double-click is recognized.

Pointers Tab

Allows you to change the appearance of the mouse pointer. For example, you can change the pointer used to indicate that Windows is busy from an hour-glass to a symbol or caricature of your choice.

The Scheme box contains the list of pointer schemes available in Windows. By selecting one, you'll see the set of pointers in the scheme displayed in the box below. You can create additional schemes by replacing the individual pointers.

Motion Tab

Controls the pointer speed and the presence of a pointer trail, which makes the mouse pointer much easier to see on LCD screens. If you select a pointer trail, you can also choose whether it is a long or a short trail.

MOVING FILES AND FOLDERS

In Windows, you can move files and folders in three ways:

- ▶ By dragging-and-dropping
- ▶ By choosing Edit ➢ Cut and Edit ➢ Paste
- ▶ By clicking the right mouse button

When you move a file or folder, you move the original to another location—no duplicate is made.

Using Drag-and-Drop

To use drag-and-drop, both the source and the destination folders must be visible, for example, in Explorer or on the Desktop. Hold down the left mouse button and drag the file or folder from one location to the other. When the file or folder reaches the correct destination folder, release the mouse button. The source and destination folders must be on the same drive. If you drag a file or a folder to a different drive, it will be copied rather than moved. If you want to move a file or folder to a different drive, you must drag using the right mouse button.

Using the Edit Menu

The Edit menu in My Computer, Explorer, or any folder window provides a Cut and Paste feature. Here are the steps to follow:

1. Select the file or folder you want to move.
2. Choose Edit ➢ Cut, or click the Cut button on the toolbar.
3. Find the destination file or folder and open it.
4. Choose Edit ➢ Paste, or click the Paste button on the toolbar.

TIP

You can select multiple contiguous files or folders to move by holding down Shift and clicking the first and last file or folder. To select noncontiguous files or folders, hold down Ctrl and click the files or folders you want.

Part ix

Using the Right Mouse Button

Right-clicking a file or folder opens the pop-up menu, which you can use to perform a variety of functions, including moving. Follow these steps:

1. Right-click the file or folder you want to move and select Cut from the pop-up menu.

2. Open the destination folder, right-click, and then select Paste.

TIP

If you drag a folder or a file with the right mouse button, a pop-up menu opens when you release the button, allowing you to copy the object, move it, or create a shortcut.

MOVING AND ARRANGING ICONS

In Windows, you can arrange icons using any of several methods. In Explorer, Control Panel, and many other windows, you can move or arrange icons using the selections in the View menu:

Large Icons   Displays the files and folders as larger-sized icons.

Small Icons   Displays the files and folders as smaller-sized icons.

List   Displays small icons alongside the names of the files and folders.

Details   Displays files and folders in the List style and adds columns for the size of file, date last modified, and type of file. To sort entries within these columns, simply click the column heading. Click once for an ascending sort (A to Z and 0 to 9); click a second time for a descending sort.

Line Up Icons   Rearranges icons into straight vertical and horizontal lines.

TIP

To rearrange icons on the Desktop, simply drag them to their new location. To tidy up the Desktop quickly, right-click an area of free space, and choose Arrange Icons.

By clicking the Views button on the Explorer toolbar, you can cycle the display through the four presentations of Large Icons, Small Icons, List, and Details; each time you click the button, the display changes to the next format.

MULTIMEDIA

Establishes the default settings for multimedia devices connected to your computer; its contents depend on which multimedia devices you have installed.

Choose Start ➢ Settings ➢ Control Panel ➢ Multimedia to open the Multimedia Properties dialog box, containing tabs appropriate to the hardware installed on your computer. You might see the following tabs:

Audio   Sets playback and recording controls.

Video   Specifies the size of the video playback window.

MIDI   Sets Musical Instruments Digital Interface controls and adds new instruments.

CD Music   Sets the drive letter and head phone volume defaults.

Devices   Lists the multimedia hardware connected to your computer and allows you to set or change properties for any of the hardware listed. Select the hardware component you want to configure, and then click Properties to open the related dialog box.

MY COMPUTER

One of the file-management tools available with Windows. You can use My Computer to locate folders, files, and disks or printers on your computer or on mapped drives on other computers connected to the network.

My Computer Folder

Click the My Computer icon on the Desktop to open the My Computer folder, showing an icon for each drive and drive-level folder on your computer. Click an icon to display the contents of one of these folders or drives in a separate window.

Finding a File or Folder with My Computer

When you open My Computer, the My Computer folder displays all the disks and folders on your computer. Follow these steps to find the file or folder you want:

1. Click the down arrow at the end of the Address toolbar to find the device or folder you want. You will see all the shared disks on your network, important folders such as Control Panel, Printers, and Dial-Up Networking, and other Windows elements, such as Internet Explorer, Network Neighborhood, Recycle Bin, and My Briefcase.

2. Click a disk or a folder to see its contents in the window.

3. Once you find the file or folder (which may be several levels down), click it to open it.

MY DOCUMENTS

A Desktop folder that provides a convenient place to store graphics, documents, or any other files you might want to access quickly. When you save a file in programs such as Paint or Word-Pad, the file is automatically saved in My Documents unless you specify a different destination folder.

To specify a different destination folder, right-click My Documents and select Properties. Type the name of the new folder in the Target field and click OK. Changing to a different folder does not move existing files stored in My Documents.

NAMING DISKS

You can give a hard or a floppy disk a name that can be a maximum of 11 characters. To name or rename a disk, follow these steps:

1. Open My Computer or Explorer.

2. Right-click the disk you want to name, and select Properties to open the Properties dialog box.

3. Select the General tab, and type the name you want to use for this disk in the Label field. Click OK.

NAMING FILES AND FOLDERS

The first time you save a file using the Save or Save As command, you are asked to provide a name for the file. When you create a new folder, it is always called New Folder until you change the name. Names for files and folders can contain a maximum of 255 characters, including spaces, but cannot contain any of these special characters: / \ ? : * " <> |

You can rename both files and folders in Explorer or My Computer. Follow these steps:

1. Open Explorer or My Computer and find the file or folder you want to rename.

2. Click the name once, pause, and then click it again. A box will enclose the name, and the name will be selected. If you move the mouse inside the box, the pointer will become an I-beam.

3. Type the new name or edit the existing name and press Enter.

NETMEETING

A conferencing application that allows people working in different locations to collaborate simultaneously on the same project, sharing Microsoft applications to edit documents. NetMeeting also supports audio and video conferencing over the Internet (as long as you have the appropriate hardware such as a video camera or microphone attached to your computer system), as well as a file-transfer function.

Choose Start ≻ Programs ≻ Internet Explorer ≻ Microsoft NetMeeting to open NetMeeting.

ONLINE SERVICES

Allows you to access several popular online services such as AOL and the Microsoft Network. Before you can use any of these services, you must first register with it. You can do this using the items in the Online Services menu; each item connects you to a specific service. You can also use the Online Services folder on the Desktop.

Before you start, connect your modem to the phone line, and close any other open applications.

Outlook Express

 Windows application used to send and receive e-mail and read and post messages to Internet news groups. To start Outlook Express, click the Outlook Express Desktop icon, or choose Start ➢ Programs ➢ Internet Explorer ➢ Outlook Express. You can also click the Launch Outlook Express button on the Quick Launch toolbar, or use the Mail menu from within Internet Explorer.

Chapters 4 and 5 show how to use Outlook Express for basic operations such as sending and receiving e-mail, as well as managing address books and mail folders. Following are additional highlights.

Reading the News

Outlook Express is also a newsreader, that you can use to access the thousands of specific-subject newsgroups on the Internet.

WARNING
Anything goes in many of these Internet newsgroups. There is absolutely no censorship, and if you are easily offended (and even if you are not), you might want to stay with the more mainstream Web pages.

In the same way that you set up an e-mail account with an ISP, you must also set up a newsgroup account, complete with password, before you can use Outlook Express as a newsreader.

Configuring Outlook Express

Configuration options for Outlook Express are quite extensive. You can customize the toolbar and add buttons for the tasks you perform most often, and you can define the rules you want Outlook Express to follow when you are creating, sending, and receiving e-mail. Choose Tools ➢ Options to open the Options dialog box. It has the following tabs:

General   Contains general-purpose settings for Outlook Express.

Send   Specifies the format for sending mail and articles to news-groups, as well as several other mail-related options, such as whether to include the text of the original message in any reply.

Read   Specifies options used when displaying articles from newsgroups.

Security   Establishes security zones and specifies how Outlook Express manages digital certificates (also known as digital IDs).

Dial Up   Specifies the options used when connecting to your ISP by dial-up connection.

Advanced   Specifies options only of interest to system administrators.

You can also choose View ➤ Layout to open the Layout Properties dialog box. Click Customize Toolbar to add or remove buttons from the Outlook Express toolbar. To return the toolbar to its original layout, click Customize Toolbar again, and then click Reset followed by Close in the Customize Toolbar dialog box.

PAINT

A program with which you can create lines and shapes, with or without color, and place text within graphics. You can also use it to create backgrounds for the Desktop. Choose Start ➤ Programs ➤ Accessories ➤ Paint to open the main Paint window.

Paint Toolbar

Provides tools for drawing and working with color and text. Below the toolbar is an area containing optional choices depending on the type of tool you chose. For example, if you choose the Brush tool, a selection of brush edges is displayed. If you choose Magnifier, a selection of magnifying strengths is displayed. At the bottom of the main window, the Color Palette displays a series of colored squares.

The toolbox contains the following buttons for drawing lines and shapes and for working with color:

 Free-Form Select   Selects an irregularly shaped area of the image to move, copy, or edit.

Select Selects a rectangular area of the image to move, copy, or edit.

Eraser/Color Eraser Erases an area of the image as you move the eraser tool over it.

Fill with Color Fills an enclosed area with the currently selected color.

Pick Color Selects the color of any object you click. It is for use with the tool that you chose immediately before you selected Pick Color.

Magnifier Enlarges the selected area.

Pencil Draws a free-hand line one pixel wide.

Brush Draws lines of different shapes and widths.

Airbrush Draws using an airbrush of the selected size.

Text Inserts text onto the drawing. Click Text, click the color you want for the text, and then drag a text box to the location where you want to insert the text. In the font window that appears, click the font, size, and style (Bold, Italic, Underline) you want. Click inside the text box, and begin typing your text.

Line Draws a straight line. After dragging the tool to create a line segment, click once to anchor the line before continuing in a different direction, or click twice to end the line.

Curve Draws a curved line where one segment ends and another begins. After dragging the tool to create a line segment, click once to anchor the line before continuing. To create a curve, click anywhere on the line and then drag it. Click twice to end the line.

Rectangle Creates a rectangle. Select the fill style from the toolbar below the main Paint window.

Polygon Creates a polygon, or figure consisting of straight lines connecting at any angle. After dragging the

Part ix

first line segment, release the mouse, place the pointer where the second line segment is to end, click the mouse button, and repeat until the drawing is complete. Click twice to end the drawing.

Ellipse   Draws an ellipse. Select the fill style from the Color Palette below the main Paint window.

Rounded Rectangle   Creates a rectangle with curved corners. Select the fill style from the Color Palette below the main Paint window.

When you create an image in Paint, first select the tool, then select the tool shape, if applicable, and then click the color you want to use from the Color Palette at the bottom of the Paint window. The currently active color is displayed in the top square on the left of the palette. To change the background color, click Pick Color, and then click the color you want. The next image you create will use the new background color.

Paint Menus

Contain many of the standard Windows options. In addition, you can set a saved paint File to be used as wallpaper, zoom in various ways, flip or rotate an image, invert its colors, define custom colors, and set various image attributes.

Passwords

 Allows you to specify a logon password. Windows maintains a set of user profiles, each containing a different user name, password, Desktop preferences, and accessibility options. When you log on to Windows, your profile ensures that your Desktop settings, including elements such as your own Desktop icons, background image, and other settings, are automatically available to you.

Enabling User Profiles

To enable user profiles, follow these steps:

1. Choose Start ➢ Settings ➢ Control Panel ➢ Passwords to open the Passwords Properties dialog box.

2. Select *Users can customize their preferences and Desktop settings.*

3. In the User Profile Settings box; you can select one option or both:

   ▶ Include Desktop icons and Network Neighborhood content in user settings.

   ▶ Include Start menu and Program groups in user settings.

4. You'll have to use Shut Down to restart your computer for these changes to be applied.

Specifying a Password

When you start Windows 98 for the first time, you are prompted to enter a user name and password and then to confirm that password. If you are connected to a network, you may also be asked to enter a network password. On all subsequent startups, this series of dialog boxes will be slightly different. You will only be asked to enter the password; you will not have to confirm it.

Changing a Password

To change a password, follow these steps:

NOTE

You must know the current password in order to change it.

1. Choose Start ➤ Settings ➤ Control Panel ➤ Passwords to open the Passwords Properties dialog box.

2. Select the Change Passwords tab, and then click the Change Windows Password button to open the Change Windows Password dialog box.

3. Type the old password (asterisks will appear as you type), and enter the new password; you will have to retype the new password to confirm it. Click OK to close the Change Windows Password dialog box.

4. Click OK to close the Passwords Properties dialog box and finalize your new password. Next time you log on to Windows, remember to use your new password.

In addition to your logon password, you can establish a password for the following resources:

Dial-Up Connections To change passwords, click My Computer, click the Dial-Up Networking icon, and select Connections ➤ Dial-Up Server. Click Allow Caller Access to enable the Change Password button.

Disks To set and change passwords, right-click the disk in the Explorer window and select Sharing from the pop-up menu.

Folders To change the password or sharing status, open Explorer or My Computer, select the folder, choose File ➤ Properties, and then click the Sharing tab.

Printers To change the password or sharing status, open the Printers folder from either Explorer, My Computer, or Control Panel. Right-click the printer and select Sharing from the pop-up menu.

Network Administration Set password access to shared devices from the Access Control tab in the Network applet in the Control Panel.

Screen Savers You can use a password to prevent others from gaining access to your files when a screen saver is active. To change a password, choose Start ➤ Settings ➤ Control Panel ➤ Display to open the Display Properties dialog box. Select the Screen Saver tab and click Password Protected, and then click the Change button.

Shared Resources To change the password or sharing status, open Explorer or My Computer, select the resource, choose File ➤ Properties to open the Properties dialog box, and select the Sharing tab. If the resource is shared, you can change the password. You can also change the sharing status from the Access Control tab in the Network applet in the Control Panel.

Click the Change Other Passwords button in the Passwords Properties dialog box to work with these other passwords.

Part ix

Allowing Remote Administration

You can specify whether a system administrator can create shared folders and shared printers on your computer, and see the user names of anyone who connects to them by using the options on the Remote Administration tab in the Passwords Properties dialog box.

PASTE COMMAND

Copies the contents of the Clipboard into the current document. It is available from the Edit menu and some pop-up menus that are displayed when you right-click a file or a folder.

PLUG AND PLAY

A Windows feature that automatically detects hardware installed in your computer system. Today, most hardware is specifically designed with Plug and Play in mind. You just install the hardware, and Windows takes care of the details, loading the appropriate device drivers and other related software automatically.

Plug and Play adapters contain configuration information stored in permanent memory on the board, including vendor information, serial number, and other configuration data. The Plug and Play hardware allows each adapter to be isolated, one at a time, until Windows identifies all the cards installed in your computer. Once this task is complete, Windows can load and configure the appropriate device drivers. After installing a new Plug and Play adapter in your computer system, Windows will often ask you to restart the system. This is so the new device drivers can be loaded into the correct part of system memory.

PRINTERS

Manages all functions related to printers and printing. From here you can add a new printer, check on a job in the print queue, change the active printer, or modify a printer's properties.

PROGRAMS

Lists the programs available in Windows, either as stand-alone applications or as collections of applications located in submenus or program groups. Any selection that has an arrow pointer to the right of the name is not a single program but a program group. Choosing one of these groups opens another menu listing the items in the group.

Follow these steps to start a program from the Programs menu:

1. Choose Start ➢ Programs to display the current list of program groups.

2. Select a program group to display a list of the programs it contains.

3. Click an application name to start it.

Adding a New Submenu to the Programs Menu

Most Windows programs are added to the Programs menu automatically as they are installed—you are generally asked to verify in which folder or program group any new program should be placed—and the Setup program takes care of the rest. However, you can create a new submenu manually if you wish. Follow these steps:

1. Right-click the Start button and choose Open to open the Start Menu folder.

2. Select the Programs folder, and then choose File ➢ New ➢ Folder. This creates an empty folder in the Program group with the name New Folder.

3. Enter the name you want to use for the submenu as the name of this new folder, press Enter, and then open the folder you just created.

4. Choose File ➢ New ➢ Shortcut to start the Create Shortcut Wizard, which guides you through the process of adding applications to your new folder.

5. Enter the path and file name for the application in the Command Line box, or click the Browse button to locate the file.

6. Type a shortcut name for the program and click Finish.

The next time you open the Programs menu, you will see the entry you just created, and when you select that entry, you will see the list of items that it contains.

PROPERTIES

Characteristics of something in Windows—a computer, a peripheral such as a printer or modem, a file, or a folder—are displayed in the Properties dialog box. The properties for any item depend on what it is. To open any Properties dialog box, follow these steps:

1. Select the item in the Explorer.

2. Choose File ➤ Properties.

You can also open the Properties dialog box by right-clicking an object and then selecting Properties from the pop-up menu.

RECYCLE BIN

 A folder that stores deleted files until they are finally removed from your hard disk. The Recycle Bin is represented on the Desktop by a wastebasket icon. Files are copied to the Recycle Bin both directly and indirectly; you can simply drag a file there, or you can send a file to the Recycle Bin by choosing Delete from a pop-up menu. When you empty the Recycle Bin, the files it contains are permanently removed from your hard disk; once you empty the bin, anything it contained is gone for good.

TIP

If the Recycle Bin contains deleted files, you will see paper protruding from the top of the wastebasket icon.

REGIONAL SETTINGS

Sets the system-wide defaults for country (and therefore language), number, currency, time, and date formatting. If you are using English in the United States, you will probably never need Regional

Settings; if you want to use a different language, this is the place to start. Choose Start ➢ Settings ➢ Control Panel ➢ Regional Settings to open the Regional Settings Properties dialog box.

Regional Tab

On the Regional Settings tab, click the down arrow and select a language and a country.

Number Tab

Sets the defaults for how positive and negative numbers are displayed, the number of decimal places, the separator between groups of numbers, and so on. This tab contains the following options:

Decimal Symbol   Establishes which symbol will be used as a decimal point. The default in the United States is a period.

No. of Digits after Decimal   Specifies how many numbers will be placed to the right of the decimal point. The default is 2.

Digit Grouping Symbol   Determines the symbol that will group digits into a larger number, such as the comma in 999,999. The default is a comma.

No. of Digits in Group   Specifies how many numbers will be grouped together into larger numbers. The default is 3, as in 9,999,999.

Negative Sign Symbol   Establishes which symbol is used to show a negative number. The default is a minus sign.

Negative Number Format   Establishes how a negative number will be displayed. The default is to display the negative sign in front of the number, such as −24.5.

Display Leading Zeroes   Determines whether a zero is shown in front of a decimal number. The default is yes, as in 0.952.

Measurement System   Determines whether the system of measurement will be U.S. or metric. The default is U.S.

List Separator   Specifies which symbol will separate items in a list or series. The default is a comma.

If you make any changes in this tab, click Apply and then OK.

Currency Tab

Determines the format for displaying currency. For example, you might want to vary the number of decimal points or the presentation of negative numbers. This tab contains the following options:

Currency Symbol   Displays the symbol of the currency, such as the dollar sign.

Position of Currency Symbol   Shows where the currency symbol is displayed in the number—usually in front of a number.

Negative Number Format   Specifies how negative numbers are displayed.

Decimal Symbol   Determines which symbol separates the whole from the fractional parts of a number, such as a period or a comma.

No. of Digits after Decimal   Specifies how many digits are shown by default after the decimal—usually two.

Digit Grouping Symbol   Shows which symbol—usually a comma—separates the number groups, such as thousands, millions, and so on.

Number of Digits in Group   Specifies how many digits determine a number group, such as 3 for thousands, millions, and so on.

Click Apply and then OK to put any changes you make into effect.

Time Tab

Establishes the default formatting for the time. The Time tab has the following options:

Time Style   Determines how the time will be formatted.

Time Separator   Determines which symbol separates the hours from the minutes and seconds; the default is a colon.

AM Symbol   Specifies the default for the morning symbol.

PM symbol   Specifies the default for the afternoon symbol.

Click Apply and then OK to activate any changes you make.

Date Tab

Establishes the default formatting for the date. The Date tab has the following options:

Calendar Type   Displays the types of calendars that you can choose from.

Short Date Style   Lists the formats available for displaying the date.

Date Separator   Lists the symbols that can be used to separate the month, day, and year.

Long Date Style   Lists the formats available for displaying a formal date notation.

Click Apply and then OK to activate any changes you make.

RESTORE

Restores an archive copy of one or more files and folders to your hard disk after a disk or controller failure or some other unforeseen event. To start the Windows 98 backup and restore program, choose Start ➣ Programs ➣ Accessories ➣ System Tools ➣ Backup. The first time you start the program, a dialog box welcomes you to Microsoft Backup and leads directly into the Restore Wizard.

Using the Restore Wizard

Using the Restore Wizard is a quick and easy way to learn about restoring backups; it gets you going quickly with a minimum of technical knowledge. Check Restore Backed up Files, and then click OK in this opening dialog box to start the Wizard. If you would rather not use the Wizard, click Close; you can always restart it from the toolbar inside the Backup program if you change your mind.

The Wizard walks you through the following sequence of dialog boxes. Click the Next button when you have made your choice to advance to the next dialog box; click Back to retrace your steps, and click Cancel if you change your mind about using the Wizard.

Restore From   Specify the type and location of the backup you want to restore.

Select Backup Sets   Select a backup set for the restore.

What to Restore   You can restore all files and folders in the backup set, or you can restore selected files and folders.

Where to Restore   Specify the target of the restore; most of the time selecting Original Location to put the file back where it came from makes the most sense.

How to Restore   Specify whether existing files on your hard disk should be overwritten during the restore.

Click the Start button to begin the restore; a small progress indicator tracks the restore as it proceeds.

Using the Restore Tab

Using the Restore tab in the Backup program involves essentially the same tasks that the Restore Wizard does for you—selecting the files, deciding where to put them, and specifying how the restore should actually be made.

NOTE
A check mark in a gray check box means that only some of the files in a folder have been selected. A check mark in a white box means that all files in a folder have been selected.

RUN

Starts a program or opens a folder when you type its path and name. You often use Run with a Setup program or installation programs or to run a program such as Scanreg that does not have a Windows shortcut. Follow these steps:

1.   Choose Start ➤ Run to open the Run dialog box.

2.   If you have run this program recently, you may find its name already entered in the Open list box. Click the down arrow, select it by name, and then click OK.

3.   If you have not run this program recently or if the Open box is blank, type the full path and program name, such as C:*Folder**Program*.

4. If you are not sure of the path or program name, click Browse to find and select the program. Then click OK to load and run the program.

ScanDisk

Checks a disk for certain common errors. Once ScanDisk detects these errors, it can fix them and recover any data in corrupted areas. Windows 98 runs ScanDisk automatically if the operating system is shut down improperly, as might happen during a power outage.

Choose Start ➤ Programs ➤ Accessories ➤ System Tools ➤ ScanDisk to open the ScanDisk dialog box.

Screen Saver

Displays an image on the screen after a fixed period of inactivity. The screen saver hides the normal information displayed by the application you are using and replaces it with another image.

You can change or select a screen saver using the Display applet in the Control Panel. You can set the speed, shape, density, and color of the screen saver, and you can set a password to get back to your work and other settings. You can also use certain active channels as screen savers.

Send To

Sends items to common destinations, such as floppy disk drives, a fax, an e-mail, or My Briefcase. You can send a file quickly to a destination by following these steps:

1. Right-click the file or folder to open the pop-up menu.

2. Select Send To.

3. Click the appropriate destination.

SETTINGS

 Choose Start ➤ Settings to access all the Windows 98 configuration tools, including the Control Panel, Printers, Taskbar & Start Menu, Folder Options, and the Active Desktop controls.

SHORTCUTS

Quick ways to open an application or access a disk, file, folder, printer, or computer without going to its permanent location using the Windows Explorer. Shortcuts are useful for applications that you use frequently; when you access a shortcut, the file, folder, printer, computer, or program is opened for you. You can create a shortcut using the File menu, pop-up menus, or drag-and-copy.

SHUT DOWN

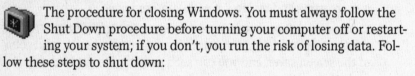 The procedure for closing Windows. You must always follow the Shut Down procedure before turning your computer off or restarting your system; if you don't, you run the risk of losing data. Follow these steps to shut down:

1. When you are ready to turn off your computer, choose Start ➤ Shut Down to open the Shut Down Windows dialog box. It contains the following options:

    Shut Down   Prepares the computer to be turned off.

    Restart   Prepares the computer for shut down and then automatically starts it again.

    Restart in MS-DOS Mode   Closes Windows and restarts the computer in MS-DOS mode.

2. Select the option you want, and then click OK.

3. Respond to any other questions that Windows displays, such as whether it is OK to disconnect network users.

When Windows 98 has finished saving data to your hard disk, it displays a final message telling you that it is now safe to turn off your computer.

SOUNDS

 Assigns sounds to certain system events, such as warning dialog boxes, and to more common events such as opening or closing windows or receiving an e-mail message. Choose Start ➤ Settings ➤ Control Panel ➤ Sounds to open the Sounds Properties dialog box.

START

⚑ Start The primary way to access files, folders, and programs on your computer. Initially, the Start button is on the bottom left of your screen at the left end of the Taskbar. Click Start to display the Start menu. Some of the options on this menu are standard with Windows 98, but you can add others to give you fast access to your favorite applications.

The Start menu contains the following options:

Shut Down   Prepares the computer to be shut down or restarted.

Log Off   Logs off the system quickly so that you can log back on with a different user profile or so that another user can log on.

Run   Opens the Run dialog box so that you can run a program or open a folder by typing its path and name.

Help   Opens the extensive Windows 98 Help system.

Find   Searches for a file, folder, device, or computer. You can also search the Internet and look for personal contact information.

Settings   Accesses the Control Panel, Printers, Taskbar & Start Menu, Folder Options, and Active Desktop controls so that you can configure the way Windows operates.

Documents   Gives you access to the last 15 documents you opened.

Favorites   Gives you access to Channels, Links, and Software Updates.

Programs   Gives you access to the program groups and files on your computer.

Windows Update   Automatically connects to the Microsoft Web site to check for updates to the Windows 98 operating system.

TIP

To add a program or a shortcut to the Start menu, simply drag its icon to the Start button.

STARTUP

An application that is activated automatically each time you start Windows. If you use certain applications frequently and do not want the bother of starting them manually every time you start Windows, simply put them in your Startup folder. Follow these steps:

1. Choose Start ➤ Settings ➤ Taskbar & Start Menu to open the Taskbar Properties dialog box.

2. Select the Start Menu Programs tab.

3. Click Add, and type the name of the path to the program you want, or click Browse to find it. Click Next.

4. Find the StartUp folder in the list of Start Menu folders, and select it. Click Next.

5. If you don't like the default, type the shortcut name that you want to appear in the StartUp folder, and click Finish.

6. If you are prompted to choose an icon, click one, and then click Finish.

7. To verify that the program you selected is now in the StartUp menu, choose Start ➤ Programs ➤ StartUp.

The next time you start Windows 98, the program you just added to the StartUp folder will be automatically loaded.

TASKBAR

Launches programs and is the primary tool for switching from one application to another. The Taskbar contains several types of icons:

Start | Exploring - E1ka5o3 | THE SYBEX HOME PAGE | 11:31 AM

▶ The Start button at the left end of the Taskbar is responsible for launching applications, opening documents, and adjusting settings.

▶ The Quick Launch toolbar contains buttons you can use to do the following:

  ▶ Open Internet Explorer

  ▶ Open Outlook Express

  ▶ Open TV Viewer

  ▶ Bring the Desktop to the front

  ▶ View channels

▶ Any shortcut buttons to the right of the Quick Launch toolbar represent the applications currently active in memory or open folders. You can use these icons to switch between the running applications.

▶ The system clock at the right end of the Taskbar displays the current time.

The Taskbar may also show other icons from time to time, indicating that an e-mail message is waiting, that you are printing a document, or the battery condition on a laptop computer.

Switching with the Taskbar

When you open a new application, the Taskbar gets another button, and by clicking that button, you can switch to the new application or folder.

Switching with Alt+Tab

You can also use the Alt+Tab key combination to switch between running applications. Press and hold down the Alt key and press the Tab key once to open a dialog box that contains an icon for each application running on your system. Each time you press the Tab key, the outline box moves one icon to the right until it wraps all the way round and reappears on the left side of the box. This outline box indicates the application that will run when you release the Alt key.

TASKBAR & START MENU

The Taskbar is the main way that you switch from one application to another in Windows 98. The default Taskbar contains two types of buttons: the Start button, and any number of shortcut buttons for the applications currently active in memory.

To change how the Taskbar looks and works, choose Start ➤ Settings ➤ Taskbar & Start Menu to open the Taskbar Properties dialog box. You can also choose a toolbar from a set of default toolbars and add it to your Taskbar; you can even create your own custom toolbar.

TIP

You don't have to leave the Windows Taskbar at the bottom of the screen; you can place it along any of the four edges. To move it, simply drag it to its new location.

Modifying the Taskbar Display

The Taskbar is usually at the bottom of the screen and is always displayed on top of other windows so that you can get to it quickly and easily. To change how the Taskbar is displayed, follow these steps:

1. Choose Start ➤ Settings ➤ Taskbar & Start Menu to open the Taskbar Properties dialog box. You can also simply right-click an empty spot on the Taskbar and select Properties from the pop-up menu.

2. Place a check mark in the box next to the options you want:

   Always on Top   Forces the Taskbar to remain on top of other windows, ensuring that it is always visible to you.

   Auto Hide   Displays the Taskbar as a small thin line on the bottom of the screen. To also display the thin line when a full-screen window is displayed, select both Always on Top and Auto Hide.

   Show Small Icons in Start Menu   Displays a small Start menu with smaller icons.

Show Clock   Displays the time in the left of the Taskbar. By double-clicking the clock, you can reset the time or date.

3. Click Apply to make the changes final, and then click OK.

Adding Toolbars

Windows 98 includes a default set of toolbars that you can add to your Taskbar if you wish:

Address   Allows you to open an Internet address without first opening Internet Explorer.

Links   Contains a set of Internet addresses.

Desktop   Contains all your Desktop icons. Because this toolbar is longer than the screen is wide, you can use the small arrows to see the other icons.

Quick Launch   Contains buttons you can use to do the following:

- ▶ Open Internet Explorer
- ▶ Open Outlook Express
- ▶ Open TV Viewer
- ▶ Bring the Desktop to the front
- ▶ View channels

To add one of these toolbars to your Taskbar, right-click an empty spot on the Taskbar, choose Toolbars from the pop-up menu, and then select the toolbar you want to add to your Taskbar.

TIP

You can also add your own shortcut to the Quick Launch toolbar. Open My Computer or Explorer, select the application you want to add, and drag it to the Quick Launch part of the Windows Taskbar. You will see that program's icon appear next to the other icons on the Quick Launch toolbar. To remove an icon from the Quick Launch toolbar, right-click it and choose Delete.

Creating a Custom Toolbar

If the default set of toolbars don't meet your needs, you can always create your own. Follow these steps:

1. Right-click an empty part of the Taskbar to open the pop-up menu.

2. Choose Toolbars ➤ New Toolbar to open the New Toolbar dialog box.

3. Select a folder from the list or type an Internet address that you want to appear as a toolbar.

Another way to build a custom toolbar is to create a new folder, add all your favorite shortcuts to it, and then choose Toolbars ➤ New Toolbar to turn it into a toolbar.

TASK SCHEDULER

A program you can use to run selected applications at specific times—daily, weekly or even monthly—without any input from you or involvement on your part. The Task Scheduler starts running in the background every time you start Windows 98; it just sits there until it is time to run one of your selected tasks, and then it moves into action.

UNDELETING FILES

When you delete a file or a folder, it is stored in the Recycle Bin, but until you actually empty the Recycle Bin, you can still retrieve any files you deleted. To recover a file from the Recycle Bin and return it to its original location, follow these steps:

1. Click the Recycle Bin on the Desktop.

2. Select the file or files you want to restore.

3. Right-click and choose Restore, or choose File ➤ Restore.

If you have chosen to display the contents of the Recycle Bin as a Web page, you can also click Restore All to return multiple files to their original locations.

TIP
To select multiple files, hold down Ctrl while you click.

UNINSTALLING APPLICATIONS

The Uninstall program removes all traces that an application was ever installed. It removes all references to the program from the Windows directories and subdirectories and from the Windows Registry.

The Uninstall feature is found in the Add/Remove Program Properties dialog box. Follow these steps to uninstall a program:

1. Choose Start ➤ Settings ➤ Control Panel ➤ Add/Remove Programs to open the Add/Remove Programs Properties dialog box.

2. If necessary, select the Install/Uninstall tab.

3. Select the software you want to remove from the list and click Add/Remove.

USERS

Windows 98 maintains a set of user profiles each containing a different user name, password, Desktop preferences, and accessibility options. When you log on to Windows 98, your profile ensures that your Desktop settings—including elements such as your own Desktop icons, background image, and other settings—are automatically available to you.

To set up a new user profile, follow these steps:

1. Choose Start ➤ Settings ➤ Control Panel ➤ Users to open the Enable Multi-User Settings dialog box.

2. Click the Next button.

3. In the Add User dialog box, enter your user name and click Next.

4. In the Enter New Password dialog box, type your password. Type it again in the Confirm Password field and click Next.

5. In the Personalized Items Settings dialog box, select the items from the list that you want to personalize, and then choose whether you want to create copies of these items or create new items in order to save hard-disk space. Click the Next button.

6. Click the Finish button to complete the creation of this new user profile and to close the Wizard.

VOLUME CONTROL

An accessory you can use to control the volume of your sound card and speakers. If you have more than one multimedia capability installed, for example, MIDI or Wave-handling capability, you can control the volume and balance for each device separately. Follow these steps to access the Volume Control:

1. Choose Start ➤ Programs ➤ Accessories ➤ Entertainment ➤ Volume Control to open the Volume Control dialog box. It contains separate features to balance volume for the devices on your computer. Depending on the hardware installed on your computer, the following features may or may not appear:

    Volume Control   Controls volume and balance for sounds coming out of your computer. This is the "master" control.

    Line-In   Controls the volume and balance for an external device that feeds sound into your computer, such as audio tape or an FM tuner.

    Wave Out   Controls the volume and balance for playing .wav files as they come into the computer.

    MIDI   Controls the volume and balance for incoming sounds from MIDI files.

    Audio-CD   Controls the volume and balance for CD-ROM audio files as they come into the computer.

    Microphone   Controls the volume and balance for sound coming in via a microphone.

2. To control the volume of the components, move the vertical slider labeled Volume up or down to increase or decrease volume.

3. To control the balance between two speakers, move the horizontal slider labeled Balance to the left or right to move the emphasis to the left or right speaker.

4. Click Mute All or Mute to silence all components' or one component's contribution to the sound.

Varying the Recording Volume

To vary the volume and balance when you are recording, follow these steps:

1. From the Volume Control dialog box, choose Options ➤ Properties to open the Properties dialog box.

2. Select Recording to display a list of devices that apply to the recording task.

3. If it is not already checked, click the check box to select the device you want.

4. Click OK to open the Recording Control dialog box for the selected device.

5. Move the Balance and Volume sliders to adjust the volume and balance of the sound.

WELCOME TO WINDOWS

Opens an interactive guide to Windows 98. Choose Start ➤ Programs ➤ Accessories ➤ System Tools ➤ Welcome to Windows. The Welcome screen contains the following options:

Register Now Runs the Windows 98 Registration Wizard so that you can register your copy of Windows 98. In the Welcome screen, click Next to proceed with online registration, or click Register Later if you don't want to register right now.

Discover Windows 98 Starts a three-part Windows 98 tutorial consisting of Computing Essentials, Windows 98 Overview, and What's New.

Tune Up Your Computer   Runs Windows Tune-Up on your system.

Release Notes   Opens WordPad on the Windows 98 Release Notes file. You should check the information in this file as it may contain late-breaking information that didn't make it into the Windows Help system.

What's This

What's This?   Provides context-sensitive help in some dialog boxes. If you right-click an item in a dialog box, a small menu opens containing the single selection What's This. Click What's This to display help text for that specific item.

Other dialog boxes have a Help button in the upper-right corner (look for the button with a question mark on it) next to the Close button. When you click this Help button, the question mark jumps onto the cursor; move the cursor to the entry on the dialog box that you want help with and click again. A small window containing the help text opens; click the mouse to close this window when you are done.

Windows Tune-Up

Optimizes your system for best performance. The Windows Tune-Up Wizard can help make your programs run faster, free up precious hard-disk space, and optimize system performance.

The Wizard actually does its work by running three other Windows system utilities—Disk Defragmenter, ScanDisk, and Disk Cleanup—in concert with Task Scheduler, which controls when the other utilities run on your system. To run Windows Tune-Up, follow these steps:

1. Choose Start ➤ Programs ➤ Accessories ➤ System Tools ➤ Windows Tune-Up to start the Windows Tune-Up Wizard. The Wizard welcome screen gives you two choices:

   Express   Uses the most common optimization settings.

   Custom   Allows you to select the tune-up settings.

2. Choose Express and click Next.

The next screen lets you schedule when the Tune-Up Wizard will run on your system. Select a time when your computer will be switched on but you won't be using it, such as in the middle of the night, very early in the morning, or during your lunch break.

3. In the final screen, you will see a list of the optimizations that the Wizard plans to execute on your system. Check the box at the bottom of the screen to run these optimizations when the Wizard closes.

4. Click Finish to close the Wizard.

If you choose Custom in the Wizard welcome screen, you can also specify in more detail how Disk Defragmenter, ScanDisk, and Disk Cleanup will operate on your system.

WINDOWS UPDATE

Connects to the Windows Update Web site and keeps your system up-to-date by automatically downloading new device drivers and Windows system updates as they are needed. Choose Start ➤ Windows Update, or choose Start ➤ Settings ➤ Windows Update. Internet Explorer opens and connects to the Web site. The Wizard scans your system looking for items that could be updated. It makes a list of any new device drivers or system patches that you need and then downloads and installs the files for any items you want to update.

You will also find current information on using Windows 98 on the Windows Update Web site as well as a set of answers to frequently asked questions about Windows. Simply follow the instructions on the screen.

Part ix

PART X

APPENDIX

Appendix A

INSTALLING MICROSOFT OFFICE 2000

Installing Microsoft Office 2000 is relatively easy if you do the necessary preparation. Before you put the Office 2000 CD in your drive, you'll want to make sure you have enough memory and hard drive capacity to use Office. Table A.1 lists Microsoft's minimum and recommended hardware requirements and our comments. If you don't have enough hard drive space, consider removing files or folders you don't use.

Adapted from *Mastering Microsoft Office 2000 Professional Edition* by Gini Courter and Annette Marquis

ISBN 0-7821-2313-9   1200 pages $39.99

TABLE A.1: Minimum and Recommended Hardware Requirements for Office 2000

REQUIREMENT	MICROSOFT RECOMMENDATION	COMMENTS
32-bit Windows OS	NT 4.0 with Service Pack 3 or Windows 95 or 98	Windows 95 does not support some Outlook functionality.
Compatible PC	Pentium 90 or faster	We suggest at least a Pentium 200 unless you only want to run one or two programs at a time.
Memory	32MB or more	We tested Office 2000 at 40, 48, 64, 96, and 128 MB. With less than 64MB, we noted performance differences— the more memory, the better.
Hard drive	250MB or more free; if you want to support more than one language, add 50MB for each language	If you don't have at least 500MB free, it's time to add another hard drive.
Registry (Windows NT only)	4MB or more free	
CD-ROM	Not indicated	At least 8X; the Office CDs would not run on the 4X drive we tested.

There are a number of versions of Office 2000, and each is supplied on one or more CDs. To begin installation, close any open applications, and then insert CD 1 in your CD-ROM drive. The CD should run automatically. If you've disabled the Windows AutoRun feature, open My Computer or

Explorer; then locate and double-click the *setup.exe* file on the CD-ROM to begin installation. The Windows Installer will load and check your computer system, and the message "Preparing to Install..." will appear in the Microsoft Office 2000 Setup dialog box on the screen. In the first step of Office 2000 setup, shown in Figure A.1, verify your name. Setup gets your name from your computer system; if it is incorrect, select and type over your name. Enter your initials and the 25-character CD key for the Office 2000 CD. Generally, you'll find the key on the CD case, but it may be included on a separate license packaged with your CD. Click Next to continue.

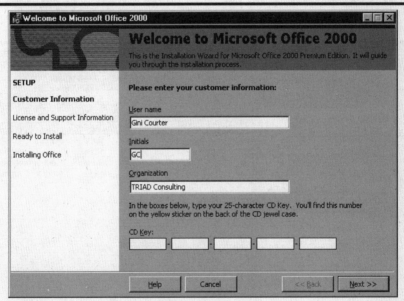

FIGURE A.1: Enter your name, initials, and CD key to begin installation.

The EULA (end user license agreement) appears on the second page. You didn't really buy Office 2000 from Microsoft—you're licensing it. Take a minute and scroll through the terms of the agreement so you understand your rights and responsibilities with the software. (If you don't indicate that you agree with the terms, you cannot install Office 2000.) When you've finished reading, click the I Accept The Terms In The License Agreement option and click Next.

The third step of installation is to choose the Typical installation (or Upgrade now if you have a prior version of Office) or indicate that you wish to customize the installation. We suggest that you choose Customize even if you don't want to make any changes to the Typical installation. Customizing is the only way you can see what features you are installing. Click Next.

In the fourth step (see Figure A.2), choose a location for the Office 2000 files. The default location is the Program Files directory on your boot drive (the hard drive that also has Windows installed). Office 2000 installs about 100MB of files on your boot drive, even if you choose to install on another hard drive; the remaining 150MB of files will be put in the drive and folder you designate here. Click Next to continue.

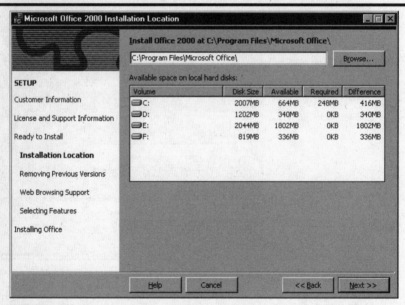

FIGURE A.2: Choose a location for Office 2000 files.

The Windows Installer searches your computer to see if you have any previous versions of Office programs installed. The applications will be listed, and you can choose to retain or remove them when Office 2000 is installed. If you are not sure you want to remove the programs right away, you can retain them. You can always remove the Office 95 or 97 applications later using Add/Remove Programs in the Windows Control Panel. Click Next to continue.

The Office 2000 CDs include Internet Explorer 5. You can install Office 2000 without installing IE 5, but there are some high-end Office features (like Presentation Broadcasting in PowerPoint) that use IE 5. Choose a Typical or Complete IE 5 upgrade or elect to retain your prior version of Internet Explorer, and then click Next.

If you chose a Custom installation, you'll now have an opportunity to review the optional application components that will be installed. The Office 2000 programs are listed in an Explorer-like tree. Click on a feature to see its description below the list. To see the options for an application, click the Expand button (the plus sign in front of the icon) to expand the view. In Figure A.3, Word has been expanded.

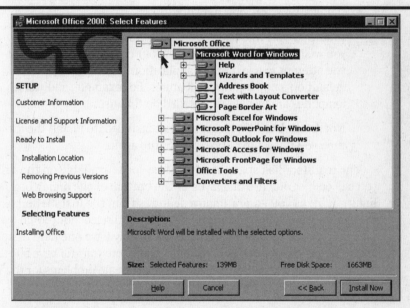

FIGURE A.3: Click the plus sign to view options for an application.

The Installer shows you the features that would have been installed if you had chosen Typical installation. With earlier versions of Office, you had an unappealing choice: either waste drive space on components you might not use or rerun Setup to add components you did not install initially. With Office 2000, you don't have to waste drive space or reinstall. A new feature called *Installation on Demand* lets you choose to install a component or feature the first time you try to use it. If there are features that you think might be needed at some point, you can make them available in the Setup program's Select Features window. Click on a feature's icon and select how, where, and when you want the feature installed from the menu:

Run From My Computer   Installs the feature on your computer now.

Run All From My Computer   Installs the feature and any related "subfeatures" on your computer now.

Run From Network   Installs the feature on your network.

Run All From Network   Installs the feature and any related "subfeatures" on your network.

Installed on First Use   Opens a message box to verify that you wish to install the feature on your computer the first time you attempt to use it in the application. This option is the default on some but not all features. For example, additional templates are by default installed on first use.

Not Available   The feature is not installed; to install the feature, you must run Office 2000 Setup again.

The required disk space and total free space available on the drive you selected earlier are displayed at the bottom of the dialog box (see Figure A.3); as you add or remove features from the installation list, these numbers change. You won't be allowed to select additional features after you exceed the free drive space. If you only have one hard drive and are installing features on your computer, make sure you still have 50–100MB free after all the features are selected or you'll create problems for the Windows virtual memory manager.

TIP

If you work in a mixed-platform office with colleagues who use other computers and other application programs, pay particular attention to the Office Tools and Converters and Filters features. If you don't know what programs your colleagues use, you can hedge by installing all the filters and converters, or indicating they should be installed on demand.

When you have finished specifying which features should be installed, click the Install Now button to begin installing Office 2000. Depending on the features you selected and your computer's system speed, installation may take up to 50 minutes. A progress meter appears in the Setup dialog box to indicate how much of the installation is completed. At times, the meter may stop completely for several minutes. Don't assume this is a problem. If installation stops for more than 10 minutes with no drive activity, press Ctrl+Alt+Del to open the Close Program dialog box to see if Setup is shown as Not Responding. If it is, select Setup and click End Task (you may have to do this two or three times) to exit Setup. Exit Windows completely, restart Windows, and then launch Office 2000 Setup again from the CD.

When the first CD is finished, the Installer will prompt you to reboot your computer. To reboot your computer, click Yes.

WARNING

Although Microsoft's installation instructions indicate that you do not have to reboot until you have installed all of the Office 2000 CDs, we recommend rebooting after each CD to avoid problems with the installation process.

After you reboot your computer, the Installer requires a few more minutes to complete the installation before you are ready to use your new Office 2000 applications.

Part x

INDEX

Note to the Reader: Page numbers in **bold** indicate the principal discussion of a topic or the definition of a term. Page numbers in *italic* indicate illustrations.

E

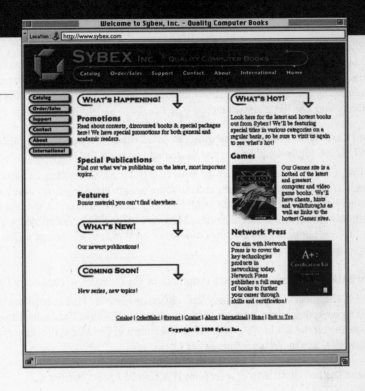

ABOUT THE CONTRIBUTORS

Pat Coleman donated chapters from *Mastering Microsoft Internet Explorer 4* (coauthored with Gene Weisskopf).

Ms. Coleman is a writer and editor. Formerly editorial director of Microsoft Press and founding editor of the Microsoft Developer Network, she also was an editor for *Encyclopedia Britannica*, *The Academic American Encyclopedia* (the first encyclopedia published online), and *The World Almanac*.

Gini Courter and **Annette Marquis** donated chapters from *Mastering Microsoft Office 2000 Professional Edition* and *Mastering Microsoft Outlook 2000*.

Ms. Courter and Ms. Marquis are co-owners of TRIAD Consulting, a consulting firm specializing in computer training and database design, including customized solutions using Microsoft Outlook and Microsoft Exchange Server. Gini and Annette are the authors of numerous books, including *Microsoft Office 2000: No Experience Required*, and several books in *The Learning Guide* series on Windows 95, Access, Office, and computers, all from Sybex.

Christian Crumlish donated a chapter from *The Internet: No Experience Required*.

Mr. Crumlish is a writer, painter, and citizen on the Net. He has been writing and editing computer books for many years and is the publisher of *Enterzone*, a hypermedia magazine on the World Wide Web. He is the author of *The Internet Dictionary: The Essential Guide to Netspeak* from Sybex.

Peter Dyson donated a chapter from *Windows 98 Instant Reference*.

Mr. Dyson is a writer and software engineer with more than twenty years of experience in software development and technical support. His more than two dozen books include *The Dictionary of Networking*, *The Unix Desk Reference*, and *Mastering Intranets*, all from Sybex.

Guy Hart-Davis donated chapters from *Word 2000: No Experience Required*.

Ron Mansfield and **J.W. Olsen** donated chapters from *Mastering Word 2000 Premium Edition*.

Mr. Mansfield is a consultant and author specializing in microcomputers. A frequent lecturer at national seminars, he has written hundreds of articles and a dozen best-selling books, including *Mastering Word 97* and *The Compact Guide to Microsoft Office Professional*, both from Sybex.

Mr. Olsen has earned his living with computers since 1985. Since 1990, he has demystified complex technical subjects as an author, a consultant, and an editor of a dozen books and more than a thousand magazine articles.

Mindy C. Martin, **Steven M. Hansen**, and **Beth Klingher**   donated chapters from *Mastering Excel 2000 Premium Edition*.

Ms. Martin is an independent developer, trainer, and author based in Chicago. She has been developing business and scientific solutions with Excel and the rest of Microsoft Office for more than eight years.

Mr. Hansen, MSCD, MBA, is president of Dakota Technology Group, Inc., a consulting firm specializing in financial and business modeling solutions that rely on Microsoft Office and Visual Basic.

Ms. Klingher is president of Willow Solutions, a consulting firm specializing in custom applications that leverage Microsoft Office. She has been working with spreadsheets since the introduction of Visi-Calc in the early 1980s.

Katherine Murray   donated chapters from *Mastering PowerPoint 2000*.

Ms. Murray is the owner of reVisions Plus, Inc., a writing and publishing services company that specializes in print and electronic communications. She has written more than 40 books on topics ranging from PowerPoint and general computing to parenting.

Celeste Robinson   donated chapters from *Access 2000: No Experience Required*.

Ms. Robinson has worked as a systems engineer, small business consultant, technical trainer, and database developer in a computing career that spans more than twenty years. A prolific writer whose work includes books on Paradox, FoxPro, and Access, she is the co-author of *Mastering Access 2000*, *Mastering Access 97*, and the forthcoming *Mastering WordPerfect Office 2000*, all from Sybex.

Gene Weisskopf   donated chapters from *Excel 2000: No Experience Required, Microsoft FrontPage 2000: No Experience Required*, and *Mastering Microsoft Internet Explorer 4* (coauthored with Pat Coleman).

Mr. Weisskopf is a software applications developer whose articles are frequently published in computer magazines. He has written several books for Sybex, including *ABCs of Excel 97*, *ABCs of FrontPage*, and *FrontPage 98: No Experience Required*. He has also taught spreadsheet and introductory computer courses.

MASTERING POWERPOINT 2000
BY KATHERINE MURRAY

400 pages
ISBN: 0-7821-2356-2
$29.99

This straightforward guide to the latest version of PowerPoint teaches new and experienced users how to make impressive presentations in a hurry. Even the simplest ideas look elegant when you effectively use wizards, multimedia, and color. Presenters who want to wow their audience will learn how to use clip art, animation, video clips, and audio.

THE INTERNET: NO EXPERIENCE REQUIRED
BY CHRISTIAN CRUMLISH

496 pages
ISBN: 0-7821-2385-6
$19.99

The explosive growth of the Internet makes having the skills to use it essential to just about anyone with a computer. Here is a no-nonsense, skills-based guide to communicating with e-mail, browsing, chatting, and publishing on the Web. Two new and unique chapters on troubleshooting make this book the most valuable and essential survival guide available. Consider it a great introduction to the Internet that also leads you through the most exciting new possibilities in e-mail, push technologies, Usenet, multimedia, and much more.

MASTERING MICROSOFT INTERNET EXPLORER 4
BY GENE WEISSKOPF AND PAT COLEMAN

960 pages
ISBN: 0-7821-2133-0
$44.99

Internet Explorer 4, the popular browser suite, paves the way to Microsoft's "active desktop," with new features and built-in push technology. Weisskopf and Coleman provide complete, in-depth coverage of all the new features and show users how to get the most out of them. Perfect for every user from beginner to advanced, Mastering Microsoft Internet Explorer 4 is an essential reference that belongs beside every Windows-based computer. The accompanying CD-ROM is loaded with valuable software, including a fully searchable, customizable electronic version of the book, Web publishing tools, and useful Net utilities.

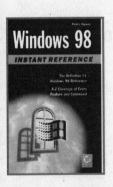

WINDOWS 98 INSTANT REFERENCE
BY PETER DYSON

336 pages
ISBN: 0-7821-2191-8
$14.99

If you're familiar with Windows, this is the best and fastest way of getting up to speed with Windows 98. If you're new to Windows, this book will be your constant companion. Easy to-use and alphabetically organized, this Guide is the key to every command, feature, menu, toolbar, and function of Windows 98. This book also provides fast answers about Internet Explorer, WebView, and all of the Internet features and functions of Windows 98. It's as easy to use as a dictionary, as authoritative as an encyclopedia, and as helpful as a Windows guru.

WORD 2000:
NO EXPERIENCE REQUIRED
BY GUY HART-DAVIS

432 pages
ISBN: 0-7821-2400-3
$19.99

Here is a comprehensive guide that teaches you all the essential skills you need to advance your career and become a truly proficient Word user. Real-world exercises and projects test your mastery and ensure that you are able to complete the tasks at hand. Just like a training course, the chapters are broken into skills and the material is presented in manageable bite-sized chunks—you learn by doing, rather than simply reading theory. With this book you are certain to get up to speed in a hurry and become an efficient Word user.

EXCEL 2000:
NO EXPERIENCE REQUIRED
BY GENE WEISSKOPF

448 pages
ISBN: 0-7821-2374-0
$19.99

Focused on the most essential Excel features, readers can quickly develop the skills they need to compete in today's workplace. Lots of graphics and step-by-step examples make it easy to grasp even the most complicated Excel concepts presented in this book. Real-world exercises and projects focus ensure that readers learn everything they need to manage workbook and spreadsheet functions. No Experience Required is designed to allow readers to pick and choose the topics that interest or challenge them most—there's no need to work through the book start to finish.